National Engineering Mathematics
Volume 3

GW00775812

Also by J. C. Yates

National Engineering Mathematics, Volume 1
National Engineering Mathematics, Volume 2
Advanced GNVQ Engineering Mathematics, Mandatory Unit

National Engineering Mathematics

Volume 3

J.C. Yates

MACMILLAN

First published 1996 by
MACMILLAN PRESS LTD
Houndmills, Basingstoke, Hampshire RG21 6XS
and London
Companies and representatives
throughout the world

ISBN 0-333-54853-1

A catalogue record for this book is available
from the British Library.

Copy-edited and typeset by Povey–Edmondson
Okehampton and Rochdale, England

Printed in Hong Kong

10   9   8   7   6   5   4   3   2   1
05 04 03 02 01 00 99 98 97 96

To Veronica, Rebecca, Charlotte and Elinor

Contents

Contents of Volume 1

Contents of Volume 2

Author's Note

This is the third and final volume covering the Mathematics required by a Higher National Certificate or Diploma student in engineering and science. It aims to complete the coverage of the BTEC and college-devised syllabi with an eye on practical applications of the subject. This means some readers may neither wish nor need to study all the chapters. Readers aiming to continue with their higher education will find most, if not all, the chapters essential. Some of the later chapters serve as useful introductions to topics where often complete texts are written upon them. The order of chapters is a possible overall order of study, though the last two stand together apart from the others.

Each chapter is introduced with an Assignment. It is a specimen example of how the mathematics within the chapter can be applied. The Assignment provides a common thread for the chapter, linking together the theory and techniques as they develop. At appropriate stages each Assignment is revisited for further attention.

An electronic calculator is used throughout the text. You may find a graphical calculator useful, but not essential. Also you should find computer software packages useful to assist with much of the work and the checking of your answers. They are to assist your solutions. The aim of the text is an understanding of the mathematics before you call upon that assistance. Beware: 'garbage in equals garbage out' is apt for those without a fundamental understanding of the processes involved.

Greek letters used

Mathematics needs more letters than those provided by the alphabet. This is why the following Greek letters have been used:

α	alpha	π	pi
β	beta	ρ	rho
γ	gamma	ϕ	phi
δ	delta	ω	omega
θ	theta	σ	sigma
λ	lambda	Σ	sigma – this is capital sigma
μ	mu	Ω	omega – this is capital omega

Acknowledgements

I am truly grateful for the help I have received whilst writing this and the previous two volumes. Again I am indebted to my wife, Veronica, for her continued and enduring patience. This is also a fitting place to thank John Winckler for his encouragement and his seemingly inexhaustible optimism. He has the ability and apt timing to lighten the darkest moments.

The author and publishers are grateful to the following organisations and individuals for permission to reproduce illustrative material: the author and publishers for tables of the normal curve in Chapter 20, from Stroud, *Engineering Mathematics*, 4th edn (1995, p. 990) and for the photographs: Barnaby's Picture Library (Chapter 5, p. 133), Blue Circle Cement (Chapter 20, p. 471), Briggs of Burton (Chapter 7, p. 160) Burton Brewery, Carlsberg-Tetley (Chapter 12, p. 277), Camera Press Ltd (Chapter 13, p. 300 and Chapter 14, p. 330), J. Allan Cash (Chapter 19, p. 451), Colorsport (Chapter 8, p. 186), D. W. Molyneux (Chapter 11, p. 265), Robinson Marshall (Europe) plc (Chapter 10, p. 238), Roxborough Electronics Ltd, © David Lee Photography Ltd, 1995 (Chapter 1, p. 2) and Science Photo Library (Chapters 3, p. 80; 4, p. 114; 6, p. 148; 9, p. 217; and 15, p. 345).

Every effort has been made to trace all copyright-holders, but if any have been inadvertently overlooked the publishers will be pleased to make the necessary arrangement at the first opportunity.

1 Complex Numbers

The objectives of this chapter are to:

1 Recall the basic ideas and operations of complex numbers.

2 Represent any complex number in one of the forms

$x + jy$	Cartesian form
$r\underline{/\theta}$	Polar form – shortened version
$r(\cos\theta + j\sin\theta)$	Polar form – trig version
$re^{j\theta}$	Exponential form

3 Define the j operator as a 90° anticlockwise rotation.

4 Perform arithmetic operations on complex numbers in their appropriate form.

5 Convert complex numbers between the four different forms.

6 State Euler's formula, $e^{j\theta} = \cos\theta + j\sin\theta$, deduce $e^{-j\theta} = \cos\theta - j\sin\theta$.

7 Derive de Moivre's theorem for positive integer powers.

8 State de Moivre's theorem for negative and fractional powers.

9 Illustrate the roots of a complex number on an Argand diagram.

10 Find the cube roots of unity in the form 1, h and h^2 where $1 + h + h^2 = 0$.

11 Apply complex numbers to engineering problems.

Introduction

We continue with the complex numbers we introduced in Volume 2, Chapter 2. Remember a complex number has 2 parts; a real part and an imaginary part. In this chapter we introduce and use some different forms of complex numbers. Also we revise some of our earlier work. Altogether we look at 4 forms;

i) the Cartesian form, $x + jy$;

ii) the polar form (trigonometrical version), $r(\cos\theta + j\sin\theta)$;

iii) the polar form (shortened version), $r\underline{/\theta}$;

iv) the exponential form, $re^{j\theta}$.

Some forms are more useful than others for addition/subtraction, multiplication/division, raising to a power and finding roots.

1

You should re-read Volume 2, Chapter 2 and refer to it as necessary. The early work of this chapter briefly revises our previous complex number work. Remember we define $\sqrt{-1}$ **to be** j. Also recall that we can represent a complex number on an Argand diagram. We can apply all the usual rules of algebra when simplifying complex numbers.

ASSIGNMENT

Our Assignment for this chapter is based on a low pass filter for a radio receiver. As the chapter progresses we shall apply our complex numbers work to the network in Fig. 1.1.

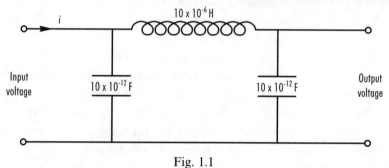

Fig. 1.1

Cartesian complex numbers

$x + jy$ **is a general Cartesian** (or **rectangular** or **algebraic**) complex number where x and y may be any numbers. x **is the real part**. y **is the imaginary part** because it is attached to the j. We often use z for the complex number written as $z = x + jy$. Fig. 1.2 shows z on an Argand diagram represented by a line vector from the origin.

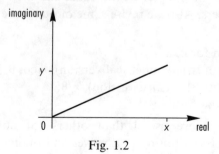

Fig. 1.2

■■■ ASSIGNMENT ■■■

In Fig. 1.3 we draw the equivalent circuit diagram of our network.

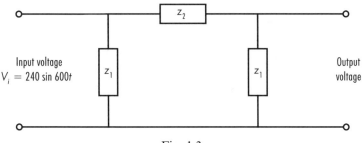

Fig. 1.3

Let us look at part of an a.c. circuit. We need to know how to represent elements of the circuit using complex numbers.

A **resistor**, ──[R]──, **has an impedance of R**. It is a real value.

A **capacitor**, ──┤(──, **has an impedance of** $\dfrac{1}{j\omega C}$.

It is an imaginary value indicated by the j. It can be re-written with the j in the numerator. We multiply both the numerator and denominator by j,

i.e. $\dfrac{1}{j\omega C} \times \dfrac{j}{j} = \dfrac{j}{j^2 \omega C} = -\dfrac{j}{\omega C} = -jX_C$

where $X_C = \dfrac{1}{\omega C}$.

> $\dfrac{j}{j}$ cancels to 1.
>
> $j^2 = -1$.

An **inductor**, ──⟨⟨⟨⟨⟨⟨⟩──, **has an impedance of** $j\omega L = jX_L$ where

$X_L = \omega L$. Again this is an imaginary value indicated by the j. As usual $\omega = 2\pi f$ where f is the frequency.

For our filter we are interested in a cut off frequency of 100 Hz, i.e. $f = 100$. Hence $\omega = 2\pi f$ gives $\omega = 628.3$. To keep the numbers relatively simple at this stage we approximate to $\omega = 600$. Using this value of ω we find the impedances z_1 and z_2.

Using $\quad z_1 = \dfrac{-j}{\omega C}$

we have $\quad z_1 = -\dfrac{j}{600 \times 10 \times 10^{-12}} = -\dfrac{j10^9}{6}$.

Using $\quad z_2 = j\omega L$

we have $\quad z_2 = j600 \times 10 \times 10^{-6} = j6 \times 10^{-3}$.

For addition and subtraction we apply the usual rules of algebra. We add and subtract like terms, i.e. separately we add and subtract real parts and imaginary parts.

Examples 1.1

Let $z_1 = 2 - j5$, $z_2 = 3 + j$ and $z_3 = -7 + j4$. We demonstrate addition and subtraction using these complex numbers.

i) $z_1 + z_2 = (2 - j5) + (3 + j)$

$= 2 - j5 + 3 + j$

$j = j1$ as usual in algebra.

$= (2 + 3) + j(-5 + 1)$

$= 5 - j4.$

Separating real and imaginary parts.

ii) $z_3 - z_1 = (-7 + j4) - (2 - j5)$

$= -7 + j4 - 2 + j5$

$= (-7 - 2) + j(4 + 5)$

Separating parts as before.

$= -9 + j9$

or $9(-1 + j)$ or $-9(1 - j)$

iii)   We can extend this technique of separating real and imaginary parts for any quantity of complex numbers.

$z_1 - z_2 + z_3 = (2 - j5) - (3 + j) + (-7 + j4)$

$= 2 - j5 - 3 - j - 7 + j4$

$= -8 - j2$

or $-2(4 + j).$

In Volume 2, Chapter 2, we also looked at addition and subtraction using the parallelogram law. You should revise this work now.

EXERCISE 1.1

In this Exercise let $z_1 = 3 + j2$, $z_2 = 2.5 - j4.5$, $z_3 = -6 - j3$ and $z_4 = 4 - j7$.

Add and subtract the following combinations of complex numbers.

1	$z_3 + z_1$	6	$z_1 - z_3 + z_4$
2	$z_2 + z_3 + z_1$	7	$z_1 - z_3 - z_4$
3	$z_4 + z_1 + z_2$	8	$-z_4 - z_1 - z_2$
4	$z_3 - z_1$	9	$z_2 - z_3 + z_4 - z_1$
5	$z_1 - z_3$	10	$z_1 + z_4 + z_3 - z_2$

For multiplication the usual rules of algebra apply. First we look at **scalar multiplication** in Examples 1.2.

Examples 1.2

i) If $z = 2 - j5$ then $2.5z = 2.5(2 - j5)$
$$= (2.5 \times 2) + (2.5 \times -j5)$$
$$= 5 - j12.5.$$

2.5 is a **scalar multiplier**. It simply changes the size of the complex number by a factor of 2.5 (Figs. 1.4). The inclinations of the complex numbers to the axes is the same.

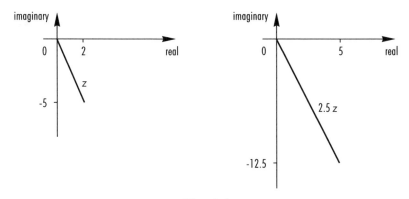

Figs. 1.4

ii) Similarly we may use a scalar multiplier of -2.5.
Now $\quad -2.5z = -2.5(2 - j5)$
$$= (-2.5 \times 2) + (-2.5 \times -j5)$$
$$= -5 + j12.5.$$

The negative sign of the scalar multiplier reverses the direction of the complex number (Figs. 1.5).

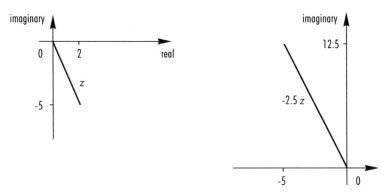

Figs. 1.5

As expected a scalar multiplier of size greater than 1 increases the size of the complex number. A scalar multiplier of size 1 leaves the complex number unchanged. A scalar multiplier of size less than 1 reduces the size of the complex number. Negative scalar multipliers reverse the direction of the complex number.

We may multiply a number by j. The j operates by rotating the number $90°$ anticlockwise. We may do this repeatedly.

Examples 1.3

i)   In Figs. 1.6 we show 8, $j8$, j^28 (i.e. -8), j^38 (i.e. $-j8$) and j^48 (i.e. 8). We saw this pattern of powers in Volume 2, Chapter 2.

$$j^2 = -1,$$
$$j^3 = j^2 \times j = -1 \times j = -j,$$
$$j^4 = j^2 \times j^2 = -1 \times -1 = 1.$$

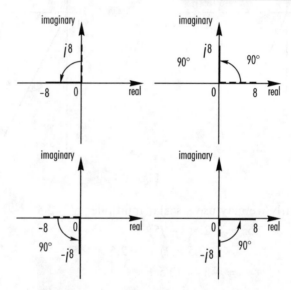

Figs. 1.6

This shows the successive multiplications by powers of j. Multiplication by j rotates the number $90°$ anticlockwise, by j^2 rotates the number $180°$ anticlockwise and by j^3 rotates the number $270°$ anticlockwise. Multiplication by j^4 rotates the number $360°$ anticlockwise, i.e. leaves it unchanged because $j^4 = 1$.

ii) We look at this idea using an example with both real and imaginary parts.

If $z = 3 + j4$ then $jz = j(3 + j4)$
$$= j3 + j^24$$
$$= j3 + (-1)4$$
$$= -4 + j3.$$

$j^2 = -1.$

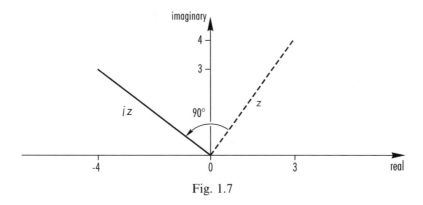

Fig. 1.7

In Fig. 1.7 we see both $3+j4$ and $-4+j3$ noticing the $90°$ anticlockwise rotation.

Generally if $z = x + jy$ then
$$jz = j(x+jy)$$
$$= jx + j^2y$$
$$= jx + (-1)y \qquad \boxed{j^2 = -1.}$$
$$= -y + jx.$$

We link both these ideas together in Examples 1.4.

Examples 1.4

We multiply together complex numbers.

i) Each part of the first complex number is multiplied by each part of the second complex number.

$$(3-j)(2+j7) = 6 - j^2 7 + j21 - j2 \qquad \boxed{\begin{aligned} j^2 &= -1, \\ -j^2 &= -(-1) = 1. \end{aligned}}$$
$$= 6 + 7 + j21 - j2$$
$$= 13 + j19.$$

ii) We apply the techniques again, using our previous result for $(3-j)(2+j7)$ so that

$$(1+j2)(3-j)(2+j7) = (1+j2)(13+j19)$$

$$= 13 + j^2 38 + j19 + j26$$
$$= 13 - 38 + j19 + j26 \qquad \boxed{-j^2 = 1.}$$
$$= -25 + j45$$

$$\text{or } 5(-5+j9) \text{ or } -5(5-j9).$$

▬▬▬ EXERCISE 1.2 ▬▬▬

Multiply together the following brackets fully simplifying your complex
number answer into $a + jb$ form.

1	$-7(3 - j2)$	**6**	$(8 + j6)(8 - j6)$
2	$(5 + j4)(3 + j7)$	**7**	$2(3 - j4)(5 + j9)$
3	$(3 - j4)(5 + j9)$	**8**	$j(5 + j4)(3 + j7)$
4	$(4 + j2)(10 - j5)$	**9**	$(2 + j3)(3 - j4)(5 + j9)$
5	$(16 - j)(2 - j3)$	**10**	$(5 - j2.5)(2 - j4)(1 + j)$

$x + jy$ and $x - jy$ **are complex
conjugate numbers of each other**.
Their real parts are identical
whilst their imaginary parts differ
by $+/-$. On the Argand diagram
(Fig. 1.8) this means they are
equally inclined to the real axis.
One of them is above and one
below the real axis.

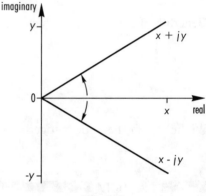

Fig. 1.8

For the complex number $8 + j6$ this means the conjugate is $8 - j6$. We saw
this in Exercise 1.2, Question **6**. Notice how the imaginary parts cancel
out, one being positive and the other being negative. This will always
happen when you multiply together a complex number and its conjugate.

We can demonstrate our numerical result more generally using a general
complex number and its complex conjugate, i.e.

$$(x + jy)(x - jy) = x^2 - j^2y^2 - jxy + jxy$$
$$= x^2 + y^2 - jxy + jxy$$
$$= x^2 + y^2$$

which is a real result.

In Volume 2, Chapter 2, we looked at the reasons behind the division
technique. You should re-read that section for revision. Here we simply
repeat the method. Remember we multiply both the numerator and the
denominator by the complex conjugate of the denominator. This always
turns the denominator into a real number.

Examples 1.5

In each case we express the answer as a complex number in the form $a + jb$.

i) $\dfrac{3-j4}{1-j2} = \dfrac{(3-j4)}{(1-j2)} \times \dfrac{(1+j2)}{(1+j2)}$

Multiplying by the complex conjugate of the denominator.

$= \dfrac{3-j^28+j6-j4}{1-j^24+j2-j2}$

$= \dfrac{3+8+j6-j4}{1+4+j2-j2}$

$j^2 = -1.$

$= \dfrac{11+j2}{5}$

$\text{or } \dfrac{11}{5} + j\dfrac{2}{5} \text{ or } 2.2 + j0.4.$

ii) We attempt multiplication before thinking about division.

$\dfrac{(5+j2)(-4-j)}{1+j2} = \dfrac{-20-j^22-j5-j8}{1+j2}$

$= \dfrac{-20+2-j5-j8}{1+j2}$

$= \dfrac{(-18-j13)}{(1+j2)} \times \dfrac{(1-j2)}{(1-j2)}$

Multiplying by the complex conjugate.

$= \dfrac{-18+j^226+j36-j13}{5}$

We know already $(1+j2)(1-j2) = 5.$

$= \dfrac{-18-26+j36-j13}{5}$

$= \dfrac{-44+j23}{5}$

$\text{or } \dfrac{-44}{5} + j\dfrac{23}{5} \text{ or } -8.8 + j4.6.$

iii) Again we attempt the multiplication before thinking about the division.

$\dfrac{4+j}{(1+j2)(3-j5)} = \dfrac{4+j}{3-j^210-j5+j6}$

$= \dfrac{4+j}{3+10-j5+j6}$

$= \dfrac{4+j}{13+j}$

$= \dfrac{(4+j)}{(13+j)} \times \dfrac{(13-j)}{(13-j)}$

Multiplying by the complex conjugate.

$$= \frac{52 - j^2 - j4 + j13}{169 - j^2 - j13 + j13}$$

$$= \frac{52 + 1 - j4 + j13}{169 + 1}$$

$$= \frac{53 + j9}{170}$$

or $0.312 + j0.053$.

ASSIGNMENT

We remind you of impedances in series and in parallel from Volume 2, Chapter 2.

For impedances in series we add when finding the resultant,

i.e. $Z = Z_1 + Z_2 + Z_3 + \ldots$

For impedances in parallel we add their reciprocals when finding the resultant,

i.e. $\dfrac{1}{Z} = \dfrac{1}{Z_1} + \dfrac{1}{Z_2} + \dfrac{1}{Z_3} \ldots$

where Z is the total impedance.

In our Assignment we have impedances z_1 and z_2 in series and then this combination in parallel with z_1.

The result of z_1 and z_2 in series is $z_1 + z_2$.

The overall impedance, Z, of the series and parallel combination is given by

$$\frac{1}{Z} = \frac{1}{z_1 + z_2} + \frac{1}{z_1}$$

$$= \frac{z_1 + z_1 + z_2}{z_1(z_1 + z_2)}$$

i.e. $\dfrac{1}{Z} = \dfrac{2z_1 + z_2}{z_1(z_1 + z_2)}.$

We can further re-arrange this equation to find Z. To do this we multiply throughout by Z, by $z_1(z_1 + z_2)$ and divide throughout by $2z_1 + z_2$. This gives

$$Z = \frac{z_1(z_1 + z_2)}{2z_1 + z_2}.$$

> i.e. turn both sides of the equation upside down.

Last time we looked at our Assignment we found $z_1 = -\dfrac{j10^9}{6}$ and $z_2 = j6 \times 10^{-3}$.

Now
$$z_1 + z_2 = -\frac{j10^9}{6} + j6 \times 10^{-3} \qquad = -j1.\bar{6} \times 10^8.$$

$$z_1(z_1 + z_2) = -\frac{j10^9}{6}(-j1.\bar{6} \times 10^8) \qquad = j^2 \frac{1.\bar{6}}{6} \times 10^{17}$$

$$= -2.\bar{7} \times 10^{16}.$$

$$2z_1 + z_2 = 2 \times \left(-\frac{j10^9}{6}\right) + j6 \times 10^{-3} = -j3.\bar{3} \times 10^8.$$

We substitute these values into our formula for Z to get

$$Z = \frac{-2.\bar{7} \times 10^{16}}{-j3.\bar{3} \times 10^8}$$

$$= \frac{2.\bar{7}}{-j3.\bar{3}} \times 10^8 \times \frac{-j}{-j}$$

$$= \frac{-j2.\bar{7}}{j^2 3.\bar{3}} \times 10^8$$

> Multiplying by $\frac{-j}{-j}$ makes the denominator real.

$$= -j8.\bar{3} \times 10^7 \quad \text{is the resultant impedance.}$$

EXERCISE 1.3

Divide and multiply as necessary the following complex numbers. Leave your answers in the form $a + jb$.

1 $\dfrac{2+j7}{4-j3}$

2 $\dfrac{8+j2}{1-j5}$

3 $\dfrac{2+j7}{8-j6}$

4 $\dfrac{3.5+j1.5}{12-j5}$

5 $\dfrac{(5-j)(3+j7)}{8-j6}$

6 $\dfrac{(5+j2)(3-j)}{1+j8}$

7 $\dfrac{(3+j)(1+j7)}{j}$

8 $\dfrac{(3+j2)(1+j10)}{j(2-j)}$

9 $\dfrac{(2+j)(3-j)}{1-j4}$

10 $\dfrac{2+j3}{(2+j2.5)(6+j8)}$

We have looked at the 4 basic arithmetic operations of addition, subtraction, multiplication and division. For the Cartesian form, $x + jy$, addition and subtraction are the easier operations. Notice that we have *not* looked at powers and roots of a complex number in Cartesian form. We need an alternative form of the complex number to do this.

Polar form – trigonometrical version

The trigonometrical version of the polar form is an alternative form for a complex number, z. In Fig. 1.9 we show a right-angled triangle with hypotenuse of length r.

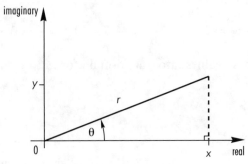

Fig. 1.9

When converting **from polar to Cartesian form**

$$x = r\cos\theta \qquad \text{gives the } \textbf{real} \text{ part}$$

and $\quad y = r\sin\theta \qquad$ gives the **imaginary** part.

> Using trigonometry in the right-angled triangle.

When converting **from Cartesian to polar** form

$$r = \sqrt{x^2 + y^2} \qquad \text{gives the } \textbf{modulus}$$

> Pythagoras' theorem. Positive root as we need only size.

and $\quad \tan\theta = \dfrac{y}{x} \qquad$ allows us to find the **argument, θ**.

r is the **modulus** (or **size** or **length** or **magnitude**). We write this as $r = |z|$, knowing that r is always positive.

> Plural of modulus is moduli.

θ is the **argument**. We write this as $\theta = \textbf{arg } z$. θ is the inclination of the complex number to the positive real axis. We label the positive real axis as $\theta = 0°$. Because θ is an angle we may use either degrees or radians. To account for all possibilities on the Argand diagram θ has a range of values. This range may be either

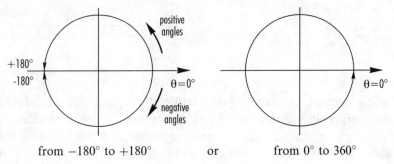

from $-180°$ to $+180°$ $\qquad$ or $\qquad$ from $0°$ to $360°$

Figs. 1.10

We have to be careful here. Now $-180°$ and $+180°$ give the same angular position. Also $0°$ and $360°$ give another similar angular position. To avoid any confusion we do not quite include one of these extreme values in each case.

We use $-180° < \theta \leqslant 180°$, | Preferring $180°$ to $-180°$. |

i.e. $-\pi < \theta \leqslant \pi$.

or $0° \leqslant \theta < 360°$, | Preferring $0°$ to $360°$. |

i.e. $0 \leqslant \theta < 2\pi$.

Our examples concentrate on the range $-180° < \theta \leqslant 180°$. This range is the **range of principal values** of θ.

In Examples 1.6 we show some conversions between the Cartesian and trigonometrical forms. We looked at this extensively in Volume 2, Chapter 2. Afterwards we look at how simply the calculator does the conversions.

███ **Examples 1.6** ████████████████████████

i) With the aid of a diagram convert
$z = 4(\cos(-120°) + j\sin(-120°))$
to Cartesian form. Fig. 1.11 is a checking aid for the calculation rather than a necessity.

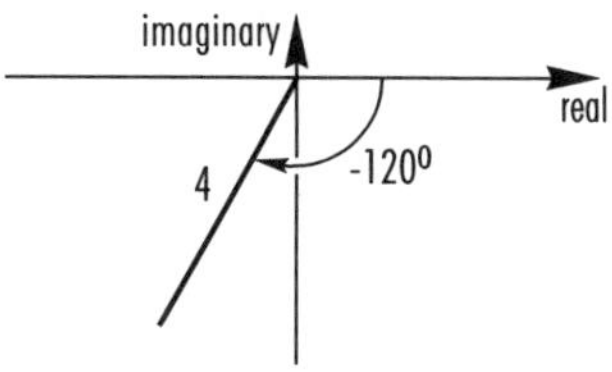

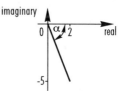

Fig. 1.11

We complete the right-angled triangle, noting that both the real and imaginary parts are negative.

$$z = 4(\cos(-120°) + j\sin(-120°))$$

i.e. $z = 4\cos(-120°) + j\,4\sin(-120°)$.

$x = 4\cos(-120°) = 4 \times -0.5 = -2.00$ is the real part.

$y = j\,4\sin(-120°) = 4 \times -0.866 = -3.46$ is the imaginary part.

Linking these together $z = x + jy$

becomes $z = -2 - j3.46$ in the Cartesian form.

ii) With the aid of a diagram convert $z = 2 - j5$ to polar form (trigonometrical version).

For this type of conversion we recommend a diagram.

Fig. 1.12

For $z = 2 - j5$

$$r = \sqrt{2^2 + (-5)^2}$$

i.e. $r = 5.39$.

We use the *sizes* of the triangles' sides so that

$$\tan \alpha = \frac{5}{2}$$

gives $\alpha = 68.20°$.

We know this clockwise direction is negative, i.e. $\theta = -\alpha = -68.20°$.
$z = 5.39(\cos(-68.20°) + j\sin(-68.20°))$.

Now we know the principles behind the conversions. In the next Examples we attempt conversions using a calculator. The function keys we need are P→R| and R→P|. The **R** stands for **rectangular** (i.e. **Cartesian**) and the **P** stands for **polar**. P→R| converts polar to Cartesian form and R→P| converts Cartesian to polar form.

▰▰▰▰ Examples 1.7 ▰▰▰▰

Using a calculator convert the following complex numbers from polar to Cartesian form: i) $5(\cos 30° + j\sin 30°)$, ii) $7.4\left(\cos\left(-\frac{\pi}{4}\right) + j\sin\left(-\frac{\pi}{4}\right)\right)$
or $7.4(\cos(-0.785\ldots) + j\sin(-0.785\ldots))$

i) First we must check that the calculator is in the degree mode. For $5(\cos 30° + j\sin 30°)$ our order of key operations is

   5| P→R| 30°| =| to display the real part 4.33

   followed by X↔Y| to display the imaginary part 2.5.

   ∴ $5(\cos 30° + j\sin 30°) = 4.33 + j2.5$.

ii) This time we need to use radian mode.
   For $7.4(\cos(-0.785) + j\sin(-0.785))$ our order of key operations is

   7.4| P→R| 0.785| ⁺/₋| =| to display the real part 5.23

   followed by X↔Y| to display the imaginary part −5.23.

   ∴ $7.4(\cos(-0.785) + j\sin(-0.785)) = 5.23 - j5.23$.

▰▰▰▰ Example 1.8 ▰▰▰▰

Using a calculator we convert the following complex numbers from Cartesian to polar form   i) $3 - j4$, ii) $-5 + j12$.

In these examples we may use either degree or radian mode.

i) For $3 - j4$ our order of key operations is

   3| R→P| 4| ⁺/₋| =| to display the modulus 5

followed by X↔Y to display the argument −53.13°. In radian mode the argument is −0.927.

$$3 - j4 = 5(\cos(-53.13°) + j\sin(-53.13°)).$$

ii) For $-5 + j12$ our order of key operations is

5 +/− R→P 12 =   to display the modulus 13

followed by X↔Y to display the argument 112.62°. In radian mode the argument is 1.966.

$$-5 + j12 = 13(\cos 112.62° + j\sin 112.62°).$$

ASSIGNMENT

Last time we looked at our Assignment we had

$$z_1 = -\frac{j10^9}{6},$$

$$z_2 = j6 \times 10^{-3}$$

and from $Z = \dfrac{z_1(z_1 + z_2)}{2z_1 + z_2}$, $Z = -j8.\bar{3} \times 10^7$.

> Remember $8.\bar{3}$ is $8.3333\ldots$, i.e. the 3 recurs.

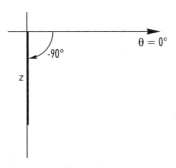

Fig. 1.13

There are no real parts to these impedances. We write Z as $Z = 0 - j8.\bar{3} \times 10^7$ before converting it to polar form. Notice how Fig. 1.13 shows the modulus and argument immediately,

i.e. $Z = 8.\bar{3} \times 10^7(\cos(-90°) + j\sin(-90°)).$

The diagram aids understanding and saves time, in this case, over the calculator. Similarly for yourself you can convert the other impedances to their polar forms (trigonometrical version).

EXERCISE 1.4

Convert the following complex numbers from Cartesian to polar form.

1 $6 + j8$
2 $7 + j7$
3 $-5 + j4$
4 $1 - j7$
5 $-4 - j3$

Convert the following complex numbers from polar to Cartesian form.

6 $2(\cos 70° + j\sin 70°)$
7 $5(\cos 110° + j\sin 110°)$
8 $1(\cos(-65°) + j\sin(-65°))$
9 $4(\cos(-115°) + j\sin(-115°))$
10 $2.5(\cos(-90°) + j\sin(-90°))$

We could add/subtract complex numbers in this form. It is *not* recommended because first we have to convert to the Cartesian form. In Examples 1.9 we show the idea only for completeness.

Examples 1.9

We use $z_1 = 4(\cos 135° + j \sin 135°)$ and $z_2 = 5(\cos(-60°) + j \sin(-60°))$.

i) $\quad z_1 + z_2 = 4(\cos 135° + j \sin 135°) + 5(\cos(-60°) + j \sin(-60°))$
$$= 4\cos 135° + j4 \sin 135° + 5\cos(-60°) + j5\sin(-60°)$$
$$= -2.83 + j2.83 + 2.50 - j4.33 \qquad \boxed{\text{Cartesian forms.}}$$
$$= -0.33 - j1.50.$$

ii) $\quad z_1 - z_2 = 4(\cos 135° + j \sin 135°) - 5(\cos(-60°) + j \sin(-60°))$
$$= 4\cos 135° + j4 \sin 135° - 5\cos(-60°) - j5\sin(-60°)$$
$$= -2.83 + j2.83 - 2.50 + j4.33 \qquad \boxed{\text{Cartesian forms.}}$$
$$= -5.33 + j7.16.$$

Next we look at multiplication in general. In our proof we apply some of the compound angle formulae from trigonometry.

We use $\qquad z_1 = r_1(\cos \theta_1 + j \sin \theta_1) = r_1 \cos \theta_1 + jr_1 \sin \theta_1$

and $\qquad z_2 = r_2(\cos \theta_2 + j \sin \theta_2) = r_2 \cos \theta_2 + jr_2 \sin \theta_2$.

Then $\qquad z_1 z_2 = (r_1 \cos \theta_1 + jr_1 \sin \theta_1)(r_2 \cos \theta_2 + jr_2 \sin \theta_2)$
$$= r_1 r_2 \cos \theta_1 \cos \theta_2 + j^2 r_1 r_2 \sin \theta_1 \sin \theta_2$$
$$+ jr_1 r_2 \sin \theta_1 \cos \theta_2 + jr_1 r_2 \sin \theta_2 \cos \theta_1$$
$$= r_1 r_2 \{\cos \theta_1 \cos \theta_2 - \sin \theta_1 \sin \theta_2$$
$$+ j(\sin \theta_1 \cos \theta_2 + \sin \theta_2 \cos \theta_1)\} \qquad \boxed{\begin{array}{l}\text{Compound}\\\text{angle formulae.}\end{array}}$$
i.e. $\qquad z_1 z_2 = r_1 r_2 \{\cos(\theta_1 + \theta_2) + j \sin(\theta_1 + \theta_2)\}.$

When we multiply complex numbers in this form we multiply their moduli and add their arguments.

Examples 1.10

We use $z_1 = 4(\cos 135° + j \sin 135°)$ and $z_2 = 5(\cos(-60°) + j \sin(-60°))$.

i) $\quad z_1 z_2 = 4 \times 5\{\cos(135° + -60°) + j \sin(135° + -60°)\}$
$$= 20\{\cos 75° + j \sin 75°\}.$$

ii) $\quad 3z_1 = 3(\cos 0° + j \sin 0°) \times 4(\cos 135° + j \sin 135°)$
$$= 3 \times 4\{\cos(0° + 135°) + j \sin(0° + 135°)\}$$
$$= 12\{\cos 135° + j \sin 135°\}.$$

Notice 3 is a scalar multiplier. It alters the length (modulus) but *not* the inclinations to the axes (*not* the arguments).

Now we turn our attention to division in general, again using z_1 and z_2. Remember we find the complex conjugate of the denominator. We multiply both the numerator and denominator by this conjugate. This makes the denominator real.

$$\frac{z_1}{z_2} = \frac{r_1 \cos\theta_1 + jr_1 \sin\theta_1}{r_2 \cos\theta_2 + jr_2 \sin\theta_2}$$

$$= \left(\frac{r_1 \cos\theta_1 + jr_1 \sin\theta_1}{r_2 \cos\theta_2 + jr_2 \sin\theta_2}\right) \times \left(\frac{r_2 \cos\theta_2 - jr_2 \sin\theta_2}{r_2 \cos\theta_2 - jr_2 \sin\theta_2}\right).$$

For ease we work out the numerator and denominator separately.

$$\text{Numerator} = r_1 r_2 \cos\theta_1 \cos\theta_2 - j^2 r_1 r_2 \sin\theta_1 \sin\theta_2$$
$$+ jr_1 r_2 \sin\theta_1 \cos\theta_2 - jr_1 r_2 \sin\theta_2 \cos\theta_1$$
$$= r_1 r_2 \{\cos\theta_1 \cos\theta_2 + \sin\theta_1 \sin\theta_2$$
$$+ j(\sin\theta_1 \cos\theta_2 - \sin\theta_2 \cos\theta_1)\}$$
$$= r_1 r_2 \{\cos(\theta_1 - \theta_2) + j\sin(\theta_1 - \theta_2)\}. \qquad \boxed{\begin{array}{l}\text{Compound}\\\text{angle formulae.}\end{array}}$$

$$\text{Denominator} = r_2{}^2 \cos^2\theta_2 - j^2 r_2{}^2 \sin^2\theta_2 + jr_2{}^2 \cos\theta_2 \sin\theta_2$$
$$- jr_2{}^2 \cos\theta_2 \sin\theta_2$$
$$= r_2{}^2 \{\cos^2\theta_2 + \sin^2\theta_2\} \qquad \boxed{\cos^2 A + \sin^2 A = 1.}$$
$$= r_2{}^2.$$

Gathering together our results we have

$$\frac{z_1}{z_2} = \frac{r_1 r_2}{r_2{}^2}\{\cos(\theta_1 - \theta_2) + j\sin(\theta_1 - \theta_2)\}$$

i.e.
$$\frac{z_1}{z_2} = \frac{r_1}{r_2}\{\cos(\theta_1 - \theta_2) + j\sin(\theta_1 - \theta_2)\} \qquad \boxed{\text{Cancelling } r_2.}$$

When we divide complex numbers in this form we divide their moduli and subtract their arguments.

■■■■ **Examples 1.11** ■■■■

We use
$$z_1 = 4(\cos 135° + j\sin 135°),$$
$$z_2 = 5(\cos(-60°) + j\sin(-60°))$$
and
$$z_3 = 2.5(\cos 50° + j\sin 50°).$$

i)
$$\frac{z_1}{z_3} = \frac{4(\cos 135° + j\sin 135°)}{2.5(\cos 50° + j\sin 50°)}$$
$$= \frac{4}{2.5}\{\cos(135° - 50°) + j\sin(135° - 50°)\}$$
$$= 1.6(\cos 85° + j\sin 85°).$$

ii) $\dfrac{z_1}{z_2} = \dfrac{4(\cos 135° + j\sin 135°)}{5(\cos(-60°) + j\sin(-60°))}$

$= \dfrac{4}{5}\{\cos(135° - -60°) + j\sin(135° - -60°)\}$

$= 0.8(\cos 195° + j\sin 195°).$

This form of a complex number is out of the range of principal values $(-180° < \theta \leqslant 180°)$. In Fig. 1.14 we show the amended argument to be $-165°$, i.e.

$\dfrac{z_1}{z_2} = 0.8(\cos(-165°) + j\sin(-165°)).$

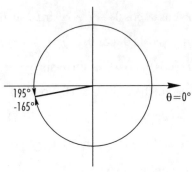

195°

-165°

$\theta = 0°$

Fig 1.14

iii)   We combine both multiplication and division. Remember the rules for the moduli (multiplying and dividing) and for the arguments (adding and subtracting).

$\dfrac{z_1 z_2}{z_3} = \dfrac{4 \times 5}{2.5}\{\cos(135° + -60° - 50°) + j\sin(135° + -60° - 50°)\}$

$= 8(\cos 25° + j\sin 25°).$

We can extend these ideas to multiplying and dividing many complex numbers; multiplying/dividing the moduli and adding/subtracting the arguments.

■■■■■■ **ASSIGNMENT** ■■■■■■

In Cartesian and polar form (trigonometrical version) we have our impedances

$$z_1 = -\dfrac{j10^9}{6} = \dfrac{10^9}{6}(\cos(-90°) + j\sin(-90°))$$

and $z_1 + z_2 = -j1.\overline{6} \times 10^8 = 1.6 \times 10^8(\cos(-90°) + j\sin(-90°))$

For $z_1(z_1 + z_2)$ we multiply the moduli and add the arguments, i.e.

$$z_1(z_1 + z_2) = \dfrac{10^9}{6} \times 1.6 \times 10^8\{\cos(-90° + -90°) + j\sin(-90° + -90°)\}$$

$$= 2.\overline{7} \times 10^{16}(\cos(-180°) + j\sin(-180°)).$$

This form of a complex number is out of the range of principal values $(-180° < \theta \leqslant 180°)$. In Fig. 1.15 we show the amended argument to be $180°$, i.e.

$$z_1(z_1 + z_2) = 2.\bar{7} \times 10^{16}(\cos 180° + j\sin 180°).$$

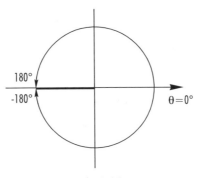

Fig 1.15

EXERCISE 1.5

Multiply and divide the complex numbers using

$z_1 = 2(\cos 45° + j\sin 45°),$
$z_2 = 6(\cos(-120°) + j\sin(-120°)),$
$z_3 = 5(\cos(-30°) + j\sin(-30°))$ and
$z_4 = 8(\cos 140° + j\sin 140°).$

1 $\quad z_1 z_2$

2 $\quad z_1 z_2 z_4$

3 $\quad z_2 z_3 z_4$

4 $\quad \dfrac{z_2}{z_4}$

5 $\quad \dfrac{z_1}{z_3}$

6 $\quad \dfrac{z_1 z_2}{z_4}$

7 $\quad \dfrac{z_1 z_2}{z_3 z_4}$

8 $\quad \dfrac{z_4}{z_2 z_1}$

9 $\quad \dfrac{1}{z_1 z_2}$

10 $\quad \dfrac{z_1}{z_2 z_3 z_4}$

Polar form – shortened version

We write the **polar form (shortened version)** of the complex number, z, as $z = r\underline{/\theta}$. We omit, but understand, the positions of the cosine and sine of the trigonometrical version. As usual r is the modulus and θ is the argument with the range of principal values. θ may be in either degrees or radians. We concentrate upon degrees just as we did for the trigonometrical version.

We *cannot* add/subtract using this shortened version of the polar form of complex numbers.

For 2 complex numbers, $z_1 = r_1\underline{/\theta_1}$ and $z_2 = r_2\underline{/\theta_2}$, we have rules for their multiplication and division. Remember the techniques when we involved cosine and sine in the trigonometrical version.

We **multiply** according to $z_1z_2 = r_1r_2\underline{/\theta_1 + \theta_2}$,

i.e. we **multiply the moduli** and **add the arguments**.

We **divide** according to $\dfrac{z_1}{z_2} = \dfrac{r_1}{r_2}\underline{/\theta_1 - \theta_2}$,

i.e. we **divide the moduli** and **subtract the arguments**.

In Examples 1.12 we demonstrate these ideas and extend them to more than 2 complex numbers.

Examples 1.12

We use $z_1 = 4\underline{/135°}$, $z_2 = 5\underline{/-60°}$ and $z_3 = 2.5\underline{/50°}$.

i) $\begin{aligned}[t] z_1z_2 &= 4\underline{/135°} \times 5\underline{/-60°} \\ &= 4 \times 5\underline{/135° + -60°} \\ &= 20\underline{/75°}. \end{aligned}$

ii) $\begin{aligned}[t] 3z_1 &= 3\underline{/0°} \times 4\underline{/135°} \\ &= 3 \times 4\underline{/0° + 135°} \\ &= 12\underline{/135°}. \end{aligned}$

Notice 3 is a scalar multiplier. It alters the length (modulus) but *not* the inclinations to the axes (*not* the arguments).

iii) $\begin{aligned}[t] \frac{z_1}{z_3} &= \frac{4\underline{/135°}}{2.5\underline{/50°}} \\ &= \frac{4}{2.5}\underline{/135° - 50°} \\ &= 1.6\underline{/85°}. \end{aligned}$

iv) $\begin{aligned}[t] \frac{z_1}{z_2} &= \frac{4\underline{/135°}}{5\underline{/-60°}} \\ &= \frac{4}{5}\underline{/135° - -60°} \\ &= 0.8\underline{/195°}. \end{aligned}$

This form of a complex number is out of the range of principal values $(-180° < \theta \leqslant 180°)$. In Examples 1.11 we amended this argument to get

$$\frac{z_1}{z_2} = 0.8\underline{/-165°}.$$

v) We combine both multiplication and division. Remember the rules for the moduli (multiplying and dividing) and for the arguments (adding and subtracting).

$$\frac{z_1 z_2}{z_3} = \frac{4\underline{/135°} \times 5\underline{/-60°}}{2.5\underline{/50°}}$$

$$= \frac{4 \times 5}{2.5}\underline{/135° + -60° - 50°}$$

$$= 8\underline{/25°}.$$

We can extend these ideas to multiplying and dividing many complex numbers; multiplying/dividing the moduli and adding/subtracting the arguments.

ASSIGNMENT

In Cartesian and polar form (trigonometrical version) we have our impedances

$$z_1 = -\frac{j10^9}{6} \qquad = \frac{10^9}{6}(\cos(-90°) + j\sin(-90°)),$$

$$z_1(z_1 + z_2) \qquad = 2.\bar{7} \times 10^{16}(\cos 180° + j\sin 180°)$$

and $\quad Z = -j8.\bar{3} \times 10^7 = 8.\bar{3} \times 10^7(\cos(-90°) + j\sin(-90°)).$

The polar forms (shortened version) are

$$z_1 = \frac{10^9}{6}\underline{/-90°},$$

$$z_1(z_1 + z_2) = 2.\bar{7} \times 10^{16}\underline{/180°}$$

and $\quad Z = 8.\bar{3} \times 10^7\underline{/-90°}.$

EXERCISE 1.6

Multiply and divide the complex numbers using
$z_1 = 6\underline{/30°}$, $z_2 = 2\underline{/-150°}$, $z_3 = 5\underline{/-60°}$ and $z_4 = 4\underline{/120°}$.

1 $\quad z_1 z_2$

2 $\quad z_1 z_2 z_4$

3 $\quad z_2 z_3 z_4$

4 $\quad \dfrac{z_2}{z_4}$

5 $\quad \dfrac{z_1}{z_3}$

6 $\quad \dfrac{z_1 z_2}{z_4}$

7 $\quad \dfrac{z_1 z_2}{z_3 z_4}$

8 $\quad \dfrac{z_4}{z_2 z_1}$

9 $\quad \dfrac{1}{z_1 z_2}$

10 $\quad \dfrac{z_1}{z_2 z_3 z_4}$

Exponential form

We write the **exponential form** of the complex number, z, as $z = re^{j\theta}$. As usual r is the modulus and θ is the argument within the range of principal values, $-\pi < \theta \leqslant \pi$ radians. In this form θ must be in radians, so you may need to apply the conversion factor $1° = \dfrac{\pi}{180}$ radians.

From Volume 2, Chapter 6, we may write an exponential function as a series of terms,

$$e^{ax} = 1 + ax + \frac{(ax)^2}{2!} + \frac{(ax)^3}{3!} + \frac{(ax)^4}{4!} + \frac{(ax)^5}{5!} \cdots$$

In this case we replace ax with $j\theta$ to get

$$e^{j\theta} = 1 + j\theta + \frac{(j\theta)^2}{2!} + \frac{(j\theta)^3}{3!} + \frac{(j\theta)^4}{4!} + \frac{(j\theta)^5}{5!} \cdots$$

$$= 1 + j\theta + \frac{j^2\theta^2}{2!} + \frac{j^3\theta^3}{3!} + \frac{j^4\theta^4}{4!} + \frac{j^5\theta^5}{5!} \cdots$$

$$= 1 + j\theta - \frac{\theta^2}{2!} - \frac{j\theta^3}{3!} + \frac{\theta^4}{4!} + \frac{j\theta^5}{5!} \cdots$$

$$\begin{aligned} j^2 &&&= -1 \\ j^3 &= j \times j^2 && = -j \\ j^4 &= j^2 \times j^2 && = 1 \\ j^5 &= j \times j^4 && = j. \end{aligned}$$

We gather together the real and imaginary parts to get

$$e^{j\theta} = \left(1 - \frac{\theta^2}{2!} + \frac{\theta^4}{4!} \cdots\right) + j\left(\theta - \frac{\theta^3}{3!} + \frac{\theta^5}{5!} \cdots\right).$$

The separate real and imaginary parts are themselves series. In Chapter 10 we shall deduce that $\cos\theta = 1 - \dfrac{\theta^2}{2!} + \dfrac{\theta^4}{4!} \cdots$ Notice after the first term the powers of θ are even. Also the terms alternate $+/-$ signs. For example the next two terms are $-\dfrac{\theta^6}{6!}$ and $+\dfrac{\theta^8}{8!}$. Also from Chapter 10 $\sin\theta = \theta - \dfrac{\theta^3}{3!} + \dfrac{\theta^5}{5!} \cdots$ with odd powers of θ and terms with alternate $+/-$ signs. For $\sin\theta$ the next terms are $-\dfrac{\theta^7}{7!}$ and $+\dfrac{\theta^9}{9!}$.

This means we have

$e^{j\theta} = \cos\theta + j\sin\theta$ which is **Euler's formula**.

Similarly we could show that

$e^{-j\theta} = \cos\theta - j\sin\theta.$

Sometimes these results are combined as

$e^{\pm j\theta} = \cos\theta \pm j\sin\theta.$

Multiplying throughout by r we have

$z = re^{j\theta} = r(\cos\theta + j\sin\theta)$

i.e. $z = re^{j\theta} = r\underline{/\theta}$

linking both polar and exponential forms of a complex number.

In Chapter 10 we shall deduce the exponential, cosine and sine series using differentiation. This implies θ must be in radians.

We *cannot* add/subtract using the exponential form of complex numbers.

For 2 complex numbers, $z_1 = r_1 e^{j\theta_1}$ and $z_2 = r_2 e^{j\theta_2}$, we have rules for their multiplication and division. The usual rules of algebra continue to apply.

We **multiply** according to $z_1 z_2 = r_1 r_2 e^{\theta_1 + \theta_2}$,

i.e. we **multiply the moduli** and **add the arguments**.

We **divide** according to $\dfrac{z_1}{z_2} = \dfrac{r_1}{r_2} e^{\theta_1 - \theta_2}$,

i.e. we **divide the moduli** and **subtract the arguments**.

Examples 1.13

We use $z_1 = 5e^{-j\,3\pi/4}$, $z_2 = 2.5e^{-j\pi/6}$ and $z_3 = 2e^{j\pi/3}$.

i) $z_1 z_2 = 5e^{-j\,3\pi/4} \times 2.5e^{-j\pi/6}$

$= 5 \times 2.5 e^{j(-3/4 - 1/6)\pi}$

$= 12.5 e^{-j11\pi/12}$.

ii) $3z_1 = 3e^{j0} \times 5e^{-j\,3\pi/4}$

$= 3 \times 5 e^{j(0 - 3\pi/4)}$

$= 15 e^{-j\,3\pi/4}$.

Notice 3 is a scalar multiplier. It alters the length (modulus) but *not* the inclinations to the axes (*not* the arguments).

iii) $\dfrac{z_1}{z_2} = \dfrac{5e^{-j\,3\pi/4}}{2.5e^{-j\pi/6}}$

$= \dfrac{5}{2.5} \times e^{j(-3/4 - -1/6)\pi}$

$= 2e^{-j\,7\pi/12}$.

iv) $\dfrac{z_1 z_3}{z_2} = \dfrac{5e^{-j\,3\pi/4} \times 2e^{j\pi/3}}{2.5e^{-j\pi/6}}$

$= \dfrac{5 \times 2}{2.5} e^{j(-3/4 + 1/3 - -1/6)\pi}$

$= 4e^{-j\pi/4}$.

We can extend these ideas to multiplying and dividing many complex numbers; multiplying/dividing the moduli and adding/subtracting the arguments.

██████ **ASSIGNMENT** ██████

Last time we looked at our Assignment we wrote down some impedances in polar form (shortened version). Their arguments in degrees must be converted to radians.

$$z_1 = \frac{10^9}{6}\underline{/-90^\circ} = \frac{10^9}{6}\underline{/-\frac{\pi}{2}}$$

$$= \frac{10^9}{6}e^{-j\pi/2},$$

$-90^\circ = -\dfrac{\pi}{2}$ radians.

$$z_1(z_1 + z_2) = 2.\overline{7} \times 10^{16}\underline{/180^\circ} = 2.\overline{7} \times 10^{16}\underline{/\pi}$$

$$= 2.\overline{7} \times 10^{16}e^{j\pi}$$

$180^\circ = \pi$ radians.

and $\quad Z = 8.\overline{3} \times 10^7\underline{/-90^\circ} = 8.\overline{3} \times 10^7 \underline{/-\frac{\pi}{2}}$

$$= 8.\overline{3} \times 10^7 e^{-j\pi/2}.$$

██████ **EXERCISE 1.7** ██████

Multiply and divide the complex numbers using $z_1 = 2e^{j\pi/6}$, $z_2 = 2.5e^{-j5\pi/6}$, $z_3 = 4e^{-j\pi/3}$, $z_4 = 5e^{j\pi/4}$ and $z_5 = 1e^{j3\pi/4}$ or $e^{j3\pi/4}$.

1 $z_1 z_2$

2 $z_1 z_2 z_4$

3 $z_2 z_3 z_4$

4 $\dfrac{z_2}{z_4}$

5 $\dfrac{z_1}{z_3}$

6 $\dfrac{z_1 z_2}{z_5}$

7 $\dfrac{z_1 z_2}{z_3 z_4}$

8 $\dfrac{z_5}{z_2 z_1}$

9 $\dfrac{1}{z_1 z_2}$

10 $\dfrac{z_1 z_5}{z_2 z_3 z_4}$

We return to Euler's formula,

$$\cos\theta + j\sin\theta = e^{j\theta}$$

and $\quad \cos\theta - j\sin\theta = e^{-j\theta}.$

Treating them as simultaneous equations we may add to get

$$2\cos\theta = e^{j\theta} + e^{-j\theta}$$

i.e. $\quad \cos\theta = \dfrac{1}{2}\left(e^{j\theta} + e^{-j\theta}\right).$

Alternatively we may subtract the simultaneous equations, i.e.

$$j2\sin\theta = e^{j\theta} - e^{-j\theta}$$

i.e. $\sin\theta = \dfrac{1}{j2}\left(e^{j\theta} - e^{-j\theta}\right).$

We may re-arrange this expression, multiplying the right hand side by $\dfrac{-j}{-j}$

(i.e. 1) so that

$$\sin\theta = \dfrac{-j}{-j^2 2}\left(e^{j\theta} - e^{-j\theta}\right)$$

i.e. $\sin\theta = -\dfrac{j}{2}\left(e^{j\theta} - e^{-j\theta}\right).$

De Moivre's theorem

Let us look at a complex number of modulus 1 and argument θ,

i.e. $z = \cos\theta + j\sin\theta$ or $1\underline{/\theta}.$ | θ in degrees or radians. |

We can multiply this complex number by itself (i.e. square it),

i.e. $(1\underline{/\theta})^2 = 1^2\underline{/2\times\theta} = 1\underline{/2\theta}$ | Multiply moduli, add arguments. |

i.e. $(\cos\theta + j\sin\theta)^2 = \cos 2\theta + j\sin 2\theta.$

Multiplying again by $1\underline{/\theta}$ we get

$$(1\underline{/\theta})^2 \times (1\underline{/\theta}) = (1\underline{/2\theta}) \times (1\underline{/\theta})$$ | Multiply moduli, add arguments. |

i.e. $(1\underline{/\theta})^3 = 1\underline{/3\theta}.$

We could continue with this technique which generalises to

$$(1\underline{/\theta})^n = 1\underline{/n\theta}$$

i.e. $(\cos\theta + j\sin\theta)^n = \cos n\theta + j\sin n\theta.$

This is **De Moivre's theorem**.

▬▬▬ Examples 1.14 ▬▬▬

Use De Moivre's theorem to find, in their simplest forms, the complex numbers: i) $(\cos 75° + j\sin 75°)^3$,   ii) $\left(\cos\dfrac{\pi}{6} + j\sin\dfrac{\pi}{6}\right)^4$,   iii) $(3 - j4)^6$.

We apply $(\cos\theta + j\sin\theta)^n = \cos n\theta + j\sin n\theta.$

i) $(\cos 75° + j\sin 75°)^3 = \cos(3\times 75°) + j\sin(3\times 75°)$ | $n = 3.$ |

$$= \cos 225° + j\sin 225°$$

$$= \cos(-135°) + j\sin(-135°),$$

remembering 225° is out of the principal value range.

ii) $\left(\cos\dfrac{\pi}{6}+j\sin\dfrac{\pi}{6}\right)^4 = \cos\dfrac{4\pi}{6}+j\sin\dfrac{4\pi}{6}$ $\boxed{n = 4.}$

$$= \cos\dfrac{2\pi}{3}+j\sin\dfrac{2\pi}{3}.$$

We may convert answers to any other complex number form using degrees or radians where appropriate. This means

$$\cos(-135°)+j\sin(-135°) = \cos\left(-\dfrac{3\pi}{4}\right)+j\sin\left(-\dfrac{3\pi}{4}\right)$$

$$= 1\underline{/-135°}$$

$$= 1\left/-\dfrac{3\pi}{4}\right.$$

$$= -0.707 + j0.707$$

$$= e^{-j\,3\pi/4}.$$

Also $\cos\dfrac{2\pi}{3}+j\sin\dfrac{2\pi}{3} = \cos 120° + j\sin 120°$

$$= 1\underline{/120°}$$

$$= 1\left/\dfrac{2\pi}{3}\right.$$

$$= -0.5 + j0.866$$

$$= e^{j\,2\pi/3}.$$

You should check these conversions for yourself.

iii)   Before attempting to apply the power 6 we need to convert $3 - j4$ to polar form. Using a calculator

$\boxed{3}\ \ \boxed{R{\to}P}\ \ \boxed{4}\ \ \boxed{^{+}\!/_{-}}\ \ \boxed{=}$ displays 5

and $\boxed{X{\leftrightarrow}Y}$ displays $-53.13°$,

i.e. $3 - j4 = 5(\cos(-53.13°)+j\sin(-53.13°))$

then $(3 - j4)^6 = \{5(\cos(-53.13°)+j\sin(-53.13°))\}^6$

$$= 5^6(\cos(-53.13°)+j\sin(-53.13°))^6$$

$$= 15625(\cos(-318.78°)+j\sin(-318.78°))$$

$$= 15625(\cos 41.22° + j\sin 41.22°).$$

Again we could convert this to any complex number form.

▄▄▄ EXERCISE 1.8 ▄▄▄

Apply De Moivre's theorem to find each complex number in its simplest form. Write your final answer in the same complex form as the question.

1 $(\cos 60° + j\sin 60°)^5$

2 $\left(\cos\dfrac{\pi}{3}+j\sin\dfrac{\pi}{3}\right)^6$

3 $(4\underline{/140°})^3$

4 $(\cos 70° + j\sin 70°)^8$

5 $\left(1\left/-\dfrac{\pi}{6}\right.\right)^5$

10 $\left(2\left/\dfrac{5\pi}{6}\right.\right)^6$

6 $\left(\cos\left(-\dfrac{3\pi}{4}\right)+j\sin\left(-\dfrac{3\pi}{4}\right)\right)^2$

11 $(1+j)^6$

12 $(1-j)^3$

7 $\left(\cos\left(-\dfrac{\pi}{4}\right)+j\sin\left(-\dfrac{\pi}{4}\right)\right)^4$

13 $(3+j4)^5$

14 $(\sqrt{3}-j)^4$

8 $(\cos(-130°)+j\sin(-130°))^3$

15 $(-5-j12)^5$

9 $(1/110°)^6$

Roots of complex numbers

We found square roots of complex numbers in Volume 2, Chapter 2. Here we extend our ideas to find other roots by applying De Moivre's theorem.

Multiplication has an inverse operation; division. Raising a number to a power has an inverse operation; finding the roots, say the q th roots. De Moivre's theorem states

$$(\cos\theta+j\sin\theta)^n = \cos n\theta + j\sin n\theta.$$

Then $\quad (\cos\theta+j\sin\theta)^{1/q} = \cos\dfrac{\theta}{q}+j\sin\dfrac{\theta}{q}$

where the qth roots are found by using the power $\dfrac{1}{q}$. For example there are

3 cube roots, found by using the power $\dfrac{1}{3}$. Remember if we cube a number and then find its cube root we return to that original number. A root is *not* unique. In Volume 2, Chapter 2, we saw there are 2 square roots. We look at non-uniqueness in Examples 1.15.

▬▬▬ **Examples 1.15** ▬▬▬

We find the cubes of i) $z_1 = 2\left(\cos\dfrac{\pi}{3}+j\sin\dfrac{\pi}{3}\right)$, ii) $z_2 = 2(\cos\pi+j\sin\pi)$,

iii) $z_3 = 2\left(\cos\dfrac{5\pi}{3}+j\sin\dfrac{5\pi}{3}\right)$, i.e. $z_3 = 2\left(\cos\left(-\dfrac{\pi}{3}\right)+j\sin\left(-\dfrac{\pi}{3}\right)\right)$.

Notice all the moduli are the same. In Fig. 1.16 we notice the arguments differ by $\dfrac{2\pi}{3}$, i.e. $120°$ which is $\dfrac{360°}{3}$.

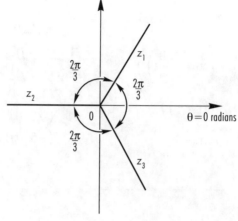

Fig. 1.16

i) Using $z_1 = 2\left(\cos\dfrac{\pi}{3} + j\sin\dfrac{\pi}{3}\right)$

we cube throughout to get

$$z_1{}^3 = \left\{2\left(\cos\dfrac{\pi}{3} + j\sin\dfrac{\pi}{3}\right)\right\}^3$$

$$= 2^3\left(\cos\dfrac{3\pi}{3} + j\sin\dfrac{3\pi}{3}\right)$$

$$= 8(\cos\pi + j\sin\pi).$$

ii) Using $z_2 = 2(\cos\pi + j\sin\pi)$

we cube throughout to get

$$z_2{}^3 = \{2(\cos\pi + j\sin\pi)\}^3$$

$$= 2^3(\cos 3\pi + j\sin 3\pi)$$

> 3π and π are the same angle on the Argand diagram.

$$= 8(\cos\pi + j\sin\pi).$$

iii) Using $z_3 = 2\left(\cos\left(-\dfrac{\pi}{3}\right) + j\sin\left(-\dfrac{\pi}{3}\right)\right)$

we cube throughout to get

$$z_3 3 = \left\{2\left(\cos\left(-\dfrac{\pi}{3}\right) + j\sin\left(-\dfrac{\pi}{3}\right)\right)\right\}^3$$

$$= 2^3\left(\cos\left(-\dfrac{3\pi}{3}\right) + j\sin\left(-\dfrac{3\pi}{3}\right)\right)$$

$$= 8(\cos(-\pi) + j\sin(-\pi))$$

> The range of principal values is $-\pi < \theta \leqslant \pi$.

$$= 8(\cos\pi + j\sin\pi).$$

As we have seen we can cube 3 different complex numbers to get the same result. The reverse operation is finding the cube roots. This means we can start with $8(\cos\pi + j\sin\pi)$ and find each of z_1, z_2 and z_3. According to

$$(\cos\theta + j\sin\theta)^{1/q} = \cos\frac{\theta}{q} + j\sin\frac{\theta}{q},$$

$$8(\cos\pi + j\sin\pi)^{1/3} = 8^{1/3}(\cos\frac{\pi}{3} + j\sin\frac{\pi}{3}) \quad \text{and others}$$

$$= 2\left(\cos\frac{\pi}{3} + j\sin\frac{\pi}{3}\right) \quad \text{and others.}$$

The type of root tells us how many answers to expect. For the power $\frac{1}{3}$, the cube root, it is the 3 that suggests we will find 3 answers. We use 3 revolutions each of 2π radians for $\cos\pi + j\sin\pi$. Notice in Figs. 1.17 that $\cos\pi + j\sin\pi$ (1st revolution), $\cos(\pi + 2\pi) + j\sin(\pi + 2\pi)$ (2nd revolution) and $\cos(\pi + 4\pi) + j\sin(\pi + 4\pi)$ (3rd revolution) all occupy the same position on the Argand diagram.

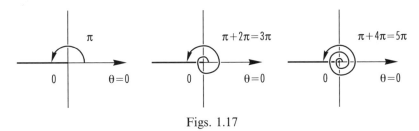

Figs. 1.17

Now we use this fact to find all the cube roots.

$$\{8(\cos\pi + j\sin\pi)\}^{1/3} = 8^{1/3}\left(\cos\frac{\pi}{3} + j\sin\frac{\pi}{3}\right),$$

$$8^{1/3}\left(\cos\left(\frac{\pi + 2\pi}{3}\right) + j\sin\left(\frac{\pi + 2\pi}{3}\right)\right),$$

$$8^{1/3}\left(\cos\left(\frac{\pi + 4\pi}{3}\right) + j\sin\left(\frac{\pi + 4\pi}{3}\right)\right).$$

$$= 2\left(\cos\frac{\pi}{3} + j\sin\frac{\pi}{3}\right),$$

$$2(\cos\pi + j\sin\pi),$$

$$2\left(\cos\left(-\frac{\pi}{3}\right) + j\sin\left(-\frac{\pi}{3}\right)\right).$$

$$\frac{\pi + 2\pi}{3} = \frac{3\pi}{3} = \pi,$$

$$\frac{\pi + 4\pi}{3} = \frac{5\pi}{3} = -\frac{\pi}{3}.$$

We drew these 3 complex numbers in Fig. 1.16 all with the same moduli but separated by $\frac{2\pi}{3}$, i.e. $\frac{360°}{3} = 120°$.

There is no need to go beyond 3 revolutions for the cube roots. The next revolution brings us back to our first answer.

━━━━━ **Example 1.16** ━━━━━

We find the 5th roots of $2\underline{/80°}$.

For the 5th roots we are looking for 5 answers, with arguments $\dfrac{360°}{5} = 72°$

apart. Also $2^{1/5} = 1.14869\ldots = 1.15$ correct to 2 decimal places. We need 5 revolutions because we are looking for 5th roots.

Now $(2\underline{/80°})^{1/5} = 2^{1/5}\underline{\Big/\dfrac{80°}{5}},\ 2^{1/5}\underline{\Big/\dfrac{80° + 360°}{5}},\ 2^{1/5}\underline{\Big/\dfrac{80° + 720°}{5}},$

$$2^{1/5}\underline{\Big/\dfrac{80° + 1080°}{5}},\ 2^{1/5}\underline{\Big/\dfrac{80° + 1440°}{5}}$$

$$= 1.15\underline{/16°},\ 1.15\underline{/88°},\ 1.15\underline{/160°},\ 1.15\underline{/232°},\ 1.15\underline{/304°}$$

$$= 1.15\underline{/16°},\ 1.15\underline{/88°},\ 1.15\underline{/160°},\ 1.15\underline{/-128°},\ 1.15\underline{/-56°}.$$

We can write these answers in order,

i.e. $(2\underline{/80°})^{1/5} = 1.15\underline{/-128°},\ 1.15\underline{/-56°},\ 1.15\underline{/16°},\ 1.15\underline{/88°},\ 1.15\underline{/160°},$

to bring our answers within the range of principal values, $-180° < \theta \leqslant 180°$. We display these complex numbers in Fig. 1.18.

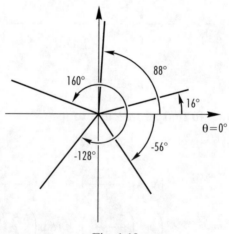

Fig. 1.18

Any Cartesian form of a complex number must be converted to its polar form before we find its roots.

━━━━━ **Example 1.17** ━━━━━

We find the 4th roots of $-2 - j6$, i.e. $(-2 - j6)^{1/4}$.

Using a calculator we convert $-2 - j6$ to polar form, i.e.

$\underline{2}\ \boxed{^{+}/_{-}}\ \boxed{R{\leftrightarrow}P}\ \boxed{6}\ \boxed{^{+}/_{-}}\ \boxed{=}$ displays $6.32\ldots$

and $\underline{X{\leftrightarrow}Y}$ displays $-108.43°$.

For the 4th roots we are looking for 4 answers, with arguments $\dfrac{360°}{4} = 90°$ apart. We need the 4th root of the modulus, i.e. $(6.32\ldots)^{1/4} = 1.59$ correct to 2 decimal places. We need 4 revolutions because we are looking for 4th roots.

Now $\quad (6.32\ldots \underline{/-108.43°})^{1/4} = \quad 6.32\ldots^{1/4} \underline{/\dfrac{-108.43°}{4}},$

$$6.32\ldots^{1/4} \underline{/\dfrac{-108.43° + 360°}{4}},$$

$$6.32\ldots^{1/4} \underline{/\dfrac{-108.43° + 720°}{4}},$$

$$6.32\ldots^{1/4} \underline{/\dfrac{-108.43° + 1080°}{4}}$$

$$= 1.59\underline{/-27.11°},\ 1.59\underline{/62.89°},$$
$$1.59\underline{/152.89°},\ 1.59\underline{/242.89°}$$
$$= 1.59\underline{/-27.11°},\ 1.59\underline{/62.89°},$$
$$1.59\underline{/152.89°},\ 1.59\underline{/-117.11°}.$$

We can write these answers in order,

i.e. $\quad (6.32\ldots \underline{/-108.43°})^{1/4} = 1.59\underline{/-117.11°},\ 1.59\underline{/-27.11°},$
$$1.59\underline{/62.89°},\ 1.59\underline{/152.89°},$$

to bring our answers within the range of principal values, $-180° < \theta \leqslant 180°$. We display these complex numbers in Fig. 1.19.

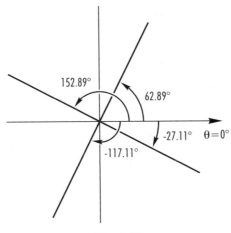

Fig. 1.19

■■■■ **ASSIGNMENT** ■■■■

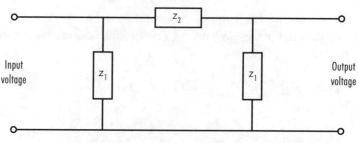

Fig. 1.20

We re-draw our circuit diagram (Fig. 1.20) for the low pass filter. The open circuit input impedance, z_{oc}, is given by $z_{oc} = \dfrac{z_1(z_1 + z_2)}{2z_1 + z_2}$. The short circuit input impedance, z_{sc}, is given by $z_{sc} = \dfrac{z_1 z_2}{z_1 + z_2}$. The characteristic impedance, z_c, is given by $z_c = \sqrt{z_{oc} z_{sc}}$.

We know we must add the Cartesian forms and need the polar forms for the square root.

Already, previously labelled Z, we have found $z_{oc} = 8.\bar{3} \times 10^7 \underline{/-90^\circ}$.

Also we have $z_1 + z_2 = 1.\bar{6} \times 10^8 \underline{/-90^\circ}$.

Using $z_1 = -\dfrac{j10^9}{6}$ and $z_2 = j6 \times 10^{-3}$ we have

$$z_1 z_2 = -j\frac{10^9}{6} \times j6 \times 10^{-3}$$
$$= 10^6 \text{ or } 10^6 \underline{/0^\circ}.$$

$$\boxed{-j \times j = -j^2 = 1.}$$

Using $z_{sc} = \dfrac{z_1 z_2}{z_1 + z_2}$

we have $z_{sc} = \dfrac{10^6 \underline{/0^\circ}}{1.\bar{6} \times 10^8 \underline{/-90^\circ}}$

$$= 6 \times 10^{-3} \underline{/90^\circ}.$$

Now $z_{oc} z_{sc} = 8.\bar{3} \times 10^7 \underline{/-90^\circ} \times 6 \times 10^{-3} \underline{/90^\circ}$

$$= 500\,000 \underline{/0^\circ}$$

so that $z_c = \sqrt{z_{oc} z_{sc}}$

gives $z_c = \sqrt{500\,000 \underline{/0^\circ}}$

$$= 500\,000^{1/2} \underline{\bigg/\frac{0^\circ}{2}}, \quad 500\,000^{1/2} \underline{\bigg/\frac{0^\circ + 360^\circ}{2}}$$
$$= 707.1 \underline{/0^\circ}, \quad 707.1 \underline{/180^\circ}.$$

We retain the first answer but reject the other one because it implies negative resistance.

▬▬▬ EXERCISE 1.9 ▬▬▬

Find the roots of each complex number giving your answers in either version of the polar form.

1 $\{25(\cos 30° + j \sin 30°)\}^{1/2}$

2 $\{27(\cos(-60°) + j \sin(-60°))\}^{1/3}$

3 $\left\{2\left(\cos\dfrac{\pi}{2} + j \sin\dfrac{\pi}{2}\right)\right\}^{1/3}$

4 $(10\underline{/100°})^{1/4}$

5 $(32\underline{/150°})^{1/5}$

6 $\left(81\underline{/-\dfrac{3\pi}{5}}\right)^{1/2}$

7 $\{81(\cos(-120°) + j \sin(-120°))\}^{1/4}$

8 $\left\{16\left(\cos\dfrac{\pi}{4} + j \sin\dfrac{\pi}{4}\right)\right\}^{1/2}$

9 $\{125(\cos \pi + j \sin \pi)\}^{1/3}$

10 $\left(32, \underline{/-\dfrac{\pi}{4}}\right)^{1/5}$

11 $(12 + j5)^{1/2}$

12 $(7 - j24)^{1/4}$

13 $(1 + j)^{1/3}$

14 $(-2 + j3)^{1/6}$

15 $(-8 - j6)^{1/5}$

The cube roots of unity

Here we are going to find the cube roots of 1. Because 'cube' is associated with 3 we expect to find 3 roots. We start with

$z = 1^{1/3} = (1 + j0)^{1/3}$ in Cartesian form;

$= (1\underline{/0°})^{1/3}$ in polar form.

Looking for roots we need to use the polar form to get

$z = 1^{1/3} \underline{\dfrac{/0°}{3}}$ and other values.

We simplify this answer to give the **principal value**, $1\underline{/0°}$. The other values differ by $\dfrac{360°}{3} = 120°$. In Fig. 1.21 we show all the roots within the range $-180° < \theta \leqslant 180°$.

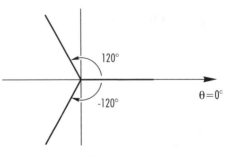

Fig. 1.21

They are $z = 1\underline{/0°}, \ 1\underline{/120°}, \ 1\underline{/-120°}$.

Suppose we let $\qquad h = 1\underline{/120°}$,

then $\qquad\qquad h^2 = (1\underline{/120°})^2 = 1^2\underline{/2 \times 120°}$

$$= 1\underline{/240°}$$

$$= 1\underline{/{-120°}}$$

within our range of $-180° < \theta \leqslant 180°$.

h is an operator. Applying h to any complex number effects an anticlockwise rotation of $120°$.

Also $\qquad 1 + h + h^2 = 1(\cos 0° + j\sin 0°) + 1(\cos 120° + j\sin 120°)$

$$+ 1(\cos 240° + j\sin 240°)$$

$$= 1 + j0 - 0.5 + j0.866 - 0.5 - j0.866$$

$$= 0.$$

We may start with $z = 1^{1/3}$ again and look at an alternative method. Cubing our equation we get

$$z^3 = 1$$

i.e. $\qquad\qquad z^3 - 1 = 0$

which factorises to

$$(z - 1)(z^2 + z + 1) = 0$$

i.e. $\quad z - 1 = 0,\ z^2 + z + 1 = 0.$

The first equation is linear, giving $z = 1$. The second equation is quadratic which will not factorise. We apply the formula to get

$$z = \frac{-1 \pm \sqrt{1^2 - 4(1)(1)}}{2(1)}$$

$$= -0.5 + j0.866,\ -0.5 - j0.866.$$

Using your calculator you should check that these 3 roots agree with our earlier ones, $z = 1\underline{/0°},\ 1\underline{/120°},\ 1\underline{/{-120°}}$.

Equal complex numbers

Suppose we have 2 complex numbers, $a + jb$ and $c + jd$, that are equal,

i.e. $\quad a + jb = c + jd$

i.e. $\quad a - c = j(d - b).$

Throughout our complex numbers work we have distinguished between real and imaginary parts. Here we seem to be making them the same. The only explanation is for the real and imaginary parts to separately have a value of zero, i.e.

$\qquad\qquad a - c = 0 \quad$ implying $a = c$

and $\quad d - b = 0 \quad$ implying $d = b$.

This means for 2 complex numbers to be equal we need their real parts to be equal and their imaginary parts to be equal. To do this we separately equate real parts and imaginary parts.

Example 1.18

Suppose $x + jy$ is the result of $z_1 + z_2 - z_3 + 2z_4$ for $z_1 = 3 + j4$, $z_2 = 5 - j2$, $z_3 = -12 - j5$ and $z_4 = -1 + j$.

Then $\quad x + jy = z_1 + z_2 - z_3 + 2z_4$

gives $\quad x + jy = 3 + j4 + 5 - j2 - (-12 - j5) + 2(-1 + j)$.

Equating the real parts

$$x = 3 + 5 + 12 - 2 = 18.$$

Equating the imaginary parts

$$y = 4 - 2 + 5 + 2 = 9.$$

We may write this as $x + jy = 18 + j9$.

For the other forms of complex numbers we can equate like terms, i.e. equating moduli and equating arguments (consistent with either degrees or radians). In Example 1.19 we show the idea for one polar form in degrees.

Example 1.19

Suppose $r\underline{/\theta}$ is the result of $\dfrac{z_1 z_2}{z_3}$ for $z_1 = 3\underline{/60°}$, $z_2 = 2.5\underline{/90°}$ and $z_3 = 1.5\underline{/180°}$.

Then $\quad r\underline{/\theta} = \dfrac{z_1 z_2}{z_3}$

gives $\quad r\underline{/\theta} = \dfrac{3\underline{/60°} \times 2.5\underline{/90°}}{1.5\underline{/180°}}$.

Equating the moduli

$$r = \frac{3 \times 2.5}{1.5} = 5.$$

Equating the arguments

$$\theta = 60° + 90° - 180° = -30°.$$

We may write this as $r\underline{/\theta} = 5\underline{/-30°}$.

The other polar form and the exponential form use degrees or radians as necessary. You should repeat Example 1.19 as an exercise for yourself using the different forms.

Powers of cos nθ and sin nθ

We apply De Moivre's theorem
$$\cos n\theta + j\sin n\theta = (\cos\theta + j\sin\theta)^n.$$

For ease of writing the algebra we shorten $(\cos\theta + j\sin\theta)^n$ to $(c + js)^n$.

> c is $\cos\theta$,
> s is $\sin\theta$.

We have seen expansions of the type $(c + js)^n$ in Volume 2, Chapter 5. There we used Pascal's triangle and the binomial theorem. To remind you we start off Pascal's triangle

$$
\begin{array}{ccccccccccc}
 & & & & & 1 & & & & & \\
 & & & & 1 & & 1 & & & & \\
 & & & 1 & & 2 & & 1 & & & \\
 & & 1 & & 3 & & 3 & & 1 & & \\
 & 1 & & 4 & & 6 & & 4 & & 1 & \\
1 & & 5 & & 10 & & 10 & & 5 & & 1 \\
\end{array}
$$

$\ldots$

Example 1.20

We find power expansions for $\cos 2\theta$ and $\sin 2\theta$.

In De Moivre's theorem,
$$\cos n\theta + j\sin n\theta = (\cos\theta + j\sin\theta)^n,$$
we use $n = 2$ so that
$$\cos 2\theta + j\sin 2\theta = (c + js)^2 = c^2 + 2cjs + j^2s^2,$$

> $j^2 = -1$,
> $s^2 j^2 = -s^2$.

i.e. $\cos 2\theta + j\sin 2\theta = c^2 - s^2 + j\,2cs$.

Equating real and imaginary parts we get

real: $\cos 2\theta = c^2 - s^2 = \cos^2\theta - \sin^2\theta$.

imag: $\sin 2\theta = 2\cos\theta\sin\theta$.

There are variations to both of these identities. We can eliminate either $\cos\theta$ or $\sin\theta$ using $\cos^2\theta + \sin^2\theta = 1$.

Example 1.21

We find power expansions for $\cos 5\theta$ and $\sin 5\theta$.

In De Moivre's theorem,
$$\cos n\theta + j\sin n\theta = (\cos\theta + j\sin\theta)^n,$$
we use $n = 5$ so that
$$\cos 5\theta + j\sin 5\theta = (c + js)^5$$
$$= c^5 + 5c^4js + 10c^3j^2s^2 + 10c^2j^3s^3 + 5cj^4s^4 + j^5s^5.$$

> Using Pascal's triangle or the Binomial theorem.

Simplifying the powers of j we get

$$\cos 5\theta + j\sin 5\theta = c^5 - 10c^3s^2 + 5cs^4$$
$$+ j(5c^4s - 10c^2s^3 + s^5).$$

$$\boxed{\begin{aligned} j^2 &= -1, \ j^3 = -j, \\ j^4 &= 1, \quad j^5 = j. \end{aligned}}$$

Equating real and imaginary parts we get

real: $\cos 5\theta = c^5 - 10c^3s^2 + 5cs^4$

$$= \cos^5\theta - 10\cos^3\theta\sin^2\theta + 5\cos\theta\sin^4\theta. \qquad\text{——①}$$

imag: $\sin 5\theta = 5c^4s - 10c^2s^3 + s^5$

$$= 5\cos^4\theta\sin\theta - 10\cos^2\theta\sin^3\theta + \sin^5\theta. \qquad\text{——②}$$

In equation ① we have cosine on the left-hand side and even powers of sine on the right-hand side. This encourages us to use $\sin^2\theta = 1 - \cos^2\theta$ to remove the sine terms. Eventually we will have only various related cosine forms.

Using $\sin^2\theta = 1 - \cos^2\theta$

we square throughout so that

$$(\sin^2\theta)^2 = (1 - \cos^2\theta)^2 = 1 - 2\cos^2\theta + \cos^4\theta.$$

Using these substitutions

$$\begin{aligned} \cos 5\theta &= \cos^5\theta - 10\cos^3\theta(1 - \cos^2\theta) \\ &\quad + 5\cos\theta(1 - 2\cos^2\theta + \cos^4\theta) \\ &= \cos^5\theta - 10\cos^3\theta + 10\cos^5\theta \\ &\quad + 5\cos\theta - 10\cos^3\theta + 5\cos^5\theta \end{aligned}$$

i.e. $\cos 5\theta = 16\cos^5\theta - 20\cos^3\theta + 5\cos\theta.$

In equation ② we have sine on the left-hand side and even powers of cosine on the right-hand side. This encourages us to use $\cos^2\theta = 1 - \sin^2\theta$ to remove the cosine terms. Eventually we will have only various related sine forms.

Using $\cos^2\theta = 1 - \sin^2\theta$

we square throughout so that

$$(\cos^2\theta)^2 = (1 - \sin^2\theta)^2 = 1 - 2\sin^2\theta + \sin^4\theta.$$

Using these substitutions

$$\begin{aligned} \sin 5\theta &= 5(1 - 2\sin^2\theta + \sin^4\theta)\sin\theta \\ &\quad - 10(1 - \sin^2\theta)\sin^3\theta + \sin^5\theta \\ &= 5\sin\theta - 10\sin^3\theta + 5\sin^5\theta \\ &\quad - 10\sin^3\theta + 10\sin^5\theta + \sin^5\theta \\ &= 16\sin^5\theta - 20\sin^3\theta + 5\sin\theta. \end{aligned}$$

EXERCISE 1.10

1   Using the power expansion for $\cos 2\theta$ find a value for $\cos 180°$ by substituting for $\theta = 90°$.

2   Work out a power expansion for $\cos 3\theta$ in terms of cosines only. Similarly find an expansion for $\sin 3\theta$ in terms of sines only.

3   Prove that $\cos 4\theta = 8\cos^4\theta - 8\cos^2\theta + 1$. Work out a parallel power expansion for $\sin 4\theta$.

4   $\sin 30° = 0.5$. Using our earlier result for $\sin 5\theta$ with $\theta = 30°$ find the value of $\sin 150°$. Check your answer with a calculator.

5   Work out power expansions for $\cos 6\theta$ and $\sin 6\theta$. If possible attempt to write them in terms of either cosines or sines only.

We complete this first chapter with a selection of practical questions.

EXERCISE 1.11

1   Convert the impedance $Z = 3 + j4$ into shortened polar form. The phasor current, $I = 6e^{j\pi/3}$, flows through this impedance. Using $V = IZ$ find the voltage, V, in shortened polar form.

2   Write the voltage $V = 2e^{j3\pi/4}$ and the current $I = 5 + j12$ in shortened polar form. Find Z from $V = IZ$ quoting your answer in all the complex forms.

3   A 60 microfarad ($C = 60 \times 10^{-6}$ F) capacitor is connected in series with 5 similar ones. The total impedance is given by $\sum \dfrac{1}{j\omega C}$. For a frequency, f, of 50 Hz where $f = \dfrac{\omega}{2\pi}$ find the total impedance in polar form. If the voltage is 240 V write this and the current both in polar form.

If the frequency is doubled what happens to your values for the impedance of one capacitor, the total impedance and the current?

4   The a.c. bridge is 'balanced' when no current flows along BD. This occurs when
$$\frac{z_{AB}}{z_{BC}} = \frac{z_{AD}}{z_{DC}}.$$
Does it balance?
If you could alter z_{DC} what value must you use to make the bridge balance?
Suppose you replace the capacitor with a variable resistor. Can you balance the bridge and if so with what resistance?

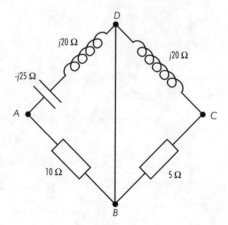

5 A voltage of $200\underline{/0°}$ V is applied to an impedance of $4+j5$ Ω (i.e. a resistance 4 and inductive reactance 5). What is the value of the current, I? If the power, P, is given by $P = |I|^2 R$ find P.

6 Convert the impedances $z_1 = 4+j3$ Ω and $z_2 = 5+j\,200$ Ω into shortened polar form.

For a transmission line the propagation constant, P, is given by the formula $P = 10^{-4} \times \sqrt{z_1 z_2}$. Find P in both polar and Cartesian forms. The correct value for P must lie in the positive quadrant so discard any other answers.

7 The characteristic impedance, Z, of a transmission line is given by

$Z = \sqrt{\dfrac{R+j\omega L}{G+j\omega C}}$. You are given $R = 1.5$ Ω, $L = 0.25 \times 10^{-3}$ H,

$G = 5 \times 10^{-6}$ Ω, $C = 10^{-9}$ F and $\omega = 110$ Hz.
Convert your complex numbers for the numerator and denominator into shortened polar form. In this form find Z.

8 The first diagram shows a star network. The admittance, Y, is related to the impedance, Z, by $Y = \dfrac{1}{Z}$.

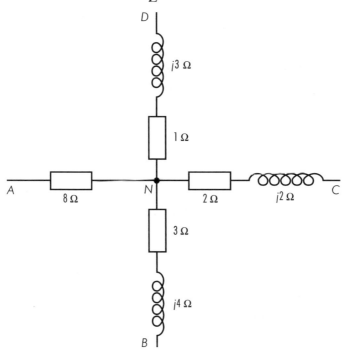

$BN,\ Y_{BN} = \dfrac{1}{3+j4} = 0.12 - j0.16 = 0.2\underline{/-53.13°}.$

Write down the admittances in AN, CN and DN in these forms. The sum of these admittances is given by $\sum Y$. Find $\sum Y$.

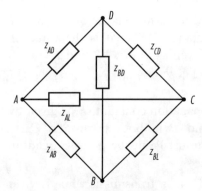

The second diagram shows the star network redrawn as an equivalent mesh network.

The admittance in AB is given by

$$Y_{AB} = \frac{Y_{AN} Y_{BN}}{\sum Y}.$$

Find all 6 admittances and impedances in this mesh network.

9 The a.c. bridge is 'balanced' when no current flows along BD. This occurs when $\dfrac{z_{AB}}{z_{BC}} = \dfrac{z_{AD}}{z_{DC}}$.
You are given values for most of the components. The only unknown is the resistance R and the inductance L in AB. Find R and L in terms of the other component values so that the bridge balances.

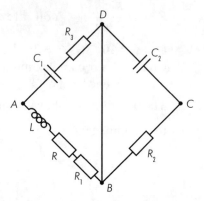

10 We redraw the 'T' network with its equivalent circuit diagram. The frequency is $f = 50$ Hz so that $\omega = 100\pi$.

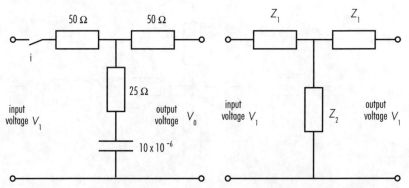

Write down the impedances in both Cartesian and polar forms. Find the short circuit impedance, z_{sc}, where

$$z_{sc} = z_1 + \frac{1}{\dfrac{1}{z_1} + \dfrac{1}{z_2}}.$$

Also find the open circuit impedance, z_{oc} where $z_{oc} = z_1 + z_2$.
Finally, use these results to find the characteristic impedance, z_c, where $z_c = (z_{sc} z_{oc})^{1/2}$.

2 Functions and Inverse Functions

The objectives of this chapter are to:

1 Decide if a graphical relationship is a function.
2 Decide if a function is one-to-one or many-to-one.
3 Decide if a function is odd or even or neither odd nor even.
4 Decide if a function is continuous or discontinuous.
5 Decide if a function is periodic.
6 Find the inverse of a one-to-one function.
7 Deduce the graph of an inverse function from the graph of the original function.
8 Define inverse trigonometric functions.
9 Define the principal values of inverse trigonometric functions.
10 Differentiate inverse trigonometric functions.

Introduction

We have introduced one type of function notation in Volume 2, Chapter 7. This is *not* the only form. For simplicity and to save confusion we will continue with this notation. We decide if graphical relationships are functions and the types of those functions. Later we attempt to find the inverses of functions, particularly trigonometric functions. Finally we differentiate inverse trigonometric functions.

◼◼◼◼ ASSIGNMENT ◼◼◼◼◼◼◼◼◼◼◼◼◼◼◼◼◼◼

We have two Assignments for this chapter.

1 A cosine voltage or waveform is rectified by a single semiconductor diode. The input is a cosine wave whilst the output is only the positive half cycles (Fig. 2.1 overleaf). This is half wave rectification.

2 Here we have a sine voltage or current waveform rectified by 2 diodes. From the sine input this output has the negative half cycles as positive half cycles. This means the complete output is all positive. This is full wave rectification.

41

1

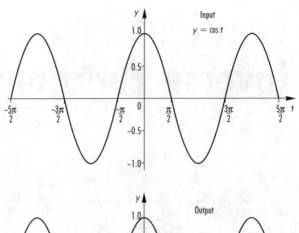

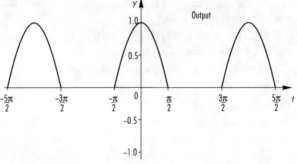

Fig. 2.1

2

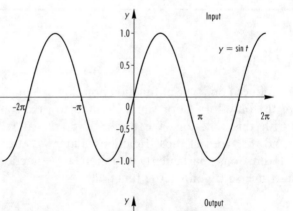

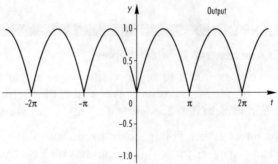

Fig. 2.2

Functions

In Mathematics we often start with an independent variable, x, and a dependent variable, y. Graphically we label the horizontal axis x and the vertical axis y. More generally the horizontal axis is the independent axis and the vertical axis is the dependent axis. We can vary the independent variable, x. In turn, through its specific relationship with y, this automatically varies y, i.e. y depends upon x. We choose our independent values from the domain and relate them to dependent values in the codomain.

We write that y is a function of x and use the notation $y = f(x)$. The first derivative, $\dfrac{dy}{dx}$, is $f'(x)$, said 'f dashed of x'. The second derivative, $\dfrac{d^2y}{dx^2}$, is $f''(x)$, said 'f double dashed of x'; the third derivative, $\dfrac{d^3y}{dx^3}$, is $f'''(x)$, said 'f treble dashed of x'. Further derivatives are:

the fourth derivative, $f^{iv}(x)$;

the fifth derivative, $f^{v}(x)$;

the sixth derivative, $f^{vi}(x)$; ...

████████ **Examples 2.1** ████████

The following are some of the simple functions we have seen in Volumes 1 and 2.

   i) $y = x$, $y = 3x$.

   ii) $y = x^3$, $y = 2x^3$, $y = 2x^3 + x - 7$.

   iii) $y = +\sqrt{x}$ (notice the positive root only).

   iv) $y = -\sqrt{x}$ (notice the negative root only).

   v) $y = \dfrac{1}{x}$, $y = \dfrac{4}{x}$.

   vi) $y = \cos 2x$, $y = \cos 2x - \sin x$.

   vii) $y = e^x$, $y = 4e^{2x}$.

   viii) $y = \ln x$, $y = \ln(\cos x)$.

████████ **Examples 2.2** ████████

Here we replace y with $f(x)$. Also we calculate some functional values.

   i) For $f(x) = 3x$, $f(2) = 3 \times 2 = 6$. $\boxed{x = 2.}$

   ii) For $f(x) = 2x^3 + x - 7$, $f(1) = 2 \times 1^3 + 1 - 7 = -4$. $\boxed{x = 1.}$

   iii) For $f(x) = \cos x$, $f(0) = \cos 0 = 1$. $\boxed{x = 0.}$

   iv) For $f(\theta) = \sin 2\theta$, $f\left(\dfrac{\pi}{8}\right) = \sin \dfrac{2\pi}{8} = \sin \dfrac{\pi}{4} = 0.707$. $\boxed{\theta = \dfrac{\pi}{8}.}$

■ EXERCISE 2.1 ■

For each function calculate the values required.

1   $f(x) = 2x$; $f(1), f(0), f(-1), f(0.5)$.
2   $f(x) = x^2 + x$; $f(2), f(-2), f(1.5)$.
3   $f(x) = +\sqrt{x}$; $f(9), f(121), f(5)$.
4   $f(\theta) = \cos\theta$; $f\left(\dfrac{\pi}{3}\right), f\left(-\dfrac{\pi}{3}\right)$.
5   $f(t) = \sin t$; $f\left(\dfrac{5\pi}{4}\right), f\left(-\dfrac{5\pi}{4}\right)$.
6   $f(x) = e^x$; $f(1), f(2), f(0), f(-2)$.
7   $f(x) = e^{-x}$; $f(1), f(2), f(0), f(-2)$.
8   $f(x) = \dfrac{4}{x}$; $f(5), f(-5)$.
9   $f(\theta) = \cos\theta + \sin\theta$; $f\left(\dfrac{\pi}{4}\right), f\left(-\dfrac{\pi}{4}\right)$.
10 $f(x) = \frac{1}{2}(e^x + e^{-x})$; $f(1), f(-1)$.

We look at some examples of possible functions, relating them to graphical sketches.

■ Example 2.3 ■

We sketch the graph of $y = x^3 + 4$ in Fig. 2.3. In functional notation this is $f(x) = x^3 + 4$. Hence we can label the vertical axis y or $f(x)$.

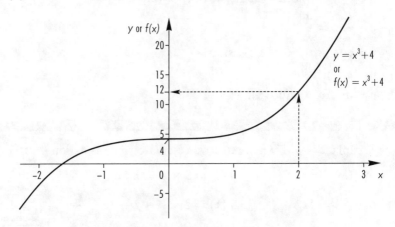

Fig. 2.3

We start from the horizontal axis (i.e. independent axis, i.e. x-axis), with a value of x. Suppose we choose $x = 2$ and move vertically from the x-axis to the graph, $y = x^3 + 4$. Then we turn through $90°$ and move horizontally to meet the y-axis at $y = 12$, (i.e. $y = 2^3 + 4 = 8 + 4 = 12$). According to our specific relationship, $y = x^3 + 4$, we have mapped one value of x to one value of y. You should try this for yourself with other values of x. Notice the graph passes through the point $(0, 4)$. This means $x = 0$ maps to $y = 4$. Also in our numerical example we moved vertically up and then horizontally to the graph. It is just as acceptable to move vertically down and then horizontally.

Example 2.4

We repeat the technique of the previous example, this time with $y = x^2 - 3$ in Fig. 2.4. In functional notation this is $f(x) = x^2 - 3$. Hence we can label the vertical axis y or $f(x)$.

As before we start from the x-axis. This time we choose two specimen values, $x = 1$ and $x = -1$, in Fig. 2.4. We move vertically down to the curve and then horizontally to the y-axis. Both mappings reach the value $y = -2$.

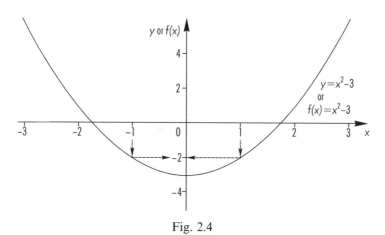

Fig. 2.4

Examples 2.3 and 2.4 show different categories of functions. **A function mapping one independent value, x, to one dependent value, y, is a one-to-one function.** This can be written as a '**1-1 function**'.

A function mapping more than one independent value to one dependent value is a many-to-one function.

Example 2.5

In Fig. 2.5 we look at the graph of $y = \pm\sqrt{x}$ (or $y^2 = x$).

As usual we start from the x-axis. This time we choose $x = 9$ as a specimen value. In Fig. 2.5 we can move both vertically up and down towards the graph. In one case we reach $y = 3$ and in the other case we

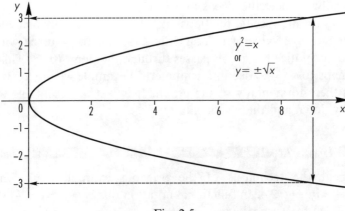

Fig. 2.5

reach $y = -3$. This is ambiguous. Which option should we choose? We could refer to this situation as many to one, but note that it is not a function.

Only mappings that are one-to-one or many-to-one are functions.

We could get around this problem in Example 2.5. If we use $y = \sqrt{x}$ then we have a function because there is no ambiguity. Similarly we have a function if we use $y = -\sqrt{x}$.

ASSIGNMENT

Let us look at our input graphs. As an exercise for yourself you can look at the output graphs.

1   In functional notation for $f(t) = \cos t$ notice we have a many-to-one function. We show some numerical examples.

. . .

$$f\left(-\frac{5\pi}{3}\right) = \cos\left(-\frac{5\pi}{3}\right) = 0.5.$$

$$f\left(-\frac{\pi}{3}\right) = \cos\left(-\frac{\pi}{3}\right) = 0.5.$$

$$f\left(\frac{\pi}{3}\right) = \cos\frac{\pi}{3} = 0.5.$$

$$f\left(\frac{5\pi}{3}\right) = \cos\frac{5\pi}{3} = 0.5.$$

. . .

We show this in Fig. 2.6.

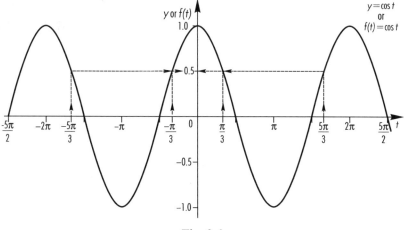

Fig. 2.6

2 Also for $f(t) = \sin t$ notice we have a many-to-one function. Again we show some numerical examples.

. . .

$$f\left(-\frac{5\pi}{4}\right) = \sin\left(-\frac{5\pi}{4}\right) = 0.707.$$

$$f\left(\frac{\pi}{4}\right) \quad = \sin\frac{\pi}{4} \quad\;\; = 0.707.$$

$$f\left(\frac{3\pi}{4}\right) \quad = \sin\frac{3\pi}{4} \quad = 0.707.$$

$$f\left(\frac{9\pi}{4}\right) \quad = \sin\frac{9\pi}{4} \quad = 0.707.$$

. . .

We show this in Fig. 2.7.

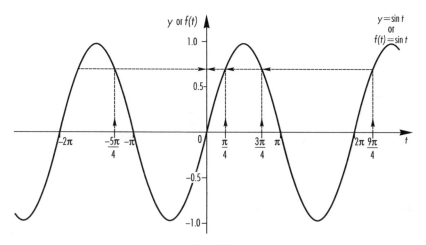

Fig. 2.7

EXERCISE 2.2

For each of the following relationships between x and y decide whether it is   i)   a 1-1 function,
or   ii)   a many-to-one function,
or   iii)   not a function.

1   $y = 2x^3$

2   $y = 2 + x^2$

3   $y = x$

4   $y = e^x$

5   $y = x^{1/4}$

6   $y = e^{-x}$

7   $y = \sin x$

8   $y = \sin^2 x$

9   $y = \cos 2x$

10   $y = \ln x$

11   $y = \pm\sqrt{25 - x^2}$

12   $xy = 2$

13   $y = \frac{1}{2}(e^x + e^{-x})$

14   $x^2 + y^2 = 9$

15   $y = \tan x$

Odd and even functions

We have seen how to put functions into categories of one-to-one and many-to-one. Also we can decide if a function is
      i)   odd,
or   ii)   even,
or   iii)   neither odd nor even.

We can test for these conditions either graphically or algebraically. A function that involves odd powers of x (or some other independent variable) is an odd function. A function that involves even powers of x (or some other independent variable) is an even function. Within the even function category we include multiples of x^0, i.e. constant values. A function that involves both odd and even powers of x is neither odd nor even. Some functions, e.g. $y = \cos x$, are not usually displayed in terms of powers of x. Other functions like this that we have met already are trigonometric, logarithmic and exponential functions. However we have seen exponential functions expressed as series in Volume 2, Chapter 6.

We define $f(x)$ to be an even function if $f(-x) = f(x)$. The graph of an even function is symmetrical about the vertical axis.

Example 2.6

Is $y = 3x^2$ an even function?

In functional notation this is $f(x) = 3x^2$.

Using the algebraic definition, $f(-x) = 3(-x)^2 = 3x^2$ | Using $-x$ in place of x. |

i.e. $f(-x) = f(x)$

i.e. $y = 3x^2$ is an even function.

For our graphical test we cover the graph to the left of the vertical axis. We reflect the exposed right-hand section about the vertical axis. If the result agrees with the covered section then the graph is even. You can test this for yourself with $y = 3x^2$ in Fig. 2.8.

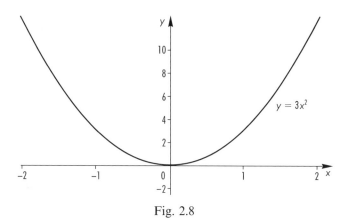

Fig. 2.8

We define $f(x)$ to be an odd function if $f(-x) = -f(x)$. The graph of an odd function is symmetrical about the origin.

▰▰ Example 2.7 ▰▰

Is $y = x^3$ an odd function?

In functional notation this is $\qquad f(x) = x^3.$

Using the algebraic definition, $f(-x) = (-x)^3 = -x^3$ Using $-x$ in place of x.

i.e. $f(-x) = -f(x)$

i.e. $y = x^3$ is an odd function.

For our graphical test we consider an axis ZZ through O perpendicular to the plane of the graph. About this axis we rotate the graph through $180°$. If the result agrees with the original graph then the function is odd. You can test this for yourself with $y = x^3$ in Fig. 2.9.

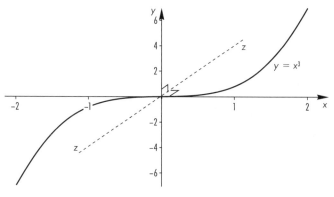

Fig. 2.9

We define $f(x)$ to be a function that is neither odd nor even if it fails the tests for odd and even functions, i.e. if $f(-x) \neq f(x)$ and $f(-x) \neq -f(x)$.

$\neq$ is 'not equal to'.

Example 2.8

Is $y = x^3 + 4$ an odd or even function?

In functional notation this is $f(x) = x^3 + 4$.

We test using the even function definition, $f(-x) = f(x)$.

$$f(-x) = (-x)^3 + 4 = -x^3 + 4$$

i.e. $f(-x) \neq f(x)$

$\neq$ is 'not equal to'.

i.e. this is *not* an even function.

We test using the odd function definition, $f(-x) = -f(x)$.

$$-f(x) = -(x^3 + 4)$$
$$= -x^3 - 4$$

i.e. $-f(x) \neq f(-x)$

i.e. this is *not* an odd function.

Combining our two test results we see that this function is neither odd nor even.

Using Fig. 2.10, the graph of $y = x^3 + 4$ you can check this result by applying each graphical test.

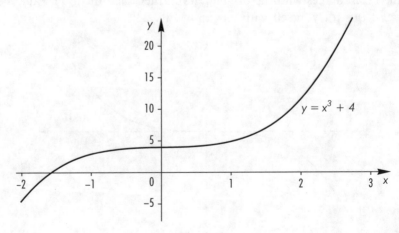

Fig. 2.10

ASSIGNMENT

1   We look at the input graph in Fig. 2.11, i.e. $f(t) = \cos t$. Notice the graph is symmetrical about the vertical axis, i.e.

$$f(-t) = \cos(-t) = \cos t = f(t).$$

We showed this numerically last time we looked at the Assignment, e.g.

$$f\left(-\frac{\pi}{3}\right) = \cos\left(-\frac{\pi}{3}\right) = 0.5 = \cos\frac{\pi}{3} = f\left(\frac{\pi}{3}\right).$$

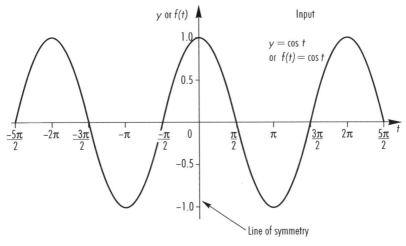

Fig. 2.11

We also look at the output graph in Fig. 2.12. Notice the graph is symmetrical about the vertical axis. Because we have *not* yet defined the output graph in functional notation we find it difficult to discuss $f(-t) = f(t)$.

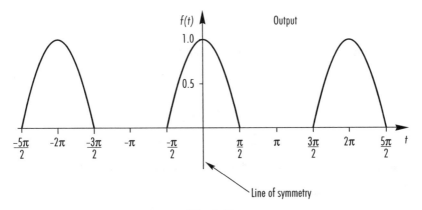

Fig. 2.12

We leave the second part of the Assignment for you as an exercise.

▇▇▇▇ EXERCISE 2.3 ▇▇▇▇

Decide whether each of the following functions is
      i) odd,
or ii) even,
or iii) neither odd nor even.

You should test using the algebraic definitions. Confirm each answer by sketching the graph of the function and applying the graphical test.

1	$y = x^2$	**9**	$y = e^{-x}$
2	$y = x^2 + 3$	**10**	$y = \sin 2x$
3	$y = x$	**11**	$y = \frac{1}{2}(e^x + e^{-x})$
4	$y = x^2 + x$	**12**	$y = \ln x$
5	$y = x^4 - x$	**13**	$xy = 3$
6	$y = e^x$	**14**	$y = x^2 + x^4$
7	$y = \cos x$	**15**	$y = \frac{1}{2}(e^x - e^{-x})$
8	$y = \tan x$		

Let us look back at some of the answers to Exercise 2.3.

$$f(x) = x \text{ is an odd function,}$$

$$f(x) = x^2 \text{ is an even function,}$$

and $f(x) = x^4$ is an even function.

Notice where you add/subtract odd and even functions (Questions **4** and **5**) the result is a function that is neither odd nor even. Where you add only even functions (e.g. Question **14**) the result is also even. You would find adding only odd functions gives a result that is also odd. The same patterns apply to subtraction.

Add/subtract even functions to give another even function.

Add/subtract odd functions to give another odd function.

Add/subtract even and odd functions to give a function that is neither odd nor even.

Now let us look at some products of functions.

▇▇▇ Examples 2.9 ▇▇▇

Test whether the functions   i) $x^2 \cos x$,   ii) $x \sin x$,   iii) $\sin x . \cos x$ are odd or even or neither odd nor even.

In each case we have a product of functions. First let us look at the individual functions in turn.

For $f(x) = x$, $f(-x) = -x$

$\qquad$ i.e. $f(-x) = -f(x)$

i.e. $f(x) = x$ is an odd function.

For $f(x) = x^2$, $f(-x) = (-x)^2 = x^2$

i.e. $\qquad\qquad\qquad f(-x) = f(x)$

i.e. $f(x) = x^2$ is an even function.

For $f(x) = \cos x$, $f(-x) = \cos(-x) = \cos x$

$\qquad$ i.e. $f(-x) = f(x)$

i.e. $f(x) = \cos x$ is an even function.

For $f(x) = \sin x$, $f(-x) = \sin(-x) = -\sin x$

$\qquad$ i.e. $f(-x) = -f(x)$

i.e. $f(x) = \sin x$ is an odd function.

Our next stage is to apply these results to each product of functions.

i) $\quad$ For $f(x) = x^2 \cos x$, $f(-x) = (-x)^2 \cos(-x)$

$$= x^2 \cos x$$

$\qquad$ i.e. $f(-x) = f(x)$.

x^2 and $\cos x$ are even functions. The function created by the product of these two functions is itself an even function.

ii) $\quad$ For $f(x) = x \sin x$, $f(-x) = (-x)\sin(-x)$

$$= (-x)(-\sin x)$$

$$= x \sin x$$

$\qquad$ i.e. $f(-x) = f(x)$.

x and $\sin x$ are odd functions. The function created by the product of these two functions is an even function.

iii) $\quad$ For $f(x) = \sin x . \cos x$, $f(-x) = \sin(-x).\cos(-x)$

$$= -\sin x . \cos x$$

$\qquad$ i.e. $f(-x) = -f(x)$.

$\sin x$ is an odd function and $\cos x$ is an even function. The function created by a product of these two functions is an odd function.

We can generalise the results of Examples 2.9. We apply the simple idea of the multiplication of $+/-$ signs.

$\qquad\qquad (+)(+) = + \qquad\qquad\qquad\qquad (-)(-) = +,$

i.e. the product of 2 like signs is a $+$.

$\qquad\qquad (-)(+) = - \qquad\qquad\qquad\qquad (+)(-) = -,$

i.e. the product of 2 unlike signs is a $-$.

In place of $+/-$ signs **we use even/odd functions**.

$$\textbf{(even)(even) = even} \qquad \textbf{(odd)(odd) = even,}$$

i.e. the product of 2 like functions is an even function.

$$\textbf{(odd)(even) = odd} \qquad \textbf{(even)(odd) = odd,}$$

i.e. the product of 2 unlike functions is an odd function.

Continuous and discontinuous functions

When the graph of a function is unbroken the function is continuous. The majority of functions are continuous.

Example 2.10

In Fig. 2.13 we show the continuous function $y = x^2 + 2$, or $f(x) = x^2 + 2$.

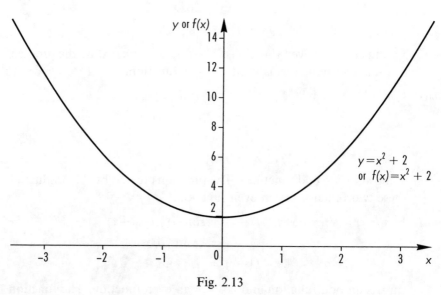

Fig. 2.13

When the graph of a function is broken the function is discontinuous.

Example 2.11

In Fig. 2.14 we show the discontinuous function $y = \dfrac{1}{x}$ or $f(x) = \dfrac{1}{x}$. It is discontinuous at $x = 0$. This is because at $x = 0$, the function implies y should be $\dfrac{1}{0}$ but $\dfrac{1}{0}$ is not defined in Mathematics.

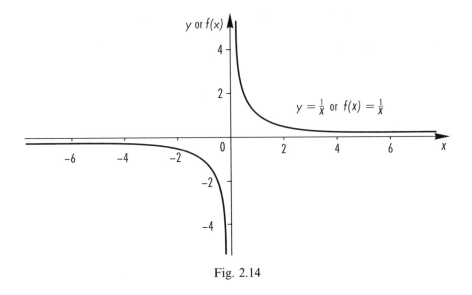

Fig. 2.14

◼ ASSIGNMENT ◼

We draw only some of the graphs here. You should also refer to Figs. 2.1 and 2.2. where both input graphs are continuous. In part 2 of Fig. 2.2 the fully rectified sine wave is also continuous.

Let us look more closely at the half rectified wave, drawn without the axes. Whether it is continuous or discontinuous depends upon how we draw it. In Fig. 2.15 we show it to be continuous. Its shape alternates between a horizontal line at zero and part of a sine wave.

Fig. 2.15

Alternatively in Fig. 2.16 we show it to be discontinuous. This is because we only draw the sections that are non-zero, i.e. part of a sine wave.

Fig. 2.16

▆▆▆▆ EXERCISE 2.4 ▆▆▆▆

Decide whether each function is continuous or discontinuous. If the function is discontinuous find a value of x where this occurs.

1 $y = \sin 2x$

2 $y = \cos \dfrac{x}{2}$

3 $y = \tan x$

4 $y = 5 \ln x$

5 $y = 3e^{2x}$

6 $xy = 4$

7 $y = 2 + \tan x$

8 $y = \frac{1}{2}(e^x + e^{-x})$

9 $y = \dfrac{6}{x-1}$

10 $y = \frac{1}{2}(e^x - e^{-x})$

Periodic functions

A function that repeats itself is a periodic function. The usual examples of periodic functions are sine and cosine waves. We have looked at the periodic nature of these trigonometrical graphs in Volume 2, Chapter 3. The next Examples are for some simple revision. They are based on the general equations $y = A \sin \omega x$ and $y = A \cos \omega x$, both with periods of $\dfrac{2\pi}{\omega}$.

▆▆▆▆ Examples 2.12 ▆▆▆▆

i) $y = 3 \sin x$ is a periodic function with $\omega = 1$. Its period is $\dfrac{2\pi}{1} = 2\pi$.

We look at some specimen values.

$$3 \sin \frac{\pi}{4} = 2.121$$

$$3 \sin \frac{9\pi}{4} = 2.121.$$

$$3 \sin \frac{17\pi}{4} = 2.121.$$

$$\frac{9\pi}{4} = \frac{\pi}{4} + 2\pi.$$

$$\frac{17\pi}{4} = \frac{\pi}{4} + 2(2\pi).$$

We will continue to get this pattern based on multiples of 2π, i.e. based on multiples of the period. Notice this pattern of repetition in Fig. 2.17.

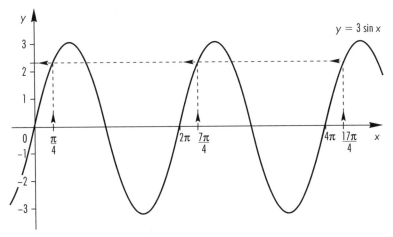

Fig. 2.17

ii) $y = 2.5\cos 2x$ is a periodic function with $\omega = 2$. Its period is $\dfrac{2\pi}{2} = \pi$.

We look at some specimen values.

$$2.5\cos\frac{2\pi}{6} = 1.25.$$

$$2.5\cos\frac{2(7\pi)}{6} = 1.25. \qquad \boxed{\begin{aligned}\frac{2(7\pi)}{6} &= 2\left(\frac{\pi}{6} + \pi\right).\end{aligned}}$$

$$2.5\cos\frac{2(13\pi)}{6} = 1.25. \qquad \boxed{\begin{aligned}\frac{2(13\pi)}{6} &= 2\left(\frac{\pi}{6} + 2(\pi)\right).\end{aligned}}$$

We will continue to get this pattern based on multiples of π, i.e. based on multiples of the period. Notice this pattern of repetition in Fig. 2.18.

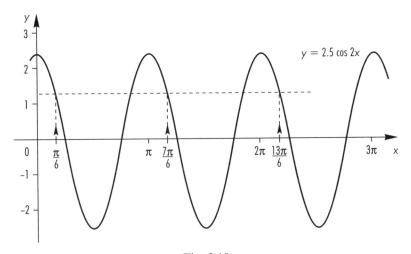

Fig. 2.18

We may write the periodic property in function notation. For some function, $f(x)$, with a period, ℓ, we have

$$f(x+\ell) = f(x).$$

ASSIGNMENT

We refer to our early diagrams in Figs. 2.1 and 2.2, and use function notation. For each graph you should choose a value of t. Note the corresponding value of $f(t)$ and its position on the graph. Check other positions differing by the period. Notice the pattern of repetition.

1   For the input graph we have $f(t) = \cos t$ which has a period of 2π.
We may write $f(t + 2\pi) = f(t)$.
For the output graph notice the period is again 2π. We may write $f(t + 2\pi) = f(t)$.

2   For the input graph we have $f(t) = \sin t$ which has a period of 2π.
We may write $f(t + 2\pi) = f(t)$.
For the output graph notice the period is π. This time we write $f(t + \pi) = f(t)$.

Notice, as for the output graphs, we do not need the definition of the function. You will find this is true in the next Exercise.

EXERCISE 2.5

1   Sketch a sine curve of period $\frac{1}{2}\pi$.
2   Sketch the graph of $y = \tan\theta$. What is the period of this graph?
3   A cosine function has a period of 4π. Write down its equation and sketch its curve.
4   Sketch the sine curve with amplitude 2 and period 4π.

In Questions 5–7 what are the periods of the functions?

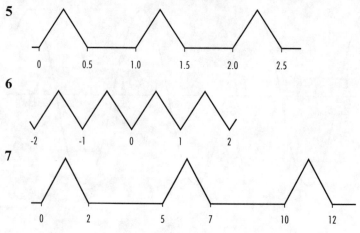

In Questions **8–10** the sketches are drawn to scale. In each case fully label the axes and state the period.

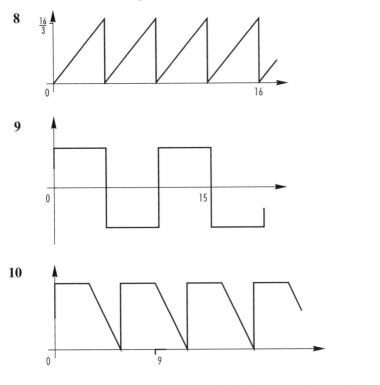

8

9

10

Inverse functions

We have met the idea of inverses with inverse matrices in both Volumes 1 and 2. In matrix notation we started with

$$AX = B$$

and multiplied throughout by the inverse of matrix A, A^{-1}, so that

$$A^{-1}AX = A^{-1}B$$

i.e. $IX = A^{-1}B$ | where $A^{-1}A = I$. |

i.e. $X = A^{-1}B$.

When we multiply a matrix by its inverse the result is the identity matrix, I. The identity matrix multiplied by any matrix leaves that matrix unchanged.

Now let us look at functions and their inverses. **For a function $f(x)$ the inverse function is $f^{-1}(x)$.**

Example 2.13

We sketch the graph of $y = x - 2$ in Fig. 2.19.

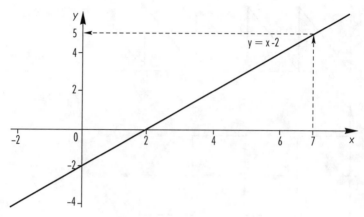

Fig. 2.19

This is a function because a value of x (e.g. $x = 7$) maps to only one value of y (i.e. $y = 5$). We move from the x-axis vertically to the graph, turn through $90°$ and move horizontally to reach the y-axis. The reverse of this process describes the inverse function. We start with one value of y (e.g. $y = 5$), move horizontally to reach the graph, turn through $90°$ and move vertically to reach the x-axis (i.e. at $x = 7$).

In Example 2.13 we start with the independent variable. The function maps this to the dependent variable and then the inverse function maps it back to the original, independent, variable. Now we look at the functional notation for $y = x - 2$. We write $f(x) = x - 2$, noticing the variable, x, is used consistently. For the inverse function we transpose $y = x - 2$ to make x the subject instead of y, i.e. $x = y + 2$. We could write $f(y) = y + 2$. However this is *not* consistent with our original, independent, variable x. Also it is not obvious that we have an inverse function. We replace y. Hence we write our original function as $f(x) = x - 2$ and its inverse function as $f^{-1}(x) = x + 2$.

We can combine the function and its inverse as a check. For $f(x) = x - 2$ we start with x, shown by x within $f(x)$. We finish with $x - 2$ on the right-hand side. For $f^{-1}f(x)$ we start with x, apply the function f (because it is next to x) and then apply the inverse function f^{-1}.

Then $f^{-1}f(x) = f^{-1}(x - 2)$ | x is processed into $x - 2$.

$\qquad\qquad = (x - 2) + 2$

$\qquad\qquad = x,$

i.e. by applying the original function to x and then its inverse function we return to x.

Alternatively we can look at $ff^{-1}(x)$.

Then $ff^{-1}(x) = f(x+2)$

$$= (x+2) - 2$$

$$= x,$$

| x is processed into $x+2$. |

i.e. by applying the inverse function to x and then the original function we return to x.

Notice the order of operations; $f^{-1}f$ and ff^{-1} have the same effect. In fact a function and its inverse are interchangeable. If we start with $f(x) = x+2$ then we would have $f^{-1}(x) = x-2$.

▮▮▮ Example 2.14 ▮▮▮

What is the inverse of the function $f(x) = \sqrt{x}$? Plot the function and its inverse on one set of axes.

You may spot immediately that the inverse function is $f(x) = x^2$. Alternatively suppose we write $y = \sqrt{x}$. To make x the subject we need to square throughout. It is the operation of squaring that tells us the inverse function is $f^{-1}(x) = x^2$. In Fig. 2.20 we have the two graphs labelled $y = \sqrt{x}$ and $y = x^2$ for the positive quadrant only. This ensures we avoid the one to many situation that is not functional. We have included the line $y = x$. Notice our curves are symmetrical about this line, i.e. if we reflect one of them in the line $y = x$ we create the other. Just as before each function is the inverse of the other, i.e. if we start with $f(x) = x^2$ then $f^{-1}(x) = \sqrt{x}$.

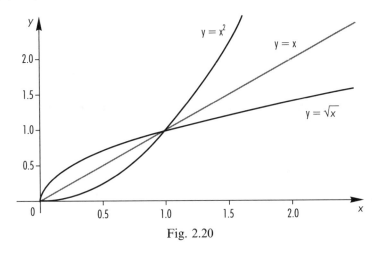

Fig. 2.20

Any function and its inverse are symmetrical about the line $y = x$. We can sketch the graph of an inverse function by reflecting the original function in the line $y = x$. Now look back at Example 2.13 and check this graphical condition for yourself.

■■■■■■ **Example 2.15** ■■■■■■

Here we look at $f(x) = e^x$ and its inverse function $f^{-1}(x) = \ln x$. In fact many calculators combine these functions using the <u>inv|</u> key.

We choose a specimen value for x, $x = 3$, so that

$$f^{-1}f(3) = f^{-1}\left(e^3\right) \qquad \text{or} \qquad ff^{-1}(3) = f(\ln 3)$$
$$= \ln\left(e^3\right) \qquad\qquad\qquad = e^{\ln 3}$$
$$= \ln(20.085537\ldots) \qquad\qquad = e^{1.0986\ldots}$$
$$= 3. \qquad\qquad\qquad\qquad = 3.$$

In Fig. 2.21 we sketch both graphs noticing their reflections in the line $y = x$. Also notice they cross the axes at $(1, 0)$ and $(0, 1)$, these coordinates being interchanged.

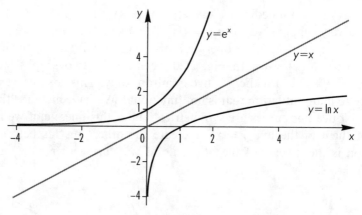

Fig. 2.21

■■■■■■ **EXERCISE 2.6** ■■■■■■

In each question work out the inverse function. Sketch the original function and reflect it in the line $y = x$. Make sure the reflection agrees with your inverse function.

1 $y = 3x$

2 $f(x) = \dfrac{x}{2}$

3 $f(x) = 2x + 1$

4 $f(x) = x$

5 $xy = 2$

6 $f(x) = x^3$

7 $y = 3\sqrt{x}$

8 $f(x) = \sqrt{3x}$

9 $y = 2x^{1/4}$

10 $y = \ln 2x$

Inverse trigonometric functions

We have several different types of notation. The inverse function of sine is $\sin^{-1} x$ or $\arcsin x$, i.e. the angle with a sine value of x.

If	$y = \sin^{-1} x$	or	if	$f(x) = \sin x$
then	$\sin y = x$.		then	$f^{-1}(x) = \sin^{-1} x$.

Linking together the inverse and original functions we get

$$f^{-1}f(x) = f^{-1}(\sin x)$$
$$= \sin^{-1}(\sin x)$$
$$= x.$$

Also we know how to create the graph of $\sin y = x$. We reflect the graph of $y = \sin x$ in the line $y = x$. In Fig. 2.22 we have done this, omitting $y = \sin x$ for clarity. As you can see the graph of $\sin y = x$ is *not* the graph of a function. This graph is many to one. In Example 2.16 we look at a numerical example.

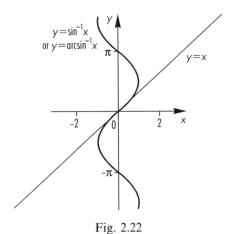

Fig. 2.22

Example 2.16

$\sin^{-1} 0.866\ldots$ = the angle with a sine value of $0.866\ldots$

$$= 60° \text{ or } \frac{\pi}{3} \text{ radians.}$$

This is a limited answer from the calculator. We know from trigonometry there are many angles with a sine value of $0.866\ldots$, e.g. $\ldots$, $-300°$, $-240°$, $60°$, $120°$, $420°$, $480°$, $\ldots$ This agrees with Fig. 2.22 but creates an ambiguity similar to the one in Example 2.5.

To overcome the one to many problem we restrict the graph of $f^{-1}(x) = \sin^{-1} x$. In Fig. 2.23 we show the inverse function restricted to the **principal values**. The range of **principal values** is $-\frac{\pi}{2} \leqslant \text{Sin}^{-1} x \leqslant \frac{\pi}{2}$. Strictly we write $y = \text{Sin}^{-1} x$ or $f^{-1}(x) = \text{Sin}^{-1} x$, the capital S emphasising the restriction. This is consistent with the restricted selection of calculator values.

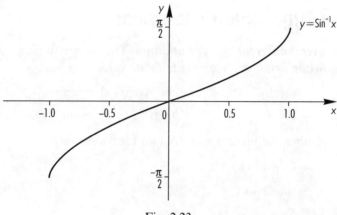

Fig. 2.23

Examples 2.17

i)   Using the calculator we find the principal value of $\sin^{-1} 0.7071$.

   0.7071| inv| sin| to display $45°$ or 0.785 radians.

ii) Using the calculator we find the principal value of $\sin^{-1}(-0.85)$.

   0.85| $^+/_-$| inv| sin| to display $-58.2°$ or -1.016 radians.

We can apply the same ideas to cosine. The inverse function of cosine is
$\cos^{-1}x$ or **arccos x**, i.e. the angle with a cosine value of x.

If $y = \cos^{-1} x$ or if $f(x) = \cos x$

then $\cos y = x$.   then $f^{-1}(x) = \cos^{-1} x$.

Linking together the inverse and original functions we get

$$f^{-1}f(x) = f^{-1}(\cos x)$$
$$= \cos^{-1}(\cos x)$$
$$= x.$$

We reflect the graph of $y = \cos x$
in the line $y = x$ to create
$\cos y = x$. In Fig. 2.24 we have
done this, omitting $y = \cos x$ for
clarity. As you can see the graph
of $\cos y = x$ is *not* the graph of a
function. This graph is many to
one. In Example 2.18 we look at
a numerical example.

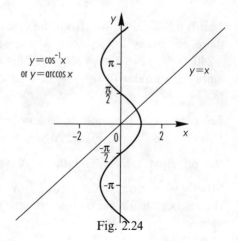

Fig. 2.24

Example 2.18

$\cos^{-1} 0.866\ldots = $ the angle with a cosine value of $0.866\ldots$

$$= 30° \text{ or } \frac{\pi}{6} \text{ radians.}$$

This is a limited answer from the calculator. We know from trigonometry there are many angles with a cosine value of $0.866\ldots$, e.g. $\ldots$, $-330°$, $-30°$, $30°$, $330°$, $\ldots$ This agrees with Fig. 2.24 but again creates an ambiguity.

To overcome the one to many problem we restrict the graph of $f^{-1}(x) = \cos^{-1} x$. In Fig. 2.25 we show the inverse function restricted to the **principal values**. The range of **principal values** is $0 \leqslant \text{Cos}^{-1} x \leqslant \pi$. Strictly we write $y = \text{Cos}^{-1} x$ or $f^{-1}(x) = \text{Cos}^{-1} x$, the capital C emphasising the restriction. This is consistent with the restricted selection of calculator values.

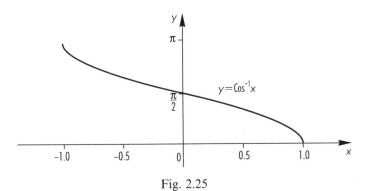

Fig. 2.25

Examples 2.19

i) Using the calculator we find the principal value of $\cos^{-1} 0.245$.

$\boxed{0.245}$ $\boxed{\text{inv}}$ $\boxed{\cos}$ to display $75.8°$ or 1.323 radians.

ii) Using the calculator we find the principal value of $\cos^{-1}(-0.77)$.

$\boxed{0.77}$ $\boxed{^{+}/_{-}}$ $\boxed{\text{inv}}$ $\boxed{\cos}$ to display $140.4°$ or 2.450 radians.

Finally we apply our ideas to tangent. The inverse function of tangent is $\tan^{-1} x$ or $\arctan x$, i.e. the angle with a tangent value of x.

If $y = \tan^{-1} x$ or   if $f(x) = \tan x$

then $\tan y = x$.   then $f^{-1}(x) = \tan^{-1} x$.

Linking together the inverse and original functions we get

$$f^{-1}f(x) = f^{-1}(\tan x)$$
$$= \tan^{-1}(\tan x)$$
$$= x.$$

We reflect the graph of $y = \tan x$ in the line $y = x$ to create $\tan y = x$. In Fig. 2.26 we have done this, omitting $y = \tan x$ for clarity. As you can see the graph of $\tan y = x$ is *not* the graph of a function. This graph is many to one. In Example 2.20 we look at a numerical example.

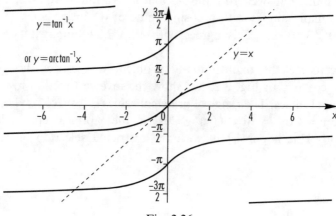

Fig. 2.26

$\tan^{-1} 1.00 =$ the angle with a tangent value of 1.00.

$$= 45° \text{ or } \frac{\pi}{4} \text{ radians.}$$

This is a limited answer from the calculator. We know from trigonometry there are many angles with a tangent value of 1.00, e.g. ..., $-315°$, $-135°$, $45°$, $225°$, ... This agrees with Fig. 2.26 but again creates an ambiguity.

To overcome the one to many problem we restrict the graph of $f^{-1}(x) = \tan^{-1} x$. In Fig. 2.27 we show the inverse function restricted to

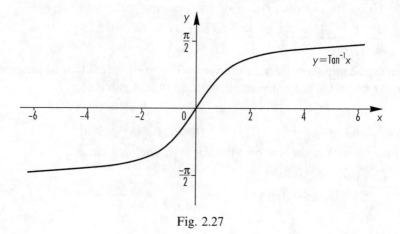

Fig. 2.27

the **principal values**. The range of **principal values** is $-\dfrac{\pi}{2} \leqslant \mathrm{Tan}^{-1}x \leqslant \dfrac{\pi}{2}$. Strictly we write $y = \mathrm{Tan}^{-1}x$ or $f^{-1}(x) = \mathrm{Tan}^{-1}x$, the capital T emphasising the restriction. This is consistent with the restricted selection of calculator values.

Examples 2.21

i)   Using the calculator we find the principal value of $\tan^{-1} 1.732$.

$\underline{1.732|}$ $\underline{\mathrm{inv}|}$ $\underline{\mathrm{tan}|}$ to display $60°$ or 1.047 radians.

ii) Using the calculator we find the principal value of $\tan^{-1}(-0.55)$.

$\underline{0.55|}$ $\underline{{}^{+}\!/\!{}_{-}|}$ $\underline{\mathrm{inv}|}$ $\underline{\mathrm{tan}|}$ to display $-28.8°$ or -0.503 radians.

Exactly the same ideas apply to the inverse functions of secant, cosecant and cotangent. Drawing the graphs of the inverse functions are left as an exercise for yourself.

ASSIGNMENT

We can look at the inverse trigonometric functions related to some of our Assignment graphs.

1   Our input is a cosine waveform (Fig. 2.1). In Fig. 2.25 we show the inverse waveform for the principal values.
    Our output graph (Fig. 2.1) is not a 1-1 function. Remember this means it *cannot* have an inverse function. We would need to restrict the output function (e.g. from 0 to $\pi/2$) to make it a 1-1 function. You should try this for yourself and draw the graph of the function and its inverse function.

2   Our input is a sine waveform (Fig. 2.2). In Fig. 2.23 we show the inverse waveform for the principal values.
    Again our output graph (Fig. 2.2) is not a 1-1 function. As an exercise for yourself restrict it so creating a 1-1 function. Reflect it in the line $y = x$ to get the graph of its inverse function.

EXERCISE 2.7

1   Find the principal angle with a sine of 0.95.
2   Find the principal angle with a cosine of -0.32.
3   Find the principal angle with a tangent of 1.65.
4   Find the principal angle, x, where $\sin x = -0.45$.
5   Find the principal angle, y, where $\sec y = 2.00$.

$$\sec y = \frac{1}{\cos y}.$$

6 Find the principal angle with a cosecant of 1.50.

7 Find the principal angle, z, where $\cot z = 0.75$.

8 Find the principal angle with a tangent of 1.33.

9 Find the principal angle, x, where $\cos x = 0.40$.

10 Find the principal angle with a secant of 1.25.

In Questions **11–20** find the principal angles for the inverse functions.

11	$\cos^{-1} 0.5$	**16**	$\sin^{-1} 0.625$
12	$\tan^{-1} 0.75$	**17**	$\tan^{-1} 1.5$
13	$\sin^{-1} 1$	**18**	$\operatorname{cosec}^{-1} 2$
14	$\cos^{-1}(-0.7)$	**19**	$\cot^{-1}(-2.5)$
15	$\sin^{-1}(-0.35)$	**20**	$\sec^{-1} 3.4$

Let us look at some more general trigonometric functions.

Example 2.22

In Fig. 2.28a we sketch the graph of $f(x) = \sin 3x$ in the range $-\dfrac{\pi}{2} \leqslant 3x \leqslant \dfrac{\pi}{2}$, i.e. $-\dfrac{\pi}{6} \leqslant x \leqslant \dfrac{\pi}{6}$. In Fig. 2.28b we reflect that graph in line $y = x$ to get the inverse function.f

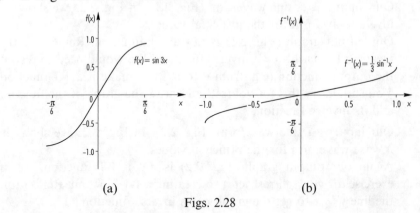

(a)   (b)

Figs. 2.28

Let us look at this algebraically with $y = \sin 3x$. We re-arrange this equation to make x the subject,

$$3x = \sin^{-1} y$$

i.e. $x = \dfrac{1}{3}\sin^{-1} y.$

For consistent notation, in terms of x, we now have $f(x) = \sin 3x$ and $f^{-1}(x) = \dfrac{1}{3}\sin^{-1} x.$

We can apply this technique to all functions and their inverses.

Example 2.23

In Fig. 2.29a we sketch the graph of $f(x) = 5 \cos \dfrac{x}{2}$ in the range $0 \leqslant \dfrac{x}{2} \leqslant \pi$, i.e. $0 \leqslant x \leqslant 2\pi$. In Fig. 2.29b we reflect that graph in line $y = x$ to get the inverse function.

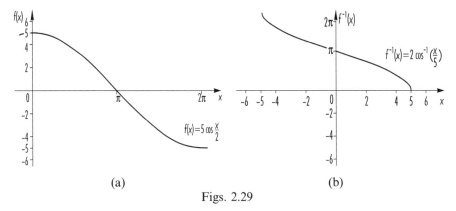

(a)   (b)

Figs. 2.29

Let us look at this algebraically with $y = 5 \cos \dfrac{x}{2}$. We re-arrange this equation to make x the subject,

$$\frac{y}{5} = \cos \frac{x}{2}$$

$$\frac{x}{2} = \cos^{-1}\left(\frac{y}{5}\right)$$

i.e. $x = 2 \cos^{-1}\left(\dfrac{y}{5}\right).$

For consistent notation, in terms of x, we now have $f(x) = 5 \cos \dfrac{x}{2}$ and

$$f^{-1}(x) = 2 \cos^{-1}\left(\frac{x}{5}\right).$$

EXERCISE 2.8

For each Question
- i)   sketch the graph of the function,
- ii) draw the line $y = x$,
- iii) reflect the function in the line $y = x$,
- iv) show the inverse function for the range of principal values,
- v)   in functional notation write down the equation of the inverse function.

1 $f(x) = \sin 2x$

2 $f(x) = \cos 4x$

3 $f(x) = \tan 3x$

4 $f(x) = 2 \sin 3x$

5 $f(x) = 4 \cos 2x$

6 $f(x) = \dfrac{1}{2} \sin 2x$

7 $f(x) = \sin\dfrac{x}{2}$ | **9** $f(x) = \tan\dfrac{3}{2}x$

8 $f(x) = 4\sin\dfrac{x}{2}$ | **10** $f(x) = 4\cos\dfrac{2}{3}x$

Differentiation of inverse trigonometric functions

In Volume 1, Chapter 18, we defined $\dfrac{dy}{dx}$ as

$$\frac{dy}{dx} = \operatorname*{Lim}_{\delta x \to 0} \frac{\delta y}{\delta x}.$$

Similarly we can define $\dfrac{dx}{dy}$ as

$$\frac{dx}{dy} = \operatorname*{Lim}_{\delta y \to 0} \frac{\delta x}{\delta y}.$$

Linking together these definitions we have

$$\frac{dy}{dx} = \frac{1}{\dfrac{dx}{dy}}.$$

We use this relationship in each of our differentiation techniques.

We may re-write $\quad y = \sin^{-1} ax$

as $\qquad\qquad ax = \sin y$

i.e. $\qquad\qquad x = \dfrac{1}{a}\sin y.$

Differentiating with respect to y we get

$$\frac{dx}{dy} = \frac{1}{a}\cos y.$$

Using $\qquad \dfrac{dy}{dx} = \dfrac{1}{\dfrac{dx}{dy}}$

we get $\qquad \dfrac{dy}{dx} = \dfrac{1}{\dfrac{1}{a}\cos y} = \dfrac{a}{\cos y}$

i.e. $\qquad \dfrac{dy}{dx} = \dfrac{a}{\pm\sqrt{1 - \sin^2 y}}$

$\boxed{\begin{array}{l} \sin^2 y + \cos^2 y = 1, \\ \cos^2 y = 1 - \sin^2 y. \end{array}}$

i.e. $\qquad \dfrac{dy}{dx} = \dfrac{a}{\sqrt{1 - a^2 x^2}}.$

$\boxed{\begin{array}{l} \text{Substituting} \quad \sin y = ax \\ \qquad \text{i.e.} \qquad \sin^2 y = a^2 x^2. \end{array}}$

Notice we use only the positive square root. For the principal values only we sketched $y = \mathrm{Sin}^{-1}x$ in Fig. 2.23. For this curve the gradient is never negative.

Examples 2.24

Find $\dfrac{dy}{dx}$ for i) $y = \sin^{-1} 3x$, ii) $y = \sin^{-1}\dfrac{x}{2}$, iii) $y = 4\sin^{-1}\dfrac{3}{2}x$.

In each case we relate our equation to $y = \sin^{-1} ax$ and then apply $\dfrac{dy}{dx} = \dfrac{a}{\sqrt{1 - a^2 x^2}}$.

i) For $y = \sin^{-1} 3x$ we have $a = 3$ so that

$$\frac{dy}{dx} = \frac{3}{\sqrt{1 - 3^2 x^2}} = \frac{3}{\sqrt{1 - 9x^2}}.$$

ii) For $y = \sin^{-1}\dfrac{x}{2}$ we have $a = \dfrac{1}{2} = 0.5$ so that

$$\frac{dy}{dx} = \frac{0.5}{\sqrt{1 - 0.5^2 x^2}} = \frac{0.5}{\sqrt{1 - 0.25x^2}}.$$

iii) For $y = 4\sin^{-1}\dfrac{3}{2}x$ we have $a = \dfrac{3}{2} = 1.5$ so that

$$\frac{dy}{dx} = 4 \times \frac{1.5}{\sqrt{1 - 1.5^2 x^2}} = \frac{6}{\sqrt{1 - 2.25x^2}}.$$

Now we repeat the technique for inverse cosine and inverse tangent and their examples.

We may re-write $\quad y = \cos^{-1} ax$

as $\qquad ax = \cos y$

i.e. $\qquad x = \dfrac{1}{a}\cos y.$

Differentiating with respect to y we get

$$\frac{dx}{dy} = -\frac{1}{a}\sin y.$$

Using $\qquad \dfrac{dy}{dx} = \dfrac{1}{\dfrac{dx}{dy}}$

we get $\qquad \dfrac{dy}{dx} = \dfrac{1}{-\dfrac{1}{a}\sin y} = -\dfrac{a}{\sin y}$

i.e. $\qquad \dfrac{dy}{dx} = -\dfrac{a}{\pm\sqrt{1 - \cos^2 y}}$

i.e. $\qquad \dfrac{dy}{dx} = -\dfrac{a}{\sqrt{1 - a^2 x^2}}.$

$$\sin^2 y + \cos^2 y = 1,$$
$$\sin^2 y = 1 - \cos^2 y.$$

Substituting $\quad \cos y = ax$

i.e. $\qquad \cos^2 y = a^2 x^2.$

Notice we use only the answer. For the principal values only we sketched $y = \text{Cos}^{-1}x$ in Fig. 2.25. For this curve the gradient is never positive.

Example 2.25

Find $\dfrac{dy}{dx}$ for $y = 5\cos^{-1} 4x$.

We relate our equation to $y = \cos^{-1} ax$ and then apply
$$\frac{dy}{dx} = -\frac{a}{\sqrt{1 - a^2x^2}}.$$
For $y = 5\cos^{-1} 4x$ we have $a = 4$ so that
$$\frac{dy}{dx} = 5 \times -\frac{4}{\sqrt{1 - 4^2x^2}} = -\frac{20}{\sqrt{1 - 16x^2}}.$$

We may re-write $\quad y = \tan^{-1} ax$

as $\qquad ax = \tan y$

i.e. $\qquad x = \dfrac{1}{a}\tan y.$

Differentiating with respect to y we get
$$\frac{dx}{dy} = \frac{1}{a}\sec^2 y.$$

Using $\qquad\qquad \dfrac{dy}{dx} = \dfrac{1}{\dfrac{dx}{dy}}$

we get $\qquad\qquad \dfrac{dy}{dx} = \dfrac{1}{\dfrac{1}{a}\sec^2 y} = \dfrac{a}{\sec^2 y}$

i.e. $\qquad\qquad \dfrac{dy}{dx} = \dfrac{a}{1 + \tan^2 y}$ $\qquad\boxed{\sec^2 y = 1 + \tan^2 y.}$

i.e. $\qquad\qquad \dfrac{dy}{dx} = \dfrac{a}{1 + a^2x^2}.$ $\qquad\boxed{\text{Substituting for } \tan^2 y.}$

Example 2.26

Find the value of the gradient to the curve $y = 3\tan^{-1}\dfrac{x}{2}$ at the points where $x = -0.8$ and 0.8.

We relate our equation to $y = \tan^{-1} ax$ and then apply $\dfrac{dy}{dx} = \dfrac{a}{1 + a^2x^2}.$

For $y = 3\tan^{-1}\dfrac{x}{2}$ we have $a = \dfrac{1}{2} = 0.5$ so that
$$\frac{dy}{dx} = 3 \times \frac{0.5}{1 + 0.5^2x^2} = \frac{1.5}{1 + 0.25x^2}.$$

We substitute our values for x into this general expression.

At $x = -0.8$, $\dfrac{dy}{dx} = \dfrac{1.5}{1 + 0.25(-0.8)^2} = 1.29.$

At $x = 0.8$, $\dfrac{dy}{dx} = \dfrac{1.5}{1 + 0.25(0.8)^2} = 1.29.$

It is no surprise to see that these answers are the same. We have squared both -0.8 and 0.8 to get the positive value 0.64. Also you can check the curve and its general curvature in Fig. 2.27.

We summarise these differentiation results.

$$y = \sin^{-1} ax, \qquad\qquad y = \cos^{-1} ax, \qquad\qquad y = \tan^{-1} ax,$$

$$\frac{dy}{dx} = \frac{a}{\sqrt{1 - a^2 x^2}}. \qquad \frac{dy}{dx} = -\frac{a}{\sqrt{1 - a^2 x^2}}. \qquad \frac{dy}{dx} = \frac{a}{1 + a^2 x^2}.$$

◼️ EXERCISE 2.9 ◼️

In Questions **1–10** find a general expression for $\dfrac{dy}{dx}$.

1 $y = \sin^{-1} 2x$

2 $y = \cos^{-1} 3x$

3 $y = \tan^{-1} \dfrac{x}{3}$

4 $y = \sin^{-1} \dfrac{x}{4}$

5 $y = 2 \sin^{-1} \dfrac{x}{4}$

6 $y = 2 \cos^{-1} \dfrac{x}{4}$

7 $y = 3 \tan^{-1} 2x$

8 $y = \dfrac{1}{4} \sin^{-1} 2x$

9 $y = 3 \cos^{-1} \dfrac{5}{4} x$

10 $y = 5 \sin^{-1} \dfrac{3}{4} x$

11 Find the value of $\dfrac{dy}{dx}$ to the curve $y = 2.5 \sin^{-1} 2x$ at the point where $x = 0.25$.

12 At the point where $x = 0.75$ on the curve $y = \sin^{-1} \dfrac{x}{2}$ find the value of $\dfrac{dy}{dx}$.

13 For the curve $y = 2 \cos^{-1} \dfrac{x}{5}$ find the values of the gradient at $x = -2$ and $x = 2$.

14 Given $y = \dfrac{1}{3} \sin^{-1} x$ what is the value of $\dfrac{dy}{dx}$ at $x = -0.5$?

15 You are given the inverse tangent curve, $y = 2 \tan^{-1} x$. At the points where $y = -\dfrac{\pi}{4}$ and $\dfrac{\pi}{4}$ find the values of x and the gradients of the curve.

We look at some slightly more complicated examples for which we could produce a list of formulae. The list may be too long and *not* particularly worthwhile. As a direct alternative we return to our basic differentiation technique.

Example 2.27

For the curve $y = 2\operatorname{cosec}^{-1} 5x$ find a general expression for the gradient. What is its value at the point $\left(0.4, \dfrac{\pi}{3}\right)$?

We re-write $y = 2\operatorname{cosec}^{-1} 5x$

as $\dfrac{y}{2} = \operatorname{cosec}^{-1} 5x$

so that $5x = \operatorname{cosec}\dfrac{y}{2} = \dfrac{1}{\sin\dfrac{y}{2}}$

$$\boxed{\operatorname{cosec}\theta = \dfrac{1}{\sin\theta}.}$$

i.e. $5x = \left(\sin\dfrac{y}{2}\right)^{-1}$

$x = 0.2\left(\sin\dfrac{y}{2}\right)^{-1}.$

We apply the function of a function rule. Differentiating with respect to y we get

$$\frac{dx}{dy} = 0.2(-1)\left(\frac{1}{2}\right)\cos\frac{y}{2}\left(\sin\frac{y}{2}\right)^{-2} = \frac{-0.1\cos\dfrac{y}{2}}{\sin^2\dfrac{y}{2}}.$$

Using $\dfrac{dy}{dx} = \dfrac{1}{\dfrac{dx}{dy}}$

we get $\dfrac{dy}{dx} = \dfrac{-10\sin^2\dfrac{y}{2}}{\cos\dfrac{y}{2}}.$

Into this general expression for the gradient we substitute for $y = \dfrac{\pi}{3}$ so that

$$\frac{dy}{dx} = \frac{-10\sin^2\dfrac{\pi}{6}}{\cos\dfrac{\pi}{6}} = \frac{-10 \times 0.5^2}{0.866} = -2.89.$$

Example 2.28

At the point $\left(0.5, \dfrac{\pi}{4}\right)$ on the curve $y = \cos^{-1}\sqrt{x}$ find the value of the gradient.

We re-write $y = \cos^{-1}\sqrt{x}$

as $\sqrt{x} = \cos y.$

Squaring both sides of this equation gives

$$x = \cos^2 y.$$

Differentiating with respect to y we get

$$\frac{dx}{dy} = -2\sin y.\cos y.$$

Using $\quad \dfrac{dy}{dx} = \dfrac{1}{\dfrac{dx}{dy}}$

we get $\quad \dfrac{dy}{dx} = \dfrac{1}{-2\sin y.\cos y}$

$$= \frac{1}{-2\sqrt{1-\cos^2 y}.\cos y}$$

$$\boxed{\begin{array}{l}\sin^2 y + \cos^2 y = 1,\\[4pt]\sin^2 y = 1 - \cos^2 y.\end{array}}$$

$$= -\frac{1}{2\sqrt{1-x}\sqrt{x}}$$

$$\boxed{\begin{array}{l}\text{Substituting for}\\[4pt]\cos y = \sqrt{x}.\end{array}}$$

$$= -\frac{1}{2\sqrt{x-x^2}}.$$

Into this general expression for the gradient we substitute for $x = 0.5$ so that

$$\frac{dy}{dx} = -\frac{1}{2\sqrt{0.5 - 0.5^2}}$$

$$= -\frac{1}{2\sqrt{0.25}}$$

$$= -1.$$

EXERCISE 2.10

In Questions **1–5** find a general expression for $\dfrac{dy}{dx}$.

1 $\quad y = \sec^{-1} 2x$

2 $\quad y = \sin^{-1}\dfrac{1}{x}$

3 $\quad y = 3\sin^{-1}\sqrt{x}$

4 $\quad y = 5\operatorname{cosec}^{-1}2x$

5 $\quad y = \cos^{-1}\dfrac{2}{x}$

6 For $y = 2\sec^{-1} x$ find the value of $\dfrac{dy}{dx}$ at the point where $x = 2$.

7 Find the gradient to the curve $y = \operatorname{cosec}^{-1}3x$ where $y = \dfrac{\pi}{3}$ radians.

8   Given $y = \cot^{-1} 2x$ what is the value of $\dfrac{dy}{dx}$ at $x = 0.25$?

9   Find the value of $\dfrac{dy}{dx}$ at the point where $y = 0.5$ radians on the curve $y = 2\sin^{-1}\dfrac{3}{x}$.

10   What are the coordinates on the curve $y = \sin^{-1}\sqrt{3x}$ where the gradient is 10.5?

Practical applications

We work through Example 2.29 involving an inverse trigonometric function. Afterwards there is a short Exercise for you to complete the chapter.

Example 2.29

In simple harmonic motion, S.H.M., the time of motion, t, can be related to the displacement, x, by $t = \dfrac{1}{n}\cos^{-1}\left(\dfrac{x}{A}\right)$. A is the amplitude of the motion and n is a constant. $T = \dfrac{2\pi}{n}$ is the time period for one complete oscillation. Find a general expression showing how time changes in relation to displacement. For a time period of 8 seconds and an amplitude of 2.50 metres find the value of $\dfrac{dt}{dx}$ where $x = 1.75$ metres.

We relate our equation to the general $y = \cos^{-1} ax$ and then apply $\dfrac{dy}{dx} = -\dfrac{a}{\sqrt{1 - a^2 x^2}}$. In place of ax we have $\dfrac{x}{A}$, i.e. $a = \dfrac{1}{A}$. $\dfrac{1}{n}$ is a multiplying factor.

This means

$$\frac{dt}{dx} = \frac{1}{n} \times -\frac{1/A}{\sqrt{1 - \dfrac{x^2}{A^2}}}$$

$$= -\frac{1}{nA\sqrt{1 - \dfrac{x^2}{A^2}}}$$

is the general expression for the change in time due to a change in displacement.

We need to find n and so substitute for $T = 8$ in

$$T = \frac{2\pi}{n}$$

i.e.

$$n = \frac{2\pi}{8} = \frac{\pi}{4}.$$

Using $n = \dfrac{\pi}{4}$, $A = 2.50$ and $x = 1.75$ we substitute into our expression for $\dfrac{dt}{dx}$,

i.e.
$$\frac{dt}{dx} = -\frac{1}{\dfrac{\pi}{4} \times 2.50\sqrt{1 - \dfrac{1.75^2}{2.50^2}}}$$

$$= -\frac{1}{1.963\ldots\sqrt{1 - 0.49}}$$

$$= -\frac{1}{1.963\ldots\sqrt{0.51}}$$

$$= -\frac{1}{1.963\ldots \times 0.714\ldots}$$

$$= -0.71 \text{ sm}^{-1}.$$

EXERCISE 2.11

1

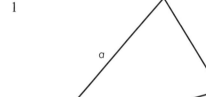

The formula for the area of a triangle, A, is given by

$$A = \frac{1}{2}ab\sin\theta.$$

For a particular isosceles triangle $a = b = 0.20$ m. Re-arrange this equation to make θ the subject. Find a general expression to show how the angle, θ, varies for different A. What is the value of $\dfrac{d\theta}{dA}$ where $A = 0.018$ m^2?

2   In computer simulation a vehicle is attempting to go around a track banked at an angle θ to the horizontal. Its path is an arc of a circle of radius r. g is the acceleration due to gravity. Where there is no tendency to side slip the velocity of the vehicle, v, is $v = \sqrt{gr\tan\theta}$. Make θ the subject of this formula and simplify it for $g = 9.81$ ms^{-2} and $r = 120$ m. The software design is concentrating upon varying v and θ. Find the value of $\dfrac{d\theta}{dv}$ for $v = 14.5$ ms^{-1}?

3   In an a.c. circuit the voltage, V, is related to time, t, by $V = V_{max}\sin\omega t$. $V_{max} = 250$ V and the frequency, f, is 50 Hz where $f = \dfrac{\omega}{2\pi}$. Substitute for V_{max} and ω in the original equation. Re-arrange that equation to make t the subject and see how t varies according to V when the voltage is 225 V.

4   A non-right-angled triangle has sides x, y and z. The angle θ is opposite side x. The cosine rule links them together according to $x^2 = y^2 + z^2 - 2yz\cos\theta$. For $y = 0.10$ m and $z = 0.20$ m show that $\theta = \cos^{-1}(1.25 - 25x^2)$. Find a general expression for $\dfrac{d\theta}{dx}$ and its value where $x = 0.15$ m.

5   During the parabolic flight of a ground to air missile we have $\theta = \sin^{-1}\left(\dfrac{gt}{2v}\right)$ and $\theta = \dfrac{1}{2}\sin^{-1}\left(\dfrac{gR}{v^2}\right)$. θ is the angle of projection to the horizontal, g is the acceleration due to gravity, t is the time from projection and v is the velocity of projection. R is the horizontal range. Investigate how θ varies over time. Also find a general expression for $\dfrac{d\theta}{dR}$ for different ranges.

3 Hyperbolic Functions

The objectives of this chapter are to:

1 Define $\cosh x$ and $\sinh x$ in terms of e^x and e^{-x}.

2 Define $\tanh x$ in terms of $\sinh x$ and $\cosh x$.

3 Using a calculator find values of $\sinh x$, $\cosh x$ and $\tanh x$.

4 Sketch the graphs of $\sinh x$, $\cosh x$ and $\tanh x$.

5 Define the reciprocal functions, $\operatorname{sech} x$, $\operatorname{cosech} x$ and $\coth x$.

6 Sketch the graphs of the reciprocal functions.

7 Prove and verify simple hyperbolic identities.

8 State Osborn's rule and use it to translate between hyperbolic and trigonometric identities.

9 Relate hyperbolic and trigonometric functions through exponential forms.

10 Differentiate hyperbolic functions.

11 Integrate hyperbolic functions.

12 Define inverse hyperbolic functions.

13 Deduce the graph of the inverse function from its hyperbolic function.

14 Understand there are logarithmic forms of the inverse hyperbolic functions.

Introduction

We define the hyperbolic functions in two stages using exponential functions. Later we link them with trigonometry and complex numbers. We show direct comparisons with trigonometry through Osborn's rule. Finally we involve calculus; both differentiating and integrating hyperbolic functions.

The trigonometric functions are linked to a circle. A similar link can be made between the hyperbolic functions and a hyperbola. Here we concentrate upon our definitions in terms of exponential functions.

■■■■ ASSIGNMENT ■■■■

Our Assignment for this chapter looks at a catenary cable. We have a uniform cable suspended between two points along the same horizontal line, Fig. 3.1. The system is symmetrical about a vertical line through the mid-point of the cable. Later we shall discuss the tension in the cable, the span and the sag of the cable.

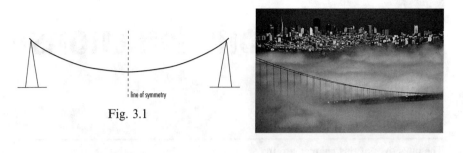

Fig. 3.1

Hyperbolic functions

We write the **hyperbolic sine** as **sinh** and say 'shine'. The **hyperbolic cosine** is **cosh** (said 'cosh') and the **hyperbolic tangent** is **tanh** (said 'thann'). Notice the h for each function to indicate 'hyperbolic' with the sin, cos and tan from trigonometry.

Using a calculator we can find the values of these hyperbolic functions. The hyperbolic key is hyp|.

Examples 3.1

We find values of i) $\sinh 2.5$, ii) $\cosh(-3.75)$, iii) $3 \tanh 0.6$.

i) For $\sinh 2.5$ we use

2.5| hyp| sin| to display 6.05 (2 decimal places).

ii) For $\cosh(-3.75)$ we use

3.75| ⁺⁄₋| hyp| cos| to display 21.27 (2 dp).

iii) For $3 \tanh 0.6$ we use

0.6| hyp| tan| ×| 3| =| to display 1.61 (2 dp).

ASSIGNMENT

We look in more detail at our cable. In Fig. 3.2 we refer a pair of axes to the origin, O, at the lowest point of the cable.

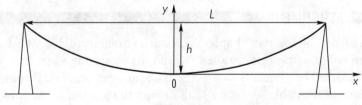

Fig. 3.2

L is the span of the cable between the two points along the same horizontal line. *h* is the sag of the cable, i.e. the greatest distance of the cable below that horizontal line. The equation of the cable is

$$y = \frac{T_0}{w}\left(\cosh\frac{wx}{T_0} - 1\right).$$

x is the horizontal distance from the centre position, O.

y is the vertical distance from the centre position, O.

w is the weight/unit length (Nm^{-1}),

T_0 is the tension in the cable at the origin.

This equation of the curve (a catenary) assumes the cable is hanging under the action of only its weight. In this case we have a maximum value for T_0 of 25 kN and a mass per metre of 10 kg. If the cable spans 400 m (i.e. $L = 400$ m so that $x = 200$ m) we can calculate the sag, *y*.

Using $y = \dfrac{T_0}{w}\left(\cosh\dfrac{wx}{T_0} - 1\right)$

we substitute to get

$$y = \frac{25 \times 10^3}{10 \times 9.81}\left(\cosh\left(\frac{10 \times 9.81 \times 200}{25 \times 10^3}\right) - 1\right)$$

$$= 254.842(\cosh 0.7848 - 1)$$

$$= 254.842(1.324\ldots - 1)$$

$$= 82.6 \text{ m, i.e. the sag of the cable.}$$

We can use the calculator to find the inverse hyperbolic function. The keys are inv| hyp|.

Examples 3.2

Find the values of *x* where i) $\sinh x = 1.52$, ii) $\cosh x = 4.66$, iii) $\tanh x = -0.75$.

i) $\sinh x = 1.52$ may be written as $x = \sinh^{-1} 1.52$ or $x = \text{arcsinh}\, 1.52$. Both $\sinh^{-1}$ and arcsinh represent the inverse hyperbolic function. We use

   1.52| inv| hyp| sin| to display 1.21 (2 dp).

   Then $x = 1.21$ or $\sinh 1.21 = 1.52$.

ii) $\cosh x = 4.66$ may be written as $x = \cosh^{-1} 4.66$ or $x = \text{arccosh}\, 4.66$. Both $\cosh^{-1}$ and arccosh represent the inverse hyperbolic function. We use

   4.66| inv| hyp| cos| to display 2.22 (2 dp).

   Then $x = 2.22$ or $\cosh 2.22 = 4.66$.

iii) $\tanh x = -0.75$ may be written as $x = \tanh^{-1}(-0.75)$ or $x = \text{arctanh}\,(-0.75)$. Both $\tanh^{-1}$ and arctanh represent the inverse hyperbolic function. We use

$\boxed{0.75}\ \boxed{+/-}\ \boxed{\text{inv}}\ \boxed{\text{hyp}}\ \boxed{\text{tan}}$ to display -0.97 (2 dp).

Then $x = -0.97$ or $\tanh(-0.97) = -0.75$.

■ ASSIGNMENT ■

We look again at our cable using its equation

$$y = \frac{T_0}{W}\left(\cosh\frac{wx}{T_0} - 1\right).$$

Again we have a maximum value for T_0 of 25 kN and a mass per metre of 10 kg. Here we wish to find the greatest possible span for a sag of 75 m.

Using $y = \dfrac{T_0}{W}\left(\cosh\dfrac{wx}{T_0} - 1\right).$

we substitute to get

$$75 = \frac{25 \times 10^3}{10 \times 9.81}\left(\cosh\left(\frac{10 \times 9.81x}{25 \times 10^3}\right) - 1\right)$$

$$0.2943 = \cosh\left(\frac{10 \times 9.81x}{25 \times 10^3}\right) - 1$$

$$1.2943 = \cosh\left(\frac{10 \times 9.81x}{25 \times 10^3}\right)$$

i.e. $\dfrac{10 \times 9.81x}{25 \times 10^3} = 0.7495\ldots$

$$x = 191 \text{ m}.$$

Because $L = 2x$ we have a span of 382 m.

■ EXERCISE 3.1 ■

Find the values of the hyperbolic functions.

1   $\sinh 2$

2   $\tanh 1.5$

3   $\cosh 0.5$

4   $\cosh(-0.5)$

5   $\sinh(-2)$

6   $\sinh 4.5$

7   $\tanh(-1.5)$

8   $2\tanh 2.5$

9   $1.5\cosh 0.75$

10   $-3\sinh 1.35$

Find the values of the inverse hyperbolic functions.

11   $\sinh^{-1} 1.5$

12   $\cosh^{-1} 1.3$

13   $\cosh^{-1} 2.6$

14   $\sinh^{-1} 3.6$

15 $\tanh^{-1} 0.475$ **18** $\tanh^{-1} 0.125$

16 $\tanh^{-1} 0.25$ **19** $\tanh^{-1} (-0.475)$

17 $\sinh^{-1} (-1.5)$ **20** $\cosh^{-1} 1$

We define the **hyperbolic sine, sinh x,** as

$$\sinh x = \frac{1}{2}(e^x - e^{-x}).$$

We define the **hyperbolic cosine, cosh x,** as

$$\cosh x = \frac{1}{2}(e^x + e^{-x}).$$

We define the **hyperbolic tangent, tanh x,** as

$$\tanh x = \frac{\sinh x}{\cosh x} = \frac{\frac{1}{2}(e^x - e^{-x})}{\frac{1}{2}(e^x + e^{-x})} = \frac{e^x - e^{-x}}{e^x + e^{-x}}.$$

We could use these definitions where a calculator has no hyperbolic functions key. In Example 3.3 we show the technique for completeness only.

Example 3.3

We find the value of $\sinh 2.5$ using $\sinh x = \frac{1}{2}(e^x - e^{-x})$ with $x = 2.5$.

$$\begin{aligned}
\text{Now} \quad \sinh 2.5 &= \frac{1}{2}\left(e^{2.5} - e^{-2.5}\right) \\
&= \frac{1}{2}(12.182\ldots - 0.082\ldots) \\
&= \frac{1}{2} \times 12.100\ldots \\
&= 6.05 \text{ (2 dp), confirming our answer to Example 3.1i)}
\end{aligned}$$

Later we shall see the inverse hyperbolic function in natural logarithmic terms.

We have series for both e^x and e^{-x} (Volume 2, Chapter 6). It is easy to apply them to our hyperbolic cosine and hyperbolic sine definitions. For the hyperbolic tangent the algebra becomes less easy and is omitted.

$$\text{Now} \quad e^x = 1 + x + \frac{x^2}{2!} + \frac{x^3}{3!} + \frac{x^4}{4!} + \frac{x^5}{5!} \ldots$$

$$\text{and} \quad e^{-x} = 1 - x + \frac{x^2}{2!} - \frac{x^3}{3!} + \frac{x^4}{4!} - \frac{x^5}{5!} \ldots$$

When we add the series alternate terms, in odd powers of x, cancel out to give

$$e^x + e^{-x} = 2 + 2\frac{x^2}{2!} + 2\frac{x^4}{4!} \cdots$$

$$\therefore \quad \frac{1}{2}(e^x + e^{-x}) = \frac{1}{2} \times 2\left(1 + \frac{x^2}{2!} + \frac{x^4}{4!} \cdots\right) \qquad \boxed{\text{Common factor of 2.}}$$

i.e. $\qquad \cosh x = 1 + \dfrac{x^2}{2!} + \dfrac{x^4}{4!} \cdots$

After the first term the powers of x are even. $\cosh x$ is an even function, i.e. $\cosh x = \cosh(-x)$. We shall see this when we sketch the graph of $y = \cosh x$. In Exercise 3.1, Questions **3** and **4** show this even function relationship.

When we subtract the series alternate terms, in even powers of x, cancel out to give

$$e^x - e^{-x} = 2x + 2\frac{x^3}{3!} + 2\frac{x^5}{5!} \cdots$$

$$\therefore \quad \frac{1}{2}(e^x - e^{-x}) = \frac{1}{2} \times 2\left(x + \frac{x^3}{3!} + \frac{x^5}{5!} \cdots\right) \qquad \boxed{\text{Common factor of 2.}}$$

i.e. $\qquad \sinh x = x + \dfrac{x^3}{3!} + \dfrac{x^5}{5!} \cdots$

The series terms have odd powers of x. $\sinh x$ is an odd function, i.e. $\sinh(-x) = -\sinh x$. We shall see this when we sketch the graph of $y = \sinh x$. In Exercise 3.1, Questions **1** and **5** show this odd function relationship.

Now $\tanh x = \dfrac{\sinh x}{\cosh x}$ is created from the division of an odd function by an even function. $\tanh x$ is also an odd function, i.e. $\tanh(-x) = -\tanh x$. We saw this in Exercise 3.1 Questions **2** and **7**.

So far we have concentrated on a simple x in our discussions. We may generalise our definitions to

$$\cosh ax = \frac{1}{2}(e^{ax} + e^{-ax}) = 1 + \frac{(ax)^2}{2!} + \frac{(ax)^4}{4!} \cdots,$$

$$\sinh ax = \frac{1}{2}(e^{ax} - e^{-ax}) = ax + \frac{(ax)^3}{3!} + \frac{(ax)^5}{5!} \cdots,$$

$$\tanh ax = \frac{\sinh ax}{\cosh ax} = \frac{e^{ax} - e^{-ax}}{e^{ax} + e^{-ax}}.$$

We can use our definitions to sketch the graphs of the hyperbolic functions. In Fig. 3.3 we sketch $y = e^x$, $y = e^{-x}$ and $y = e^x + e^{-x}$. We multiply the third curve by $\frac{1}{2}$ (or divide by 2) to get $y = \cosh x$, i.e. $y = \frac{1}{2}(e^x + e^{-x})$ (Fig. 3.5a).

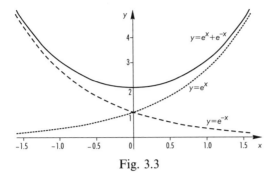

Fig. 3.3

In Fig. 3.4 we sketch $y = e^x$, $y = e^{-x}$ and $y = e^x - e^{-x}$. We multiply the third curve by $\frac{1}{2}$ (or divide by 2) to get $y = \sinh x$, i.e. $y = \frac{1}{2}(e^x - e^{-x})$ (Fig. 3.5b).

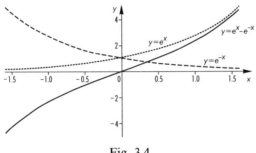

Fig. 3.4

For clarity we show the graphs of $y = \cosh x$ and $y = \sinh x$ separately in Figs. 3.5. Apply the graphical tests for odd and even functions for yourself as a check.

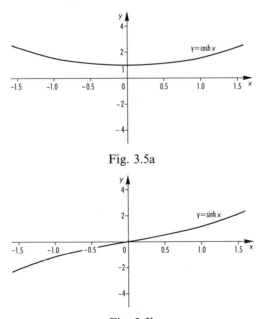

Fig. 3.5a

Fig. 3.5b

For $\tanh x = \dfrac{\sinh x}{\cosh x}$ we look to what happens at $x = 0$, as $x \to \infty$ and as $x \to -\infty$. In Fig. 3.6 we see asymptotes at $y = 1$ and $y = -1$ for the graph of $y = \tanh x$. Again you can apply the graphical test for an odd function as a check.

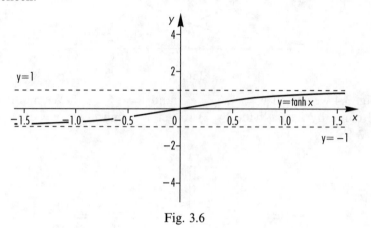

Fig. 3.6

Finally for comparison of size we show the 3 graphs together in Fig. 3.7.

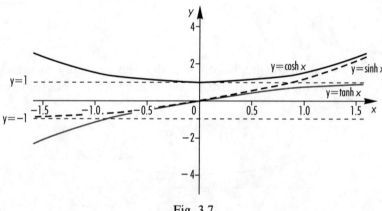

Fig. 3.7

You can use these graphs for an approximate check of your calculator values in Exercise 3.1.

Let us look again at Example 3.2ii) together with the graph of $y = \cosh x$ in Fig. 3.5a.

Example 3.4

We find the values of x where $\cosh x = 4.66$.

In Fig. 3.8 we have a horizontal line, $y = 4.66$, crossing the graph of $y = \cosh x$ in 2 places. The calculator gives us $x = 2.22$. Knowing that the hyperbolic cosine is an even function we have $x = -2.22$ as another answer. This applies to even functions.

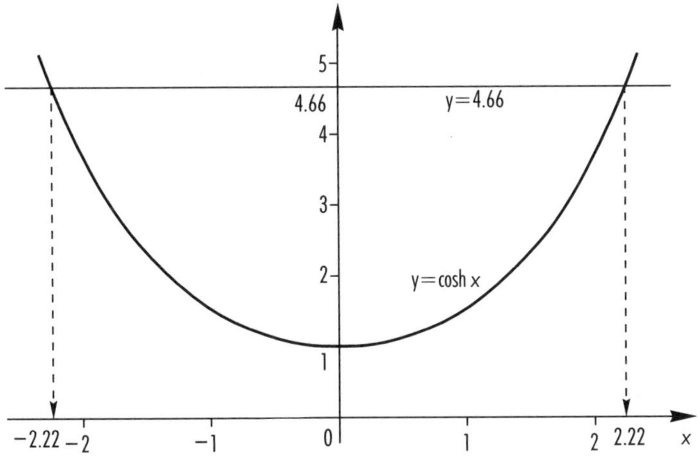

Fig. 3.8

Reciprocal hyperbolic functions

We write the **hyperbolic secant** as **sech** and say 'sheck'. The **hyperbolic cosecant** is **cosech** (said 'cosheck') and the **hyperbolic cotangent** is **coth** (said 'coth'). Again the h indicates the function is hyperbolic. We define

$$\operatorname{sech} ax = \frac{1}{\cosh ax}, \qquad \operatorname{cosech} ax = \frac{1}{\sinh ax}, \qquad \coth ax = \frac{1}{\tanh ax}.$$

Using our exponential definitions for the hyperbolic functions we may write

$$\operatorname{sech} ax = \frac{1}{\cosh ax} = \frac{1}{\frac{1}{2}(e^{ax} + e^{-ax})} = \frac{2}{e^{ax} + e^{-ax}},$$

$$\operatorname{cosech} ax = \frac{1}{\sinh ax} = \frac{1}{\frac{1}{2}(e^{ax} - e^{-ax})} = \frac{2}{e^{ax} - e^{-ax}},$$

$$\coth ax = \frac{1}{\tanh ax} = \frac{1}{\frac{\sinh ax}{\cosh ax}} = \frac{\cosh ax}{\sinh ax} = \frac{e^{ax} + e^{-ax}}{e^{ax} - e^{-ax}}.$$

When we use a calculator we need to involve the reciprocal key, 1/x|.

Examples 3.5

We find values of i) sech 1.25, ii) 2 cosech 2.9, iii) 4.4 coth(−0.8).

i) $\operatorname{sech} 1.25 = \dfrac{1}{\cosh 1.25}$. We use

1.25| hyp| cos| to display 1.888...

and 1/x| to display 0.53 (2 decimal places),

i.e. sech 1.25 = 0.53.

ii) $2 \operatorname{cosech} 2.9 = 2 \times \dfrac{1}{\sinh 2.9}$. We use

$\underline{2.9|}$ $\underline{\text{hyp}|}$ $\underline{\sin|}$ to display $9.059\ldots$

and $\underline{1/x|}$ $\underline{\times|}$ $\underline{2|}$ $\underline{=|}$ to display 0.22 (2 dp),

i.e. $2 \operatorname{cosech} 2.9 = 0.22$.

iii) $4.4 \coth(-0.8) = 4.4 \times \dfrac{1}{\tanh(-0.8)}$. We use

$\underline{0.8|}$ $\underline{^{+}/_{-}|}$ $\underline{\text{hyp}|}$ $\underline{\tan|}$ to display $-0.664\ldots$

and $\underline{1/x|}$ $\underline{\times|}$ $\underline{4.4|}$ $\underline{=|}$ to display -6.63 (2 dp),

i.e. $4.4 \coth(-0.8) = -6.63$.

We use the calculator to find the inverse hyperbolic function.

Examples 3.6

Find the values of y where i) $\operatorname{sech} y = 0.35$, ii) $\operatorname{cosech} y = -2.25$, iii) $\coth y = 1.5$.

i)   We use the definition of hyperbolic secant to rewrite

$$\operatorname{sech} y = 0.35$$

as $\dfrac{1}{\cosh y} = 0.35$

i.e. $\cosh y = \dfrac{1}{0.35}$.

$\cosh y = \dfrac{1}{0.35}$ may be written as $y = \cosh^{-1} \dfrac{1}{0.35}$ or $y = \operatorname{arccosh} \dfrac{1}{0.35}$.

Both $\cosh^{-1}$ and arccosh represent the inverse hyperbolic function. We use

$\underline{1|}$ $\underline{\div|}$ $\underline{0.35|}$ $\underline{=|}$ to display $2.857\ldots$

and $\underline{\text{inv}|}$ $\underline{\text{hyp}|}$ $\underline{\cos|}$ to display 1.71 (2 dp).

Then $y = 1.71$ or $\operatorname{sech} 1.71 = 0.35$.

ii)   We use the definition of hyperbolic cosecant to rewrite

$$\operatorname{cosech} y = -2.25$$

as $\dfrac{1}{\sinh y} = -2.25$

i.e. $\sinh y = \dfrac{1}{-2.25}$.

$\sinh y = \dfrac{1}{-2.25}$ may be written as $y = \sinh^{-1} \dfrac{1}{-2.25}$ or

$y = \operatorname{arcsinh} \dfrac{1}{-2.25}$. We use

$$\boxed{1} \quad \boxed{\div} \quad \boxed{2.25} \quad \boxed{^+/_-} \quad \boxed{=} \quad \text{to display } -0.444\ldots$$

and $\qquad \boxed{\text{inv}} \quad \boxed{\text{hyp}} \quad \boxed{\text{sin}} \quad$ to display -0.43 (2 dp).

Then $y = -0.43$ or $\operatorname{cosech}(-0.43) = -2.25$.

iii) We use the definition of hyperbolic cotangent to rewrite

$$\coth y = 1.5$$

as $\qquad \dfrac{1}{\tanh y} = 1.5$

i.e. $\tanh y = \dfrac{1}{1.5}.$

$\tanh y = \dfrac{1}{1.5}$ may be written as $y = \tanh^{-1}\dfrac{1}{1.5}$ or $y = \operatorname{arctanh}\dfrac{1}{1.5}.$ We use

$$\boxed{1} \quad \boxed{\div} \quad \boxed{1.5} \quad \boxed{=} \quad \text{to display } 0.666\ldots$$

and $\qquad \boxed{\text{inv}} \quad \boxed{\text{hyp}} \quad \boxed{\text{tan}} \quad$ to display 0.80 (2 dp).

Then $y = 0.80$ or $\coth 0.80 = 1.5$.

■■■■■ EXERCISE 3.2 ■■■■■

Find the values of the hyperbolic functions.

1	$\operatorname{cosech} 3.5$	**6**	$\operatorname{cosech}(-3.5)$
2	$\coth 1.4$	**7**	$\coth(-1.4)$
3	$\operatorname{sech} 1.75$	**8**	$3.5\operatorname{sech} 2$
4	$\operatorname{sech}(-1.75)$	**9**	$-\operatorname{cosech} 3.5$
5	$4\operatorname{cosech} 1.5$	**10**	$2\coth 4.25$

Find the values of the inverse hyperbolic functions.

11	$\operatorname{sech}^{-1} 0.55$	**16**	$\operatorname{sech}^{-1} 0.10$
12	$\coth^{-1} 2.55$	**17**	$\operatorname{sech}^{-1} 0.435$
13	$\operatorname{cosech}^{-1} 2.7$	**18**	$\operatorname{cosech}^{-1} 3.45$
14	$\coth^{-1}(-2.55)$	**19**	$\operatorname{cosech}^{-1}(-2.7)$
15	$\coth^{-1} 5.65$	**20**	$\coth^{-1} 3.7$

We can use the hyperbolic functions to sketch the graphs of the reciprocal hyperbolic functions. Using $\operatorname{sech} x = \dfrac{1}{\cosh x}$ we note that $\cosh x$ has a minimum at $(0, 1)$. Hence $\operatorname{sech} x$ has a maximum at this point. As $x \to \pm\infty$, $\cosh x \to \pm\infty$ and so $\operatorname{sech} x \to 0$. In Fig 3.9 we sketch the graph of $y = \operatorname{sech} x$. Notice this is an even function.

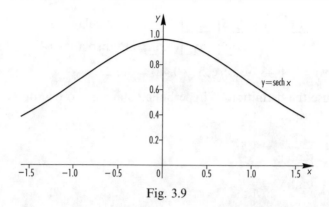

Fig. 3.9

Using $\cosech x = \dfrac{1}{\sinh x}$ we note that the graph of $\sinh x$ passes through $(0,0)$. Hence as $x \to 0$ $\cosech x \to \infty$. Also as $x \to \pm\infty$, $\sinh x \to \pm\infty$ and so $\cosech x \to 0$. In Fig 3.10 we sketch the graph of $y = \cosech x$. Notice this is an odd function.

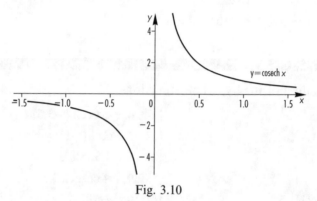

Fig. 3.10

Using $\coth x = \dfrac{1}{\tanh x}$ we have asymptotes at $y = \pm 1$ in both cases. The graph of $\tanh x$ passes through $(0,0)$. Hence as $x \to 0$ $\coth x \to \infty$. Also as $x \to \pm\infty$, $\tanh x \to \pm 1$ and so $\coth x \to \pm 1$. In Fig 3.11 we sketch the graph of $y = \coth x$. Notice this is an odd function.

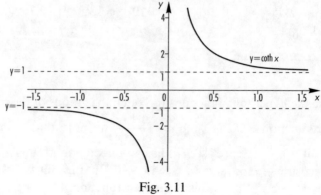

Fig. 3.11

You can use these graphs for an approximate check of your calculator values in Exercise 3.2.

Let us look again at Example 3.6i) together with the graph of $y = \text{sech}\,x$ in Fig. 3.9.

███████ **Example 3.7** ███████████████████████████████

We find the values of x where $\text{sech}\,x = 0.35$.

In Fig. 3.12 we have a horizontal line, $y = 0.35$, crossing the graph of $y = \text{sech}\,x$ in 2 places. The calculator gives us $x = 1.71$. Knowing that the hyperbolic cosine is an even function we have $x = -1.71$ as another answer. We know this applies to even functions.

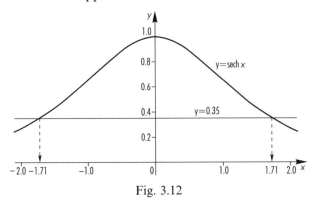

Fig. 3.12

Hyperbolic identities

We have seen trigonometric identities (formulae) in Volume 2, Chapter 4. An identity is a relationship that is true for all values. Here we may deduce hyperbolic identities using the definitions in terms of exponentials.

███████ **Example 3.8** ███████████████████████████████

We prove that $\cosh^2 x - \sinh^2 x = 1$.

We start with the left-hand side because it is the more complicated of the 2 sides. Our aim is to reach the right-hand side using algebraic simplification.

$$\text{Now} \quad \cosh^2 x - \sinh^2 x = \left\{\frac{1}{2}(e^x + e^{-x})\right\}^2 - \left\{\frac{1}{2}(e^x - e^{-x})\right\}^2$$

$$= \frac{1}{4}\left(e^{2x} + e^{-2x} + 2e^0\right) - \frac{1}{4}\left(e^{2x} + e^{-2x} - 2e^0\right)$$

$$= \frac{1}{4}\left(e^{2x} + e^{-2x} + 2 - e^{2x} - e^{-2x} + 2\right) \quad \boxed{e^0 = 1.}$$

$$= \frac{1}{4} \times 4 = 1, \text{ which is the right-hand side.}$$

Starting with one side and reaching the other side by algebraic simplification means we have proven the identity.

████ **Examples 3.9** ████

We prove that   i) $\cosh x$ is an even function
         and ii) $\coth ax$ is an odd function.

i)   We use the definition of $\cosh x$ and replace x with $-x$.

Then $\cosh x = \dfrac{1}{2}(e^x + e^{-x})$

becomes $\cosh(-x) = \dfrac{1}{2}\left(e^{-x} + e^{-(-x)}\right)$

$$= \dfrac{1}{2}(e^{-x} + e^{x})$$

$$= \dfrac{1}{2}(e^{x} + e^{-x})$$

i.e. $\cosh(-x) = \cosh x$

which is a specific case of $f(-x) = f(x)$, the condition for an even function.

ii)   We use the definition of $\coth ax$ and replace x (i.e. ax) with $-x$ (i.e. $-ax$).

Then $\coth ax = \dfrac{e^{ax} + e^{-ax}}{e^{ax} - e^{-ax}}$

becomes $\coth(-ax) = \dfrac{e^{-ax} + e^{-(-ax)}}{e^{-ax} - e^{-(-ax)}}$

$$= \dfrac{e^{-ax} + e^{ax}}{e^{-ax} - e^{ax}}$$

$$= \dfrac{e^{ax} + e^{-ax}}{-e^{ax} + e^{-ax}}$$

$$= \dfrac{e^{ax} + e^{-ax}}{-(e^{ax} - e^{-ax})}$$

$$= -\left(\dfrac{e^{ax} + e^{-ax}}{e^{ax} - e^{-ax}}\right)$$

i.e. $\coth(-ax) = -\coth ax$

which is a specific case of $f(-x) = -f(x)$, the condition for an odd function.

████ **Example 3.10** ████

We prove $\tanh 2x = \dfrac{2\tanh x}{1 + \tanh^2 x}$.

We start with the right-hand side because it is the more complicated of the 2 sides. Our aim is to reach the left-hand side using algebraic simplification.

Now $\dfrac{2\tanh x}{1+\tanh^2 x} = \dfrac{2\left(\dfrac{e^x - e^{-x}}{e^x + e^{-x}}\right)}{1 + \left(\dfrac{e^x - e^{-x}}{e^x + e^{-x}}\right)^2}$

$$= \dfrac{2\left(\dfrac{e^x - e^{-x}}{e^x + e^{-x}}\right)}{1 + \dfrac{(e^x - e^{-x})^2}{(e^x + e^{-x})^2}}$$

1 added to a fraction; we use a common denominator.

$$= \dfrac{2\left(\dfrac{e^x - e^{-x}}{e^x + e^{-x}}\right)}{\dfrac{(e^x + e^{-x})^2 + (e^x - e^{-x})^2}{(e^x + e^{-x})^2}}$$

Invert the dividing fraction and multiply.

$$= \dfrac{2(e^x - e^{-x})}{(e^x + e^{-x})} \times \dfrac{(e^x + e^{-x})^2}{\left\{(e^x + e^{-x})^2 + (e^x - e^{-x})^2\right\}}$$

$(e^x + e^{-x})$ cancels from the numerator and denominator.

$$= \dfrac{2(e^x - e^{-x})(e^x + e^{-x})}{e^{2x} + e^{-2x} + 2e^0 + e^{2x} + e^{-2x} - 2e^0}$$

$$= \dfrac{2\left(e^{2x} + e^0 - e^0 - e^{-2x}\right)}{2(e^{2x} + e^{-2x})}$$

Common factors of 2s cancel.

$$= \dfrac{e^{2x} - e^{-2x}}{e^{2x} + e^{-2x}}$$

$$= \tanh 2x.$$

Notice the format of these exponentials compared with our definition for $\tanh ax$, i.e. with $a = 2$.

Example 3.11

We prove $\sinh(x + y) = \sinh x . \cosh y + \cosh x . \sinh y$.

Again we start with the right-hand side because it is the more complicated of the 2 sides.

$\sinh x . \cosh y + \cosh x . \sinh y$

$$= \frac{1}{2}(e^x - e^{-x})\frac{1}{2}(e^y + e^{-y}) + \frac{1}{2}(e^x + e^{-x})\frac{1}{2}(e^y - e^{-y}).$$

During multiplication of the same bases, e, we add the indices, e.g.

$$(-e^{-x})(+e^{-y})$$
$$= -e^{-x-y}$$

For all the multiplication we get

$$\frac{1}{4}\left(e^{x+y} + e^{x-y} - e^{-x+y} - e^{-x-y} + e^{x+y} - e^{x-y} + e^{-x+y} - e^{-x-y}\right)$$

$$= \frac{1}{4}\left(2e^{x+y} - 2e^{-x-y}\right)$$

$$= \frac{1}{4} \times 2\left(e^{x+y} - e^{-(x+y)}\right)$$

> The common factor of 2 cancels.

$$= \frac{1}{2}\left(e^{x+y} - e^{-(x+y)}\right)$$

$$= \sinh(x+y).$$

Notice the pattern of the exponentials. In our definition of $\sinh ax$ we have exponentials with ax and $-ax$. Here, for $\sinh(x+y)$ we have exponentials with $(x+y)$ and $-(x+y)$.

■■■■ EXERCISE 3.3 ■■■■

Using the hyperbolic definitions in terms of exponentials prove the identities in Questions **1–9**.

1 $\sinh 2x = 2\sinh x . \cosh x$

2   i) $\cosh 2x = 2\cosh^2 x - 1$
   ii) $\cosh 2x = 1 + 2\sinh^2 x$

3 $\sinh(x - y) = \sinh x . \cosh y - \cosh x . \sinh y$

4 $\cosh(x + y) = \cosh x . \cosh y + \sinh x . \sinh y$

5 $\operatorname{sech}^2 x = 1 - \tanh^2 x$

6 $\operatorname{cosech}^2 x = \coth^2 x - 1$

7 $\sinh 3x = 3\sinh x + 4\sinh^3 x$

8 $\cosh 3x = 4\cosh^3 x - 3\cosh x$

9 $\tanh(x + y) = \dfrac{\tanh x + \tanh y}{1 + \tanh x . \tanh y}$

10   Simplify   i) $\cosh x . \cosh y - \sinh x . \sinh y$
   ii) $\cosh^2 x + \sinh^2 x$

We can verify an identity, i.e. we can check that it is true for a specimen value.

■■■■ Example 3.12 ■■■■

Using $x = 0.70$ and $y = 1.34$ we can verify that

$$\tanh(x + y) = \frac{\tanh x + \tanh y}{1 + \tanh x . \tanh y}.$$

We work out the left- and right-hand sides separately.

$$\tanh(x+y) = \tanh(0.70 + 1.34)$$
$$= \tanh 2.04$$
$$= 0.967 \text{ (3 dp)}.$$

Now $\quad \tanh x + \tanh y = \tanh 0.70 + \tanh 1.34$
$$= 0.6043\ldots + 0.8716\ldots = 1.4760\ldots$$

Also $\quad 1 + \tanh x.\tanh y = 1 + (\tanh 0.70)(\tanh 1.34)$
$$= 1 + (0.6043\ldots)(0.8716\ldots) = 1.5268\ldots$$

We link together these results so that
$$\frac{\tanh x + \tanh y}{1 + \tanh x.\tanh y} = \frac{1.4760\ldots}{1.5268\ldots}$$
$$= 0.967 \text{ (3 dp)},$$

agreeing with our result for $\tanh(x+y)$. Hence we have checked the relatioship is true for these values.

You can choose specimen values and verify the other identities of Exercise 3.3 for yourself.

We have hyperbolic identities from both earlier Examples and Exercise 3.3. This gives us an alternative to always proving identities using the definitions in terms of exponentials. Knowing an identity is true for all values we can apply them in further proofs.

Example 3.13

Prove $\tanh 2x = \dfrac{2\tanh x}{1 + \tanh^2 x}$.

This is a repeat of Example 3.10 using some identities. We start with the right-hand side because it is the more complicated of the 2 sides.

$$\frac{2\tanh x}{1 + \tanh^2 x} = \frac{\dfrac{2\sinh x}{\cosh x}}{1 + \dfrac{\sinh^2 x}{\cosh^2 x}}$$

$$= \frac{\dfrac{2\sinh x}{\cosh x}}{\dfrac{\cosh^2 x + \sinh^2 x}{\cosh^2 x}}$$

$$= \frac{2\sinh x}{\cosh x} \times \frac{\cosh^2 x}{(\cosh^2 x + \sinh^2 x)}$$

> $\cosh x$ cancels from the numerator and denominator.

$$= \frac{2\sinh x.\cosh x}{\cosh^2 x + \sinh^2 x}$$

$$= \frac{\sinh 2x}{\cosh 2x}$$

> Exercise 3.3, Qn **1**.
> Exercise 3.3, Qn **10ii**).

i.e. $\dfrac{2\tanh x}{1 + \tanh^2 x} = \tanh 2x.$

Osborn's rule

We might compare some of the identities in Exercise 3.3 with some of the trigonometric identities of Volume 2, Chapter 4. In many cases they are similar. Sometimes there is a change of $+/-$ sign. We may convert between hyperbolic and trigonometric identities using Osborn's rule. **Change each trigonometric ratio** (say tan) **into the corresponding hyperbolic function** (say tanh). **Wherever we have a product of 2 sines we change the $+/-$ sign**. For a product of cosines there is no sign change. The same $+/-$ sign rule applies in the reverse direction from hyperbolic functions to trigonometric ratios.

We do need to be careful. Some trigonometric ratios, e.g. tangent, have sine hidden. Remember tangent $= \dfrac{\text{sine}}{\text{cosine}}$.

Examples 3.14

Apply Osborn's rule to the trigonometric identities

i) $\cos^2 x + \sin^2 x = 1$,

ii) $\cos(x + y) = \cos x . \cos y - \sin x . \sin y$.

i)   In $\cos^2 x + \sin^2 x = 1$ we have a product of 2 sines, i.e. $\sin^2 x = \sin x \times \sin x$. This means we convert $\sin^2 x$ to $-\sinh^2 x$. The $\cos^2 x$ is a simple conversion to $\cosh^2 x$. Hence the equivalent hyperbolic identity is $\cosh^2 x - \sinh^2 x = 1$. We saw this in Example 3.8.

ii) In $\cos(x + y) = \cos x . \cos y - \sin x . \sin y$ we have a product of 2 sines, i.e. $\sin x . \sin y$. This means we convert $\sin x . \sin y$ to $-\sinh x . \sinh y$. $\cos x$ converts to $\cosh x$, $\cos y$ to $\cosh y$ and $\cos(x + y)$ to $\cosh(x + y)$. Hence the equivalent hyperbolic identity is $\cosh(x + y) = \cosh x . \cosh y + \sinh x . \sinh y$.

Examples 3.15

Apply Osborn's rule to the hyperbolic identities

i) $\operatorname{cosech}^2 x = \coth^2 x - 1$,

ii) $\sinh 3x = 3 \sinh x + 4 \sinh^3 x$.

i)   In $\operatorname{cosech}^2 x = \coth^2 x - 1$ we have $\operatorname{cosech} x = \dfrac{1}{\sinh x}$ so $\operatorname{cosech}^2 x = \dfrac{1}{\sinh^2 x}$. Also $\coth x = \dfrac{\cosh x}{\sinh x}$ so $\coth^2 x = \dfrac{\cosh^2 x}{\sinh^2 x}$. This means $\dfrac{1}{\sinh^2 x}$ converts to $-\dfrac{1}{\sin^2 x}$ and $\dfrac{\cosh^2 x}{\sinh^2 x}$ converts to $\dfrac{\cos^2 x}{-\sin^2 x}$.

Hence we have the equivalent trigonometric identity $-\operatorname{cosec}^2 x = -\cot^2 x - 1$, i.e. $\operatorname{cosec}^2 x = \cot^2 x + 1$. We met this in Volume 2, Chapter 4.

ii) In $\sinh 3x = 3\sinh x + 4\sinh^3 x$ we pay attention to $4\sinh^3 x$ written as $4\sinh x.\sinh^2 x$. $\mathrm{Sinh}^2 x$ converts to $-\sin^2 x$ according to Osborn's rule. $4\sinh x$ is a single function and so Osborn's rule is not needed. Then $\sin 3x = 3\sin x - 4\sin^3 x$ is the equivalent trigonometric identity.

▬▬ EXERCISE 3.4 ▬▬

Apply Osborn's rule to the hyperbolic identities.

1 $\cosh 2x = 1 + 2\sinh^2 x$

2 $\sinh(x - y) = \sinh x.\cosh y - \cosh x.\sinh y$

3 $\sinh 2x = 2\sinh x.\cosh x$

4 $\mathrm{sech}^2 x = 1 - \tanh^2 x$

5 $\tanh(x + y) = \dfrac{\tanh x + \tanh y}{1 + \tanh x.\tanh y}$

Apply Osborn's rule to the trigonometric identities.

6 $\cos(x - y) = \cos x.\cos y + \sin x.\sin y$

7 $\cos 2x = 2\cos^2 x - 1$

8 $\tan 2x = \dfrac{2\tan x}{1 - \tan^2 x}$

9 $\sin(x + y) = \sin x.\cos y + \cos x.\sin y$

10 $\sin 2x = \dfrac{2\tan x}{1 + \tan^2 x}$

Now we have applied Osborn's rule we look at the link in more detail. It is based on exponential definitions using real and imaginary indices. We recall Euler's formulae (p. 22),

$$\cos\theta + j\sin\theta = e^{j\theta}$$

and $\cos\theta - j\sin\theta = e^{-j\theta}$.

We add these to give

$$2\cos\theta = e^{j\theta} + e^{-j\theta}$$

i.e. $\cos\theta = \dfrac{1}{2}\left(e^{j\theta} + e^{-j\theta}\right)$.

We compare this expression for cosine with the definition for the hyperbolic cosine, i.e.

$$\cosh x = \dfrac{1}{2}\left(e^x + e^{-x}\right).$$

They both involve the addition of positive and negative exponentials. The trigonometric expression has imaginary powers; the hyperbolic definition has real powers.

Suppose we start with our expression for cosine and replace the real θ with the imaginary jx, i.e.

$$\cos\theta = \frac{1}{2}\left(e^{j\theta} + e^{-j\theta}\right)$$

becomes

$$\cos jx = \frac{1}{2}\left(e^{j(jx)} + e^{-j(jx)}\right)$$

$$= \frac{1}{2}\left(e^{j^2 x} + e^{-j^2 x}\right)$$

$$= \frac{1}{2}(e^{-x} + e^x) \qquad \boxed{j^2 = -1.}$$

$$= \frac{1}{2}(e^x + e^{-x})$$

i.e. $\cos jx = \cosh x.$

Alternatively we can start with our expression for the hyperbolic cosine replacing x with $j\theta$, i.e.

$$\cosh x = \frac{1}{2}(e^x + e^{-x})$$

becomes

$$\cosh j\theta = \frac{1}{2}\left(e^{j\theta} + e^{-j\theta}\right)$$

i.e. $\cosh j\theta = \cos\theta.$

Again we use Euler's formulae,

$$\cos\theta + j\sin\theta = e^{j\theta}$$

and $\cos\theta - j\sin\theta = e^{-j\theta}.$

We subtract these to give

$$j2\sin\theta = e^{j\theta} - e^{-j\theta}$$

i.e. $j\sin\theta = \frac{1}{2}\left(e^{j\theta} - e^{-j\theta}\right).$

We compare this expression for sine with the definition for the hyperbolic sine, i.e.

$$\sinh x = \frac{1}{2}(e^x - e^{-x}).$$

They both involve the subtraction of positive and negative exponentials. The trigonometric expression has imaginary powers; the hyperbolic definition has real powers.

Suppose we start with our expression for sine and replace the real θ with the imaginary jx, i.e.

$$j\sin\theta = \frac{1}{2}\left(e^{j\theta} - e^{-j\theta}\right)$$

becomes

$$j\sin jx = \frac{1}{2}\left(e^{j(jx)} - e^{-j(jx)}\right)$$

$$= \frac{1}{2}\left(e^{j^2 x} - e^{-j^2 x}\right)$$

$$= \frac{1}{2}(e^{-x} - e^{x})$$

$$= -\frac{1}{2}(e^{x} - e^{-x})$$

$\boxed{j^2 = -1.}$

i.e. $\quad j\sin jx = -\sinh x$

or $\quad -j \times j \sin jx = -j \times -\sinh x$

i.e. $\quad \sin jx = j\sinh x.$

Multiplying both sides by $-j$.
$j^2 = -1.$

Alternatively we may show that $j\sin x = \sinh jx$. We leave this as an exercise for yourself. We could extend this idea to tangent and the various trigonometric formulae we saw in Volume 2, Chapter 4.

We gather together our results, quoting them in terms of x for consistency, i.e.

$$\cos jx = \cosh x \qquad \sin jx = j\sinh x$$
$$\cos x = \cosh jx \qquad j\sin x = \sinh jx$$

We have used Osborn's rule without a complete explanation. It is based upon these relationships between the sine and hyperbolic sine. When we move between the 2 forms we are really replacing sinh with j sin. Squaring them we get $\sinh^2$ to give us $(j\sin)^2 = j^2 \sin^2 = -\sin^2$.

Differentiation

All the usual differentiation rules continue to apply. If you are in any doubt you should refer to Volume 2, Chapter 7 in particular. You need to recall the function of a function, product and quotient rules.

To start we derive some simple differentiation rules for hyperbolic functions based upon their exponential definitions. We know that for

$$y = e^{ax} \qquad \text{and} \quad y = e^{-ax}$$

that $\quad \dfrac{dy}{dx} = ae^{ax} \qquad \dfrac{dy}{dx} = -ae^{-ax}.$

Using these ideas and the exponential definition for the hyperbolic cosine

$$y = \cosh ax$$

becomes $\quad y = \dfrac{1}{2}(e^{ax} + e^{-ax})$

so that $\quad \dfrac{dy}{dx} = \dfrac{1}{2}(ae^{ax} - ae^{-ax})$

$$= a \times \dfrac{1}{2}(e^{ax} - e^{-ax})$$

Common factor of a.

i.e. $\quad \dfrac{dy}{dx} = a\sinh ax.$

Similarly for the hyperbolic sine,

$$y = \sinh ax$$

becomes $\quad y = \dfrac{1}{2}(e^{ax} - e^{-ax})$

so that $\quad \dfrac{dy}{dx} = \dfrac{1}{2}(ae^{ax} - -ae^{-ax})$

$$= a \times \dfrac{1}{2}(e^{ax} + e^{-ax}) \qquad \boxed{\text{Common factor of } a.}$$

i.e. $\quad \dfrac{dy}{dx} = a \cosh ax.$

When we differentiated the simple trigonometric function cosine we needed to be careful with the sign of $\dfrac{dy}{dx}$. Notice that the hyperbolic equivalent function is positive.

Example 3.16

We use our results and the quotient rule to differentiate the hyperbolic tangent. Recall the result for the trigonometric function and compare the results.

Using $\quad y = \tanh ax$

i.e. $\quad y = \dfrac{\sinh ax}{\cosh ax} \qquad \boxed{y = \dfrac{u}{v}.}$

we let $\quad u = \sinh ax \quad$ and $\quad v = \cosh ax.$

Differentiating both parts we get

$$\dfrac{du}{dx} = a \cosh ax \quad \text{and} \quad \dfrac{dv}{dx} = a \sinh ax.$$

We substitute them into

$$\dfrac{dy}{dx} = \dfrac{v\dfrac{du}{dx} - u\dfrac{dv}{dx}}{v^2}$$

to get $\quad \dfrac{dy}{dx} = \dfrac{(\cosh ax)(a \cosh ax) - (\sinh ax)(a \sinh ax)}{(\cosh ax)^2}$

$$= \dfrac{a(\cosh^2 ax - \sinh^2 ax)}{\cosh^2 ax} \qquad \boxed{\begin{array}{l}\cosh^2 ax - \sinh^2 ax = 1,\\ \text{Example 3.8.}\end{array}}$$

$$= a \times \dfrac{1}{\cosh^2 ax}$$

$$= a \operatorname{sech}^2 ax.$$

We gather together our 3 results:

$$\dfrac{d}{dx}(\cosh ax) = a \sinh ax \qquad \dfrac{d}{dx}(\sinh ax) = a \cosh ax$$

$$\dfrac{d}{dx}(\tanh ax) = a \operatorname{sech}^2 ax$$

▬▬▬▬ **Examples 3.17** ▬▬▬▬▬▬▬▬▬▬▬▬▬▬▬▬▬▬▬▬▬

We apply the basic differentiation rules to some hyperbolic functions, replacing a with numerical values.

i) For $y = \sinh 2x$

$$\frac{dy}{dx} = 2\cosh 2x.$$

ii) For $y = 3\cosh 5x$

$$\frac{dy}{dx} = 3 \times 5 \sinh 5x = 15 \sinh 5x.$$

iii) For $y = 2.5 \tanh \frac{1}{2} x$ or $2.5 \tanh \frac{x}{2}$

$$\frac{dy}{dx} = 2.5 \times \frac{1}{2} \operatorname{sech}^2 \frac{1}{2} x$$

$$= 1.25 \operatorname{sech}^2 \frac{1}{2} x.$$

In the next set of examples we apply the product, function of a function and quotient rules. We also find the gradient at a particular point.

▬▬▬▬ **Examples 3.18** ▬▬▬▬▬▬▬▬▬▬▬▬▬▬▬▬▬▬▬▬▬

i) For $y = \sinh 2x \cosh 5x$ we find the gradient at the point where $x = 0.5$.

We have two hyperbolic functions multiplied together. We differentiate using the product rule and then substitute for $x = 0.5$.

Using $y = \sinh 2x \cosh 5x$ | $y = uv.$ |

we let $u = \sinh 2x$ and $v = \cosh 5x$.

Differentiating both parts we get

$$\frac{du}{dx} = 2\cosh 2x \quad \text{and} \quad \frac{dv}{dx} = 5\sinh 5x.$$

We substitute them into

$$\frac{dy}{dx} = u\frac{dv}{dx} + v\frac{du}{dx}$$ | Product rule. |

to get $\dfrac{dy}{dx} = (\sinh 2x)(5\sinh 5x) + (\cosh 5x)(2\cosh 2x).$

Given $x = 0.5$ we have $2x = 1$ and $5x = 2.5$ so that

$$\frac{dy}{dx} = 5 \sinh 1 \sinh 2.5 + 2 \cosh 2.5 \cosh 1$$

$$= 5(1.175\ldots)(6.050\ldots) + 2(6.132\ldots)(1.543\ldots)$$

$$= 35.551 + 18.925$$

$$= 54.48.$$

ii) We relate y to time, t, according to $y = \ln(\sinh 1.25t)$ and find the rate of change of y after 0.75 seconds.

We apply the function of a function rule to

$$y = \ln(\sinh 1.25t).$$

Making a substitution we have

$$y = \ln u \quad \text{where} \quad u = \sinh 1.25t.$$

Differentiating in both cases we get

$$\frac{dy}{du} = \frac{1}{u} \quad \text{and} \quad \frac{du}{dt} = 1.25 \cosh 1.25t.$$

Using $\quad \dfrac{dy}{dt} = \dfrac{dy}{du} \times \dfrac{du}{dt}$

we get $\quad \dfrac{dy}{dt} = \dfrac{1}{u} \times 1.25 \cosh 1.25t$

$$\frac{dy}{dt} = \frac{1}{\sinh 1.25t} \times 1.25 \cosh 1.25t.$$

We could simplify these to the hyperbolic cotangent. However substituting for $t = 0.75$, i.e. $1.25t = 0.9375$ we get

$$\frac{dy}{dx} = \frac{1.25 \cosh 0.9375}{\sinh 0.9375}$$

$$= \frac{1.25 \times 1.472\ldots}{1.080\ldots}$$

$$= 1.70.$$

Example 3.19

We use a result from Example 3.18ii) and differentiate again using the quotient rule. This gives us the second derivative.

Quoting $\quad \dfrac{dy}{dt} = 1.25 \dfrac{\cosh 1.25t}{\sinh 1.25t}$ $\qquad \boxed{y = \dfrac{u}{v}.}$

we let $\quad u = \cosh 1.25t \quad$ and $\quad v = \sinh 1.25t.$

Differentiating both parts we get

$$\frac{du}{dt} = 1.25 \sinh 1.25t \quad \text{and} \quad \frac{dv}{dt} = 1.25 \cosh 1.25t.$$

As before we substitute into the formula for the quotient rule $\qquad \boxed{\text{Using} \quad \dfrac{v\dfrac{du}{dt} - u\dfrac{dv}{dt}}{v^2}.}$

to get $\quad \dfrac{d^2y}{dt^2} = 1.25 \times \dfrac{1.25\left(\sinh^2 1.25t - \cosh^2 1.25t\right)}{\left(\sinh 1.25t\right)^2}$

$$= \frac{-1.25^2\left(\cosh^2 1.25t - \sinh^2 1.25t\right)}{\sinh^2 1.25t}$$

$$= -1.25^2 \times \frac{1}{\sinh^2 1.25t} \qquad \boxed{\cosh^2 at - \sinh^2 at = 1,\ \text{Example 3.8.}}$$

We can re-write this as $-1.25^2 \operatorname{cosech}^2 1.25t$. Also we can make numerical substitutions in the usual way.

ASSIGNMENT

Let us look again at our cable with equation
$$y = \frac{T_0}{w}\left(\cosh\frac{wx}{T_0} - 1\right).$$

x is the horizontal distance from the centre,

y is the vertical distance from the centre,

w is the weight/unit length (Nm^{-1}),

T_0 is the tension in the cable at the origin.

In this case we have a maximum value for T_0 of 25 kN and a mass per metre of 10 kg. In Fig. 3.2 the cable spans 400 m (i.e. $L = 400$ m so that $x = 200$ m). $\frac{dy}{dx}$ shows how the depth changes as we move horizontally. Recall that the diagram is symmetrical about a vertical line through the minimum point of the cable. The gradient to the left of this line of symmetry is negative and to the right it is positive.

Using $y = \frac{T_0}{w}\left(\cosh\frac{wx}{T_0} - 1\right)$

we differentiate to get
$$\frac{dy}{dx} = \frac{T_0}{w}\left(\frac{w}{T_0}\sinh\frac{wx}{T_0}\right) = \sinh\frac{wx}{T_0}.$$

Suppose we find the gradient where $x = 50$ m, substituting so that
$$\frac{dy}{dx} = \sinh\left(\frac{10 \times 9.81 \times 50}{25 \times 10^3}\right)$$
$$= \sinh 0.1962$$
$$= 0.2,$$

i.e. at the point where $x = 50$ m the gradient is 0.2.

Again referring to the symmetry of Fig. 3.2 the gradient at $x = -50$ m is -0.2.

We could continue to discuss the changes, perhaps with the minumum point at O (Fig. 3.2). However reference to the diagram's symmetry and the equation is quicker in this case than a standard maximum/minimum exercise.

EXERCISE 3.5

In Questions **1–20** differentiate the functions once. Think about what you are differentiating. Some examples are simpler than you might think!

1 $y = \sinh 4x$

2 $y = \cosh 3x$

3 $y = \tanh 3t$

4 $y = \cosh\left(\dfrac{x}{2}\right)$

5 $y = \sinh^2 t$

6 $y = \cosh^2 t$

7 $y = \operatorname{sech} x$

8 $y = \operatorname{cosech} 2x$

9 $y = \coth ax$

10 $y = \sinh x \cosh x$

11 $y = 3\cosh^2 t - 3\sinh^2 t$

12 $y = \cosh^2 x + \sinh^2 x$

13 $y = \dfrac{\sinh 2x}{\cosh 2x}$

14 $y = \ln(\cosh 3t)$

15 $y = \ln(\sinh 3t)$

16 $y = \sinh x \tanh x$

17 $y = \tanh x \cosh x$

18 $y = \dfrac{\sinh x}{\tanh x}$

19 $y = \ln(\tanh t)$

20 $y = \tanh^2 t$

21 Given $x = \sinh t \cosh 2t$ find the value of the gradient at $t = 0.65$.

22 At $x = 0.25$, given $y = \cosh 2x - \sinh^2 x$, find the value of $\dfrac{dy}{dx}$.

23 Find the value of $\dfrac{d^2 y}{dt^2}$ at $t = 0.30$ given $y = \ln(\tanh 2t)$.

24 What is the value of the second derivative of $y = \sinh^2 4x$ at the point where $x = 0.15$?

25 Without differentiating explain why $\cosh^2 4X - \sinh^2 4X$ has neither a local maximum nor minimum.

Integration

Remember that integration is the reverse process to differentiation. We looked at many techniques in Volume 2. They continue to apply. We derive the integral of the hyperbolic sine knowing that

$$\int e^{ax}\, dx = \frac{1}{a} e^{ax} + c \quad \text{and} \quad \int e^{-ax}\, dx = -\frac{1}{a} e^{-ax} + c$$

Using these ideas and the exponential definition for the hyperbolic sine

$$\int \sinh ax \, dx = \int \frac{1}{2}(e^{ax} - e^{-ax})\, dx$$

$$= \frac{1}{2}\left(\frac{1}{a} e^{ax} - \frac{1}{-a} e^{-ax}\right) + c$$

$$= \frac{1}{a} \times \frac{1}{2}(e^{ax} + e^{-ax}) + c \qquad \boxed{\frac{-}{-} = +,}$$

$$\frac{1}{a} \text{ is a common factor.}$$

i.e. $\displaystyle\int \sinh ax\, dx = \frac{1}{a}\cosh ax + c.$

Similarly we can show that

$$\int \cosh ax\, dx = \frac{1}{a}\sinh ax + c$$

and $\displaystyle\int \operatorname{sech}^2 ax\, dx = \frac{1}{a}\tanh ax + c.$

Now compare these results with those you know for the trigonometrical equivalent functions. Notice we have no worries about any minus sign.

■ Examples 3.20 ■

We apply the basic integration rules to some hyperbolic functions, replacing a with numerical values.

i) $\displaystyle\int \sinh 5x\, dx = \frac{1}{5}\cosh 5x + c.$

ii) $\displaystyle\int \operatorname{sech}^2 4x\, dx = \frac{1}{4}\tanh 4x + c.$

iii) $\displaystyle\int_0^{1/2} \sinh 2x\, dx = \left[\frac{1}{2}\cosh 2x\right]_0^{1/2}$

$$= \frac{1}{2}\cosh 1 - \frac{1}{2}\cosh 0 \qquad \boxed{x = \frac{1}{2},\ 2x = 2 \times \frac{1}{2} \\ = 1}$$

$$= \frac{1}{2}(1.543\ldots - 1) = 0.272.$$

■ ASSIGNMENT ■

Let us look again at our cable with equation

$$y = \frac{T_0}{w}\left(\cosh \frac{wx}{T_0} - 1\right).$$

x is the horizontal distance from the centre,

y is the vertical distance from the centre,

w is the weight/unit length (Nm^{-1}), 10×9.81 N,

T_0 is the tension in the cable at the origin, 25 kN.

Fig. 3.2 shows the cable spanning 400 m (i.e. $L = 400$ m so that x varies from -200 m to 200 m). We know from Volume 2, Chapter 10, that the mean value from $x = a$ to $x = b$ is given by

$$\bar{y} = \frac{1}{b-a}\int_a^b y\, dx.$$

Using $\quad y = \dfrac{T_0}{w}\left(\cosh\dfrac{wx}{T_0} - 1\right)$

we substitute to get

$$\bar{y} = \frac{1}{200 - -200}\int_{-200}^{200} \frac{T_0}{w}\left(\cosh\frac{wx}{T_0} - 1\right)dx$$

$$= \frac{1}{400}\frac{T_0}{w}\int_{-200}^{200}\left(\cosh\frac{wx}{T_0} - 1\right)dx$$

$$= \frac{T_0}{400w}\left[\frac{T_0}{w}\sinh\frac{wx}{T_0} - x\right]_{-200}^{200}.$$

The next step is to substitute our constant values, $T_0 = 25 \times 10^3$ and $w = 10 \times 9.81$, together with $x = 200$ and $x = -200$. For ease we do this in stages.

$$\frac{T_0}{w} = \frac{25 \times 10^3}{10 \times 9.81} = 254.842$$

and so

$$\frac{T_0}{400w} = \frac{25 \times 10^3}{400 \times 10 \times 9.81} = 0.6371\ldots$$

Also when $x = 200$, $\quad \sinh\dfrac{wx}{T_0} = \sinh\left(\dfrac{10 \times 9.81 \times 200}{25 \times 10^3}\right)$

$$= \sinh 0.7848 = 0.86\overline{78}.$$

Remember the hyperbolic sine is an odd function (Chapter 2). Hence when $x = -200$ its value is $-0.86\overline{78}$.

Substituting all these staged results we get

$$\bar{y} = 0.6371\ldots[254.842(0.86\overline{78}) - 200 - 254.842(-0.86\overline{78}) - -(-200)]$$

$$= 0.6371\ldots[221.17\ldots - 200 + 221.17\ldots - 200]$$

$$= 26.9775\ldots,$$

i.e. the average value is just under 27 m.

EXERCISE 3.6

Integrate the following indefinite and definite integrals as appropriate.

1 $\displaystyle\int \cosh 3x\, dx$

2 $\displaystyle\int \sinh\frac{1}{2}x\, dx$

3 $\displaystyle\int\left(\sinh\frac{x}{3} + \sinh\frac{3x}{2}\right)dx$

4 $\displaystyle\int\frac{1}{2}\operatorname{sech}^2 2x\, dx$

5 $\displaystyle\int \sinh 3x \cosh 3x\, dx$

6 $\displaystyle\int_0^4 \cosh\frac{x}{2}\, dx$

7 $\displaystyle\int_0^1 \operatorname{sech}^2 x\, dx$

8 $\displaystyle\int_{0.25}^{0.5} \cosh 4x\, dx$

9 $\displaystyle\int_{1.5}^{5.1} \sinh\frac{x}{3}\, dx$

10 Prove that $\dfrac{1}{\cosh x + \sinh x} = \cosh x - \sinh x$. Use your result to find

the value of $\displaystyle\int_0^1 \dfrac{1}{\cosh x + \sinh x}\, dx$.

Inverse hyperbolic functions

We have different types of notation, just like we saw for inverse trigonometric functions in Chapter 2. The inverse function of the hyperbolic sine is $\sinh^{-1} x$ or **arcsinh** x, i.e. the value with a hyperbolic sine of x.

If $x = \sinh y$ then $y = \sinh^{-1} x$ or $y = \operatorname{arcsinh} x$.
If $x = \cosh y$ then $y = \cosh^{-1} x$ or $y = \operatorname{arccosh} x$.
If $x = \tanh y$ then $y = \tanh^{-1} x$ or $y = \operatorname{arctanh} x$.

The graph of an inverse function is a reflection of the original function in the line $y = x$. In Figs. 3.13 we show the original function and its inverse.

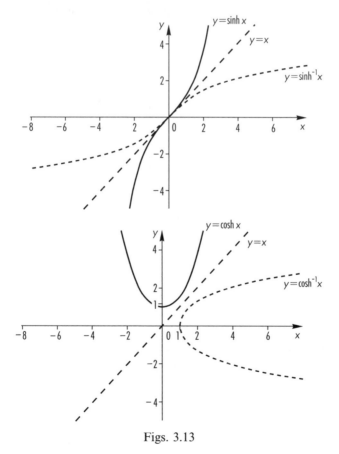

Figs. 3.13

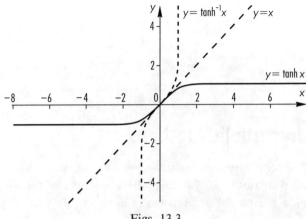

Figs. 13.3

We need a little more care with the graph of $y = \cosh^{-1} x$. Strictly a function and its inverse must be 'one-to-one', i.e. one value of x must correspond to one value of y. This means that the true graph of $y = \cosh^{-1} x$ should be only that portion above the horizontal axis.

Also in Fig. 3.14 we show together the graphs of $y = \sinh^{-1} x$ and $y = \cosh^{-1} x$. As x increases notice how they converge.

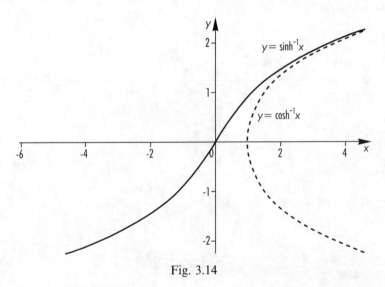

Fig. 3.14

We can look at the graphs of the reciprocal hyperbolic functions in the same way. They are $y = \text{sech}^{-1} x$, $y = \text{cosech}^{-1} x$ and $y = \coth^{-1} x$. We show them in Figs. 3.15. Again we could discuss them in strict 'one-to-one' terms.

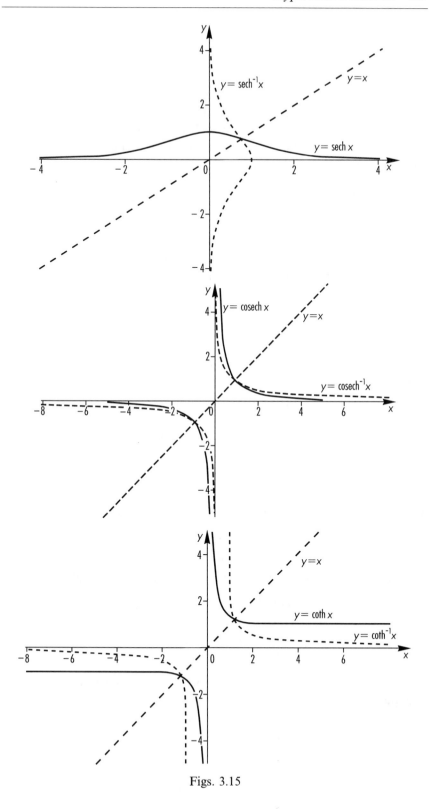

Figs. 3.15

Notice that the graphs of $y = \text{cosech}\, x$ and $y = \text{arccoshec}\, x$ are discontinuous and *not* that different from each other. The same can be written about the graphs of $y = \coth x$ and $y = \text{arccoth}\, x$.

Electronic calculators are very sophisticated, the majority having hyperbolic functions. Previously we needed to use logarithmic formulae for the inverse hyperbolic functions. Without looking at every line of mathematics here are some steps towards one of them. As an exercise you can work out the missing steps.

We start with $\quad y = \sinh^{-1}\dfrac{x}{a}$ where a is some constant and re-write it as

$$\frac{x}{a} = \sinh y.$$

Using the exponential definition for $\sinh y$ we multiply throughout by e^{-y}. This eliminates the negative exponential and creates a quadratic equation

$$e^{2y} - \frac{2x}{a}e^{y} - 1 = 0.$$

We apply the quadratic equation formula to get

$$e^{y} = \frac{x}{a} \pm \sqrt{1 + \left(\frac{x}{a}\right)^2}.$$

e^{y} is always positive. Look under the square root and appreciate that

$$1 + \left(\frac{x}{a}\right)^2 > \left(\frac{x}{a}\right)^2$$

i.e. $\quad \sqrt{1 + \left(\frac{x}{a}\right)^2} > \dfrac{x}{a}.$

For the $\pm$ this means we can only use the positive square root,

i.e. $\quad e^{y} = \dfrac{x}{a} + \sqrt{1 + \left(\frac{x}{a}\right)^2}.$

We take natural logarithms of both sides and adjust the algebra to give y.

Using $\quad y = \sinh^{-1}\dfrac{x}{a}$, i.e.

$$\sinh^{-1}\frac{x}{a} = \ln\left(\frac{x + \sqrt{a^2 + x^2}}{a}\right).$$

There are similar expressions for the other inverse hyperbolic functions. We quote

$$\cosh^{-1}\frac{x}{a} = \ln\left(\frac{x + \sqrt{x^2 - a^2}}{a}\right)$$

and $\quad \tanh^{-1}\dfrac{x}{a} = \dfrac{1}{2}\ln\left(\dfrac{a+x}{a-x}\right).$

You have the opportunity to work out these formulae in the last Exercise. We include a final example to demonstrate the logarithmic formula for $\sinh^{-1}\dfrac{x}{a}$.

Example 3.21

Using the logarithmic form for $\sinh^{-1}\dfrac{x}{a}$ solve the equation

$$2 + 3\sinh\frac{z}{4} = 10.$$

We re-arrange this equation, i.e.

$$3\sinh\frac{z}{4} = 10 - 2$$

$$\sinh\frac{z}{4} = \frac{8}{3}$$

i.e. $\qquad \dfrac{z}{4} = \sinh^{-1}\dfrac{8}{3}.$

We apply our logarithmic formula to $\sinh^{-1}\dfrac{8}{3}$ so that

$$\sinh^{-1}\frac{x}{a} = \ln\left(\frac{x + \sqrt{a^2 + x^2}}{a}\right).$$

becomes $\quad \sinh^{-1}\dfrac{8}{3} = \ln\left(\dfrac{8 + \sqrt{3^2 + 8^2}}{3}\right)$

$x = 8$,
$a = 3$.

$$= \ln\left(\frac{8 + \sqrt{73}}{3}\right)$$

$$= \ln 5.514\ldots$$

$$= 1.7074\ldots$$

In $\qquad \dfrac{z}{4} = \sinh^{-1}\dfrac{8}{3}$

we get $\quad z = 4 \times 1.7074 = 6.83$ (2 dp).

We can check this result using a calculator;

8		÷		3		=		to display 2.6
inv		hyp		sin				to display 1.7074...
×		4		=				to give the answer 6.83 (2 dp).

EXERCISE 3.7

1   λ is the increase in resistance of strip conductors due to eddy currents at power frequencies. If $\lambda = \dfrac{\alpha t}{2}\left(\dfrac{\sinh \alpha t + \sin \alpha t}{\cosh \alpha t - \cos \alpha t}\right)$ find its value at $t = 1.10$ for $\alpha = 1.0775$.

2   A cable is suspended between two pylons each of height 90 m. The vertical height of the cable above the ground is given by $y = 75\cosh\dfrac{x}{75}$. **Sketch** this curve. If the maximum sag is 15 m find the span of the cable. Briefly explain why the coefficient of the hyperbolic cosine must be 75.

3   The voltage, V_R, across a resistor, R, is Ri where i is the current. The voltage, V_L, across an inductor, L, is $L\dfrac{di}{dt}$. A resistor of 120 Ω and an inductor of 15 H are connected in series. This means the total voltage is the sum of the individual voltages. You are given $i = 2\cosh 0.25t$. Find a general expression for that total voltage and its value after 0.5 s.

4   Sketch the graph of $y = \sinh 2x$. Find the mean value of y between the origin and $x = 1.25$. Explain why the mean value for $-1.25 \leqslant x \leqslant 1.25$ is zero.

5   a)   Sketch the graphs of $y = \tanh x$ and $y = \tanh^{-1} x$ on the same axes. In the chapter text we discussed the logarithmic form for the inverse hyperbolic sine. Similarly show that
$$\tanh^{-1}\frac{x}{a} = \frac{1}{2}\ln\left(\frac{a+x}{a-x}\right).$$

   b)   Based on the graph of $y = \cosh x$ sketch the graph of $y = \cosh^{-1} x$. Find the area under the hyperbolic cosine curve from $(0, 1)$ to $(1.5, 2.35\ldots)$. By subtraction from the appropriate rectangle find the area bounded by the curve, the vertical axis and the line $y = 2.35\ldots$ Reflect this area in the line $y = x$ to show a similar area associated with the curve $y = \cosh^{-1} x$.

4 Implicit Differentiation

The objectives of this chapter are to:

1 Distinguish between explicit and implicit functions.

2 State that $\dfrac{d}{dx}\left(f(y)\right) = \dfrac{d}{dy}\left(f(y)\right)\dfrac{dy}{dx}$ based on the function of a function rule.

3 Differentiate with respect to x an implicit function, $f(x,y) = 0$ term by term.

4 Obtain an expression for $\dfrac{d}{dx}\left((f_1(x)f_2(y)\right)$ using the product rule.

5 Discuss the quotient rule where appropriate.

6 Find an expression for $\dfrac{dy}{dx}$ using **3** and **4**.

7 Evaluate $\dfrac{dy}{dx}$ for given values of x and y.

Introduction

We learned how to differentiate in Volume 1, Chapter 18. Later, in Volume 2, we introduced more techniques, i.e.

     i)   function of a function (substitution) rule,

     ii) product rule,

and iii) quotient rule.

Generally we used y in terms of x, i.e. y as a function of x, i.e. $y = f(x)$. Then we found $\dfrac{dy}{dx}, \dfrac{d^2y}{dx^2}, \ldots$ Where we can write $y = f(x)$ y is given **explicitly** in terms of x. This may not always be possible. Alternatively it may be more difficult and the expression may be too complicated to write y **directly** in terms of x. Generally in all our functions so far we have written y **directly** (i.e. **explicitly**) in terms of x. Obviously we have also used other independent and dependent variables in place of x and y.

Examples 4.1

The following are explicit functions, i.e. y is given directly in terms of x.

i) $3y + 2x - 3 = 0$, i.e. $y = -\dfrac{2}{3}x + 1$.

ii) $y = \sin x + 2\cos x$.

iii) $y = \ln(\cos(3x^2 + 2))$.

iv) $y = e^{3+\cos x}$.

ASSIGNMENT

The Assignment for this chapter looks at a simple pendulum. A small mass is attached to the lower end of a string. The upper end of the string is fixed. We consider the string to be light (i.e. of negligible weight compared with the small attached weight) and inextensible (i.e. non-elastic). Initially it hangs vertically in equilibrium. We are going to pull the mass slightly to one side of the vertical central line and then release it. If you try this for yourself you will see it oscillate about that vertical line. Later in the chapter we will discuss the energy of the system.

Implicit functions

Sometimes x and y are combined together. Where we do not or cannot separate them y is given **indirectly** (i.e. **implicitly**) in terms of x, i.e. $f(x, y) = 0$. For example we have seen the general equation for a circle, $x^2 + y^2 = r^2$, several times in Volumes 1 and 2. y is given implicitly in terms of x. We could re-write this equation as $y = \pm\sqrt{r^2 - x^2}$. In this case y is alone on one side of '=', i.e. y is given explicitly in terms of x.

Let us look at another example, $\sin xy - \cos(2x + y) = 0$. Again y is mixed with x, i.e. y is implicit with x. Because this example is a complicated mixture we would not attempt to separate x and y.

████ **Examples 4.2** ████

The following are implicit functions, i.e. y is given indirectly in terms of x.

i) $xy = 4$.

ii) $\dfrac{x^2}{4} + \dfrac{y^2}{25} = 9$.

iii) $x^3 + y^3 = 2xy$.

iv) $xy^2 + x^2 - y + 7 = 0$.

v) $\sin xy + 2 = 0$.

Using your experience from Examples 4.1 and 4.2 you should attempt this exercise.

████ **EXERCISE 4.1** ████

Decide which of the following functions are explicit and which are implicit. You may prefer to re-write some of them in a slightly different form. In each case y is the dependent variable, x, θ and t are the independent variables.

1   $2x^2 + y - 3 = 0$

2   $xy - 24 = 0$

3   $x^2 + y^2 = 9$

4   $y = \ln(t + y)$

5   $x^2 + y^2 - 2x - 4y = 0$

6   $y + \dfrac{1}{t} - 7 = 0$

7   $\sin \theta y + e^{\theta + y} = 0$

8   $x^2 + 3xy + y^2 = 2$

9   $x^3 + 2x^2y + y^3 - 4 = 0$

10 $\cos(y + \theta) - \sin y\theta = 0$

Differentiation

As we mentioned in the Introduction all the usual rules apply. If you are unsure of them you should refer to Volume 2, Chapter 7. We demonstrate the basic technique in Example 4.3. In the later Examples we extend our ideas by applying other rules of differentiation.

████ **Example 4.3** ████

Given $x^2 + y^2 = 16$ find $\dfrac{dy}{dx}$.

We can think of this equation having 3 terms; x^2, y^2 and 16. We intend to differentiate each term with respect to x.

$$\frac{d}{dx}\left(x^2\right) = 2x, \text{ applying } \frac{d}{dx}\left(ax^n\right) = anx^{n-1}.$$

Also $\frac{d}{dx}(16) = 0$ because 16 is a constant and so never changes.

We take care with $\frac{d}{dx}\left(y^2\right)$.

Suppose we let $q = y^2$ so that $\frac{dq}{dy} = 2y$.

In place of $\frac{d}{dx}(y^2)$ we have $\frac{dq}{dx}$.

Using the function of a function rule,

$$\frac{dq}{dx} = \frac{dq}{dy} \times \frac{dy}{dx}$$

we get $\qquad \frac{dq}{dx} = 2y\frac{dy}{dx}$

i.e. $\qquad \frac{d}{dx}\left(y^2\right) = 2y\frac{dy}{dx}.$

> Substituting
> $\frac{dq}{dx} = 2y.$

Let us look closely at this differentiation. When we differentiate y^2 the power of 2 comes forward as a coefficient. Also the original power is reduced by 1. Using y instead of x this is still basic differentiation. The extra $\frac{dy}{dx}$ is included because we are differentiating y with respect to x. For any terms in x, when we differentiate with respect to x we do *not* need $\frac{dy}{dx}$.

Linking together all 3 parts of our solution we have

$$x^2 + y^2 = 16$$

and differentiating with respect to x we get

$$2x + 2y\frac{dy}{dx} = 0$$

i.e. $\qquad 2y\frac{dy}{dx} = -2x$

> 2s cancel.

i.e. $\qquad \frac{dy}{dx} = -\frac{x}{y}.$

Notice our expression for $\frac{dy}{dx}$ includes both variables. This differs from answers for explicit functions. In those cases our answers were always in terms of x (or some other independent variable).

Let us look more closely at the style of $\frac{d}{dx}\left(y^2\right) = 2y\frac{dy}{dx}.$

Remember we obey the basic rules of differentiation. This is a specific example of the general rule

$$\frac{d}{dx}\left(f(y)\right) = \frac{d}{dy}\left(f(y)\right)\frac{dy}{dx}.$$

In the next Examples we demonstrate this idea.

Examples 4.4

i) $\dfrac{d}{dx}\left(y^3 + 2y^4\right) = \left(3y^2 + 8y^3\right)\dfrac{dy}{dx}$

ii) $\dfrac{d}{dx}\left(3\sin y\right) = 3\cos y.\dfrac{dy}{dx}$

iii) $\dfrac{d}{dx}\left(\cos 2y\right) = -2\sin 2y.\dfrac{dy}{dx}$

iv) $\dfrac{d}{dx}\left(3e^{2y}\right) = 6e^{2y}\dfrac{dy}{dx}$

v) $\dfrac{d}{dx}\left(\ln(\cos y)\right) = -\dfrac{\sin y}{\cos y}.\dfrac{dy}{dx} = -\tan y.\dfrac{dy}{dx}$

Examples 4.5

Find an expression for $\dfrac{dy}{dx}$ given i) $y^2 + x^2 - y + 7 = 0$,

$$\text{ii) } xy^2 + x^2 - 2y - 16 = 0.$$

In each example we differentiate term by term.

i) For $\qquad\qquad\qquad\qquad y^2 + x^2 - y + 7 = 0$

we differentiate with respect to x,

i.e. $\dfrac{d}{dx}\left(y^2\right) + \dfrac{d}{dx}\left(x^2\right) - \dfrac{d}{dx}\left(y\right) + \dfrac{d}{dx}\left(7\right) = \dfrac{d}{dx}\left(0\right)$

i.e. $\qquad\qquad\qquad 2y\dfrac{dy}{dx} + 2x - \dfrac{dy}{dx} = 0$

$$(2y - 1)\dfrac{dy}{dx} = -2x$$

$$\dfrac{dy}{dx} = \dfrac{-2x}{2y - 1} \text{ or } \dfrac{2x}{1 - 2y}.$$

We reach the alternative answer multiplying each term by -1.

ii) In $xy^2 + x^2 - 2y - 16 = 0$

$$u\frac{dv}{dx} + v\frac{du}{dx}.$$

we have a product, xy^2.

We differentiate with respect to x,

i.e. $$\frac{d}{dx}\left(xy^2\right) + \frac{d}{dx}\left(x^2\right) - \frac{d}{dx}\left(2y\right) - \frac{d}{dx}\left(16\right) = \frac{d}{dx}\left(0\right)$$

$$x\frac{d}{dx}\left(y^2\right) + y^2\frac{d}{dx}\left(x\right) + \frac{d}{dx}\left(x^2\right) - \frac{d}{dx}\left(2y\right) - \frac{d}{dx}\left(16\right) = \frac{d}{dx}\left(0\right)$$

i.e. $$x^2y\frac{dy}{dx} + y^2\left(1\right) + 2x - 2\frac{dy}{dx} = 0$$

$$2(xy - 1)\frac{dy}{dx} = -y^2 - 2x$$

$$\frac{dy}{dx} = \frac{-y^2 - 2x}{2(xy - 1)}.$$

Again we can amend our answer by multiplying each term by -1 to get $\dfrac{y^2 + 2x}{2(1 - xy)}.$

We can generalise the differentiation of a product with the rule

$$\frac{d}{dx}\left(f_1(x)f_2(y)\right) = f_1(x)\frac{d}{dx}\left(f_2(y)\right) + f_2(y)\frac{d}{dx}\left(f_1(x)\right)$$

$$= f_1(x)\frac{d}{dy}\left(f_2(y)\right)\frac{dy}{dx} + f_2(y)(f_1'(x)).$$

This rule looks complicated because of all the brackets and functional notation. As Example 4.4ii) showed it is *not* difficult. In the next Exercise you can practise these techniques.

◼◼◼◼ ASSIGNMENT ◼◼◼◼

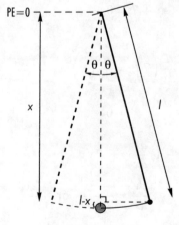

Fig. 4.1

In Fig. 4.1 we show a mass attached to the lower end of a string of length ℓ. This is a simple pendulum. The upper end is fixed and so we use this as a level of zero potential energy. The mass is slightly displaced from the central vertical line and released. It oscillates about that line. Fig. 4.1 shows the mass and string displaced at some general angle θ during its motion. The mass traces out an arc of a circle. Because this is circular motion we have angular velocity rather than linear velocity. Angular velocity, ω, is related to linear velocity, v, and radius, r, by $v = r\omega$. In this case the radius of the circle is the string length ℓ. The angular velocity is variable so we use $\dfrac{d\theta}{dt}$ (i.e. the rate of change of angle, θ, with respect to time, t). This gives $v = \ell\dfrac{d\theta}{dt}$.

Let us look at the energy (i.e. kinetic and potential energy) of the system. We calculate them at the general position shown in Fig. 4.1.

Potential energy $= mgh$ J.

Kinetic energy $= \dfrac{1}{2}mv^2$ J.

As usual we use m for the mass (kg),

$\qquad g$ for the acceleration due to gravity, 9.81 ms^{-2},

$\qquad h$ for the height (m),

$\qquad v$ for the velocity (ms^{-1}).

In our case the mass is below the level of zero potential energy. Hence the height is negative.

$$\text{PE} = -mgx = -mg\ell\cos\theta.$$

$$\text{KE} = \frac{1}{2}mv^2 = \frac{1}{2}m\left(\ell\frac{d\theta}{dt}\right)^2 = \frac{1}{2}m\ell^2\left(\frac{d\theta}{dt}\right)^2.$$

Because there is no external force acting on the system the total energy is constant, i.e.

$$\text{PE} + \text{KE} = \text{constant}$$

so that

$$-mg\ell\cos\theta + \frac{1}{2}m\ell^2\left(\frac{d\theta}{dt}\right)^2 = \text{constant}$$

We differentiate with respect to t to get

$$-mg\ell\frac{d}{dt}\left(\cos\theta\right) + \frac{1}{2}m\ell^2\frac{d}{dt}\left(\left(\frac{d\theta}{dt}\right)^2\right) = \frac{d}{dt}\left(\text{constant}\right)$$

i.e. $\quad mg\ell\sin\theta.\dfrac{d\theta}{dt} + \dfrac{1}{2}m\ell^2 2\dfrac{d\theta}{dt}.\dfrac{d}{dt}\left(\dfrac{d\theta}{dt}\right) = 0 \qquad \boxed{\begin{array}{l} m,\ g,\ \ell \text{ are constant} \\ \text{multipliers.} \end{array}}$

$$mg\ell\sin\theta.\frac{d\theta}{dt} + m\ell^2\frac{d\theta}{dt}.\frac{d^2\theta}{dt^2} = 0$$

$$g\sin\theta + \ell\frac{d^2\theta}{dt^2} = 0. \qquad \boxed{m,\ \ell \text{ and } \dfrac{d\theta}{dt} \text{ cancel.}}$$

For small angles in radians $\sin\theta \approx \theta$ so that

$$g\theta + \ell\frac{d^2\theta}{dt^2} = 0$$

i.e.

$$\frac{d^2\theta}{dt^2} = -\frac{g\theta}{\ell},$$

i.e. this motion of our simple pendulum approximates to simple harmonic motion (S.H.M.) for small angular displacements. Acceleration is directly proportional to its displacement from a fixed point in its path, and is always directed towards that fixed point. We must emphasise this is an approximation. In practice the pendulum will slow due to friction at the upper end's fixing and air resistance. Over a period of time it will eventually stop. This is consistent with damped harmonic motion described in Volume 2, Chapter 7.

■■■■ EXERCISE 4.2 ■■■■

In each question find an expression for $\dfrac{dy}{dx}$.

1   $x^2 + y^2 = 9$

2   $x^2 + y^2 - 2x - 4y = 0$

3   $xy = 24$

4   $y^3 + 2x^{-2} - 7 = 0$

5   $y^3 + x + e^{3y} = 0$

6   $\dfrac{x^2}{4} + \dfrac{y^2}{25} = 9$

7   $x^3 + y^3 = 2xy$

8   $y + \sin y + \cos x = 0$

9   $x^3 + 2x^2 y + y^3 - 4 = 0$

10   $y = x \cos y$

We could also apply the quotient rule we introduced in Volume 2, Chapter 7. However there is a way to avoid it. Suppose we have $\dfrac{\sin y}{x} + 2\cos y = 0$. We could apply the quotient rule to $\dfrac{\sin y}{x}$ and differentiate $2\cos y$ as usual. Alternatively in $\dfrac{\sin y}{x} + 2\cos y = 0$ we could multiply throughout by x to get $\sin y + 2x\cos y = 0$. Now we would simply apply the product rule to $2x\cos y$ and differentiate $\sin y$ as usual. For implicit differentiation this means the quotient rule is redundant. In fact you could avoid it in explicit differentiation too. Using multiplication you could turn an explicit function into an implicit function. We do this in the next Example.

■■■■ Examples 4.6 ■■■■

For $y = \dfrac{x \sin x}{1 + x^2}$ find an expression for $\dfrac{dy}{dx}$.

We look at this differentiation twice; explicitly and implicitly.

i)   For the explicit method we have a product in the numerator and a quotient overall. Remember for u and v as functions of x

$$y = uv, \quad \frac{dy}{dx} = u\frac{dv}{dx} + v\frac{du}{dx};$$

Product rule.

$$y = \frac{u}{v}, \quad \frac{dy}{dx} = \frac{v\frac{du}{dx} - u\frac{dv}{dx}}{v^2}.$$

Quotient rule.

$$\frac{dy}{dx} = \frac{(1+x^2)\{(x)(\cos x) + (\sin x)(1)\} - (x\sin x)\{2x\}}{(1+x^2)^2}$$

which eventually simplifies to

$$\frac{dy}{dx} = \frac{x(1+x^2)\cos x + (1-x^2)\sin x}{(1+x^2)^2}.$$

ii) For the implicit method we multiply throughout by $(1+x^2)$ to get

$$y(1+x^2) = x\sin x.$$

This gives a product on each side of the '=' sign.

We differentiate with respect to x, i.e.

$$\frac{d}{dx}\left(y(1+x^2)\right) = \frac{d}{dx}\left(x\sin x\right).$$

This gives

$$y\frac{d}{dx}\left(1+x^2\right) + (1+x^2)\frac{d}{dx}\left(y\right) = x\frac{d}{dx}\left(\sin x\right) + \sin x.\frac{d}{dx}\left(x\right)$$

i.e. $\quad y2x + (1+x^2)\frac{dy}{dx} = x\cos x + \sin x.\text{(1)}$

$$(1+x^2)\frac{dy}{dx} = x\cos x + \sin x - 2xy$$

$$\frac{dy}{dx} = \frac{x\cos x + \sin x - 2xy}{1+x^2}.$$

For yourself check the two expressions for $\dfrac{dy}{dx}$ are the same. This involves some algebraic manipulation. Notice how the implicit answer includes both x and y. The explicit answer is in terms of only x.

Let us look more deeply, applying the function of a function rule to trigonometric and exponential functions. Our next Examples show sine functions. Exactly the same ideas apply to any trigonometric functions.

Examples 4.7

Find an expression for $\dfrac{dy}{dx}$ given

i) $\sin(x+y) + y^2 - x^3 - 9 = 0$,
ii) $\sin(xy) + y^2 - x^3 - 9 = 0$.

In both examples we know how to differentiate y^2, x^3 and 9. We need to look more closely at the sine functions.

i)   In $\sin(x + y)$ we let $\qquad q = x + y$

so that $\qquad\qquad \dfrac{dq}{dx} = \dfrac{d}{dx}\left(x + y\right) = 1 + \dfrac{dy}{dx}.$

Then $\qquad \dfrac{d}{dx}\left(\sin(x + y)\right) = \dfrac{d}{dx}\left(\sin q\right)$

$$= \cos q \cdot \dfrac{dq}{dx}$$

$$= \cos(x + y) \cdot \left(1 + \dfrac{dy}{dx}\right)$$

which we write as $\left(1 + \dfrac{dy}{dx}\right)\cos(x + y)$. This ensures cosine applies

only to $(x + y)$. Notice the derivative of sine is cosine as usual. Also

the derivative of $(x + y)$ is $\left(1 + \dfrac{dy}{dx}\right)$. Now we use this result.

For $\qquad \sin(x + y) + y^2 - x^3 - 9 = 0$

we differentiate with respect to x, i.e.

$$\left(1 + \dfrac{dy}{dx}\right)\cos(x + y) + 2y\dfrac{dy}{dx} - 3x^2 = 0.$$

For yourself check this simplifies to

$$\dfrac{dy}{dx} = \dfrac{3x^2 - \cos(x + y)}{2y + \cos(x + y)}.$$

ii) In $\sin(xy)$ we let $\quad q = xy$ and apply the product rule so

$$\dfrac{dq}{dx} = x\dfrac{d}{dx}\left(y\right) + y\dfrac{d}{dx}\left(x\right) \qquad \boxed{u\dfrac{dv}{dx} + v\dfrac{du}{dx}.}$$

$$= x\dfrac{dy}{dx} + y.(1)$$

$$= x\dfrac{dy}{dx} + y.$$

Then $\qquad \dfrac{d}{dx}\left(\sin(xy)\right) = \dfrac{d}{dx}\left(\sin q\right)$

$$= \cos q \cdot \dfrac{dq}{dx}$$

$$= \cos(xy) \cdot \left(x\dfrac{dy}{dx} + y\right)$$

which we write as $\left(x\dfrac{dy}{dx} + y\right)\cos(xy)$. This ensures cosine applies

only to (xy). Notice the derivative of sine is cosine as usual. Also the

derivative of (xy) is $\left(x\dfrac{dy}{dx} + y\right)$. Now we use this result.

For $\qquad \sin(xy) + y^2 - x^3 - 9 = 0$

we differentiate with respect to x, i.e.

$$\left(x\frac{dy}{dx} + y \right) \cos(xy) + 2y\frac{dy}{dx} - 3x^2 = 0.$$

For yourself check this simplifies to

$$\frac{dy}{dx} = \frac{3x^2 - y\cos(xy)}{2y + x\cos(xy)}.$$

Examples 4.8

Find an expression for $\dfrac{dy}{dx}$ given

i) $\quad e^{(2x+3y)} + 5y^3 - 4x^2 = 0,$

ii) $\quad e^{(4xy^2)} + 5y^3 - 4x^2 = 0.$

In both examples we know how to differentiate $5y^3$ and $4x^2$. We need to look more closely at the exponential functions.

i) In $e^{(2x+3y)}$ we let $\quad q = 2x + 3y$

so that $\qquad \dfrac{dq}{dx} = \dfrac{d}{dx}\left(2x + 3y \right) = 2 + 3\dfrac{dy}{dx}.$

Then $\quad \dfrac{d}{dx}\left(e^{(2x+3y)} \right) = \dfrac{d}{dx}\left(e^q \right)$

$$= e^q \frac{dq}{dx}$$

$$= e^{(2x+3y)}\left(2 + 3\frac{dy}{dx} \right).$$

Notice the derivative of an exponential is an exponential as usual. Also the derivative of $(2x + 3y)$ is $\left(2 + 3\dfrac{dy}{dx} \right)$. Now we use this result.

For $\qquad e^{(2x+3y)} + 5y^3 - 4x^2 = 0$

we differentiate with respect to x, i.e.

$$\left(2 + 3\frac{dy}{dx} \right)e^{(2x+3y)} + 15y^2\frac{dy}{dx} - 8x = 0.$$

For yourself check this simplifies to

$$\frac{dy}{dx} = \frac{2\left(4x - e^{(2x+3y)} \right)}{3\left(5y^2 + e^{(2x+3y)} \right)}.$$

ii) In $e^{(4xy^2)}$ we let $q = 4xy^2$ and apply the product rule so

$$\frac{dq}{dx} = 4x\frac{d}{dx}\left(y^2\right) + y^2\frac{d}{dx}\left(4x\right) \qquad \boxed{u\frac{dv}{dx} + v\frac{du}{dx}.}$$

$$= 4x2y\frac{dy}{dx} + y^2 4$$

$$= 8xy\frac{dy}{dx} + 4y^2 \quad \text{or} \quad 4y\left(2x\frac{dy}{dx} + y\right).$$

Then $\quad \dfrac{d}{dx}\left(e^{(4xy^2)}\right) = \dfrac{d}{dx}\left(e^q\right)$

$$= e^q\frac{dq}{dx}$$

$$= e^{(4xy^2)}\left(8xy\frac{dy}{dx} + 4y^2\right).$$

Notice the derivative of an exponential is an exponential as usual.

Also the derivative of $\left(4xy^2\right)$ is $\left(8xy\dfrac{dy}{dx} + 4y^2\right)$. Now we use this result.

For $\qquad\qquad e^{(4xy^2)} + 5y^3 - 4x^2 = 0$

we differentiate with respect to x, i.e.

$$\left(8xy\frac{dy}{dx} + 4y^2\right)e^{(4xy^2)} + 15y^2\frac{dy}{dx} - 8x = 0.$$

For yourself check this simplifies to

$$\frac{dy}{dx} = \frac{4\left(2x - y^2 e^{(4xy^2)}\right)}{15y^2 + 8xye^{(4xy^2)}}.$$

When we differentiate logarithms implicitly we follow a similar pattern for $\ln(x+y)$. However for $\ln(xy)$ we recall a law of logarithms, $\ln xy = \ln x + \ln y$.

■ EXERCISE 4.3 ■

In each question find an expression for $\dfrac{dy}{dx}$.

1   $\sin(3x + y) = 6x^2 + x$

2   $e^{(2x+y)} = y - x$

3   $\cos(x + 5y) + 9x + y = 0$

4   $\tan(x + y) = \ln(\cos y)$

5   $e^{(3x-y)} + 4x^2 - 3y + x = 0$

6   $e^{(3y-2x)} + (2x + y)(x - y) = 0$

7   $\sin(xy) - x + 5y = 0$

8   $\cos(xy^2) - x - y = 0$

9   $\ln(2x^3 + y) - 4x = 0$

10   $\ln(6 - 2y^2) = 4xy$

11 $\ln(xy^2) = 2x^2 + y$

12 $e^{(xy)} - 7x + y = 0$

13 $e^{(3x^2y)} - 6x^3 = 0$

14 $\ln\left(\dfrac{x}{y}\right) - 2x + 4y = 0$

15 $e^{(2x^2y^3)} - 2x^2 + 5y = 0$

Gradient at a point

We follow the usual methods, making our numerical substitutions into a general expression for $\dfrac{dy}{dx}$.

Examples 4.9

i) Find the value of $\dfrac{dy}{dx}$ at the point $(1, 5)$ on the curve
$xy^2 + x^2 - 2y - 16 = 0$.

ii) At the point $(0, 3)$ on the curve $\sin(xy) + y^2 - x^3 - 9 = 0$ find the value of the gradient.

i) We use our general result from Example 4.5ii),
$$\frac{dy}{dx} = \frac{y^2 + 2x}{2(1 - xy)}$$
Given $x = 1$ and $y = 5$ we substitute to get
$$\frac{dy}{dx} = \frac{5^2 + 2(1)}{2(1 - 1 \times 5)}$$
$$= \frac{25 + 2}{2(-4)} = \frac{27}{-8} = -3.375.$$

ii) We use our general result from Example 4.7ii),
$$\frac{dy}{dx} = \frac{3x^2 - y\cos(xy)}{2y + x\cos(xy)}.$$
Given $x = 0$ and $y = 3$ we substitute to get
$$\frac{dy}{dx} = \frac{3(0)^2 - 3\cos 0}{2(3) + 0}$$

Using radians.

$$= \frac{0 - 3}{6} = -0.5.$$

Example 4.10

A charged particle moves in a magnetic field subject to exponential decay. Its path in the x direction in terms of time, t, is given by $xe^{0.25t} - \sin 12t = (5 - 2t)e^{0.25t}$. Find the initial speed of the particle in this direction (i.e. $\dfrac{dx}{dt}$ at $t = 0$).

Because we are going to differentiate implicitly we expect our answer to contain both variables, x and t. We need to find the initial value of x for later substitution.

Using $$xe^{0.25t} - \sin 12t = (5 - 2t)e^{0.25t}$$

we substitute for $t = 0$, i.e.

$$xe^0 - \sin 0 = (5 - 0)e^0$$
$$x - 0 = 5$$
$$x = 5.$$

$$\boxed{e^0 = 1.}$$

Now using $$xe^{0.25t} - \sin 12t = (5 - 2t)e^{0.25t}$$

we differentiate with respect to t, i.e.

$$\frac{d}{dt}\left(xe^{0.25t}\right) - \frac{d}{dt}\left(\sin 12t\right) = \frac{d}{dt}\left((5 - 2t)e^{0.25t}\right)$$

$$x(0.25e^{0.25t}) + e^{0.25t}\frac{dx}{dt} - 12\cos 12t = (5 - 2t)(0.25e^{0.25t}) + e^{0.25t}(-2).$$

In our general equation we substitute for $t = 0$, $x = 5$ to get

$$5(0.25e^0) + e^0\frac{dx}{dt} - 12\cos 0 = (5 - 0)(0.25e^0) - 2e^0.$$

$$1.25 + \frac{dx}{dt} - 12 = 1.25 - 2$$

i.e. $$\frac{dx}{dt} = 10$$

is the initial speed in the x direction.

ASSIGNMENT

We know the motion of our simple pendulum approximates to simple harmonic motion. Its angular acceleration, $\frac{d^2\theta}{dt^2}$, is given by $\frac{d^2\theta}{dt^2} = -\frac{g\theta}{\ell}$.

Remember the acceleration due to gravity is $g = 9.81$ ms^{-2}. For a string of length $\ell = 0.50$ m we can calculate the angular acceleration at any small angle, say $\theta = 1.5°$. Because our earlier Assignment work involved trigonometry and differentiation we convert this angle into radians, i.e.

$$1.5° = 1.5 \times \frac{\pi}{180} \text{ radians.}$$

Then $$\frac{d^2\theta}{dt^2} = -\frac{9.81}{0.5} \times 1.5 \times \frac{\pi}{180} = 0.51 \text{ rads}^{-2}.$$

EXERCISE 4.4

1   Find an expression for the velocity of a body where the displacement, x, is related to the time of motion, t, according to $2 + xe^t = t^2$.

2   If $y\theta = 4\cos\theta$ what is the value of $\frac{dy}{d\theta}$ at the point where $\theta = \frac{\pi}{3}$?

3 Cargo is pushed from a military transport aircraft during flight. It falls subject to air resistance and the effects of its parachutes. During its descent the vertical displacement from the aircraft, y metres, is connected to time, t seconds, by $ye^{2t} - 49t = 24.5$. Find a general expression for the velocity.

4 The velocity, v ms^{-1}, of a missile is related to time, t seconds, by $v(1 + t) - 35t - 35\ln(1 + t) = 0$. Find the acceleration, $\dfrac{dv}{dt}$, after 1.25 seconds.

5 In a water treatment installation the height of effluent, y metres, is related to time, t hours. During a period of 24 hours timed from midnight this relationship is $(3y - 2)(t - 24)^2 = 10t + 25$.

$\dfrac{dy}{dt}$ represents the rate of change of this height. Find a general expression for $\dfrac{dy}{dt}$ and find its value at 7.30 am.

Inverse trigonometric functions

We learned about inverse trigonometric functions, including differentiation, in Chapter 2. Now we show an alternative method, applying implicit differentiation.

████████ **Example 4.11** ████████

Find a general expression for the gradient to the curve $y = \sin^{-1} x$.

We start with $y = \sin^{-1} x$ and rewrite it as

$$x = \sin y.$$

We differentiate with respect to x, i.e.

$$\frac{d}{dx}\left(x\right) = \frac{d}{dx}\left(\sin y\right) = \frac{d}{dy}\left(\sin y\right)\frac{dy}{dx}$$

$$1 = \cos y . \frac{dy}{dx}.$$

We re-arrange this equation to get

$$\frac{dy}{dx} = \frac{1}{\cos y} = \frac{1}{\sqrt{1 - \sin^2 y}}$$

i.e. $\dfrac{dy}{dx} = \dfrac{1}{\sqrt{1 - x^2}}$

$$\boxed{\begin{aligned} &\sin^2 y + \cos^2 y = 1, \\ &\cos^2 y = 1 - \sin^2 y. \end{aligned}}$$

$$\boxed{\begin{aligned} &\text{Substituting} \quad \sin y = x, \\ &\text{i.e.} \qquad\qquad \sin^2 y = x^2. \end{aligned}}$$

Similarly we can find $\dfrac{dy}{dx}$ for both $y = \cos^{-1} x$ and $y = \tan^{-1} x$. Remember

$$x = \tan y = \frac{\sin y}{\cos y} \quad \text{or} \quad x\cos y = \sin y.$$

■■■■■■ **Example 4.12** ■■■■■■

Find a general expression for the gradient to the curve $y = \sec^{-1} x$.

We start with $\qquad\qquad y = \sec^{-1} x$

and rewrite it as $\quad \sec y = x$

and $\qquad\qquad \dfrac{1}{\cos y} = x$

i.e. $\qquad\qquad\qquad 1 = x \cos y.$

We differentiate with respect to x, i.e.

$$\frac{d}{dx}(1) = \frac{d}{dx}\left(x \cos y\right)$$

> Applying the product rule to $x \cos y$.

$$\frac{d}{dx}(1) = x\frac{d}{dx}\left(\cos y\right) + \left(\cos y\right).\frac{d}{dx}\left(x\right)$$

$$0 = x(-\sin y)\frac{dy}{dx} + \cos y.(1)$$

i.e. $\qquad\qquad x \sin y.\dfrac{dy}{dx} = \cos y$

$$\frac{dy}{dx} = \frac{\cos y}{x \sin y} = \frac{1}{x \tan y} \quad \text{or} \quad \frac{\cot y}{x}.$$

We can re-arrange this general expression for the gradient,

i.e. $\qquad\qquad \dfrac{dy}{dx} = \dfrac{1}{x\sqrt{\sec^2 y - 1}}$

> $1 + \tan^2 y = \sec^2 y$,
> $\tan^2 y = \sec^2 y - 1$.

$$\frac{dy}{dx} = \frac{1}{x\sqrt{x^2 - 1}}.$$

> Substituting for $\sec^2 y = x^2$.

Similarly we can find $\dfrac{dy}{dx}$ for both $y = \operatorname{cosec}^{-1}x$ and $y = \cot^{-1} x$. Again remember $\cot y = \dfrac{\cos y}{\sin y}$.

■■■■■■ **Example 4.13** ■■■■■■

Find the value of the gradient at the point $\left(\dfrac{1}{3}, \dfrac{\pi}{8}\right)$ on the curve $2y = \tan^{-1}(3x)$.

We start with $\quad 2y = \tan^{-1}(3x) \quad$ and rewrite it as
$$3x = \tan 2y.$$

We differentiate with respect to x, i.e.

$$\frac{d}{dx}\left(3x\right) = \frac{d}{dx}\left(\tan 2y\right) = \frac{d}{dy}\left(\tan 2y\right)\frac{dy}{dx}$$

$$3 = 2 \sec^2 2y.\frac{dy}{dx}$$

i.e. $\dfrac{dy}{dx} = \dfrac{3}{2\sec^2 2y}$

$\boxed{\sec^2 2y = 1 + \tan^2 2y.}$

$= \dfrac{3}{2(1 + \tan^2 2y)}.$

We could further re-arrange this equation. Alternatively we choose to substitute $y = \dfrac{\pi}{8}$ to get

$\dfrac{dy}{dx} = \dfrac{3}{2\left(1 + \tan^2\left(\dfrac{2\pi}{8}\right)\right)}$

$\boxed{\tan^2\left(\dfrac{2\pi}{8}\right) = \tan^2\dfrac{\pi}{4} = 1.}$

i.e. $\dfrac{dy}{dx} = \dfrac{3}{2(1 + 1)}$

$= 0.75.$

EXERCISE 4.5

In Questions **1–6** find $\dfrac{dy}{dx}$ in terms of i) y only or x and y,

ii) x only.

1 $y = \cos^{-1} x$

2 $y = \tan^{-1} x$

3 $y = {}^{-1} x$

4 $y = \cot^{-1} x$

5 $3y = \sin^{-1} x$

6 $y = \cos^{-1}(2x)$

7 Find the value of $\dfrac{dy}{dx}$ at the point $\left(2, \dfrac{\pi}{4}\right)$ on the curve $y = \tan^{-1}\left(\dfrac{x}{2}\right)$.

8 For $2y = \sin^{-1}(4x)$ what is the value of $\dfrac{dy}{dx}$ at the point $\left(\dfrac{1}{4}, \dfrac{\pi}{4}\right)$?

9 Using the curve $y = 2\cos^{-1}\left(\dfrac{x}{3}\right)$ find the value of the gradient where $x = -1.5$.

10 At the point where $y = \pi$ on the curve $y = 4\sin^{-1}(2x)$ find the value of the gradient.

Local maximum and minimum

We have looked at this topic in detail in Volume 2, Chapter 9. You may find it useful to revise the basic ideas of that chapter before continuing with this section. We show one Example and provide you with a short Exercise.

■■■ **Example 4.14** ■■■

Find the turning points of the curve $x^2 + y^2 - 2x - 4y = 4$ and distinguish between them.

Using
$$x^2 + y^2 - 2x - 4y = 4$$

we differentiate with respect to x, i.e.

$$\frac{d}{dx}\left(x^2\right) + \frac{d}{dx}\left(y^2\right) - \frac{d}{dx}\left(2x\right) - \frac{d}{dx}\left(4y\right) = \frac{d}{dx}\left(4\right)$$

$$2x + 2y\frac{dy}{dx} - 2 - 4\frac{dy}{dx} = 0.$$

At turning points $\dfrac{dy}{dx} = 0$,

i.e. $2x - 2 = 0$

to give $x = 1.$

Implicit differentiation generally gives answers involving both variables. We find the corresponding y values by substitution.

Using $x^2 + y^2 - 2x - 4y = 4$

we substitute for $x = 1$, i.e.

$$1^2 + y^2 - 2 - 4y = 4$$

i.e. $y^2 - 4y - 5 = 0$

factorising to $(y + 1)(y - 5) = 0$

i.e. $y + 1 = 0$ or $y - 5 = 0$

so that $y = -1$ or $5.$

This means we have turning points at both $(1, -1)$ and $(1, 5)$. The next stage is to find the nature of those turning points from the second derivatives.

> $2y\dfrac{dy}{dx}$ is a product.

Using $2x + 2y\dfrac{dy}{dx} - 2 - 4\dfrac{dy}{dx} = 0$

we differentiate again with respect to x, i.e.

$$2 + (2y)\left(\frac{d^2y}{dx^2}\right) + \left(\frac{dy}{dx}\right)\left(2\frac{dy}{dx}\right) - 4\frac{d^2y}{dx^2} = 0.$$

At a turning point $\dfrac{dy}{dx} = 0$ to give

$$2 + 2y\frac{d^2y}{dx^2} - 4\frac{d^2y}{dx^2} = 0$$

i.e. $2(y - 2)\dfrac{d^2y}{dx^2} = -2$

$$\frac{d^2y}{dx^2} = \frac{-2}{2(y - 2)} = \frac{1}{2 - y}.$$

We substitute our values into this general expression.

At $y = -1$, $\qquad \dfrac{d^2y}{dx^2} = \dfrac{1}{2+1} = \dfrac{1}{3}$, i.e. positive.

This means we have a minimum turning point at $(1, -1)$.

At $y = 5$, $\qquad \dfrac{d^2y}{dx^2} = \dfrac{1}{2-5} = -\dfrac{1}{3}$, i.e. negative.

This means we have a maximum turning point at $(1, 5)$.

We confirm these turning points in Fig. 4.2. As you can see the equation $x^2 + y^2 - 2x - 4y = 4$ is a circle with centre $(1, 2)$ and radius 3.

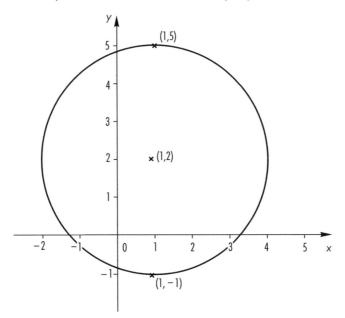

Fig. 4.2

ASSIGNMENT

Remember we have an expression for the angular acceleration of our simple pendulum. Also angular acceleration is the rate of change of angular velocity with respect to time, i.e.

$$\frac{d^2\theta}{dt^2} = \frac{d}{dt}\left(\frac{d\theta}{dt}\right).$$

As an exercise for yourself investigate the simple harmonic motion of this pendulum. We suggest a maximum angular displacement of 4° on each side of a central vertical line. Your tasks should include calculations relating to angular displacement, velocity and acceleration. You may or may not wish to represent these graphically as well.

1   The curve $y^2 - x + 4x^2 = 0$ has two turning points. Using differentiation find the coordinates of those points. Also identify which is the local maximum and the local minimum.

2   For the curve $ye^{2\theta} = 2\sin\theta$ find the coordinates of the turning point in the range $0 \leqslant \theta \leqslant \dfrac{\pi}{2}$. Is it a maximum or a minimum turning point?

3   There is thought to be a turning point where $x = -3$ on the curve $xy + x^3 = 54$. By differentiation check that this is true and find the corresponding y coordinate. Is it a local maximum or minimum point?

4   Find the coordinates of the local minimum point on the curve $2ye^x = e^{2x} + 1$.

5   A compound pendulum displays damped harmonic motion according to $20ye^{0.5t} - \sin 3t = 0$. y is the displacement at time t. Find its first maximum and the first minimum turning points.

5 Parametric Differentiation

The objectives of this chapter are to:

1 Understand the role of a parameter (e.g. t) when defining a relationship between 2 variables (e.g. x and y).

2 State $\dfrac{dy}{dx} = \dfrac{dy}{dt} \times \dfrac{dt}{dx} = \dfrac{dy}{dt} \Big/ \dfrac{dx}{dt}$.

3 Use the rule in **2** to obtain $\dfrac{dy}{dx}$ from given parametric equations.

4 Extend the rule in **2** to give $\dfrac{d^2y}{dx^2}$ as $\dfrac{d}{dt}\left(\dfrac{dy}{dx}\right) \Big/ \dfrac{dx}{dt}$.

5 Obtain and evaluate $\dfrac{dy}{dx}$ and $\dfrac{d^2y}{dx^2}$ for given parametric equations and given values of the parameter.

Introduction

We have used functional notation in many cases already. Typically $y = f(x)$ expresses the dependent variable, y, in terms of the independent variable, x. Simple systems have two variables, though generally systems are more complicated than this. A **parameter** is an **auxiliary variable**. It may be there but hidden if not currently being considered. Often time, t, or some angle, θ, act as parameters.

ASSIGNMENT

Our Assignment for this chapter looks at a circle and its parametric equations. Later we differentiate those equations, linking them together and to simple harmonic motion.

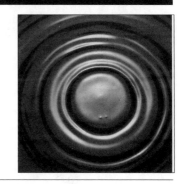

Parametric equations

Suppose we have $y = f(x)$. It is *not* unusual for both x and y to vary according to time, t. We may write

$$x = f_1(t) \quad \text{and} \quad y = f_2(t)$$

or

$$x = g(t) \quad \text{and} \quad y = h(t).$$

We might use g and h because they follow f alphabetically. Be careful *not* to confuse this g with the acceleration due to gravity.

This format means t is a parameter. It is a hidden variable we do not need to think about if simply working with x and y.

▄▄▄▄ Example 5.1 ▄▄▄▄

In Fig. 5.1 we show the path of a projectile fired with a velocity, v_0, at an angle, α, above the horizontal. g is the acceleration due to gravity.

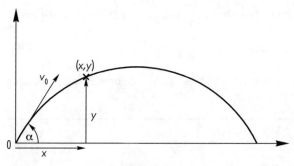

Fig. 5.1

After some time, t, the coordinates of the projectile's position are (x, y),

i.e. $\left(v_0 t \cos \alpha, \ v_0 t \sin \alpha - \dfrac{1}{2} g t^2 \right)$.

When we write $\quad x = v_0 t \cos \alpha$

$$\text{and} \quad y = v_0 t \sin \alpha - \frac{1}{2} g t^2$$

we have the parametric equations of this projectile. For constants v_0, α and g both x and y vary according to time, t.

▄▄▄▄ Example 5.2 ▄▄▄▄

In Fig. 5.2 we have a capacitor with capacitance, C, and charge, q. We know the voltage, V, across the capacitor is given by $V = \dfrac{q}{C}$. Suppose $C = 5 \times 10^{-5}$ F and $q = 4 \times 10^{-3} e^{-50t}$. By substitution

$$V = \frac{4 \times 10^{-3} e^{-50t}}{5 \times 10^{-5}} = 80 e^{-50t}.$$

Fig. 5.2

We have 3 equations:

i) $q = 4 \times 10^{-3}e^{-50t}$ relates the charge, q, to time, t;

ii) $V = 80e^{-50t}$ relates the voltage, V, across the capacitor to time, t;

iii) $V = \dfrac{q}{C}$ relates the variables q and V. From our previous work we know that each is related to the parameter t. However, in the equation $V = \dfrac{q}{C}$ that auxiliary variable (the parameter, t) is hidden.

In Example 5.2 we showed we can eliminate a parameter. This produces a relationship in terms of the other variables only. Sometimes this is easy, as in Example 5.2. Sometimes, if it is more difficult, we choose not to make the elimination.

Example 5.3

We know from Example 5.1 that x and y can be given in terms of the parameter, t. We can eliminate t to leave y in terms of x. Because t appears once only in $x = v_0 t \cos \alpha$ we re-arrange this equation to get $t = \dfrac{x}{v_0 \cos \alpha}$.

In $y = v_0 t \sin \alpha - \dfrac{1}{2}gt^2$

we substitute for t,

i.e. $y = v_0 \left(\dfrac{x}{v_0 \cos \alpha} \right) \sin \alpha - \dfrac{1}{2}g \dfrac{x^2}{v_0{}^2 \cos^2 \alpha}$.

We re-arrange and simplify this equation into a known form,

i.e. $y = x \tan \alpha - \dfrac{gx^2}{2v_0{}^2} \sec^2 \alpha$,

$$\boxed{\dfrac{\sin \alpha}{\cos \alpha} = \tan \alpha, \quad \dfrac{1}{\cos^2 \alpha} = \sec^2 \alpha.}$$

i.e. $y = x \tan \alpha - \dfrac{gx^2}{2v_0{}^2}\left(1 + \tan^2 \alpha\right)$.

There are other forms, but this is a common one for the path of a projectile.

ASSIGNMENT

Fig. 5.3 shows a circle with centre $(0,0)$ and radius, r. We show a typical point (x, y) on the circle. The radius to that point is inclined at some general angle, θ, to the horizontal axis. As we move around the circle r remains constant. The position of (x, y) changes in relation to the angle, θ. This means θ is a parameter.

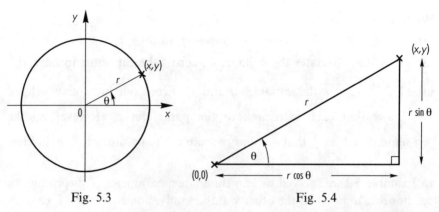

Fig. 5.3   Fig. 5.4

We complete a right-angled triangle from Fig. 5.3 and apply some trigonometry. Fig. 5.4 shows

$$x = r\cos\theta$$

and $y = r\sin\theta$.

These are the parametric equations of the circle.

As we showed in the earlier Examples we can eliminate the parameter. For a circle the standard method is to square and add the parametric equations, i.e.

$$x^2 = r^2\cos^2\theta \qquad \text{and} \qquad y^2 = r^2\sin^2\theta$$

so that $x^2 + y^2 = r^2\cos^2\theta + r^2\sin^2\theta$

$$= r^2(\cos^2\theta + \sin^2\theta)$$

i.e. $x^2 + y^2 = r^2.$ $\boxed{\cos^2\theta + \sin^2\theta = 1.}$

This is the general Cartesian equation of a circle with centre $(0,0)$ and radius r.

We can apply this method to a circle with any centre and radius. Suppose the centre is $(1,2)$ and the radius is 3.

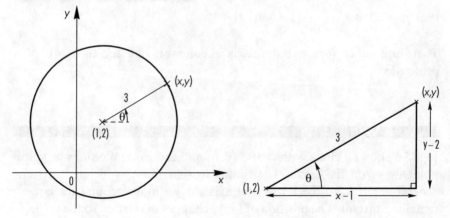

Figs. 5.5

In Figs. 5.5 we show the circle and a general right-angled triangle. Again we choose a general point on the circle. We apply similar trigonometry to the right-angled triangle to get

$$x - 1 = 3\cos\theta \quad \text{and} \quad y - 2 = 3\sin\theta.$$

Again we square and add these equations, i.e.

$$(x - 1)^2 = 3^2 \cos^2\theta \quad \text{and} \quad (y - 2)^2 = 3^2 \sin^2\theta$$

so that $(x - 1)^2 + (y - 2)^2 = 3^2 \cos^2\theta + 3^2 \sin^2\theta$

$$= 3^2 (\cos^2\theta + \sin^2\theta)$$

i.e. $\qquad (x - 1)^2 + (y - 2)^2 = 3^2.$

There are other versions of this equation. Expanding the brackets we get

$$x^2 - 2x + 1 + y^2 - 4y + 4 = 9$$

i.e. $\qquad x^2 + y^2 - 2x - 4y = 4.$

This is the circle we discussed in Example 4.14. There we found its maximum and minimum turning points.

■ EXERCISE 5.1 ■

In each question write down the parameter. Eliminate that parameter from the parametric equations. Simplify the algebra in the resulting equation of two variables.

1 $x = t^2,\ y = 2t$

2 $x = 2t^2,\ y = 3t$

3 $x = 2t,\ y = 4t^2 - 1$

4 $x = 5\cos\theta,\ y = 5\sin\theta$

5 $x = \cos\theta,\ y = 2\sin\theta$

6 $x = 2t,\ y = \dfrac{2}{t}$

7 $x = 3\sin\phi,\ y = 3\cos\phi$

8 $x = 2t,\ y = \dfrac{4}{t}$

9 $x = 2\cos\theta,\ y = \sin\theta$

10 $x = 6t^2,\ y = 4t^3$

Differentiation

In Volume 1, Chapter 18, we defined $\dfrac{dy}{dx}$ as $\dfrac{dy}{dx} = \underset{\delta x \to 0}{\text{Lim}} \dfrac{\delta y}{\delta x}$.

Similarly we can define $\dfrac{dy}{dt}$ and $\dfrac{dx}{dt}$ as $\delta t \to 0$.

In each case as $\delta t \to 0$ so $\delta x \to 0$ and $\delta y \to 0$. We use this with

$$\frac{dx}{dt} = \operatorname*{Lim}_{\delta t \to 0} \frac{\delta x}{\delta t} \quad \text{and} \quad \frac{dt}{dx} = \operatorname*{Lim}_{\delta x \to 0} \frac{\delta t}{\delta x} \quad \text{or} \quad \frac{1}{\operatorname*{Lim}_{\delta t \to 0} \dfrac{\delta x}{\delta t}}.$$

This means we have

$$\frac{dt}{dx} = \frac{1}{\dfrac{dx}{dt}}, \quad \text{i.e. } 1 \bigg/ \frac{dx}{dt}.$$

We can apply this to the function of a function rule, i.e.

$$\frac{dy}{dx} = \frac{dy}{dt} \times \frac{dt}{dx}$$

becomes $\dfrac{dy}{dx} = \dfrac{dy}{dt} \times \dfrac{1}{\dfrac{dx}{dt}}$ or $\dfrac{dy}{dt} \bigg/ \dfrac{dx}{dt}$.

████ **Examples 5.4** ████

Find $\dfrac{dy}{dx}$ for i) $x = 3t^2$, $y = 2t^3$; ii) $x = 2\sin 2\theta$, $y = 5\cos 2\theta$.

i)   Using $y = 2t^3$ and $x = 3t^2$

we simply differentiate with respect to t, i.e.

$$\frac{dy}{dt} = 6t^2 \quad \text{and} \quad \frac{dx}{dt} = 6t.$$

Using $\dfrac{dy}{dx} = \dfrac{dy}{dt} \bigg/ \dfrac{dx}{dt}$

we get $\dfrac{dy}{dx} = \dfrac{6t^2}{6t} = t.$

Notice our derivative, $\dfrac{dy}{dx}$, is in terms of the parameter, t.

ii) Using $y = 5\cos 2\theta$ and $x = 2\sin 2\theta$

we simply differentiate with respect to θ, i.e.

$$\frac{dy}{d\theta} = -10\sin 2\theta \quad \text{and} \quad \frac{dx}{d\theta} = 4\cos 2\theta.$$

Using $\dfrac{dy}{dx} = \dfrac{dy}{d\theta} \bigg/ \dfrac{dx}{d\theta}$

we get $\dfrac{dy}{dx} = \dfrac{-10\sin 2\theta}{4\cos 2\theta} = -2.5\tan 2\theta.$

Again our differential, $\dfrac{dy}{dx}$, is in terms of the parameter, θ.

████████ **Example 5.5** ████████████████████████████████████

We extend the projectile problem of Example 5.1. Suppose a missile is fired with an initial speed of 280 ms^{-1} at an angle of 55° to the horizontal. (We know the acceleration due to gravity, g, is 9.81 ms^{-2}.) We are interested in the missile $\frac{1}{2}$ minute (i.e. 30 seconds) after firing.

In $x = v_0 t \cos \alpha$

we substitute to get

$$x = 280 \times 30 \times \cos 55°$$

$$= 4818.0 \ldots \text{ m}$$

$$= 4.82 \text{ km,}$$

i.e. after 30 seconds the missile has travelled 4.82 km horizontally.

In $y = v_0 t \sin \alpha - \dfrac{1}{2} g t^2$

we substitute to get

$$y = (280 \times 30 \times \sin 55°) - (0.5 \times 9.81 \times 30^2)$$

$$= 2466.3 \ldots \text{ m}$$

$$= 2.47 \text{ km,}$$

i.e. after 30 seconds the missile has travelled 2.47 km vertically.

Our two values give the horizontal and vertical displacements after 30 seconds. Alternatively we may think of them as coordinates through which the missile is passing at $t = 30$ seconds.

Also, we find the horizontal and vertical components of velocity by differentiation.

Using $x = v_0 t \cos \alpha$

$$\frac{dx}{dt} = v_0 \cos \alpha$$

is the general expression for the horizontal component of velocity.

In our case, by substitution,

$$\frac{dx}{dt} = 280 \times \cos 55°$$

$$= 160.6 \text{ ms}^{-1}$$

is the horizontal component of velocity after 30 seconds.

Using $y = v_0 t \sin \alpha - \dfrac{1}{2} g t^2$

$$\frac{dy}{dt} = v_0 \sin \alpha - gt$$

$$\boxed{\tfrac{1}{2} g(2t) = gt.}$$

is the general expression for the vertical component of velocity.

Again in our case, by substitution,

$$\frac{dy}{dt} = 280 \times \sin 55° - 9.81 \times 30$$

$$= -64.9 \text{ ms}^{-1}$$

is the vertical component of velocity after 30 seconds. We interpret the negative sign to mean vertically downwards, i.e. 64.9 ms^{-1} vertically downwards. Perhaps the missile may have missed its airborne target or may be approaching its land based one.

Using $\quad \dfrac{dy}{dx} = \dfrac{dy}{dt} \Big/ \dfrac{dx}{dt}$

we get $\quad \dfrac{dy}{dx} = \dfrac{-64.9\ldots}{160.6\ldots}$

$$= -0.4043\ldots$$

Remember that $\dfrac{dy}{dx}$ can represent the gradient of a tangent to a curve. In Fig. 5.6 we show the tangent below the horizontal consistent with our negative sign. The inverse tangent of $-0.4043\ldots$ is $-22°$, i.e. $22°$ below the horizontal.

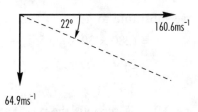

Fig. 5.6

▮▮▮▮ ASSIGNMENT ▮▮▮▮

For our circle we know $y = r\sin\theta$ and $x = r\cos\theta$.

Differentiating with respect to θ we get

$$\frac{dy}{d\theta} = r\cos\theta \quad \text{and} \quad \frac{dx}{d\theta} = -r\sin\theta.$$

Then using $\quad \dfrac{dy}{dx} = \dfrac{dy}{d\theta} \Big/ \dfrac{dx}{d\theta}$

we get $\quad \dfrac{dy}{dx} = \dfrac{r\cos\theta}{-r\sin\theta} = -\cot\theta.$

However there is an alternative version of this result.

We can link together $\dfrac{dy}{d\theta} = r\cos\theta$ and $x = r\cos\theta$

to give $\dfrac{dy}{d\theta} = x.$

> Eliminating $r\cos\theta$.

Similarly we can link together $\dfrac{dx}{d\theta} = -r\sin\theta$

and $y = r\sin\theta$ to give $\dfrac{dx}{d\theta} = -y.$

> Eliminating $r\sin\theta$.

Finally using $\dfrac{dy}{dx} = \dfrac{dy}{d\theta} \Big/ \dfrac{dx}{d\theta}$

we get $\dfrac{dy}{dx} = -\dfrac{x}{y}.$

Notice that this answer agrees with the one from Example 4.3.

■ EXERCISE 5.2 ■

In Questions **1–10** differentiate each parametric equation with respect to the parameter. Use your results to find $\dfrac{dy}{dx}$.

1 $x = t^2, y = 3t$

2 $x = 3t, y = 2t^2$

3 $x = 4t, y = 2t^2 - 1$

4 $x = 3\sin\theta, y = 3\cos\theta$

5 $x = \dfrac{1}{2}\cos\theta, y = 2\sin\theta$

6 $x = 3t, y = \dfrac{3}{t}$

7 $x = 6\sin\phi, y = 3\cos\phi$

8 $x = 2t^2, y = \dfrac{4}{t^2}$

9 $x = 2\sin 3\theta, y = \cos 3\theta$

10 $x = 2t^3, y = 3t^2$

11 A curve is given in terms of a parameter θ by $x = 1 - \sin\theta$ and $y = \theta + \cos\theta$. Find an expression for the gradient to this curve. What is the value of the gradient at $\theta = \dfrac{\pi}{6}$?

12 During a particular motion the position is (x, y) at some time t. Given $x = t\cos t - \sin t$ and $y = t\sin t + \cos t$ find expressions for the horizontal and vertical components of velocity, (v_x, v_y). The speed is given by $\sqrt{v_x^2 + v_y^2}$. Find the value of the speed after 1.5 seconds.

13 A capacitor's charge, q, is related to time, t, by $q = 4 \times 10^{-3} e^{-50t}$. Current, i, is related to charge, q, by $i = \dfrac{dq}{dt}$. Write down an expression for the current at time, t. If the voltage, V, is $V = 80e^{-50t}$ work out the change in voltage with respect to current. What is its value?

14 A curve is defined by $x = \dfrac{t^2 - 1}{t}$, $y = \dfrac{t^2 + 1}{t}$. Find an expression for $\dfrac{dy}{dx}$. At what values of t are there turning points?

15 The position of a projectile is given by (x, y). If $x = 10t$ and $y = 35t - 15t^2$ work out expressions for the horizontal and vertical components of velocity. At what time is the projectile horizontal?

Further differentiation

In parametric differentiation we know $\dfrac{dy}{dx}$ is usually expressed in terms of the parameter, often t. If we wish to differentiate again we take this into account. We write

$$\frac{d^2y}{dx^2} = \frac{d}{dx}\left(\frac{dy}{dx}\right)$$

$$= \frac{d}{dt}\left(\frac{dy}{dx}\right) \times \frac{dt}{dx}$$

> Function of a function rule.

i.e. $\dfrac{d^2y}{dx^2} = \dfrac{d}{dt}\left(\dfrac{dy}{dx}\right) \bigg/ \dfrac{dx}{dt}.$

Example 5.6

We find the second derivative, $\dfrac{d^2y}{dx^2}$, for the parametric equations $y = 2t^2 - t$ and $x = 3t$. Also we look at the turning point(s) of the curve $y = f(x)$. Notice we do not need to state the exact relationship between x and y. It is sufficient to quote the parametric equations.

Using $y = 2t^2 - t$ and $x = 3t$

we simply differentiate with respect to t, i.e.

$$\frac{dy}{dt} = 4t - 1 \quad \text{and} \quad \frac{dx}{dt} = 3.$$

Using $\dfrac{dy}{dx} = \dfrac{dy}{dt} \bigg/ \dfrac{dx}{dt}$

we get $\dfrac{dy}{dx} = \dfrac{4t - 1}{3}.$

As usual our derivative, $\dfrac{dy}{dx}$, is in terms of the parameter, t.

Then using $\dfrac{d^2y}{dx^2} = \dfrac{d}{dt}\left(\dfrac{dy}{dx}\right) \bigg/ \dfrac{dx}{dt}.$

we get $\dfrac{d^2y}{dx^2} = \dfrac{d}{dt}\left(\dfrac{4t - 1}{3}\right) \bigg/ \dfrac{dx}{dt}$

$$= \frac{4}{3} \bigg/ 3$$

$$= \frac{4}{9}.$$

Also at any turning point we know $\dfrac{dy}{dx} = 0$,

i.e. $0 = \dfrac{4t - 1}{3}$

to give $t = 0.25.$

Because $\dfrac{d^2y}{dx^2}$ is positive we know the turning point is a local minimum. By substitution we find the coordinates of this local minimum, i.e.

$$x = 3t \qquad = 3 \times 0.25 \qquad\qquad = 0.75$$

and $\quad y = 2t^2 - t = 2 \times 0.25^2 - 0.25 = -0.125,$

i.e. the coordinates are $(0.75, -0.125)$.

■■■■ ASSIGNMENT ■■■■

For our circle we know $\qquad \dfrac{dy}{dx} = -\dfrac{\cos\theta}{\sin\theta}.$

To find the second derivative we apply

$$\frac{d^2y}{dx^2} = \frac{d}{d\theta}\left(\frac{dy}{dx}\right) \bigg/ \frac{dx}{d\theta}.$$

When we attempt $\qquad \dfrac{d}{d\theta}\left(\dfrac{dy}{dx}\right) = \dfrac{d}{d\theta}\left(-\dfrac{\cos\theta}{\sin\theta}\right)$

we apply the quotient rule to get

$$\frac{d}{d\theta}\left(-\frac{\cos\theta}{\sin\theta}\right) = \frac{(\sin\theta)(\sin\theta) - (-\cos\theta)(\cos\theta)}{(\sin\theta)^2}$$

$$= \frac{\sin^2\theta + \cos^2\theta}{\sin^2\theta} \qquad\boxed{\dfrac{v\dfrac{du}{d\theta} - u\dfrac{dv}{d\theta}}{v^2}.}$$

$$= \frac{1}{\sin^2\theta}.$$

We substitute into our formula for $\dfrac{d^2y}{dx^2}$ to get

$$\frac{d^2y}{dx^2} = \frac{1}{\sin^2\theta} \bigg/ (-r\sin\theta) = -\frac{1}{r\sin^3\theta}.$$

We can also discuss the turning points of our circle.

Remember we use $\qquad \dfrac{dy}{dx} = 0 \quad$ which in our case gives

$$-\frac{\cos\theta}{\sin\theta} = 0$$

i.e. $\qquad\qquad \cos\theta = 0$

so that $\qquad\qquad \theta = \dfrac{\pi}{2}, \dfrac{3\pi}{2}, \ldots$

When $\theta = \dfrac{\pi}{2}, \quad \dfrac{d^2y}{dx^2} = -\dfrac{1}{r\sin^3\dfrac{\pi}{2}} = -\dfrac{1}{r}$, i.e. negative. $\qquad\boxed{\sin\dfrac{\pi}{2} = 1.}$

This means we have a maximum turning point where $\theta = \dfrac{\pi}{2}$.

When $\theta = \dfrac{3\pi}{2}$, $\dfrac{d^2y}{dx^2} = -\dfrac{1}{r\sin^3\dfrac{3\pi}{2}} = -\dfrac{1}{r(-1)^3}$ $\boxed{\sin\dfrac{3\pi}{2} = -1.}$

$$= \dfrac{-1}{-r} = \dfrac{1}{r}, \text{ i.e. positive.}$$

This means we have a minimum turning point where $\theta = \dfrac{3\pi}{2}$.

We re-draw our circle in Fig. 5.7. Notice that these turning points are at $\theta = \dfrac{\pi}{2}$ and $\theta = \dfrac{3\pi}{2}$.

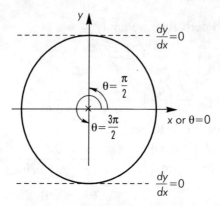

Fig. 5.7

We can apply this method to the case of our numerical circle,

$$x - 1 = 3\cos\theta \quad \text{and} \quad y - 2 = 3\sin\theta$$

so that $\dfrac{dx}{d\theta} = -3\sin\theta$ and $\dfrac{dy}{d\theta} = 3\cos\theta.$

Notice this is the same idea as the general case but with $r = 3$. This suggests we should have the same ideas for the turning points. You can check this against Fig. 5.8 as an exercise for yourself. The only things that alter are the coordinates themselves. This is because they are based upon $x - 1 = 3\cos\theta$ and $y - 2 = 3\sin\theta$.

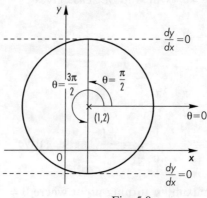

Fig. 5.8

▬▬▬ EXERCISE 5.3 ▬▬▬

In Questions **1–4** use your results from Exercise 5.2 to find $\dfrac{d^2y}{dx^2}$.

1 $x = 4t,\ y = 2t^2 - 1$

2 $x = t^2,\ y = 3t$

3 $x = \dfrac{1}{2}\cos\theta,\ y = 2\sin\theta$

4 $x = 6\sin\phi,\ y = 3\cos\phi$

In Questions **5–8** find $\dfrac{d^2y}{dx^2}$ by parametric differentiation.

5 $y = t,\ x = \dfrac{2}{t^2}$

6 $y = \dfrac{t}{t+2},\ x = \dfrac{t^2}{t+2}$

7 $y = \dfrac{1-t^2}{1+t^2},\ x = \dfrac{2t}{1+t^2}$

8 $y = \theta\sin\theta,\ x = \cos\theta$

9 A curve is given in terms of a parameter θ by $x = 2 - \sin\theta$ and $y = \theta + \cos\theta$. Find expressions for $\dfrac{dy}{dx}$ and $\dfrac{d^2y}{dx^2}$. What are their values where $\theta = \dfrac{\pi}{4}$?

10 During a particular motion the position is (x, y) at some time t. Given $y = t\cos t - \sin t$ and $x = t\sin t + \cos t$ find expressions for the horizontal and vertical components of velocity, (v_x, v_y). When is the vertical velocity 0? The inclination of the resultant velocity to the horizontal is θ. $\dfrac{dy}{dx} = \tan\theta$. Find an expression for the change in $\dfrac{dy}{dx}$ with respect to time, t. Hence find an expression for $\dfrac{d^2y}{dx^2}$. What is the value of $\dfrac{d^2y}{dx^2}$ after 0.75 seconds?

▬▬▬ ASSIGNMENT ▬▬▬

We take a final look at the Assignment. Here we look at the differentiation of x and y separately.

We have $\qquad x = r\cos\theta \qquad$ and $\qquad y = r\sin\theta$

so that $\qquad \dfrac{dx}{d\theta} = -r\sin\theta \quad$ and $\quad \dfrac{dy}{d\theta} = r\cos\theta.$

Also $\qquad \dfrac{d^2x}{d\theta^2} = -r\cos\theta \quad$ and $\quad \dfrac{d^2y}{d\theta^2} = -r\sin\theta.$

Look at the first and last lines of mathematics for both x and y. From x and $\dfrac{d^2x}{d\theta^2}$ we can eliminate $r\cos\theta$. From y and $\dfrac{d^2y}{d\theta^2}$ we can eliminate $r\sin\theta$.

These give

$$\frac{d^2x}{d\theta^2} = -x \qquad \text{and} \qquad \frac{d^2y}{d\theta^2} = -y.$$

Each of these equations represents simple harmonic motion (SHM). Remember the x and y axes are perpendicular. Together this means we can create circular motion by simultaneously applying 2 perpendicular simple harmonic motions.

6 Logarithmic Differentiation

The objectives of this chapter are to:

1 Express relationships such as $y = \dfrac{f_1(x).f_2(x)}{f_3(x)}$ in logarithmic form.

2 Express $\ln\left(\dfrac{f_1(x).f_2(x)}{f_3(x)}\right)$ as $\ln f_1(x) + \ln f_2(x) - \ln f_3(x)$.

3 State $\dfrac{d}{dx}\left(\ln f(x)\right) = \dfrac{f'(x)}{f(x)}$.

4 State $\dfrac{d}{dx}\left(\ln y\right) = \dfrac{1}{y}\dfrac{dy}{dx}$.

5 Differentiate logarithmic forms obtained in **2** term by term.

6 Obtain expressions and values for the derivatives obtained in **5**.

Introduction

In this chapter we bring together a number of techniques from all three volumes. They include

 i) the laws of logarithms (Volume 1, Chapter 10),
 ii) differentiation of logarithms (Volume 2, Chapter 7) and
 iii) implicit differentiation (Volume 3, Chapter 4).

We concentrate on the differentiation once we have applied the laws of logarithms. We use natural logarithms because the differentiation rules are defined for them. The alternative common logarithms need a change of base from 10 to e. All the usual differentiation rules apply.

■ ASSIGNMENT ■

The Assignment for this chapter is a simple pendulum performing small oscillations about the vertical. This takes place in a fluid, so involving a resistive force to the motion. The angular displacement, y, from the vertical is given in terms of time, t, by the formula

$$y = 0.05e^{-0.5t}\sin 3t.$$

Later in this chapter we will look at how y varies depending upon time.

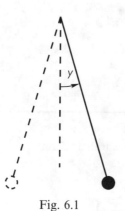

Fig. 6.1

Laws of logarithms

We remind you of the laws of logarithms to the base e. This is because we differentiate only natural logarithms.

1   $\ln MN = \ln M + \ln N$

2   $\ln \dfrac{M}{N} = \ln M - \ln N$

3   $\ln N^p = p\,(\ln N)$

Differentiation of a natural logarithm

We remind you how to differentiate a natural logarithm. It is based upon the function of a function rule.

If $y = \ln f(x)$

we make a substitution to give

$y = \ln u$ where $u = f(x)$.

Differentiating in both cases we get

$$\frac{dy}{du} = \frac{1}{u} \quad \text{and} \quad \frac{du}{dx} = f'(x).$$

$f'(x)$ is the first derivative of $f(x)$.

We substitute into the function of a function rule

$$\frac{dy}{dx} = \frac{dy}{du} \times \frac{du}{dx}$$

to get $\dfrac{dy}{dx} = \dfrac{1}{u} \times f'(x)$

i.e. $\dfrac{dy}{dx} = \dfrac{f'(x)}{f(x)}.$

> Substituting for
> $u = f(x)$.

Because $y = \ln f(x)$ we may write

$$\frac{d}{dx}\left(\ln f(x)\right) = \frac{f'(x)}{f(x)}.$$

We need to take care with $\dfrac{d}{dx}\left(\ln y\right)$.

Suppose we let $q = \ln y$ so that $\dfrac{dq}{dy} = \dfrac{1}{y}$.

In place of $\dfrac{d}{dx}\left(\ln y\right)$ we have $\dfrac{dq}{dx}$.

Using the function of a function rule,

$$\frac{dq}{dx} = \frac{dq}{dy} \times \frac{dy}{dx}$$

we get $\dfrac{dq}{dx} = \dfrac{1}{y}\dfrac{dy}{dx}$

i.e. $\dfrac{d}{dx}\left(\ln y\right) = \dfrac{1}{y}\dfrac{dy}{dx}.$

> Substituting for
> $\dfrac{dq}{dx} = \dfrac{1}{y}.$

Let us look closely at this differentiation. When we differentiate $\ln y$ the y appears in the denominator. Its derivative, 1, appears in the numerator. Using y instead of x this is still basic differentiation. The extra $\dfrac{dy}{dx}$ is included because we are differentiating y with respect to x. For any terms in x, when we differentiate with respect to x we do not need $\dfrac{dy}{dx}$.

We look at examples using differentiation and each of the three logarithmic laws.

▬▬ Example 6.1 ▬▬

For $y = (4 + x^2)\cos x$ find $\dfrac{dy}{dx}$ using logarithmic differentiation.

We have a product of $(4 + x^2)$ and $\cos x$.

Using $y = (4 + x^2)\cos x$

we take natural logarithms of both sides so that

$$\ln y = \ln\left\{(4 + x^2)\cos x\right\}$$
$$= \ln(4 + x^2) + \ln(\cos x).$$

> 1st logarithmic law.

Differentiating each logarithm with respect to x we get

$$\frac{1}{y}\frac{dy}{dx} = \frac{2x}{4+x^2} + \frac{-\sin x}{\cos x}$$

i.e. $$\frac{dy}{dx} = \left(\frac{2x}{4+x^2} - \tan x\right)y.$$

$$\boxed{\frac{\sin x}{\cos x} = \tan x.}$$

We may leave the answer in this form or replace y with its original function of x,

i.e. $$\frac{dy}{dx} = \left(\frac{2x}{4+x^2} - \tan x\right)(4+x^2)\cos x.$$

We could amend this answer by multiplying out the brackets and simplifying the algebra. To avoid algebraic errors we choose *not* to do so.

In Volume 2 we would have attempted this problem using the product rule for differentiation. That answer would have been equivalent, but in a slightly different form.

Example 6.2

For $y = 2xe^x$ using logarithmic differentiation find the value of $\dfrac{dy}{dx}$ where $x = 2.5$.

We have a product of $2x$ and e^x.
Using $y = 2xe^x$
we take natural logarithms of both sides so that

$$\ln y = \ln 2xe^x$$

$$= \ln 2x + \ln e^x$$

$$= \ln 2x + x \ln e$$

i.e. $\ln y = \ln 2x + x.$

$$\boxed{\begin{array}{l}\text{1st logarithmic law.}\\ \text{3rd logarithmic law.}\\ \ln e = 1.\end{array}}$$

Also we could apply the 1st logarithmic law to $\ln 2x$, i.e. $\ln 2 + \ln x$. Because this is so simple we choose to leave it as $\ln 2x$.

Differentiating each term with respect to x we get

$$\frac{1}{y}\frac{dy}{dx} = \frac{2}{2x} + 1$$

i.e. $$\frac{dy}{dx} = \left(\frac{1}{x}+1\right)y = \left(\frac{1}{x}+1\right)2xe^x.$$

We substitute for $x = 2.5$ to get

$$\frac{dy}{dx} = \left(\frac{1}{2.5}+1\right)2 \times 2.5 \times e^{2.5}$$

$$= (0.4+1)5 \times 12.182\ldots$$

$$= 85.28 \text{ (2 dp)}.$$

ASSIGNMENT

Our simple pendulum has an angular displacement, y, in terms of time, t, according to $y = 0.05e^{-0.5t} \sin 3t$. Let us look at the graph of y against t in Fig. 6.2

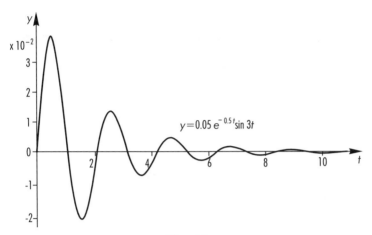

Fig. 6.2

The curve oscillates above and below the horizontal axis. Each successive peak or trough is closer to the axis than the previous one. Physically we would see the pendulum swinging a smaller and smaller distance away from the vertical. These distances would alternate either side of that vertical. Eventually the pendulum would stop, hanging in line with the central vertical line. Because the graph continually varies in shape so does its gradient. The most useful way to look at the gradient is through differentiation.

In $y = 0.05e^{-0.5t} \sin 3t$ we have a product of 0.05, $e^{-0.5t}$ and $\sin 3t$.

Using $\quad y = 0.05e^{-0.5t} \sin 3t$

we take natural logarithms of both sides so that

$$\ln y = \ln\left(0.05e^{-0.5t} \sin 3t\right)$$
$$= \ln 0.05 + \ln e^{-0.5t} + \ln(\sin 3t)$$
$$= \ln 0.05 - 0.5t \ln e + \ln(\sin 3t)$$
$$= \ln 0.05 - 0.5t + \ln(\sin 3t).$$

Differentiating each term with respect to t we get

$$\frac{1}{y}\frac{dy}{dt} = 0 \qquad - 0.5 + \frac{3\cos 3t}{\sin 3t}$$

i.e. $\quad \dfrac{dy}{dt} = \left(-0.5 + \dfrac{3\cos 3t}{\sin 3t}\right)y.$

y is the angular displacement from the vertical measured in radians. t is the time for the motion measured in seconds. This means that $\dfrac{dy}{dt}$ is the change in angular displacement with respect to time or the rate of change of angular displacement, i.e. the angular velocity, measured in rads^{-1}.

■■■■■ EXERCISE 6.1 ■■■■■

In each question write the equation in terms of natural logarithms as simply as possible. Find the first derivative using logarithmic differentiation.

1 For $y = (2x^3 + 5x^2)(x^2 + 7x^4)$ find the value of both y and $\dfrac{dy}{dx}$ at $x = 1$.

2 Find the rate of change of y with respect to time, t, after 1.5 seconds given $y = (1 + 2t^3)\sin t$.

3 At the point where $\theta = \dfrac{\pi}{3}$ find the value of $\dfrac{dy}{d\theta}$ for $y = e^\theta \cos \theta$.

4 Find the value of y and its first derivative at $x = 4$ given $y = (7 - \sqrt{x})(2x + x^3)$.

5 At $t = 0.5$ find the value of the gradient to the curve $y = e^{2t}\sin(2t + \pi)$.

■■■■■ Example 6.3 ■■■■■

For $y = \dfrac{2x - 1}{7 - x}$ find $\dfrac{dy}{dx}$ using logarithmic differentiation.

We have a quotient and so will subtract the logarithms on that right-hand side.

Using $y = \dfrac{2x - 1}{7 - x}$

we take natural logarithms of both sides so that

$$\ln y = \ln\left(\frac{2x - 1}{7 - x}\right)$$

$$= \ln(2x - 1) - \ln(7 - x). \qquad \boxed{\text{2nd logarithmic law.}}$$

Differentiating each logarithm with respect to x we get

$$\frac{1}{y}\frac{dy}{dx} = \frac{2}{2x - 1} - \frac{-1}{7 - x}$$

i.e. $\dfrac{dy}{dx} = \left(\dfrac{2}{2x - 1} + \dfrac{1}{7 - x}\right)y.$

Again we may leave the answer in this form or substitute for $y = \dfrac{2x - 1}{7 - x}$.

███ **ASSIGNMENT** ███████████████████████

Let us have another look at our simple pendulum. We can re-write our equation $y = 0.05e^{-0.5t} \sin 3t$ as $y = \dfrac{0.05 \sin 3t}{e^{0.5t}}$.

When we re-position the exponential we amend the sign in the power position. Now we have a quotient.

Using $\quad y = \dfrac{0.05 \sin 3t}{e^{0.5t}}$

we take natural logarithms of both sides so that

$$\ln y = \ln\left(\dfrac{0.05 \sin 3t}{e^{0.5t}}\right)$$

$$= \ln 0.05 + \ln(\sin 3t) - \ln e^{0.5t}$$

$$= \ln 0.05 + \ln(\sin 3t) - 0.5t \ln e$$

$$= \ln 0.05 + \ln(\sin 3t) - 0.5t.$$

This is the same relationship we had last time we looked at the Assignment. Hence we know

$$\frac{dy}{dt} = \left(-0.5 + \frac{3 \cos 3t}{\sin 3t}\right) y.$$

Using this general expression for $\dfrac{dy}{dt}$ we can substitute for values of t and y. We find y and then the angular velocity after 4 seconds.

Using $\qquad y = \dfrac{0.05 \sin 3t}{e^{0.5t}}$

we substitute for $t = 4$ to get

$$y = \frac{0.05 \sin 12}{e^2}$$

> Using radians for the sine.

$$= \frac{0.05 \times (-0.5356\ldots)}{7.3890\ldots}$$

$$= -0.0036\ldots \text{ rad.}$$

Now in our expression for $\dfrac{dy}{dt}$,

$$\frac{dy}{dt} = \left(-0.5 + \frac{3 \cos 3t}{\sin 3t}\right) y,$$

becomes $\quad \dfrac{dy}{dt} = \left(-0.5 + \dfrac{3 \cos 12}{\sin 12}\right)(-0.0036\ldots)$

$$= \left(-0.5 + \frac{3 \times 0.8438\ldots}{-0.5365\ldots}\right)(-0.0036\ldots)$$

$$= 0.019 \text{ rads}^{-1}$$

i.e. the angular velocity after 4 seconds is 0.019 rads^{-1}.

In the second case we look at when the pendulum stops, i.e. when the angular velocity is zero as shown by $\dfrac{dy}{dt} = 0$. We put our general expression for $\dfrac{dy}{dt}$ equal to 0, i.e.

$$\left(-0.5 + \frac{3\cos 3t}{\sin 3t}\right) y = 0$$

i.e. $\left(-0.5 + \dfrac{3\cos 3t}{\sin 3t}\right)\left(\dfrac{0.05\sin 3t}{e^{0.5t}}\right) = 0.$

Because $e^{0.5t} \neq 0$ and $0.05 \neq 0$ we can write

$$\left(-0.5 + \frac{3\cos 3t}{\sin 3t}\right)(\sin 3t) = 0.$$

Multiplying out the brackets gives us
$$-0.5\sin 3t + 3\cos 3t = 0.$$

We combine the trigonometric functions by dividing throughout by $0.5\cos 3t$, i.e.

$$\frac{-0.5\sin 3t}{0.5\cos 3t} + \frac{3\cos 3t}{0.5\cos 3t} = 0$$

i.e. $\qquad -\tan 3t + 6 = 0$

i.e. $\qquad \tan 3t = 6$

so that $\qquad 3t = \tan^{-1}(6) = 1.4056$

i.e. $\qquad t = 0.47.$

This means the pendulum stops after 0.47 seconds.

EXERCISE 6.2

In each question write the equation in terms of natural logarithms as simply as possible. Find the first derivative using logarithmic differentiation.

1   For $y = \dfrac{1 + 3x + x^2}{1 - x^2}$ find the value of both y and $\dfrac{dy}{dx}$ at $x = 0.75$.

2   Find the rate of change of y with respect to time, t, after 2.5 seconds given $y = \dfrac{\sin t}{1 + t}$.

3   At the point where $\theta = \dfrac{\pi}{4}$ find the value of $\dfrac{dy}{d\theta}$ for $y = \dfrac{2\sin 3\theta}{e^{2\theta}}$.

4   Find the value of θ and its first derivative at $t = 1.25$ given $\theta = \dfrac{\sin 2t + \cos t}{3t}$.

5   At $\theta = 0.5$ find the value of the gradient to the curve $y = \cot\theta$, i.e. $y = \dfrac{\cos\theta}{\sin\theta}$.

You should have found these examples relatively easy. We now apply this method to examples using more than a simple product or quotient.

━━━━━ **Examples 6.4** ━━━━━

Using logarithmic differentiation find $\dfrac{dy}{dx}$ for

i) $y = (4 + x^2)x^2 \cos x$, ii) $y = \dfrac{(4 + x^2)\cos x}{e^x}$,

iii) $y = \dfrac{\sqrt{4 + x^2}.\cos x}{e^x}$.

i) If we attempt this problem using the product rule we would need to apply that rule twice. Using the logarithmic method on
$$y = (4 + x^2)x^2 \cos x$$
we take natural logarithms of both sides so that

$$\ln y = \ln\{(4 + x^2)x^2 \cos x\}$$

$$= \ln(4 + x^2) + \ln x^2 + \ln(\cos x) \quad \boxed{\text{1st law.}}$$

$$= \ln(4 + x^2) + 2\ln x + \ln(\cos x). \quad \boxed{\text{3rd law.}}$$

Differentiating each logarithm with respect to x we get

$$\frac{1}{y}\frac{dy}{dx} = \frac{2x}{4 + x^2} + 2 \times \frac{1}{x} + -\frac{\sin x}{\cos x}$$

i.e. $\quad \dfrac{dy}{dx} = \left(\dfrac{2x}{4 + x^2} + \dfrac{2}{x} - \tan x\right)y.$

ii) This problem involves a product, $(4 + x^2)$ and $\cos x$, in the numerator within the overall quotient.

Using $\quad y = \dfrac{(4 + x^2)\cos x}{e^x}$

we take natural logarithms of both sides so that

$$\ln y = \ln\left(\frac{(4 + x^2)\cos x}{e^x}\right)$$

$$= \ln(4 + x^2) + \ln(\cos x) - \ln e^x \quad \boxed{\text{1st and 2nd laws.}}$$

$$= \ln(4 + x^2) + \ln(\cos x) - x\ln e \quad \boxed{\text{3rd law.}}$$

$$= \ln(4 + x^2) + \ln(\cos x) - x. \quad \boxed{\ln e = 1.}$$

Differentiating each term with respect to x we get

$$\frac{1}{y}\frac{dy}{dx} = \frac{2x}{4 + x^2} + \frac{-\sin x}{\cos x} - 1$$

i.e. $\quad \dfrac{dy}{dx} = \left(\dfrac{2x}{4 + x^2} - \tan x - 1\right)y.$

iii) Finally we have a mixture of function of a function, product and quotient rules. The logarithmic method is much easier than the alternative combination of those 3 rules.

Using $\quad y = \dfrac{\sqrt{4 + x^2} . \cos x}{e^x}$

we take natural logarithms of both sides so that

$$\ln y = \ln\left(\frac{\sqrt{4 + x^2} . \cos x}{e^x}\right)$$

$$= \ln(4 + x^2)^{1/2} + \ln(\cos x) - \ln e^x \quad \boxed{\text{1st and 2nd laws.}}$$

$$= \frac{1}{2}\ln(4 + x^2) + \ln(\cos x) - x \ln e \quad \boxed{\text{3rd law.}}$$

$$= \frac{1}{2}\ln(4 + x^2) + \ln(\cos x) - x. \quad \boxed{\ln e = 1.}$$

Differentiating each term with respect to x we get

$$\frac{1}{y}\frac{dy}{dx} = \frac{1}{2} \times \frac{2x}{4 + x^2} + \frac{-\sin x}{\cos x} - 1$$

i.e. $\quad \dfrac{dy}{dx} = \left(\dfrac{x}{4 + x^2} - \tan x - 1\right) y.$

▮▮▮▮▮▮ EXERCISE 6.3 ▮▮▮▮▮▮

In each question write the equation in terms of natural logarithms as simply as possible. Find the first derivative using logarithmic differentiation.

1 $y = (x + 2)(3 - x^2)\sin x$

2 $y = \dfrac{2x - 1}{(x + 2)(3 + 4x)}$

3 $y = (t^2 - 2)e^{t\sin t}$

4 $y = 2\theta e^{-2\theta}\cos 4\theta$

5 $y = (\sin t)e^{t\cos t}$

6 $y = \dfrac{\cos t}{te^t}$

7 $y = \dfrac{\theta \sin 2\theta}{\theta^2 + 2}$

8 $y = \sqrt{(1 + 2x)\sin 2x}$

9 $y = \dfrac{(1 + 2x)\cos 2x}{e^{4x}}$

10 $y = \sqrt{\dfrac{1 + \cos x}{x + \sin x}}$

▮▮▮▮▮▮ Example 6.5 ▮▮▮▮▮▮

Find the value of y where $t = 1$ given $y = e^{e^t}$. Using logarithmic differentiation find the value of the first derivative at $t = 1$.

In $y = e^{e^t}$ we substitute for $t = 1$, i.e. $y = e^{e^t} = e^{2.718...} = 15.154\ldots$

We have *not* met this type of calculation before. The order of calculator operations is

$\underline{1|}$ $\quad e^x|$ $\qquad$ to display 2.718...

and $\qquad e^x|$ $\qquad$ to display the answer of 15.154 (3 dp).

For the differentiation we use

$$y = e^{e^t}$$

and take natural logarithms of both sides so that

$\ln y = \ln e^{(e^t)}$

$\quad = e^t . \ln e$ $\qquad\qquad$ | 3rd law.

$\quad = e^t.$ $\qquad\qquad\qquad$ | $\ln e = 1.$

Differentiating simply with respect to t we get

$$\frac{1}{y}\frac{dy}{dt} = e^t$$

i.e. $\quad \dfrac{dy}{dt} = e^t.y.$

When $t = 1$ we substitute to get

$$\frac{dy}{dt} = e^1 \times 15.154\ldots = 41.19 \text{ (2 dp)}.$$

Example 6.6

The current, i A, flowing through a coil is given in terms of time, t seconds, by $i = 5te^{-t}\sin t$. Find the rate of change of current after 0.5 seconds.

Using $\quad i = 5te^{-t}\sin t$

we take natural logarithms of both sides so that

$\ln i = \ln(5te^{-t}\sin t)$

$\quad = \ln 5 + \ln t + \ln e^{-t} + \ln(\sin t)$ $\quad$ | 1st law.

$\quad = \ln 5 + \ln t - t\ln e + \ln(\sin t)$ $\qquad$ | 3rd law.

$\quad = \ln 5 + \ln t - t + \ln(\sin t).$ $\qquad$ | $\ln e = 1.$

Differentiating each term with respect to t we get

$$\frac{1}{i}\frac{di}{dt} = \frac{1}{t} - 1 + \frac{\cos t}{\sin t}$$

i.e. $\quad \dfrac{di}{dt} = \left(\dfrac{1}{t} - 1 + \dfrac{\cos t}{\sin t}\right)i$ or $\left(\dfrac{1}{t} - 1 + \dfrac{\cos t}{\sin t}\right)5te^{-t}\sin t.$

Into our general expression for the rate of change of current we substitute for $t = 0.5$ to get

$$\frac{di}{dt} = \left(\frac{1}{0.5} - 1 + \frac{\cos 0.5}{\sin 0.5}\right)5 \times 0.5 \times e^{-0.5}\sin 0.5$$

$$= 2.830\ldots \times 2.5 \times 0.606\ldots \times 0.479\ldots = 2.06 \text{ As}^{-1}.$$

▇▇▇▇▇ EXERCISE 6.4 ▇▇▇▇▇▇▇▇▇▇

1 A body is subject to damped harmonic oscillations. Its distance, x, from its equilibrium position during time, t, is given by $x = \dfrac{5\cos(2t + \pi/4)}{e^{2t}}$. Find an expression for $\dfrac{dx}{dt}$ and find its value after 1.25 seconds.

2 Find an expression for the velocity of a body where the displacement, s, is related to the time of motion, $t > 0$, according to $s = \dfrac{4 + 3t^2}{2te^{-3t}}$.

3 The gradient, g, to a curve is given in terms of the independent variable, θ, by $g = 3\cos\theta.\sin^2\theta$. Write this equation in terms of natural logarithms.

Find a general expression for the change in gradient with respect to θ.

Find the value of your derivative where $\theta = \dfrac{\pi}{4}$ radians.

In the range $0 \leqslant \theta \leqslant \dfrac{\pi}{2}$ radians where is the gradient 0?

At these points find the value of $\dfrac{dg}{d\theta}$.

4 $\theta = \dfrac{\sin^2 3t}{5(t+1)^3}$ gives the angular displacement, θ radians, in terms of time, t seconds. Using logarithmic differentiation find an equation for the angular velocity, $\dfrac{d\theta}{dt}$, only in terms of t. Show that the initial angular velocity is 0. What is the value of the angular velocity after 1.5 seconds?

5 A charged particle moves in a magnetic field subject to exponential decay. In the y direction on a pair of axes during time, t, the path is given by $y = 2te^{-0.25t}\cos 6t$.

Find a general expression for $\dfrac{dy}{dt}$ and its specific value after 1 second.

In the x direction for the particle we have $x = -2te^{-0.25t}\sin 6t$.

Find the value of $\dfrac{dx}{dt}$ at that same time.

7 Partial Differentiation

The objectives of this chapter are to:

1 Define the first order partial derivatives $\dfrac{\partial z}{\partial x}$ and $\dfrac{\partial z}{\partial y}$ for $z = f(x, y)$.

2 Find the partial derivatives for simple functions of two independent variables.

3 Define the meaning and notation of second order partial derivatives.

4 State and verify by example that $\dfrac{\partial^2 z}{\partial x \partial y} = \dfrac{\partial^2 z}{\partial y \partial x}$ at points where z and its derivatives are continuous.

5 Find the second order partial derivatives for simple functions of two variables.

6 Derive the formula for calculating small changes (or errors) of $z = f(x, y)$ due to small changes in x and y.

7 Derive the formula for the rate of change of $z = f(x, y)$ when both x and y vary with time.

8 State the formula for the total differential of $z = f(x, y)$.

9 Extend the formulae in **6**, **7** and **8** to more than two variables.

Introduction

In Volumes 1 and 2 we looked at functions and differentiation. Often x was the independent variable and y was the dependent variable. We stated y in terms of x, i.e. y being a function of x, i.e. $y = f(x)$. Then $\dfrac{dy}{dx}$ represented the change in y due to a change in x.

In this chapter we look at more than one independent variable. Also we see how changes in the independent variables affect the dependent variable. Generally we look at two independent variables and one dependent variable. Our methods can be extended to many independent variables. All our differentiation rules continue to apply.

■■■■ ASSIGNMENT ■■■■

The Assignment for this chapter looks at a cylindrical stainless steel canister. It is to be used for storage at the end of food processing. An

important design element is a series of small motors to alter the dimensions of the cylinder. These are to ensure minimum air contact with the food when the canister is only partly filled.

Our Assignment is based on the features of a cylinder (see Fig. 7.1). For a radius, r, and height, h, we have a volume, V, and a total inside surface area, A.

$$V = \pi r^2 h.$$

Total surface area = Curved surface area + Area of 2 ends

i.e. $A = 2\pi r h + 2\pi r^2$

or $A = 2\pi r(h + r).$

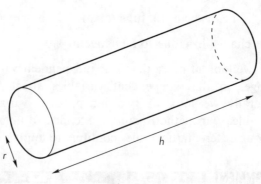

Fig. 7.1

Functional notation

We start with 2 independent variables, x and y, and a dependent variable z, i.e. $z = f(x,y)$. x or y or both x and y may vary to affect z. This creates 3 dimensions rather than the 2 dimensions we have used previously. To start we find some values of functions.

███████ **Examples 7.1** ███████

i) $z = x^2 + y^2$, or $f(x,y) = x^2 + y^2$, is a function of 2 independent variables, x and y.
    We may find the value of z, or $f(x,y)$.
    At $x = -1$, $y = 0$ we have $f(-1,0) = (-1)^2 + 0^2$
    $$= 1.$$

ii) $z = 3\sin x.\cos y$, or $f(x,y) = 3\sin x.\cos y$, is a function of 2 independent variables.
    At $x = \dfrac{\pi}{4}$, $y = \dfrac{\pi}{3}$ we have $f\left(\dfrac{\pi}{4},\dfrac{\pi}{3}\right) = 3\sin\dfrac{\pi}{4}.\cos\dfrac{\pi}{3}$
    $$= 3 \times 0.7071\ldots \times 0.5$$
    $$= 1.061.$$

We may extend this idea to more than 2 independent variables. Perhaps z varies according to time, t, as well as varying according to x and y. Then $z = f(x,y,t)$ is a function of 3 independent variables, x, y and t. When we have many independent variables we often use subscript notation,

e.g $z = f(x_1, x_2, x_3, \ldots, x_n,)$ or maybe
    $z = f(x_1, x_2, x_3, \ldots, x_n, t)$.

We have already seen functions of more than 1 independent variable in practical cases in Volumes 1 and 2.

███████ **Examples 7.2** ███████

i)   The area of a rectangle, A, is given by $A = \ell w$ where ℓ is the length and w is the width. ℓ and w are the independent variables and A is the dependent variable.

ii) For a current I flowing through a resistor of resistance R the power, P, is given by $P = I^2 R$. I and R are the independent variables and P is the dependent variable.

iii) A uniform heavy beam has length $2a$ and weight $2W$. Its bending moment, M, is given by $M = \dfrac{Wx}{2a}(2a - x)$ where x is the distance from one end. W, a and x are the independent variables. M is the dependent variable.

■ ASSIGNMENT ■

Suppose the electric motors on our stainless steel canister have altered both dimensions. At present the radius, r, is 1.10 m and the height, h, is 3.50 m. We can simply calculate the volume, V, and total inside surface area, A, of the canister.

Then $V = \pi r^2 h$

becomes $V = \pi \times 1.10^2 \times 3.50$

$= 13.30$ m^3.

Also $A = 2\pi r(h + r)$

becomes $A = 2\pi \times 1.10 \times (3.50 + 1.10)$

$= 31.79$ m^2.

■ EXERCISE 7.1 ■

1 For $z = (x + y)^2$ find the value of z where i) $x = 2$ and $y = 0$, ii) $x = 0$ and $y = -2$, iii) $x = 1$ and $y = 1$.

2 Given $z = 2x \sin y$ what is the value of z at $x = 1.5$ and $y = 2$ radians?

3 Find the value of $f(1,0)$ for $f(x, y) = (3x^2 + \cos y)^2$.

4 $f(r, h) = \dfrac{1}{3}\pi r^2 h$ represents the volume of a cone in terms of its radius, r, and height, h. Find the value of $f(2, 5)$.

5 $f(r, \theta) = \dfrac{1}{2} r^2 \theta$ is the formula for the area of a sector of angle θ radians cut from a circle of radius r. Find the value of $f\left(3, \dfrac{\pi}{6}\right)$.

6 An engineering company invests £500 000 at a rate of $R\%$ over n years. The value of its investment is given by the formula $f(R, n) = £500\,000\left(1 + \dfrac{R}{100}\right)^n$. What is the value of $f(8.5, 3.5)$?

7 In the electrical circuit the current, i A, is related to the e.m.f., E V, and time, t s, by $i = \dfrac{E}{100}\left(1 - e^{-40t}\right)$. Decide which variables are independent/dependent.

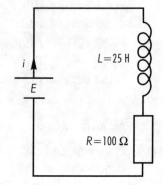

i $L = 25$ H

E

$R = 100\ \Omega$

8 A mass is in contact with a rough plane. The total reaction, $f(R, \mu)$, is a function of the normal reaction, R N, and the coefficient of friction, μ. Given that $f(R, \mu) = R\sqrt{1 + \mu^2}$ find the value of $f(250, 0.275)$.

9 The resonant frequency, $f(L, C)$, is given in terms of capacitance, C, and inductance, L, by $f(L, C) = \dfrac{1}{2\pi\sqrt{LC}}$

Find the value of the frequency when L is 4 H and C is 2×10^{-3} F.

10 The volume of a spherical frustum is given by

$$f(r, R, h) = \frac{\pi}{6}h\big(h^2 + 3\big(r^2 + R^2\big)\big).$$

r is the radius of the top circle and R is the radius of the base circle. The radii are a distance h apart. The units for r, R and h are metres. Calculate the values of $f(0.30, 0.50, 0.40)$ and $f(0.50, 0.30, 0.40)$. Comment on any similarity/difference in your answers.

First order partial differentiation

All our usual differentiation rules continue to apply.

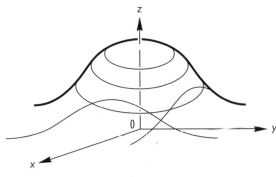

Fig. 7.2

Fig. 7.2 shows a 3 dimensional right-handed system of axes with origin O. We also show an example of a surface where $z = f(x, y)$.

Suppose we wish to insert a new light bulb into a ceiling rose. As we turn from the x-axis towards the y-axis we move upwards along the z-axis.

For $z = f(x, y)$ x or y may change or they may both change. $\dfrac{\partial z}{\partial x}$ **represents the partial change in z due to some change in x while y is held constant.** We say $\dfrac{\partial z}{\partial x}$ as 'partial dee zed by dee x'. Suppose we slice through our surface parallel to the xz plane, i.e. perpendicular to the y axis.

Looking at the cross-section, Fig. 7.3, z changes due to changes in x. This is true for each particular value of y, i.e. y is constant.

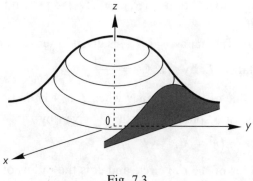

Fig. 7.3

$\dfrac{\partial z}{\partial y}$ **represents the partial change in z due to some change in y while x is held constant**. We say $\dfrac{\partial z}{\partial y}$ as 'partial dee zed by dee y'. This time suppose we slice through our surface parallel to the yz plane, i.e. perpendicular to the x axis. Looking at the cross-section, Fig. 7.4, z changes due to changes in y. This is true for each particular value of x, i.e. x is constant.

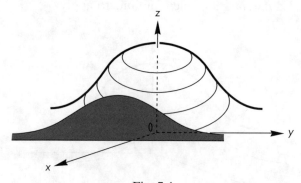

Fig. 7.4

An alternative notation for $\dfrac{\partial z}{\partial x}$ may be $\left[\dfrac{dz}{dx}\right]_{y\text{ constant}}$ and for $\dfrac{\partial z}{\partial y}$ may be $\left[\dfrac{dz}{dy}\right]_{x\text{ constant}}$.

In our examples we tend to show both $\dfrac{\partial z}{\partial x}$ and $\dfrac{\partial z}{\partial y}$ for extra practice. This is *not* always necessary. Read each question carefully to see which variables are changing.

In Examples 7.3 and 7.4 we show both ordinary and partial differentiation. You need to understand which parts of the equations are constant and which parts are variable.

███ **Examples 7.3** ███

i) Using $\quad z = 27x^2$

or $\qquad z = 3^3x^2$ or $x^2 3^3$

> 27 is constant, a multiplying factor.

we have $\quad \dfrac{dz}{dx} = 3^3 \times 2x.$

For $\qquad z = x^2 y^3$

> y^3 is constant when we discuss $\dfrac{\partial z}{\partial x}.$

we have $\quad \dfrac{\partial z}{\partial x} = 2xy^3.$

ii) Using $\quad z = 25y^3$

or $\qquad z = 5^2 y^3$

> 25 is constant, a multiplying factor.

we have $\quad \dfrac{dz}{dy} = 5^2 \times 3y^2.$

For $\qquad z = x^2 y^3$

> x^2 is constant when we discuss $\dfrac{\partial z}{\partial y}.$

we have $\quad \dfrac{\partial z}{\partial y} = x^2 \times 3y^2$

$\qquad\qquad\quad = 3x^2 y^2.$

███ **Examples 7.4** ███

i) Using $\quad z = x^2 + 27$

> 27 is constant.

we have $\quad \dfrac{dz}{dx} = 2x.$

For $\qquad z = x^2 + y^3$

> y^3 is constant when we discuss $\dfrac{\partial z}{\partial x}.$

we have $\quad \dfrac{\partial z}{\partial x} = 2x.$

ii) Using $\quad z = 25 + y^3$

> 25 is constant.

we have $\quad \dfrac{dz}{dy} = 3y^2.$

For $\qquad z = x^2 + y^3$

> x^2 is constant when we discuss $\dfrac{\partial z}{\partial y}.$

we have $\quad \dfrac{\partial z}{\partial y} = 3y^2.$

███ **Example 7.5** ███

For $\qquad z = 2x\cos y$ or $(2\cos y)x$

> $2\cos y$ is constant when we discuss $\dfrac{\partial z}{\partial x}.$

we have $\quad \dfrac{\partial z}{\partial x} = 2\cos y.$

Also $\qquad \dfrac{\partial z}{\partial y} = 2x \times (-\sin y)$

> $2x$ is constant when we discuss $\dfrac{\partial z}{\partial y}.$

$\qquad\qquad\quad = -2x\sin y.$

We may find the values of these derivatives at specific points.

Where $x = 2$ and $y = \dfrac{\pi}{4}$, $\dfrac{\partial z}{\partial x} = 2\cos\dfrac{\pi}{4} = 1.414.$

Where $x = 3$ and $y = \dfrac{\pi}{6}$, $\dfrac{\partial z}{\partial y} = -2 \times 3 \times \sin\dfrac{\pi}{6} = -3.$

ASSIGNMENT

In our previous look at the cylindrical canister we found the values of the volume and inside surface area. The calculations were based on $r = 1.10$ m and $h = 3.50$ m. Now we look at the change in the volume, V m^3, while the electric motors are operating. By way of example we do this just before the position is reached, say at $r = 1.05$ m and $h = 3.40$ m.

$\dfrac{\partial V}{\partial r}$ is the change in volume due to a change in the radius whose units are

$\dfrac{\text{m}^3}{\text{m}} = \text{m}^2.$

Using $\qquad V = \pi r^2 h \quad$ or $\quad (\pi h)r^2$

we have $\qquad \dfrac{\partial V}{\partial r} = \pi h \times 2r$

$\boxed{\text{Derivative of } r^2 \text{ is } 2r.}$

$\qquad\qquad\quad = 2\pi rh,$

which is a general expression for the change in volume due to a change in radius.

At the moment where $r = 1.05$ m and $h = 3.40$ m we have

$\qquad \dfrac{\partial V}{\partial r} = 2\pi \times 1.05 \times 3.40 = 22.4 \text{ m}^2.$

$\dfrac{\partial V}{\partial h}$ is the change in volume due to a change in the height whose units are

$\dfrac{\text{m}^3}{\text{m}} = \text{m}^2.$

Using $\qquad V = \pi r^2 h$

we have $\qquad \dfrac{\partial V}{\partial h} = \pi r^2 \times 1$

$\boxed{\text{Derivative of } h \text{ is } 1.}$

$\qquad\qquad\quad = \pi r^2,$

which is a general expression for the change in volume due to a change in height.

Also at the moment where $r = 1.05$ m and $h = 3.40$ m we have

$\qquad \dfrac{\partial V}{\partial h} = \pi \times 1.05^2 = 3.46 \text{ m}^2.$

■ EXERCISE 7.2 ■

In Questions **1–10** find expressions for $\dfrac{\partial z}{\partial x}$ and $\dfrac{\partial z}{\partial y}$.

1 $z = x^5 y$

2 $z = x + y^5$

3 $z = \dfrac{x}{y}$

4 $z = x^2 \ln y$

5 $z = \sin xy$

6 $z = x^3 y^2 + x^2 y^3$

7 $z = 3x \sin y$

8 $z = \ln(x + y)$

9 $z = \ln(2x + 3y)$

10 $z = \ln(2xy)$

11   The volume, V, of a cone of radius, r, and vertical height, h, is given by $V = \dfrac{1}{3}\pi r^2 h$. Find a general expression for $\dfrac{\partial V}{\partial r}$ and its value where $r = 0.25$ m and $h = 0.65$ m.

12   A variable mass is in contact with a plane of varying roughness. The total reaction, S N, is a function of the normal reaction, R N, and the coefficient of friction, μ. Given that $S = R\sqrt{1 + \mu^2}$ find an expression for $\dfrac{\partial S}{\partial R}$. What is the value of this partial derivative where $R = 255$ N and $\mu = 0.28$?

13   The resonant frequency, f, is given in terms of capacitance, C, and inductance, L, by $f = \dfrac{1}{2\pi\sqrt{LC}}$. For variable capacitance and inductance find $\dfrac{\partial f}{\partial L}$ when L is 3.25 H and C is 1.75×10^{-3} F.

14   The diagram shows the cross-section through a steel girder. The second moment of area about XX is given by $I = \dfrac{BD^3 - bd^3}{12}$.

It is possible for B, b, D and d to be varied in manufacture. Find a general expression for $\dfrac{\partial I}{\partial D}$. What is its value where $B = 0.35$ m, $D = 0.65$ m, $d = 0.55$ m and $b = 0.10$ m?

Briefly explain why some of these dimensions are unnecessary for this particular calculation.

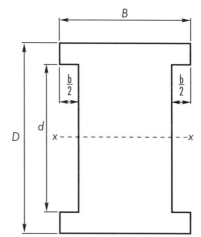

15 $Q = \dfrac{kAT}{x}$ relates the rate of heat energy transfer, Q, between two faces of material to the variables k, A, T and x. k is the coefficient of thermal conductivity. A is the conducting area. T is the temperature difference between the two faces. x is the thickness of the material. Find a general expression for $\dfrac{\partial Q}{\partial x}$. Also find its specific value for mild steel of conducting area 1.4 m^2 when its faces are 0.035 m apart. $k = 55$ Wm^{-1}K^{-1} and the temperature difference is 70°K.

We continue our first order partial differentiation. We remind you of the 3 general rules we used extensively in Volume 2:

  i)   function of a function (or chain) rule,
  ii) product rule

and iii) quotient rule.

▮▮▮ Example 7.6 ▮

For $z = e^{2x+3y}$ find $\dfrac{\partial z}{\partial x}$ and $\dfrac{\partial z}{\partial y}$ where $x = 0.50$ and $y = 0.20$.

We apply the function of a function rule for each partial derivative. Making a substitution we have

$$z = e^{u} \qquad \text{where} \qquad u = 2x + 3y.$$

Differentiating in both cases we get

$$\frac{dz}{du} = e^{u} \qquad \text{and} \qquad \frac{\partial u}{\partial x} = 2 \text{ and } \frac{\partial u}{\partial y} = 3.$$

We substitute into

$$\frac{\partial z}{\partial x} = \frac{dz}{du} \times \frac{\partial u}{\partial x} \qquad \text{and} \qquad \frac{\partial z}{\partial y} = \frac{dz}{du} \times \frac{\partial u}{\partial y}$$

to get $\quad \dfrac{\partial z}{\partial x} = e^{u} \times 2 \qquad\qquad \dfrac{\partial z}{\partial y} = e^{u} \times 3$

$$= 2e^{2x+3y}. \qquad\qquad = 3e^{2x+3y}.$$

Substituting for
$u = 2x + 3y$.

We find the specific values of these derivatives by substituting for $x = 0.50$ and $y = 0.20$ so that

$$\frac{\partial z}{\partial x} = 2e^{1+0.6} \qquad \text{and} \qquad \frac{\partial z}{\partial y} = 3e^{1+0.6}$$

$$= 2e^{1.6} \qquad\qquad\qquad = 3e^{1.6}$$

$$= 9.91. \qquad\qquad\qquad = 14.9.$$

■■■■■ **Example 7.7** ■■■■■

For $z = x \sin xy$ we find a general expression for $\dfrac{\partial z}{\partial x}$.

In $z = x \sin xy$ we have a product of x and $\sin xy$. This is a product of functions of x, but not of y. When we find $\dfrac{\partial z}{\partial x}$ we apply the product rule.

Finding $\dfrac{\partial z}{\partial y}$ uses the simple differentiation we have seen earlier in this chapter.

Let $\qquad u = x \qquad$ and $\qquad v = \sin xy$.

Differentiating both parts we get

$$\frac{\partial u}{\partial x} = 1 \qquad \text{and} \qquad \frac{\partial v}{\partial x} = y \cos xy.$$

We substitute into the formula for the product rule

$$\frac{\partial z}{\partial x} = u\frac{\partial v}{\partial x} + v\frac{\partial u}{\partial x}$$

to get $\qquad \dfrac{\partial z}{\partial x} = (x)(y \cos xy) + (\sin xy)(1)$

$$= xy \cos xy + \sin xy.$$

■■■■■ **Example 7.8** ■■■■■

In optics the focal length of a lens, f, is related to a and b by $\dfrac{1}{a} + \dfrac{1}{b} = \dfrac{1}{f}$. a is the distance of the object from the lens. b is the distance of the image from the lens. We can vary a, b and f. Our interest is how the image distance varies for different focal lengths, keeping a constant. We re-arrange the original formula to get $b = \dfrac{af}{a - f}$.

Let $\qquad u = af \qquad$ and $\qquad v = a - f$.

Differentiating both parts we get

$$\frac{\partial u}{\partial f} = a \qquad \text{and} \qquad \frac{\partial v}{\partial f} = -1.$$

We substitute into the formula for the quotient rule

$$\frac{\partial b}{\partial f} = \frac{v\dfrac{\partial u}{\partial f} - u\dfrac{\partial v}{\partial f}}{v^2}$$

to get $\qquad \dfrac{\partial b}{\partial f} = \dfrac{(a - f)(a) - (af)(-1)}{(a - f)^2}$

$$= \frac{a^2}{(a - f)^2}.$$

■ ASSIGNMENT ■

In an early look at the cylindrical canister we found the values of the volume and inside surface area. The calculations were based on $r = 1.10$ m and $h = 3.50$ m. Now we look at the change in the inside surface area, A m^2, while the electric motors are operating. Again this example is just before the position is reached, say at $r = 1.05$ m and $h = 3.40$ m. $\dfrac{\partial A}{\partial r}$ is the change in area due to a change in the radius whose units are $\dfrac{\text{m}^2}{\text{m}} = \text{m}$.

Using $A = 2\pi r(h + r)$ we have a product of functions of r.

Let $\qquad u = 2\pi r \qquad$ and $\qquad v = h + r$.

Differentiating both parts we get

$$\frac{\partial u}{\partial r} = 2\pi \qquad \text{and} \qquad \frac{\partial v}{\partial r} = 1.$$

We substitute into the formula for the product rule

$$\frac{\partial A}{\partial r} = u\frac{\partial v}{\partial r} + v\frac{\partial u}{\partial r}$$

to get $\qquad \dfrac{\partial A}{\partial r} = (2\pi r)(1) + (h + r)(2\pi)$

$$= 2\pi(2r + h),$$

which is a general expression for the change in area due to a change in radius.

At the moment where $r = 1.05$ m and $h = 3.40$ m we have

$$\frac{\partial A}{\partial r} = 2\pi(2 \times 1.05 + 3.40) = 2\pi(2.10 + 3.40) = 34.6 \text{ m}.$$

The calculation for $\dfrac{\partial A}{\partial h}$ is slightly quicker.

$\dfrac{\partial A}{\partial h}$ is the change in inside surface area due to a change in the height whose units are $\dfrac{\text{m}^2}{\text{m}} = \text{m}$.

Using $\qquad A = 2\pi r(h + r)$

we have $\qquad \dfrac{\partial A}{\partial h} = 2\pi r,$

which is a general expression for the change in area due to a change in height.

Also at the moment where $r = 1.05$ m and $h = 3.40$ m we have

$$\frac{\partial A}{\partial h} = 2\pi \times 1.05 = 6.60 \text{ m}.$$

■ EXERCISE 7.3 ■

In Questions **1–10** find expressions for $\dfrac{\partial z}{\partial x}$ and $\dfrac{\partial z}{\partial y}$.

1 $z = \sin(x^2 + 3y)$

2 $z = e^{3xy^2}$

3 $z = 4\cos(2x - 5y^2)$

4 $z = xy\ln(x - y)$

5 $z = (x + y)\sin 2xy$

6 $z = (x^2 - y^2)^4$

7 $z = \dfrac{x^2y}{x + y}$

8 $z = \dfrac{x - y}{e^{xy}}$

9 $z = \dfrac{x^2 + y^2}{x - y}$

10 $z = \dfrac{x^2(y - x)}{x + y}$

11 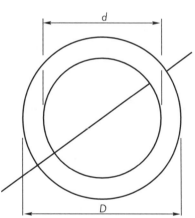 Two capacitors, C_1 and C_2, which can be varied are in series. Their total capacitance, C_T, is given by $\dfrac{1}{C_T} = \dfrac{1}{C_1} + \dfrac{1}{C_2}$. Re-arrange this formula to get $C_T = \dfrac{C_1 C_2}{C_1 + C_2}$. Find an expression for $\dfrac{\partial C_T}{\partial C_1}$. Hence write down the comparable expression for $\dfrac{\partial C_T}{\partial C_2}$.

Find the value of each partial derivative when $C_1 = 5 \times 10^{-5}$ F and $C_2 = 4.5 \times 10^{-5}$ F.

12 The polar second moment of area is given by

$$I = \frac{\pi}{32}(D^2 - d^2)(D^2 + d^2).$$

For variables D and d find an expression for $\dfrac{\partial I}{\partial D}$ and its value where $D = 0.45$ m and $d = 0.35$ m.

13 A resistor, R, inductor, L, and capacitor, C are connected in series as shown. Respectively the voltages across them are V_R, V_L and V_C. The values of all 3 may be varied. Given that

$$V = \sqrt{V_R{}^2 + (V_L - V_C)^2}$$ find a general expression for $\dfrac{\partial V}{\partial V_R}$.

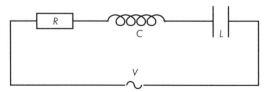

14 The diagram shows a rubber ring used to dampen the transmission of vibrations. It is elliptical with an approximate perimeter, C, given by

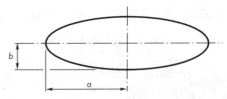

$C = 2\pi \ \sqrt{\frac{1}{2}(a^2 + b^2)}$. When it is stretched find a general expression for $\frac{\partial C}{\partial a}$ and its value where $a = 0.15$ m and $b = 0.05$ m.

15 Design engineers of a civil engineering company are investigating the design of a banked track. They are simulating a vehicle attempting to go around a track banked at an angle θ to the horizontal. Its path is an arc of a circle of radius r. g is the acceleration due to gravity. The engineers can vary the radius, angle of banking and velocity of the vehicle. Where there is no tendency to side slip the velocity of the vehicle, v, is $v = \sqrt{gr\tan\theta}$. Find general expressions for $\frac{\partial v}{\partial r}$ and $\frac{\partial v}{\partial \theta}$. What are their values for $g = 9.81$ ms^{-2}, $r = 120$ m and $\theta = 0.175$ radians?

Now the banked track is rough with a tendency for the vehicle to slip up the banking. The velocity, v, is amended to

$$v^2 = gr\left(\frac{\sin\theta + \mu\cos\theta}{\cos\theta - \mu\sin\theta}\right) \quad \text{where } \mu \text{ is the coefficient of friction.}$$

Find a general expression for $\frac{\partial}{\partial\theta}(v^2)$.

Second order partial differentiation

For one independent and one dependent variable, say $y = f(x)$, we can find $\frac{dy}{dx}, \frac{d^2y}{dx^2}, \ldots$ Now $\frac{d^2y}{dx^2}$ may be written as $\frac{d}{dx}\left(\frac{dy}{dx}\right)$, i.e. the change in the first derivative due to a change in x. In partial differentiation we have 2 or more independent variables. This gives us more variations for second order differentiation and beyond.

Suppose we have $z = f(x, y)$. We know how to find $\frac{\partial z}{\partial x}$ and $\frac{\partial z}{\partial y}$. For $\frac{\partial z}{\partial x}$ we can further differentiate partially with respect to either x or y, i.e. $\frac{\partial}{\partial x}\left(\frac{\partial z}{\partial x}\right)$ and $\frac{\partial}{\partial y}\left(\frac{\partial z}{\partial x}\right)$ respectively. We can simplify these to $\frac{\partial^2 z}{\partial x^2}$ and $\frac{\partial^2 z}{\partial y\partial x}$ respectively, i.e.

$$\frac{\partial}{\partial x}\left(\frac{\partial z}{\partial x}\right) = \frac{\partial^2 z}{\partial x^2} \quad \text{and} \quad \frac{\partial}{\partial y}\left(\frac{\partial z}{\partial x}\right) = \frac{\partial^2 z}{\partial y\partial x}$$

For the mixed derivative notice the order of partial differentiation. First we differentiate partially with respect to x and then we differentiate partially with respect to y.

A similar pattern applies to $\dfrac{\partial z}{\partial y}$. Again we can further differentiate partially with respect to either x or y, i.e. $\dfrac{\partial}{\partial x}\left(\dfrac{\partial z}{\partial y}\right)$ and $\dfrac{\partial}{\partial y}\left(\dfrac{\partial z}{\partial y}\right)$ respectively. We can simplify these to $\dfrac{\partial^2 z}{\partial x \partial y}$ and $\dfrac{\partial^2 z}{\partial y^2}$ respectively, i.e.

$$\frac{\partial}{\partial x}\left(\frac{\partial z}{\partial y}\right) = \frac{\partial^2 z}{\partial x \partial y} \quad \text{and} \quad \frac{\partial}{\partial y}\left(\frac{\partial z}{\partial y}\right) = \frac{\partial^2 z}{\partial y^2}.$$

Again for the mixed derivative notice the order of partial differentiation. First we differentiate partially with respect to y and then we differentiate partially with respect to x.

Strictly we have 4 second order partial derivatives. In many cases this reduces to 3 where $\dfrac{\partial^2 z}{\partial x \partial y} = \dfrac{\partial^2 z}{\partial y \partial x}$. This is true provided the function is continuous at the point(s) where we are calculating these mixed partial derivatives. A continuous function in this case would be modelled by a continuous surface.

▬▬▬▬ **Example 7.9** ▬▬▬▬

We apply an earlier result to find expressions for $\dfrac{\partial^2 z}{\partial x^2}$ and $\dfrac{\partial^2 z}{\partial y^2}$.

From Examples 7.3 if $z = x^2 y^3$

then $\dfrac{\partial z}{\partial x} = 2xy^3$.

Differentiating partially again with respect to x,

$$\frac{\partial}{\partial x}\left(\frac{\partial z}{\partial x}\right) = \frac{\partial}{\partial x}\left(2xy^3\right)$$

i.e. $\dfrac{\partial^2 z}{\partial x^2} = 2 \times y^3 = 2y^3$. $\boxed{\text{Derivative of } 2x \text{ is } 2.}$

Also $\dfrac{\partial z}{\partial y} = 3x^2 y^2$

so that differentiating partially again with respect to y gives

$$\frac{\partial}{\partial y}\left(\frac{\partial z}{\partial y}\right) = \frac{\partial}{\partial y}\left(3x^2 y^2\right)$$

i.e. $\dfrac{\partial^2 z}{\partial y^2} = 3x^2 \times 2y = 6x^2 y$. $\boxed{\text{Derivative of } y^2 \text{ is } 2y.}$

███ **Example 7.10** ███

We apply the same earlier result to find expressions for the mixed derivatives, $\dfrac{\partial^2 z}{\partial x \partial y}$ and $\dfrac{\partial^2 z}{\partial y \partial x}$. Also we see if they are equal.

Using $\qquad z = x^2 y^3$

and $\qquad \dfrac{\partial z}{\partial y} = 3x^2 y^2$

we differentiate partially again, now with respect to x,

i.e. $\qquad \dfrac{\partial}{\partial x}\left(\dfrac{\partial z}{\partial y}\right) = \dfrac{\partial}{\partial x}\left(3x^2 y^2\right)$

so that $\qquad \dfrac{\partial^2 z}{\partial x \partial y} = 6x \times y^2 = 6xy^2.$

Also for $\qquad \dfrac{\partial z}{\partial x} = 2xy^3$

we differentiate partially, now with respect to y,

i.e. $\qquad \dfrac{\partial}{\partial y}\left(\dfrac{\partial z}{\partial x}\right) = \dfrac{\partial}{\partial y}\left(2xy^3\right)$

so that $\qquad \dfrac{\partial^2 z}{\partial y \partial x} = 2x \times 3y^2 = 6xy^2.$

For this example we see the mixed derivatives are indeed equal.

███ **EXERCISE 7.4** ███

In each question find general expressions for $\dfrac{\partial^2 z}{\partial x^2}, \dfrac{\partial^2 z}{\partial y^2}, \dfrac{\partial^2 z}{\partial x \partial y}$ and $\dfrac{\partial^2 z}{\partial y \partial x}$.

1   $z = 2x^3 \ln y$

2   $z = \cos(x + y)$

3   $z = e^{(4x - 3y)}$

4   $z = \sin 2xy$

5   $z = 2x^2 \cos y$

6   $z = (2x + 3y)^3$

7   $z = 2xy(x^2 + y^2)$

8   $z = \dfrac{x + y}{e^{xy}}$

9   $z = x^2 y^2 (x + y)$

10   $z = \dfrac{x^2 + y^2}{xy}$

Small changes

We apply the ideas of partial differentiation to small changes or errors. In Volume 2, Chapter 5, we did look at these using the binomial series. Here these small changes may be incremental changes. Later numerical substitutions will show increases as positive and decreases as negative, consistent with Volume 2, Chapter 5.

Generally we have looked at z as a function of x and y, i.e. $z = f(x, y)$. Then $\dfrac{\partial z}{\partial x}$ discusses the changing x while y is constant. Also $\dfrac{\partial z}{\partial y}$ discusses the changing y while x is constant. Now we look at how z changes due to changes in both x and y.

We concentrate upon the Assignment to show the basic ideas in a practical sense.

▆▆▆▆▆▆ ASSIGNMENT ▆▆▆▆▆▆

For our cylindrical canister we recall the formula for the volume, $V = \pi r^2 h$. Let us look at small changes in the radius, r, and height, h.

δr is a small change in the radius from r to $r + \delta r$.

δh is a small change in the height from h to $h + \delta h$.

Together these changes cause some change in the volume from V to $V + \delta V$. This means

$$V = \pi r^2 h$$

changes to $\quad V + \delta V = \pi \{r + \delta r\}^2 \{h + \delta h\}$

$$= \pi \left\{ r^2 + 2r(\delta r) + (\delta r)^2 \right\} \{h + \delta h\}$$

i.e. $\quad \pi r^2 h + \delta V = \pi \left\{ r^2 h + 2rh(\delta r) + h(\delta r)^2 + r^2(\delta h) \right.$

$$\left. + 2r(\delta r)(\delta h) + (\delta r)^2(\delta h) \right\}.$$

Because δr and δh are small $(\delta r)^2$, $(\delta r)(\delta h)$, and $(\delta r)^2(\delta h)$ are yet smaller. This means we may neglect these 3 terms as a first approximation,

i.e. $\quad \pi r^2 h + \delta V \approx \pi \{r^2 h + 2rh(\delta r) + r^2(\delta h)\}$

i.e. $\quad \delta V \approx 2\pi rh(\delta r) + \pi r^2(\delta h).$

> Subtracting $\pi r^2 h$ from both sides.

We know from our earlier Assignment work that $\dfrac{\partial V}{\partial r} = 2\pi rh$ and $\dfrac{\partial V}{\partial h} = \pi r^2$. This means we have

$$\delta V \approx \frac{\partial V}{\partial r} . \delta r + \frac{\partial V}{\partial h} . \delta h.$$

Earlier we used $r = 1.10$ m and $h = 3.50$ m to calculate $V = 13.30$ m³. Later we looked at $r = 1.05$ m and $h = 3.40$ m to calculate $\dfrac{\partial V}{\partial r} = 22.4$ m²

and $\dfrac{\partial V}{\partial h} = 3.46$ m².

Using our formula for δV we are going to calculate the change in volume. This is from where $r = 1.05$ m, $h = 3.40$ m to where $r = 1.10$ m, $h = 3.50$ m.

$$\delta r = 1.10 - 1.05 = 0.05 \text{ m}.$$

$$\delta h = 3.50 - 3.40 = 0.10 \text{ m}.$$

Then $\quad \delta V \approx \dfrac{\partial V}{\partial r}.\delta r + \dfrac{\partial V}{\partial h}.\delta h$

becomes $\quad \delta V \approx (22.4)(0.05) + (3.46)(0.10)$

$$\approx 1.47 \text{ m}^3,$$

i.e. during these changes the approximate increase in the volume is 1.47 m^3.

Similarly we can look at the inside surface area, A. We have changes in r, δr, and in h, δh. It means

$$A = 2\pi r(h + r)$$

changes to $\quad A + \delta A = 2\pi\{r + \delta r\}\{h + \delta h + r + \delta r\}$

i.e. $\quad 2\pi r(h + r) + \delta A = 2\pi\{rh + r(\delta h) + r^2 + r(\delta r) + h(\delta r)$

$$+ (\delta r)(\delta h) + r(\delta r) + (\delta r)^2\}.$$

Again neglecting very small terms we have

$$2\pi r(h + r) + \delta A \approx 2\pi\{rh + r(\delta h) + r^2 + 2r(\delta r) + h(\delta r)\}$$

i.e $\quad\quad\quad\quad \delta A \approx 2\pi(2r + h)(\delta r) + 2\pi r(\delta h).$

> Subtracting $2\pi r(h + r)$ from both sides.

Also we know from the Assignment that $\dfrac{\partial A}{\partial r} = 2\pi(2r + h)$ and $\dfrac{\partial A}{\partial h} = 2\pi r.$

This means we have

$$\delta A \approx \dfrac{\partial A}{\partial r}.\delta r + \dfrac{\partial A}{\partial h}.\delta h.$$

Using $\delta r = 0.05$ m, $\delta h = 0.10$ m, and our earlier results of $\dfrac{\partial A}{\partial r} = 34.6$ m

and $\dfrac{\partial A}{\partial h} = 6.60$ m we have

$$\delta A \approx (34.6)(0.05) + (6.60)(0.10)$$

$$\approx 2.39 \text{ m}^2,$$

i.e. during these changes the approximate increase in the inside surface area is 2.39 m^2.

We may return to $z = f(x, y)$ and write generally

$$\delta z \approx \frac{\partial z}{\partial x}.\delta x + \frac{\partial z}{\partial y}.\delta y.$$

Often the approximately equals symbol ($\approx$) is replaced to give

$$\delta z = \frac{\partial z}{\partial x}.\delta x + \frac{\partial z}{\partial y}.\delta y.$$

If we expanded our system to n independent variables so that $z = f(x_1, x_2, \ldots x_n)$ then

$$\delta z = \frac{\partial z}{\partial x_1}.\delta x_1 + \frac{\partial z}{\partial x_2}.\delta x_2 + \ldots + \frac{\partial z}{\partial x_n}.\delta x_n$$

δz is the overall change in z for changes in all the independent variables together.

Remember that increases are positive and decreases are negative. It is possible for an increase in one independent variable and a decrease in another independent variable to create no overall change.

Examples 7.11

In an electrical circuit the voltage, V, and the resistance, R, are related to power, P, by $P = \dfrac{V^2}{R}$. Initially the voltage is 240 V and the resistance is 20 Ω. Find the approximate change in power when

i)   the voltage decreases to 238 V and the resistance decreases to 19 Ω,

ii) the voltage decreases to 238.5 V and the resistance increases to 20.5 Ω,

iii) the voltage decreases to 237 V and the resistance decreases to 19.5 Ω,

iv) the voltage increases by 1% and the resistance decreases by 0.5%.

Using $\qquad P = \dfrac{V^2}{R} = V^2 R^{-1}$

we have $\qquad \dfrac{\partial P}{\partial V} = \dfrac{2V}{R}$ and $\dfrac{\partial P}{\partial R} = -V^2 R^{-2} = -\dfrac{V^2}{R^2}.$

We can find the values of $\dfrac{\partial P}{\partial V}$ and $\dfrac{\partial P}{\partial R}$ at the initial or final values of V and R. Remember our change in P, δP, is an approximate change. For consistent reference we use the initial values.

$$\frac{\partial P}{\partial V} = \frac{2 \times 240}{20} = 24 \qquad \text{and} \qquad \frac{\partial P}{\partial R} = -\frac{240^2}{20^2} = -144.$$

We compare our example with the general $z = f(x, y)$ and

$$\delta z \approx \frac{\partial z}{\partial x}.\delta x + \frac{\partial z}{\partial y}.\delta y$$

i.e. $\qquad \delta P \approx \dfrac{\partial P}{\partial V}.\delta V + \dfrac{\partial P}{\partial R}.\delta R.$

i) V changes from 240 to 238, i.e. $\delta V = -2$.

R changes from 20 to 19, i.e. $\delta R = -1$.

We substitute into our formula for δP to get

$$\delta P \approx (24)(-2) + (-144)(-1)$$
$$\approx -48 + 144$$
$$\approx 96,$$

i.e. the approximate change in the power is an increase of 96 W.

Notice how in this case two decreases create a final increase. This is because of the composition of the formula.

ii) V changes from 240 to 238.5, i.e. $\delta V = -1.5$.

R changes from 20 to 20.5, i.e. $\delta R = +0.5$.

We substitute into our formula for δP to get

$$\delta P \approx (24)(-1.5) + (-144)(0.5)$$
$$\approx -36 - 72$$
$$\approx -108,$$

i.e. the approximate change in the power is a decrease of 108 W.

iii) V changes from 240 to 237, i.e. $\delta V = -3$.

R changes from 20 to 19.5, i.e. $\delta R = -0.5$.

We substitute into our formula for δP to get

$$\delta P \approx (24)(-3) + (-144)(-0.5)$$
$$\approx -72 + 72$$
$$\approx 0,$$

i.e. there is no approximate change in the power.

Notice how in this case two decreases compensate for each other to leave the power approximately as before.

iv)   This time we are dealing with percentage changes. Our substitutions into the formula for δP are slightly different.

The change in the voltage is an increase of 1%,

i.e. $\delta V = 1\%$ of $V = \dfrac{1}{100} \times V = \dfrac{V}{100}$.

The change in the resistance is a decrease of 0.5%,

i.e. $\delta R = -0.5\%$ of $R = -\dfrac{0.5}{100} \times R = -\dfrac{0.5R}{100}$.

Now $\delta P \approx \dfrac{\partial P}{\partial V}.\delta V + \dfrac{\partial P}{\partial R}.\delta R$

becomes $\delta P \approx \left(\dfrac{2V}{R}\right)\left(\dfrac{V}{100}\right) + \left(-\dfrac{V^2}{R^2}\right)\left(-\dfrac{0.5R}{100}\right)$

$$\delta P \approx \left(\frac{2}{100} + \frac{0.5}{100}\right) \frac{V^2}{R}$$

i.e. $\delta P \approx \frac{2.5}{100} \times P$, $\boxed{\text{Substituting for } P = \frac{V^2}{R}.}$

i.e. this is an approximate increase in power of 2.5%.

EXERCISE 7.5

1   The surface area, A, of a solid cone is $A = \pi r(\ell + r)$ where ℓ is the slant height and r is the base radius. Find the approximate change in A when r changes from 0.600 m to 0.625 m and ℓ changes from 0.800 m to 0.780 m.

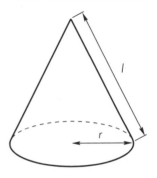

2   The resonant frequency, f, is given in terms of capacitance, C, and inductance, L, by $f = \frac{1}{2\pi\sqrt{LC}}$. For variable capacitance and inductance find $\frac{\partial f}{\partial L}$ and $\frac{\partial f}{\partial C}$ when L is 3.00 H and C is 1.75×10^{-3} F. Find the approximate change in the frequency when L increases to 3.15 H and C increases to 1.80×10^{-3} F.

3   In optics the focal length of a lens, f, is related to a and b by $\frac{1}{a} + \frac{1}{b} = \frac{1}{f}$. a is the distance of the object from the lens. b is the distance of the image from the lens. We can vary a, b and f. Show that $b = \frac{af}{a - f}$. Find the approximate change in b for a decrease in a from 0.550 m to 0.525 m and an increase in f from 0.25 m to 0.255 m.

4   The periodic time, T, of a simple pendulum is related to its length, ℓ, by $T = 2\pi\sqrt{\frac{\ell}{g}}$. g is the acceleration due to gravity. If ℓ is measured 2.5% too small and g is over-estimated by 2% what is the approximate percentage change in the periodic time?

5   $Q = \frac{kAT}{x}$ relates the rate of heat energy transfer, Q, between two faces of material to the variables k, A, T and x. k is the coefficient of thermal conductivity. A is the conducting area. T is the temperature difference between the two faces. x is the thickness of the material.

Find a general expression for $\frac{\partial Q}{\partial x}$. Also find its specific value for mild steel of conducting area 1.4 m^2 when its faces are 0.035 m apart. $k = 55$ Wm^{-1}K^{-1} and the temperature difference is 70°K. Similarly find general expressions for $\frac{\partial Q}{\partial A}$ and $\frac{\partial Q}{\partial T}$ and their values. What is the approximate change in Q when the distance between the faces is decreased to 0.0325 m, the area is decreased to 1.38 m^2 and the temperature difference is decreased to 65°K?

Rates of change

For $z = f(x, y)$ we know that $\delta z = \frac{\partial z}{\partial x}.\delta x + \frac{\partial z}{\partial y}.\delta y$. δx is some small change in x. This change occurs over some small time, δt, i.e. we have a change in x due to a change in t, $\frac{\delta x}{\delta t}$.

Similarly δy is some small change in y. Again this change occurs over some small time, δt, to give us $\frac{\delta y}{\delta t}$. Together these changes cause the small change in z, δz, over that small time,

i.e. $\quad \frac{\delta z}{\delta t} = \frac{\partial z}{\partial x}.\frac{\delta x}{\delta t} + \frac{\partial z}{\partial y}.\frac{\delta y}{\delta t}$

In the limiting case as $\delta t \to 0$ we apply our definition for differentiation,

i.e. $\quad \frac{dx}{dt} = \lim_{\delta t \to 0} \frac{\delta x}{\delta t}$.

We have similar definitions for $\frac{dy}{dt}$ and $\frac{dz}{dt}$ so that

$$\frac{dz}{dt} = \frac{\partial z}{\partial x}.\frac{dx}{dt} + \frac{\partial z}{\partial y}.\frac{dy}{dt}.$$

$\frac{dz}{dt}$ is the **total derivative**. Notice that it involves a mixture of types of differentiation.

If we expand our system to n independent variables so that $z = f(x_1, x_2, \ldots, x_n)$ then

$$\frac{dz}{dt} = \frac{\partial z}{\partial x_1}.\frac{dx_1}{dt} + \frac{\partial z}{\partial x_2}.\frac{dx_2}{dt} + \ldots + \frac{\partial z}{\partial x_n}.\frac{dx_n}{dt}.$$

We use the Assignment to look at rates of change.

ASSIGNMENT

Using $\delta V = \dfrac{\partial V}{\partial r}.\delta r + \dfrac{\partial V}{\partial h}.\delta h$ and our ideas for rates of change we have

$$\frac{dV}{dt} = \frac{\partial V}{\partial r}.\frac{dr}{dt} + \frac{\partial V}{\partial h}.\frac{dh}{dt}.$$

We use some of the values from before, i.e. $r = 1.05$ m, $h = 3.40$ m, $\dfrac{\partial V}{\partial r} = 22.4$ m^2 and $\dfrac{\partial V}{\partial h} = 3.46$ m^2.

Suppose the motors are increasing both the radius and the height at 0.01 ms^{-1}, i.e. $\dfrac{dr}{dt} = 0.01$ ms^{-1} and $\dfrac{dh}{dt} = 0.01$ ms^{-1}.

We substitute these values into our formula for $\dfrac{dV}{dt}$,

i.e. $\quad \dfrac{dV}{dt} = (22.4)(0.01) + (3.46)(0.01)$

$\qquad\qquad = 0.26$ m^{3}s^{-1},

i.e. the volume is increasing at a rate of 0.26 m^3 each second.
As an exercise for yourself work out the rate of change of the inside surface area, $\dfrac{dA}{dt}$.

Examples 7.12

In Fig. 7.5 we have a segment of a circle of centre O. The length of its straight side is x and its area is A. The distance of its centroid from O is $\bar{y}$ where $\bar{y} = \dfrac{x^3}{12A}$. This segment is changing over time. When x is 0.75 m it is increasing at a rate of 0.005 ms^{-1}. When A is 0.20 m^2 it is increasing at a rate of 0.010 m^{2}s^{-1}. What is the rate of change of $\bar{y}$?

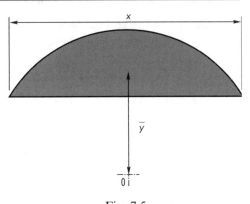

Fig. 7.5

We relate our problem to the general $z = f(x, y)$ and

$$\frac{dz}{dt} = \frac{\partial z}{\partial x}.\frac{dx}{dt} + \frac{\partial z}{\partial y}.\frac{dy}{dt}.$$

This means we have

$$\frac{d\bar{y}}{dt} = \frac{\partial \bar{y}}{\partial x}.\frac{dx}{dt} + \frac{\partial \bar{y}}{\partial A}.\frac{dA}{dt}.$$

Using $\qquad \bar{y} = \dfrac{x^3}{12A}$ $\qquad$ or $\qquad \bar{y} = \dfrac{x^3 A^{-1}}{12}$

we have $\quad \dfrac{\partial \bar{y}}{\partial x} = \dfrac{3x^2}{12A} = \dfrac{x^2}{4A}$ $\quad$ and $\quad \dfrac{\partial \bar{y}}{\partial A} = -\dfrac{x^3 A^{-2}}{12}$.

Where $x = 0.75$ m and $A = 0.20$ m^2 we find the values of these partial derivatives, i.e.

$$\dfrac{\partial \bar{y}}{\partial x} = \dfrac{0.75^2}{4 \times 0.20} \qquad \text{and} \qquad \dfrac{\partial \bar{y}}{\partial A} = -\dfrac{0.75^3 \times 0.20^{-2}}{12}$$

$$= 0.7031 \ldots \qquad\qquad\qquad = -0.8789 \ldots$$

In this example we are given

$$\dfrac{dx}{dt} = 0.005 \qquad \text{and} \qquad \dfrac{dA}{dt} = 0.010.$$

We substitute into our general expression for $\dfrac{d\bar{y}}{dt}$, i.e.

$$\dfrac{d\bar{y}}{dt} = (0.7031 \ldots)(0.005) + (-0.8789 \ldots)(0.010)$$

$$= -0.00527,$$

i.e. the distance of the centroid from O is decreasing at a rate of 0.00527 ms^{-1}.

EXERCISE 7.6

1   The volume, V, of a conical shell is $V = \dfrac{1}{3}\pi r^2 h$

where h is the vertical height and r is the base radius. Find the change in volume with respect to time, t, when r is 0.50 m, $\dfrac{dr}{dt}$ is 0.025 ms^{-1},

h is 1.20 m and $\dfrac{dh}{dt}$ is -0.015 ms^{-1}.

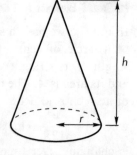

2   $W = Fs$ is the work done, W J, by a force, F N, moving a displacement, s m. When $F = 400$ N it is decreasing at 2 Ns^{-1}. Correspondingly when $s = 35$ m the velocity $\left(\text{i.e. } v = \dfrac{ds}{dt}\right)$ is 1.75 ms^{-1}. Find the rate of working, $\dfrac{dW}{dt}$.

3   In an electrical circuit the current, i A, is given by $i = \dfrac{V}{R}$. When the voltage, V, is 237.5 V it is decreasing at a rate of 0.01Vs^{-1}. At this time the resistance, R, is 25 Ω and decreasing at 0.02 Ωs^{-1}. Find the rate of change of current, $\dfrac{di}{dt}$.

4   A vehicle's speed, v, on a curved horizontal road is related to the radius of the curve, r, by $v = \sqrt{g\mu r}$. $g = 9.81$ ms^{-2} is the acceleration due to gravity and μ is the coefficient of friction. The radius of the curved road and its roughness are variable. When $r = 120$ m, $\mu = 0.28$, $\dfrac{dr}{dt} = 0.5$ ms^{-1} and $\dfrac{d\mu}{dt} = 0.01$ s^{-1} find $\dfrac{dv}{dt}$.

5   In optics the focal length of a lens, f, is related to a and b by $\dfrac{1}{a} + \dfrac{1}{b} = \dfrac{1}{f}$. a is the distance of the object from the lens. b is the distance of the image from the lens. We can vary a, b and f. We know that $b = \dfrac{af}{a-f}$.

When a is 0.750 m it is increasing at a rate of 0.01 ms^{-1}. Also when f is 0.30 m it is decreasing at a rate of 0.0075 ms^{-1}. Find $\dfrac{db}{dt}$.

Total differentials

We have looked at a mixture of types of differentiation for small changes and rates of change. A total differential is another similar idea. For $z = f(x, y)$ dz **is a total differential** where

$$dz = \frac{\partial z}{\partial x} . dx + \frac{\partial z}{\partial y} . dy.$$

Again we may extend it for many independent variables. If $z = f(x_1, x_2, \ldots, x_n)$ then

$$dz = \frac{\partial z}{\partial x_1} . dx_1 + \frac{\partial z}{\partial x_2} . dx_2 + \ldots + \frac{\partial z}{\partial x_n} . dx_n.$$

■ ASSIGNMENT ■

We compare our Assignment with the general $z = f(x, y)$ and

$$dz = \frac{\partial z}{\partial x} . dx + \frac{\partial z}{\partial y} . dy.$$

In our case $V = f(r, h)$ so that

$$dV = \frac{\partial V}{\partial r} . dr + \frac{\partial V}{\partial h} . dh.$$

For $V = \pi r^2 h$ we know that $\dfrac{\partial V}{\partial r} = 2\pi r h$ and $\dfrac{\partial V}{\partial h} = \pi r^2$. We substitute into our formula for the total differential, dV,

i.e. $dV = 2\pi r h.dr + \pi r^2.dh.$

Alternatively we may compare dV to the volume, V, so that

$$\frac{dV}{V} = \frac{2\pi rh}{V} dr + \frac{\pi r^2}{V} dh$$

> Dividing throughout by V.

i.e. $$\frac{dV}{V} = \frac{2\pi rh}{\pi r^2 h} dr + \frac{\pi r^2}{\pi r^2 h} dh$$

> Substituting for $V = \pi r^2 h$.

i.e. $$\frac{dV}{V} = 2\frac{dr}{r} + \frac{dh}{h}.$$

8 Vectors

The objectives of this chapter are to:

1   Define and apply scalar product.

2   Understand that scalar product is commutative.

3   Define and apply vector product.

4   Find a vector product using a determinant.

5   Understand that vector product is *not* commutative.

6   Define and apply triple scalar product.

7   Define and apply triple vector product.

8   Appreciate the cyclical properties of triple products.

9   Differentiate variable vectors.

10   Introduce the ∇ operator.

11   Apply ∇ in the form of div, grad and curl.

Introduction

We introduced some early vector work in Volume 1, Chapter 13. Here, in Volume 3, we develop it further in three dimensional Cartesian form. The bulk of this chapter looks at types of products. Their titles indicate the type of solution we get in each case. For each type we show some sample applications. Final sections link together differentiation (including partial differentiation) and vectors using the operator ∇. This is an elementary introduction to vector analysis. Though we use Cartesian vector forms throughout the chapter you need to appreciate there are other forms, e.g. spherical polars and cylindrical polars.

We assume the early vector work you have seen before. You may find a brief look at Volume 1, Chapter 13, useful. Remember a **scalar** has **magnitude only**. A **vector** has both **magnitude and direction**.

▬▬ ASSIGNMENT ▬▬▬▬▬▬▬▬▬▬▬▬▬▬▬▬▬

The Assignment for this chapter looks at a force in vector format. The early applications are for a constant force. Using scalar product we look at its components and work done. Using vector product we look at its turning effect, i.e. its vector moment.

Scalar product

Scalar product is different from scalar multiplication. This idea links 2 vectors using multiplication (i.e. product) and gives a scalar answer: hence the title of scalar product. To denote the operation of scalar product we use a dot, .. It leads to the alternative title of **dot product**.

The scalar (dot) product of 2 vectors, a and b, is defined as the product of their magnitudes and the cosine of the angle between them, i.e.

$$\boldsymbol{a}.\boldsymbol{b} = ab\cos\theta \qquad \text{or} \qquad \boldsymbol{a}.\boldsymbol{b} = |\boldsymbol{a}||\boldsymbol{b}|\cos\theta.$$

As you see in Figs. 8.1 the angle between the vectors may be either acute or obtuse. In Fig. 8.1a) θ is an acute angle so $\cos\theta$ is positive and $\boldsymbol{a}.\boldsymbol{b}$ is also positive. In Fig. 8.1b) θ is an obtuse angle so $\cos\theta$ is negative and $\boldsymbol{a}.\boldsymbol{b}$ is also negative.

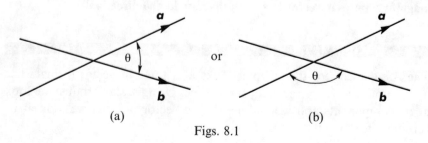

(a)   (b)

Figs. 8.1

Remember i is a unit vector (i.e. the magnitude is 1) in the x direction,
                   j is a unit vector (i.e. the magnitude is 1) in the y direction
and k is a unit vector (i.e. the magnitude is 1) in the z direction.

This means i, j and k are mutually perpendicular vectors (Fig. 8.2), i.e. each is at $90°$ to the others. Later we will use $\sin 0° = 0$, $\sin 90° = 1$, $\cos 0° = 1$ and $\cos 90° = 0$.

Also $|i| = |j| = |k| = 1$.

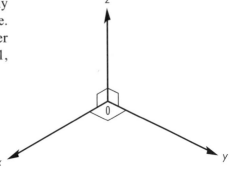

Let us look at 2 general vectors,

$$a = a_1 i + a_2 j + a_3 k$$

and $b = b_1 i + b_2 j + b_3 k,$

Fig. 8.2

where a_1, a_2, a_3, b_1, b_2, and b_3 are values in the respective directions.

Now $a.b = (a_1 i + a_2 j + a_3 k).(b_1 i + b_2 j + b_3 k).$

When we multiply together these brackets we have $3 \times 3 = 9$ terms,

i.e. $a.b = a_1 b_1 i.i + a_1 b_2 i.j + a_1 b_3 i.k+$

              $a_2 b_1 j.i + a_2 b_2 j.j + a_2 b_3 j.k+$

              $a_3 b_1 k.i + a_3 b_2 k.j + a_3 b_3 k.k.$

Now $i.i = (1)(1)\cos 0° = 1.$ | $\cos 0° = 1.$ |

Similarly $j.j = 1$ and $k.k = 1.$

Also $i.j = (1)(1)\cos 90° = 0.$ | $\cos 90° = 0.$ |

Similarly the remaining scalar products are zero.

This leaves us with

$$a.b = a_1 b_1 + a_2 b_2 + a_3 b_3.$$

This is an easier version of the definition. Notice we start with 2 vectors and apply the **scalar product** to reach a **scalar answer**.

Scalar product is commutative, i.e. the order of a and b does *not* matter. In basic arithmetic the order of addition and multiplication do *not* matter, e.g. $24 + 7 = 7 + 24$ and $3 \times 5 = 5 \times 3$. This means we can write

$$a.b = a_1 b_1 + a_2 b_2 + a_3 b_3$$

$$= b_1 a_1 + b_2 a_2 + b_3 a_3$$

| The commutative law for scalar product. |

i.e. $a.b = b.a.$

■■■■■ Examples 8.1 ■■■■■

We use $a = 4i - 2j + 3k$ and $b = 1.5i - k$. Notice b has no j component and the coefficient of k is -1.

i)   Using $a.b = a_1b_1 + a_2b_2 + a_3b_3$
             $a.b = (4i - 2j + 3k).(1.5i - k)$
     gives us $a.b = (4)(1.5) + (-2)(0) + (3)(-1)$
                   $= 6 + 0 - 3$
     i.e. $a.b = 3.$
     Also $15a.b = 15 \times 3 = 45.$

ii) Now $5a = 5(4i - 2j + 3k) = 20i - 10j + 15k$
     and $3b = 3(1.5i - k) = 4.5i - 3k$
     so that $5a.3b = (20i - 10j + 15k).(4.5i - 3k)$
                    $= (20)(4.5) + (-10)(0) + (15)(-3)$
                    $= 90 + 0 - 45$
                    $= 45,$ as before.

For yourself you can move around the scalar multipliers of 3 and 5 to achieve the same result.

■■■■■ EXERCISE 8.1 ■■■■■

In this Exercise we use $a = 2i + 2j + 4k$, $b = i + 2j + 3k$, $c = 4i - 5j + 6k$, $d = 0.5i - 2k$, and $e = -3j + 2k$.

In each case find the value of the scalar product.

1	$a.b$	6	$6(a.b)$
2	$b.c$	7	$(4c).b$
3	$e.d$	8	$d.7e$
4	$a.(2b)$	9	$0.5e.6a$
5	$(2a).(3b)$	10	$2b.2c$

The angle between 2 vectors

We use our definition for scalar product, making $\cos \theta$ the subject of the formula, i.e. dividing throughout by ab, so that

$$\cos \theta = \frac{a.b}{ab}.$$

Examples 8.2

i) We use $a = 4i - 2j + 3k$ and $b = 1.5i - k$. From Example 8.1i) we know that $a.b = 3$. For our angle formula we need the sizes of a and b, i.e.

$$a = \sqrt{4^2 + (-2)^2 + 3^2} \qquad \text{and} \qquad b = \sqrt{1.5^2 + (-1)^2}$$
$$= \sqrt{16 + 4 + 9} \qquad\qquad\qquad = \sqrt{2.25 + 1}$$
$$= \sqrt{29} \qquad\qquad\qquad\qquad = \sqrt{3.25}$$
$$\text{or} \quad 5.385. \qquad\qquad\qquad \text{or} \quad 1.803.$$

Using $\qquad \cos\theta = \dfrac{a.b}{ab}$

$$\cos\theta = \frac{3}{(5.3851\ldots)(1.8027\ldots)}$$
$$= 0.309\ldots$$

to give $\qquad \theta = 72°$ as the angle between a and b.

ii) Using $\qquad a.b = a_1 b_1 + a_2 b_2 + a_3 b_3$

let $\qquad d.e = (0.5i - 2k).(-3j + 2k)$

to give us $\quad d.e = (0.5)(0) + (0)(-3) + (-2)(2)$
$$= 0 + 0 - 4$$
$$= -4.$$

Also $\qquad d = \sqrt{0.5^2 + (-2)^2} \qquad \text{and} \qquad e = \sqrt{(-3)^2 + 2^2}$
$$= \sqrt{0.25 + 4} \qquad\qquad\qquad = \sqrt{9 + 4}$$
$$= \sqrt{4.25} \qquad\qquad\qquad\qquad = \sqrt{13}$$
$$\text{or} \quad 2.062. \qquad\qquad\qquad \text{or} \quad 3.606.$$

Using $\qquad \cos\theta = \dfrac{a.b}{ab}$

$$\cos\theta = \frac{-4}{(2.0615\ldots)(3.6055\ldots)}$$
$$= -0.538\ldots$$

to give $\qquad \theta = 122.6°$ as the obtuse angle between d and e.

Hence the acute angle is $180° - 122.6° = 57.4°$.

EXERCISE 8.2

In this Exercise we use $a = 2i + 2j + 4k$, $b = i + 2j + 3k$, $c = 4i - 5j + 6k$, $d = 0.5i - 2k$, and $e = -3j + 2k$.

In each case find the angle between the vectors using scalar product.

1   a and b 3 $2e$ and d

2   b and c 4 a and d

5 *a* and *c*	8 3*a* and *e*
6 *e* and *b*	9 4*c* and *d*
7 *c* and *e*	10 *b* and *d*

We can further apply our definition for the angle between 2 vectors, $a.b = ab \cos\theta$. For **perpendicular vectors** $\theta = 90°$ so $\cos\theta = 0$, i.e

$$a.b = 0.$$

Examples 8.3

i)   Using $a = 4i - 2j + 3k$ and $b = 1.5i - k$ we know from Example 8.1i) that *a* and *b* are *not* perpendicular because $a.b = 3 \neq 0$.

ii)   For $a = 4i - 2j + 3k$ and $b = 1.5i - 2k$ then
$$a.b = (4i - 2j + 3k).(1.5i - 2k)$$
gives us $a.b = (4)(1.5) + (-2)(0) + (3)(-2)$
$$= 6 + 0 - 6$$
i.e. $a.b = 0$,   i.e. *a* and *b* are perpendicular.

Resolution

In Volume 1, Chapter 13, we looked at simple resolution. Here we concentrate upon applying scalar product. Any vector, say $v = 7i + 2j - 8k$, has components. In this case they are 7 along the x-axis, 2 along the y-axis and 8 along the negative z-axis (or -8 along the z-axis).
Now $v.i = (7i + 2j - 8k).(1i + 0j + 0k)$
gives us $v.i = (7)(1) + (2)(0) + (-8)(0)$
$$= 7,$$

i.e. $v.i$, where *i* is a unit vector, gives the component in the x direction. The unit vector is important here.
Similarly $v.j = 2$ and $v.k = -8$.
We can link this idea with right-angled triangle trigonometry.

In Fig. 8.3 $\dfrac{x}{v} = \cos\theta$,

i.e. $x = v\cos\theta$ is the horizontal
                       component
$$= (v)(1)\cos\theta$$
$$= v.i.$$

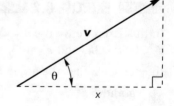

Fig. 8.3

We can generalise this right-angled triangle so the perpendicular sides do *not* align with the axes. Then we need to consider a general unit vector. The component of a vector, v, in the direction, d, is given by $v.\hat{d}$. $\hat{d}$ is a unit vector in the direction of d. $\hat{d}$ ('d hat') is expressed as $\dfrac{d}{d}$.

Example 8.4

We find the component of v in the direction of d where $v = 7i + 2j - 8k$ and $d = 4i + 3j$.

Given $d = 4i + 3j$

$$d = \sqrt{4^2 + 3^2} = 5,$$

i.e. the size of d is 5 units, yet we need it to be of size 1 unit (unit vector). This is why we scale down, dividing by the size, d, so that

$$\hat{d} = \frac{d}{d}$$

gives us $\hat{d} = \dfrac{4i + 3j}{5}$.

or $\dfrac{4}{5}i + \dfrac{3}{5}j$ or $0.8i + 0.6j$.

The component of v in the direction of d is

$$v.\hat{d} = (7i + 2j - 8k).\frac{(4i + 3j)}{5}$$
$$= \frac{(7)(4) + (2)(3) + (-8)(0)}{5}$$
$$= 6.8.$$

Sometimes we may wish to find both parallel and perpendicular components of a vector. This implies we need a direction perpendicular to d, say d_1, where $d.d_1 = 0$. In Fig. 8.4 we show d and 2 possible (opposite) directions for d_1.

or

Fig. 8.4

We can achieve these for d_1 quite simply. We reverse the coefficients of d and change one of the $+/-$ signs.

For $d = 4i + 3j$ then $d_1 = 3i - 4j$ or $d_1 = -3i + 4j$.

$$d.d_1 = (4i + 3j).(3i - 4j) \qquad \text{or} \qquad d.d_1 = (4i + 3j).(-3i + 4j)$$

Then
$$= (4)(3) + (3)(-4) \qquad\qquad\qquad = (4)(-3) + (3)(4)$$

$$= 0. \qquad\qquad\qquad\qquad\qquad\quad = 0.$$

Example 8.5

We find the component of v perpendicular to the direction d where $v = 7i + 2j - 8k$ and $d = 4i + 3j$.

Given $\qquad d = 4i + 3j$

we have already noted a possible d_1, i.e.

$$d_1 = 3i - 4j.$$

$$d_1 = 5$$

and $\qquad \hat{d}_1 = \dfrac{3i - 4j}{5}.$ $\boxed{d = d_1.}$

The component of v in the direction of d_1 (i.e. perpendicular to d) is

$$v.\hat{d}_1 = (7i + 2j - 8k).\frac{(3i - 4j)}{5}$$

$$= \frac{(7)(3) + (2)(-4) + (-8)(0)}{5}$$

$$= 2.6.$$

For this level of Mathematics requiring parallel and perpendicular components we concentrate upon 2 dimensional direction vectors. If d is 3 dimensional then there is a plane containing an infinite number of vectors perpendicular to it.

ASSIGNMENT

For this part of the Assignment we look at a force, $F = 12i + 4j + 3k$ N.

Its size is $F = \sqrt{12^2 + 4^2 + 3^2} = 13$ N.

Also a unit vector in the force's direction is $\dfrac{12i + 4j + 3k}{13}.$

If a force, F N, acts upon an object it can move it some displacement, s m. The work done is the product of that force and displacement. In vector form

Work done $= F.s.$

Suppose $\qquad s = 3i + 2j - 5k$

then the Work done $= (12i + 4j + 3k).(3i + 2j - 5k)$

$$= (12)(3) + (4)(2) + (3)(-5)$$
$$= 29 \text{ J.}$$

In this case the answer is positive, showing the force is doing work. Where the answer is negative work is being done upon the force.

A force *cannot* do work where the displacement is perpendicular to it, i.e. F and s would be at $90°$ and so $F.s = 0$.

EXERCISE 8.3

In this Exercise we use $a = 2i - 2j + 4k$, $b = i + 2j - 3k$, $c = 4i - 5j + 6k$, $d = 0.5i - 2k$, and $e = -3j + 2k$.

For Questions **1–5** find the vector component in the stated direction.

1 a in the direction $2i + 5j$.

2 b in the direction $i - 5j + 3k$.

3 c in the direction $4i + 6k$.

4 d in the direction $i - j + k$.

5 e in the direction $4i + j + 7k$.

In Questions **6–10** use the vector, $v = 2i - 3j + 4k$. Find the components of v parallel and perpendicular to d in each case.

6 $d = i + j$.

7 $d = 2i + k$.

8 $d = -(i + j)$.

9 $d = 3i + 2j$.

10 $d = 2i - 3k$.

Applications of scalar product

Having introduced an application of scalar product in the Assignment we look at applications in 2 more examples.

Example 8.6

A shadow, $s = 2i + 1.5j + 0.5k$ m, is cast along a slope of direction $d = i + j - 3k$. The projection of the shadow on the slope is given by $s.\hat{d}$. We find the length of this projection.

Given $\qquad d = i + j - 3k$

$$d = \sqrt{1^2 + 1^2 + (-3)^2} = 3.3166\ldots.$$

$$\hat{d} = \frac{d}{d}$$

gives us $\quad \hat{d} = \dfrac{i + j - 3k}{3.3166\ldots}.$

The length of the projection is

$$s.\hat{d} = (2i + 1.5j + 0.5k).\frac{(i + j - 3k)}{3.3166\ldots}$$

$$= \frac{(2)(1) + (1.5)(1) + (0.5)(-3)}{3.3166\ldots}$$

$$= 0.603 \text{ m.}$$

Example 8.7

In Volume 1, Chapter 7, we introduced the difference of 2 squares, $a^2 - b^2 = (a + b)(a - b)$. In vector form, using scalar product, this is $a.a - b.b = (a + b).(a - b)$. Here we use $a = 6i - j$ and $b = 2i - 5j + 4k$ to show that it is true. Remember this is *not* a proof because we are using specific numerical examples for a and b. A proof depends upon generalities.

We look at the left-hand side first.

$$a.a = (6i - j).(6i - j) \qquad \text{and} \qquad b.b = (2i - 5j + 4k).(2i - 5j + 4k)$$
$$= (6)(6) + (-1)(-1) \qquad\qquad\qquad = (2)(2) + (-5)(-5) + (4)(4)$$
$$= 37. \qquad\qquad\qquad\qquad\qquad = 45.$$

Then $a.a - b.b = 37 - 45$
$$= -8.$$

Now for the right-hand side.

$$a + b = 8i - 6j + 4k \qquad \text{and} \qquad a - b = 4i + 4j - 4k = 4(i + j - k)$$
so that
$$(a + b).(a - b) = 4(8i - 6j + 4k).(i + j - k)$$
$$= 4\{(8)(1) + (-6)(1) + (4)(-1)\}$$
$$= -8.$$

We see that both sides give the same value, -8. This shows that $a.a - b.b = (a + b).(a - b)$.

Example 8.4

1   Find the work done by a force, $F = 4i - 4j + 7k$ N, moving an object through a displacement $s = 3i - 3j$ m. What happens when the displacement is changed to $3i + 3j$ m and why?

2   The scalar product is distributive over addition, i.e. $a.(b + c) = (a.b) + (a.c)$. (Note: We do not really need the brackets around $a.b$ and $a.c$.) Using $a = 2i - j - 12k$, $b = 6i + 2k$ and $c = i + 3j + 5k$ separately work out each side of this law to show it is true.

3   Apply the distributive law for scalar product over addition to find the total work done by forces F_1 and F_2 moving a mass through

a displacement s. You are given $F_1 = 2i - 7j + 6k$ N and $F_2 = 3i + 2j + k$ N together with $s = i + 4j + k$ m.

4 The power, P (W), of a force, F (N), with a velocity, v (ms^{-1}), are connected by $P = F.v$. When $F = -i + 2j + 5k$ N, and $v = i + j + 4k$ ms^{-1} find the value of the power.
The kinetic energy in vector form is given by KE $= \frac{1}{2}mv.v$ (J). For a mass of 0.125 kg find the value of the kinetic energy at this instant.

5 The scalar product of any vector, v and itself is $v.v = v^2$.
For any triangle with sides a, b and c the cosine rule is $a^2 = b^2 + c^2 - 2bc \cos\theta$ (Volume 1, Chapter 6). In vector notation we may write this rule as $a.a = b.b + c.c - 2b.c$. The vertices of the triangle are $A(2, 3, 6)$, $B(4, 3, -1)$ and $C(7, 1, 0)$. Using $a = BC$, $b = CA$ and $c = BA$ show this is true.
Another version of the cosine rule is $a.a = (b - c).(b - c)$. Using the same values for a, b and c show that this is also true.

Vector product

Vector product links 2 vectors using multiplication (i.e. product) and gives a vector answer: hence the title of vector product. To denote the operation of vector product we use a cross, $\times$. It leads to the alternative title of **cross product**.

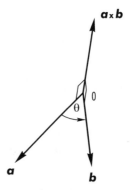

Fig. 8.5

The vector (cross) product of 2 vectors, a and b (Fig. 8.5), is defined as the product of their magnitudes and the sine of the angle between them ($\sin\theta$). It acts in a direction that is perpendicular to both of the original vectors, i.e.

$$a \times b = (ab \sin\theta)\hat{n},$$

where $\hat{n}$ is unit vector perpendicular to both a and b.

We include the brackets for safety, but they are not really necessary.

Note the direction of θ, moving from a to b.

Later we will use $\sin 0° = 0$ and $\sin 90° = 1$. Again let us look at 2 general vectors,

$$a = a_1 i + a_2 j + a_3 k$$

and $\quad b = b_1 i + b_2 j + b_3 k,$

where a_1, a_2, a_3, b_1, b_2, and b_3 are values in the respective directions.
Now $\quad a \times b = (a_1 i + a_2 j + a_3 k) \times (b_1 i + b_2 j + b_3 k)$.

When we multiply together these brackets we have $3 \times 3 = 9$ terms,

i.e.
$$\begin{aligned}
a{\times}b &= a_1b_1i{\times}i + a_1b_2i{\times}j + a_1b_3i{\times}k + \\
&\quad a_2b_1j{\times}i + a_2b_2j{\times}j + a_2b_3j{\times}k + \\
&\quad a_3b_1k{\times}i + a_3b_2k{\times}j + a_3b_3k{\times}k.
\end{aligned}$$

Now $i{\times}i = (1)(1)\sin 0°\hat{n} = 0.$

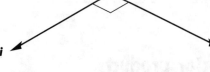

$\boxed{\sin 0° = 0.}$

Similarly $j{\times}j = 0$ and $k{\times}k = 0.$

Also $i{\times}j = (1)(1)\sin 90°\hat{n} = 1\hat{n} = k,$

$\boxed{\sin 90° = 1.}$

following the cyclical pattern in Fig. 8.6, moving from i to j and then on to k.

Similarly $j{\times}k = i$

and $k{\times}i = j.$

Notice the reverse spiral leads to negative vectors in

$$i{\times}k = -j,$$
$$k{\times}j = -i$$

and $j{\times}i = -k.$

Fig. 8.6

This leaves us with

$$a{\times}b = a_1b_2k - a_1b_3j - a_2b_1k + a_2b_3i + a_3b_1j - a_3b_2i.$$

We gather these terms and notice a pattern

$$a{\times}b = (a_2b_3 - a_3b_2)i - (a_1b_3 - a_3b_1)j + (a_1b_2 - a_2b_1)k.$$

We recall both 2 and 3 order determinants from Volumes 1 and 2, e.g.

$$a_2b_3 - a_3b_2 = \begin{vmatrix} a_2 & a_3 \\ b_2 & b_3 \end{vmatrix}$$

i.e. $$a{\times}b = \begin{vmatrix} i & j & k \\ a_1 & a_2 & a_3 \\ b_1 & b_2 & b_3 \end{vmatrix}.$$

This is a more user-friendly version of the original definition. Remember we start with 2 vectors and apply the **vector product** to reach a **vector answer**.

When we interchange two rows of a determinant we alter its sign $+/-$ (Volume 2, Chapter 1), i.e.

$$\begin{vmatrix} i & j & k \\ a_1 & a_2 & a_3 \\ b_1 & b_2 & b_3 \end{vmatrix} = - \begin{vmatrix} i & j & k \\ b_1 & b_2 & b_3 \\ a_1 & a_2 & a_3 \end{vmatrix}$$

i.e. $a{\times}b = -b{\times}a,$

i.e. $a{\times}b \neq b{\times}a.$

Vector product is *not* commutative, i.e. the order of a and b does matter.

Examples 8.8

We use $a = j + 2k$ and $b = -2.5i + 4j - 0.5k$.

i) Using $a \times b = \begin{vmatrix} i & j & k \\ a_1 & a_2 & a_3 \\ b_1 & b_2 & b_3 \end{vmatrix}$

$$a \times b = \begin{vmatrix} i & j & k \\ 0 & 1 & 2 \\ -2.5 & 4 & -0.5 \end{vmatrix}$$

$$= \{(1)(-0.5) - (2)(4)\}i - \{(0)(-0.5) - (2)(-2.5)\}j$$
$$+ \{(0)(4) - (1)(-2.5)\}k$$
$$= -8.5i - 5j + 2.5k.$$

ii) Also $b \times a = \begin{vmatrix} i & j & k \\ -2.5 & 4 & -0.5 \\ 0 & 1 & 2 \end{vmatrix}$

$$= \{(4)(2) - (-0.5)(1)\}i - \{(-2.5)(2) - (-0.5)(0)\}j$$
$$+ \{(-2.5)(1) - (4)(0)\}k$$
$$= 8.5i + 5j - 2.5k.$$

These two examples demonstrate the relationship $a \times b = -b \times a$, or $a \times b \neq b \times a$.

iii) We can test that the vector product is perpendicular to each of the original vectors, e.g.

$$(a \times b).a = (-8.5i - 5j + 2.5k).(j + 2k)$$
$$= (-8.5)(0) + (-5)(1) + (2.5)(2)$$
$$= 0,$$

i.e. using scalar product to give us a zero answer we confirm the perpendicularity.

For yourself test that $(a \times b).b = 0$.

EXERCISE 8.5

In this Exercise we use $a = -7j + k$, $b = 0.5i - 2j - 3k$, $c = i - j + 6k$, $d = 2.5i - 4k$, and $e = -3i + 2.5k$.

In each case find the value of the vector product.

1	$a \times b$	6	$15(a \times b)$
2	$d \times c$	7	$(4c) \times b$
3	$e \times c$	8	$b \times 7e$
4	$a \times (2b)$	9	$0.5e \times 6c$
5	$(3a) \times (5b)$	10	$2b \times 2c$

Vector moment

We apply vector moment to the vector moment of a force. Remember that moment is a turning effect. In 2 dimensions the moment of a force about a point is the product of that force and the perpendicular distance of the force from that point. Here it is a generalisation, using vectors, into 3 dimensions of the moment of a force in 2 dimensions. F is a force having magnitude and direction. Let A and B be any 2 points on its line of action, and r be the position vector of A from the origin, O (Fig. 8.7). The **vector moment**, M, of the force, F, about the origin is $M = r \times F$.

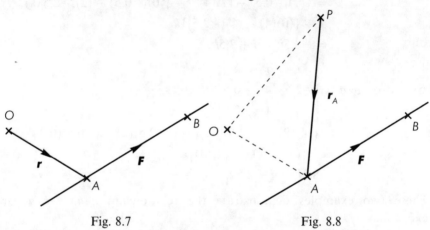

Fig. 8.7   Fig. 8.8

We can generalise this idea from the origin, O, to any point, P. Again F is a force having magnitude and direction with A and B being any 2 points on its line of action. r_A is the position vector of A from P (Fig. 8.8). This is less helpful because we usually refer vectors to the origin so we amend the formula. Now the **vector moment**, M_P, of the force, F, about some point P is

$$M_P = r_A \times F.$$

As we can see in Fig. 8.8
$$PA = PO + OA$$
$$= -OP + OA$$
$$= r - OP$$

to give
$$M_P = r_A \times F$$

as
$$M_P = (r - OP) \times F.$$

We apply vector moments in our Assignment.

■■■■■ ASSIGNMENT ■■■■■

For this part of the Assignment we look at the turning effect of the force, $F = 12i + 4j + 3k$ N. Suppose it acts through a point (A) with position vector $r = i + 2j + k$. Using the vector moment, M, of the force, F, about the origin as $M = r \times F$ we have

$$M = \begin{vmatrix} i & j & k \\ 1 & 2 & 1 \\ 12 & 4 & 3 \end{vmatrix}$$
$$= (6 - 4)i - (3 - 12)j + (4 - 24)k$$
$$= 2i + 9j - 20k.$$

Suppose we need the vector moment about some point $P(1.5, 0, 3.5)$. Then $OP = 1.5i + 3.5k$ so that

$$r - OP = (i + 2j + k) - (1.5i + 3.5k)$$
$$= -0.5i + 2j - 2.5k.$$

Using $\quad M_P = (r - OP) \times F$

we have $\quad M_P = \begin{vmatrix} i & j & k \\ -0.5 & 2 & -2.5 \\ 12 & 4 & 3 \end{vmatrix}$

$$= (6 - -10)i - (-1.5 - -30)j + (-2 - 24)k$$
$$= 16i - 28.5j - 26k.$$

EXERCISE 8.6

In Questions **1–3** F acts through the point with position vector r. Find the vector moment of F about the origin.

1 $F = i + j + k$, $r = 2i + 3j - 4k$.

2 $F = 0.5i + 2j - k$, $r = i + 5j + k$.

3 $F = 6i - j + k$, $r = 12i + 9j + 3k$.

In Questions **4** and **5** F acts through the point A with position vector r. Write r in vector form given the coordinates of A. Find the vector moment of F about the origin.

4 $F = -i + 5j + 2.5k$, $A(1, 4, 2)$.

5 $F = i + 7j + 3k$, $A(0, 2, 0)$.

In Questions **6–8** F acts through the point with position vector r. Find the vector moment of F about the given point P.

6 $F = i + j + k$, $r = 2i + 3j - 4k$, $P(4, 6, 3)$.

7 $F = 2.5i + 6.5j + 1.5k$, $r = i + 2j - k$, $P(-3, 0, 1)$.

8 $F = 3i - j + k$, $r = 2i - j - 3k$, $OP = 2i - 9j + 3k$.

In Questions **9** and **10** F acts through the point A with position vector r. Find the vector moment of F about the given point P.

9 $F = -i - 1.5j + 2k$, $A(1, -4, 0)$, $P(3, 2, 1)$

10 $F = 2i + 5j + k$, $A(10, 2, 0)$, $P(-3, 0, 4)$.

Further applications of vector product

In Fig. 8.9 we have a triangle ABC with $A(1,0,5)$, $B(3,2,-2)$ and $C(4,-1,6)$. In Volume 1, Chapter 6, we looked at different formulae for the area of a triangle. Here we have one of those formulae in vector format. The previous formula may be written as

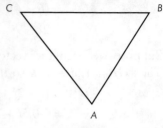

Fig. 8.9

$$\text{Area} = \frac{1}{2}ab\sin C$$

or $$\text{Area} = \frac{1}{2}(CA)(CB)\sin C$$

which translates to

$$\text{Area} = \frac{1}{2}|(\boldsymbol{a}-\boldsymbol{c})\times(\boldsymbol{b}-\boldsymbol{c})|.$$

Now $A(1,0,5)$ in vector form is $\boldsymbol{a} = \boldsymbol{i}+5\boldsymbol{k}$,
         $B(3,2,-2)$ in vector form is $\boldsymbol{b} = 3\boldsymbol{i}+2\boldsymbol{j}-2\boldsymbol{k}$
and $C(4,-1,6)$ in vector form is $\boldsymbol{c} = 4\boldsymbol{i}-\boldsymbol{j}+6\boldsymbol{k}$;
so that $\boldsymbol{a}-\boldsymbol{c} = -3\boldsymbol{i}+\boldsymbol{j}-\boldsymbol{k}$
and $\boldsymbol{b}-\boldsymbol{c} = -\boldsymbol{i}+3\boldsymbol{j}-8\boldsymbol{k}$.

From $$\text{Area} = \frac{1}{2}|(\boldsymbol{a}-\boldsymbol{c})\times(\boldsymbol{b}-\boldsymbol{c})|$$

we have $$(\boldsymbol{a}-\boldsymbol{c})\times(\boldsymbol{b}-\boldsymbol{c}) = \begin{vmatrix} \boldsymbol{i} & \boldsymbol{j} & \boldsymbol{k} \\ -3 & 1 & -1 \\ -1 & 3 & -8 \end{vmatrix}$$

$$= (-8--3)\boldsymbol{i} - (24-1)\boldsymbol{j} + (-9--1)\boldsymbol{k}$$
$$= -(5\boldsymbol{i}+23\boldsymbol{j}+8\boldsymbol{k}).$$

Then $$|(\boldsymbol{a}-\boldsymbol{c})\times(\boldsymbol{b}-\boldsymbol{c})| = \sqrt{5^2+23^2+8^2} = \sqrt{618} = 24.859\ldots$$

so that $$\text{Area} = \frac{1}{2} \times 24.859\ldots = 12.43 \text{ unit}^2.$$

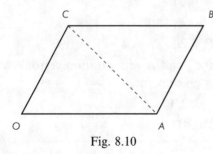

Fig. 8.10

We can extend this idea to find the area of a parallelogram. In Fig. 8.10 $OABC$ is a parallelogram which we have bisected with the line AC.

Area of $OABC = 2 \times$ Area of ABC
$$= |(\boldsymbol{a}-\boldsymbol{c})\times(\boldsymbol{b}-\boldsymbol{c})|.$$

Congruent triangles.

We mention 2 more applications.

1 Suppose a body is rotating with angular velocity ω. A part of the body at some position vector *r* from the axis of rotation (containing the origin) has a linear velocity *v* where *v* = ω×*r*.

2 In electromagnetic theory suppose we have a current *I* flowing along a straight wire in a constant magnetic field *B*. The force *F* is given by *F* = *I*×*B*.

■ EXERCISE 8.7 ■

1 Find the area of the i) triangle OAB where $A(1,2,3)$ and $B(-2,7,4)$; ii) parallelogram $OABC$ where $A(5,0,0)$, $B(7,4,0)$ and $C(2,4,0)$.

2 The vector product is distributive over addition, i.e. $a \times (b+c) = (a \times b) + (a \times c)$.
Using $a = 2i - 5j - 2k$, $b = i + 3k$ and $c = 1.5i + j + 4k$ separately work out each side of this law to show it is true.

3 From the definition of vector product we know $a \times a = 0$. Using a determinant with $a = -2i + j + 5k$ show that it is true. Also using the general vector $a = a_1 i + a_2 j + a_3 k$ repeat the technique.

4 A body is rotating with angular velocity ω. A part of it at some position vector *r* from the axis of rotation (containing the origin) has a linear velocity *v* where *v* = ω×*r*.
Using $\omega = -i + 0.2j + 0.5k$ rads^{-1}, and $r = 0.25i + j + 0.4k$ m find the value *v*.

5 The vector moment of a couple is given by $AB \times F$ where *F* is one of the forces. One force acts through A while the other force acts through B. For $F = 2i + 13j + 6k$ N, $OB = i + 3.5j - 1.5k$ m and $OA = i + j + 2k$ m find this vector moment.

Triple scalar product

Triple scalar product, as its title implies, links 3 vectors using multiplication (i.e. product) to give a scalar answer. $a.b \times c$ is an example of a triple scalar product. We could include brackets around $b \times c$ but they are *not* necessary. Because of the separate definitions for scalar and vector products we must find $b \times c$ first. Any other alternative would give a scalar part way through which we *cannot* then combine with the remaining vector.

███████ **Examples 8.10** ███████

We use $a = i + k$, $b = 2i - j + 4k$ and $c = 5i + 3j$.

i) Now $b \times c = \begin{vmatrix} i & j & k \\ 2 & -1 & 4 \\ 5 & 3 & 0 \end{vmatrix} = -12i + 20j + 11k$.

Then $a.b \times c = (i + k).(-12i + 20j + 11k)$

$= (1)(-12) + (0)(20) + (1)(11)$

$= -1.$

ii) Alternatively we can use a determinant to find the triple scalar product in one step, i.e.

$$a.b \times c = \begin{vmatrix} 1 & 0 & 1 \\ 2 & -1 & 4 \\ 5 & 3 & 0 \end{vmatrix}$$

$$= 1(0 - 12) - 0(0 - 20) + 1(6 - -5)$$

$$= -1.$$

iii) Similarly $a \times b.c = -1$. You can try this for yourself using both alternatives above.

Using general versions of a, b and c there is a variety of equal triple scalar products.

Already we know $a.b \times c = a \times b.c$.

Also $a.b \times c$ has a meaning $a.(b \times c)$ and scalar product is commutative, i.e.

$a.(b \times c) = (b \times c).a,$

i.e. $a.b \times c = b \times c.a$, dispensing with the brackets.

Vector product is *not* commutative and we know $b \times c = -c \times b$. Then $a.b \times c = -a.c \times b$. There are yet more permutations of a, b and c that give equivalent triple scalar products.

███████ **EXERCISE 8.8** ███████

In this Exercise we use $a = i + 3j + k$, $b = 2i + 2j + 4k$, $c = 4i - 1.5j + 6k$, $d = 2.5i - 2j$, and $e = 3j + k$.

In each case find the value of the triple scalar product.

1	$a.b \times c$	6	$c.a \times b$
2	$a \times b.c$	7	$(4c) \times a.b$
3	$a \times e.d$	8	$d.b \times e$
4	$a.b \times e$	9	$e.c \times a$
5	$a.b \times d$	10	$2b \times 2a.2c$

Application of triple scalar product

We can apply triple scalar product to find the volume of a parallelepiped (Fig. 8.11) and a tetrahedron (Fig. 8.12). The ideas are similar. The parallelogram sides of a parallelepiped are deformed into triangles to create a tetrahedron.

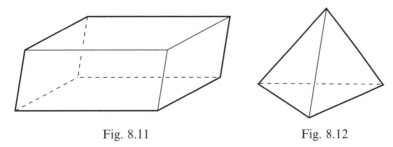

Fig. 8.11   Fig. 8.12

Example 8.11

In Fig. 8.13 we show a parallelepiped with some marked vertices A, B, C and D. Taken in order we move from b to c and on to d where $b = AB$, $c = AC$ and $d = AD$. In this Example we use $A(0,0,1)$, $B(2,1,4)$, $C(7,0,1)$ and $D(0,5,1)$.

Then $\quad b = AB = 2i + j + 3k,$

$\qquad c = AC = 7i$

and $\quad d = AD = 5j.$

The volume, V, of the parallelepiped is given by

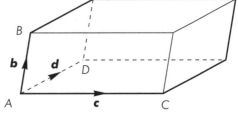

Fig. 8.13

$$V = |b.c \times d|$$

$$= \begin{vmatrix} 2 & 1 & 3 \\ 7 & 0 & 0 \\ 0 & 5 & 0 \end{vmatrix}$$

$$= 2(0-0) - 1(0-0) + 3(35-0)$$

$$= 105 \text{ unit}^3.$$

Triple vector product

Triple vector product, as its title implies, links 3 vectors using multiplication (i.e. product) to give a vector answer. $(a \times b) \times c$ is an example of a triple vector product. We include brackets because order is important in any vector product. $(a \times b) \times c$ is different from $a(b \times c)$ as we see in Examples 8.12.

▰▰▰▰ **Examples 8.12** ▰▰▰▰

We use $a = i + j + k$, $b = 2i - j + k$ and $c = i + 2j + 5k$.

i) In $(a \times b) \times c$ we have $\quad a \times b = \begin{vmatrix} i & j & k \\ 1 & 1 & 1 \\ 2 & -1 & 1 \end{vmatrix} = 2i + j - 3k$

and $\qquad (a \times b) \times c = \begin{vmatrix} i & j & k \\ 2 & 1 & -3 \\ 1 & 2 & 5 \end{vmatrix} = 11i - 13j + 3k.$

ii) In $a \times (b \times c)$ we have $\quad b \times c = \begin{vmatrix} i & j & k \\ 2 & -1 & 1 \\ 1 & 2 & 5 \end{vmatrix} = -7i - 9j + 5k$

and $\qquad a \times (b \times c) = \begin{vmatrix} i & j & k \\ 1 & 1 & 1 \\ -7 & -9 & 5 \end{vmatrix} = 14i - 12j - 2k.$

This Example shows that $(a \times b) \times c \neq a \times (b \times c)$. Indeed they are totally different, without any hint of commonality.

It is possible to express a triple vector product in terms of 2 scalar products. We omit the proof as it is rather long and not necessary at this level. We could prove

$$(a \times b) \times c = (a.c)b - (b.c)a$$

and $\quad a \times (b \times c) = (a.c)b - (a.b)c.$

As an alternative we use a numerical example to show the first relationship and leave you the second to try for yourself.

▰▰▰▰ **Example 8.13** ▰▰▰▰

We use $a = i + j + k$, $b = 2i - j + k$ and $c = i + 2j + 5k$ to show that $(a \times b) \times c = (a.c)b - (b.c)a$.

From Examples 8.12i) we know that $(a \times b) \times c = 11i - 13j + 3k$.

Separately we look at the right-hand side.

$$a.c = (i + j + k).(i + 2j + 5k) = 1 + 2 + 5 = 8$$

so that $\qquad (a.c)b = 8b.$

Also $\qquad b.c = (2i - j + k).(i + 2j + 5k) = 2 - 2 + 5 = 5$

so that $\qquad (b.c)a = 5a.$

Then $\quad (a.c)b - (b.c)a = 8b - 5a = 8(2i - j + k) - 5(i + j + k)$

$$= 11i - 13j + 3k \text{ as before,}$$

i.e. $\qquad (a \times b) \times c = (a.c)b - (b.c)a.$

In this Exercise we use $a = i + 3j + k$, $b = 2i + 2j + 4k$, $c = 4i - 1.5j + 6k$, and $d = 2.5i - 2j$.

In each case find the value of the triple vector product.

1 $(a \times b) \times c$

2 $a \times (b \times c)$

3 $a \times (c \times d)$

4 $(a \times b) \times d$

5 $c \times (b \times d)$

Application of triple vector product

We apply the triple vector product when we look at the operator ∇.

Differentiation of vectors

All the usual rules apply to each component in turn. We take care with the order and meaning of the derivatives in the following examples.

■■■■ **Example 8.14** ■■■■

For $r = x^3 i - 4x^2 j + (\ln x)k$

$$\frac{dr}{dx} = 3x^2 i - 8xj + \frac{1}{x}k$$

and $\frac{d^2 r}{dx^2} = 6xi - 8j - \frac{1}{x^2}k.$

We can continue differentiating each component. Notice the j component is now a constant so the third derivative would have only i and k components.

■■■■ **Examples 8.15** ■■■■

We distinguish between vector and scalar derivatives starting with $r = (\sin t)i + (\cos t)j - tk$.

i) $\frac{dr}{dt} = (\cos t)i - (\sin t)j - k.$ | Vector answer.

ii) Then $\left|\frac{dr}{dt}\right| = \sqrt{(\cos t)^2 + (-\sin t)^2 + (-1)^2}$

$= \sqrt{\cos^2 t + \sin^2 t + 1}$ | $\cos^2 t + \sin^2 t = 1.$

$= \sqrt{2}$ or 1.414. | Scalar answer.

iii) Also from $r = (\sin t)\mathbf{i} + (\cos t)\mathbf{j} - t\mathbf{k}$

$$r = \sqrt{\sin^2 t + \cos^2 t + (-t)^2}$$

i.e. $r = (1 + t^2)^{1/2}$

so that $\dfrac{dr}{dt} = \dfrac{1}{2}(2t)(1 + t^2)^{-1/2}$

$$= t(1 + t^2)^{-1/2}.$$

> Function of a function rule.
>
> Scalar answer.

Notice the different orders of calculation in ii) and iii). In ii) we differentiated and then found the scalar. In iii) the order was reversed; i.e. we found a scalar and then differentiated it.

Vector differentiation applied to kinematics

Kinematics is the study of motion. If we start with displacement, r, then $\dfrac{dr}{dt}$ is the velocity, v, and $\dfrac{d^2r}{dt^2}$ is the acceleration. For a displacement, r, the distance is r and for a velocity v the speed is $\left|\dfrac{dr}{dt}\right|$ or v. We can also quote acceleration as a scalar, $\left|\dfrac{d^2r}{dt^2}\right|$.

Example 8.16

For a displacement $r = (\sin 2t)\mathbf{i} + e^{2t}\mathbf{j} + 2t\mathbf{k}$ m

$$\frac{dr}{dt} = (2\cos 2t)\mathbf{i} + 2e^{2t}\mathbf{j} + 2\mathbf{k} \text{ ms}^{-1}$$

or $2\{(\cos 2t)\mathbf{i} + e^{2t}\mathbf{j} + \mathbf{k}\}$ ms^{-1} is the velocity

and $\dfrac{d^2r}{dt^2} = (-4\sin 2t)\mathbf{i} + 4e^{2t}\mathbf{j} \text{ ms}^{-2}$

or $4\{(-\sin 2t)\mathbf{i} + e^{2t}\mathbf{j}\}$ ms^{-2} is the acceleration.

When $t = 0$ we find the initial velocity, i.e.

$$\frac{dr}{dt} = 2\{(\cos 0)\mathbf{i} + e^0\mathbf{j} + \mathbf{k}\} = 2\{\mathbf{i} + \mathbf{j} + \mathbf{k}\} \text{ ms}^{-1}.$$

The initial speed is the size of the initial velocity, i.e.

$$\left|\frac{dr}{dt}\right| = 2\sqrt{1^2 + 1^2 + 1^2}$$

$$= 2\sqrt{3} \text{ ms}^{-1}$$

or 3.46 ms^{-1}.

EXERCISE 8.10

Differentiate the following vectors once.

1 $r = (x^3 + 6)i + 3x^2j + x^4k$

2 $r = x^3i + (2x^2 + x)j - (7 + 2x)k$

3 $r = \theta i + (\cos 2\theta)j + (\sin 2\theta)k$

4 $r = (t^3 + 5)i - t^4j + 5t^2k$

5 $r = (4 - x^2)i + (2 + 3x^2)j + (x^4 + 1)k$

For the displacement vector, r, find vectors for the velocity and acceleration.

6 $r = e^{3t}i + (\sin 3t)k$

7 $r = (1 + t^3)j + (3t^2 + t)k$

8 $r = 3t^3i + (4t^2 - t)j - (7t + 2.5)k$

9 $r = (2t^3 + t)i + (2t - 3t^2)j + 0.5t^2k$

10 $r = (e^{3t}\cos t)i + (e^{3t}\sin t)j + tk$

Example 8.17

We apply our vector differentiation application. Here we look at motion in a circle, of radius a.
Motion around this circle involves an angular velocity, ω, and a linear velocity, v. In Fig. 8.14 we show the circle with some general point P. If we complete a right-angled triangle with a hypotenuse OP then the horizontal side is $a\cos\theta$ and the vertical side is $a\sin\theta$. In vector form we have

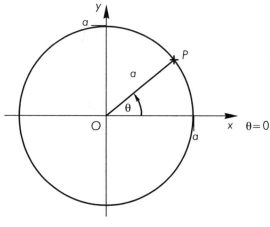

Fig. 8.14

$$r = OP$$

and $r = a\{(\cos\theta)i + (\sin\theta)j\}.$

The general angle θ and the angular velocity ω are related to time by $\omega = \dfrac{\theta}{t}$, i.e. $\theta = \omega t$, so that

$$r = a\{(\cos\omega t)i + (\sin\omega t)j\}. \qquad \boxed{\text{Substituting for } \theta = \omega t.}$$

Then $v = \dfrac{dr}{dt} = a\{(-\omega\sin\omega t)i + (\omega\cos\omega t)j\}.$

In Fig. 8.15 we see the components of v at P.

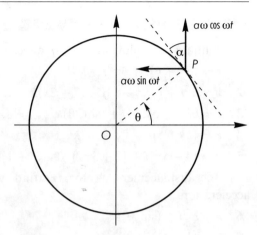

$$\tan \alpha = \frac{a\omega \sin \omega t}{a\omega \cos \omega t} = \tan \omega t$$

i.e. $\alpha = \omega t = \theta$,

i.e. the linear velocity acts tangentially.

Also we can find the speed, i.e.

Fig. 8.15

$$\left|\frac{dr}{dt}\right| = \sqrt{a^2\{(-\omega \sin \omega t)^2 + (\omega \cos \omega t)^2\}}$$

$$= \sqrt{a^2\omega^2\{\sin^2 \omega t + \cos^2 \omega t\}}$$

$$= \sqrt{a^2\omega^2}$$

$$= a\omega.$$

> $\sin^2 \omega t + \cos^2 \omega t = 1.$

Linking together these 2 features: the size of the linear velocity is $a\omega$ and it acts tangentially.

Now for the acceleration we differentiate $\dfrac{dr}{dt}$ to get

$$\frac{d^2r}{dt^2} = a\{(-\omega^2 \cos \omega t)i + (-\omega^2 \sin \omega t)j\}$$

$$= -a\omega^2\{(\cos \omega t)i + (\sin \omega t)j\}$$

$$= -\omega^2r.$$

This relationship involving the negative sign shows the acceleration is directed towards O (remember $r = OP$). The size of the acceleration is

$$\left|\frac{d^2r}{dt^2}\right| = |-\omega^2r|$$

$$= \omega^2|r|$$

$$= a\omega^2.$$

> $r = OP = a$ is the radius of the circle.

ASSIGNMENT

In our previous looks at the Assignment we used a force, F N, where $F = 12i + 4j + 3k$ N. There it was a constant force. Remember, according to Newton's laws, $F = ma$ where m is the mass and a is the acceleration.

Suppose we have a mass of 0.25 kg and a displacement vector

$$r = (24t^2 + 8t)i + (8t^2 + 16t)j + (6t^2 + 24)k.$$

Differentiating and applying $F = ma$ we get

$$\frac{dr}{dt} = (48t + 8)i + (16t + 16)j + 12tk$$

and $\quad \dfrac{d^2r}{dt^2} = 48i + 16j + 12k$

so that $\quad F = 0.25(48i + 16j + 12k)$

$$= 12i + 4j + 3k \text{ N}.$$

EXERCISE 8.11

1 A position vector is given in terms of time, t, by $r = 3ti + (\ln 3t)j$. Find general vector expressions for the velocity and acceleration. Find their particular values after 4 seconds.

2 A position vector is given in terms of time, t, by

$$r = (2 \sin pt)i + (2 \cos pt)k$$

where p is a constant. Find the vector values for the velocity and acceleration after $\dfrac{\pi}{6p}$ seconds. Repeat the mathematics for $r = (\sin^2 pt)i + (\cos^2 pt)k$.

3 The position vector is $r = e^{2t}i + 3tj - 6k$ where t represents time. Show the acceleration vector has no j and k components. Also find the *speed* after 0.25 seconds.

4 For $r = (\sin t)i + tj - (\cos t)k$ find expressions for $\dfrac{dr}{dt}, \dfrac{d^2r}{dt^2}, \left|\dfrac{dr}{dt}\right|, \left|\dfrac{d^2r}{dt^2}\right|$, $r, \dfrac{dr}{dt}, \dfrac{d^2r}{dt^2}$.

5 A body has a vector moment, M, about the origin, O, given by $M = r{\times}F$ where F is the force, acting upon the body, passing through a point with position vector r. m is the constant mass of the body and according to Newton's laws $F = ma$ where $a = \dfrac{dv}{dt} = \dfrac{d^2r}{dt^2}$.

Differentiating using the product rule show that

$$\frac{d}{dt}\left(r{\times}mv\right) = r{\times}\frac{d}{dt}\left(mv\right).$$ Link this with $M = r{\times}F$ to show that

$M = \dfrac{dh}{dt}$ where h is the angular momentum (i.e. the moment of the linear momentum).

6 The relative velocity of a body, A, to a body, B, is given by $v_A - v_B$. The position vectors of A and B are given by

$$r_A = (2 \cos t)j + (2 \sin t)k \quad \text{and} \quad r_B = 2tj + t^2k.$$

Find this relative velocity and the relative speed.

7   Using the postion vector $r = (e^t \cos t)i + (e^t \sin t)j$ find the angle between it and the velocity vector.

8   Check the differentiation of a product rule applied to scalar products, i.e. $\dfrac{d}{dt}\left(r.s\right) = r.\dfrac{ds}{dt} + \dfrac{dr}{dt}. s$, using $r = 2t^2 i + 3tj - (2 + t)k$ and $s = (3t - 2)i + (\ln t)j + 7tk$.

9   $r = a(1 + \cos\theta)$ is the polar equation of a curve and a is a constant. $\omega = \dfrac{d\theta}{dt}$ is the constant angular velocity. The radial and transverse components of both velocity, v, and acceleration, $\dfrac{dv}{dt}$, are aligned to the i and j directions respectively. These are $v = \left(\dfrac{dr}{dt}\right)i + \left(r\dfrac{d\theta}{dt}\right)j$ and $\dfrac{dv}{dt} = \left(\dfrac{d^2 r}{dt^2} - r\left(\dfrac{d\theta}{dt}\right)^2\right)i + \left(r\dfrac{d^2\theta}{dt^2} + 2\dfrac{dr}{dt}\dfrac{d\theta}{dt}\right)j$. Using these relationships find the velocity and acceleration.

10 Check the differentiation of a product rule applied to vector products, i.e. $\dfrac{d}{dt}(r \times s) = r \times \dfrac{ds}{dt} - s \times \dfrac{dr}{dt}$, using $r = t^3 i - 4tj - e^t k$ and $s = (t + 4)i + 6t^2 k$.

Vector analysis

We briefly introduce some 'simple' early work in this topic area, mixing vectors and partial differentiation. It is vital that you are familiar with the work in Chapter 7 (Partial Differentiation). Vector analysis is used extensively in potential theory (e.g. fluid mechanics and electromagnetic theory). We start with the vector operator ∇ (called **nabla** or **del**), in 3 dimensional Cartesian coordinates. In other coordinate systems, e.g. spherical polars and cylindrical polars, it is less easy to apply. ∇ operates in each component direction in turn, partially differentiating with respect to x or y or z. ∇ is defined as

$$\nabla = \frac{\partial}{\partial x}i + \frac{\partial}{\partial y}j + \frac{\partial}{\partial z}k.$$

We look at ∇ operating in 3 different ways:

1   the gradient (grad),
2   the divergence (div),
3   the curl (curl) (or rotation).

1   The gradient

Where ϕ is a scalar (technically 'a differentiable scalar field') then grad ϕ (i.e. $\nabla\phi$) is defined as

$$\nabla\phi = \left(\frac{\partial}{\partial x}i + \frac{\partial}{\partial y}j + \frac{\partial}{\partial z}k\right)\phi$$

i.e. $\nabla\phi = \frac{\partial\phi}{\partial x}i + \frac{\partial\phi}{\partial y}j + \frac{\partial\phi}{\partial z}k.$

Notice that ϕ is a scalar but that $\nabla\phi$ is a vector.

Example 8.18

For the scalar $\phi = x^2y^3 + y\sin z$ we differentiate partially to get

$$\frac{\partial\phi}{\partial x} = 2xy^3, \quad \frac{\partial\phi}{\partial y} = 3x^2y^2 + \sin z, \quad \frac{\partial\phi}{\partial z} = y\cos z.$$

Using $\nabla\phi = \frac{\partial\phi}{\partial x}i + \frac{\partial\phi}{\partial y}j + \frac{\partial\phi}{\partial z}k$

we have $\nabla\phi = 2xy^3 i + (3x^2y^2 + \sin z)j + (y\cos z)k.$

Then we can find the gradient at any point, say at $(1,2,0)$, so that

$$\nabla\phi = 2(1)(2^3)i + (3(1^2)(2^2) + \sin 0)j + (2\cos 0)k$$

$$= 16i + 12j + 2k.$$

2   The divergence

Where V is a vector, i.e. $V = V_1 i + V_2 j + V_3 k$ (technically 'a differentiable vector field'), then div V (i.e. $\nabla.V$) is defined as

$$\nabla.V = \left(\frac{\partial}{\partial x}i + \frac{\partial}{\partial y}j + \frac{\partial}{\partial z}k\right).(V_1 i + V_2 j + V_3 k)$$

$$= \frac{\partial V_1}{\partial x}i + \frac{\partial V_2}{\partial y}j + \frac{\partial V_3}{\partial z}k.$$

Notice that V is a vector and $\nabla.V$ is a scalar.

Example 8.19

For the vector $V = 2x^3 i + 4x^2 y j + (\sin 2z)k$ using

$$\nabla.V = \frac{\partial V_1}{\partial x}i + \frac{\partial V_2}{\partial y}j + \frac{\partial V_3}{\partial z}k$$

then $\nabla.V = \frac{\partial}{\partial x}\left(2x^3\right)i + \frac{\partial}{\partial y}\left(4x^2y\right)j + \frac{\partial}{\partial z}\left(\sin 2z\right)k$

$$= 6x^2 + 4x^2 + 2\cos 2z$$

$$= 10x^2 + 2\cos 2z.$$

3   The curl

Again V is a vector, i.e. $V = V_1 i + V_2 j + V_3 k$ (technically 'a differentiable vector field'), then curl V (i.e. $\nabla \times V$) is defined as

$$\nabla \times V = \left(\frac{\partial}{\partial x} i + \frac{\partial}{\partial y} j + \frac{\partial}{\partial z} k \right) \times (V_1 i + V_2 j + V_3 k)$$

which we write as a determinant

$$\nabla \times V = \begin{vmatrix} i & j & k \\ \dfrac{\partial}{\partial x} & \dfrac{\partial}{\partial y} & \dfrac{\partial}{\partial z} \\ V_1 & V_2 & V_3 \end{vmatrix}$$

Notice that V is a vector and $\nabla \times V$ is also a vector.

▬▬▬▬ **Examples 8.20** ▬▬▬▬

i)   For the vector $V = 2x^3 i + 4x^2 y j + (\sin 2z) k$ using

$$\nabla \times V = \begin{vmatrix} i & j & k \\ \dfrac{\partial}{\partial x} & \dfrac{\partial}{\partial y} & \dfrac{\partial}{\partial z} \\ V_1 & V_2 & V_3 \end{vmatrix}$$

we have $\nabla \times V = \begin{vmatrix} i & j & k \\ \dfrac{\partial}{\partial x} & \dfrac{\partial}{\partial y} & \dfrac{\partial}{\partial z} \\ 2x^3 & 4x^2 y & \sin 2z \end{vmatrix}$

$$= \left\{ \frac{\partial}{\partial y} \left(\sin 2z \right) - \frac{\partial}{\partial z} \left(4x^2 y \right) \right\} i$$

$$- \left\{ \frac{\partial}{\partial x} \left(\sin 2z \right) - \frac{\partial}{\partial z} \left(2x^3 \right) \right\} j$$

$$+ \left\{ \frac{\partial}{\partial x} \left(4x^2 y \right) - \frac{\partial}{\partial y} \left(2x^3 \right) \right\} k$$

$$= \{0 - 0\} i - \{0 - 0\} j + \{8xy - 0\} k$$

$$= 8xy k.$$

Notice how many parts of this solution gave 0. Now we make a slight amendments to V and practise using the determinant and partial differentiation again when finding curl V.

ii)   This time we use $V = 2x^3 i + 4x^2 yz j + (xy + \sin 2z) k$ and again substitute into

$$\nabla \times V = \begin{vmatrix} i & j & k \\ \dfrac{\partial}{\partial x} & \dfrac{\partial}{\partial y} & \dfrac{\partial}{\partial z} \\ V_1 & V_2 & V_3 \end{vmatrix}$$

$$\text{to get} \quad \nabla \times V = \begin{vmatrix} \boldsymbol{i} & \boldsymbol{j} & \boldsymbol{k} \\ \dfrac{\partial}{\partial x} & \dfrac{\partial}{\partial y} & \dfrac{\partial}{\partial z} \\ 2x^3 & 4x^2 yz & xy + \sin 2z \end{vmatrix}$$

$$= \left\{ \frac{\partial}{\partial y}\left(xy + \sin 2z\right) - \frac{\partial}{\partial z}\left(4x^2 yz\right) \right\} \boldsymbol{i}$$

$$- \left\{ \frac{\partial}{\partial x}\left(xy + \sin 2z\right) - \frac{\partial}{\partial z}\left(2x^3\right) \right\} \boldsymbol{j}$$

$$+ \left\{ \frac{\partial}{\partial x}\left(4x^2 yz\right) - \frac{\partial}{\partial y}\left(2x^3\right) \right\} \boldsymbol{k}$$

$$= \{x - 4x^2 y\}\boldsymbol{i} - \{y - 0\}\boldsymbol{j} + \{8xyz - 0\}\boldsymbol{k}$$

$$= \{x - 4x^2 y\}\boldsymbol{i} - yj + 8xyz\boldsymbol{k}.$$

■ EXERCISE 8.12 ■

In Questions **1–5** you are given the scalar ϕ. In each case find an expression for grad ϕ (i.e. $\nabla\phi$).

1 $\phi = x^2 y + 2xz + 5$

2 $\phi = x^3 y^2 z + 3xy^3 z^2$

3 $\phi = \sin 3x + x^2 z^3 + 2y$

4 $\phi = e^{2x}\cos 4y$

5 $\phi = \dfrac{x^2 - z}{x^2 + y^2}$

In Questions **6–10** you are given the vector V. In each case find div V (i.e. $\nabla . V$).

6 $V = x\boldsymbol{i} + y\boldsymbol{j} + z\boldsymbol{k}$

7 $V = x\boldsymbol{i} - 3y\boldsymbol{j} + 2z\boldsymbol{k}$

8 $V = x^2 y\boldsymbol{i} + xy\boldsymbol{j} + xyz\boldsymbol{k}$

9 $V = \sin(x + y)\boldsymbol{i} + \cos(y - z)\boldsymbol{j} + 3xyz\boldsymbol{k}$

10 $V = e^{xy}\boldsymbol{i} + e^{yz}\boldsymbol{j} + e^{yx}\boldsymbol{k}$

In Questions **11–15** you are given the vector V. In each case find curl V (i.e. $\nabla \times V$).

11 $V = xy\boldsymbol{i} + (x + y)\boldsymbol{j}$

12 $V = 2x^2\boldsymbol{i} + 3y\boldsymbol{j} + xz\boldsymbol{k}$

13 $V = (x^2 + y)\boldsymbol{i} + xy\boldsymbol{j} - yz\boldsymbol{k}$

14 $V = \cos(x - y)\boldsymbol{i} + (\cos xy)\boldsymbol{j} + (x + y + z)\boldsymbol{k}$

15 $V = e^{x+y}\boldsymbol{i} + e^{y+z}\boldsymbol{j} + e^{z+x}\boldsymbol{k}$

16 Decide whether the following are scalars or vectors.

    i) $\nabla \times V$,   ii) $\nabla . V$,   iii) $V.\boldsymbol{j}$

    iv) $V \times \boldsymbol{k}$ v) grad V vi) $V.V$

17 ϕ is a scalar field where $\phi = 4x^3y^2 + y^3z^2$. Find the value of $\nabla\phi$ at the point $(2, -1, 0)$.

18 $r = xi + yj + zk$ is a position vector and $s = 2xi + yj - zk$. Find $r.s$. Why can you *not* find $\nabla.(r.s)$ and $\nabla\times(r.s)$? Hence find $\nabla(r.s)$.

19 For $r = xi + yj + zk$ find r. If $\phi = \dfrac{1}{r}$ find $\nabla\phi$ (i.e. $\nabla\left(\dfrac{1}{r}\right)$) in terms of x, y and z. Hence show that $\nabla\phi = \dfrac{-r}{r^3}$. (Note: this may remind you of Newton's law of gravitation; the vector form being $F = \dfrac{-Gm_1m_2r}{r^3}$ and the scalar form being $F = \dfrac{Gm_1m_2}{r^2}$.

20 Using $v = (2x + \sin y)i + (x\cos z)k$ find div v and curl v. w is another vector, related to v according to $w = \nabla\times v$. Find curl w. Why can you *not* find grad w?

Towards the end of Exercise 8.12 we have mixed together the operator ∇ and more than one vector. Your solutions have been staged, gently led by the question style. Now we look at mixing ∇ and vectors more openly; for example applying the triple vector product we met earlier. We list some formulae involving the operator ∇, 2 vectors, r and s, and 2 scalars, ϕ and ψ.

1 The distributive law, showing in turn, that grad, div and curl are distributive over addition, i.e.
$$\nabla(\phi + \psi) = \nabla\phi + \nabla\psi,$$
$$\nabla.(\phi + \psi) = \nabla.\phi + \nabla.\psi,$$
$$\nabla\times(\phi + \psi) = \nabla\times\phi + \nabla\times\psi.$$

2 The product rule for differentiation in vector analysis, i.e.
$$\nabla(\phi\psi) = \phi(\nabla\psi) + \psi(\nabla\phi),$$
$$\nabla.(\phi r) = \phi(\nabla.r) + r.(\nabla\phi),$$
$$\nabla\times(\phi r) = \phi(\nabla\times r) - r\times(\nabla\phi).$$

3 $\nabla\times(\nabla\phi) = 0.$

4 $\nabla.(\nabla\times r) = 0.$

We omit the formulae for many more variations, including those for $\nabla.(r\times s)$, $\nabla\times(r\times s)$, $\nabla(r.s)$, and $\nabla\times(\nabla\times r)$.

We use $r = x^2zi + xyj + xzk$ and $s = 2xi + 3zj$ to demonstrate triple vector product applied to i) $\nabla \times (r \times s)$, ii) $\nabla \times (\nabla \times r)$.

i) We start with $\quad r \times s = \begin{vmatrix} i & j & k \\ x^2z & xy & xz \\ 2x & 3z & 0 \end{vmatrix}$

$$= (0 - 3xz^2)i - (0 - 2x^2z)j + (3x^2z^2 - 2x^2y)k$$

$$= -3xz^2i + 2x^2zj + (3x^2z^2 - 2x^2y)k.$$

Then $\quad \nabla \times (r \times s) = \begin{vmatrix} i & j & k \\ \dfrac{\partial}{\partial x} & \dfrac{\partial}{\partial y} & \dfrac{\partial}{\partial z} \\ -3xz^2 & 2x^2z & (3x^2z^2 - 2x^2y) \end{vmatrix}$

$$= \left\{ \frac{\partial}{\partial y}\left(3x^2z^2 - 2x^2y\right) - \frac{\partial}{\partial z}\left(2x^2z\right) \right\}i$$

$$- \left\{ \frac{\partial}{\partial x}\left(3x^2z^2 - 2x^2y\right) - \frac{\partial}{\partial z}\left(-3xz^2\right) \right\}j$$

$$+ \left\{ \frac{\partial}{\partial x}\left(2x^2z\right) - \frac{\partial}{\partial y}\left(-3xz^2\right) \right\}k$$

$$= \{-2x^2 - 2x^2\}i - \{6xz^2 - 4xy + 6xz\}j$$

$$+ \{4xz - 0\}k$$

$$= -4x^2i + 2x\left(2y - 3z - 3z^2\right)j + 4xzk.$$

ii) We start with $\quad \nabla \times r = \begin{vmatrix} i & j & k \\ \dfrac{\partial}{\partial x} & \dfrac{\partial}{\partial y} & \dfrac{\partial}{\partial z} \\ x^2z & xy & xz \end{vmatrix}$

$$= \left\{ \frac{\partial}{\partial y}\left(xz\right) - \frac{\partial}{\partial z}\left(xy\right) \right\}i$$

$$- \left\{ \frac{\partial}{\partial x}\left(xz\right) - \frac{\partial}{\partial z}\left(x^2z\right) \right\}j$$

$$+ \left\{ \frac{\partial}{\partial x}\left(xy\right) - \frac{\partial}{\partial y}\left(x^2z\right) \right\}k$$

$$= \{0 - 0\}i - \{z - x^2\}j + \{y - 0\}k$$

$$= (x^2 - z)j + yk.$$

Then

$$\nabla \times (\nabla \times r) = \begin{vmatrix} i & j & k \\ \dfrac{\partial}{\partial x} & \dfrac{\partial}{\partial y} & \dfrac{\partial}{\partial z} \\ 0 & x^2 - z & y \end{vmatrix}$$

$$= \left\{ \frac{\partial}{\partial y}(y) - \frac{\partial}{\partial z}(x^2 - z) \right\} i$$

$$- \left\{ \frac{\partial}{\partial x}(y) - \frac{\partial}{\partial z}(0) \right\} j$$

$$+ \left\{ \frac{\partial}{\partial x}(x^2 - z) - \frac{\partial}{\partial y}(0) \right\} k$$

$$= \{1 - -1\} i - \{0 - 0\} j + \{2x - 0\} k$$

$$= 2i + 2xk.$$

We could continue with more intricate vector analysis but it generally becomes more abstract. Before the final short Exercise we mention some applications. In fluid mechanics (where v is the velocity vector) for irrotational motion curl $v = 0$ implying $v = \operatorname{grad} \phi$ is the velocity potential. Also for an incompressible fluid the equation of continuity is div $v = 0$. In an electromagnetic field Maxwell's equations are div $D = 4\pi\rho$, div $B = 0$, curl $H = 4\pi j + \dfrac{1}{c}\dfrac{\partial D}{\partial t}$, curl $E = -\dfrac{1}{c}\dfrac{\partial B}{\partial t}$.

■ EXERCISE 8.13 ■

1   Using $\phi = x \sin y$ show that $\nabla \times (\nabla \phi) = \mathbf{0}$.

2   For $v = xe^y i + xj + yz^2 k$ show that $\nabla . (\nabla \times v) = 0$.

3   If $v = xi + yj$ is the vector flow irrotational ?

4   $r = xi + yj + zk$ and $V = \dfrac{1}{r}$. Find the value of curl (grad V).

5   Is the vector flow for $v = \left(y\sqrt{x^2 + y^2} \right) i - \left(x\sqrt{x^2 + y^2} \right) j$ incompressible?

We have curtailed our simple introduction to vector analysis. It goes more deeply into the application of the operator ∇ and extensively into integration. There you meet such delights as line integrals, double integrals and triple integrals; beyond the scope of this text.

9 Integration

Introduction

Remember that integration is the reverse process to differentiation. Indeed you should notice the reversal of the differentiation of a function of a function rule in many examples. Originally we looked at integration in Volume 1, Chapter 19. We extended our ideas and techniques in Volume 2, Chapters 10–14. There we also looked at numerical integration. Later we used integration to solve some simple differential equations. We use plenty of integration techniques in the later chapters of this volume as well.

In Chapter 9 we concentrate upon some standard forms of integrals. Many of the integrals can also be solved using integration by substitution or numerical integration. Using standard forms saves time. However these forms depend upon recognition of the required type. Sometimes you may not instantly recognise the correct form and need to use an alternative, equally valid, method.

You may find it useful to skim through Volume 2, Chapters 10, 12, 13 and 14, again. To save time and space we assume all the techniques and applications learned there.

▬▬▬ ASSIGNMENT ▬▬▬

Previously we have seen the calculus links between displacement, s, velocity, v, and acceleration. In this Assignment we link them once more for a variety of different functions for the velocity. Each choice enables us to demonstrate an integration technique. Remember how they are linked with force (Newton's laws) and with work done and power.

Integration of $(ax + b)^n$

$$\int (ax + b)^n dx = \frac{1}{a} \times \frac{(ax + b)^{n+1}}{n+1} + c$$

where a, b, c and n are constants.

This integral is valid for $n \neq -1$.

Notice the power of x is 1 and the complete bracket is raised to the power of n.

Examples 9.1

i) $\int (2x - 3)^4 dx = \frac{1}{2} \times \frac{(2x - 3)^{4+1}}{4+1} + c$

$a = 2$, $b = -3$, $n = 4$.

$\qquad = \frac{1}{10}(2x - 3)^5 + c.$

$2 \times (4 + 1) = 2 \times 5$
$= 10.$

ii) $\int 7(2x - 3)^4 dx = 7 \times \frac{1}{2} \times \frac{(2x - 3)^{4+1}}{4+1} + c$

$a = 2$, $b = -3$, $n = 4$.

$\qquad = \frac{7}{10}(2x - 3)^5 + c.$

i.e. $7\times$ the previous result.

iii) $\int 5(2x - 3)^{1.5} dx = 5 \times \frac{1}{2} \times \frac{(2x - 3)^{1.5+1}}{1.5+1} + c$

$a = 2$, $b = -3$, $n = 1.5$.

$\qquad = (2x - 3)^{2.5} + c.$

$5 \times \frac{1}{2} \times \frac{1}{1.5+1} = 5 \times \frac{1}{2} \times \frac{1}{2.5}$
$= 1.$

We look at some negative powers for n using exactly the same idea.

Examples 9.2

i) $\int \frac{1}{(4x + 1)^3} dx = \int (4x + 1)^{-3} dx$

$a = 4$, $b = 1$, $n = -3$.

$\qquad = \frac{1}{4} \times \frac{(4x + 1)^{-3+1}}{-3+1} + c$

$\qquad = -\frac{1}{8} \times (4x + 1)^{-2} + c$

$4 \times (-3 + 1) = 4 \times -2$
$= -8.$

$\qquad$ or $\quad -\frac{1}{8(4x + 1)^2} + c.$

ii) Notice in this case only the bracket moves and hence only the power changes. The $\frac{16}{3}$ is a simple multiplying factor.

$$\int \frac{16}{3(4x+1)^3} \, dx = \frac{16}{3} \int (4x+1)^{-3} \, dx$$

> $a = 4, b = 1, n = -3.$

$$= \frac{16}{3} \times -\frac{1}{8(4x+1)^2} + c$$

> Using the previous result.

$$= -\frac{2}{3(4x+1)^2} + c.$$

Example 9.3

We find the mean value of $y = \dfrac{1}{\sqrt{x+5}}$ between $x = 1$ and $x = 2$.

We have a formula for mean value,

$$\bar{y} = \frac{1}{b-a} \int_a^b y \, dx.$$

> Volume 2, Chapter 10.

Do *not* confuse the a and b of this formula with those of our standard integral.

We substitute for y, our lower limit of 1 and our upper limit of 2 so that

$$\bar{y} = \frac{1}{2-1} \int_1^2 \frac{1}{\sqrt{x+5}} \, dx$$

$$= \frac{1}{1} \int_1^2 (x+5)^{-0.5} \, dx$$

> $\dfrac{1}{\sqrt{x+5}} = \dfrac{1}{(x+5)^{0.5}}$
> $= (x+5)^{-0.5}.$

$$= \left[\frac{(x+5)^{-0.5+1}}{-0.5+1} \right]_1^2$$

$$= \left[2(x+5)^{0.5} \right]_1^2$$

> The denominator simplifies to 0.5 and $\dfrac{1}{0.5} = 2.$

$$= 2(2+5)^{0.5} - 2(1+5)^{0.5}$$

$$= 2 \times 2.645\ldots - 2 \times 2.449\ldots$$

$$= 0.39.$$

ASSIGNMENT

We look at a velocity, $v = (5s+1)^2$ ms^{-1}, where s (m) is the displacement. The acceleration, $\dfrac{dv}{dt}$, introduces another variable, time, t. To bring us back to only 2 variables we apply the function of a function rule to the acceleration, i.e.

$$\frac{dv}{dt} = \frac{dv}{ds} \times \frac{ds}{dt} = v\frac{dv}{ds}.$$

> $v = \dfrac{ds}{dt}.$

Now using $\qquad v = (5s + 1)^2$

we differentiate to get $\quad \dfrac{dv}{ds} = 2 \times 5(5s + 1)$

so that our expression for acceleration is

$$v\dfrac{dv}{ds} = (5s + 1)^2 \times 10(5s + 1)$$

$$= 10(5s + 1)^3.$$

If we have a mass of 0.25 kg, then using $F = ma$ we have a force of

$$F = 0.25 \times 10(5s + 1)^3$$

$$= 2.5(5s + 1)^3 \text{ N}.$$

We can look at the work done during the first 0.5 m of this motion by applying the formula

$$\text{Work done} = \int_a^b F\, ds$$

> Work done is the area under a force–displacement graph.

i.e. $\qquad$ Work done $= \displaystyle\int_0^{0.5} 2.5(5s + 1)^3\, ds$

$$= \left[2.5 \times \dfrac{1}{5} \times \dfrac{(5s + 1)^4}{4} \right]_0^{0.5}$$

$$= \left[\dfrac{(5s + 1)^4}{8} \right]_0^{0.5}$$

$$= \dfrac{3.5^4}{8} - \dfrac{1^4}{8}$$

$$= 18.63 \text{ J}$$

EXERCISE 9.1

Find the following indefinite integrals.

1 $\displaystyle\int (2x - 1)^3\, dx$

2 $\displaystyle\int \dfrac{4}{3}(2x - 1)^3\, dx$

3 $\displaystyle\int \dfrac{2}{(3 + 7x)^2}\, dx$

4 $\displaystyle\int 5\sqrt{x - 3}\, dx$

5 $\displaystyle\int \dfrac{4}{(3x + 2)^{1/2}}\, dx$

Find the values of the following definite integrals.

6 $\displaystyle\int_0^{0.25} (2+x)^4 \, dx$

9 $\displaystyle\int_5^{7.5} \frac{4}{(2x-7)^3} \, dx$

7 $\displaystyle\int_{1.5}^{2.0} (3x-2)^3 \, dx$

10 $\displaystyle\int_1^{3.5} \frac{1}{\sqrt{7x-1}} \, dx$

8 $\displaystyle\int_0^{0.2} \frac{3}{4}\sqrt{2x+5} \, dx$

Integration of $\dfrac{1}{ax+b}$

This is the exception to the previous rule where $n \neq -1$.

$$\int \frac{1}{ax+b} \, dx = \frac{1}{a} \ln\,(ax+b) + c$$

where a, b and c are constants.

Examples 9.4

i) $\displaystyle\int \frac{1}{2x-3} \, dx = \frac{1}{2}\ln(2x-3) + c.$ | $a = 2, b = -3.$

ii) $\displaystyle\int \frac{3}{4(2x-3)} \, dx = \frac{3}{4}\int \frac{1}{2x-3} \, dx$ | $a = 2, b = -3.$

$$= \frac{3}{4} \times \frac{1}{2}\ln(2x-3) + c$$

$$= \frac{3}{8}\ln(2x-3) + c.$$ | Using the previous result.

Example 9.5

We find the value of $\displaystyle\int_1^{1.5} \frac{1}{x+0.25} \, dx.$

$$\int_1^{1.5} \frac{1}{x+0.25} \, dx = \left[\frac{1}{1}\ln(x+0.25) \right]_1^{1.5}$$ | $a = 1, b = 0.25.$

$$= \ln(1.5+0.25) - \ln(1+0.25)$$

$$= \ln 1.75 - \ln 1.25$$

$$= 0.5596\ldots - 0.2231\ldots$$

$$= 0.34.$$

■■■ EXERCISE 9.2 ■■■

Find the values of the following definite integrals.

1    $\displaystyle\int_{1}^{1.5} \frac{1}{3x-2}\, dx$

4    $\displaystyle\int_{5}^{10} \frac{2}{3(x+5)}\, dx$

2    $\displaystyle\int_{0}^{0.45} \frac{1}{3-2x}\, dx$

5    $\displaystyle\int_{3}^{6} \frac{1}{2(3x-5)}\, dx$

3    $\displaystyle\int_{2}^{5} \frac{2}{4x+1}\, dx$

Integration of $f'(x)[f(x)]^n$

$$\int f'(x)[f(x)]^n\, dx = \frac{[f(x)]^{n+1}}{n+1} + c$$

where a, b, c and n are constants.

This integral is valid for $n \neq -1$. It is the reverse process to differentiation using the function of a function rule. The first integral type of the chapter, $\int (ax+b)^n\, dx$, is a specific example of this general case. There we have a minor adjustment using a factor of a.

■■■ Examples 9.6 ■■■

i) $\displaystyle\int 2x(x^2-1)^4\, dx = \frac{(x^2-1)^{4+1}}{4+1} + c$

$$= \frac{(x^2-1)^5}{5} + c.$$

$f(x) = x^2 - 1,$
$f'(x) = 2x,$
$n = 4.$

ii)   We use the previous result, just removing a factor of 4.5 to create $f'(x) = 2x$.

$$\int 9x(x^2-1)^4\, dx = 4.5 \int 2x(x^2-1)^4\, dx$$

$$= 4.5 \times \frac{(x^2-1)^5}{5} + c$$

Using the previous result.

$$= 0.9(x^2-1)^5 + c.$$

We look at fractional and negative powers for n using exactly the same idea.

Examples 9.7

i) $\int (2+5x)(2x+2.5x^2)^{3/2}\,dx = \dfrac{(2x+2.5x^2)^{3/2+1}}{3/2+1} + c$

> $f(x) = 2x+2.5x^2,$
> $f'(x) = 2+5x,$
> $n = 3/2.$

$$= \frac{2}{5}(2x+2.5x^2)^{5/2} + c.$$

> $\dfrac{1}{3/2+1} = \dfrac{1}{5/2} = \dfrac{2}{5}.$

ii) $\displaystyle \int \frac{2+5x}{(2x+2.5x^2)^3}\,dx = \int (2+5x)(2x+2.5x^2)^{-3}\,dx$

$$= \frac{(2x+2.5x^2)^{-3+1}}{-3+1} + c$$

> $f(x) = 2x+2.5x^2,$
> $f'(x) = 2+5x,$
> $n = -3.$

$$= -\frac{(2x+2.5x^2)^{-2}}{2} + c$$

$$\text{or} \quad -\frac{1}{2(2x+2.5x^2)^2} + c.$$

Example 9.8

We find the value of $\displaystyle\int_{0.75}^{1} \frac{12}{7}x^2(x^3+5)^2\,dx.$

We remove a factor of $\dfrac{4}{7}$ to create the correct $f'(x)$, i.e.

$$\int_{0.75}^{1} \frac{12}{7}x^2(x^3+5)^2\,dx = \frac{4}{7}\int_{0.75}^{1} 3x^2(x^3+5)^2\,dx$$

> $f(x) = x^3+5,$
> $f'(x) = 3x^2,$
> $n = 2.$

$$= \frac{4}{7}\left[\frac{(x^3+5)^3}{3}\right]_{0.75}^{1}$$

> Increase the power by 1 and divide by the new power.

$$= \frac{4}{21}\left[(1^3+5)^3 - (0.75^3+5)^3\right]$$

> $\dfrac{4}{7} \times \dfrac{1}{3} = \dfrac{4}{21}$ is a common factor.

$$= \frac{4}{21}\left[6^3 - 5.421\ldots^3\right]$$

$$= \frac{4}{21}[216 - 159.385\ldots]$$

$$= 10.78.$$

ASSIGNMENT

Previously we looked at a velocity, $v = (5s + 1)^2$ ms^{-1}, where s (m) is the displacement. This time we make a minor change and apply this standard integral. We let $v = (5s^2 + 1)^2$ ms^{-1}. All the same method continues using this adjusted velocity. Again we start with the acceleration.

$$\frac{dv}{dt} = \frac{dv}{ds} \times \frac{ds}{dt} = v\frac{dv}{ds}.$$

$$v = \frac{ds}{dt}.$$

Now using

$$v = (5s^2 + 1)^2$$

we differentiate to get $\dfrac{dv}{ds} = 2 \times 10s(5s^2 + 1)$

Function of a function rule.

so that our expression for acceleration is

$$v\frac{dv}{ds} = (5s^2 + 1)^2 \times 20s(5s^2 + 1)$$

$$= 20s(5s^2 + 1)^3.$$

If we have a mass of 0.25 kg, then using $F = ma$, we have a force of

$$F = 0.25 \times 20s(5s^2 + 1)^3$$

$$= 5s(5s^2 + 1)^3 \text{ N}.$$

We can look at the work done during the first 0.5 m of this motion by applying the formula

$$\text{Work done} = \int_a^b F\, ds$$

i.e. $\text{Work done} = \displaystyle\int_0^{0.5} 5s(5s^2 + 1)^3 \, ds.$

$$f(s) = 5s^2 + 1,$$
$$f'(s) = 10s,$$
$$n = 3.$$

We need to remove a factor of 0.5 to create the required $f'(s) = 10s$, i.e.

$$= 0.5\int_0^{0.5} 10s(5s^2 + 1)^3 \, ds$$

$$= \left[\frac{0.5(5s^2 + 1)^4}{4}\right]_0^{0.5}$$

Increase the power by 1 and divide by the new power.

$$= \left[\frac{(5s^2 + 1)^4}{8}\right]_0^{0.5}$$

$$= \frac{2.25^4}{8} - \frac{1^4}{8}$$

$$= 3.08 \text{ J}$$

EXERCISE 9.3

Find the following indefinite integrals.

1 $\displaystyle\int 6x(3x^2 - 5)^3\, dx$

4 $\displaystyle\int x(2x^2 - 1)^2\, dx$

2 $\displaystyle\int 6x(5 - 3x^2)^3\, dx$

5 $\displaystyle\int \frac{x^2}{2}(x^3 - 5)^4\, dx$

3 $\displaystyle\int 2x(x^2 + 7)^{3/4}\, dx$

Find the values of the following definite integrals.

6 $\displaystyle\int_0^1 12x^2(1 + x^3)^4\, dx$

9 $\displaystyle\int_{0.5}^{0.6} \frac{5x^4}{(x^5 + 2)^3}\, dx$

7 $\displaystyle\int_{0.8}^{1.0} x^3(5 - x^4)^2\, dx$

10 $\displaystyle\int_2^{2.5} \frac{x^3}{(x^4 - 2)^{1/2}}\, dx$

8 $\displaystyle\int_{0.9}^{1.1} 4x(x^2 + 7)^{1/3}\, dx$

Integration of $\dfrac{f'(x)}{f(x)}$

This is the exception to an earlier rule, $\int f'(x)[f(x)]^n\, dx$ where $n \neq -1$. Notice that $f'(x)$, the first derivative of $f(x)$, lies in the numerator. $f(x)$ lies in the denominator. This pattern gives us the standard integral

$$\int \frac{f'(x)}{f(x)}\, dx = \ln f(x) + c.$$

The earlier integration type is a specific example of this general case. Here we concentrate upon the denominator, $f(x)$. Then we look at the numerator to see if it is the first derivative, $f'(x)$. Sometimes we may need a slight adjustment with a multiplying factor.

Examples 9.9

i) We concentrate upon the denominator, looking for $f(x)$. Then we look for $f'(x)$ in the numerator.

$\displaystyle\int \frac{2 + 5x}{2x + 2.5x^2}\, dx = \ln(2x + 2.5x^2) + c.$

$\boxed{\begin{aligned} f(x) &= 2x + 2.5x^2, \\ f'(x) &= 2 + 5x. \end{aligned}}$

ii) $\displaystyle \int \frac{\sin\theta}{\cos\theta}\,d\theta = -\int -\frac{\sin\theta}{\cos\theta}\,d\theta$

> $f(\theta) = \cos\theta$ and $f'(\theta) = -\sin\theta$ so we need to adjust for the negative sign.

$$= -\ln(\cos\theta) + c.$$

This is one version of the solution. Also remember $\ln 1 = 0$.

Now $-\ln(\cos\theta) = 0 - \ln(\cos\theta)$

$$= \ln 1 - \ln(\cos\theta)$$

> Law of logarithms.

$$= \ln\left(\frac{1}{\cos\theta}\right)$$

$$= \ln(\sec\theta).$$

Example 9.10

We find the area under the curve $y = \tan 2\theta$ bounded by the θ-axis from $\theta = 0$ to $\theta = \dfrac{\pi}{6}$ radians.

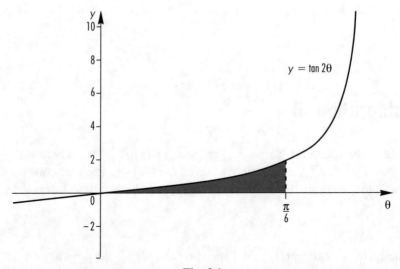

Fig. 9.1

For revision we sketch the curve in Fig. 9.1. The area formula is

$$\text{Area} = \int_a^b y\,dx$$

which we apply as

$$\text{Area} = \int_0^{\pi/6} -\frac{\sin 2\theta}{\cos 2\theta}\,d\theta.$$

> Remember $\tan 2\theta = \dfrac{\sin 2\theta}{\cos 2\theta}$

We need to adjust the integral, looking at the form of $f(\theta)$ and $f'(\theta)$, i.e.

$$\text{Area} = -\frac{1}{2}\int_0^{\pi/6}\frac{2\sin 2\theta}{\cos 2\theta}\,d\theta$$

$$\boxed{\begin{array}{l} f(\theta) = \cos 2\theta, \\ f'(\theta) = -2\sin 2\theta. \end{array}}$$

$$= -\frac{1}{2}\Big[\ln(\cos 2\theta)\Big]_0^{\pi/6}$$

$$= -\frac{1}{2}\Big[\ln\Big(\cos\frac{2\pi}{6}\Big) - \ln(\cos 0)\Big]$$

$$= -0.5[\ln 0.5 - \ln 1]$$

$$= -0.5(-0.693\ldots) + 0$$

$$= 0.35 \text{ unit}^2.$$

EXERCISE 9.4

Find the values of the following definite integrals.

1 $\displaystyle\int_0^{1.5}\frac{2x}{x^2+1}\,dx$

2 $\displaystyle\int_{0.25}^{0.5}\frac{2x}{1-x^2}\,dx$

3 $\displaystyle\int_{\pi/4}^{\pi/3}\cot\theta\,d\theta$ Hint: $\cot\theta = \dfrac{\cos\theta}{\sin\theta}$.

4 $\displaystyle\int_{2.5}^{3.0}\frac{2x^3}{x^4+3}\,dx$

5 $\displaystyle\int_{1.5}^{4.5}\frac{2x^3+3x^2}{2+2x^3+x^4}\,dx$

Integration of $\dfrac{f'(x)}{\sqrt{f(x)}}$

Notice how the square root sign in the denominator affects the standard integral, i.e.

$$\int\frac{f'(x)}{\sqrt{f(x)}}\,dx = 2\sqrt{f(x)} + c.$$

This is a specific example of $\displaystyle\int f'(x)[f(x)]^n\,dx$ with $n = -\frac{1}{2}$ to save time.

Examples 9.11

i) $\int \dfrac{2+5x}{\sqrt{2x+2.5x^2}}\,dx = 2\sqrt{2x+2.5x^2}+c.$

$\boxed{\begin{array}{l} f(x)=2x+2.5x^2, \\ f'(x)=2+5x. \end{array}}$

ii) $\int 5(2x-3)^{-0.5}\,dx = 5\int \dfrac{1}{\sqrt{2x-3}}\,dx$

$\boxed{\begin{array}{l} (2x-3)^{-0.5}=\dfrac{1}{(2x-3)^{0.5}} \\[2mm] \phantom{(2x-3)^{-0.5}}=\dfrac{1}{\sqrt{2x-3}} \end{array}}$

$ = \dfrac{5}{2}\int \dfrac{2}{\sqrt{2x-3}}\,dx$

$\boxed{\begin{array}{l} f(x)=2x-3, \\ f'(x)=2. \end{array}}$

$ = \dfrac{5}{2}\times 2\sqrt{2x-3}+c$

$ = 5\sqrt{2x-3}+c.$

Example 9.12

We find the mean value of $y = \dfrac{1}{\sqrt{x+5}}$ between $x=1$ and $x=2$.

This is a repeat of Example 9.3 using this standard integral.

We have a formula for mean value,

$\bar{y} = \dfrac{1}{b-a}\displaystyle\int_a^b y\,dx.$ $\boxed{\text{Volume 2, Chapter 10.}}$

Do *not* confuse the a and b of this formula with those of our standard integral.

We substitute for y, our lower limit of 1 and our upper limit of 2 so that

$\bar{y} = \dfrac{1}{2-1}\displaystyle\int_1^2 \dfrac{1}{\sqrt{x+5}}\,dx$

$\phantom{\bar{y}} = \displaystyle\int_1^2 \dfrac{1}{\sqrt{x+5}}\,dx$ $\boxed{\begin{array}{l} f(x)=x+5, \\ f'(x)=1. \end{array}}$

$\phantom{\bar{y}} = \Big[2\sqrt{x+5}\,\Big]_1^2$

$\phantom{\bar{y}} = 0.39,\ \text{as before.}$

ASSIGNMENT

Previously we looked at a velocity, v. This time our minor change is to $v=(5s+1)^{-1/2}$ ms^{-1}, where s (m) is the displacement, i.e. $v=\dfrac{1}{\sqrt{5s+1}}$.

For this application we find the mean velocity over the first 0.5 m of the motion.

Using the formula for mean value,

$$\bar{y} = \frac{1}{b-a}\int_a^b y\,dx$$

Volume 2, Chapter 10.

we substitute to get

$$\bar{v} = \frac{1}{0.5 - 0}\int_0^{0.5} \frac{1}{\sqrt{5s+1}}\,ds$$

$f(s) = 5s + 1,$
$f'(s) = 5.$

$$\bar{v} = \frac{2}{5}\int_0^{0.5} \frac{5}{\sqrt{5s+1}}\,ds$$

Adjusting for $f'(s)$.

$$= 0.4 \times \left[2\sqrt{5s+1}\right]_0^{0.5}$$

$$= 0.4\left[2\sqrt{2.5+1} - 2\sqrt{0+1}\right]$$

$$= 0.4[2(1.870\ldots) - 2(1)]$$

$$= 0.4 \times 1.74\ldots$$

$$= 0.70 \text{ ms}^{-1}.$$

■ EXERCISE 9.5 ■

Find the values of the following definite integrals.

1 $\displaystyle\int_0^4 \frac{2x}{\sqrt{x^2+1}}\,dx$

4 $\displaystyle\int_2^3 \frac{2x^3}{\sqrt{x^4-4}}\,dx$

2 $\displaystyle\int_1^{1.5} \frac{1}{\sqrt{4+x}}\,dx$

5 $\displaystyle\int_0^{\pi/4} \frac{\sec^2\theta}{\sqrt{3-\tan\theta}}\,d\theta$

3 $\displaystyle\int_0^{\pi/6} \frac{\sin\theta}{\sqrt{4-\cos\theta}}\,d\theta$

Integration of $\dfrac{1}{x^2 - a}$

$$\int \frac{1}{x^2 - a^2}\,dx = \frac{1}{2a}\ln\left(\frac{x-a}{x+a}\right) + c \quad \text{where the coefficient of } x^2 \text{ is } 1$$

and similarly

$$\int \frac{1}{a^2 - x^2}\,dx = \frac{1}{2a}\ln\left(\frac{a+x}{a-x}\right) + c \quad \text{where the coefficient of } x^2 \text{ is } -1.$$

a and c are constants.

We can prove these standard integrals using partial fractions. $x^2 - a^2$ factorises and we can write

$$\frac{1}{x^2 - a^2} \equiv \frac{1}{(x-a)(x+a)} \equiv \frac{A}{x-a} + \frac{B}{x+a}$$

where A and B are constants to be found.

Using the partial fraction techniques (Volume 2, Chapter 12) we get $A = \dfrac{1}{2a}$ and $B = -\dfrac{1}{2a}$. We remove this common factor of $\dfrac{1}{2a}$ and integrate to get logarithmic functions. These we combine using a law of logarithms. You can try this for yourself, knowing the above general result. Again these standard integrals save time and effort compared with the partial fraction techniques.

Examples 9.13

We find the values of three definite integrals,

i) $\displaystyle\int_4^6 \frac{4}{x^2 - 9}\, dx,$ ii) $\displaystyle\int_2^3 \frac{1}{2x^2 - 32}\, dx,$ iii) $\displaystyle\int_2^3 \frac{1}{11 - x^2}\, dx$

i) Using $\displaystyle\int \frac{1}{x^2 - a^2}\, dx = \frac{1}{2a}\ln\left(\frac{x-a}{x+a}\right) + c$

we have $\displaystyle\int_4^6 \frac{4}{x^2 - 9}\, dx = \frac{4}{2(3)}\left[\ln\left(\frac{x-3}{x+3}\right)\right]_4^6$

> $a^2 = 9$,
> $a = 3$.

$$= \frac{2}{3}\left[\ln\left(\frac{6-3}{6+3}\right) - \ln\left(\frac{4-3}{4+3}\right)\right]$$

$$= \frac{2}{3}\left[\ln\frac{3}{9} - \ln\frac{1}{7}\right]$$

$$= \frac{2}{3}\left[\ln\left(\frac{3}{9}\bigg/\frac{1}{7}\right)\right]$$

> Law of logarithms.

$$= \frac{2}{3}\ln\frac{7}{3}$$

> Dividing by a fraction – invert and multiply.

$$= \frac{2}{3} \times 0.847\ldots$$

$$= 0.565.$$

ii) Using $\displaystyle\int \frac{1}{x^2 - a^2}\, dx = \frac{1}{2a}\ln\left(\frac{x-a}{x+a}\right) + c$

we have $\displaystyle\int_2^3 \frac{1}{2x^2 - 32}\, dx = \frac{1}{2}\int_2^3 \frac{1}{x^2 - 16}\, dx$

> $a^2 = 16$,
> $a = 4$.

> Removing a factor of 2 so the coefficient of x^2 is 1.

$$= \frac{1}{2} \times \frac{1}{2(4)} \left[\ln \left(\frac{x-4}{x+4} \right) \right]_2^3$$

$$= \frac{1}{16} \left[\ln \left(\frac{3-4}{3+4} \right) - \ln \left(\frac{2-4}{2+4} \right) \right]$$

$$= \frac{1}{16} \left[\ln \left(\frac{-1}{7} \right) - \ln \left(\frac{-2}{6} \right) \right].$$

Remember a logarithm is defined only for positive values. We can remove the negative signs during division by applying a logarithmic law, i.e.

$$\frac{1}{16} \left[\ln \left(\frac{-1}{7} \middle/ \frac{-1}{3} \right) \right]$$

> Dividing by a fraction – invert and multiply.

$$= \frac{1}{16} \ln \frac{3}{7}$$

$$= -0.053.$$

iii) Using $\displaystyle\int \frac{1}{a^2 - x^2} \, dx = \frac{1}{2a} \ln \left(\frac{a+x}{a-x} \right) + c$

we have

$$\int_2^3 \frac{1}{11 - x^2} \, dx = \frac{1}{2(3.3166)} \left[\ln \left(\frac{3.3166 + x}{3.3166 - x} \right) \right]_2^3$$

> $a^2 = 11,$
> $a = 3.3166.$

$$= \frac{1}{6.6332} \left[\ln \left(\frac{3.3166 + 3}{3.3166 - 3} \right) - \ln \left(\frac{3.3166 + 2}{3.3166 - 2} \right) \right]$$

$$= 0.150 \ldots [\ln 19.949 \ldots - \ln 4.038 \ldots]$$

$$= 0.24.$$

■■■■ EXERCISE 9.6 ■■■■

Find the values of the following definite integrals.

1 $\displaystyle\int_2^3 \frac{1}{x^2 - 1} \, dx$

2 $\displaystyle\int_{7.5}^{10} \frac{1}{x^2 - 25} \, dx$

3 $\displaystyle\int_0^{1.5} \frac{1}{4 - x^2} \, dx$

4 $\displaystyle\int_4^8 \frac{3}{4x^2 - 9} \, dx$

5 $\displaystyle\int_0^{\pi/6} \frac{1}{1 - \sin^2 \theta} \, d\theta$

Integration with inverse trigonometric results

Remember integration is the reverse process to differentiation. In Chapter 2 we saw how to differentiate inverse trigonometric functions. Here we look at the integration.

$$\int \frac{1}{\sqrt{a^2 - x^2}} \, dx = \sin^{-1}\left(\frac{x}{a}\right) + c \qquad \text{where the coefficient of } x^2 \text{ is } -1.$$

$$\int \frac{-1}{\sqrt{a^2 - x^2}} \, dx = \cos^{-1}\left(\frac{x}{a}\right) + c \qquad \text{where the coefficient of } x^2 \text{ is } -1.$$

$$\int \frac{1}{a^2 + x^2} \, dx = \frac{1}{a}\tan^{-1}\left(\frac{x}{a}\right) + c \qquad \text{where the coefficient of } x^2 \text{ is } 1.$$

████ Examples 9.14 ████

i) $\displaystyle \int \frac{1}{\sqrt{4 - x^2}} \, dx = \sin^{-1}\left(\frac{x}{2}\right) + c.$

$a^2 = 4,$
$a = 2.$

ii) $\displaystyle \int \frac{-1}{\sqrt{9 - x^2}} \, dx = \cos^{-1}\left(\frac{x}{3}\right) + c.$

$a^2 = 9,$
$a = 3.$

iii) $\displaystyle \int \frac{-1}{\sqrt{36 - 4x^2}} \, dx = \int \frac{-1}{\sqrt{4(9 - x^2)}} \, dx$

$a^2 = 9,$
$a = 3.$

$$= \frac{1}{\sqrt{4}} \int \frac{-1}{\sqrt{9 - x^2}} \, dx$$

$$= \frac{1}{2}\cos^{-1}\left(\frac{x}{3}\right) + c.$$

Using the previous result.

iv) $\displaystyle \int \frac{7}{\sqrt{36 - 4x^2}} \, dx = 7\int \frac{1}{\sqrt{36 - 4x^2}} \, dx$

$a^2 = 9,$
$a = 3.$

$$= \frac{7}{2}\sin^{-1}\left(\frac{x}{3}\right) + c.$$

Using a positive version of the previous result.

████ Example 9.15 ████

We use the answer to Example 9.14iv) to find the value of a definite integral, i.e.

$$\int_2^3 \frac{7}{\sqrt{36 - 4x^2}} \, dx = 3.5\left[\sin^{-1}\left(\frac{x}{3}\right)\right]_2^3$$

$$= 3.5\left[\sin^{-1}\left(\frac{3}{3}\right) - \sin^{-1}\left(\frac{2}{3}\right)\right]$$

$$= 3.5[1.570\ldots - 0.729\ldots] \qquad \text{Using radians.}$$

$$= 2.94.$$

Examples 9.16

i) $\int \dfrac{1}{x^2+9}\,dx = \int \dfrac{1}{3^2+x^2}\,dx$

Notice the order within the denominator does *not* matter. $a^2 = 9$, $a = 3$.

$$= \frac{1}{3}\tan^{-1}\left(\frac{x}{3}\right) + c.$$

ii) $\int \dfrac{4}{x^2+9}\,dx = 4\int \dfrac{1}{3^2+x^2}\,dx$

$$= \frac{4}{3}\tan^{-1}\left(\frac{x}{3}\right) + c.$$

Using the previous result.

iii) $\int \dfrac{4}{45+5x^2}\,dx = 4\int \dfrac{1}{5(9+x^2)}\,dx$

$$= \frac{4}{5}\int \frac{1}{3^2+x^2}\,dx$$

$$= \frac{4}{5} \times \frac{1}{3}\tan^{-1}\left(\frac{x}{3}\right) + c$$

Using the previous result.

$$= \frac{4}{15}\tan^{-1}\left(\frac{x}{3}\right) + c.$$

EXERCISE 9.7

Find the following indefinite integrals.

1 $\displaystyle\int \frac{1}{\sqrt{25-x^2}}\,dx$

2 $\displaystyle\int \frac{-7}{\sqrt{1-x^2}}\,dx$

3 $\displaystyle\int \frac{5}{4+x^2}\,dx$

4 $\displaystyle\int \frac{4}{\sqrt{9-x^2}}\,dx$

5 $\displaystyle\int \frac{1}{4x^2+64}\,dx$

Find the values of the following definite integrals.

6 $\displaystyle\int_{0.5}^{1.5} \frac{9}{\sqrt{4-x^2}}\,dx$

7 $\displaystyle\int_{2.5}^{3.5} \frac{-1}{\sqrt{20-x^2}}\,dx$

8 $\displaystyle\int_{3}^{5} \frac{1}{121+x^2}\,dx$

9 $\displaystyle\int_{0.2}^{0.3} \frac{14}{\sqrt{0.25-x^2}}\,dx$

10 $\displaystyle\int_{1}^{2} \frac{1/2}{2x^2+8}\,dx$

We can combine these standard integrals. It is possible to split a question based on the common denominator.

▮▮▮▮▮ **Example 9.17** ▮▮▮▮▮

$\int \dfrac{6x+2}{3x^2+12}\,dx$ does not exactly match any of the standard integrals. However we split it using the common denominator, $3x^2+12$, to get

$$\int \frac{6x}{3x^2+12}\,dx + \int \frac{2}{3x^2+12}\,dx.$$

The first integral matches $\int \dfrac{f'(x)}{f(x)}\,dx$. The second integral, with adjustment, gives an inverse tangent.

$$\int \frac{6x}{3x^2+12}\,dx + \frac{2}{3}\int \frac{1}{x^2+4}\,dx = \ln(3x^2+12) + \frac{2}{3}\times\frac{1}{2}\tan^{-1}\left(\frac{x}{2}\right) + c$$

$$= \ln(3x^2+12) + \frac{1}{3}\tan^{-1}\left(\frac{x}{2}\right) + c.$$

▮▮▮▮▮ **EXERCISE 9.8** ▮▮▮▮▮

Find the following indefinite integrals.

1 $\int \dfrac{1+2x}{9+x^2}\,dx$

2 $\int \dfrac{8x+1}{\sqrt{4-x^2}}\,dx$

3 $\int \dfrac{x-4}{18+2x^2}\,dx$

4 $\int \dfrac{1-x}{\sqrt{1-x^2}}\,dx$

5 $\int \dfrac{2x+5}{8+2x^2}\,dx$

Improper integrals

An integral with infinite limit(s) is an improper integral. An improper integral is convergent if we can find its value. We concentrate on this type. An improper integral is divergent if its value is infinite. In Chapter 10 we look in detail at convergence and divergence.

We apply improper integrals in Chapter 16 (Laplace Transforms).

Let us look at some general integral, $\int_a^b f(x)\,dx$. We know how to find its value. Suppose the upper limit is ∞. Instead of writing $\int_a^\infty f(x)\,dx$ we write the **improper integral** as $\displaystyle\lim_{b\to\infty}\int_a^b f(x)\,dx$. **Lim** is short for **limit**.

■■■■■■ **Example 9.18** ■■■■■■

We find the value of $\int_0^\infty e^{-3x}\,dx$.

$$\int_0^\infty e^{-3x}\,dx = \lim_{b\to\infty} \int_0^\infty e^{-3x}\,dx$$

$$= \lim_{b\to\infty}\left[\frac{-1}{3}e^{-3x}\right]_0^b$$

$$= \lim_{b\to\infty}\left[\frac{-1}{3}e^{-3b} - \frac{-1}{3}e^0\right]$$

$$= \lim_{b\to\infty}\frac{1}{3}\left[-\frac{1}{e^{3b}} + 1\right].$$

As $b\to\infty$, $3b\to\infty$, $e^{3b}\to\infty$, $\dfrac{1}{e^{3b}}\to 0$.

$$\therefore \int_0^\infty e^{-3x}\,dx = \frac{1}{3}\left[0+1\right] = \frac{1}{3}.$$

■■■■■ **EXERCISE 9.9** ■■■■■

Find the values of the improper integrals.

1 $\int_0^\infty e^{-2x}\,dx$ **3** $\int_1^\infty \frac{1}{x^4}\,dx$

2 $\int_1^\infty e^{-2x}\,dx$ **4** $\int_{-\infty}^2 e^{3x}\,dx$

5 $\int_2^\infty 4xe^{-x}\,dx$ using integration by parts.

The final exercise gives you the chance to apply some of the techniques from this chapter. The integration formula is included in each question to remind you of the application.

■■■■■ **EXERCISE 9.10** ■■■■■

1 The area under a velocity-time graph represents displacement, s, i.e.

$$s = \int_a^b v\,dt.$$

You are given the velocity function $v = \dfrac{3t}{1+t^2}$ in terms of time, t. Find the displacement over the first 5 seconds and over the first 10 seconds.

2   The length, S, of a curve is given by the integral

$$S = \int_a^b \sqrt{1 + \left(\frac{dy}{dx}\right)^2}\, dx.$$

For the curve $y = 2x^{3/2}$ find an expression for $\sqrt{1 + \left(\frac{dy}{dx}\right)^2}$. Now find the length along the curve from $x = 0$ to $x = 2.5$.

3 $F = ma$ connects the force, F, to the mass, m, and the acceleration, a or $\frac{dv}{dt}$.

For a velocity, $v = \left(5t^2 + 2t\right)^{3/2}$ find an expression for acceleration and for force where the mass is unity. Hence use

$$\text{Mean force} = \frac{1}{b - a}\int_a^b F\, dt$$

to find the mean force over the first 10 seconds.

4   In thermodynamics we look at the expansion of a gas in a cylinder against a piston. Pressure, p, and volume, V, are connected in the adiabatic case by $pV^n = C$ where C is a constant. The work done expanding the volume from V_1 to V_2 is given by

$$\text{Work done} = \int_{V_1}^{V_2} p\, dV.$$

Find a formula for the work done in terms of C, n, V_1 and V_2. Hence find a formula for the work done in doubling the original volume, V_1.

5   Rotating a curve through 2π radians about the x-axis creates a volume, V, given by

$$V = \pi \int_a^b y^2\, dx.$$

In each case find the volume generated between the lines $x = 0$ and $x = 1.5$

i) $y = \dfrac{1}{\sqrt{1 + 4x}}$,

ii) $y = \dfrac{1}{(1 + 4x)^{1/4}}$,

iii) $y = \left(\dfrac{x^2}{1 + 4x^2}\right)^{1/4}.$

Summary of standard integrals

y	$\int y\,dx$	
$(ax+b)^n$	$\dfrac{1}{a} \times \dfrac{(ax+b)^{n+1}}{n+1} + c$	for $n \neq -1$.
$\dfrac{1}{ax+b}$	$\dfrac{1}{a}\ln(ax+b) + c$	
$f'(x)[f(x)]^n$	$\dfrac{[f(x)]^{n+1}}{n+1} + c$	for $n \neq -1$.
$\dfrac{f'(x)}{f(x)}$	$\ln f(x) + c$	
$\dfrac{f'(x)}{\sqrt{f(x)}}$	$2\sqrt{f(x)} + c$	
$\dfrac{1}{x^2 - a^2}$	$\dfrac{1}{2a}\ln\left(\dfrac{x-a}{x+a}\right) + c$	where the coefficient of x^2 is 1.
$\dfrac{1}{a^2 - x^2}$	$\dfrac{1}{2a}\ln\left(\dfrac{a+x}{a-x}\right) + c$	where the coefficient of x^2 is -1.
$\dfrac{1}{\sqrt{a^2 - x^2}}$	$\sin^{-1}\left(\dfrac{x}{a}\right) + c$	where the coefficient of x^2 is -1.
$\dfrac{-1}{\sqrt{a^2 - x^2}}$	$\cos^{-1}\left(\dfrac{x}{a}\right) + c$	where the coefficient of x^2 is -1.
$\dfrac{1}{a^2 + x^2}$	$\dfrac{1}{a}\tan^{-1}\left(\dfrac{x}{a}\right) + c$	where the coefficient of x^2 is 1.

10 Series

The objectives of this chapter are to:

1. Describe the concept of convergence of a sequence to a limit.
2. Describe, by examples, sequences that diverge and oscillate.
3. Describe the conditions for convergence of series.
4. Use the ratio and comparison tests for convergence of series.
5. State Taylor's theorem and use the expansion to find the series for a function, $f(x)$, about any point $x = a$.
6. State Maclaurin's theorem and use the expansion to find the series for a function, $f(x)$.
7. Deduce that Maclaurin's theorem is a special case of Taylor's theorem.
8. Define the radius of convergence of a power series.
9. Use Maclaurin's series to find combinations of series.
10. Apply series to find derivatives and to find approximate values of definite integrals.

Introduction

In both Volumes 1 and 2 we have seen sequences and series. They have been arithmetic and geometric progressions and series (Volume 1, Chapter 15), the binomial series (Volume 2, Chapter 5) and the exponential series (Volume 2, Chapter 6). Here we look to see if sequences and series converge or diverge or oscillate. Using differentiation we see how to derive series by applying Taylor's theorem and Maclaurin's theorem. Towards the end of the chapter we apply our results to calculus.

◼ ASSIGNMENT ◼

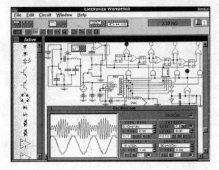

Our Assignment for this chapter is based on the electrical circuit in Fig. 10.1. We have an emf of 96 V together with an inductor of 8 H, a capacitor of 5×10^{-3} F and a resistor of 64 Ω in series. We may mathematically model this circuit using a differential equation. The solution of that differential equation relates the current, i A, to the time, t s, by $i = 4e^{-4t} \sin 3t$. The exponential decay in this solution indicates a damping effect on the electrical oscillations.

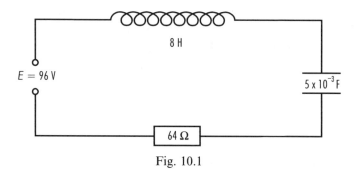

Fig. 10.1

During the chapter we will look at the exponential and trigonometric parts separately and then together. Using integration we will calculate the mean current.

Convergence of sequences

A sequence is a list of terms connected by some pattern. Suppose we have a general sequence, $u_1, u_2, u_3, \ldots, u_n, \ldots$. A general term in the sequence would be u_n. We write the nth term as u_n and the $(n+1)$th term as u_{n+1}. A simple numerical sequence is $1, 2, 3, 4, \ldots$. The general arithmetic progression; $a, a+d, a+2d, \ldots$; and the general geometric progression; $a, ar, ar^2, \ldots$; are algebraic examples of sequences.

A sequence may either converge or not converge. It may converge to some value, i.e. it may converge to a limit, ℓ. Mathematically we write $\underset{n \to \infty}{\text{Lim}}\, u_n = \ell$.

Any sequence that does *not* converge is said to diverge. Within the divergence category we also have sequences that oscillate. For a sequence that strictly diverges $\underset{n \to \infty}{\text{Lim}}\, u_n = \infty$ or $\underset{n \to \infty}{\text{Lim}}\, u_n = -\infty$.

The sequence $1, -1, 1, -1, 1, -1, \ldots$ oscillates between 1 and -1. Sometimes its sum will be 0 and sometimes its sum will be 1. We have already seen the oscillation of graphs. The sine and cosine graphs oscillate about the horizontal axis.

We may be interested in all these types of sequences for various reasons. Often we aim to control a sequence. This we can do for a convergent one, working to where it converges.

Examples 10.1

i) $\dfrac{2}{1}, \dfrac{3}{2}, \dfrac{4}{3}, \dfrac{5}{4}, \ldots$ is a sequence with a general term $\dfrac{n+1}{n}$.

Notice how each successive term is smaller than the previous term. The decimal equivalents of these fractions confirm that as $n \to \infty$ the terms in the sequence tend to 1, i.e. the sequence converges to 1. You can see this in Fig. 10.1 with the graph of

$$y = \dfrac{x+1}{x}.$$

> Using x in place of n graphically.

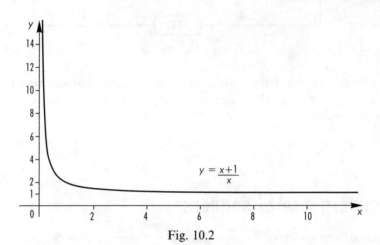

Fig. 10.2

ii) $1^2, 2^2, 3^2, 4^2, \ldots$ is a sequence with a general term n^2.

Each term is bigger than the term before it. As n increases, n^2 increases yet faster, i.e. as $n \to \infty$ $n^2 \to \infty$. This shows the sequence is divergent. You can see this in Fig. 10.2 with the graph of $y = x^2$.

> Using x in place of n graphically.

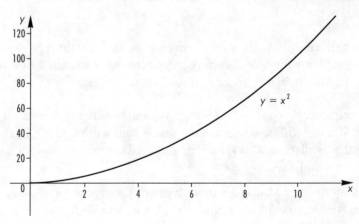

Fig. 10.3

iii) $-1^2, -2^2, -3^2, \ldots$ is a sequence with a general term $-n^2$.
As $n \to \infty$ $-n^2 \to -\infty$. This shows the sequence is divergent. You
can see this in Fig. 10.3 with the graph of
$y = -x^2$.

> Using x in place of n
> graphically.

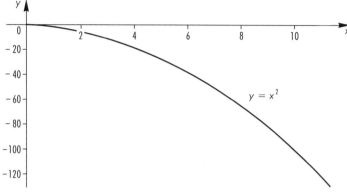

Fig. 10.4

iv) $\cos \pi, \cos 2\pi, \cos 3\pi, \ldots$ is a sequence with a general term $\cos n\pi$.
As $n \to \infty$ the terms oscillate between -1 and 1. Because this
sequence is not convergent we label it divergent.

We look further at the general nth and $(n+1)$th terms of a sequence.
Monotonic terms are terms that follow on from one to another.

When $u_{n+1} \geqslant u_n$ the sequence is said to be monotonic increasing.
When $u_{n+1} > u_n$ the sequence is said to be strictly monotonic increasing.
When $u_{n+1} \leqslant u_n$ the sequence is said to be monotonic decreasing.
When $u_{n+1} < u_n$ the sequence is said to be strictly monotonic decreasing.

████████ **Examples 10.2** ████████

i) $1, 2, 3, 4, 5, \ldots$ is a sequence. The nth term is n and the $(n+1)$th term
is $n+1$, i.e. $u_n = n$ and $u_{n+1} = n+1$.

Because $n+1 > n$,

i.e. $u_{n+1} > u_n$,

the sequence is strictly monotonic increasing.

ii) $1, \dfrac{1}{2}, \dfrac{1}{3}, \dfrac{1}{4}, \ldots$ is a sequence. The nth term is $\dfrac{1}{n}$ and the $(n+1)$th term is

$\dfrac{1}{n+1}$, i.e. $u_n = \dfrac{1}{n}$ and $u_{n+1} = \dfrac{1}{n+1}$.

Because $\dfrac{1}{n+1} < \dfrac{1}{n}$,

i.e. $u_{n+1} < u_n$,

the sequence is strictly monotonic decreasing.

iii) $3, -4, 5, -6, 7, -8, \ldots$ is a sequence. The nth term is $(-1)^{n+1}(n+2)$ and the $(n+1)$th term is $(-1)^{n+2}(n+2+1)$, i.e. $u_n = (-1)^{n+1}(n+2)$ and $u_{n+1} = (-1)^{n+2}(n+3)$.

The signs of both the nth and $(n+1)$th terms alternate $+/-$. This means we *cannot* determine if the sequence is increasing or decreasing.

■■■■ EXERCISE 10.1 ■■■■

In Questions **1–5** decide if each sequence is convergent or not convergent.

1 $2, 4, 6, 8, \ldots$

2 $\dfrac{1}{3}, \dfrac{1}{3^2}, \dfrac{1}{3^3}, \ldots$

3 $1, \dfrac{1}{\sqrt{2}}, \dfrac{1}{\sqrt{3}}, \dfrac{1}{\sqrt{4}}, \ldots$

4 $5, -10, 20, -40, \ldots$

5 $\dfrac{1}{2}, \dfrac{2}{3}, \dfrac{3}{4}, \dfrac{4}{5}, \ldots$

In Questions **6–10** you are given the nth term, u_n. Write down the $(n+1)$th term. Decide if the sequence is (strictly) monotonic increasing or decreasing.

6 $\dfrac{1}{n}$

7 $\dfrac{1}{n(n+2)}$

8 $\sqrt{n+2}$

9 $(n+1)(n+2)$

10 $\dfrac{n}{2^n}$

Limiting values

We are interested in both sequences and series when we consider more and more terms. For a general, nth term, u_n we are interested as $n \to \infty$. We know that as $n \to \infty$, $n^2 \to \infty$, $2^n \to \infty$, $\ldots$. Also as $n \to \infty$, $\dfrac{1}{n} \to 0$.

When terms tend to infinity we have no control. In contrast we do have control when they tend to a specific, finite, limit. Because of this we will attempt to divide by n (or perhaps by n^2).

Examples 10.3

As $n \to \infty$ find the limiting values of   i) $\dfrac{2n-3}{3n+5}$,   ii) $\dfrac{n^2-13n+5}{2n^2+4n-1}$.

i) $\dfrac{2n-3}{3n+5} = \dfrac{2n/n - 3/n}{3n/n + 5/n}$

> Dividing each term by n.

$$= \dfrac{2 - \dfrac{3}{n}}{3 + \dfrac{5}{n}}.$$

As $n \to \infty$, $\dfrac{1}{n} \to 0$ so also $\dfrac{3}{n} \to 0$ and $\dfrac{5}{n} \to 0$. Then we can write

$$\operatorname*{Lim}_{n\to\infty} \left\{ \dfrac{2n-3}{3n+5} \right\} = \operatorname*{Lim}_{n\to\infty} \left\{ \dfrac{2 - \dfrac{3}{n}}{3 + \dfrac{5}{n}} \right\}$$

$$= \dfrac{2}{3}.$$

ii) $\dfrac{n^2-13n+5}{2n^2+4n-1} = \dfrac{n^2/n^2 - 13n/n^2 + 5/n^2}{2n^2/n^2 + 4n/n^2 - 1/n^2}$

> Dividing each term by n^2.

$$= \dfrac{1 - \dfrac{13}{n} + \dfrac{5}{n^2}}{2 + \dfrac{4}{n} - \dfrac{1}{n^2}}.$$

As $n \to \infty$, $\dfrac{1}{n} \to 0$ and $\dfrac{1}{n^2} \to 0$. Then we can write

$$\operatorname*{Lim}_{n\to\infty} \left\{ \dfrac{n^2-13n+5}{2n^2+4n-1} \right\} = \operatorname*{Lim}_{n\to\infty} \left\{ \dfrac{1 - \dfrac{13}{n} + \dfrac{5}{n^2}}{2 + \dfrac{4}{n} - \dfrac{1}{n^2}} \right\}$$

$$= \dfrac{1}{2}.$$

Examples 10.4

As $n \to \infty$ find the limiting values of   i) $\dfrac{n-2}{n^2-n-2}$,   ii) $\dfrac{n^2-n-2}{n-2}$.

We notice the quadratic expression factorises, i.e.
$$n^2 - n - 2 = (n-2)(n+1).$$
Both the numerator and the denominator have a common factor of $n-2$.
In each example we cancel this to leave $n+1$.

i) $\displaystyle \text{Lim}_{n \to \infty} \left\{ \frac{n-2}{n^2 - n - 2} \right\} = \text{Lim}_{n \to \infty} \left\{ \frac{n-2}{(n-2)(n+1)} \right\}$

$\displaystyle = \text{Lim}_{n \to \infty} \left\{ \frac{1}{n+1} \right\}.$

As $n \to \infty$, $(n+1) \to \infty$ so that $\dfrac{1}{n+1} \to 0$.

ii) $\displaystyle \text{Lim}_{n \to \infty} \left\{ \frac{n^2 - n - 2}{n-2} \right\} = \text{Lim}_{n \to \infty} \left\{ \frac{(n-2)(n+1)}{n-2} \right\}$

$\displaystyle = \text{Lim}_{n \to \infty} \left\{ n+1 \right\}.$

As $n \to \infty$, also $(n+1) \to \infty$.

EXERCISE 10.2

In each question find the limiting values as $n \to \infty$.

1 $\displaystyle \text{Lim}_{n \to \infty} \left\{ \frac{n+1}{n+2} \right\}$

2 $\displaystyle \text{Lim}_{n \to \infty} \left\{ \frac{n-4}{2n+1} \right\}$

3 $\displaystyle \text{Lim}_{n \to \infty} \left\{ \frac{2n-5}{3n-3} \right\}$

4 $\displaystyle \text{Lim}_{n \to \infty} \left\{ \frac{2n^2 + 3n + 1}{n^2 - 2n + 3} \right\}$

5 $\displaystyle \text{Lim}_{n \to \infty} \left\{ \frac{4n^2 - 3}{5n^2 + 2n} \right\}$

6 $\displaystyle \text{Lim}_{n \to \infty} \left\{ \frac{n^2 - 3n}{n^2 - n - 6} \right\}$

7 $\displaystyle \text{Lim}_{n \to \infty} \left\{ \frac{n-3}{n^2 - n - 6} \right\}$

8 $\displaystyle \text{Lim}_{n \to \infty} \left\{ \frac{n^2 - 3n - 4}{n - 4} \right\}$

9 $\displaystyle \text{Lim}_{n \to \infty} \left\{ \frac{n^2 - 9}{n^2 - 2n - 3} \right\}$

10 $\displaystyle \text{Lim}_{n \to \infty} \left\{ \frac{2n^2 + 3n + 1}{n^2 - 2n - 3} \right\}$

Series

Examples 10.1 show a selection of sequences. As the Chapter title states we are interested in series. We form a series by adding the terms of a sequence.

Example 10.5

$\dfrac{2}{1}, \dfrac{3}{2}, \dfrac{4}{3}, \dfrac{5}{4}, \ldots$ is a sequence.

$\dfrac{2}{1} + \dfrac{3}{2} + \dfrac{4}{3} + \dfrac{5}{4} + \ldots$ is a series.

When we look at the convergence (or divergence) of a series we avoid looking at individual terms. The terms may look to be getting smaller, but the series may be diverging rather than converging.

In the remainder of the chapter we continue with series.

Convergent and divergent series

For a series of n terms we may find its sum, S_n.

As $n \to \infty$ if S_n tends to some limit, ℓ, then the series is convergent, i.e. $\text{Lim}_{n \to \infty} S_n \to \ell$.

As $n \to \infty$ if S_n does *not* tend to a limit then the series is *not* convergent, i.e. it is divergent. We label oscillatory series as divergent series.

▰▰▰▰ **Examples 10.6** ▰▰▰▰▰▰▰▰▰▰▰▰▰▰▰▰

i) $1 + \dfrac{1}{2} + \dfrac{1}{4} + \dfrac{1}{8} + \ldots$ is a geometric series. Its sum, S_n, is given by the formula

$$S_n = \frac{a(1 - rn)}{1 - r}$$

i.e. $$S_n = \frac{1\left(1 - \left(\frac{1}{2}\right)^n\right)}{1 - \frac{1}{2}}$$

> First term, $a = 1$.
> Common ratio, $r = \frac{1}{2}$.

$$= \frac{1(1 - 1/2^n)}{\frac{1}{2}}$$

$$= 2\left(1 - \frac{1}{2^n}\right).$$

As $n \to \infty$, $2^n \to \infty$ and $\dfrac{1}{2^n} \to 0$.

This means $S_n \to 2(1 - 0)$

i.e. $S_n \to 2$.

Using our general statement for convergence, $\text{Lim}_{n \to \infty} S_n \to \ell$, our limit, ℓ, is 2. This means $\text{Lim}_{n \to \infty} S_n \to 2$, i.e. the series is convergent.

ii) $1 + 3 + 9 + 27 \ldots$ is a geometric series. Its sum, S_n, is given by the formula

$$S_n = \frac{a(1 - r^n)}{1 - r}$$

i.e. $$S_n = \frac{1(1 - 3^n)}{1 - 3}$$

> First term, $a = 1$.
> Common ratio, $r = 3$.

$$S_n = \frac{1(1 - 3^n)}{-2}$$

$$= \frac{1}{2}\left(3^n - 1\right)$$

As $n \to \infty$, $3^n \to \infty$.

This means $S_n \to \infty$, i.e. there is no limit for the sum, S_n. Hence the series is divergent.

iii) $1 - 1 + 1 - 1 + 1 \ldots$ is an oscillatory series, i.e. a divergent series. Sometimes its sum, S_n, is 1 and sometimes it is 0, i.e. it does *not* tend to a specific limit.

We look alternatively at Example 10.6i); this time in stages. Including more terms at each subsequent calculation we find the value of the sum.

Example 10.7

Our series is $1 + \frac{1}{2} + \frac{1}{4} + \frac{1}{8} + \ldots$

Sum of the first term only, S_1 $= 1.0000$

Sum of the first two terms, $S_2 = 1 + \frac{1}{2}$ $= 1.5000$

Sum of the first three terms, $S_3 = 1 + \frac{1}{2} + \frac{1}{4}$ $= 1.7500$

Sum of the first four terms, $S_4 = 1.7500 + \frac{1}{8}$ $= 1.8750$

Sum of the first five terms, $S_5 = 1.8750 + \frac{1}{16}$ $= 1.9375$

Sum of the first six terms, $S_6 = 1.9375 + \frac{1}{32}$ $= 1.96875$

Sum of the first seven terms, $S_7 = 1.96875 + \frac{1}{64}$ $= 1.9844$

This staged method is one of looking at the partial sum of the series. As $n \to \infty$ the sum appears to be approaching 2. We can find the sum to infinity of a geometric series using the formula

$$S_\infty = \frac{a}{1 - r}$$

$$= \frac{1}{1 - \frac{1}{2}}$$

$$= 2, \quad \text{as expected.}$$

A series cannot be convergent unless its terms eventually tend to 0, i.e. as
$n \to \infty$ $u_n \to 0$. This statement needs care. If we start with $n \to \infty$ $u_n \to 0$
then this does *not* guarantee the series to be convergent.

If the terms do not tend to 0 then the series is *not* convergent, i.e. as
$n \to \infty$ $u_n \not\to 0$. Hence we use this to test if a series is not convergent.

We look at this necessary condition in Examples 10.8. You will see that it
is not sufficient to decide if the series is convergent or divergent.

Examples 10.8

i) In the series $1 + \frac{1}{2} + \frac{1}{4} + \frac{1}{8} + \frac{1}{16} + \frac{1}{32} + \dots$ each term is getting
    smaller. In fact as $n \to \infty$ $u_n \to 0$. We have shown already using two
    methods that this series is convergent. Later we will apply other tests
    for convergence to demonstrate some of the alternatives available.

ii) In the series $1 + \frac{1}{2} + \frac{1}{3} + \frac{1}{4} + \frac{1}{5} + \frac{1}{6} + \dots$ again each term is getting
    smaller. Again as $n \to \infty$ $u_n \to 0$. However, later we will show this
    series is divergent.

A more rigorous test is the **ratio test** which compares the $(n+1)$th term
(u_{n+1}) to the nth term (u_n). It uses a modulus sign to allow for series with
terms of alternating signs.

If $\lim\limits_{n \to \infty} \left| \frac{u_{n+1}}{u_n} \right| < 1$ **then the series is convergent.**

If $\lim\limits_{n \to \infty} \left| \frac{u_{n+1}}{u_n} \right| > 1$ **then the series is divergent.**

If $\lim\limits_{n \to \infty} \left| \frac{u_{n+1}}{u_n} \right| = 1$ **then we *cannot* determine if the series is convergent or divergent.** In this case we need to apply another test.

Examples 10.9

i) We re-write the series $1 + \frac{1}{2} + \frac{1}{4} + \frac{1}{8} + \frac{1}{16} + \frac{1}{32} + \dots$

    as powers of 2, i.e. $\frac{1}{2^0} + \frac{1}{2^1} + \frac{1}{2^2} + \frac{1}{2^3} + \frac{1}{2^4} + \frac{1}{2^5} + \dots$

    Notice the power of 2 is always 1 less than the number of the term.
    Now $u_n = \frac{1}{2^{n-1}}$ and $u_{n+1} = \frac{1}{2^n}$ so that

$$\left| \frac{u_{n+1}}{u_n} \right| = \frac{\frac{1}{2^n}}{\frac{1}{2^{n-1}}} = \frac{1}{2^n} \times \frac{2^{n-1}}{1} = \frac{1}{2^n} \times \frac{2^n}{2} = \frac{1}{2}.$$

Using the ratio test we have

$$\lim_{n\to\infty} \left| \frac{u_{n+1}}{u_n} \right| = \frac{1}{2}.$$

Because this limiting value is less than 1 the series converges. Notice the ratio test has *not* given the sum to which it converges, only that the series does converge.

ii) We re-write the series $-3 + 9 - 27 + 81 \ldots$ as powers of 3, i.e. $-3^1 + 3^2 - 3^3 + 3^4 \ldots$

Now $u_n = (-1)^n 3^n$ and $u_{n+1} = (-1)^{n+1} 3^{n+1}$ so that

$$\left| \frac{u_{n+1}}{u_n} \right| = \left| \frac{(-1)^{n+1} 3^{n+1}}{(-1)^n 3^n} \right| = \frac{3^n \times 3}{3^n} = 3.$$

Using the ratio test we have

$$\lim_{n\to\infty} \left| \frac{u_{n+1}}{u_n} \right| = 3.$$

Because this limiting value is greater than 1 the series diverges.

iii) For the series $1 + \dfrac{1}{2} + \dfrac{1}{3} + \dfrac{1}{4} + \dfrac{1}{5} + \dfrac{1}{6} + \ldots$ we write down general terms. $u_n = \dfrac{1}{n}$ and $u_{n+1} = \dfrac{1}{n+1}$ so that

$$\left| \frac{u_{n+1}}{u_n} \right| = \frac{\frac{1}{n+1}}{\frac{1}{n}} = \frac{1}{n+1} \times \frac{n}{1} = \frac{n}{n+1}.$$

We divide each term by n and apply the ratio test, i.e.

$$\lim_{n\to\infty} \left| \frac{u_{n+1}}{u_n} \right| = \lim_{n\to\infty} \left| \frac{1}{1 + \frac{1}{n}} \right| = 1.$$

The ratio test cannot determine if this series converges or diverges. We need to apply an alternative test.

An alternative test is a **comparison test**. Here we test an infinite series against another known infinite series, both of positive terms. Suppose the series under test has a general term u_n and a sum $\sum u_n$. The known series has a general term v_n and a sum $\sum v_n$.

If $u_n < v_n$ and $\sum v_n$ is convergent then $\sum u_n$ is also convergent.

If $u_n > v_n$ and $\sum v_n$ is divergent then $\sum u_n$ is also divergent.

━━━━ **Example 10.10** ━━━━━━━━━━━━━

We return to the series of Example 10.8ii),

$$1 + \frac{1}{2} + \frac{1}{3} + \frac{1}{4} + \frac{1}{5} + \frac{1}{6} + \ldots \quad \text{This is the harmonic series.}$$

After the first and second terms we group subsequent terms together, i.e.

$$1 + \frac{1}{2} + \left(\frac{1}{3} + \frac{1}{4}\right) + \left(\frac{1}{5} + \frac{1}{6} + \frac{1}{7} + \frac{1}{8}\right) + \left(\frac{1}{9} + \ldots + \frac{1}{16}\right) + \ldots$$

We compare this series against a known series,

$$1 + \frac{1}{2} + \left(\frac{1}{4} + \frac{1}{4}\right) + \left(\frac{1}{8} + \frac{1}{8} + \frac{1}{8} + \frac{1}{8}\right) + \left(\frac{1}{16} + \ldots + \frac{1}{16}\right) + \ldots$$

Comparing bracketed terms we have

$$\left(\frac{1}{3} + \frac{1}{4}\right) > \left(\frac{1}{4} + \frac{1}{4}\right), \quad \left(\frac{1}{5} + \frac{1}{6} + \frac{1}{7} + \frac{1}{8}\right) > \left(\frac{1}{8} + \frac{1}{8} + \frac{1}{8} + \frac{1}{8}\right),$$

$$\left(\frac{1}{9} + \ldots + \frac{1}{16}\right) > \left(\frac{1}{16} + \ldots + \frac{1}{16}\right), \quad \ldots$$

We simplify the brackets in the known series to give

$$1 + \frac{1}{2} + \frac{1}{2} + \frac{1}{2} + \frac{1}{2} + \ldots \quad \text{which is clearly } not \text{ convergent. This comparison}$$

test shows that our harmonic series is also *not* convergent.

Suppose we have an infinite series of positive and negative terms. It has a general term u_n and a sum $\sum u_n$.

If the sum of the moduli is convergent then the series is absolutely convergent, i.e. if $\sum |u_n|$ is convergent then $\sum u_n$ is absolutely convergent.

If the sum of the moduli is *not* convergent yet the sum of the series is convergent then the series is conditionally convergent, i.e. if $\sum |u_n|$ is *not* convergent yet $\sum u_n$ is convergent then $\sum u_n$ is conditionally convergent.

━━━━ **Examples 10.11** ━━━━━━━━━━━━━

i) We re-write the series $\quad 1 - \frac{1}{2} + \frac{1}{4} - \frac{1}{8} + \frac{1}{16} - \frac{1}{32} \ldots$

as powers of 2, i.e. $\quad \frac{1}{2^0} - \frac{1}{2^1} + \frac{1}{2^2} - \frac{1}{2^3} + \frac{1}{2^4} - \frac{1}{2^5} \ldots$

Using our result from Example 10.9i) the sum of the moduli, $\frac{1}{2^0} + \frac{1}{2^1} + \frac{1}{2^2} + \frac{1}{2^3} + \frac{1}{2^4} + \frac{1}{2^5} + \ldots$ is convergent. This means that our series of alternate positive and negative terms is absolutely convergent.

ii)   Let us look at the series $1 - \dfrac{1}{2} + \dfrac{1}{3} - \dfrac{1}{4} + \dfrac{1}{5} - \dfrac{1}{6} \cdots$

Using our result from Example 10.10 we know the sum of the moduli, $1 + \dfrac{1}{2} + \dfrac{1}{3} + \dfrac{1}{4} + \dfrac{1}{5} + \dfrac{1}{6} + \ldots$, is divergent.

We could prove that the series $1 - \dfrac{1}{2} + \dfrac{1}{3} - \dfrac{1}{4} + \dfrac{1}{5} - \dfrac{1}{6} \cdots$ is convergent. Hence it is conditionally convergent.

ASSIGNMENT

We show the graph of current, i, against time, t, in Fig. 10.5. It appears to tend to zero current within several seconds. Later we will look in greater detail at the exponential and trigonometric parts in terms of their series.

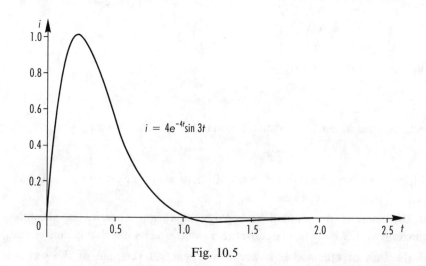

$$i = 4e^{-4t}\sin 3t$$

Fig. 10.5

EXERCISE 10.3

Decide which series are convergent.

In Questions **1–5** we give the series based on the nth term, u_n and in Questions **6–10** we give the early terms of the series.

1 $\displaystyle\sum \frac{3^n}{n(n+1)}$

2 $\displaystyle\sum \frac{2^n}{n}$

3 $\displaystyle\sum n e^{-n}$

4 $\displaystyle\sum \frac{n}{3^n}$

5 $\displaystyle\sum \frac{4^n}{n!}$

6 $1 + \dfrac{1}{3} + \dfrac{1}{9} + \dfrac{1}{27} + \dfrac{1}{81} + \ldots$

7 $\quad 3 + \dfrac{9}{2} + 9 + \dfrac{81}{4} + \dfrac{243}{5} + \ldots$

8 $\quad 2 + \dfrac{2}{2} + \dfrac{2}{3} + \dfrac{2}{4} + \dfrac{2}{5} + \dfrac{2}{6} \ldots$

9 $\quad 10 - 5 + 2.5 - 1.25 + \ldots$

10 $\quad 1 + \dfrac{1}{1/2} + \dfrac{1}{1/3} + \dfrac{1}{1/4} \ldots$

Taylor's series

Taylor's theorem allows us to write a function, $f(x)$, as a power series. We do this near some given point, say $x = a$. This means $(x - a)$ is a small value. It is based upon the assumption we know what happens to the function and its derivatives at $x = a$. We can write that 'we expand the function about $x = a$'.

We start with a general power series based upon $(x - a)$, i.e.

$$f(x) = \alpha_0 + \alpha_1(x - a) + \alpha_2(x - a)^2 + \alpha_3(x - a)^3 + \ldots$$

where the αs are constants. The theorem is based upon the series being convergent. Also the function and all its derivatives must exist. We apply this, using successive differentiation.

To begin we substitute for $x = a$ in the general power series to give

$$f(a) = \alpha_0.$$

i.e. $x - a = 0$.

Differentiating we get

$$f'(x) = \alpha_1 + 2\alpha_2(x - a) + 3\alpha_3(x - a)^2 + 4\alpha_4(x - a)^3 + \ldots$$

Again we substitute $x = a$ to give

$$f'(a) = \alpha_1.$$

Differentiating again we get

$$f''(x) = 2\alpha_2 + 6\alpha_3(x - a) + 12\alpha_4(x - a)^2 + \ldots$$

Again we substitute $x = a$ to give

$$f''(a) = 2\alpha_2$$

i.e. $\quad \dfrac{f''(a)}{2!} = \alpha_2.$

2! establishes a better pattern than a simple 2.

Differentiating yet again we get

$$f'''(x) = 6\alpha_3 + 24\alpha_4(x - a) + \ldots$$

Again we substitute $x = a$ to give

$$f'''(a) = 6\alpha_3$$

i.e. $\quad \dfrac{f'''(a)}{3!} = \alpha_3$

3! = 6.

We continue with this technique finding values for all the αs. According to Taylor's theorem this gives the following expansion (or series)

$$f(x) = f(a) + (x - a)f'(a) + (x - a)^2\dfrac{f''(a)}{2!} + (x - a)^3\dfrac{f'''(a)}{3!} + \ldots$$

━━━━━━ **Example 10.12** ━━━━━━

Using Taylor's series find a power series for $\ln x$ in terms of $(x - a)$ up to and including the $(x - a)^3$ term.

Our function is $f(x) = \ln x$. We need to differentiate it and substitute for $x = a$. We do this in columns. The general differentiation is to the left and the specific substitution is to the right.

$$f(x) = \ln x \qquad\qquad f(a) = \ln a$$

$$f'(x) = \frac{1}{x} \qquad\qquad f'(a) = \frac{1}{a}$$

$$f''(x) = -\frac{1}{x^2} \qquad\qquad f''(a) = -\frac{1}{a^2}$$

$$f'''(x) = \frac{2}{x^3}\dots \qquad\qquad f'''(a) = \frac{2}{a^3}\dots$$

We substitute these values into Taylor's series, i.e.

$$f(x) = f(a) + (x - a)f'(a) + (x - a)^2\frac{f''(a)}{2!} + (x - a)^3\frac{f'''(a)}{3!} + \dots$$

which becomes

$$\ln x = \ln a + \frac{(x - a)}{a} - \frac{(x - a)^2}{2a^2} + \frac{(x - a)^3}{3a^3}\dots$$

Notice there is some numerical cancellation. For example in the fourth term $\dfrac{2}{3!} = \dfrac{2}{3 \times 2 \times 1} = \dfrac{1}{3}$.

This is a general power series for $\ln x$. Now we can substitute a numerical value for a, as in Example 10.13.

━━━━━━ **Example 10.13** ━━━━━━

Find the value of $\ln 1.05$ using Taylor's series.

From the previous example we have a general series for $\ln x$ about the point where $x = a$. Comparing $\ln x$ and $\ln 1.05$ we have $x = 1.05$. Remember the expansion is valid close to a specific value. For $x = 1.05$ we use $a = 1$ so that $(x - a)$ is 0.05, a small value.

Then $$\ln x = \ln a + \frac{(x - a)}{a} - \frac{(x - a)^2}{2a^2} + \frac{(x - a)^3}{3a^3}\dots$$

becomes

$$\ln 1.05 = \ln 1 + \frac{0.05}{1} - \frac{0.05^2}{2} + \frac{0.05^3}{3}\dots$$

$$= 0 + 0.05 - 0.00125 + 0.0000416\dots$$

$$= 0.04879\dots$$

This compares with the calculator value of $0.0487901\dots$, agreeing with the first five decimal places.

There is an alternative version of Taylor's series. Compared with the first version we replace x with $x+h$ and a with x. This means that $x - a = x + h - x = h$. Now we have

$$f(x + h) = f(x) + hf'(x) + h^2\frac{f''(x)}{2!} + h^3\frac{f'''(x)}{3!} + \cdots$$

Example 10.14

We apply the alternative version of Taylor's series to the function $f(x + h) = (x + h)^n$.

This means that $f(x) = x^n$.

We differentiate several times to build up a pattern, i.e.

$$f'(x) = nx^{n-1}$$
$$f''(x) = n(n - 1)x^{n-2}$$
$$f'''(x) = n(n - 1)(n - 2)x^{n-3} \ldots$$

Notice, in contrast to the first version, there is no substitution for x. We simply substitute for the functions and derivatives into

$$f(x + h) = f(x) + hf'(x) + h^2\frac{f''(x)}{2!} + h^3\frac{f'''(x)}{3!} + \cdots$$

to get $(x + h)^n = x^n + nhx^{n-1} + \dfrac{n(n - 1)h^2x^{n-2}}{2!}$

$$+ \frac{n(n - 1)(n - 2)h^3x^{n-3}}{3!} + \cdots$$

You ought to recognise this as the binomial theorem (Volume 2, Chapter 5).

ASSIGNMENT

We could look at our equation for current, i, in terms of time, t, i.e. $i = 4e^{-4t}\sin 3t$. This would be about some general point, say $t = 1$ or 0.5 or $\ldots$. First we would find separate series for each of e^{-4t} and $\sin 3t$. Then the resultant series is a product of 4 and those series. In the next section, Maclaurin's theorem, we look at this in detail.

EXERCISE 10.4

1   Using Taylor's series establish a pattern for $\cosh x$ as a series of powers of $(x - 1)$. This means you are expanding $\cosh x$ about the point where $x = 1$.

2   Expand the function $f(x) = \dfrac{1}{x}$ in terms of $(x - a)$ and its powers as far as the power 3.

3 a) Find the first 4 terms of the following series

i) $\cos(x + \alpha)$, ii) $\sin(x + \alpha)$, iii) $\cos(x - \alpha)$,
iv) $\sin(x - \alpha)$.

b) Use your results to find the approximate values of

i) $\cos 92°$ as $\cos(90° + 2°)$, ii) $\sin 275°$,
iii) $\cos 177°$ as $\cos(180° - 3°)$, iv) $\sin 357.5°$.

Because Taylor's series is derived using calculus remember to convert the degrees to radians.

4 Find the Taylor series expansion for $x^2 \ln x$ in powers of $(x - 1)$ to the term $(x - 1)^4$.

5 Given $y = x^x$ show that $\ln y = x \ln x$. Using logarithmic differentiation find the first and second derivatives of y with respect to x. Using Taylor's series find the first three terms of x^x as powers of $(x - 1)$.

Maclaurin's series

Maclaurin's theorem also allows us to write a function, $f(x)$, as a power series. We do this about $x = 0$. It is based upon the assumption we know what happens to the function and its derivatives at $x = 0$. We can write that 'we expand the function about $x = 0$'.

We start with a general power series,

$$f(x) = \alpha_0 + \alpha_1 x + \alpha_2 x^2 + \alpha_3 x^3 + \alpha_4 x^4 \ldots$$

The theorem is based upon the series being convergent. Also the function and all its derivatives exist. We apply this, using successive differentiation.

To begin we substitute for $x = 0$ in the general power series to give

$$f(0) = \alpha_0.$$

Differentiating we get

$$f'(x) = \alpha_1 + 2\alpha_2 x + 3\alpha_3 x^2 + 4\alpha_4 x^3 + \ldots$$

Again we substitute $x = 0$ to give

$$f'(0) = \alpha_1.$$

Differentiating again we get

$$f''(x) = 2\alpha_2 + 6\alpha_3 x + 12\alpha_4 x^2 + \ldots$$

Again we substitute $x = 0$ to give

$$f''(0) = 2\alpha_2$$

i.e. $\dfrac{f''(0)}{2!} = \alpha_2.$

2! establishes a better pattern than a simple 2.

Differentiating yet again we get

$$f'''(x) = 6\alpha_3 + 24\alpha_4 x + \ldots$$

Again we substitute $x = 0$ to give

$$f'''(0) = 6\alpha_3$$

i.e. $\dfrac{f'''(0)}{3!} = \alpha_3$

$3! = 6.$

We continue with this technique finding values for all the αs. According to Maclaurin's theorem this gives the following expansion (or series)

$$f(x) = f(0) + xf'(0) + x^2\frac{f''(0)}{2!} + x^3\frac{f'''(0)}{3!} + \cdots$$

You can see that Maclaurin's series is a special case of Taylor's series, replacing $x = a$ with $x = 0$. This means we could derive Taylor's series and replace a with 0. Like Taylor's series we show the first few terms to establish the pattern.

Remember that we *cannot* divide by zero in Mathematics. Sometimes this can stop us using Maclaurin's series. This has been the case already. In Example 10.12 the function, $f(x) = \ln x$, and its derivatives are not defined for $x = 0$. This means we need an alternative series for some natural logarithms using Maclaurin's series.

■■■■ ASSIGNMENT ■■■■

We are going to apply Maclaurin's series twice. This is to find series for both e^{-4t} and $\sin 3t$.

Our function is $f(t) = e^{-4t}$. We need to differentiate it and substitute for $x = 0$. We do this in columns. The general differentiation is to the left and the specific substitution is to the right.

$$f(t) = e^{-4t} \qquad\qquad f(0) = e^0 \quad\; = 1$$
$$f'(t) = -4e^{-4t} \qquad\qquad f'(0) = -4e^0 = -4$$
$$f''(t) = 16e^{-4t} \qquad\qquad f''(0) = 16e^0 = 16$$
$$f'''(t) = -64e^{-4t} \ldots \qquad f'''(0) = -64e^0 = -64 \ldots$$

We substitute these values into Maclaurin's series, i.e.

$$f(t) = f(0) + tf'(0) + t^2\frac{f''(0)}{2!} + t^3\frac{f'''(0)}{3!} + \cdots$$

which becomes

$$e^{-4t} = 1 + t(-4) + t^2\frac{(16)}{2!} + t^3\frac{(-64)}{3!} + \cdots$$

i.e. $e^{-4t} = 1 - 4t + \dfrac{(-4t)^2}{2!} + \dfrac{(-4t)^3}{3!} + \cdots$

$(-4)^2 = 16,$
$(-4)^3 = -64.$

or $e^{-4t} = 1 - 4t + 8t^2 - \dfrac{32}{3}t^3 \ldots$

Following this pattern the next term is $\dfrac{(-4t)^4}{4!}$. You can check that it simplifies to $\dfrac{32}{3}t^4$.

This time our function is $f(t) = \sin 3t$. Again we differentiate it and substitute for $x = 0$ in columns. Notice we use more terms than for the exponential series.

$$
\begin{aligned}
f(t) &= \sin 3t & f(0) &= \sin 0 & &= 0\\
f'(t) &= 3\cos 3t & f'(0) &= 3\cos 0 & &= 3\\
f''(t) &= -9\sin 3t & f''(0) &= -9\sin 0 & &= 0\\
f'''(t) &= -27\cos 3t & f'''(0) &= -27\cos 0 & &= -27\\
f^{iv}(t) &= 81\sin 3t & f^{iv}(0) &= 81\sin 0 & &= 0\\
f^{v}(t) &= 243\cos 3t \ldots & f^{v}(0) &= 243\cos 0 & &= 243\ldots
\end{aligned}
$$

We substitute these values into Maclaurin's series, i.e.

$$
f(t) = f(0) + tf'(0) + t^2\frac{f''(0)}{2!} + t^3\frac{f'''(0)}{3!} + \cdots
$$

which becomes

$$
\sin 3t = 0 + t(3) + t^2\frac{(0)}{2!} + t^3\frac{(-27)}{3!} + t^4\frac{(0)}{4!} + t^5\frac{(243)}{5!}\cdots
$$

i.e. $\sin 3t = 3t - \dfrac{(3t)^3}{3!} + \dfrac{(3t)^5}{5!}\cdots$

or $\sin 3t = 3t - \dfrac{9}{2}t^3 + \dfrac{81}{40}t^5\ldots$

We have used more terms than usual in the Maclaurin's series. This is because some of them have reduced to zero. The remaining terms all have odd powers. Remember that sine is an odd function.

EXERCISE 10.5

Using Maclaurin's series find the series for the following functions up to and including the term in x^5.

1	$\sin 2x$	9	$\sinh 2x$
2	$\cos 3x$	10	$\cosh 3x$
3	e^{2x}	11	$\cos(-3x)$
4	$\ln(1+x)$	12	$\sin\dfrac{x}{2}$
5	e^{-2x}		
6	e^{-x}	13	$\dfrac{1}{1+x}$ or $(1+x)^{-1}$
7	$(1+x)^n$	14	$e^{x/2}$
8	$\ln(1-x)$	15	$\ln(1+2x)$

Radius of convergence

Earlier in this chapter we have seen series either converge or diverge. Here we are interested in convergence. Remember that Taylor's and Maclaurin's theorems only apply to convergent series. The **radius of convergence** is the range of values for which a series converges. For some series we do *not* need to give a radius of convergence. This is because the series is convergent for all values of x.

Summary of series

We list some examples of commonly used series. The list is *not* supposed to be exhaustive.

$$e^x = 1 + x + \frac{x^2}{2!} + \frac{x^3}{3!} + \frac{x^4}{4!} \cdots \qquad \text{for all values of } x.$$

$$e^{-x} = 1 - x + \frac{x^2}{2!} - \frac{x^3}{3!} + \frac{x^4}{4!} \cdots \qquad \text{for all values of } x.$$

$$\sin x = x - \frac{x^3}{3!} + \frac{x^5}{5!} - \frac{x^7}{7!} \cdots \qquad \text{for all } x \text{ in radians.}$$

$$\cos x = 1 - \frac{x^2}{2!} + \frac{x^4}{4!} - \frac{x^6}{6!} \cdots \qquad \text{for all } x \text{ in radians.}$$

$$\sinh x = x + \frac{x^3}{3!} + \frac{x^5}{5!} \cdots \qquad \text{for all values of } x.$$

$$\cosh x = 1 + \frac{x^2}{2!} + \frac{x^4}{4!} \cdots \qquad \text{for all values of } x.$$

$$\ln(1 + x) = x - \frac{x^2}{2} + \frac{x^3}{3} - \frac{x^4}{4} \cdots \qquad \text{for } -1 < x \leqslant 1.$$

$$\ln(1 - x) = -x - \frac{x^2}{2} - \frac{x^3}{3} - \frac{x^4}{4} \cdots \qquad \text{for } -1 \leqslant x < 1.$$

$$(a + x)^n = a^n + na^{n-1}x + \frac{n(n-1)a^{n-2}x^2}{2!}$$
$$+ \frac{n(n-1)(n-2)a^{n-3}x^3}{3!}$$
$$+ \frac{n(n-1)(n-2)(n-3)a^{n-4}x^4}{4!} \cdots$$

$$(1 + x)^n = 1 + nx + \frac{n(n-1)x^2}{2!} + \frac{n(n-1)(n-2)x^3}{3!}$$
$$+ \frac{n(n-1)(n-2)(n-3)x^4}{4!} \cdots \qquad \text{for } -1 < x < 1.$$

$$(1 + x)^{-1} = 1 - x + x^2 - x^3 + x^4 \cdots \qquad \text{for } -1 < x < 1.$$

$$(1 - x)^{-1} = 1 + x + x^2 + x^3 + x^4 \cdots \qquad \text{for } -1 < x < 1.$$

Combinations of series

We use our earlier results and multiply them together. You will notice that we do *not* divide series.

Examples 10.15

In these examples we show you some algebraic manipulations. You will be able to practise them in the next Exercise.

i)   To find the series for $\ln\left(\dfrac{1+x}{1-x}\right)$ we apply a law of logarithms, i.e.

$$\ln\left(\frac{1+x}{1-x}\right) = \ln(1+x) - \ln(1-x).$$

We work out the series for $\ln(1+x)$. For the $\ln(1-x)$ series we compare $\ln(1-x)$ with $\ln(1+x)$ and replace x with $-x$. Finally we subtract the 2 series.

ii) This technique is similar to the previous one.

$$\begin{aligned}\ln(1-x^2) &= \ln(1+x)(1-x)\\ &= \ln(1+x) + \ln(1-x).\end{aligned}$$

We apply the basic series results for $\ln(1+x)$ and $\ln(1-x)$ and then add them.

iii) $(1+x)^2 \sin 2x$ needs only the series for $\sin 2x$. We can expand the bracket, i.e. $(1+x)^2 = 1 + 2x + x^2$. Finally we multiply together $(1 + 2x + x^2)$ and the series for $\sin 2x$.

iv) We re-write $\dfrac{\cos 3x}{e^{2x}}$ as $e^{-2x}\cos 3x$. The resulting series is the product of the separate series for e^{-2x} and $\cos 3x$.

ASSIGNMENT

Last time we looked at the Assignment we found separate series for the exponential and sine parts of $i = 4e^{-4t}\sin 3t$. Here we apply those results, multiplying together the series. The exponential series has been worked only to the term in t^3. This level of accuracy limits the overall accuracy of our result. To increase that accuracy we would need to include more terms in the exponential or both series. We use

$$e^{-4t} = 1 - 4t + 8t^2 - \frac{32}{3}t^3 \ldots$$

and $\sin 3t = 3t - \dfrac{9}{2}t^3 \ldots$

Multiplying together each term in the first bracket with each term in the second bracket we get

$$4e^{-4t}\sin 3t = 4\left(1 - 4t + 8t^2 - \frac{32}{3}t^3 \ldots\right)\left(3t - \frac{9}{2}t^3 \ldots\right).$$

When we expand these brackets we stop at the terms in t^3 because this is the limit of our accuracy.

$$4e^{-4t}\sin 3t = 4\left(3t \qquad\qquad -\frac{9}{2}t^3\ldots\right.$$
$$-12t^2\ldots$$
$$\left.+24t^3\ldots\right)$$
$$= 12t - 48t^2 + 78t^3\ldots$$

There is an alternative approach using Maclaurin's series. We start with $f(t) = 4e^{-4t}\sin 3t$ and differentiate repeatedly using the product rule. We substitute for $t = 0$ and use the series to achieve the same result as above.

<hr>

▰▰▰ Example 10.16 ▰▰▰

We find a series for $\tan x$.

Remember that $\tan x = \dfrac{\sin x}{\cos x} = (\sin x)(\cos x)^{-1}$ and we *cannot* divide by a series. We know that

$$\sin x = x - \frac{x^3}{3!} + \frac{x^5}{5!}\ldots$$

and
$$\cos x = 1 - \frac{x^2}{2!} + \frac{x^4}{4!}\ldots = 1 + \left(-\frac{x^2}{2!} + \frac{x^4}{4!}\ldots\right)$$

We need $(\cos x)^{-1}$ and so write

$$(\cos x)^{-1} = \left(1 + \left(-\frac{x^2}{2!} + \frac{x^4}{4!}\ldots\right)\right)^{-1}$$

This means we can apply the series

$$(1 + X)^{-1} = 1 - X + X^2 - X^3 + X^4\ldots$$

and by comparison replace X with $\left(-\dfrac{x^2}{2!} + \dfrac{x^4}{4!}\ldots\right)$.

The limit of powers in the cosine series restricts the terms we consider.

$$\text{Now}\quad (\cos x)^{-1} = \left(1 + \left(-\frac{x^2}{2!} + \frac{x^4}{4!}\ldots\right)\right)^{-1}$$

$$= 1 - \left(-\frac{x^2}{2!} + \frac{x^4}{4!}\ldots\right) + \left(-\frac{x^2}{2!} + \frac{x^4}{4!}\ldots\right)^2\ldots$$

$$= 1 - \left(-\frac{x^2}{2} + \frac{x^4}{24}\ldots\right) + \left(\frac{x^4}{4}\ldots\right)\ldots \qquad \boxed{\begin{array}{l}4! = 24.\\ (2!)^2 = 2^2.\end{array}}$$

$$= 1 + \frac{x^2}{2} + \frac{5}{24}x^4\ldots$$

Now $\qquad \tan x = \dfrac{\sin x}{\cos x} = (\sin x)(\cos x)^{-1}$

becomes $\quad \tan x = \left(x - \dfrac{x^3}{6} + \dfrac{x^5}{120} \cdots \right) \left(1 + \dfrac{x^2}{2} + \dfrac{5}{24} x^4 \cdots \right)$

$$= x + \dfrac{x^3}{2} + \dfrac{5}{24} x^5 \cdots$$

$$- \dfrac{x^3}{6} - \dfrac{x^5}{12} \cdots$$

$$+ \dfrac{x^5}{120} \cdots$$

$$= x + \dfrac{x^3}{3} + \dfrac{2}{15} x^5 \cdots$$

> Multiplying together the brackets and limiting up to the x^5 terms.

EXERCISE 10.6

Use your earlier results or Maclaurin's series. Find the series for the following combinations up to and including the term in x^5.

1 $\ln\left(\dfrac{1+x}{1-x}\right)$

2 $(1+x)^2 \sin 2x$

3 $\sin^2 x$

4 $\ln(1 - x^2)$

5 $\dfrac{e^x}{1+x}$

6 $\cos^2 x$

7 $\ln(1+x)^2$

8 $\sec 2x$

9 $\dfrac{\cos 3x}{e^{2x}}$

10 $\ln\left(\dfrac{1-x}{1+x}\right)$

Applications to calculus

There are various applications for both Taylor's and Maclaurin's series. We cannot hope to cover them all and so offer a selection.

We can use together some earlier results from both Taylor's and Maclaurin's series.

Example 10.17

We are going to find an alternative expression for $\sin(x + \alpha)$.

Using the second version of Taylor's series,

$$f(x+h) = f(x) + hf'(x) + h^2 \dfrac{f''(x)}{2!} + h^3 \dfrac{f'''(x)}{3!} + \cdots$$

we let $f(x+h) = \sin(x + \alpha)$.

> Replacing h with α.

Then $\qquad f(x) = \sin x$

so that $\qquad f'(x) = \cos x$

$$f''(x) = -\sin x$$
$$f'''(x) = -\cos x$$
$$f^{iv}(x) = \sin x$$
$$f^{v}(x) = \cos x, \ldots$$

We substitute into Taylor's series to get

$$\sin(x + \alpha) = \sin x + \alpha \cos x + \alpha^2 \frac{(-\sin x)}{2!} + \alpha^3 \frac{(-\cos x)}{3!}$$
$$+ \alpha^4 \frac{(\sin x)}{4!} + \alpha^5 \frac{(\cos x)}{5!} \cdots$$

Notice the terms of this series alternate between $\sin x$ and $\cos x$. We use them as common factors, i.e.

$$\sin(x + \alpha) = \left(1 - \frac{\alpha^2}{2!} + \frac{\alpha^4}{4!} \cdots \right) \sin x + \left(\alpha - \frac{\alpha^3}{3!} + \frac{\alpha^5}{5!} \cdots \right) \cos x.$$

From our Summary of series we recognise the first bracket as the cosine series, $\cos \alpha$. Similarly the second bracket is the sine series, $\sin \alpha$. These give

$$\sin(x + \alpha) = \sin x . \cos \alpha + \cos x . \sin \alpha.$$

This is one of the compound angle formulae we introduced in Volume 2, Chapter 4.

When we express a function as a series it is a series of terms, i.e. a polynomial. We know from very early differentiation work that we may differentiate term by term.

▮▮▮▮ Example 10.18 ▮▮▮▮

Using the Taylor's series expansion for $\ln x$ find a series for $\frac{1}{x}$.

We recall we *cannot* divide by zero in Mathematics. This means, in this case, we must apply Taylor's series rather than Maclaurin's series. From Example 10.12 we have

$$\ln x = \ln a + \frac{(x - a)}{a} - \frac{(x - a)^2}{2a^2} + \frac{(x - a)^3}{3a^3} - \frac{(x - a)^4}{4a^4} \cdots$$

For each term we differentiate with respect to x, i.e.

$$\frac{1}{x} = 0 + \frac{1}{a} - \frac{2(x - a)}{2a^2} + \frac{3(x - a)^2}{3a^3} - \frac{4(x - a)^3}{4a^4} \cdots$$

i.e. $\qquad \dfrac{1}{x} = \dfrac{1}{a} - \dfrac{(x - a)}{a^2} + \dfrac{(x - a)^2}{a^3} - \dfrac{(x - a)^3}{a^4} \cdots$

Notice we have used one series to deduce another series. You can check this agrees with your answer to Exercise 10.4, Question 2.

■■■■■■■ **Example 10.19** ■■■■■■■

We use our $\dfrac{1}{x}$ series from Example 10.18 to find an approximate value

for $\dfrac{1}{1.5}$.

By comparison with our series and $\dfrac{1}{1.5}$ we have $x = 1.5$. Letting $a = 1$ we are 'expanding the function about 1'. We substitute into

$$\frac{1}{x} = \frac{1}{a} - \frac{(x-a)}{a^2} + \frac{(x-a)^2}{a^3} - \frac{(x-a)^3}{a^4} \cdots$$

i.e. $\quad \dfrac{1}{1.5} = \dfrac{1}{1} - \dfrac{0.5}{1^2} + \dfrac{0.5^2}{1^3} - \dfrac{0.5^3}{1^4} + \dfrac{0.5^4}{1^5} - \dfrac{0.5^5}{1^6} + \dfrac{0.5^6}{1^7} \cdots$

$= 1 - 0.5 + 0.25 - 0.125 + 0.0625 - 0.03125 + 0.015625 \ldots$

$= 0.671875$ after 7 terms.

You can continue this pattern for yourself seeing the sum approach $0.\overline{6}$. After 8 terms we had $0.6640\ldots$, after 9 terms we had $0.6679\ldots$ and after 10 terms we had $0.6660\ldots$.

We can integrate a series term by term. This is valid provided the limits lie within the radius of convergence. Remember each series is an approximation of an infinite series, giving only the first few terms. This means each definite integral is also an approximation.

■■■■■■■ **Example 10.20** ■■■■■■■

Using Maclaurin's series we have a series for $\ln(1 + x)$ which is valid for $-1 < x \leqslant 1$. This means, using the logarithmic series, we can find the value of $\displaystyle\int_{0.5}^{0.75} \ln(1 + x)\, dx$. Notice both limits lie within the range $-1 < x \leqslant 1$.

Now $\displaystyle\int_{0.5}^{0.75} \ln(1 + x)\, dx = \int_{0.5}^{0.75} \left(x - \frac{x^2}{2} + \frac{x^3}{3} - \frac{x^4}{4} \cdots \right) dx$

$$= \left[\frac{x^2}{2} - \frac{x^3}{6} + \frac{x^4}{12} - \frac{x^5}{20} \cdots \right]_{0.5}^{0.75}$$

$$= 0.225 - 0.108$$

$$= 0.12.$$

In Volume 2 we saw how to integrate a natural logarithm using integration by parts. This is an alternative method.

Notice we cannot find the value of $\displaystyle\int_{0.5}^{1.5} \ln(1 + x)\, dx$ using Maclaurin's series because 1.5 lies outside the radius of convergence, $-1 < x \leqslant 1$.

ASSIGNMENT

Our original task was to find the mean current where $i = 4e^{-4t} \sin 3t$. So far we have found separate series for the exponential and sine parts. Also during our previous look at the Assignment we combined these together to give

$$i = 4e^{-4t} \sin 3t$$

$$= 12t - 48t^2 + 78t^3 \ldots$$

Now we are going to find the mean current during the first 5 hundredths of a second. We apply the formula for mean value,

i.e. mean value $= \dfrac{1}{b-a} \displaystyle\int_a^b i \, dt,$

to give

mean current, $\quad \bar{i} = \dfrac{1}{0.05 - 0} \displaystyle\int_0^{0.05} \left(12t - 48t^2 + 78t^3 \ldots \right) dt$

$$= 20 \left[\frac{12t^2}{2} - \frac{48t^3}{3} + \frac{78t^4}{4} \ldots \right]_0^{0.05}$$

$$= 20[0.015 - 0.002 + 0.00012 \ldots]$$

$$= 0.262 \text{ A.}$$

We could have integrated the original expression, $4e^{-4t} \sin 3t$, by parts as an alternative method.

The final Exercise links together our series work and these last 3 techniques.

EXERCISE 10.7

1 Using Maclaurin's and Taylor's series work out the compound angle formulae for i) $\sin(x - \alpha)$, ii) $\cos(x + \alpha)$, iii) $\cos(x - \alpha)$.

2 For small angles we have approximations for $\sin x$, $\cos x$ and $\tan x$. They are $\sin x \approx x$, $\cos x \approx 1 - \dfrac{x^2}{2}$ and $\tan x \approx x$. Use the series for each trigonometric function to check those approximations are correct. Check their accuracies when $x = 0.175$ radians. By including the next term in each series re-check their accuracies.

3 Show that $\sin^2 x \approx x^2 \left(1 - \dfrac{x^2}{3} \right)$ for small angles in radians.

4 Using the sine series in the Summary write down a series for $\sin 2x$. Differentiate that series for $\sin 2x$ to find a series for $\cos 2x$. Apply Maclaurin's series starting with $f(x) = \cos 2x$ to check your answer. Repeat this technique based on $\sin ax$, where a is a constant, in place of $\sin 2x$.

5 In Example 10.16 we found a series for $\tan x$.

    i) Generalise this to a series for $\tan ax$ where a is a constant. Using differentiation find a general series for $\sec^2 ax$ and a particular series for $\sec^2 3x$.

    ii) Integrate the series for $\tan x$ to find a series for $\ln(\cos x)$.

6 A variable force, F N, is related to displacement, x m, by $F = \dfrac{2-x}{1-x}$. Find a series for $(1-x)^{-1}$ up to the term in x^3. Use this result to find a series for F. Find the mean value of the force between 0.24 m and 0.72 m.

7 The work done by a force, F, is given by the integral

$$\int_a^b F\, ds. \quad F = (10-s)e^{0.2s}, \quad \text{where } s \text{ is the displacement.}$$

Use the exponential series to find a series for F up to the term in s^3. Find the work done over the first 10 metres.

8 Find the value of the integral $\displaystyle\int_0^{0.5} \sqrt{1-x^2}\, dx$ using the series for $(1-x^2)^{1/2}$.

9 A voltage, V, over time, t, is given by $V = 2t\sin t$. Using the sine series find a series for V up to the term in t^6. Find the mean value of this voltage in the first second.

10 A variable force, F (N), is related to distance, s (m), by $F = 5s^2e^{-s}$. The mean force is given by

$$\text{Mean force} = \frac{1}{b-a}\int_a^b F\, ds.$$

Use the exponential series to write down a series for F up to the term in s^4. Calculate the mean force from $s = 0$ to $s = 2.5$ m.

11 Numerical Methods: 1 – Newton– Raphson Method

The objectives of this chapter are to:

1 Recognise that if $f(x)$ changes sign between $x = a$ and $x = b$ then $f(x) = 0$ has a root between $x = a$ and $x = b$.

2 Select a suitable approximation to the required root of a given equation.

3 Understand the iterative process of the Newton–Raphson method.

4 Apply the Newton–Raphson method to reach an approximate root to the required degree of accuracy.

Introduction

We look at a numerical method for solving equations; the Newton–Raphson method. There are other methods (e.g. the secant and bisection methods). It is an iterative technique, refining a solution until the necessary degree of accuracy is reached. An **iteration** is a repetition of the technique. A solution requiring 10 iterations means you have had to work through the method 10 times. The Newton–Raphson method is used to solve single equations for which there may *not* be a standard method. By way of comparison our Assignment applies the method to an equation type we have seen before. For an easier solution computer software can be written.

▰▰▰ ASSIGNMENT ▰▰▰

Our Assignment for this chapter looks at a pair of parallel a.c. voltages, $v_1 = 15 \sin 5t$ and $v_2 = 8 \cos 5t$. The total voltage, v, is the sum of v_1 and v_2, i.e.  $v = 15 \sin 5t + 8 \cos 5t$. We looked at this in Volume 2, Chapters 3 and 4. Here, as an alternative, we apply the Newton–Raphson method to find when the voltage is 10 V.

Roots of an equation

In Volume 1 we saw how to solve an equation graphically. This was where the graph crossed the horizontal axis. We remind you with some simple sketches, omitting the tables of values.

Example 11.1

In Fig. 11.1 we show the graph of $y = x(x-4)$. It crosses the horizontal axis where $y = 0$, i.e. at $x = 0$ and $x = 4$. All along the horizontal axis $y = 0$.

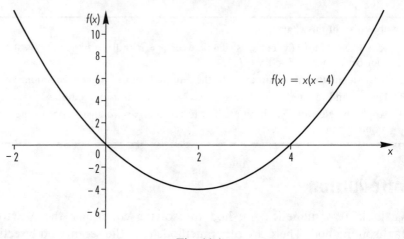

Fig. 11.1

If we use functional notation we have $f(x) = x(x-4)$ crossing the horizontal axis where $f(x) = 0$. Above the axis $f(x)$ is positive and below it is negative, i.e. $f(x)$ changes sign as it crosses that axis.

Example 11.2

In Fig. 11.2 we show the graph of $f(x) = 4x^3 - 3x^2 - 11x + 2.5$. It is not immediately obvious for the equation $4x^3 - 3x^2 - 11x + 2.5 = 0$ where the exact roots lie. We see the graph crosses the the horizontal axis in 3 places. $f(x)$ changes sign between $x = -2.00$ (here $f(x)$ is negative) and $x = -1.00$ (here $f(x)$ is positive). It changes sign between $x = 0.00$ (here $f(x)$ is positive) and $x = 0.50$ (here $f(x)$ is negative). Finally it changes sign between $x = 1.50$ (here $f(x)$ is negative) and $x = 2.00$ (here $f(x)$ is positive). With a graphical software package we could zoom in to find more accurately where the function crosses the horizontal axis.

The Newton–Raphson method is an alternative iterative mathematical technique.

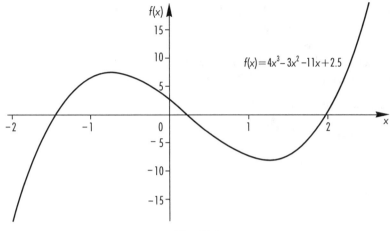

Fig. 11.2

Newton–Raphson method

Let us look at some Mathematics to support the Newton–Raphson method. At the end we show the general formula we apply to each problem. Always sketch a graph (or graphs) before attempting the method. This will give you some clue to the approximate location of the root(s).

In Fig. 11.3 we sketch the graph of some general function. It has a root at the point Q which we need to locate. We guess where Q might be, say a

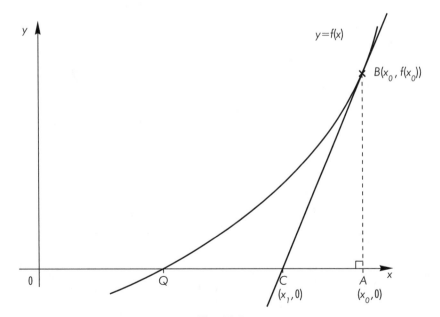

Fig. 11.3

point A, where $x = x_0$. The point B is vertically above A, lying on the graph. Its coordinates are $(x_0, f(x_0))$. At B we approximate the curve to a tangent. This crosses the horizontal axis at C, with coordinates $(x_1, 0)$. C lies closer to Q than does A. This means $x = x_1$ is a better approximation to the true root than $x = x_0$.

The gradient of the tangent at B is given by

$$\text{gradient} = \frac{\text{vertical change}}{\text{horizontal change}}$$

i.e. $$f'(x_0) = \frac{f(x_0) - 0}{x_0 - x_1}$$

i.e. $$x_0 - x_1 = \frac{f(x_0)}{f'(x_0)}$$

which re-arranges to

$$x_1 = x_0 - \frac{f(x_0)}{f'(x_0)}.$$

We repeat the process, i.e. we go through another iteration. Remember we have improved our estimate of the true root to $x = x_1$ at C. In Fig. 11.4 we show our graph and the point C. The point D is vertically above C, lying on the graph. Its coordinates are $(x_1, f(x_1))$. At D we approximate the curve to a tangent. This crosses the horizontal axis at E, with

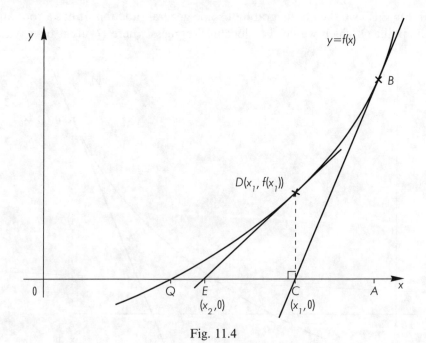

Fig. 11.4

coordinates $(x_2, 0)$. E lies closer to Q than do C and A. This means $x = x_2$ is a better approximation to the true root than both $x = x_1$ and $x = x_0$.

The gradient of the tangent at D is given by

$$\text{gradient} = \frac{\text{vertical change}}{\text{horizontal change}}$$

i.e. $\quad f'(x_1) = \dfrac{f(x_1) - 0}{x_1 - x_2}$

i.e. $\quad x_1 - x_2 = \dfrac{f(x_1)}{f'(x_1)}$

which re-arranges to

$$x_2 = x_1 - \frac{f(x_1)}{f'(x_1)}.$$

We could continue with further iterations getting closer and closer to the true root at Q. Following the pattern of the first and second iterations we generalise the formula to

$$x_{n+1} = x_n - \frac{f(x_n)}{f'(x_n)}.$$

Example 11.3

We know from Example 11.2 that $4x^3 - 3x^2 - 11x + 2.5 = 0$ has three roots (solutions). From Fig. 11.2 we can see the middle root lies close to $x = 0.00$. We are going to find this root correct to 2 decimal places. This means we will work with 3 decimal places confident of the accuracy to 2 decimal places, i.e. one decimal place less.

Let $\quad f(x) = 4x^3 - 3x^2 - 11x + 2.5$

$\therefore \quad f'(x) = 12x^2 - 6x - 11.$

We use the general formula

$$x_{n+1} = x_n - \frac{f(x_n)}{f'(x_n)}.$$

Starting with $x_0 = 0.000$,

$$f(0.000) = 2.5$$

and $\quad f'(0.000) = -11$

we have $\quad x_1 = 0.000 - \dfrac{2.5}{-11} = 0.227.$

Using $x_1 = 0.227$,

$$f(0.227) = 4(0.227)^3 - 3(0.227)^2 - 11(0.227) + 2.5$$

$$= -0.105$$

and $f'(0.227) = 12(0.227)^2 - 6(0.227) - 11 = -11.744$

we have $x_2 = 0.227 - \dfrac{(-0.105)}{(-11.744)} = 0.218.$

Using $x_2 = 0.218$,

$$f(0.218) = 4(0.218)^3 - 3(0.218)^2 - 11(0.218) + 2.5$$

$$= 0.0009$$

and $f'(0.218) = 12(0.218)^2 - 6(0.218) - 11 = -11.738$

we have $x_3 = 0.218 - \dfrac{0.0009}{-11.738} = 0.218.$

The last and previous iterations are the same correct to 3 decimal places. This shows the last iteration is as close to the true root as the previous iteration. Working to 3 decimal places we suggest a true root of 0.218, or 0.22 correct to 2 decimal places, i.e. one decimal place less than the working.

We always need the last and previous iterations to be the same to our degree of accuracy.

We can test our result by substituting into the original function, i.e.

$$f(0.22) = 4(0.22)^3 - 3(0.22)^2 - 11(0.22) + 2.5$$

$$= -0.02 \ldots$$

This small difference of the function from 0 shows that 0.22 is a close approximation to the true root. Similarly we saw earlier that $f(0.218) = 0.0009$, i.e. $x = 0.218$ is a yet closer approximation.

Now look back at the solution in Example 11.3. You will see the magnitude of $f(x)$ getting very small with successive iterations. Also the magnitude of $\dfrac{f(x)}{f'(x)}$ is getting yet smaller. These features show we are getting successively closer to the true root, i.e. we are converging to that root.

Sometimes it is *not* easy to sketch the function with one graph. Perhaps it is easier to sketch it in sections, say 2 separate graphs. Where they cross, as for simultaneous equations, we have a solution. We do this in the Assignment.

ASSIGNMENT

We wish to know when the voltage is 10 V, i.e. we need to solve the equation $15 \sin 5t + 8 \cos 5t = 10$. Separately we know about sine and cosine curves. We re-arrange our equation to read $15 \sin 5t - 10 = -8 \cos 5t$. This is one re-arrangement; there are others. In Fig. 11.5 we draw the sine curve shifted vertically down by 10 and the negative cosine curve. For this portion they cross several times, the first time at approximately $t = 0.02$ s.

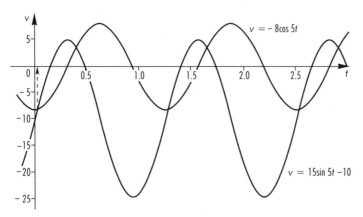

Fig. 11.5

Example 11.4

Solve the equation $e^{-t} - t - 2 = 0$ correct to 3 decimal places.

We use the variable t as an alternative to x for variety. As in earlier Examples we may sketch the complete curve. In this case the graph of $f(t) = e^{-t} - t - 2$ is difficult to sketch. Alternatively we can re-write our original equation as $e^{-t} = t + 2$. Now we sketch $f_1(t) = e^{-t}$ and $f_2(t) = t + 2$ in Fig. 11.6. We are interested in where one value of t satisfies both graphs, i.e. a simultaneous solution. This occurs where the graphs cross.

They cross at the point A. The horizontal coordinate of A is not far from $t = -0.5$. We use this as our first estimate of the solution. We return to our original equation and apply the Newton–Raphson method.

Let $\qquad f(t) = e^{-t} - t - 2$

$\therefore \qquad f'(t) = -e^{-t} - 1.$

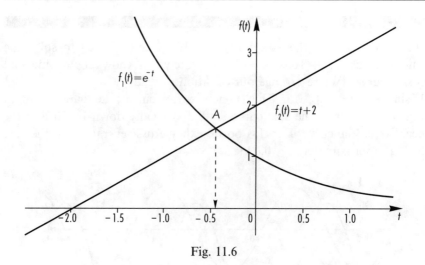

Fig. 11.6

We use the general formula

$$t_{n+1} = t_n - \frac{f(t_n)}{f'(t_n)}.$$

Starting with $t_0 = -0.5000$,

$$f(-0.5000) = e^{0.5000} + 0.5000 - 2 = 0.1487$$

and $f'(-0.5000) = -e^{0.5000} - 1 \qquad = -2.6487$

we have $\qquad t_1 = -0.5000 - \dfrac{0.1487}{-2.6487} = -0.4439.$

Using $t_1 = -0.4439$,

$$f(-0.4439) = e^{0.4439} + 0.4439 - 2 = 0.0027$$

and $f'(-0.4439) = -e^{0.4439} - 1 \qquad = -2.5588$

we have $\qquad t_2 = -0.4439 - \dfrac{0.0027}{-2.5588} = -0.4429.$

Using $t_2 = -0.4429$,

$$f(-0.4429) = e^{0.4429} + 0.4429 - 2 = 0.0001$$

and $f'(-0.4429) = -e^{0.4429} - 1 \qquad = -2.5572$

we have $\quad t_3 = -0.4429 - \dfrac{0.0001}{-2.5572} = -0.4429.$

The last and previous iterations are the same correct to 4 decimal places. We have confidence to write the solution as $t = -0.443$. Again, like in Example 11.3, we can test this result in our function. We can repeat our comments about the magnitudes of $f(t)$ and $\dfrac{f(t)}{f'(t)}$.

◼️ ASSIGNMENT ◼️

We know from our previous look at the Assignment that the first solution is close to $t = 0.02$ s. We re-arrange our original equation from $15 \sin 5t + 8 \cos 5t = 10$ to $15 \sin 5t + 8 \cos 5t - 10 = 0$.

Let $\qquad f(t) = 15 \sin 5t + 8 \cos 5t - 10$

$\therefore \qquad f'(t) = 75 \cos 5t - 40 \sin 5t.$

We use the general formula

$$t_{n+1} = t_n - \frac{f(t_n)}{f'(t_n)}.$$

Starting with $t_0 = 0.020,$

$f(0.020) = 15 \sin 0.1 + 8 \cos 0.1 - 10 = -0.542$

and $\quad f'(0.020) = 75 \cos 0.1 - 40 \sin 0.1 = 70.632$

> $5t_0 = 5 \times 0.020$
> $\quad = 0.1.$
>
> Using radians.

we have $\qquad t_1 = 0.020 - \dfrac{(-0.542)}{70.632} = 0.028.$

Using $t_1 = 0.028,$

$f(0.028) = 15 \sin 0.14 + 8 \cos 0.14 - 10 = 0.015$

and $\quad f'(0.028) = 75 \cos 0.14 - 40 \sin 0.14 = 68.684$

> $5t_1 = 5 \times 0.028$
> $\quad = 0.14.$

we have $\qquad t_2 = 0.028 - \dfrac{0.015}{68.684} = 0.028.$

The last and previous iterations are the same correct to 3 decimal places. This means we do *not* need to iterate again, i.e. we are confident this is our solution.

Remember our original equation has various forms, e.g.

$$15 \sin 5t + 8 \cos 5t = 10$$

$$15 \sin 5t + 8 \cos 5t - 10 = 0.$$

We have used $f(t) = 15 \sin 5t + 8 \cos 5t - 10$ and solved $f(t) = 0$. In fact we have found only one of the solutions associated with this periodic waveform. To find the next solution you need to repeat the process based on its graphical estimate. Because this is a periodic waveform you should notice a pattern of solutions quite quickly.

The Newton–Raphson method links with Taylor's series. Let us remind ourselves of Taylor's series from Chapter 10, i.e.

$$f(x + h) = f(x) + hf'(x) + h^2 \frac{f''(x)}{2!} + h^3 \frac{f'''(x)}{3!} \cdots$$

Remember h is small so that $x + h$ is close to x. Because h is small we may neglect terms involving h^2, h^3, h^4, ... as a first approximation. This leaves

$$f(x + h) = f(x) + hf'(x).$$

Just like our graphical approach using tangents to approximate we could use x_0 and x_1, ... Eventually this would lead to the general situation involving x_n and x_{n+1}, a small distance apart. In our approximation to Taylor's series we can substitute x_{n+1} for $x + h$ and x_n for x to get

$$f(x_{n+1}) = f(x_n) + (x_{n+1} - x_n)f'(x_n).$$

$$\boxed{x_n + h = x_{n+1}.}$$

The Newton–Raphson method is based upon x_{n+1} being a solution of $f(x_{n+1}) = 0$, i.e.

$$0 = f(x_n) + (x_{n+1} - x_n)f'(x_n).$$

We can re-arrange this equation so that

$$x_{n+1} = x_n - \frac{f(x_n)}{f'(x_n)} \text{ as before.}$$

You are now in a position to attempt the Exercise. All our calculations have been based upon a few iterations to show the technique. They have used a graphical sketch to estimate the solution to the equation. You can expect to use more iterations in some questions. Also it is possible that the method may fail if your estimate is too close to the true solution. Another failure may result if the true root and the estimate are separated by a turning point. At a turning point the gradient, $f'(x)$, is zero and the Newton–Raphson formula has $f'(x)$ in the denominator. Remember division by zero is not allowed in Mathematics.

■ EXERCISE 11.1 ■

1 A disc is spun from rest. It spins through $y°$ in t seconds according to $y = 100t - 5t^3$. Using the Newton–Raphson method when is $y = 150°$?

2 A hollow cylinder with closed ends is made from 6×10^4 mm^2 of sheet metal. For a cylinder of radius, r, and volume, V, this means they are related by the formula $V = 3 \times 10^4 r - \pi r^3$. For what radius, to 1 decimal place, is the volume 10^6 mm^3?

3 Sketch the graphs of $f_1(x) = x^4$ and $f_2(x) = 2x + 1$ on a set of axes. Estimate that the graphs intersect at x values of approximately -0.5 and 1.5. You will need two applications of the Newton–Raphson method. Find the roots of the equation $x^4 - 2x - 1 = 0$ to 3 decimal places.

4 Use the Newton–Raphson method to find the two solutions of the equation $e^x + e^{-x} = 2.5$. You can check your answers by solving either a quadratic equation in e^x or using hyperbolics.

5   The formula for the area of a sector, A_1, is given by $A_1 = \frac{1}{2}r^2x$ where x is the angle subtended in radians. A formula for the area of an isosceles triangle, A_2, is given by $A_2 = \frac{1}{2}R^2 \sin x$. In this particular case $r = 0.8R$. For what value of x are these areas equal?

6   Using sketches of cubic and quadratic graphs estimate the x value at the intersection of $f_1(x) = x^3$ and $f_2 = x^2 - 0.5$. Solve the equation $x^3 - x^2 + 0.5 = 0$ by applying the Newton–Raphson method.

7   Apply the Newton–Raphson method twice to solve the equation $e^x = 2x^2$. We have a power series for the exponential, i.e. $e^x = 1 + x + \frac{x^2}{2!} + \frac{x^3}{3!} \ldots$ Using the first three terms only of that series re-write the original equation as a quadratic equation. You should find an approximate check for your answer by solving this quadratic equation.

8   A chemical process plant can produce up to 5 tonnes each week. Its costs, y_1, are related to the tonnage produced, x, by $y_1 = 10 + 3x - x^2$. Its sales income, y_2, is also related to tonnage by $y_2 = 0.2x^3$. The units for y_1 and y_2 are £,000 (thousands of pounds). The break even point is where costs and income are the same. Apply the Newton–Raphson method based on an estimate of $x = 3$ to show that $x = 3.47$.

9   In a submarine cable the speed of the signal, v, is related to the radius of the cable's covering, R, by $v = \frac{25}{R^2} \ln \frac{R}{5}$. You are given $v = 0.165$.

For ease of calculation let $x = \frac{R}{5}$ and show that $0.165x^2 = \ln x$.

Sketch the graphs of the appropriate quadratic and logarithmic functions. From your sketch check these graphs cross at approximately $x = 1.3$. Apply the Newton–Raphson method to improve upon this estimate. Hence write down the value of R.

10   A local engineering company borrows £250 000 to invest in new plant. The company repays £8500 each month over 3 years (i.e. 36 repayments) according to the formula
$$250000I + 8500((1 + I)^{-36} - 1) = 0.$$
I is the monthly interest rate. Starting with an estimate of 1% per month (i.e. $I_0 = 0.01$) improve the accuracy of this figure to 3 significant figures.

12 Numerical Methods: 2 – Simultaneous Equations

The objectives of this chapter are to:

1 Solve simultaneous linear equations using Jacobi's method.
2 Solve simultaneous linear equations using the Gauss–Seidel method.
3 Solve simultaneous linear equations by Gaussian elimination.

Introduction

In the earlier volumes we have learned to solve systems of simultaneous linear equations by various methods. Most recently we have used determinants and matrices. Remember that linear equations are represented by straight lines. The solution of simultaneous equations is the point at which all the graphs intersect. By way of example we use sets of 3 different equations in 3 unknowns (variables). The methods are easily extended. As the number of unknowns increases so must the number of different equations for a solution.

The first and second methods are iterative techniques. We try specimen values for our unknowns and then refine them repeatedly.

■ ASSIGNMENT ■

A major UK brewer has three breweries of different ages using different levels of technology. As a first step towards possible upgrades it is evaluating the times involved prior to costing. The brewing process for super lager can be split into three basic sections. These are: fermentation, which takes x days, cold conditioning, which takes y days and kegging

and despatch which takes z days. For the three different breweries, x, y and z are related by the simultaneous equations

$$3x + y + z = 49,$$
$$x + 5y + 2z = 40,$$
and $\quad x + y + 4z = 30.$

We are going to use this set of 3 equations to demonstrate the 3 methods of solution. Our aim is to find the optimum (best) solution for x, y and z.

Jacobi's method

Suppose we have a general set of equations in unknowns x, y and z. The as and bs represent numbers. For the as we apply the double suffix notation first introduced in Volume 1, Chapter 14. We write

$$a_{11}x + a_{12}y + a_{13}z = b_1,$$
$$a_{21}x + a_{22}y + a_{23}z = b_2$$
and $\quad a_{31}x + a_{32}y + a_{33}z = b_3$

or in matrix form
$$\begin{pmatrix} a_{11} & a_{12} & a_{13} \\ a_{21} & a_{22} & a_{23} \\ a_{31} & a_{32} & a_{33} \end{pmatrix} \begin{pmatrix} x \\ y \\ z \end{pmatrix} = \begin{pmatrix} b_1 \\ b_2 \\ b_3 \end{pmatrix}.$$

We highlight the leading diagonal of the 3×3 matrix containing a_{11}, a_{22} and a_{33}. We need our solution to converge to the true values for x, y and z. For this to happen we need the size of the leading diagonal element to dominate the other elements in its row. The sizes are emphasised by the use of moduli. This will happen if the following conditions are satisfied, i.e. $|a_{11}| > |a_{12}| + |a_{13}|,$

$\quad |a_{22}| > |a_{21}| + |a_{23}|$

and $\quad |a_{33}| > |a_{31}| + |a_{32}|.$

> Row ① elements
> Row ② elements
> Row ③ elements.

You must always test that these 3 conditions are true before continuing with the method. The greater the inequalities the more quickly the solution will converge.

It is possible that *not* all 3 conditions are true in a particular case. If this happens try to interchange the original equations. Unfortunately this may not always help. If only one of the conditions just fails then the solution will probably converge, but more slowly.

Example 12.1

Solve the simultaneous equations $\quad 6x - 2y + z = 7,$

$$x - 10y + 4z = -20,$$

and $\quad 5x \quad + 9z = -17.$

We re-write them in matrix form, i.e.

$$\begin{pmatrix} 6 & -2 & 1 \\ 1 & -10 & 4 \\ 5 & 0 & 9 \end{pmatrix} \begin{pmatrix} x \\ y \\ z \end{pmatrix} = \begin{pmatrix} 7 \\ -20 \\ -17 \end{pmatrix}.$$

According to our earlier conditions we highlight the leading diagonal elements. We compare them with the other elements in each row.

$a_{11} = 6, \therefore |a_{11}| = 6.$

$a_{12} = -2, a_{13} = 1,$ then $\quad |a_{12}| + |a_{13}| = |-2| + |1|$

$$= 2 + 1$$

$$= 3;$$

i.e. $\quad |a_{11}| > |a_{12}| + |a_{13}|.$

$a_{22} = -10, \therefore |a_{22}| = 10.$

$a_{21} = 1, a_{23} = 4,$ then $\quad |a_{21}| + |a_{23}| = |1| + |4|$

$$= 1 + 4$$

$$= 5;$$

i.e. $\quad |a_{22}| > |a_{21}| + |a_{23}|.$

$a_{33} = 9, \therefore |a_{33}| = 9.$

$a_{31} = 5, a_{32} = 0,$ then $\quad |a_{31}| + |a_{32}| = |5| + |0|$

$$= 5;$$

i.e. $\quad |a_{33}| > |a_{31}| + |a_{32}|.$

All 3 conditions are satisfied so we may continue.

In the first equation the leading diagonal element is associated with $6x$, i.e. $6x$ is the dominant term. We re-arrange the first equation to make x the subject, i.e.

$$6x = 7 + 2y - z$$

i.e.
$$x = \frac{1}{6}\left(7 + 2y - z\right). \quad\text{———①}$$

In the second equation the leading diagonal element is associated with $-10y$, i.e. $-10y$ is the dominant term. We re-arrange the second equation to make y the subject, i.e.

$$-10y = -20 - x - 4z$$

$$y = \frac{1}{-10}\left(-20 - x - 4z\right)$$

i.e.
$$y = \frac{1}{10}\left(20 + x + 4z\right). \quad\text{———②}$$

> Simplifying the minus signs.

In the third equation the leading diagonal element is associated with $9z$, i.e. $9z$ is the dominant term. We re-arrange the third equation to make z the subject, i.e.

$$9z = -17 - 5x$$

i.e.
$$z = \frac{1}{9}\left(-17 - 5x\right). \quad\text{———③}$$

We need to choose some specimen values for x, y and z. Without any idea of the solution it is convenient to start with $x = 0$, $y = 0$ and $z = 0$. We substitute for these values in equations ①, ② and ③.

$$x = \frac{1}{6}\left(7\right) \quad = \quad 1.167,$$

$$y = \frac{1}{10}\left(20\right) \quad = \quad 2.000,$$

> All correct to 3 decimal places.

$$z = \frac{1}{9}\left(-17\right) = -1.889.$$

These new values for x, y and z complete the first iteration. They are improvements upon our original choices. Now we substitute for them in equations ①, ② and ③.

$$x = \frac{1}{6}\left(7 + 2(2) - (-1.889)\right) \quad = \frac{12.889}{6} \quad = \quad 2.148,$$

$$y = \frac{1}{10}\left(20 + 1.167 + 4(-1.889)\right) = \frac{13.611}{10} \quad = \quad 1.361,$$

$$z = \frac{1}{9}\left(-17 - 5(1.167)\right) \quad = -\frac{22.835}{9} = -2.537.$$

This is the second iteration complete. Again we substitute into our equations using these refined values for x, y and z.

$$x = \frac{1}{6}\Big(7 + 2(1.361) - (-2.537)\Big) \quad = \frac{12.259}{6} \quad = \quad 2.043,$$

$$y = \frac{1}{10}\Big(20 + 2.148 + 4(-2.537)\Big) = \frac{12.000}{10} \quad = \quad 1.200,$$

$$z = \frac{1}{9}\Big(-17 - 5(2.148)\Big) \qquad\qquad = -\frac{27.740}{9} = -3.082.$$

Again we substitute for x, y and z in equations ①, ② and ③ in turn. After five more iterations we reach

$$x = \quad 2.000,$$
$$y = \quad 0.998,$$
$$z = -3.003.$$

Once again we substitute, i.e.

$$x = \frac{1}{6}\Big(7 + 2(0.998) - (-3.003)\Big) \quad = \frac{11.999}{6} \quad = \quad 2.000,$$

$$y = \frac{1}{10}\Big(20 + 2.000 + 4(-3.003)\Big) = \frac{9.988}{10} \quad = \quad 0.999,$$

$$z = \frac{1}{9}\Big(-17 - 5(2.000)\Big) \qquad\qquad = -\frac{27.000}{10} = -3.000.$$

We have worked correct to 3 decimal places. With confidence, correct to 2 decimal places (1 less than the working) we can write $x = 2.00$, $y = 1.00$ and $z = -3.00$. You can test the accuracy of these values by substituting into any of the original equations.

▬▬▬ ASSIGNMENT ▬▬▬

We are going to apply Jacobi's method to solve our simultaneous equations

$$3x + y + z = 49,$$
$$x + 5y + 2z = 40,$$
and
$$x + y + 4z = 30.$$

We re-write them in matrix form, i.e.

$$\begin{pmatrix} 3 & 1 & 1 \\ 1 & 5 & 2 \\ 1 & 1 & 4 \end{pmatrix} \begin{pmatrix} x \\ y \\ z \end{pmatrix} = \begin{pmatrix} 49 \\ 40 \\ 30 \end{pmatrix}.$$

According to our convergence conditions we highlight the leading diagonal elements. We compare them with the other elements in each row.

$|a_{11}| = 3.$

Also $|a_{12}| + |a_{13}| = |1| + |1|$

$$= 2;$$

i.e. $|a_{11}| > |a_{12}| + |a_{13}|.$

$|a_{22}| = 5.$

Also $|a_{21}| + |a_{23}| = |1| + |2|$

$$= 3;$$

i.e. $|a_{22}| > |a_{21}| + |a_{23}|.$

$|a_{33}| = 4.$

Also $|a_{31}| + |a_{32}| = |1| + |1|$

$$= 2;$$

i.e. $|a_{33}| > |a_{31}| + |a_{32}|.$

All 3 conditions are satisfied so we may continue. Notice the inequalities are *not* great. This means the solution will converge slowly.

In the first equation the leading diagonal element is associated with $3x$, i.e. $3x$ is the dominant term. We re-arrange the first equation to make x the subject, i.e.

$$3x = 49 - y - z$$

i.e. $x = \dfrac{1}{3}\left(49 - y - z\right).$ ———①

In the second equation the leading diagonal element is associated with $5y$, i.e. $5y$ is the dominant term. We re-arrange the second equation to make y the subject, i.e.

$$5y = 40 - x - 2z$$

$$y = \dfrac{1}{5}\left(40 - x - 2z\right).$$ ———②

In the third equation the leading diagonal element is associated with $4z$, i.e. $4z$ is the dominant term. We re-arrange the third equation to make z the subject, i.e.

$$4z = 30 - x - y$$

i.e. $z = \dfrac{1}{4}\left(30 - x - y\right).$ ———③

We choose specimen values for x, y and z. Without any idea of the solution it is convenient to start with $x = 0$, $y = 0$ and $z = 0$. We substitute for these values in equations ①, ② and ③.

$$x = \frac{1}{3}\left(49\right) = 16.333,$$

$$y = \frac{1}{5}\left(40\right) = 8.000,$$

All correct to 3 decimal places.

$$z = \frac{1}{4}\left(30\right) = 7.500.$$

These new values for x, y and z complete the first iteration. They are improvements upon our original choices. Now we substitute for them in equations ①, ② and ③.

$$x = \frac{1}{3}\left(49 - 8.000 - 7.500\right) = \frac{33.500}{3} = 11.167,$$

$$y = \frac{1}{5}\left(40 - 16.333 - 2(7.500)\right) = \frac{8.667}{5} = 1.733,$$

$$z = \frac{1}{4}\left(30 - 16.333 - 8.000\right) = \frac{5.667}{4} = 1.417.$$

This is the second iteration complete. Again we substitute into our equations using these refined values for x, y and z.

$$x = \frac{1}{3}\left(49 - 1.733 - 1.417\right) = \frac{45.850}{3} = 15.283,$$

$$y = \frac{1}{5}(40 - 11.167 - 2(1.417)) = \frac{25.999}{5} = 5.200,$$

$$z = \frac{1}{4}\left(30 - 11.167 - 1.733\right) = \frac{17.100}{4} = 4.275.$$

Again we substitute for x, y and z in equations ①, ② and ③ in turn. After many more iterations we reach $x = 14$, $y = 4$ and $z = 3$. These occur in the following iteration to confirm we have converged upon the solution. We can check the values by substituting into any one of our three original equations. Our results mean the fermentation takes 14 days, the cold conditioning takes 4 days and the kegging and despatch takes 3 days.

Rather than showing all the working you can use the calculator's memories and tabulate the results. The table shows this for the Assignment.

Iteration	x	y	z
	0	0	0
First	16.333	8.000	7.500
Second	11.167	1.733	1.417
Third	15.283	5.200	4.275
. . .			
	14	4	3

■■■■■ EXERCISE 12.1 ■■■■■

In this Exercise apply Jacobi's method to solve the sets of simultaneous equations.

1 Solve this set of 3 simultaneous equations correct to 2 decimal places.

$$23x + 3y + 4z = 5,$$
$$5x + 67y + 7z = 6,$$
and $$7x + 5y + 34z = 7.$$

2 The following set of simultaneous equations needs re-arranging. Briefly explain the reason for this.

$$9V_1 + V_2 = 10,$$
$$V_1 - V_2 + 7V_3 = 7,$$
and $$7V_2 - 2V_3 = 5.$$

Write down the equations in the correct sequence. Solve them using 3 decimal places in your working.

3 The electrical circuit may be modelled by the accompanying set of simultaneous equations.

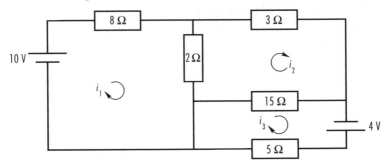

By iteration find the values of the currents i_1, i_2, and i_3 to 2 decimal places.

$$5i_1 - i_2 = 5,$$
$$-2i_1 + 20i_2 - 15i_3 = 0,$$
$$-15i_2 + 20i_3 = 4.$$

4 Two aircraft will collide if they attempt to occupy the same coordinates (x, y, z) in space at the same time. These coordinates are measured in kilometres from navigation beacons. They are connected by the simultaneous equations

$$6x + y - 3z = 3,$$
$$3x + 7y - 2z = 20,$$
and $$-5x - 10y + 24z = 13.$$

Find the coordinates for a potential collision to occur working to 2 decimal places.

5 An engineering company part-manufactures and assembles 3 models of steel cabinets. The table shows the number of minutes per item allocated to part-manufacture and both assemblies.

	Manufacturing	*Sub-assembly*	*Final assembly*
Model One	12	4	3
Model Two	7	10	5
Model Three	3	4	11

For these products the production manager generally allocates daily timings. These are 415 minutes for manufacturing, 390 minutes each for sub-assembly and final assembly. Within these times the company produces x number of Model One, y number of Model Two and z number of Model Three. x, y and z are connected by the simultaneous equations

$$12x + 7y + 3z = 415,$$
$$4x + 10y + 4z = 390,$$
and $$3x + 5y + 11z = 390.$$

Use 1 decimal place in your working. After 5 complete iterations show that approximately x, y and z are 22, 31 and 26 respectively.

In Exercise 12.1, Question **5**, the solution converges slowly. Notice the leading diagonal elements are *not* very dominant. The true values are $x = 15$, $y = 25$ and $z = 20$. Obviously there need to be many more iterations to reach these values. We might suggest in this question the method of solution has not been particularly useful. There are alternative methods.

Gauss–Seidel method

The Gauss–Seidel method is a refined version of Jacobi's method. It updates a value each time the appropriate equation is used rather than in sets of three. Again we start with a general set of equations in unknowns x, y and z. The as and bs represent numbers. We write

$$a_{11}x + a_{12}y + a_{13}z = b_1,$$
$$a_{21}x + a_{22}y + a_{23}z = b_2,$$
and $$a_{31}x + a_{32}y + a_{33}z = b_3$$

or in matrix form $$\begin{pmatrix} a_{11} & a_{12} & a_{13} \\ a_{21} & a_{22} & a_{23} \\ a_{31} & a_{32} & a_{33} \end{pmatrix} \begin{pmatrix} x \\ y \\ z \end{pmatrix} = \begin{pmatrix} b_1 \\ b_2 \\ b_3 \end{pmatrix}.$$

As for Jacobi's method we highlight the leading diagonal of the 3×3 matrix containing a_{11}, a_{22} and a_{33}. We need our solution to converge to the true values for x, y and z. For this to happen we need the size of the leading diagonal element to dominate the other elements in its row. The sizes are emphasised by the use of moduli. This will happen if the following conditions are satisfied, i.e.

$$|a_{11}| > |a_{12}| + |a_{13}|,$$
$$|a_{22}| > |a_{21}| + |a_{23}|$$
$$\text{and} \quad |a_{33}| > |a_{31}| + |a_{32}|.$$

Row ① elements

Row ② elements

Row ③ elements.

You must always test that these 3 conditions are true before continuing with the method. The greater the inequalities the more quickly the solution will converge.

It is possible that *not* all 3 conditions are true in a particular case. If this happens try to interchange the original equations. Unfortunately this may not always help. If only one of the conditions just fails then the solution will probably converge, but more slowly.

▬▬▬ Example 12.2 ▬▬▬

The electrical circuit, Fig. 12.1, may be modelled by the accompanying set of simultaneous equations;

$$5i_1 - i_2 \qquad = 5,$$
$$-2i_1 + 20i_2 - 15i_3 = 0,$$
$$-15i_2 + 20i_3 = 4.$$

We use the Gauss–Seidel method to find the values of i_1, i_2 and i_3.

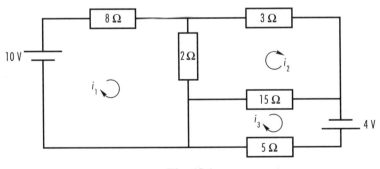

Fig. 12.1

We re-write our equations in matrix form, i.e.

$$\begin{pmatrix} 5 & -1 & 0 \\ -2 & 20 & -15 \\ 0 & -15 & 20 \end{pmatrix} \begin{pmatrix} i_1 \\ i_2 \\ i_3 \end{pmatrix} = \begin{pmatrix} 5 \\ 0 \\ 4 \end{pmatrix}.$$

According to our earlier conditions we highlight the leading diagonal elements. We compare them with the other elements in each row.

$a_{11} = 5, \therefore |a_{11}| = 5.$

$a_{12} = -1, a_{13} = 0$, then $\quad |a_{12}| + |a_{13}| = |-1| + |0|$

$$= 1;$$

i.e. $\qquad\qquad\qquad\qquad |a_{11}| > |a_{12}| + |a_{13}|.$

$a_{22} = 20, \therefore |a_{22}| = 20.$

$a_{21} = -2, a_{23} = -15$, then $|a_{21}| + |a_{23}| = |-2| + |-15|$

$$= 2 + 15$$

$$= 17;$$

i.e. $\qquad\qquad\qquad\qquad |a_{22}| > |a_{21}| + |a_{23}|.$

$a_{33} = 20, \therefore |a_{33}| = 20.$

$a_{31} = 0, a_{32} = -15$, then $\quad |a_{31}| + |a_{32}| = |0| + |-15|$

$$= 15;$$

i.e. $\qquad\qquad\qquad\qquad |a_{33}| > |a_{31}| + |a_{32}|.$

All 3 conditions are satisfied so we may continue.

In the first equation the leading diagonal element is associated with $5i_1$, i.e. $5i_1$ is the dominant term. We re-arrange the first equation to make i_1 the subject, i.e.

$$5i_1 = 5 + i_2$$

i.e. $\qquad i_1 = \dfrac{1}{5}\left(5 + i_2\right).$ ————①

In the second equation the leading diagonal element is associated with $20i_2$, i.e. $20i_2$ is the dominant term. We re-arrange the second equation to make i_2 the subject, i.e.

$$20i_2 = 2i_1 + 15i_3$$

i.e. $\qquad i_2 = \dfrac{1}{20}\left(2i_1 + 15i_3\right).$ ————②

In the third equation the leading diagonal element is associated with $20i_3$, i.e. $20i_3$ is the dominant term. We re-arrange the third equation to make i_3 the subject, i.e.

$$20i_3 = 4 + 15i_2$$

i.e. $\qquad i_3 = \dfrac{1}{20}\left(4 + 15i_2\right).$ ————③

We need to choose some specimen values for i_1, i_2 and i_3. Without any idea of the solution it is convenient to start with $i_1 = 0$, $i_2 = 0$ and $i_3 = 0$. We substitute into equation ①. Remember we update a value after using each equation.

Using equation ① $i_1 = \dfrac{1}{5}\left(5 + 0\right)$ $= 1.000.$

Immediately we apply this new value of i_1.

Using equation ② $i_2 = \dfrac{1}{20}\left(2(1.000) + 0\right)$ $= 0.100.$

Again, immediately we use this new value of i_2.

Using equation ③ $i_3 = \dfrac{1}{20}\left(4 + 15(0.100)\right) = 0.275.$

This is the first iteration complete. We continue with the second iteration updating the values immediately we have calculated them.

$$i_1 = \frac{1}{5}\left(5 + 0.100\right) \qquad = \frac{5.100}{5} = 1.020.$$

$$i_2 = \frac{1}{20}\left(2(1.020) + 15(0.275)\right) = \frac{6.165}{20} = 0.308.$$

$$i_3 = \frac{1}{20}\left(4 + 15(0.308)\right) \qquad = \frac{8.620}{20} = 0.431.$$

We continue with the third iteration.

$$i_1 = \frac{1}{5}\left(5 + 0.308\right) \qquad = \frac{5.308}{5} = 1.062.$$

$$i_2 = \frac{1}{20}\left(2(1.062) + 15(0.431)\right) = \frac{8.589}{20} = 0.429.$$

$$i_3 = \frac{1}{20}\left(4 + 15(0.429)\right) \qquad = \frac{10.435}{20} = 0.522.$$

We could continue with the iterations to converge upon the solution. There are some further values in the table for you to check. Now we have seen the method we tabulate the values. The layout of the table differs slightly from that used in Jacobi's method. This is simply to distinguish between the methods. If you wish you may compress this table of Gauss–Seidel method values.

Iteration	i_1	i_2	i_3
First	1.000		
		0.100	
			0.275
Second	1.020		
		0.308	
			0.431
Third	1.062		
		0.429	
			0.522
Fourth	1.086		
		0.500	
			0.575
Fifth	1.100		
		0.541	
			0.606
Sixth	1.108		
		0.565	
			0.624
. . .			
	1.12		
		0.60	
			0.65

Eventually we reach values for i_1, i_2 and i_3 that do not change for the next iteration. This means we have $i_1 = 1.12$ A, $i_2 = 0.60$ A and $i_3 = 0.65$ A.

We look at examples that need more care. We have already hinted at this in Exercise 12.1, Question **2**.

Examples 12.3

In each case we have to be careful.

i)
$$2x \qquad + 3z = 16,$$
$$x + 4y - \ z = -14,$$
and $\quad -2x - \ y \qquad = -1$

needs to be re-arranged before attempting either the Jacobi or Gauss–Seidel methods. The leading diagonal elements are *not* dominant. We interchange the first and third equations to get

$$-2x - \ y \qquad = -1,$$
$$x + 4y - \ z = -14,$$
and $\quad 2x \qquad + 3z = 16.$

Now the solution will converge because all 3 conditions based upon the leading diagonal are satisfied.

ii) $12x + 8y + 4z = 46,$

$6x + 10y + 5z = 44,$

and $4x + 6y + 11z = 43$

look to be ordered correctly. When you check the conditions for convergence they just fail in the first equation. They also fail in the second equation. With one condition just failing we might expect the solution to converge very slowly. Two failures means there is *no* convergence so we do *not* get a solution.

ASSIGNMENT ████████████████████████████

We are going to apply the Gauss–Seidel method to solve our simultaneous equations

$3x + y + z = 49,$

$x + 5y + 2z = 40,$

and $x + y + 4z = 30.$

From our work with Jacobi's method we know about writing them in matrix form and checking the convergence conditions. There is no need to repeat this work. We go to the re-arranged equations ①, ② and ③,

$$x = \frac{1}{3}\left(49 - y - z\right), \qquad ①$$

$$y = \frac{1}{5}\left(40 - x - 2z\right), \qquad ②$$

$$\text{and} \quad z = \frac{1}{4}\left(30 - x - y\right). \qquad ③$$

Again we choose specimen values for x, y and z. Without any idea of the solution it is convenient to start with $x = 0$, $y = 0$ and $z = 0$. We substitute into equation ①.

$$x = \frac{1}{3}\left(49\right) \qquad\qquad = 16.333,$$

$$y = \frac{1}{5}\left(40 - 16.333\right) \qquad = \frac{23.667}{5} = 4.733,$$

Correct to 3 decimal places.

$$z = \frac{1}{4}\left(30 - 16.333 - 4.733\right) = \frac{8.934}{4} = 2.2335.$$

These new values for x, y and z complete the first iteration. We start the second iteration.

$$x = \frac{1}{3}\left(49 - 4.733 - 2.2335\right) \quad = \frac{42.033}{3} = 14.011,$$

$$y = \frac{1}{5}\left(40 - 14.011 - 2(2.2335)\right) = \frac{21.522}{5} = 4.304,$$

$$z = \frac{1}{4}\left(30 - 14.011 - 4.304\right) \quad = \frac{11.685}{4} = 2.921.$$

This is the second iteration complete. Again we substitute into our equations refining the values for x, y and z.

$$x = \frac{1}{3}\left(49 - 4.304 - 2.921\right) \quad = \frac{41.775}{3} = 13.925,$$

$$y = \frac{1}{5}\left(40 - 13.925 - 2(2.921)\right) = \frac{20.233}{5} = 4.047,$$

$$z = \frac{1}{4}\left(30 - 13.925 - 4.047\right) \quad = \frac{12.028}{4} = 3.007.$$

Rather than continue with all the working we tabulate the iterations.

Iteration	x	y	z
	0	0	0
First	16.333		
		4.733	
			2.2335
Second	14.011		
		4.304	
			2.921
Third	13.925		
		4.047	
			3.007
Fourth	13.982		
		4.001	
			3.004
Fifth	13.998		
		3.999	
			3.001
Sixth	14.000		
		4.000	
			3.000
Seventh	14	4	3

In fact the solution converges more quickly using the Gauss–Seidel method than using Jacobi's method.

Remember we can always check our solution by substituting into one of our original equations.

◼◼◼◼ EXERCISE 12.2 ◼◼◼◼◼◼◼◼◼◼◼◼

In this Exercise apply the Gauss–Seidel method to solve the sets of simultaneous equations.

1   Solve this set of 3 simultaneous equations working with 2 decimal places.

$$4x - y - z = 11,$$
$$-6x + 15y + 3z = -21,$$
and $$-x + 2y + 6z = 5.$$

2   Solve the 3 simultaneous equations with the hint that the solutions are whole numbers.

$$3x - y + z = 5,$$
$$5x + 2y - 12z = 4,$$
and $$-x + 4y - z = 33.$$

3   The electrical circuit shows 2 emfs together with various resistors. The sums of the relevant voltages produce the simultaneous equations.

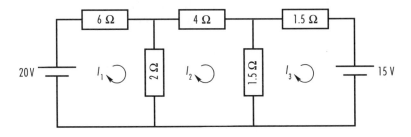

They are in terms of the currents, I_1, I_2 and I_3 amps.

$$6I_1 + 2(I_1 - I_2) = 20,$$
$$2(I_2 - I_1) + 4I_2 + 1.5(I_2 - I_3) = 0$$
and $$1.5I_3 + 1.5(I_3 - I_2) = 15.$$

These equations will simplify. Show that they may be reduced to

$$8I_1 - 2I_2 = 20,$$
$$-2I_1 + 7.5I_2 - 1.5I_3 = 0,$$
and $$-1.5I_2 + 3I_3 = 15.$$

Now solve these simultaneous equations for I_1, I_2 and I_3.

4 Two aircraft will collide if they attempt to occupy the same coordinates (x, y, z) in space at the same time. These coordinates are measured in kilometres from navigation beacons. They are connected by the simultaneous equations

$$6x + y - 3z = 3,$$
$$3x + 7y - 2z = 20$$

and $-5x - 10y + 24z = 13.$

Find the coordinates for a potential collision to occur working to 2 decimal places.

5 The electrical circuit shows various resistors.

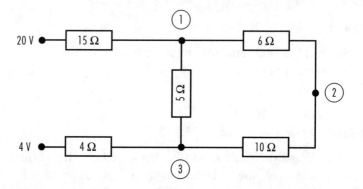

At the marked nodes the voltages are V_1, V_2 and V_3. We can apply Kirchoff's current law to obtain the equations

$$\frac{1}{15}\left(V_1 - 20\right) + \frac{1}{6}\left(V_1 - V_2\right) + \frac{1}{5}\left(V_1 - V_3\right) = 0 \quad \text{for node ①,}$$

$$\frac{1}{6}\left(V_2 - V_1\right) + \frac{1}{10}\left(V_2 - V_3\right) = 0 \quad \text{for node ②,}$$

$$\frac{1}{4}\left(V_3 - 4\right) + \frac{1}{10}\left(V_3 - V_2\right) + \frac{1}{5}\left(V_3 - V_1\right) = 0 \quad \text{for node ③.}$$

Re-arrange these equations to obtain

$$13V_1 - 5V_2 - 6V_3 = 40,$$
$$-5V_1 + 8V_2 - 3V_3 = 0,$$

and $-4V_1 - 2V_2 + 11V_3 = 20.$

Notice the convergence condition just fails for the second equation. However with care show the solution converges to $V_1 = 9.5$ V, $V_2 = 8.5$ V and $V_3 = 6.8$ V.

Gaussian elimination

Gaussian elimination is more efficient than the classical methods we have seen in both Volumes 1 and 2. This is particularly so when the number of unknowns increase. The aim of the method is to create a triangle of zeroes within an augmented (greater) matrix. The method may be refined to reduce the errors by 'pivoting'. We concentrate upon the method in its first version.

Example 12.4

Solve the simultaneous equations

$$4x - 2y + z = 3,$$
$$x - 10y + 4z = -6,$$
and $$5x + 4y - 9z = -7.$$

In matrix form these equations are $\begin{pmatrix} 4 & -2 & 1 \\ 1 & -10 & 4 \\ 5 & 4 & -9 \end{pmatrix} \begin{pmatrix} x \\ y \\ z \end{pmatrix} = \begin{pmatrix} 3 \\ -6 \\ -7 \end{pmatrix}.$

We gather the numerical values to one side of this matrix equation to create the **augmented matrix**, i.e.

$$\left(\begin{array}{ccc:c} 4 & -2 & 1 & 3 \\ 1 & -10 & 4 & -6 \\ 5 & 4 & -9 & -7 \end{array} \right).$$

Row ①
Row ②
Row ③.

The vertical ⋮ line reminds us where the fourth column has come from. We learned how to work with equations early in Volume 1. 'What we do to one side we do to the other', i.e. we need to be consistent; to maintain a balance about the '=' sign. This idea of consistency applies here.

From the first column we identify $a_{11} = 4$, $a_{21} = 1$ and $a_{31} = 5$. Now $\dfrac{a_{21}}{a_{11}} = \dfrac{1}{4}$. Multiplying row ① by $\dfrac{1}{4}$ we make the coefficients of x the same in rows ① and ②, i.e. $(1 - 0.5\ 0.25 \vdots 0.75)$. Next we subtract this from row ②,

i.e. $\left(\begin{array}{ccc:c} 4 & -2 & 1 & 3 \\ 0 & -9.5 & 3.75 & -6.75 \\ 5 & 4 & -9 & -7 \end{array} \right)$

New row ②= Old row ②
$-\dfrac{1}{4}$Row ①.

Now $\dfrac{a_{31}}{a_{11}} = \dfrac{5}{4}$. Multiplying row ① by $\dfrac{5}{4}$ we make the coefficients of x the same in rows ① and ③, i.e. $(5 - 2.5\ 1.25 \vdots 3.75)$. Next we subtract this from row ③,

i.e. $\left(\begin{array}{ccc:c} 4 & -2 & 1 & 3 \\ 0 & -9.5 & 3.75 & -6.75 \\ 0 & 6.5 & -10.25 & -10.75 \end{array} \right).$

New row ③= Old row ③
$-\dfrac{5}{4}$Row ①.

From the second column we identify $a_{22} = -9.5$ and $a_{32} = 6.5$. Now $\dfrac{a_{32}}{a_{22}} = \dfrac{6.5}{-9.5}$. Multiplying row ② by $\dfrac{6.5}{-9.5}$ we make the coefficients of y the same in rows ② and ③, i.e. $(0\ 6.5\ -2.56\ldots\ \vdots\ 4.61\ldots)$. Next we subtract this from row ③,

i.e.
$$\begin{pmatrix} 4 & -2 & 1 & \vdots & 3 \\ 0 & -9.5 & 3.75 & \vdots & -6.75 \\ 0 & 0 & -7.68\ldots & \vdots & -15.36\ldots \end{pmatrix}.$$

New row ③ =

Old row ③ $- \dfrac{6.5}{-9.5}$ Row ②.

Notice we have created a lower triangle of zeroes in the augmented matrix. This has eliminated some unknowns from our equations. We move back from our augmented matrix and re-write our equations as

$$4x - 2y + z = 3, \qquad \text{———(1.1)}$$
$$-9.5y + 3.75z = -6.75 \qquad \text{———(2.2)}$$
$$\text{and} \qquad -7.68\ldots z = -15.36\ldots \text{———(3.3)}$$

From equation ③.③ $\quad z = \dfrac{-15.36\ldots}{-7.68\ldots} = 2.$

Using equation ②.②
$$-9.5y + 3.75z = -6.75$$
we substitute for $z = 2$ to get
$$-9.5y + 3.75(2) = -6.75$$
$$-9.5y = -6.75 - 7.5$$

i.e. $\qquad y = \dfrac{-14.25}{-9.5} = 1.5.$

Finally, using equation ③.③
$$4x - 2y + z = 3$$
we substitute for both $y = 1.5$ and $z = 2$ to get
$$4x - 2(1.5) + 2 = 3$$
$$4x = 3 + 3 - 2$$

i.e. $\quad x = \dfrac{4}{4} = 1.$

■ ASSIGNMENT ■

We return to our Assignment simultaneous equations,
$$3x + y + z = 49,$$
$$x + 5y + 2z = 40$$
$$\text{and} \quad x + y + 4z = 30.$$

In matrix form these equations are
$$\begin{pmatrix} 3 & 1 & 1 \\ 1 & 5 & 2 \\ 1 & 1 & 4 \end{pmatrix} \begin{pmatrix} x \\ y \\ z \end{pmatrix} = \begin{pmatrix} 49 \\ 40 \\ 30 \end{pmatrix}.$$

We gather the numerical values to one side of this matrix equation to create the **augmented matrix**,

i.e.
$$\begin{pmatrix} 3 & 1 & 1 & \vdots & 49 \\ 1 & 5 & 2 & \vdots & 40 \\ 1 & 1 & 4 & \vdots & 30 \end{pmatrix}$$

Row ①
Row ②
Row ③.

From the first column we identify $a_{11} = 3$, $a_{21} = 1$ and $a_{31} = 1$. Now $\frac{a_{21}}{a_{11}} = \frac{1}{3}$. Multiplying row ① by $\frac{1}{3}$ we make the coefficients of x the same in rows ① and ②, i.e. $(1\ 0.\bar{3}\ 0.\bar{3} \vdots 16.\bar{3})$. Next we subtract this from row ②,

i.e.
$$\begin{pmatrix} 3 & 1 & 1 & \vdots & 49 \\ 0 & 4.\bar{6} & 1.\bar{6} & \vdots & 23.\bar{6} \\ 1 & 1 & 4 & \vdots & 30 \end{pmatrix}.$$

New row ② = Old row ②
$-\frac{1}{3}$ Row ①.

Now $\frac{a_{31}}{a_{11}} = \frac{1}{3}$. Multiplying row ① by $\frac{1}{3}$ we make the coefficients of x the same in rows ① and ③, i.e. $(1\ 0.\bar{3}\ 0.\bar{3} \vdots 16.\bar{3})$. Next we subtract this from row ③,

i.e.
$$\begin{pmatrix} 3 & 1 & 1 & \vdots & 49 \\ 0 & 4.\bar{6} & 1.\bar{6} & \vdots & 23.\bar{6} \\ 0 & 0.\bar{6} & 3.\bar{6} & \vdots & 13.\bar{6} \end{pmatrix}.$$

New row ③ = Old row ③
$-\frac{1}{3}$ Row ①.

From the second column we identify $a_{22} = 4.\bar{6}$ and $a_{32} = 0.\bar{6}$. Now $\frac{a_{32}}{a_{22}} = \frac{0.\bar{6}}{4.\bar{6}}$. Multiplying row ② by $\frac{0.\bar{6}}{4.\bar{6}}$ we make the coefficients of y the same in rows ② and ③, i.e. $(0\ 0.\bar{6}\ 0.238\ldots \vdots 3.38\ldots)$. Next we subtract this from row ③,

i.e.
$$\begin{pmatrix} 3 & 1 & 1 & \vdots & 49 \\ 0 & 4.\bar{6} & 1.\bar{6} & \vdots & 23.\bar{6} \\ 0 & 0 & 3.42\ldots & \vdots & 10.28\ldots \end{pmatrix}.$$

New row ③ = Old row ③
$-\frac{0.\bar{6}}{4.\bar{6}}$ Row ②.

Again we have created a lower triangle of zeroes in the augmented matrix. We move back from our augmented matrix and re-write our equations as

$$3x + y + z = 49, \qquad\text{(1.1)}$$
$$4.\bar{6}y + 1.\bar{6}z = 23.\bar{6} \qquad\text{(2.2)}$$
$$\text{and} \qquad 3.42\ldots z = 10.28\ldots \qquad\text{(3.3)}$$

From equation ③.③ $\quad z = \dfrac{10.28\ldots}{3.42\ldots} = 3.$

Using equation ②.②

$$4.\bar{6}y + 1.\bar{6}z = 23.\bar{6}$$

we substitute for $z = 3$ to get

$$4.\overline{6}y + 1.\overline{6}(3) = 23.\overline{6}$$
$$4.\overline{6}y = 23.\overline{6} - 5$$

i.e. $$y = \frac{18.\overline{6}}{4.\overline{6}} = 4.$$

Finally, using equation ③.③
$$3x + y + z = 49$$
we substitute for both $y = 4$ and $z = 3$ to get
$$3x + 4 + 3 = 49$$
$$3x = 42$$

i.e. $$x = \frac{42}{3} = 14.$$

These values confirm our earlier results. The fermentation takes 14 days, the cold conditioning takes 4 days and the kegging and despatch takes 3 days.

Comparison of methods

By way of illustration we have looked at a selection of numerical methods for solving simultaneous linear equations. They are all extendible to more than the 3 unknowns we have used for demonstration. The Jacobi and Gauss–Seidel methods are iterative methods. This means they automatically correct the numerical approximation errors during the process. The Gauss–Seidel method is a refinement of Jacobi's method. However they have a major disadvantage. The convergence conditions may not always be satisfied. When this is the case we need to use another technique, e.g. the Gaussian elimination method. It needs more care with the arithmetic than do iterative methods. There is no pattern showing convergence to a solution. As with any numerical method it is subject to approximation errors. We can overcome these by working with more decimal places than required for the final answer. There is another refinement termed 'pivoting'. This reduces the approximation errors by exchanging rows to make the scaling as small as possible. A further development is the Gaussian–Jordan method.

■■■■ EXERCISE 12.3 ■■■■

In this Exercise apply the Gaussian elimination method to solve the sets of simultaneous equations.

1   Solve this set of 3 simultaneous equations
$$4x + y - 2z = 0,$$
$$4x - 5y + 4z = 3,$$
and $$x + 2y - z = 1.$$

2 Solve the 3 simultaneous equations
$$3x + y + z = 6,$$
$$x + 3y = 11,$$
and $2x - y + z = 2.$

3 This question is based upon an Assignment from Volume 2, Chapter 1 for a company assembling personal computers. It uses 3 assembly teams of differing skill levels to produce its 3 models; the PC/SD, PC/DD and PC/HD. The following table shows the hourly assembly rates for each team for each model.

Hourly production	PC/SD	PC/DD	PC/HD
Assembly Team North	3	4	5
Assembly Team East	3.5	3	2.5
Assembly Team West	5.5	6	5.5

The company has a large order book for these relatively new models. A longstanding customer has placed an urgent valuable order which will need to be met by overtime working. It is for 28 of the PC/SD, 30 of the PC/DD and 29 of the PC/HD. We want to know how to schedule this order using all the assembly teams.

Suppose the order will be met by the teams working x, y and z hours of overtime respectively. Combining the hourly production rates with these hours of overtime gives

Order production	PC/SD	PC/DD	PC/HD
Assembly Team North	$3x$	$4x$	$5x$
Assembly Team East	$3.5y$	$3y$	$2.5y$
Assembly Team West	$5.5z$	$6z$	$5.5z$
Total	28	30	29

We mathematically model this using 3 simultaneous equations
$$3x + 3.5y + 5.5z = 28,$$
$$4x + 3y + 6z = 30$$
and $5x + 2.5y + 5.5z = 29.$

Solve them for x, y and z.

4 An engineering company part-produces and assembles 2 models of paint spraying equipment. The table shows the number of minutes per item allocated to part-manufacture, assembly and packaging/warehousing.

	Manufacturing	Assembly	Pack/Warehouse
Model One	8	12	10
Model Two	10	7	10

For these products the production manager generally allocates daily timings. These are 395 minutes for manufacturing and 380 minutes for assembly each including slack time of z minutes. The 400 minutes for packaging/warehousing is exact. Within these times the company produces x number of Model One and y number of Model Two. x, y and z are connected by the simultaneous equations

$$8x + 10y + z = 395,$$
$$12x + 7y + z = 380,$$
$$\text{and} \quad 10x + 10y \quad = 400.$$

By solving these equations decide how many of each model are made and the slack time involved.

5   The electrical circuit shows an emf together with various resistors. The sums of the relevant voltages produce the simultaneous equations.

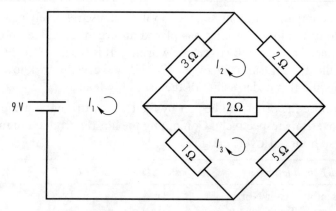

They are in terms of the currents, I_1, I_2 and I_3 amps and form the simultaneous equations

$$4I_1 - 3I_2 - I_3 = 9,$$
$$-3I_1 + 7I_2 - 2I_3 = 0,$$
$$\text{and} \quad -I_1 - 2I_2 + 8I_3 = 0.$$

Solve these simultaneous equations for I_1, I_2 and I_3.

We have given a selection of Exercise questions. You may wish to further practise the methods by using questions from another Exercise.

13 Differential Equations: Numerical Solutions

The objectives of this chapter are to:

1 Understand the idea of iterative techniques to solve first order differential equations.

2 Derive Euler's method from a truncated Taylor's series.

3 Appreciate Euler's method is a severe approximation.

4 Apply Euler's method to solve first order differential equations.

5 Improve upon Euler's method with the Euler–Cauchy method.

6 Apply the Euler–Cauchy method to solve first order differential equations.

7 Appreciate the Runge–Kutta method is the most accurate of the 3 numerical methods in this chapter.

8 Apply the fourth-order Runge–Kutta method to solve first order differential equations.

Introduction

We have solved differential equations using analytical techniques, and will do so again when we use Laplace transforms. However, not all differential equations may be solved using these techniques. Many of them may be solved only using numerical methods. We have already seen examples of numerical solutions (e.g. Newton–Raphson) in Volume 3. Also in Volume 2, Chapter 11, we looked at numerical integration. There we used the mid-ordinate, trapezoidal and Simpson's rules.

In this chapter we concentrate upon solving only first order differential equations to demonstrate the techniques. The methods can be extended to higher order differential equations. Also they can be solved using computer software written for one of the methods. We look at 3 numerical methods, though there are many more alternatives:

1 Euler's method,

2 The Euler–Cauchy method,

3 The Runge–Kutta method.

ASSIGNMENT

Our Assignment for this chapter looks at the flight path (trajectory) of a missile. To demonstrate the techniques we look at just the first 5 seconds of the motion. A first model would exclude any form of resistance to the motion. In this case we have a simple projectile whose flight path is a parabola. The vertical height, y, and the horizontal distance, x, both vary in terms of time, t. Eliminating the parameter, t, we have y as a quadratic function in terms of x.

A more realistic mathematical model includes some resistance. If we apply $F = ma$ we obtain a pair of second order differential equations to describe the horizontal and vertical components of motion. The resistance may be due to a number of factors. Mathematically it is acceptable to say that it is proportional to the speed. We choose our constant of proportionality to involve the mass, m, of the missile. This enables us to simplify our differential equations to

$$\frac{d^2x}{dt^2} = -k\frac{dx}{dt}$$

$\dfrac{dx}{dt}$ is the velocity and $\dfrac{d^2x}{dt^2}$ is the acceleration in the x direction (horizontally), and

$$\frac{d^2y}{dt^2} = -k\frac{dy}{dt} - g$$

where g is the acceleration due to gravity. $\dfrac{dy}{dt}$ is the velocity and $\dfrac{d^2y}{dt^2}$ is the acceleration in the y direction (vertically).

From this pair of differential equations we are going to look at the vertical motion. You can attempt a similar solution for the horizontal component of this model.

Vertically $\dfrac{dy}{dt}$ is the component of the speed, say v.

Then we have $\dfrac{d^2y}{dt^2} = \dfrac{d}{dt}\left(\dfrac{dy}{dt}\right) = \dfrac{dv}{dt}$.

This relationship turns our second order differential equation from

$$\frac{d^2y}{dt^2} = -k\frac{dy}{dt} - g$$

into the first order differential equation

$$\frac{dv}{dt} = -kv - g.$$

In fact there is an analytical solution to this equation, but we shall choose a value for k and solve it numerically.

Euler's method

This is a simple method for solving differential equations. To show how it works we apply it to first order differential equations. It is based upon Taylor's series, i.e.

$$f(x+h) = f(x) + hf'(x) + \frac{h^2}{2!}f''(x) + \frac{h^3}{3!}f'''(x)\ldots$$

where h is a small increment in x.

Euler uses only the early terms of this series; neglecting later, smaller, terms, i.e.

$$f(x+h) \approx f(x) + hf'(x).$$

This approximation can be rather inaccurate. As we see in the next section Euler's method is refined by Cauchy to give the Euler–Cauchy method. The $\approx$ tends to be overlooked. It is replaced with $=$ so that **Euler's method** is quoted as

$$\boldsymbol{f(x+h) = f(x) + hf'(x)}$$

where h is a small increment in x.

The approximation of Euler's method is lessened by using smaller intervals for h. We look at this in Example 13.2.

In each problem we have a first order differential equation with some boundary conditions. These conditions are our starting point for x and y, i.e. in function notation for x and $f(x)$. If h is *not* given we decide upon the small increment. We substitute for them in the right-hand side of Euler's method. This gives us a value for $f(x+h)$, i.e. the y value having moved along from x to $x + h$. Then we use this new value to estimate y by adding a further increment, h, to x. We repeat the method to estimate more values of the function. Remember they must be estimates rather than true values because Euler's method is an approximation, neglecting terms in Taylor's series.

We look at a graphical interpretation In Fig. 13.1. We show $y = f(x)$ to be some general function so that $\dfrac{dy}{dx} = f'(x)$.

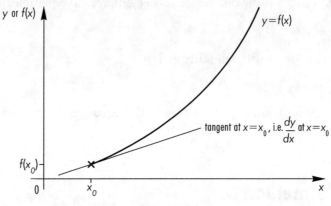

Fig. 13.1

Suppose we have a first order differential equation $\left(\text{i.e. involving}\right.$
$\dfrac{dy}{dx}$ $\left.(\text{or } f'(x))\right)$ which has the true solution $y = f(x)$ in Fig. 13.1. Because *we have not* solved the differential equation *we do not* really know the true shape of $y = f(x)$.

We are given the boundary conditions $x = x_0$ and $y = y_0$ (i.e. in function notation $x = x_0$ and $f(x) = f(x_0)$). They must lie on the curve. We move a small increment, h, to a new value $x_0 + h$. This horizontal move consequently affects the vertical value. We look at the gradient,

$$\text{Gradient} = \frac{\text{vertical change}}{\text{horizontal change}}$$
$$= \frac{f(x_0 + h) - f(x_0)}{(x_0 + h) - x_0} = \frac{f(x_0 + h) - f(x_0)}{h}.$$

This is a straight line joining the points $(x_0, f(x_0))$ to $(x_0 + h, f(x_0 + h))$. We have not solved the differential equation and so do *not* know if $(x_0 + h, f(x_0 + h))$ lies on our curve. $f(x_0 + h)$ is an estimate rather than a true value.

In our equation involving gradient what 'value' do we choose for 'gradient'? Because $f(x_0 + h)$ is an estimate we do not know the gradient at the point $(x_0 + h, f(x_0 + h))$. Also we do not know the gradient of the line joining $(x_0, f(x_0))$ to $(x_0 + h, f(x_0 + h))$. The only alternative is to use the gradient at $(x_0, f(x_0))$, i.e. $f'(x_0)$, from the original differential equation. As you can see in Fig. 13.2 this is also slightly inaccurate. However we can find its value from our original differential equation.

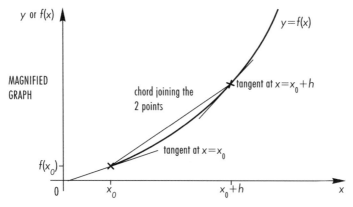

Fig. 13.2

$$\therefore \quad \frac{f(x_0 + h) - f(x_0)}{h} \approx f'(x_0)$$

Multiplying through by h.

i.e. $\quad f(x_0 + h) - f(x_0) \approx hf'(x_0)$

$$f(x_0 + h) \approx f(x_0) + hf'(x_0).$$

Accepting errors created by amending $\approx$ to $=$ we write

$$f(x_0 + h) = f(x_0) + hf'(x_0).$$

Also, rather than the specific x_0 we generalise this to **Euler's method**,

$$f(x + h) = f(x) + hf'(x).$$

In Fig. 13.3 we show the curve, $y = f(x)$, and the gradient at $(x_0, f(x_0))$. Then at the point where $x = x_0 + h$ we see the difference between the true value for $f(x_0 + h)$ and Euler's estimate for $f(x_0 + h)$. Our diagram is magnified because h is a small increment.

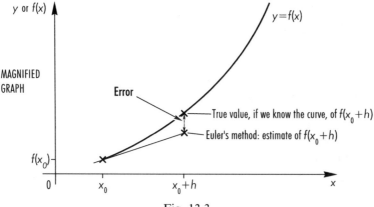

Fig. 13.3

The process of Euler's method involves repetition. In Fig. 13.4 we see it creating a series of straight lines based on gradients. They are estimates for the true curve, i.e. approximating curve to a series of straight lines. The smaller the value of h the closer these lines are to the curve, i.e. the better the approximation.

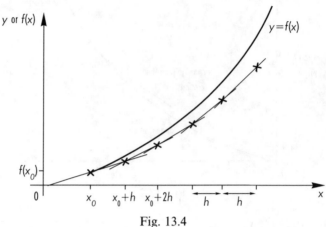

Fig. 13.4

Now we apply the technique to some first order differential equations. You will see the repetitions and a pattern to the numbers.

<hr>

Example 13.1

Find an approximate solution to the differential equation $\dfrac{dy}{dy} = x^2 + y$ given that it passes through the point $(1, 2.15)$.

We are going to work with increments of 0.2 from $x = 1$ to $x = 2$ and quote our answers to 3 decimal places. You may find it convenient to retain more places in your calculator memory. In function notation our differential equation is

$$f'(x) = x^2 + f(x). \quad\text{———}\textcircled{A}$$

Euler's method is

$$f(x + h) = f(x) + hf'(x). \quad\text{———}\textcircled{B}$$

We substitute for $h = 0.2$ with our starting values of $x = 1$ and $f(x) = 2.150$.

Hence $f'(1) = 1^2 + 2.15 = 3.150$

which we use in Euler's method, i.e.

$$f(1.2) = 2.15 + 0.2 \times 3.150 = 2.780.$$

Using Equation $\textcircled{A}$.
$x + h = 1 + 0.2 = 1.2$.
Using Equation $\textcircled{B}$.

We use these values to estimate the function's value at the next increment.

$h = 0.2$, $x = 1.2$, $f(x) = 2.780$.

Hence $f'(1.2) = 1.2^2 + 2.780 = 4.220$

which we use in Euler's method, i.e.

$f(1.4) = 2.780 + 0.2 \times 4.220 = 3.624$.

> Using Equation Ⓐ.
> $x + h = 1.2 + 0.2 = 1.4$.
> Using Equation Ⓑ.

Again we use these values to estimate the function's value at the next increment.

$h = 0.2$, $x = 1.4$, $f(x) = 3.624$.

Hence $f'(1.4) = 1.4^2 + 3.624 = 5.584$

which we use in Euler's method, i.e.

$f(1.6) = 3.624 + 0.2 \times 5.584 = 4.741$.

> Using Equation Ⓐ.
> $x + h = 1.4 + 0.2 = 1.6$.
> Using Equation Ⓑ.

Once again we use these values to estimate the function's value at the next increment.

$h = 0.2$, $x = 1.6$, $f(x) = 4.741$.

Hence $f'(1.6) = 1.6^2 + 4.741 = 7.301$

which we use in Euler's method, i.e.

$f(1.8) = 4.741 + 0.2 \times 7.301 = 6.201$.

> Using Equation Ⓐ.
> $x + h = 1.6 + 0.2 = 1.8$.
> Using Equation Ⓑ.

Finally $h = 0.2$, $x = 1.8$, $f(x) = 6.201$.

Hence $f'(1.8) = 1.8^2 + 6.201 = 9.441$

which we use in Euler's method, i.e.

$f(2.0) = 6.201 + 0.2 \times 9.441 = 8.089$.

> Using Equation Ⓐ.
> $x + h = 1.8 + 0.2 = 2.0$.
> Using Equation Ⓑ.

For ease we present our results in a table

x	$f(x)$ *or* y
1.0	2.150
1.2	2.780
1.4	3.624
1.6	4.741
1.8	6.201
2.0	8.089

In Fig. 13.5 we show these estimated points joined by a series of straight lines. They approximate to the curve of the true, but unknown, function.

You need to understand that we have 2 sources of errors. They are Euler's method itself and the rounding errors caused by using only 3 decimal places.

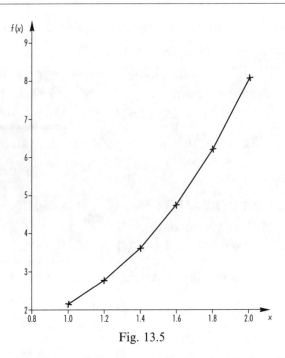

Fig. 13.5

In Example 13.2 we repeat the technique. Here we have chosen a differential equation that we have solved algebraically and quoted values in the final table. This allows us to compare them to our approximate answers using Euler's method. Also we use Euler's method twice, with different increments (h), to show its effect upon accuracy.

Example 13.2

Find an approximate solution to the differential equation

$$2\frac{dy}{dx} + 5y = 9e^{2x}$$

given that it passes through the point $(0, 1)$.

i) We are going to work with increments of 0.1 from $x = 0$ to $x = 0.5$ and quote our answers to 3 decimal places. You may find it convenient to retain more places in your calculator memory. In our differential equation we move the $5y$ term from the left- to the right-hand side and then divide throughout by 2. This leaves $\frac{dy}{dx}$ alone on the left-hand side.

In function notation our differential equation is

$$f'(x) = 4.5e^{2x} - 2.5f(x). \quad\text{——Ⓐ}$$

Euler's method is

$$f(x + h) = f(x) + hf'(x). \quad\text{——Ⓑ}$$

We substitute for $h = 0.1$ with our starting values of $x = 0$ and $f(x) = 1$.

Hence $f'(0) = 4.5e^0 - 2.5 \times 1 = 2$

Using Equation Ⓐ.
$x + h = 0 + 0.1 = 0.1$.
Using Equation Ⓑ.

which we use in Euler's method, i.e.

$\quad f(0.1) = 1 + 0.1 \times 2 = 1.200$.

We use these values to estimate the function's value at the next increment.

$h = 0.1, x = 0.1, f(x) = 1.200$.

Hence $f'(0.1) = 4.5e^{0.2} - 2.5 \times 1.200$

$\qquad\qquad = 2.496$

which we use in Euler's method, i.e.

$\quad f(0.2) = 1.200 + 0.1 \times 2.496 = 1.450$.

Using Equation Ⓐ.
$x + h = 0.1 + 0.1 = 0.2$.
Using Equation Ⓑ.

Again we use these values to estimate the function's value at the next increment.

$h = 0.1, x = 0.2, f(x) = 1.450$.

Hence $f'(0.2) = 4.5e^{0.4} - 2.5 \times 1.450$

$\qquad\qquad = 3.088$

which we use in Euler's method, i.e.

$\quad f(0.3) = 1.450 + 0.1 \times 3.088 = 1.759$.

Using Equation Ⓐ.
$x + h = 0.2 + 0.1 = 0.3$.
Using Equation Ⓑ.

Once again we use these values to estimate the function's value at the next increment.

$h = 0.1, x = 0.3, f(x) = 1.759$.

Hence $f'(0.3) = 4.5e^{0.6} - 2.5 \times 1.759$

$\qquad\qquad = 3.802$

which we use in Euler's method, i.e.

$\quad f(0.4) = 1.759 + 0.1 \times 3.802 = 2.139$.

Using Equation Ⓐ.
$x + h = 0.3 + 0.1 = 0.4$.
Using Equation Ⓑ.

Finally $h = 0.1, x = 0.4, f(x) = 2.139$

Hence $f'(0.4) = 4.5e^{0.8} - 2.5 \times 2.139$

$\qquad\qquad = 4.667$

which we use in Euler's method, i.e.

$\quad f(0.5) = 2.139 + 0.1 \times 4.667 = 2.606$.

Using Equation Ⓐ.
$x + h = 0.4 + 0.1 = 0.5$.
Using Equation Ⓑ.

For ease we present our results in a table

x	$f(x)$ or y
0.0	1.000
0.1	1.200
0.2	1.450
0.3	1.759
0.4	2.139
0.5	2.606

ii) We repeat the solution from the same boundary conditions, this time using $h = 0.05$, i.e. only half the original increment. For clarity we omit the words, simply giving the calculations. As an exercise you should work through this part, checking your values against the quoted ones. In function notation our differential equation is
$$f'(x) = 4.5e^{2x} - 2.5f(x).$$
Euler's method is
$$f(x + h) = f(x) + hf'(x).$$
$$f'(0) = 4.5e^0 - 2.5 \times 1 = 2$$
$$f(0.05) = 1 + 0.05 \times 2 = 1.100$$
$$f'(0.05) = 4.5e^{0.1} - 2.5 \times 1.1 = 2.223$$
$$f(0.10) = 1.100 + 0.05 \times 2.223 = 1.211$$
$$f'(0.10) = 4.5e^{0.2} - 2.5 \times 1.211 = 2.469$$
$$f(0.15) = 1.211 + 0.05 \times 2.469 = 1.334$$
$$f'(0.15) = 4.5e^{0.3} - 2.5 \times 1.334 = 2.739$$
$$f(0.20) = 1.334 + 0.05 \times 2.739 = 1.471$$
$$f'(0.20) = 4.5e^{0.4} - 2.5 \times 1.471 = 3.036$$
$$f(0.25) = 1.471 + 0.05 \times 3.036 = 1.623$$
$$f'(0.25) = 4.5e^{0.5} - 2.5 \times 1.623 = 3.362$$
$$f(0.30) = 1.623 + 0.05 \times 3.362 = 1.791$$
$$f'(0.30) = 4.5e^{0.6} - 2.5 \times 1.791 = 3.722$$
$$f(0.35) = 1.791 + 0.05 \times 3.722 = 1.977$$
$$f'(0.35) = 4.5e^{0.7} - 2.5 \times 1.977 = 4.119$$
$$f(0.40) = 1.977 + 0.05 \times 4.119 = 2.183$$
$$f'(0.40) = 4.5e^{0.8} - 2.5 \times 2.183 = 4.557$$
$$f(0.45) = 2.183 + 0.05 \times 4.557 = 2.411$$
$$f'(0.45) = 4.5e^{0.9} - 2.5 \times 2.411 = 5.041$$
$$f(0.50) = 2.411 + 0.05 \times 5.041 = 2.663.$$

In this example we could have found the true, rather than the approximate numerical, solution. The example has been chosen and worked through twice so we may look at the errors. In the following table we show the true values for $f(x)$ together with our calculated numerical values. We include columns for the percentage errors.

x	True $f(x)$	i) Euler	% error	ii) Euler	% error
0	1.000				
0.05	1.105			1.100	−0.5
0.10	1.221	1.200*	−1.7	1.211	−0.8
0.15	1.350			1.334	−1.2
0.20	1.492	1.450	−2.8	1.471	−1.4
0.25	1.649			1.623	−1.6
0.30	1.822	1.759	−3.5	1.791	−1.7
0.35	2.014			1.977	−1.8
0.40	2.226	2.139	−3.9	2.183	−1.9
0.45	2.460			2.411	−2.0
0.50	2.718	2.606	−4.1	2.663**	−2.0

The percentage errors are based from the true values. We show some specimen calculations for the table.

$$* \% \text{ error} = \frac{1.200 - 1.221}{1.221} \times 100\% \quad ** \% \text{ error} = \frac{2.663 - 2.718}{2.718} \times 100\%$$
$$= -1.7\%. \qquad = -2.0\%.$$

Notice the errors in the table are rising as we work through with the values of x. The errors from the true value are compounding themselves. On the same set of axes the graphs of these table values would be diverging. (With care you could plot the graphs for yourself to see this.) However the sizes of the errors are smaller for the smaller increment. This shows we can improve our accuracy with smaller increments.

ASSIGNMENT

Let us look at our mathematical model of the missile. Remember we have a first order differential equation,

$$\frac{dv}{dt} = -kv - g.$$

v is the vertical component of speed in terms of the time, t. k is a constant and the acceleration due to gravity is $g = 9.81$ ms^{-2}. For a mathematical model we would make an educated guess for the value of k and test it experimentally. For the first few seconds we expect the missile to accelerate from rest. Our mathematical model is too simple for this part of the motion. Where our differential equation applies we are going to assume that it has reached a speed with a vertical component of 200 ms^{-1}.

To demonstrate the technique we look at a 5 second period in increments of 1 second. Also we suggest a value for k of 0.001. In function notation our first order differential equation is

$$f'(t) = -0.001f(t) - 9.81$$

and Euler's method is

$$f(t+h) = f(t) + hf'(t)$$

We work with increments of 1 from $t = 0$ to $t = 5$ and quote our answers to 5 significant figures. You may find it convenient to retain more places in your calculator memory.

We substitute for $h = 1$ with our starting values of $t = 0$ and $f(t) = 200$

Hence $f'(0) = -0.001 \times 200 - 9.81 = -10.01$

which we use in Euler's method, i.e.

$$f(1) = 200 + 1(-10.01) = 189.99.$$

We use these values to estimate the function's value at the next increment.

$h = 1, t = 2, f(t) = 189.99.$

Hence $f'(1) = -0.001 \times 189.99 - 9.81 = -9.999\ldots$

which we use in Euler's method, i.e.

$$f(2) = 189.99 + 1(-9.999\ldots) = 179.99\ldots$$

Again we use these values to estimate the function's value at the next increment.

$h = 1, t = 3, f(t) = 179.99\ldots$

Hence $f'(2) = -0.001 \times 179.99\ldots - 9.81 = -9.989\ldots$

which we use in Euler's method, i.e.

$$f(3) = 179.99\ldots + 1(-9.989\ldots) = 170.00\ldots.$$

Once again we use these values to estimate the function's value at the next increment.

$h = 1, t = 4, f(t) = 170.00\ldots$

Hence $f'(3) = -0.001 \times 170.00\ldots - 9.81 = -9.98$

which we use in Euler's method, i.e.

$$f(4) = 170.00\ldots + 1(-9.98) = 160.02\ldots$$

Finally $h = 1, t = 5, f(t) = 160.02\ldots$

Hence $f'(4) = -0.001 \times 160.02\ldots - 9.81 = -9.97\ldots$

which we use in Euler's method, i.e.

$$f(5) = 160.02\ldots + 1(-9.97\ldots) = 150.05.$$

For ease we present our results in a table

Time, *t* (s)	Vertical speed component, *v* or $f(t)$ (ms^{-1})
0	200.00
1	189.99
2	179.99
3	170.00
4	160.02
5	150.05

▬▬▬ EXERCISE 13.1 ▬▬▬

Use Euler's method to find a numerical solution for each first order differential equation. Each question requires a few increments of evaluation for you to practise the method.

1 $\dfrac{dy}{dx} = x + y$ given that $y = 1.5$ at $x = 0$. Use increments of 0.2 from $x = 0$ to $x = 1$. Quote your answers to 3 decimal places.

2 $\dfrac{dy}{dx} = x - 2y$ from $x = 0$ to $x = 0.5$ at increments of 0.1 based on zero initial conditions. Quote your answers to 3 decimal places.

3 $\dfrac{dy}{dx} = \dfrac{x}{y} + 1$ using 5 increments of 0.1 from $(1, 2.5)$. Maintain as many decimal places as your calculator will allow so that you can quote your answers to 4 decimal places.

4 $2\dfrac{dy}{dx} + y = \sqrt{x}$ from $x = 0$ to $x = 0.3$ using increments of 0.05. We know the solution passes through $y = 0.8$ at $x = 0$. Give your answers to 4 decimal places.

5 $(y + t)\dfrac{dy}{dt} - \sin t = 0$ from $t = 1$ to 1.5 radians in increments of 0.1. At $t = 1$, $y = 0$. Quote your answers to 5 decimal places.

The Euler–Cauchy method

Euler's method, $f(x + h) = f(x) + hf'(x)$, involves an incremental change of h from x to $x + h$. The estimate for $f(x + h)$ is an estimate at the end of the interval. However it is based upon what happens to the function, $f(x)$, and its derivative, $f'(x)$, at the beginning of that interval. This creates an error. Because Euler neglected most of the terms in Taylor's series the estimate for $f(x + h)$ is very rarely exact. We saw this error in Fig. 13.3. Using the Euler–Cauchy method the objective is to reduce that error.

The Euler–Cauchy method improves upon Euler's method using estimates for the gradients at the beginning, $f'(x)$, and the end, $f'(x + h)$, of the interval. In place of $f'(x)$ in Euler's method, this method uses the arithmetic average of these estimates for gradients, i.e.

$$\frac{f'(x) + f'(x + h)}{2}.$$

We see this graphically in Fig. 13.6. We split the incremental interval, h, into halves. Over the first half (x_0 to $x_0 + \frac{1}{2}h$) we use the gradient at the beginning of the interval, $f'(x_0)$. Over the second half ($x_0 + \frac{1}{2}h$ to $x_0 + h$) we use the gradient at the end of the interval, $f'(x_0 + h)$.

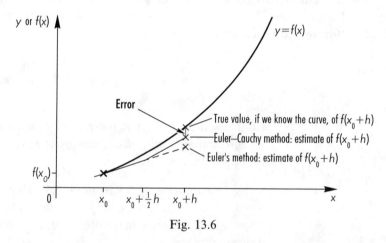

Fig. 13.6

Compare Figs. 13.3 and 13.6. Notice how the error from Euler's method is reduced when using the Euler–Cauchy method. Also the compounding of the errors is reduced. This improved accuracy is at the expense of a slightly more complicated method. We quote the formula in terms of a general x rather than x_0. Replacing $f'(x)$ in Euler's method we have the **Euler–Cauchy method**

$$f(x + h) = f(x) + \frac{h(f'(x) + f'(x + h))}{2}.$$

This is more usually written as

$$f(x + h) = f(x) + \frac{1}{2}h(f'(x) + f'(x + h)).$$

Remember, like Euler's method, these are estimates once we have used our boundary conditions. Again we estimate a series of points which we may wish to plot. Then we can use them to attempt to draw a smooth curve approximating to the function.

For ease we split our method into a set of labelled equations. We use them in turn for each iteration. You will see we need Euler's method in Ⓑ to estimate $f'(x+h)$. The idea is similar to the previous method, just being slightly longer to achieve a more accurate result.

Example 13.3

Find an approximate solution to the differential equation $\dfrac{dy}{dx} = x + 2y$ given that it passes through the point $(1.5, 4)$.

We are going to work with increments of 0.1 from $x = 1.5$ to $x = 2$ and quote our answers to 3 decimal places. You may find it convenient to retain more places in your calculator memory. In function notation our differential equation at $(x, f(x))$ is

$$f'(x) = x + 2f(x). \quad\text{——Ⓐ}$$

Euler's method is

$$f(x+h) = f(x) + hf'(x). \quad\text{——Ⓑ}$$

In function notation our differential equation at $(x+h, f(x+h))$ is

$$f'(x+h) = x + h + 2f(x+h). \quad\text{——Ⓒ}$$

The Euler–Cauchy method gives

$$f(x+h) = f(x) + \frac{1}{2}h(f'(x) + f'(x+h)). \quad\text{——Ⓓ}$$

Before we work through this example we explain the relationships Ⓐ, Ⓑ, Ⓒ and Ⓓ.

Ⓐ is the estimate of the gradient using the original differential equation evaluated at the beginning of each interval.

Ⓑ is the estimate of the function at the end of the interval using Euler's method.

Ⓒ is the estimate of the gradient at the end of each interval.

Ⓓ is the improved estimate of the function at the end of the interval using the Euler–Cauchy method.

We substitute for $h = 0.1$ with our starting values of $x = \mathbf{1.5}$ and $f(x) = \mathbf{4}$ so that $x + h = 1.6$.

Hence $f'(1.5) = 1.5 + 2 \times 4 = 9.500$ | Using Equation Ⓐ.

$f(1.6) = 4 + 0.1 \times 9.500 = 4.950$ | Using Equation Ⓑ.

$f'(1.6) = 1.6 + 2 \times 4.950 = 11.500$ | Using Equation Ⓒ.

$f(\mathbf{1.6}) = 4 + \dfrac{0.1}{2}(9.500 + 11.500)$ | Using Equation Ⓓ.

$$= \mathbf{5.050}.$$

We use these values to estimate the function's value at the next increment.

$h = 0.1$, $x = 1.6$, $f(x) = 5.050$.

Hence $f'(1.6) = 1.6 + 2 \times 5.050 = 11.700$ Using Equation (A).

  $f(1.7) = 5.050 + 0.1 \times 11.700 = 6.220$ Using Equation (B).

  $f'(1.7) = 1.7 + 2 \times 6.220 = 14.1400$ Using Equation (C).

  $f(\mathbf{1.7}) = 5.050 + \dfrac{0.1}{2}(11.700 + 14.140)$ Using Equation (D).

  $= \mathbf{6.342}$.

Again we use these values to estimate the function's value at the next increment.

$h = 0.1$, $x = 1.7$, $f(x) = 6.342$.

Hence $f'(1.7) = 1.7 + 2 \times 6.342 = 14.384$ Using Equation (A).

  $f(1.8) = 6.342 + 0.1 \times 14.384 = 7.780$ Using Equation (B).

  $f'(1.8) = 1.8 + 2 \times 7.780 = 17.361$ Using Equation (C).

  $f(\mathbf{1.8}) = 6.342 + \dfrac{0.1}{2}(14.384 + 17.361)$ Using Equation (D).

  $= \mathbf{7.929}$.

Once again we use these values to estimate the function's value at the next increment.

$h = 0.1$, $x = 1.8$, $f(x) = 7.929$.

Hence $f'(1.8) = 1.8 + 2 \times 7.929 = 17.658$ Using Equation (A).

  $f(1.9) = 7.929 + 0.1 \times 17.658 = 9.695$ Using Equation (B).

  $f'(1.9) = 1.9 + 2 \times 9.695 = 21.290$ Using Equation (C).

  $f(\mathbf{1.9}) = 7.929 + 0.1(17.658 + 21.290)$ Using Equation (D).

  $= \mathbf{9.876}$.

Finally $h = 0.1$, $x = 1.9$, $f(x) = 9.876$.

Hence $f'(1.9) = 1.9 + 2 \times 9.876 = 21.653$ Using Equation (A).

  $f(2.0) = 9.876 + 0.1 \times 21.653 = 12.041$ Using Equation (B).

  $f'(2.0) = 2.0 + 2 \times 12.041 = 26.083$ Using Equation (C).

  $f(\mathbf{2.0}) = 9.876 + \dfrac{0.1}{2}(21.653 + 26.083)$ Using Equation (D).

  $= \mathbf{12.263}$.

For ease we present our results in a table

x	$f(x)$ *or* y
1.5	4.000
1.6	5.050
1.7	6.342
1.8	7.929
1.9	9.876
2.0	12.263

■ ASSIGNMENT ■

Let us look again at our mathematical model of the missile. Remember we have a first order differential equation,

$$\frac{dv}{dt} = -kv - g.$$

v is the vertical component of speed in terms of the time, t. k is a constant and the acceleration due to gravity is $g = 9.81 \text{ ms}^{-2}$. Where our differential equation applies we assume again that it has reached a speed with a vertical component of 200 ms^{-1}. To demonstrate the technique we look at a 5 second period in increments of 1 second. Also we suggest a value for k of 0.001. In function notation our differential equation at $(t, f(t))$ is

$$f'(t) = -0.001f(t) - 9.81. \quad\text{——}Ⓐ$$

Euler's method is

$$f(t + h) = f(t) + hf'(t). \quad\text{——}Ⓑ$$

In function notation our differential equation at $(t + h, f(t + h))$ is

$$f'(t + h) = -0.001f(t + h) - 9.81. \quad\text{——}Ⓒ$$

The Euler–Cauchy method gives

$$f(t + h) = f(t) + \frac{1}{2}h(f'(t) + f'(t + h)) \quad\text{——}Ⓓ$$

We work with increments of 1 from $t = 0$ to $t = 5$ and quote our answers to 5 significant figures. You may find it convenient to retain more places in your calculator memory.

We substitute for $h = 1$ with our starting values of $t = 0$ and $f(t) = 200$.

Hence $f'(0) = -0.001 \times 200 - 9.81 = -10.010$ Using Equation Ⓐ.

$f(1) = 200 + 1 \times -10.010 = 189.99$ Using Equation Ⓑ.

$f'(1) = -0.001 \times 189.99 - 9.81$ Using Equation Ⓒ.

$= -9.999\ldots$

$f(1) = 200 + \frac{1}{2}(-10.010 - 9.999\ldots)$ Using Equation Ⓓ.

$= \mathbf{190.00}.$

We use these values to estimate the function's value at the next increment.

$h = 1, t = 1, f(t) = 190.00.$

Hence $f'(1) = -0.001 \times 190 - 9.81 = -9.999\ldots$ Using Equation Ⓐ.

$f(2) = 190.00 + 1 \times -9.999\ldots = 180.00$ Using Equation Ⓑ.

$f'(2) = -0.001 \times 180.00 - 9.81 = -9.99$ Using Equation Ⓒ.

$f(2) = 190.00 + \frac{1}{2}(-9.999\ldots - 9.99)$ Using Equation Ⓓ.

$= \mathbf{180.01}.$

Again we use these values to estimate the function's value at the next increment.

$h = 1$, $t = 2$, $f(t) = 180.01$.

Hence $f'(2) = -0.001 \times 180.01 - 9.81$

$\qquad = -9.990\ldots$ Using Equation (A).

$\qquad f(3) = 180.01 + 1 \times -9.990\ldots$

$\qquad\quad = 170.01\ldots$ Using Equation (B).

$\qquad f'(3) = -0.001 \times 170.01\ldots - 9.81$

$\qquad\quad = -9.980\ldots$ Using Equation (C).

$\qquad f(3) = 180.01 + \dfrac{1}{2}(-9.990\ldots - 9.980\ldots)$ Using Equation (D).

$\qquad\quad = \mathbf{170.01}.$

Once again we use these values to estimate the function's value at the next increment.

$h = 1$, $t = 3$, $f(t) = 170.01$.

Hence $f'(3) = -0.001 \times 170.01 - 9.81$

$\qquad = -9.980\ldots$ Using Equation (A).

$\qquad f(4) = 170.01 + 1 \times -9.980\ldots$

$\qquad\quad = 160.03\ldots$ Using Equation (B).

$\qquad f'(4) = -0.001 \times 160.03\ldots - 9.81$

$\qquad\quad = -9.970\ldots$ Using Equation (C).

$\qquad f(4) = 170.01 + \dfrac{1}{2}(-9.980\ldots - 9.970\ldots)$ Using Equation (D).

$\qquad\quad = \mathbf{160.03}.$

Finally $h = 1$, $t = 4$, $f(t) = 160.03$.

Hence $f'(4) = -0.001 \times 160.03 - 9.81$

$\qquad = -9.970\ldots$ Using Equation (A).

$\qquad f(5) = 160.03 + 1 \times -9.970\ldots$

$\qquad\quad = 150.059\ldots$ Using Equation (B).

$\qquad f'(5) = -0.001 \times 150.059\ldots - 9.81$

$\qquad\quad = -9.960\ldots$ Using Equation (C).

$\qquad f(5) = 160.03 + \dfrac{1}{2}(-9.970\ldots - 9.960\ldots)$ Using Equation (D).

$\qquad\quad = \mathbf{150.07}.$

Again we present our results in a table. Compare these results with those using Euler's method. In this case there is no great benefit in terms of accuracy.

Time, t (s)	Vertical speed component, v or $f(t)$ (ms^{-1})
0	200.00
1	190.00
2	180.01
3	170.01
4	160.03
5	150.07

▆▆▆▆ EXERCISE 13.2 ▆▆▆▆

Use the Euler–Cauchy method to find a numerical solution for each first order differential equation. Each question requires a few increments of evaluation for you to practise the method.

1 $\dfrac{dy}{dx} = x^2 + y$ given that $y = 2.15$ at $x = 1$. Use increments of 0.2 from $x = 1$ to $x = 2$. Quote your answers to 3 decimal places. Compare your results with those in Example 13.1 where we used Euler's method.

2 $\dfrac{dy}{dx} = 2x + 3y$ from $x = 0$ to $x = 0.5$ at increments of 0.1 given $f(0) = 1.5$. Quote your answers to 4 decimal places.

3 $\dfrac{dy}{dx} = x^2 + y^2$ using 5 increments of 0.1 from $(1, 1)$. Maintain as many decimal places as your calculator will allow so that you can quote your answers to 4 decimal places.

4 $2\dfrac{dy}{dt} = \sqrt{t - y}$ from $t = 1$, $y = 0.5$ to $t = 2$ using increments of 0.2. Give your answers to 4 decimal places.

5 $xy\dfrac{dy}{dx} - x = y$ from $x = 0.5$, $y = 2$, to $x = 1$ in increments of 0.1. Quote your answers to 3 decimal places.

The Runge–Kutta method

This is considered to be a more accurate method than Euler's and Euler–Cauchy's methods. To achieve this accuracy the method is rather long. It is widely used in industry to solve equations numerically. Again we demonstrate the techniques by solving first order differential equations. We use the **fourth order** Runge–Kutta method, i.e. a method with

4 intermediate calculations. We start with a general first order differential equation, say $\dfrac{dy}{dx} = f(x, y)$, i.e. $f'(x) = f(x, y)$. This format for the first derivative, $f'(x)$, in function terms, $f(x, y)$, is important.

Remember this is an iterative method. We start with some boundary conditions and use them together with our differential equation to estimate values at successive small increments. In function notation suppose we are given x and $f(x)$. Remember $y = f(x)$. After some small increment, h, we estimate $f(x + h)$ to be

$$f(x + h) = f(x) + \frac{1}{6}(k_1 + 2k_2 + 2k_3 + k_4)$$

where $k_1 = hf(x, y) = hf'(x).$ | Notice the link between $f(x, y)$ and $f'(x)$.

Also $k_2 = hf(x + \frac{1}{2}h, y + \frac{1}{2}k_1),$

$$k_3 = hf(x + \frac{1}{2}h, y + \frac{1}{2}k_2),$$

$$k_4 = hf(x + h, y + k_3).$$

Again throughout these relationships we can make similar links between the functions and derivatives. The 4 intermediate calculations are shown to be values of k_1, k_2, k_3 and k_4.

Example 13.4

Find an approximate solution to the differential equation $\dfrac{dy}{dx} + y + 2x = 0$ given that it passes through the point where $x = 0$ and $y = -1$.

In this example we are going to work to 4 decimal places. To demonstrate the method we start from $x = 0$ and finish at $x = 1$ using increments of 0.2. Rather than quoting again the relationships for the ks we refer to them above. Also we re-arrange our differential equation. Replacing y with $f(x)$ we write it in function notation

$$f'(x) = -f(x) - 2x$$

i.e. $f'(x) = -(f(x) + 2x).$

We use $h = 0.2$, $\frac{1}{2}h = 0.1$, $x = 0$, $f(x) = -1$.

Hence $k_1 = 0.2f(0, -1)$

$\qquad = 0.2f'(0)$

$\qquad = -0.2(f(0) + 2 \times 0)$ | Using $f'(x) = -(f(x) + 2x).$

$\qquad = -0.2(-1 + 0)$

$\qquad = 0.2,$ $\therefore \quad \frac{1}{2}k_1 = 0.1.$

To find k_2 we use $x + \frac{1}{2}h = 0 + 0.1 = 0.1$ and $y + \frac{1}{2}k_1 = -1 + 0.1$
$= -0.9$.

Hence $k_2 = 0.2f(0.1, -0.9)$

$\qquad = 0.2f'(0.1)$

$\qquad = -0.2(f(0.1) + 2 \times 0.1)$ $\boxed{\text{Using } f'(x) = -(f(x) + 2x).}$

$\qquad = -0.2(-0.9 + 0.2) = -0.2(-0.7)$

$\qquad = 0.14,$ $\therefore \quad \frac{1}{2}k_2 = 0.07.$

To find k_3 we use $x + \frac{1}{2}h = 0 + 0.1 = 0.1$ and $y + \frac{1}{2}k_2 = -1 + 0.07$
$= -0.93$.

Hence $k_3 = 0.2f(0.1, -0.93)$

$\qquad = 0.2f'(0.1)$

$\qquad = -0.2(f(0.1) + 2 \times 0.1)$ $\boxed{\text{Using } f'(x) = -(f(x) + 2x).}$

$\qquad = -0.2(-0.93 + 0.2)$

$\qquad = 0.146.$

To find k_4 we use $x + h = 0 + 0.2 = 0.2$ and $y + k_3 = -1 + 0.146$
$= -0.854$.

Hence $k_4 = 0.2f(0.2, -0.854)$

$\qquad = 0.2f'(0.2)$

$\qquad = -0.2(f(0.2) + 2 \times 0.2)$ $\boxed{\text{Using } f'(x) = -(f(x) + 2x).}$

$\qquad = -0.2(-0.854 + 0.4)$

$\qquad = 0.0908.$

Using $f(x + h) = f(x) + \frac{1}{6}(k_1 + 2k_2 + 2k_3 + k_4)$ we have

$$y_1 = -1 + \frac{1}{6}(0.2 + 2(0.14) + 2(0.146) + 0.0908)$$

$$= -1 + \frac{1}{6}(0.8628)$$

$$= -0.8562, \qquad \text{i.e. } y_1 = -0.8562 \text{ corresponds to } x_1 = 0.2.$$

This has been only the first iteration. We repeat the technique to find y_2.

We use $h = 0.2$, $\frac{1}{2}h = 0.1$, $x = 0.2$, $f(x) = -0.8562$.

Hence $k_1 = 0.2f(0.2, -0.8562)$

$\qquad = 0.2f'(0.2)$

$\qquad = -0.2(f(0.2) + 2 \times 0.2)$ $\boxed{\text{Using } f'(x) = -(f(x) + 2x).}$

$\qquad = -0.2(-0.8562 + 0.4)$

$\qquad = 0.0912,$ $\therefore \quad \frac{1}{2}k_1 = 0.0456.$

To find k_2 we use $x + \dfrac{1}{2}h = 0.2 + 0.1 = 0.3$ and

$y + \dfrac{1}{2}k_1 = -0.8562 + 0.0456 = -0.8106.$

Hence $\quad k_2 = 0.2f(0.3, -0.8106)$

$\qquad = 0.2f'(0.3)$

$\qquad = -0.2(f(0.3) + 2 \times 0.3) \qquad \boxed{\text{Using } f'(x) = -(f(x) + 2x).}$

$\qquad = -0.2(-0.8106 + 0.6)$

$\qquad = 0.0421, \qquad\qquad \therefore \quad \dfrac{1}{2}k_2 = 0.0211.$

To find k_3 we use $x + \dfrac{1}{2}h = 0.2 + 0.1 = 0.3$ and

$y + \dfrac{1}{2}k_2 = -0.8562 + 0.0211 = -0.8351.$

Hence $\quad k_3 = 0.2f(0.3, -0.8351)$

$\qquad = 0.2f'(0.3)$

$\qquad = -0.2(f(0.3) + 2 \times 0.3) \qquad \boxed{\text{Using } f'(x) = -(f(x) + 2x).}$

$\qquad = -0.2(-0.8351 + 0.6)$

$\qquad = 0.0470.$

To find k_4 we use $x + h = 0.2 + 0.2 = 0.4$ and $y + k_3 = -0.8562 + 0.0470 = -0.8092.$

Hence $\quad k_4 = 0.2f(0.4, -0.8092)$

$\qquad = 0.2f'(0.4)$

$\qquad = -0.2(f(0.4) + 2 \times 0.4) \qquad \boxed{\text{Using } f'(x) = -(f(x) + 2x).}$

$\qquad = -0.2(-0.8092 + 0.8)$

$\qquad = 0.0018.$

Using $f(x + h) = f(x) + \dfrac{1}{6}(k_1 + 2k_2 + 2k_3 + k_4)$ we have

$$y_2 = -0.8562 + \frac{1}{6}(0.0912 + 2(0.0421) + 2(0.0470) + 0.0018)$$

$$= -0.8562 + \frac{1}{6}(0.2712)$$

$$= -0.8110, \qquad \text{i.e. } y_2 = -0.8110 \text{ corresponds to } x_2 = 0.4.$$

This has been the second iteration. Once again we repeat the technique to find y_3.

We use $h = 0.2$, $\frac{1}{2}h = 0.1$, $x = 0.4$, $f(x) = -0.8110$.

Hence $k_1 = 0.2f(0.4, -0.8110)$

$\qquad = 0.2f'(0.4)$

$\qquad = -0.2(f(0.4) + 2 \times 0.4)$ ⬛ Using $f'(x) = -(f(x) + 2x)$.

$\qquad = -0.2(-0.8110 + 0.8)$

$\qquad = 0.0022,$ $\qquad\qquad \therefore \; \frac{1}{2}k_1 = 0.0011.$

To find k_2 we use $x + \frac{1}{2}h = 0.4 + 0.1 = 0.5$ and

$y + \frac{1}{2}k_1 = -0.8110 + 0.0011 = -0.8099.$

Hence $k_2 = 0.2f(0.5, -0.8099)$

$\qquad = 0.2f'(0.5)$

$\qquad = -0.2(f(0.5) + 2 \times 0.5)$ ⬛ Using $f'(x) = -(f(x) + 2x)$.

$\qquad = -0.2(-0.8099 + 1.0)$

$\qquad = -0.0380,$ $\qquad\qquad \therefore \; \frac{1}{2}k_2 = -0.0190.$

To find k_3 we use $x + \frac{1}{2}h = 0.4 + 0.1 = 0.5$ and

$y + \frac{1}{2}k_2 = -0.8110 - 0.0190 = -0.8300.$

Hence $k_3 = 0.2f(0.5, -0.8300)$

$\qquad = 0.2f'(0.5)$

$\qquad = -0.2(f(0.5) + 2 \times 0.5)$ ⬛ Using $f'(x) = -(f(x) + 2x)$.

$\qquad = -0.2(-0.8300 + 1.0)$

$\qquad = -0.0340.$

To find k_4 we use $x + h = 0.4 + 0.2 = 0.6$ and $y + k_3 = -0.8110 - 0.0340$
$= -0.8450.$

Hence $k_4 = 0.2f(0.6, -0.8450)$

$\qquad = 0.2f'(0.6)$

$\qquad = -0.2(f(0.6) + 2 \times 0.6)$ ⬛ Using $f'(x) = -(f(x) + 2x)$.

$\qquad = -0.2(-0.8450 + 1.2)$

$\qquad = -0.0710.$

Using $f(x+h) = f(x) + \dfrac{1}{6}(k_1 + 2k_2 + 2k_3 + k_4)$ we have

$$y_3 = -0.8110 + \frac{1}{6}(0.0022 + 2(-0.0380) + 2(-0.0340) - 0.0710)$$

$$= -0.8110 + \frac{1}{6}(-0.2128)$$

$$= -0.8465, \qquad \text{i.e. } y_3 = -0.8465 \text{ corresponds to } x_3 = 0.6.$$

This has been the third iteration. Once again we repeat the technique to find y_4.

We use $h = 0.2$, $\dfrac{1}{2}h = 0.1$, $x = 0.6$, $f(x) = -0.8465$.

Hence $k_1 = 0.2f(0.6, -0.8465)$

$$= 0.2f'(0.6)$$

$$= -0.2(f(0.6) + 2 \times 0.6) \qquad \boxed{\text{Using } f'(x) = -(f(x) + 2x).}$$

$$= -0.2(-0.8465 + 1.2)$$

$$= -0.0707, \qquad\qquad \therefore \ \frac{1}{2}k_1 = -0.0353.$$

To find k_2 we use $x + \dfrac{1}{2}h = 0.6 + 0.1 = 0.7$ and

$y + \dfrac{1}{2}k_1 = -0.8465 - 0.0353 = -0.8819.$

Hence $k_2 = 0.2f(0.7, -0.8819)$

$$= 0.2f'(0.7)$$

$$= -0.2(f(0.7) + 2 \times 0.7) \qquad \boxed{\text{Using } f'(x) = -(f(x) + 2x).}$$

$$= -0.2(-0.8819 + 1.4)$$

$$= -0.1036, \qquad\qquad \therefore \ \frac{1}{2}k_2 = -0.0518.$$

To find k_3 we use $x + \dfrac{1}{2}h = 0.6 + 0.1 = 0.7$ and

$y + \dfrac{1}{2}k_2 = -0.8465 - 0.0518 = -0.8983.$

Hence $k_3 = 0.2f(0.7, -0.8983)$

$$= 0.2f'(0.7)$$

$$= -0.2(f(0.7) + 2 \times 0.7) \qquad \boxed{\text{Using } f'(x) = -(f(x) + 2x).}$$

$$= -0.2(-0.8983 + 1.4)$$

$$= -0.1003.$$

To find k_4 we use $x + h = 0.6 + 0.2 = 0.8$ and $y + k_3 = -0.8465 - 0.1003$
$= -0.9468$.

Hence $k_4 = 0.2f(0.8, -0.9468)$

$= 0.2f'(0.8)$

$= -0.2(f(0.8) + 2 \times 0.8)$ Using $f'(x) = -(f(x) + 2x)$.

$= -0.2(-0.9468 + 1.6)$

$= -0.1306$.

Using $f(x + h) = f(x) + \dfrac{1}{6}(k_1 + 2k_2 + 2k_3 + k_4)$ we have

$$y_4 = -0.8465 + \frac{1}{6}(-0.0707 + 2(-0.1036) + 2(-0.1003) - 0.1306)$$

$$= -0.8465 + \frac{1}{6}(-0.6091)$$

$= -0.9480$,   i.e. $y_4 = -0.9480$ corresponds to $x_4 = 0.8$.

This has been the fourth iteration. We show one more iteration to find y_5.

We use $h = 0.2$, $\dfrac{1}{2}h = 0.1$, $x = 0.8$, $f(x) = -0.9480$.

Hence $k_1 = 0.2f(0.8, -0.9480)$

$= 0.2f'(0.8)$

$= -0.2(f(0.8) + 2 \times 0.8)$ Using $f'(x) = -(f(x) + 2x)$.

$= -0.2(-0.9480 + 1.6)$

$= -0.1304$, $\therefore \dfrac{1}{2}k_1 = -0.0652$.

To find k_2 we use $x + \dfrac{1}{2}h = 0.8 + 0.1 = 0.9$ and

$y + \dfrac{1}{2}k_1 = -0.9480 - 0.0652 = -1.0132$.

Hence $k_2 = 0.2f(0.9, -1.0132)$

$= 0.2f'(0.9)$

$= -0.2(f(0.9) + 2 \times 0.9)$ Using $f'(x) = -(f(x) + 2x)$.

$= -0.2(-1.0132 + 1.8)$

$= -0.1574$, $\therefore \dfrac{1}{2}k_2 = -0.0787$.

To find k_3 we use $x + \dfrac{1}{2}h = 0.8 + 0.1 = 0.9$ and

$y + \dfrac{1}{2}k_2 = -0.9480 - 0.0787 = -1.0269.$

Hence $\quad k_3 = 0.2f(0.9, -1.0269)$

$\qquad = 0.2f'(0.9)$

$\qquad = -0.2(f(0.9) + 2 \times 0.9)$ $\qquad$ $\boxed{\text{Using } f'(x) = -(f(x) + 2x).}$

$\qquad = -0.2(-1.0269 + 1.8)$

$\qquad = -0.1546.$

To find k_4 we use $x + h = 0.8 + 0.2 = 1.0$ and $y + k_3 = -0.9480 - 0.1546$
$= -1.1026$

Hence $\quad k_4 = 0.2f(1.0, -1.1026)$

$\qquad = 0.2f'(1.0)$

$\qquad = -0.2(f(1.0) + 2 \times 1.0)$ $\qquad$ $\boxed{\text{Using } f'(x) = -(f(x) + 2x).}$

$\qquad = -0.2(-1.1026 + 2.0)$

$\qquad = -0.1795.$

Using $f(x + h) = f(x) + \dfrac{1}{6}(k_1 + 2k_2 + 2k_3 + k_4)$ we have

$$y_5 = -0.9480 + \frac{1}{6}(-0.1304 + 2(-0.1573) + 2(-0.1546) - 0.1795)$$

$$= -0.9480 + \frac{1}{6}(-0.9337)$$

$$= -1.1036, \quad \text{i.e. } y_5 = -1.1036 \text{ corresponds to } x_5 = 1.0.$$

We collect our iteration results together in the table below

x	y
0	-1
0.2	-0.8562
0.4	-0.8110
0.6	-0.8465
0.8	-0.9480
1.0	-1.1036

ASSIGNMENT

We take a final look at our mathematical model of the missile. Remember
we have a first order differential equation,

$$\frac{dv}{dt} = -0.001v - 9.81.$$

v is the vertical component of speed in terms of the time, t. Where our differential equation applies we assume again that it has reached a speed with a vertical component of 200 ms^{-1}. To demonstrate previous techniques we looked at a 5 second period in increments of 1 second. Here we look at a single iteration, having just worked through 5 iterations in the previous example. In function notation our differential equation at $(t, f(t))$ is

$$f'(t) = -0.001f(t) - 9.81.$$

In the previous example we removed a common minus sign. As an alternative we do not amend this differential equation.

The Runge–Kutta method uses

$$f(t + h) = f(t) + \frac{1}{6}(k_1 + 2k_2 + 2k_3 + k_4)$$

where $\qquad k_1 = hf(t, v) = hf'(t),$

$$k_2 = hf(t + \frac{1}{2}h, v + \frac{1}{2}k_1),$$

$$k_3 = hf(t + \frac{1}{2}h, v + \frac{1}{2}k_2),$$

$$k_4 = hf(t + h, v + k_3).$$

We use $h = 1$, $\frac{1}{2}h = 0.5$, $t = 0$, $f(t) = 200$.

Hence $\quad k_1 = f(0, 200)$

$\qquad = f'(0)$

$\qquad = -0.001f(0) - 9.81$ $\qquad$ | Using $f'(t) = -0.001f(t) - 9.81$.

$\qquad = -0.001 \times 200 - 9.81$

$\qquad = -10.010, \qquad\qquad \therefore \quad \frac{1}{2}k_1 = -5.005.$

To find k_2 we use $t + \frac{1}{2}h = 0 + 0.5 = 0.5$ and $v + \frac{1}{2}k_1 = 200 - 5.005$
$= 194.995.$

Hence $\quad k_2 = f(0.5, 194.995)$

$\qquad = f'(0.5)$

$\qquad = -0.001f(0.5) - 9.81$ $\qquad$ | Using $f'(t) = -0.001f(t) - 9.81$.

$\qquad = -0.001 \times 194.995 - 9.81$

$\qquad = -10.005, \qquad\qquad \therefore \quad \frac{1}{2}k_2 = -5.0025.$

To find k_3 we use $t + \dfrac{1}{2}h = 0 + 0.5 = 0.5$ and $v + \dfrac{1}{2}k_2 = 200 - 5.0025$
$= 194.9975$.

Hence $k_3 = f(0.5, 194.9975)$

$\qquad = f'(0.5)$

$\qquad = -0.001f(0.5) - 9.81$ $\qquad$ Using $f'(t) = -0.001f(t) - 9.81.$

$\qquad = -0.001 \times 194.9975 - 9.81$

$\qquad = -10.005$.

To find k_4 we use $t + h = 0 + 1 = 1$ and $y + k_3 = 200 - 10.005 = 189.995$.

Hence $k_4 = f(1.0, 189.995)$

$\qquad = f'(1.0)$

$\qquad = -0.001f(1.0) - 9.81$ $\qquad$ Using $f'(t) = -0.001f(t) - 9.81.$

$\qquad = -0.001 \times 189.995 - 9.81$

$\qquad = -9.999 \ldots, \quad$ i.e. $\ -10.000$

Using $f(t + h) = f(t) + \dfrac{1}{6}(k_1 + 2k_2 + 2k_3 + k_4)$ we have

$v_1 = 200 + 1(-10.010 + 2(-10.005) + 2(-10.005) - 10.000)$

$\quad = 200 + \dfrac{1}{6}(-60.030)$

$\quad = 189.995, \qquad$ i.e. $v_1 = 189.995$ corresponds to $t_1 = 1.0$.

This tells us the velocity is estimated to be 189.995 ms^{-1} after 1.0 s. Remember this has been only the first iteration. We can repeat the technique to estimate other velocities. Notice the closeness of the answers to all 3 numerical methods we have looked at.

EXERCISE 13.3

Use the Runge–Kutta method to find a numerical solution for each first order differential equation. Each question requires a few increments of evaluation for you to practise the method.

1 $\dfrac{dy}{dx} = x^2 + y$ $\qquad$ given that $y = 2.15$ at $x = 1$. Use increments of 0.2 from $x = 1$ to $x = 2$. Quote your answers to 4 decimal places.

2 $\dfrac{dy}{dx} = x^2 + xy$ $\qquad$ given $x = 0.5$, $y = 1$. Use four iterations from $x = 0.5$ in increments of 0.1.

3 $2y\dfrac{dy}{dx}+y^2=3$ from a starting point of $(0,2)$ and using three iterations of increment 0.1. Before you start the iterations you should re-arrange this differential equation to make $\dfrac{dy}{dx}$ the subject.

4 $\dfrac{dy}{dx}=y+3(1-x)$ from $x=0.5$ to $x=0.6$ in increments of 0.02. At $x=0.5$ y has a value of 4.80.

5 $\dfrac{dy}{d\theta}+\dfrac{\cos\theta}{\theta-y}=0$ for three iterations from $\theta=0$ rad, $y=1.5$, in increments of 0.1 rad.

We have reached a final Exercise of practical problems. You should attempt the questions using a selection of the 3 methods introduced in the chapter. For variety and experience you should repeat questions using an alternative method.

■■■■ EXERCISE 13.4 ■■■■

1 This question deals with a vessel cooling and its surrounding environment. (In Chapter 16 a similar example applies to a human corpse, when the body is still warm, to estimate the time of death.) In this case the law is represented by the differential equation

$$\frac{dT}{dt}=-0.2\left(T-\sqrt{T}\right).$$

T is the temperature of the vessel (°C) and t is the time (hours).

Originally the vessel has a temperature of 65°C. Estimate its temperature at quarter hour intervals over the first hour.

2 A large portion of a rocket's mass, m kg, is fuel so that during flight this mass changes significantly. The mass, m, is related to the velocity, v ms^{-1}, of the rocket according to the differential equation

$$\frac{dm}{dv}+\frac{mv}{2000+\sqrt{v}}=0.$$

The original mass of the rocket, when resting on the launch pad, is 13 500 kg. Estimate the mass for the first three increments of 10 ms^{-1}.

3 The needle deflection from the vertical, θ, in a meter is initially zero. Its movement is modelled by the differential equation

$$\frac{d\theta}{dt}=4t^2e^{-3t}.$$

Estimate the deflection at intervals of 0.1 s during the first half second.

4 y is the displacement of a damper, modelled by the first order differential equation

$$e^t \frac{dy}{dt} + \frac{4}{\sqrt{3}} \cos \frac{t}{\sqrt{3}} = 0$$

where t represents time. Initially there is a displacement of approximately 1.75 mm. Estimate the displacements after 0.2 s, 0.4 s and 0.6 s.

5   The resistance $R \, \Omega$ of a conductor varies with temperature $\theta°C$ according to the first order differential equation

$$\frac{dR}{d\theta} = \frac{0.04R}{1 + R}.$$

Estimate the resistance at positive intervals of 2.5°C based upon it being 45.6 Ω at 75°C. For practice use 4 iterations.

14 First Order Differential Equations

The objectives of this chapter are to:

1. Recognise a first order differential equation which is homogeneous in $\frac{y}{x}$.

2. Apply the $y = vx$ substitution to the differential equation.

3. Separate the variables, v and x, and integrate.

4. Express the solution of y in terms of x.

5. Derive the integrating factor for $\frac{dy}{dx} + Py = Q$.

6. Multiply the differential equation by the integrating factor and integrate throughout.

7. Obtain a solution to the differential equation.

Introduction

We introduced some simple differential equations in Volume 2, Chapter 15. They were simple first and second order differential equations. In our solutions we used direct integration and separation of variables.

In this chapter we concentrate upon first order differential equations, i.e. the highest derivative is $\frac{dy}{dx}$, or similar. We look at 2 further types:

1. Homogeneous equations
2. Linear equations.

In Chapter 15 we move on to look at some types of second order differential equations.

■ ASSIGNMENT ■

Our Assignment for this chapter looks at the flight path (trajectory) of a missile. To demonstrate the techniques we look at just the first 5 seconds of the motion. A first model would exclude any form of resistance to the

motion. In this case we have a simple projectile whose flight path is a parabola. The vertical height, y, and the horizontal distance, x, both vary in terms of time, t. Eliminating the parameter, t, we have y as a quadratic function in terms of x.

A more realistic mathematical model includes some resistance. If we apply $F = ma$ we obtain a pair of second order differential equations to describe the horizontal and vertical components of motion. The resistance may be due to a number of factors. Mathematically it is acceptable to say that it is proportional to the speed. We choose our constant of proportionality to involve the mass, m, of the missile. This enables us to simplify our differential equations to

$$\frac{d^2x}{dt^2} = -k\frac{dx}{dt};$$

$\dfrac{dx}{dt}$ is the velocity and $\dfrac{d^2x}{dt^2}$ is the acceleration in the x direction (horizontally) and

$$\frac{d^2y}{dt^2} = -k\frac{dy}{dt} - g$$

where g is the acceleration due to gravity. $\dfrac{dy}{dt}$ is the velocity and $\dfrac{d^2y}{dt^2}$ is the acceleration in the y direction (vertically).

From this pair of differential equations we are going to look at the vertical motion. You can attempt a similar solution for the horizontal component of this model.

Vertically $\dfrac{dy}{dt}$ is the component of the speed, say v.

Then we have $\dfrac{d^2y}{dt^2} = \dfrac{d}{dt}\left(\dfrac{dy}{dt}\right) = \dfrac{dv}{dt}$.

This relationship turns our second order differential equation from

$$\frac{d^2y}{dt^2} = -k\frac{dy}{dt} - g$$

into the first order differential equation

$$\frac{dv}{dt} = -kv - g.$$

In this chapter we obtain an analytical solution. Previously, in Chapter 13, we found an alternative numerical solution.

Homogeneous differential equations

A first order differential equation that is homogeneous may be written in the form $\dfrac{dy}{dx} = f\left(\dfrac{y}{x}\right)$, i.e. the derivative is some divisible function of x and y. The standard approach is to write $y = vx$ and substitute into the differential equation. If the differential equation is indeed homogeneous then all the x terms cancel. For this to happen we need the same common factors of x terms in both the numerator and denominator.

Example 14.1

We show that $\dfrac{dy}{dx} = \dfrac{xy}{x^2 + y^2}$ is a homogeneous differential equation.

By recognition we see that $\dfrac{dy}{dx} = f\left(\dfrac{y}{x}\right)$ where $f\left(\dfrac{y}{x}\right) = \dfrac{xy}{x^2 + y^2}$.

Substituting $y = vx$ we have $\dfrac{dy}{dx} = \dfrac{x(vx)}{x^2 + v^2x^2}$

$$= \frac{x^2v}{x^2(1 + v^2)} \qquad \boxed{x^2 \text{ terms cancel.}}$$

$$= \frac{v}{1 + v^2}.$$

In Example 14.1 we see that now the differential equation involves 3 variables; x, y and v. This needs our attention. We look at $y = vx$ and differentiate using the product rule, i.e.

$$\frac{dy}{dx} = v\frac{d}{dx}(x) + x\frac{d}{dx}(v)$$

$$= v + x\frac{dv}{dx}.$$

> Product rule, $y = uv$
>
> $$\frac{dy}{dx} = u\frac{dv}{dx} + v\frac{du}{dx},$$
>
> and $\frac{d}{dx}(x) = 1.$

This is a standard result we apply in the following Examples.

Example 14.2

Substituting for the first derivative in $\dfrac{dy}{dx} = \dfrac{v}{1+v^2}$

we get
$$v + x\frac{dv}{dx} = \frac{v}{1+v^2}$$

$$x\frac{dv}{dx} = \frac{v}{1+v^2} - v$$

$$= \frac{v - v(1+v^2)}{1+v^2}$$

$$= \frac{v - v - v^3}{1+v^2}$$

i.e.
$$x\frac{dv}{dx} = \frac{-v^3}{1+v^2}.$$

Example 14.3

The format of our original differential equation, $\dfrac{dy}{dx} = \dfrac{xy}{x^2 + y^2}$, is now

$$x\frac{dv}{dx} = \frac{-v^3}{1+v^2}.$$

The original format was *not* in an integrable form. This amended format is useful, separating the variables and integrating. The position of the dv is important, indicating we gather the v terms on the left. On the right-hand side we gather the x terms, i.e.

$$\left(\frac{1+v^2}{-v^3}\right)\frac{dv}{dx} = \frac{1}{x}.$$

We integrate with respect to x, i.e.

$$\int\left(\frac{1+v^2}{-v^3}\right)\frac{dv}{dx}\,dx = \int\frac{1}{x}\,dx.$$

On the left-hand side the dxs appear to cancel, i.e. $\dfrac{dv}{dx}dx$ simplifies to dv.

We have the variables exclusively on separate sides of the = sign. Also we simplify the variables, v, on the left to write

$$\int \left(\frac{-1}{v^3} - \frac{v^2}{v^3} \right) dv = \int \frac{1}{x} \, dx$$

i.e. $\quad \displaystyle\int \left(-v^{-3} - \frac{1}{v} \right) dv = \int \frac{1}{x} \, dx$

so that $\quad \displaystyle \frac{-v^{-2}}{-2} - \ln v = \ln x + c$

i.e. $\quad \displaystyle \frac{1}{2v^2} - \ln v = \ln x + c.$

In Example 14.4 we go further, using limits of integration and replacing v according to $y = vx$.

▮▮▮▮ **Example 14.4** ▮▮▮▮

Solve the first order differential equation $\dfrac{dy}{dx} = \dfrac{xy}{x^2 + y^2}$ given that $y = 1$ at $x = 1$.

The boundary conditions are the lower limits for x and y. We substitute for them into $y = vx$ to obtain the lower limit for v, i.e. 1. The upper limits are based on the variables, as we saw in Volume 2, Chapter 15.

We link together the previous Examples.

In $\qquad\qquad\qquad\qquad \dfrac{dy}{dx} = \dfrac{xy}{x^2 + y^2}$

we substitute for $y = vx$ and the first derivative to get

$$v + x\frac{dv}{dx} = \frac{v}{1 + v^2}.$$

This simplifies to $\qquad\qquad x\dfrac{dv}{dx} = \dfrac{-v^3}{1 + v^2}.$

We separate the variables and integrate, using the limits of integration to write

$$\int_1^v \left(-v^{-3} - \frac{1}{v} \right) dv = \int_1^x \frac{1}{x} \, dx$$

i.e. $\qquad\qquad \left[\dfrac{1}{2v^2} - \ln v \right]_1^v = \left[\ln x \right]_1^x$

$$\left[\frac{1}{2v^2} - \ln v \right] - \left[\frac{1}{2 \times 1^2} - \ln 1 \right] = \ln x - \ln 1$$

i.e. $\qquad\qquad \dfrac{1}{2v^2} - \ln v - \dfrac{1}{2} = \ln x.$ $\qquad$ ▮ $\boxed{\ln 1 = 0.}$

There are various ways we might choose to simplify these variables, x and v. Here we might choose to gather together the natural logarithms, i.e.

$$\frac{1}{2}\left(\frac{1}{v^2} - 1\right) = \ln v + \ln x$$

$$\frac{1}{v^2} - 1 = 2\ln vx. \qquad \boxed{\text{Law of logarithms.}}$$

The original variables were x and y linked by $y = vx$. To return to those variables we replace v using $v = \dfrac{y}{x}$, i.e.

$$\frac{1}{\left(\frac{y}{x}\right)^2} - 1 = 2\ln\left(\frac{y}{x}x\right)$$

i.e. $\dfrac{x^2}{y^2} - 1 = 2\ln y.$

y is implicitly related to x. It is not unusual to have implicit solutions. Alternatively you may wish to express x in terms of y. You can work through the steps for yourself to get $x = y\sqrt{1 + 2\ln y}$. We work through a problem linking together the techniques we have demonstrated so far.

Example 14.5

We solve the first order differential equation $\dfrac{dy}{dx} = \dfrac{2y - x}{x}$ given the solution passes through the point $(3, 2)$.

We start with $y = vx.$

Differentiating with respect to x, using the product rule, we get

$$\frac{dy}{dx} = v\frac{d}{dx}(x) + x\frac{d}{dx}(v)$$

i.e. $\dfrac{dy}{dx} = v + x\dfrac{dv}{dx}.$ $\qquad \boxed{\dfrac{d}{dx}(x) = 1.}$

In $\dfrac{dy}{dx} = \dfrac{2y - x}{x}$

we substitute for the first derivative and for $y = vx$ so that

$$v + x\frac{dv}{dx} = \frac{2vx - x}{x} = \frac{x(2v - 1)}{x}$$

i.e. $x\dfrac{dv}{dx} = 2v - 1 - v$

i.e. $x\dfrac{dv}{dx} = v - 1.$

The position of the dv dictates that we move v terms to the left. Hence, separating the variables, we move the x to the right, i.e.

$$\left(\frac{1}{v - 1}\right)\frac{dv}{dx} = \frac{1}{x}.$$

Separating the variables and integrating with respect to x

$$\int \left(\frac{1}{v-1} \right) \frac{dv}{dx} \, dx = \int \frac{1}{x} \, dx.$$

On the left-hand side $\frac{dv}{dx} dx$ simplifies to dv. Also we have our boundary condition of $x = 3$ and $y = 2$. In $y = vx$ they substitute to give $v = \frac{2}{3}$.

Our integrals become

$$\int_{2/3}^{v} \left(\frac{1}{v-1} \right) dv = \int_{3}^{x} \frac{1}{x} \, dx.$$

i.e. $$\left[\ln(v-1) \right]_{2/3}^{v} = \left[\ln x \right]_{3}^{x}$$

$$\ln(v-1) - \ln\left(\frac{-1}{3} \right) = \ln x - \ln 3.$$

Strangely we have the logarithm of a negative number, yet it is *not* supposed to be defined. We can adjust our logarithms to remove this problem.

$$\ln(v-1) - \ln\left(\frac{-1}{3} \right) = \ln\left(\frac{v-1}{-1/3} \right)$$

> Law of logarithms.

$$= \ln\left(\frac{-(-v+1)}{-1/3} \right)$$

> Removing a negative sign as a common factor in the numerator.

$$= \ln 3(1-v).$$

> Cancelling the negative factors and inverting a fraction from division to multiplication.

Remember our original definition for logarithms is based upon positive numbers only. This result, $\ln 3(1-v)$, is only defined for $1 - v > 0$, i.e. for $1 > v$.

Now $\ln 3(1-v) = \ln \frac{x}{3}$

i.e. $3(1-v) = \frac{x}{3}$

> Cancelling the logarithms consistently applied on both sides.

$$1 - v = \frac{x}{9}$$

and using $y = vx$, i.e. $v = \frac{y}{x}$, we have

$$1 - \frac{y}{x} = \frac{x}{9}.$$

y appears once only implying that we can write *y* explicitly in terms of *x*. We omit a few steps, leaving you to fill them in for yourself, to reach

$$y = \frac{(9-x)x}{9}.$$

ASSIGNMENT

Let us look at our mathematical model of the missile. Remember we have a first order differential equation,

$$\frac{dv}{dt} = -kv - g.$$

v is the vertical component of speed in terms of the time, *t*. *k* is a constant and the acceleration due to gravity is $g = 9.81 \text{ ms}^{-2}$. For a mathematical model we would make an educated guess for the value of *k* and test it experimentally. For the first few seconds we expect the missile to accelerate from rest. Our mathematical model is too simple for this part of the motion. Where our differential equation applies we are going to assume that it has reached a speed with a vertical component of 200 ms^{-1}.

A first order differential equation that is homogeneous has the form

$$\frac{dy}{dx} = f\left(\frac{y}{x}\right).$$

The variables *x* and *y* are replaced by *t* and *v*. In this Assignment we need

$$\frac{dv}{dx} = f\left(\frac{v}{t}\right).$$

Comparing the general form with our original differential equation we see that $-kv - g$ does *not* have the form $f(v)$. Hence $\frac{dv}{dt} = -kv - g$ is *not* homogeneous. We need an alternative method of solution.

EXERCISE 14.1

Solve the following first order differential equations. Questions **1** and **2** require general solutions only. Questions **3**, **4** and **5** include boundary conditions and so require particular solutions.

1 $\quad \dfrac{dy}{dx} = -\dfrac{(x+2y)}{2x}$

2 $\quad \dfrac{dy}{dx} = \dfrac{-2y}{2x+y}$

3 $\quad x\dfrac{dy}{dx} = y + 2x \qquad$ given $y = 0$ at $x = 2$.

4 $\quad \dfrac{dy}{dx} = \dfrac{(x+y)y}{(y-2x)x} \qquad$ provided that $y = 1$ at $x = 1$.

5 $\quad \dfrac{dy}{dx} = \dfrac{-(x^2+y^2)}{2x^2} \qquad$ with the boundary condition $y = \frac{1}{2}$ at $x = 1$.

Linear differential equations

Here we look at another specific type of first order differential equation. Generally we may write

$$\frac{dy}{dx} + Py = Q.$$

Both P and Q are functions of x (including numerical values) but *not* of y. In each example it is vital we identify P and Q, particularly P. We form $\int P \, dx$ and then $e^{\int P \, dx}$. When we do so we ignore the constant of integration, c; including it later in the general solution. This exponential is called an **integrating factor**. We multiply our original differential equation throughout by the integrating factor. It always creates a perfect differential on the left-hand side based upon the product rule.

Example 14.6

Solve the first order differential equation $2\frac{dy}{dx} - 4y = 6x$.

Notice we will get a general solution because there are no boundary conditions. Also to create the correct format we divide throughout by 2 to write

$$\frac{dy}{dx} - 2y = 3x.$$

We compare this differential equation with the standard

$$\frac{dy}{dx} + Py = Q$$

and by recognition write $P = -2$ and $Q = 3x$.

Then $\qquad \int P \, dx = \int -2 \, dx = -2x$

> Ignoring the constant of integration at this stage.

so that $\qquad e^{\int P \, dx} = e^{-2x}$.

Using $\qquad \dfrac{dy}{dx} - 2y = 3x$

we multiply throughout by e^{-2x}, i.e.

$$e^{-2x}\frac{dy}{dx} - 2ye^{-2x} = 3xe^{-2x}.$$

The left-hand side is a perfect differential, i.e. $\dfrac{d}{dx}\left(ye^{-2x}\right)$. Differentiate using the product rule to check this for yourself.

We can amend our differential equation from

$$e^{-2x}\frac{dy}{dx} - 2ye^{-2x} = 3xe^{-2x}$$

to $$\frac{d}{dx}\left(ye^{-2x}\right) = 3xe^{-2x}.$$

Integration is the reverse process to differentiation so that

$$ye^{-2x} = \int 3xe^{-2x}\,dx.$$

We saw this type of integration, also involving a product, in Volume 2 Chapter 13. It often, but *not* always, happens. This is 'integration by parts' which has a formula

$$\int u\frac{dv}{dx}\,dx = uv - \int v\frac{du}{dx}\,dx.$$

Let $u = 3x$ and $\dfrac{dv}{dx} = e^{-2x}$

$\therefore$ $\dfrac{du}{dx} = 3$ and $v = -\dfrac{1}{2}e^{-2x}.$

Using the integration by parts formula we have

$$\int 3xe^{-2x}\,dx = (3x)\left(-\frac{1}{2}e^{-2x}\right) - \int\left(-\frac{1}{2}e^{-2x}\right)(3)\,dx$$

$$= -\frac{3}{2}xe^{-2x} + \frac{3}{2}\int e^{-2x}\,dx$$

$$= -\frac{3}{2}xe^{-2x} - \frac{3}{4}e^{-2x} + c$$

which we link with our left-hand side to write

$$ye^{-2x} = -\frac{3}{2}xe^{-2x} - \frac{3}{4}e^{-2x} + c.$$

To simplify we divide by e^{-2x}. Some of the exponentials cancel to leave

$$\frac{c}{e^{-2x}} = ce^{2x},$$

i.e. $$y = -\frac{3}{2}x - \frac{3}{4} + ce^{2x}$$

written as $$y = ce^{2x} - \frac{3}{2}x - \frac{3}{4}.$$

Example 14.7

Solve the first order differential equation $\dfrac{dy}{dx} - y\tan x = 2\sin x$ given that $y = 1$ at $x = \dfrac{\pi}{3}$.

We compare this differential equation with the standard $\dfrac{dy}{dx} + Py = Q$ and by recognition write $P = -\tan x$ and $Q = 2\sin x$.

Then $\displaystyle\int P\,dx = \int -\tan x\,dx = \int -\frac{\sin x}{\cos x}\,dx = \ln(\cos x)$

so that $e^{\int P\,dx} = e^{\ln(\cos x)}$.

> Ignoring the constant of
> integration at this stage.

Let us investigate $e^{\ln(\cos x)}$. Suppose we have a value for x. To find the value of $e^{\ln(\cos x)}$ the order of calculator operations is

$$\boxed{x}\quad \boxed{\cos}\quad \boxed{\ln}\quad \boxed{e^x}.$$

Now $\ln$ and e^x are inverse operations of each other, i.e. their effects balance out each other. This means that $e^{\ln(\cos x)} = \cos x$. You should try this for yourself, using say $x = \dfrac{\pi}{4}$ rad.

We return to our differential equation

$$\frac{dy}{dx} - y\tan x = 2\sin x$$

and multiply throughout by the integrating factor, $\cos x$, i.e.

$$\cos x\frac{dy}{dx} - y\tan x.\cos x = 2\sin x.\cos x$$

> $\tan x.\cos x = \dfrac{\sin x}{\cos x}.\cos x$
> $\qquad\qquad = \sin x.$
>
> Double angle formula,
> $2\sin x.\cos x = \sin 2x.$

i.e. $\cos x\dfrac{dy}{dx} - y\sin x = \sin 2x.$

As expected the left-hand side is a perfect differential so we write

$$\frac{d}{dx}\left(y\cos x\right) = \sin 2x.$$

Integration is the reverse process to differentiation so that

$$y\cos x = \int \sin 2x\,dx$$

i.e. $y\cos x = -\dfrac{1}{2}\cos 2x + c.$

> General solution.

We substitute for our boundary condition $y = 1$ and $x = \dfrac{\pi}{3}$ to get

$$1\cos\frac{\pi}{3} = -\frac{1}{2}\cos\frac{2\pi}{3} + c$$

i.e. $\dfrac{1}{2} = -\dfrac{1}{2}\left(-\dfrac{1}{2}\right) + c$

$$c = \frac{1}{4}.$$

> $\dfrac{1}{2} - \dfrac{1}{4} = \dfrac{1}{4}.$

Substituting for c in the general solution we have the particular solution

$$y\cos x = \frac{1}{4} - \frac{1}{2}\cos 2x.$$

━━━━━ **ASSIGNMENT** ━━━━━

Let us look at our mathematical model of the missile. Remember we have a first order differential equation,

$$\frac{dv}{dt} = -kv - g.$$

v is the vertical component of speed in terms of the time, t. k is a constant and the acceleration due to gravity is $g = 9.81$ ms^{-2}. For a mathematical model we would make an educated guess for the value of k and test it experimentally. For the first few seconds we expect the missile to accelerate from rest. Our mathematical model is too simple for this part of the motion. Where our differential equation applies we are going to assume that it has reached a speed with a vertical component of 200 ms^{-1}. Also we suggest a value for k of 0.001.

We substitute for these values in our first order differential equation to write

$$\frac{dv}{dt} = -0.001v - 9.81$$

i.e. $$\frac{dv}{dt} + 0.001v = -9.81$$

which we compare with

$$\frac{dy}{dx} + Py = Q.$$

Of course we have replaced the general variables of x and y with t and v. By recognition we have $P = 0.001$ to give

$$\int P \, dt = \int 0.001 \, dt = 0.001t$$

> Ignoring the constant of integration at this stage.

so that $$e^{\int P \, dt} = e^{0.001t}.$$

Using $$\frac{dv}{dt} + 0.001v = -9.81$$

we multiply throughout by $e^{0.001t}$, i.e.

$$e^{0.001t}\frac{dv}{dt} + 0.001ve^{0.001t} = -9.81e^{0.001t}.$$

The left-hand side is a perfect differential, i.e. $\frac{d}{dt}\left(ve^{0.001t}\right)$, to give

$$\frac{d}{dt}\left(ve^{0.001t}\right) = -9.81e^{0.001t}.$$

Integration is the reverse process to differentiation so that

$$ve^{0.001t} = \int -9.81e^{0.001t} \, dt.$$

Unlike Example 14.6 this does *not* require a solution using 'integration by parts'. It is a simple standard integral, i.e.

$$ve^{0.001t} = \frac{-9.81}{0.001}e^{0.001t} + c.$$

We simplify the division and substitute for our boundary condition, $v = 200$ at $t = 0$, i.e.

$$200e^0 = -9810e^0 + c$$

$$c = 10010.$$

$$\boxed{e^0 = 1.}$$

Substituting for c and then dividing throughout by the exponential we get

$$ve^{0.001t} = 10010 - 9810e^{0.001t}$$

i.e. $$v = 10010e^{-0.001t} - 9810$$

gives the vertical component of velocity, v, in terms of time, t.

■■■■ EXERCISE 14.2 ■■■■

Find the particular solutions to the following first order differential equations.

1 $\dfrac{dy}{dx} + y = \dfrac{1}{2}e^{-x}$ given $y = -\dfrac{1}{2}$ where $x = 0$.

2 $\dfrac{dy}{dx} + \dfrac{y}{x} = \dfrac{2}{x}$ provided that $y = 3$ at $x = 1$.

3 $\dfrac{dy}{dx} + y + 2\sin x = 0$ given $y = 2$ at $x = 0$.

4 $2\dfrac{dy}{dx} + 2y = 3e^{2x} + x - 2$ provided that $y = -1$ at $x = 0$.

5 $\dfrac{dy}{dx} + y\cot x = \cos x$ with the boundary condition $y = 1$ at $x = \dfrac{\pi}{6}$.

We have seen a practical application of a first order differential equation in the Assignment. Here is a final Exercise for you to try.

■■■■ EXERCISE 14.3 ■■■■

1 The circuit diagram shows an inductance of 1 H in series with a resistance of 5 Ω and an emf of 125 V. The voltage drop across the inductor is $1\dfrac{di}{dt}$ and across the resistor is $5i$. Our differential equation models the sum of these voltage drops being equal to the emf, i.e.

$$\frac{di}{dt} + 5i = 125.$$

Apply an integrating factor to find a solution to this differential equation, given the initial current is zero. Find the current after 0.05 seconds.

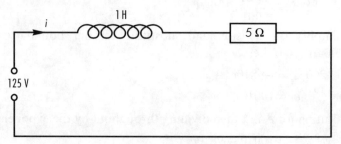

2 A small car of mass 800 kg is parked, facing down a gentle incline, when suddenly it is hit from behind. Its initial speed is 5 ms^{-1} down the incline. The car has a forward force of 400 N and a resistive force of twice its speed, v. Using $F = ma$ we model this scenario with the first order differential equation

$$800\frac{dv}{dt} = 400 - 2v \qquad \text{where } t \text{ represents time.}$$

Using an integrating factor solve the differential equation for v in terms of t. Monitor the car's progress by finding the speed after 5, 10 and 15 seconds. Eventually it crashes into a wall at 45 mph. (Remember to convert mph to ms^{-1}.) Find the time between the two crashes.

3 A body of mass 0.2 kg moves along the x-axis. It is subject to 2 forces; one of attraction to the origin ($0.2a^2x$ where a is a constant) and one being a frictional resistance ($0.2kv$ where k is a constant and v is the velocity). The differential equation modelling the body is

$$-(0.2kv + 0.2a^2x) = 0.2\frac{dv}{dt}.$$

Explain why we use $v\dfrac{dv}{dx}$ in place of $\dfrac{dv}{dt}$ and demonstrate the connection between them. Using $v\dfrac{dv}{dx}$ decide if that version of the differential equation is homogeneous, but do *not* solve it.

4 A resistance of 500 Ω is connected in series with a capacitor of 10^{-5} F and an emf of 100 V. $500\dfrac{dq}{dt} + 100\,000q = 100$, where q is the charge, models this electrical circuit. Initially the current, i, where $i = \dfrac{dq}{dt}$, is 0.02 A. Substitute into the differential equation to find the initial charge. Using an integrating factor and this newly found initial condition solve the differential equation.

5   A body of mass m moves along the x-axis. It is subject to 2 forces; one of attraction to the origin (ma^2x where a is a constant) and one being a frictional resistance (mkv^2 where k is a constant and v is the velocity). The differential equation modelling the body is

$$-(mkv^2 + ma^2x) = mv\frac{dv}{dx}.$$

Make a substitution of $y = v^2$ to simplify the equation. Given the body starts from rest at some distance $x = b$ from the origin solve this differential equation.

15 Second Order Differential Equations

The objectives of this chapter are to:

1 Solve a differential equation of the type $\dfrac{d^2y}{dx^2} = f(x)$.

2 Solve a differential equation of the type $\dfrac{d^2y}{dx^2} = f(y)$.

3 Obtain the auxiliary equation $am^2 + bm + c = 0$ to solve a differential equation of the type $a\dfrac{d^2y}{dx^2} + b\dfrac{dy}{dx} + cy = 0$.

4 Solve the differential equation in **3** for the auxiliary equation having
    i) real and different roots,
    ii) repeated roots,
    iii) complex roots.

5 Solve a differential equation of the type $a\dfrac{d^2y}{dx^2} + b\dfrac{dy}{dx} + cy = f(x)$ using complementary functions and particular integrals.

6 Use differential equations in mathematical models of practical applications.

Introduction

We have seen differential equations in Volume 2, Chapter 15, and developed our solution of more first order ones in the previous chapter of this Volume. A second order differential equation contains $\dfrac{d^2y}{dx^2}$ (or similar) as the highest derivative. Remember we use the reverse process to differentiation, i.e. integration, to solve differential equations. As usual we can find a general solution, and then a particular solution if we are given boundary conditions. Here they are linear differential equations. This means $\dfrac{d^2y}{dx^2}, \dfrac{dy}{dx}$ and y are *not* raised to any power beyond the power 1, i.e.

as we see them written here. Also all the coefficients of these terms are constant. In this chapter we look at 4 forms of second order differential equations:

1 $\quad \dfrac{d^2y}{dx^2} = f(x),$

2 $\quad \dfrac{d^2y}{dx^2} = f(y),$

3 $\quad \dfrac{d^2y}{dx^2} + a\dfrac{dy}{dx} + by = 0,$

4 $\quad \dfrac{d^2y}{dx^2} + a\dfrac{dy}{dx} + by = f(x).$

a and b are constant values in each question.

The auxiliary equation we introduce is a quadratic equation and so may have 1 of 3 different solutions. Each solution determines the nature of the solution of the differential equation. Exponential functions together with other functions are specifically associated with each of them.

■■■■■■ ASSIGNMENT ■■■■■■

In Volume 2, Chapter 7, we looked at differentiation applied to a simple pendulum. We return to a similar type of problem, but here concentrate on differential equations to model the pendulum. Remember we looked at modelling using differential equations in Chapter 15 of that Volume.

In Fig. 15.1 we have a simple pendulum oscillating about a central vertical line. They are small oscillations. Our first, approximate, mathematical model of this motion is simple harmonic. Later we refine our model to include a resistive force. This is damped harmonic motion.

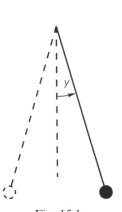
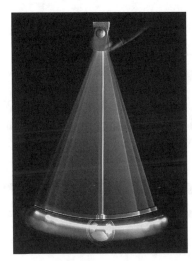

Fig. 15.1

Equations of the type $\dfrac{d^2y}{dx^2} = f(x)$

Notice that we have only the second derivative together with some function of x, $f(x)$. $f(x)$ is the important feature in the solution. Remember the meaning of $\dfrac{d^2y}{dx^2}$ is $\dfrac{d}{dx}\left(\dfrac{dy}{dx}\right)$. We integrate the second derivative with respect to x to find the first derivative. We integrate the first derivative to find y as a function of x. Because we are integrating twice we expect to include 2 constants of integration in our general solution. Hence we need 2 sets of boundary conditions to find a particular solution.

Example 15.1

We find the general solution to the second order differential equation $\dfrac{d^2y}{dx^2} = 1 + x^2 + 8\sin 2x$.

We start with $\quad \dfrac{d^2y}{dx^2} = 1 + x^2 + 8\sin 2x$

and integrate with respect to x, i.e.

$$\frac{dy}{dx} = x + \frac{x^3}{3} + -\frac{8}{2}\cos 2x + c_1$$

> c_1 is a constant of integration.

i.e. $\quad \dfrac{dy}{dx} = x + \dfrac{x^3}{3} - 4\cos 2x + c_1.$

We integrate again with respect to x, i.e.

$$y = \frac{x^2}{2} + \frac{x^4}{3 \times 4} - \frac{4}{2}\sin 2x + c_1 x + c_2$$

> c_2 is another constant of integration.

i.e. $\quad y = -2\sin 2x + \dfrac{x^4}{12} + \dfrac{x^2}{2} + c_1 x + c_2$

is a general solution of y in terms of x.

Notice we have re-ordered the terms, bringing the polynomial terms (x to the powers 4, 2 and 1) together in descending order.

Example 15.2

We find the particular solution to the second order differential equation $\dfrac{d^2y}{dx^2} = e^{-x} + 2\cos x$ given boundary conditions $\dfrac{dy}{dx} = 4$ at $x = 0$ and $y = 6$ at $x = 1$.

We start with $\dfrac{d^2 y}{dx^2} = e^{-x} + 2\cos x$

and integrate with respect to x, i.e.

$$\frac{dy}{dx} = -e^{-x} + 2\sin x + c_1.$$

> c_1 is a constant of integration.

To find a value for c_1 we substitute using $\dfrac{dy}{dx} = 4$ at $x = 0$,

i.e. $\qquad 4 = -e^{-0} + 2\sin 0 + c_1$

> $e^{-0} = e^0 = 1.$

$\qquad 4 + 1 = c_1$

$\qquad 5 = c_1.$

We substitute for c_1, i.e.

$$\frac{dy}{dx} = -e^{-x} + 2\sin x + 5.$$

Again we integrate with respect to x, i.e.

$$y = e^{-x} - 2\cos x + 5x + c_2.$$

> Remember to use radians for the cosine.

To find a value for c_2 we substitute using $y = 6$ at $x = 1$,

$$6 = e^{-1} - 2\cos 1 + 5(1) + c_2$$

i.e. $\qquad 6 = 0.3679 - 2(0.5403) + 5 + c_2$

to give $\quad c_2 = 1.71.$

Finally we substitute for c_2 to give the particular solution

$$y = e^{-x} - 2\cos x + 5x + 1.71.$$

Example 15.3

We find the particular solution to the second order differential equation $\dfrac{d^2 y}{dx^2} = 1 + x^2 + 8\sin 2x$ given that $y = 2$ at $x = 1$ and $y = 5$ at $x = -1$.

We know from Example 15.1 that the general solution is

$$y = -2\sin 2x + \frac{x^4}{12} + \frac{x^2}{2} + c_1 x + c_2.$$

Because we have no boundary condition for $\dfrac{dy}{dx}$ we cannot substitute part way through the solution. Instead we substitute for our x and y boundary conditions to create a pair of simultaneous equations in c_1 and c_2.

Substituting for $y = 2$, $x = 1$ we have

$$2 = -2\sin 2 + \frac{1^4}{12} + \frac{1^2}{2} + c_1 + c_2.$$

> Using radians for the sine.

i.e. $\quad 3.235 = c_1 + c_2.$ ——————①

Substituting for $y = 5$, $x = -1$ we have

$$5 = -2\sin(-2) + \frac{(-1)^4}{12} + \frac{(-1)^2}{2} + c_1(-1) + c_2.$$

i.e. $2.598 = -c_1 + c_2.$ ————————②

Equations ① and ② are a pair of simultaneous equations in c_1 and c_2.

Adding we get   Subtracting we get

$\qquad\qquad 5.833 = 2c_2$ $\qquad\qquad 0.637 = 2c_1$

$\qquad\qquad c_2 = 2.92.$ $\qquad\qquad c_1 = 0.32.$

Substituting for these values into our general solution we have the particular solution

$$y = -2\sin 2x + \frac{x^4}{12} + \frac{x^2}{2} + 0.32x + 2.92.$$

ASSIGNMENT

In the next section we shall see a differential equation of the type $\frac{d^2y}{dx^2} = f(y)$ models simple harmonic motion rather than $\frac{d^2y}{dx^2} = f(x)$.

EXERCISE 15.1

In Question **1** you can find only the general solution of the differential equation. For the remaining questions use the boundary conditions to find each particular solution.

1 $\dfrac{d^2y}{dx^2} = x^2 + e^{2x}.$

2 $\dfrac{d^2y}{dx^2} = x + \dfrac{2}{x^2}$ given $\dfrac{dy}{dx} = 0$ at $x = 2$ and $y = \dfrac{1}{6}$ at $x = 1$.

3 $\dfrac{d^2y}{dx^2} - \cos 2x = e^{-x}$ given $x = 0$, $y = \dfrac{3}{4}$ and $x = \dfrac{\pi}{2}$, $y = 0$.

4 $\dfrac{d^2y}{dt^2} = \dfrac{1}{\cos^2 t}$ given all initial values are zero.

5 $\dfrac{d^2x}{dt^2} = \sin\dfrac{t}{2}$ given that initially $x = 0$ and then $x = 1$ at $t = \pi$.

Equations of the type $\dfrac{d^2y}{dx^2} = f(y)$

We may see this type of second order differential equation as $\dfrac{d^2y}{dx^2} \pm f(y) = 0$. In this case we simply move the function of y to write $\dfrac{d^2y}{dx^2} = \mp f(y)$.

We look briefly at a general solution, starting with

$$\frac{d^2y}{dx^2} = f(y) \qquad \text{or} \qquad f''(y) = f(y)$$

and multiplying throughout by $2\dfrac{dy}{dx}$, or $2f'(y)$, i.e.

$$2\frac{dy}{dx}\frac{d^2y}{dx^2} = 2f(y)\frac{dy}{dx} \qquad \text{or} \qquad 2f'(y)f''(y) = 2f(y)f'(y).$$

Using the function of a function rule we have

$$\frac{d}{dx}\left(\frac{dy}{dx}\right)^2 = 2\frac{dy}{dx}\frac{d^2y}{dx^2} \qquad \text{or} \qquad \frac{d}{dx}\left(f'(y)\right)^2 = 2f'(y)f''(y).$$

This means we can re-write

$$2\frac{dy}{dx}\frac{d^2y}{dx^2} = 2f(y)\frac{dy}{dx} \qquad \text{or} \qquad 2f'(y)f''(y) = 2f(y)f'(y)$$

as $\quad \dfrac{d}{dx}\left(\dfrac{dy}{dx}\right)^2 = 2f(y)\dfrac{dy}{dx} \qquad \text{or} \qquad \dfrac{d}{dx}\left(f'(y)\right)^2 = 2f(y)f'(y).$

We integrate throughout with respect to x. On the left-hand side the derivative $\dfrac{d}{dx}$ is balanced by the integration with respect to x, leaving $\left(\dfrac{dy}{dx}\right)^2$. On the right-hand side we need to look carefully at the form of $f(y)$. This indicates how it will integrate. Integrating generally we get

$$\left(\frac{dy}{dx}\right)^2 = \int 2f(y)\frac{dy}{dx}\,dx$$

> $\dfrac{dy}{dx}dx$ simplifies to dy.

i.e. $\quad \left(\dfrac{dy}{dx}\right)^2 = \displaystyle\int 2f(y)\,dy.$

As usual we can use this idea to find both general and particular solutions.

Example 15.4

We solve the second order differential equation $\dfrac{d^2y}{dx^2} = y^2$ given the boundary conditions $\dfrac{dy}{dx} = 0$ at $y = 0$ and $y = 4$ at $x = \sqrt{3}$.

We start with $\dfrac{d^2y}{dx^2} = y^2$

and multiply throughout by $2\dfrac{dy}{dx}$, i.e.

$$2\frac{dy}{dx}\frac{d^2y}{dx^2} = 2y^2\frac{dy}{dx}.$$

We know the left-hand side may be re-written and substituted to give

$$\frac{d}{dx}\left(\frac{dy}{dx}\right)^2 = 2y^2\frac{dy}{dx}.$$

Integrating throughout with respect to x we get

$$\left(\frac{dy}{dx}\right)^2 = \int 2y^2\frac{dy}{dx}\,dx = 2\int y^2\,dy$$

i.e. $$\left(\frac{dy}{dx}\right)^2 = \frac{2y^3}{3} + c_1.$$

Using our first boundary condition we substitute to get

$$0 = c_1$$

so that $$\left(\frac{dy}{dx}\right)^2 = \frac{2y^3}{3}.$$

$$\boxed{0^2 = \frac{2 \times 0^3}{3} + c_1.}$$

We take the square root of both sides to find a simple relationship only for $\dfrac{dy}{dx}$, i.e.

$$\frac{dy}{dx} = \pm\sqrt{\frac{2}{3}}y^{3/2}$$

$$\boxed{\sqrt{y^3} = (y^3)^{1/2} = y^{3/2}.}$$

We need to separate the variables and integrate with respect to x. The position of $\dfrac{dy}{dx}$ dictates we gather y terms on the left. Hence we gather x terms, if any, on the right. Then

$$\frac{1}{y^{3/2}}\frac{dy}{dx} = \pm\sqrt{\frac{2}{3}}.$$

Integrating with respect to x we have

$$\int y^{-3/2}\frac{dy}{dx}\,dx = \pm\int\sqrt{\frac{2}{3}}\,dx$$

i.e. $$\int y^{-3/2}\,dy = \pm\int\sqrt{\frac{2}{3}}\,dx$$

$$\boxed{\frac{dy}{dx}dx \text{ simplifies to } dy.}$$

so that $\dfrac{y^{-1/2}}{-1/2} = \pm\sqrt{\dfrac{2}{3}}x + c_2$

i.e. $-2y^{-1/2} = \pm\sqrt{\dfrac{2}{3}}x + c_2.$

Using our second boundary condition we substitute to get

$$-2 \times \dfrac{1}{\sqrt{4}} = \pm\sqrt{\dfrac{2}{3}} \times \sqrt{3} + c_2.$$

> For $y = 4$ then $y^{-1/2} = 4^{-1/2}$
> $$= \dfrac{1}{4^{1/2}}.$$

Using the positive square root and simplifiying the arithmetic we get
$c_2 = -2.414.$

We substitute for c_2 and re-arrange the algebra to get

$$y = \left(\dfrac{2}{2.414 - 0.816x}\right)^2.$$

> Fill in the missing
> stages for yourself.

■ ASSIGNMENT ■

Our first, approximate, mathematical model of the pendulum's motion is simple harmonic motion. We can model using either forces or energy. In this case we look at the energy at some general angle θ (Fig. 15.2) increasing from the central vertical line. At the top point from where the pendulum is suspended we state the potential energy is zero. We always refer potential energy to some fixed horizontal line. Because the pendulum is below this horizontal line its potential energy is negative. The pendulum travels through an arc, i.e. its motion is circular. This means the velocity, v, is given by $v = \ell\dfrac{d\theta}{dt}$. The system is conservative, i.e. it does no work, the total energy (kinetic and potential) is constant. Just the proportion of each type changes throughout the motion.

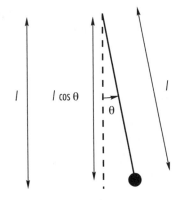

Fig. 15.2

Mass of the pendulum $= m$.

Acceleration due to gravity $= g$.

Length of string $= \ell$.

Potential energy $= mgh = -mg\ell\cos\theta.$

Kinetic energy $= \dfrac{1}{2}mv^2 = \dfrac{1}{2}m\left(\ell\dfrac{d\theta}{dt}\right)^2 = \dfrac{1}{2}m\ell^2\left(\dfrac{d\theta}{dt}\right)^2.$

Applying the conservation of energy principle we have

kinetic energy + potential energy = constant

i.e. $\frac{1}{2}m\ell^2\left(\frac{d\theta}{dt}\right)^2 + -mg\ell\cos\theta = \text{constant}.$

We differentiate with respect to time, t, i.e.

$$\frac{d}{dt}\left(\frac{1}{2}m\ell^2\left(\frac{d\theta}{dt}\right)^2\right) + \frac{d}{dt}\left(-mg\ell\cos\theta\right) = \frac{d}{dt}(\text{constant})$$

$$\frac{d}{dt}\left(\frac{1}{2}m\ell^2\left(\frac{d\theta}{dt}\right)^2\right) + \frac{d}{d\theta}\left(-mgl\cos\theta\right)\frac{d\theta}{dt} = \frac{d}{dt}(\text{constant})$$

> Implicit differentiation for θ.

$$\frac{1}{2}m\ell^2 2\left(\frac{d\theta}{dt}\right)\frac{d^2\theta}{dt^2} + mg\ell\sin\theta\frac{d\theta}{dt} = 0$$

> m, g and ℓ are constants.

We can cancel and simplify the terms so that

$$\frac{d^2\theta}{dt^2} = -\frac{g}{\ell}\sin\theta.$$

> Cancelling $m\ell^2\frac{d\theta}{dt}$ and moving the second term to the right.

For small angles $\sin\theta \approx \theta$. $\frac{g}{\ell}$ is a constant and we replace it with n^2 to ease the later integration.

$$\frac{d^2\theta}{dt^2} = -n^2\theta.$$

> We use a numerical value for n later.

Compared with our general differential equation type we have replaced y with θ and x with t.

To solve this differential equation we let $\frac{d\theta}{dt} = q,$

then $\frac{d^2\theta}{dt^2} = \frac{dq}{dt} = \frac{d\theta}{dt} \times \frac{dq}{d\theta} = q\frac{dq}{d\theta}.$

The introduction of this dummy variable, q, allows us to separate the variables and integrate. However it increases the number of variables from 2 (i.e θ and t) to 3 (i.e. θ, t and q). We apply the function of a function rule to eliminate t and return to only 2 variables. Hence we have

$$q\frac{dq}{d\theta} = -n^2\theta.$$

Then $\int q\frac{dq}{d\theta}\,d\theta = \int -n^2\theta\,d\theta$

i.e. $\int q\,dq = \int -n^2\theta\,d\theta$

$$\frac{q^2}{2} = -\frac{n^2\theta^2}{2} + c_1$$

or $\frac{1}{2}\left(\frac{d\theta}{dt}\right)^2 = -\frac{n^2\theta^2}{2} + c_1.$

At the maximum angular displacement, α (amplitude), from the central vertical line the pendulum momentarily stops. It reverses its direction and swings back. We interpret this as $\dfrac{d\theta}{dt} = 0$ at $\theta = \alpha$ and use it as a boundary condition.

$$0 = -\frac{n^2\alpha^2}{2} + c_1$$

> Later we use $n = 1.2$ and $\alpha = 0.08$ radians.

i.e.
$$\frac{n^2\alpha^2}{2} = c_1.$$

We substitute for c_1 and simplify to get

$$\left(\frac{d\theta}{dt}\right)^2 = n^2\alpha^2\left(1 - \frac{\theta^2}{\alpha^2}\right)$$

> Cancelling through by $\frac{1}{2}$ and removing α^2 as a factor for easy integration later.

i.e.
$$\frac{d\theta}{dt} = n\alpha\sqrt{1 - \frac{\theta^2}{\alpha^2}}.$$

> Using the positive square root.

Separating the variables and integrating

$$\frac{1}{\sqrt{1 - \dfrac{\theta^2}{\alpha^2}}}\frac{d\theta}{dt} = n\alpha$$

becomes
$$\int \frac{1}{\sqrt{1 - \dfrac{\theta^2}{\alpha^2}}}\frac{d\theta}{dt}\,dt = \int n\alpha\,dt$$

i.e.
$$\int \frac{1/\alpha}{\sqrt{1 - \dfrac{\theta^2}{\alpha^2}}}\,d\theta = \int n\,dt$$

> Integration gives an inverse sine.

so that
$$\sin^{-1}\left(\frac{\theta}{\alpha}\right) = nt + c_2$$

i.e.
$$\frac{\theta}{\alpha} = \sin(nt + c_2).$$

From where we start timing dictates the value of c_2. In this case we use $\theta = 0$ at $t = 0$,

i.e.
$$0 = \sin c_2$$

i.e.
$$0 = c_2.$$

Substituting for c_2 we get $\theta = \alpha \sin nt$ to be our particular solution. In this case we suggest appropriate values for α and n may be $n = 1.2$ and $\alpha = 0.08$ radians,

i.e.
$$\theta = 0.08 \sin 1.2t.$$

Now we have an Exercise for you to try. Some solutions involve exponentials and/or logarithms. For revision you should sketch the graphs of these functions, noting they are defined for specific positive values in each case.

■■■■■ EXERCISE 15.2 ■■■■■

Find the particular solutions to the second order differential equations.

1 $\dfrac{d^2y}{dx^2} = e^{2y}$ given $\dfrac{dy}{dx} = 1$ and $y = 0$ at $x = 1$.

2 $\dfrac{d^2y}{dx^2} + \dfrac{1}{y^3} = 0$ given $\dfrac{dy}{dx} = 1$ at $y = 1$ and $y = 2$ at $x = 0$.

3 $\dfrac{d^2y}{dx^2} + y = 0$ given $\dfrac{dy}{dx} = 1$ at $y = 0$ and $y = \dfrac{1}{2}$ at $x = 0$.

4 $\dfrac{d^2y}{dx^2} + \dfrac{1}{2}\cos^3 y . \sin y = 0$ given $\dfrac{dy}{dx} = \dfrac{1}{2}$ at $y = \pi$ and $y = \dfrac{\pi}{4}$ at $x = 1$.

5 $\dfrac{d^2y}{dx^2} + 2e^{-y} = 0$ given $\dfrac{dy}{dx} = 2$, $y = 0$ and $x = 1$.

Equations of the type $a\dfrac{d^2y}{dx^2} + b\dfrac{dy}{dx} + cy = 0$

a, b and c are constants.

This second order differential equation can have a solution of the form $y = e^{mx}$. In this case $\dfrac{dy}{dx} = me^{mx}$ and $\dfrac{d^2y}{dx^2} = m^2e^{mx}$. Substituting into

$$a\dfrac{d^2y}{dx^2} + b\dfrac{dy}{dx} + cy = 0$$

we get $am^2e^{mx} + bme^{mx} + ce^{mx} = 0$

i.e. $(am^2 + bm + c)e^{mx} = 0$.

We recall the graph of the exponential function, e^{mx}, always lies above the horizontal axis, i.e. $e^{mx} \neq 0$.

$\therefore$ $am^2 + bm + c = 0$.

$am^2 + bm + c = 0$ is the **auxiliary equation**. It is a quadratic equation in m which we may solve by either factorisation or the formula

$$m = \dfrac{-b \pm \sqrt{b^2 - 4ac}}{2a}.$$ | or by completing the square. |

There are 3 cases of interest to us:

1 $b^2 > 4ac$ gives two different real solutions (roots),
2 $b^2 = 4ac$ gives one repeated real solution,
3 $b^2 < 4ac$ gives two different complex solutions.

For case **1** where $b^2 > 4ac$ the auxiliary equation has different real roots. Suppose these roots are $m = m_1$ and $m = m_2$. The general solution of the differential equation

$$a\frac{d^2y}{dx^2} + b\frac{dy}{dx} + cy = 0$$

is $y = Ae^{m_1 x} + Be^{m_2 x}.$

As usual we need boundary conditions to find values for the constants A and B, and hence a particular solution.

■■■■■ **Example 15.5** ■■■■■

Find the general solution to the differential equation

$$\frac{d^2y}{dx^2} - 2\frac{dy}{dx} - 24y = 0.$$

Using the boundary conditions of $y = 2$ and $\frac{dy}{dx} = 0$ at $x = 0$ find the particular solution.

We know $\dfrac{d^2y}{dx^2} - 2\dfrac{dy}{dx} - 24y = 0$

has an auxiliary equation $m^2 - 2m - 24 = 0$

which factorises to $(m + 4)(m - 6) = 0$

so that $m = -4, 6.$

Using $y = Ae^{m_1 x} + Be^{m_2 x}$

we have $y = Ae^{-4x} + Be^{6x}$

as the general solution.

Two unknown constants, A and B, mean we need 2 simultaneous equations for a complete solution.

Substituting for the boundary condition $y = 2$, $x = 0$ we have

$$2 = Ae^0 + Be^0$$

i.e. $2 = A + B.$ ⎯⎯⎯①

> $e^0 = 1.$

Before substituting for the boundary condition $\dfrac{dy}{dx} = 0$, $x = 0$ we

differentiate

$$y = Ae^{-4x} + Be^{6x}$$

to get $\dfrac{dy}{dx} = -4Ae^{-4x} + 6Be^{6x}$

and then $0 = -4Ae^0 + 6Be^0$

i.e. $0 = -4A + 6B.$ ———②

Solving equations ① and ② simultaneously we get $A = 1.2$ and $B = 0.8$.
Substituting into our general solution gives

$$y = 1.2e^{-4x} + 0.8e^{6x} \text{ as the particular solution.}$$

Example 15.6

Find the general solution to the differential equation

$$3\frac{d^2y}{dx^2} - 2\frac{dy}{dx} - 12y = 0.$$

Using the boundary conditions of $y = 5.665$ at $x = 1$ and $y = 10.885$ at $x = -1$ find the particular solution.

We know $3\dfrac{d^2y}{dx^2} - 2\dfrac{dy}{dx} - 12y = 0$

has an auxiliary equation $3m^2 - 2m - 12 = 0$

which, using the quadratic equation formula, gives

$$m = -1.69, 2.36.$$

Using $y = Ae^{m_1 x} + Be^{m_2 x}$

we have $y = Ae^{-1.69x} + Be^{2.36x}$ as the general solution.

Substituting for the boundary condition $y = 5.665$, $x = 1$ we have

$$5.665 = Ae^{-1.69} + Be^{2.36}$$

i.e. $5.665 = 0.185A + 10.591B.$ ———①

Substituting for the boundary condition $y = 10.885$, $x = -1$ we have

$$10.885 = Ae^{1.69} + Be^{-2.36}$$

i.e. $10.885 = 5.419A + 0.094B.$ ———②

Solving equations ① and ② simultaneously we get $A = 2$ and $B = 0.5$.
Substituting into our general solution gives

$$y = 2e^{-1.69x} + 0.5e^{2.36x} \text{ as the particular solution.}$$

For case **2** where $b^2 = 4ac$ the auxiliary equation has repeated real roots.
Suppose the root is m. The general solution of the differential equation

$$a\frac{d^2y}{dx^2} + b\frac{dy}{dx} + cy = 0$$

is $y = (Ax + B)e^{mx}.$

Again we need boundary conditions to find values for the constants A and B, and hence a particular solution.

Find the general solution to the differential equation $\dfrac{d^2y}{dx^2} - 6\dfrac{dy}{dx} + 9y = 0$.
Using the boundary conditions of $y = -2$ at $x = 0$ and $y = 0$ at $x = 0.5$
find the particular solution.

We know $\qquad\qquad\qquad \dfrac{d^2y}{dx^2} - 6\dfrac{dy}{dx} + 9y = 0$

has an auxiliary equation $\quad m^2 - 6m + 9 = 0$

which factorises to $\qquad\qquad (m - 3)^2 = 0$

so that $\qquad\qquad\qquad\qquad m = 3$ repeated.

Using $\qquad\qquad\qquad\qquad y = (Ax + B)e^{mx}$

we have $\qquad\qquad\qquad\qquad y = (Ax + B)e^{3x}$

as the general solution.

Substituting for the boundary condition $y = -2$, $x = 0$ we have

$$-2 = (0 + B)e^0$$

i.e. $\qquad\qquad\qquad -2 = B.$

Substituting for the other boundary condition $y = 0$, $x = 0.5$ we have

$$0 = (0.5A - 2)e^{1.5}.$$

Now $e^{mx} \neq 0$ so $\quad 0 = 0.5A - 2$

i.e. $\qquad\qquad\qquad A = 4.$

We substitute into our general solution to get

$$y = (4x - 2)e^{3x} \text{ as the particular solution.}$$

For case **3** where $b^2 < 4ac$ the auxiliary equation has different complex
roots. Suppose these roots are $m = p \pm jq$ (i.e. $p + jq$ and $p - jq$). The
general solution of the differential equation

$$a\dfrac{d^2y}{dx^2} + b\dfrac{dy}{dx} + cy = 0$$

is $\qquad\qquad\qquad y = c_1e^{(p+jq)x} + c_2e^{(p-jq)x}$

$$= e^{px}(c_1e^{jqx} + c_2e^{-jqx}).$$

We recall the link between trigonometry and complex numbers in
Chapter 1. More usually we write this type of solution as

$$y = e^{px}(A\cos qx + B\sin qx).$$

As usual we need boundary conditions to find values for the constants A
and B, and hence a particular solution.

Example 15.8

Find the general solution to the differential equation

$$\frac{d^2y}{dx^2} - 6\frac{dy}{dx} + 25y = 0.$$

Using the boundary conditions of $y = 1$ at $x = 0$ and $y = 2.5$ at $x = \frac{\pi}{8}$ find the particular solution.

We know
$$\frac{d^2y}{dx^2} - 6\frac{dy}{dx} + 25y = 0$$

has an auxiliary equation $m^2 - 6m + 25 = 0$

which has complex solutions $m = 3 + j4,\ 3 - j4.$

Using $y = e^{px}(A\cos qx + B\sin qx)$

we have $y = e^{3x}(A\cos 4x + B\sin 4x)$

as the general solution.

Substituting for the boundary condition $y = 1$, $x = 0$ we have

$$1 = e^0(A\cos 0 + B\sin 0)$$

i.e. $1 = A.$

> $e^0 = 1,\ \cos 0 = 1,\ \sin 0 = 0.$

Substituting for the other boundary condition $y = 2.5$, $x = \frac{\pi}{8}$ we have

$$2.5 = e^{3\pi/8}\left(1\cos\frac{4\pi}{8} + B\sin\frac{4\pi}{8}\right)$$

so that $B = 0.77.$

> $\cos\frac{4\pi}{8} = 0,\ \sin\frac{4\pi}{8} = 1.$

Substituting into our general solution gives

$$y = e^{3x}(\cos 4x + 0.77\sin 4x)$$

as the particular solution.

ASSIGNMENT

We refine our first, approximate, mathematical model of the pendulum's motion. We suggest it is damped harmonic motion, which we model using forces. The pendulum travels through an arc either side of a central vertical line.

Mass of the pendulum $= m$.

General angular displacement from the central line $= \theta$.

There is a force acting on m proportional to the angular displacement from the central line and acting towards that line, i.e. in this case $-1.69m\theta$.

There is a resistive force (i.e. damping the motion) proportional to the angular velocity, i.e. in this case $-m\dfrac{d\theta}{dt}$.

Using $$F = ma$$

$$-1.69m\theta - m\frac{d\theta}{dt} = m\frac{d^2\theta}{dt^2}.$$

Notice the ms cancel and we gather all the terms to one side of the equation, i.e.

$$\frac{d^2\theta}{dt^2} + \frac{d\theta}{dt} + 1.69\theta = 0$$

which has an auxiliary equation

$$m^2 + m + 1.69 = 0$$

and complex solutions $m = -0.5 + j1.2, \; -0.5 - j1.2$.

Using $$y = e^{px}(A\cos qx + B\sin qx)$$

we have $$\theta = e^{-0.5t}(A\cos 1.2t + B\sin 1.2t)$$

as the general solution.

EXERCISE 15.3

Solve the following second order differential equations. In Questions **1–10** find the general solutions.

1 $\dfrac{d^2y}{dx^2} - 5\dfrac{dy}{dx} + 6y = 0$

2 $\dfrac{d^2y}{dx^2} + 2\dfrac{dy}{dx} - 8y = 0$

3 $\dfrac{d^2y}{dx^2} + 6\dfrac{dy}{dx} + 9y = 0$

4 $\dfrac{d^2y}{dx^2} + 3\dfrac{dy}{dx} - 2y = 0$

5 $\dfrac{d^2x}{dt^2} - 2\dfrac{dx}{dt} + 10x = 0$

6 $\dfrac{d^2y}{dx^2} + 3\dfrac{dy}{dx} + 2y = 0$

7 $\dfrac{d^2y}{dx^2} - 10\dfrac{dy}{dx} + 25y = 0$

8 $2\dfrac{d^2y}{dx^2} + 12\dfrac{dy}{dx} + 20y = 0$

9 $15\dfrac{d^2x}{dt^2} - 9\dfrac{dx}{dt} + x = 0$

10 $\dfrac{d^2y}{dt^2} + 4\dfrac{dy}{dt} + 5y = 0$

In Questions **11–15** substitute the boundary conditions into the general solutions to find the particular solutions.

11 $4\dfrac{d^2y}{dx^2} - 4\dfrac{dy}{dx} + y = 0$ given the curve passes through $(0, 1)$ and $(1, 4.95)$.

12 $\dfrac{d^2x}{dt^2} + 7\dfrac{dx}{dt} + 12x = 0$ given $x = 5$ and $\dfrac{dx}{dt} = -18$ at $t = 0$.

13 $\dfrac{d^2x}{dt^2} + 2\dfrac{dx}{dt} + 5x = 0$ given $x = -0.21$ at $t = \dfrac{\pi}{2}$ and $x = 0$ at $t = \dfrac{\pi}{4}$.

14 $\dfrac{d^2y}{dx^2} - 3\dfrac{dy}{dx} = 10y$ given $y = 2$ and $\dfrac{dy}{dx} = 3$ at $x = 0$.

15 $\dfrac{d^2y}{dt^2} - \dfrac{dy}{dt} - y = 0$ knowing that $y = 3.70$ at $t = 1$ and $y = -4.45$ at $t = -1$.

Equations of the type $\mathbf{a\dfrac{d^2y}{dx^2} + b\dfrac{dy}{dx} + cy = f(x)}$

a, b and c are constants.

This looks similar to the previous type of second order differential equations. Here we have $f(x)$ rather than 0 on the right-hand side. The solution is made up of 2 parts, $y = y_{CF} + y_{PI}$. The first part, y_{CF}, is the solution of $a\dfrac{d^2y}{dx^2} + b\dfrac{dy}{dx} + cy = 0$. It is called the **complementary function, y_{CF}**.

The second part depends upon the format of $f(x)$. It is called the **particular integral, y_{PI}**. We look at possible formats for $f(x)$ using the following examples. Always work out the solution part y_{CF} first.

1 $f(x)$ **is an exponential function.** Generally for y_{PI} we try $y_{PI} = \alpha e^{\beta x}$, where α and β are constants. This type of solution works provided β is *not* a root of the auxiliary equation. This is why we work out y_{CF} first.

▮▮▮▮ Example 15.9 ▮▮▮▮

Find the general solution to the differential equation

$\dfrac{d^2y}{dx^2} - 2\dfrac{dy}{dx} - 24y = 2e^{-3x}$.

We know $\dfrac{d^2y}{dx^2} - 2\dfrac{dy}{dx} - 24y = 0$

gives $y_{CF} = Ae^{-4x} + Be^{6x}$.

Because of the format for $f(x) = 2e^{-3x}$ we know the particular integral part of the solution must have the format $y_{PI} = \alpha e^{\beta x}$. Comparing both exponentials we see that $\beta x = -3x$, i.e. $\beta = -3$ so that

$$y_{PI} = \alpha e^{-3x}.$$

We differentiate to get $\dfrac{dy_{PI}}{dx} = -3\alpha e^{-3x}$

and $\dfrac{d^2y_{PI}}{dx^2} = 9\alpha e^{-3x}$

and substitute into $\qquad \dfrac{d^2y}{dx^2} - 2\dfrac{dy}{dx} - 24y = 2e^{-3x}$

to get $\qquad 9\alpha e^{-3x} - 2(-3\alpha e^{-3x}) - 24(\alpha e^{-3x}) = 2e^{-3x}$

i.e. $\qquad\qquad\qquad\quad 9\alpha + 6\alpha - 24\alpha = 2$

> We cancel e^{-3x} because $e^{-3x} \neq 0$.

i.e. $\qquad\qquad\qquad\qquad\qquad\qquad \alpha = -\dfrac{2}{9}.$

The complete general solution is $\qquad\qquad y = y_{CF} + y_{PI}$

i.e. $\qquad\qquad\qquad\qquad\qquad\qquad y = Ae^{-4x} + Be^{6x} - \dfrac{2}{9}e^{-3x}.$

Only at this stage do we attempt to find the particular solution.

Example 15.10

Find the general solution to the differential equation
$\dfrac{d^2y}{dx^2} - 2\dfrac{dy}{dx} - 24y = 2e^{-3x}.$

Using the boundary conditions of $y = 4$ and $\dfrac{dy}{dx} = 6$ at $x = 0$ find the particular solution.

We know the general solution is $\quad y = Ae^{-4x} + Be^{6x} - \dfrac{2}{9}e^{-3x}.$

Substituting for the boundary condition $y = 4$, $x = 0$ we have

$\qquad 4 = Ae^0 + Be^0 - \dfrac{2}{9}e^0$

i.e. $\quad 4 = A + B - \dfrac{2}{9}.$ ———① $\qquad\qquad$ | $e^0 = 1.$

We differentiate our general solution to get

$\qquad \dfrac{dy}{dx} = -4Ae^{-4x} + 6Be^{6x} + \dfrac{2}{3}e^{-3x}$

and substitute for the boundary condition $\dfrac{dy}{dx} = 6$, $x = 0$, to get

$\qquad 6 = -4Ae^0 + 6Be^0 + \dfrac{2}{3}e^0$

i.e. $\quad 3 = -2A + 3B + \dfrac{1}{3}.$ ———② $\qquad\qquad$ | $e^0 = 1.$

We solve equations ① and ② simultaneously to get $A = 2$ and $B = \dfrac{20}{9}$ so our particular solution is

$\qquad y = 2e^{-4x} + \dfrac{20}{9}e^{6x} - \dfrac{2}{9}e^{-3x}.$

2 $f(x)$ is an exponential function. We look at $y_{PI} = \alpha e^{\beta x}$, where α and β are constants and β **is a root of the auxiliary equation.** Again this is why we work out y_{CF} first. For this case we try $\boldsymbol{y_{PI} = \alpha x e^{\beta x}}$ or maybe $\boldsymbol{y_{PI} = \alpha x^2 e^{\beta x}}$. Once more we show the techniques based on earlier work in Example 15.5.

■■■■■ **Example 15.11** ■■■■■

Find the general solution to the differential equation

$$\frac{d^2y}{dx^2} - 2\frac{dy}{dx} - 24y = 5e^{-4x}.$$

We know $\dfrac{d^2y}{dx^2} - 2\dfrac{dy}{dx} - 24y = 0$

gives $y_{CF} = Ae^{-4x} + Be^{6x}$

and e^{-4x} features in both y_{CF} and y_{PI}. Hence we try

$$y_{PI} = \alpha x e^{-4x}.$$

> If this fails we would need to try $y_{PI} = \alpha x^2 e^{-4x}$.

We differentiate to get $\dfrac{dy_{PI}}{dx} = -4\alpha x e^{-4x} + \alpha e^{-4x}$

> Product rule.

and $\dfrac{d^2y_{PI}}{dx^2} = 16\alpha x e^{-4x} - 8\alpha e^{-4x}$

> Product rule again.

We substitute into $\dfrac{d^2y}{dx^2} - 2\dfrac{dy}{dx} - 24y = 5e^{-4x}$

to get $16\alpha x e^{-4x} - 8\alpha e^{-4x} - 2(-4\alpha x e^{-4x} + \alpha e^{-4x}) - 24(\alpha x e^{-4x}) = 5e^{-4x}$

i.e. $16\alpha x - 8\alpha + 8\alpha x - 2\alpha - 24\alpha x = 5$

> We cancel e^{-4x} because $e^{-4x} \neq 0$.

i.e. $\alpha = -\dfrac{1}{2}.$

The complete general solution is $y = y_{CF} + y_{PI}$

i.e. $y = Ae^{-4x} + Be^{6x} - \dfrac{1}{2}xe^{-4x}$

or $y = Be^{6x} + (A - 0.5x)e^{-4x}.$

Again at this stage we could attempt to fnd the particular solution.

■■■■ EXERCISE 15.4 ■■■■■■■

Solve the following second order differential equations. In Questions **1** and **2** find the general solutions.

1 $\dfrac{d^2y}{dx^2} + 5\dfrac{dy}{dx} + 6y = 4e^x$

2 $\dfrac{d^2y}{dx^2} - 3\dfrac{dy}{dx} + 2y = 3e^{2x}$

In Questions **3–5** substitute the boundary conditions into the general solutions to find the particular solutions.

3 $\dfrac{d^2y}{dx^2} + 10\dfrac{dy}{dx} + 25y = e^{-x}$ given both y and $\dfrac{dy}{dx}$ are $\dfrac{1}{16}$ at $x = 0$.

4 $\dfrac{d^2y}{dx^2} + 3\dfrac{dy}{dx} - 10y = 2e^{2x}$ with $y = \dfrac{13}{7}$ and $\dfrac{dy}{dx} = -3$ where $x = 0$.

5 $\dfrac{d^2y}{dt^2} + 4\dfrac{dy}{dt} + 5y = e^{-3t}$ given $y = 1.5$ initially and $y = 0.0477$ when $t = \dfrac{\pi}{2}$.

---

3 $f(x)$ **is either a sine or a cosine.** We use $y_{PI} = \alpha\cos rx + \beta\sin rx$ where α, β and r are constants. This type of solution works provided β is *not* a root of the auxiliary equation.

4 $f(x)$ **is either a sine or a cosine.** If $\cos rx$ and/or $\sin rx$ are in the complementary function we try $y_{PI} = x(\alpha\cos rx + \beta\sin rx)$. Notice these ideas are similar to those we saw for the exponential function.

■■■■ Example 15.12 ■■■■

Find the general solution to the differential equation $\dfrac{d^2y}{dt^2} + y = 6\sin 2t$.

Using the boundary conditions of $y = 4$ at $x = \dfrac{\pi}{2}$ and $y = 3$ at $x = \pi$ find the particular solution.

Rather than use earlier work we solve this second order differential equation from the beginning. We start with the complementary function.

We know $\dfrac{d^2y}{dt^2} + y = 0$

has an auxiliary equation $m^2 + 1 = 0$

         i.e. $m^2 = -1 = j^2$

which has complex solutions $m = j, -j$ or $0 + j, 0 - j$.

Using $y_{CF} = e^{px}(A\cos qx + B\sin qx)$

we have $y_{CF} = e^{0t}(A\cos t + B\sin t)$

i.e. $y_{CF} = A\cos t + B\sin t$

$p = 0, q = 1.$
$e^0 = 1.$

Because of the format for $f(t) = 6\sin 2t$ we know the particular integral part of the solution must have the format $y_{PI} = \alpha\cos rt + \beta\sin rt$. Comparing rt with $2t$ we have $r = 2$ so that

$$y_{PI} = \alpha\cos 2t + \beta\sin 2t.$$

We differentiate to get

$$\frac{dy_{PI}}{dt} = -2\alpha\sin 2t + 2\beta\cos 2t$$

and

$$\frac{d^2y_{PI}}{dt^2} = -4\alpha\cos 2t - 4\beta\sin 2t$$

and substitute into

$$\frac{d^2y}{dt^2} + y = 6\sin 2t$$

to get $\quad -4\alpha\cos 2t - 4\beta\sin 2t + \alpha\cos 2t + \beta\sin 2t = 6\sin 2t$.

For the same **general** angle cosine and sine *cannot* be equal. Hence we can equate cosine and sine terms,

i.e. $-4\alpha\cos 2t + \alpha\cos 2t = 0$

and $-4\beta\sin 2t + \beta\sin 2t = 6\sin 2t$,

and then the coefficients so that $-3\alpha = 0$ and $-3\beta = 6$. They give $\alpha = 0$ and $\beta = -2$.

The complete general solution is $\quad y = y_{CF} + y_{PI}$

i.e. $\qquad\qquad\qquad\qquad\qquad y = A\cos t + B\sin t - 2\sin 2t.$

Substituting for the boundary condition $y = 4$, $t = \dfrac{\pi}{2}$ we have

$$4 = A\cos\frac{\pi}{2} + B\sin\frac{\pi}{2} - 2\sin\frac{2\pi}{2}$$

i.e. $\qquad\qquad\qquad\qquad\qquad 4 = B.$

Substituting for the boundary condition $y = 3$, $t = \pi$ we have

$$3 = A\cos\pi + B\sin\pi - 2\sin 2\pi$$

i.e. $\qquad\qquad\qquad\qquad\qquad -3 = A.$

Our particular solution is $\qquad y = 4\sin t - 3\cos t - 2\sin 2t.$

■ EXERCISE 15.5 ■

Solve the following second order differential equations. In Questions **1** and **2** find the general solutions.

1 $\dfrac{d^2y}{dx^2} - 2\dfrac{dy}{dx} + 10y = \cos 2x$

2 $\dfrac{d^2y}{dx^2} - 2\dfrac{dy}{dx} - 24y = \sin x + \cos x$

In Questions **3–5** substitute the boundary conditions into the general solutions to find the particular solutions.

3 $\dfrac{d^2y}{dt^2} + 4\dfrac{dy}{dt} + 4y = 6\sin 2t$ given all initial conditions are zero.

4 $\dfrac{d^2y}{dt^2} + 6\dfrac{dy}{dt} + 10y = 20\cos 3t - 35\sin 3t$

     with $y = 2$ at $t = 2\pi$ and $\dfrac{dy}{dt} = 0$ at $t = \dfrac{\pi}{4}$.

5 $\dfrac{d^2y}{dt^2} + 4y = 9\cos t + 3\sin t$ given $y = 2$ when $t = \dfrac{\pi}{2}$ and $y = 0$

                           when $t = \dfrac{\pi}{4}$.

---

5 $f(x)$ **is a polynomial of degree** n.

We use $y_{PI} = \alpha_0 + \alpha_1 x + \alpha_2 x^2 + \ldots + \alpha_n x^n$ where the αs are constants. The highest powers of x in $f(x)$ and y_{PI} must agree.

████████ **Example 15.13** ████████

Find the general solution to the differential equation $\dfrac{d^2y}{dx^2} + 4y = 2x + x^2$.

Using the boundary conditions of $y = -0.125$ and $\dfrac{dy}{dx} = 1.5$ at $x = 0$ find the particular solution.

From Exercise 15.5, Question **5**, we have

$$y_{CF} = A\cos 2x + B\sin 2x.$$

Because of the format for $f(x)$ we use a polynomial up to and including a term in x^2, i.e.

$$y_{PI} = a + bx + cx^2$$

where a, b and c are constants.

We differentiate to get $\dfrac{dy_{PI}}{dx} = b + 2cx$

and $\dfrac{d^2y_{PI}}{dx^2} = 2c$

and substitute into $\dfrac{d^2y}{dx^2} + 4y = 2x + x^2$

to get $2c + 4(a + bx + cx^2) = 2x + x^2.$

Equating the coefficients of like terms we have

constants: $2c + 4a = 0,$

x: $4b = 2,$

x^2: $4c = 1.$

They give us the values $a = -0.125$, $b = 0.5$ and $c = 0.25$.

The complete general solution is

$$y = y_{CF} + y_{PI}$$

i.e. $y = A\cos 2x + B\sin 2x - 0.125 + 0.5x + 0.25x^2.$

Substituting for the boundary condition $y = -0.125$, $x = 0$ we have

$$-0.125 = A\cos 0 + B\sin 0 - 0.125 + 0 + 0$$

i.e. $A = 0.$

We substitute for A and differentiate our general solution to get

$$\frac{dy}{dx} = 2B\cos 2x + 0.5 + 0.5x.$$

Substituting for the boundary condition $\frac{dy}{dx} = 1.5$, $x = 0$ we have

$$1.5 = 2B\cos 0 + 0.5 + 0$$

i.e. $B = 0.5.$

Our particular solution is $y = 0.5\sin 2x - 0.125 + 0.5x + 0.25x^2.$

■■■■ EXERCISE 15.6 ■■■■

Solve the following second order differential equations. In Questions **1** and **2** find the general solutions.

1 $\dfrac{d^2y}{dx^2} + 8\dfrac{dy}{dx} + 16y = 12x - 4$ | **2** $\dfrac{d^2y}{dx^2} + 5\dfrac{dy}{dx} + 6y = \dfrac{5}{6} + 6x^3$

In Questions **3–5** substitute the boundary conditions into the general solutions to find the particular solutions.

3 $2\dfrac{d^2y}{dx^2} + 6\dfrac{dy}{dx} + 4y = 4x^2 + 2$ given $y = 4$ and $\dfrac{dy}{dx} = -2$ where $x = 0.$

4 $\dfrac{d^2y}{dt^2} - 2\dfrac{dy}{dt} + 10y = 20t$ with $y = 0.4$ at $t = 0$ and $y = 0$ at $t = \dfrac{\pi}{2}.$

5 $\dfrac{d^2x}{dt^2} + 7\dfrac{dx}{dt} + 12x = 6t^2 - t + 3$ given $x = 1.5$ and $\dfrac{dx}{dt} = 2.5$ initially.

6   If $f(x)$ is a combination of trigonometry, an exponential and a polynomial then we use a similar combination for y_{PI}.

We complete this chapter with some general applications.

■ EXERCISE 15.7 ■

1   The circuit diagram shows a capacitor of 0.05 F, a resistor of 8 Ω and an inductor of 1 H in series with an emf of 125 V. The second order differential equation models the charge, q, over time, t,

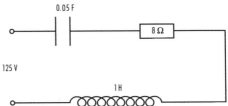

$$\frac{d^2q}{dt^2} + 8\frac{dq}{dt} + 20q = 125.$$

Find q in terms of t given zero initial conditions.

2   A mass, m (1 kg), is attached to a coiled spring. The force in a spring is proportional to its extension or compression, x, according to Hooke's law. In this case the proportionality constant is 25 Nm^{-1} so that the force is $25x$. The motion of the mass is damped by a force proportional to its velocity, $6\frac{dx}{dt}$. Using $F = m\frac{d^2x}{dt^2}$ to model this motion we create the differential equation

$$-25x - 6\frac{dx}{dt} = 1\frac{d^2x}{dt^2}.$$

You are given the initial boundary conditions that the extension is 0 m and the velocity is 6 ms^{-1}. Solve this second order differential equation for x in terms of t.

3   The circuit diagram shows a capacitor of 0.025 F, a resistor of 40 Ω and an inductor of 10 H in series with an emf of 84.1sin 5t V.

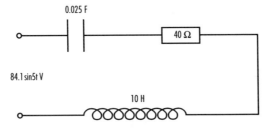

The second order differential equation models the current, i, over time, t,

$$10\frac{d^2i}{dt^2} + 40\frac{di}{dt} + 40i = 420.5\cos 5t.$$

Find i in terms of t given the initial conditions are zero.

4   Two capacitors (0.05 F and 0.2 F) each have a plate earthed. The two insulated plates are connected initially by a wire of resistance R (10 Ω) and inductance L (1 H). One capacitor has a charge q while the other capacitor is uncharged so that a current i flows in the wire. It is modelled by the second order differential equation

$$1\frac{d^2i}{dt^2} + 10\frac{di}{dt} + \left(\frac{1}{0.05} + \frac{1}{0.2}\right)i = 0.$$

Initially $i = 0$ and $\dfrac{di}{dt} = \alpha$, some general constant. Hence solve this differential equation.

5   The basis of this question has some similarities with Question **2**. A mass, m (2 kg), is attached to a coiled spring. The force in a spring is proportional to its extension or compression, x, according to Hooke's law. In this case the proportionality constant is 34 Nm^{-1} so that the force is $34x$. The motion of the mass is damped by a force proportional to its velocity, $4\dfrac{dx}{dt}$. Here we apply an external sinusoidal force, $13\sin 4t$. This causes forced vibrations. Using $F = m\dfrac{d^2x}{dt^2}$ to model this motion we create the differential equation

$$\frac{d^2x}{dt^2} + 2\frac{dx}{dt} + 17x = 6.5\sin 4t.$$

You are given the initial boundary conditions that the extension is 0 m and the velocity is 2 ms^{-1}. Solve this second order differential equation for x in terms of t.

16 Laplace Transforms: 1

The objectives of this chapter are to:

1 Define the Laplace transform of $f(t)$ and apply it to some sample functions.

2 Use a table of standard transforms for both Laplace transforms and inverse Laplace transforms.

3 Use partial fractions to create the correct format for inverse Laplace transforms.

4 Apply the techniques to solve first order differential equations.

5 State and use the initial and final value theorems.

6 Identify the transfer function and analyse it in terms of poles and zeroes.

7 Discuss the stability of a transfer function.

Introduction

In this chapter we introduce Laplace transforms through the integral definition. We show how to find the transforms of some simple functions and give a table of the more commonly used transforms (at the end of the chapter). For a first reading you may wish to omit the section that derives some simple Laplace transforms. Later we concentrate on using the transforms table and apply it to solve first order differential equations. Because this is a large topic we have split it into 2 chapters. However, there are indeed complete books covering Laplace transforms in detail.

████ **ASSIGNMENT** ████

Our Assignment looks at electrical circuits; first with a constant e.m.f., then with a sinusoidal one. In each case we create a differential equation, solving it by applying Laplace transforms. The numbers have been simplified to concentrate on using the transforms rather than on the particular circuit problem. Each differential equation is in the time, t, domain. The Laplace transforms change this to the s domain for us to work within. In that domain we apply some algebraic techniques, often involving partial fractions. Finally, when we have created the correct format we transform back from the s domain. This uses inverse Laplace transforms allowing us to quote our answer in the original t domain.

The definition

We use the symbol $\mathcal{L}$ to mean the 'Laplace transform of'. For any function, $F(t)$, its Laplace transform, $\mathcal{L}\{F(t)\}$, is defined by

$$\mathcal{L}\{F(t)\} = \int_0^\infty e^{-st} F(t)\, dt.$$

s is a parameter that we use throughout this work. In the integration it is assumed to be large and positive. This ensures we can find a value for the integral as $t \to \infty$, i.e. the integral converges to some value of s. To show we have actually transformed $F(t)$ we may write $\mathcal{L}\{F(t)\} = f(s)$, i.e. $f(s)$ is the transform of the function of t.

At the end of this chapter we give a table of transforms. You should refer to these. Here for reference we apply the integral to obtain some specimen transforms.

Example 16.1

We find the Laplace transform of 2.5, i.e. an example of a constant.

In the formula $\mathcal{L}\{F(t)\} = \displaystyle\int_0^\infty e^{-st} F(t)\, dt$ $\boxed{F(t) = 2.5.}$

we have $\mathcal{L}\{2.5\} = \displaystyle\int_0^\infty 2.5 e^{-st}\, dt$

$$= \mathrm{Lim}_{n\to\infty} \int_0^n 2.5 e^{-st}\, dt$$

$$\mathcal{L}\{2.5\} = \mathrm{Lim}_{n\to\infty} \left[\frac{-2.5}{s} e^{-st} \right]_0^n$$

$$= \mathrm{Lim}_{n\to\infty} \left[-\frac{2.5}{s} e^{-sn} - -\frac{2.5}{s} e^0 \right] \qquad \boxed{e^0 = 1.}$$

$$= \mathrm{Lim}_{n\to\infty} \frac{2.5}{s} \left[1 - \frac{1}{e^{sn}} \right]$$

As $n \to \infty$, $sn \to \infty$, $e^{sn} \to \infty$ and so $\dfrac{1}{e^{sn}} \to 0$

Hence $\mathcal{L}\{2.5\} = \dfrac{2.5}{s}.$

Example 16.2

We find the Laplace transform of $3t$.

In the formula $\mathscr{L}\{F(t)\} = \int_0^\infty e^{-st} F(t)\, dt$ $\boxed{F(t) = 3t.}$

we have $\mathscr{L}\{3t\} = \int_0^\infty 3te^{-st}\, dt$

$$= \operatorname*{Lim}_{n\to\infty} \int_0^n 3te^{-st}\, dt.$$

We need to use integration by parts to solve this integral.

Let $u = 3t$ and $\dfrac{dv}{dt} = e^{-st}$

$\therefore \quad \dfrac{du}{dt} = 3$ and $v = -\dfrac{1}{s}e^{-st}$

Using our formula for integration by parts

$$\int u\frac{dv}{dx}dx = uv - \int v\frac{du}{dx}dx$$

we get $\mathscr{L}\{3t\} = \operatorname*{Lim}_{n\to\infty}\left[-\dfrac{3t}{s}e^{-st}\right]_0^n - \int_0^n -\dfrac{3}{s}e^{-st}\, dt$

$$= \operatorname*{Lim}_{n\to\infty}\left[-\frac{3t}{se^{st}}\right]_0^n - \left[\frac{3}{s^2e^{st}}\right]_0^n$$

$$= \operatorname*{Lim}_{n\to\infty}\left[-\frac{3n}{se^{sn}} - \frac{-3(0)}{se^0} - \frac{3}{s^2e^{sn}} - \frac{-3}{s^2e^0}\right] \quad \boxed{e^0 = 1.}$$

As $n \to \infty$, $sn \to \infty$, $e^{sn} \to \infty$ and so $\dfrac{1}{e^{sn}} \to 0$.

In the term $\dfrac{-3n}{se^{sn}}$, $\dfrac{1}{e^{sn}}$ dominates the simple n. Hence this term tends to 0.

Hence $\mathscr{L}\{3t\} = 0 + 0 - 0 + \dfrac{3}{s^2}$

i.e. $\mathscr{L}\{3t\} = \dfrac{3}{s^2}.$

Example 16.3

We find the Laplace transform of $\sin \omega t$ where ω is a constant.

In the formula $\mathscr{L}\{F(t)\} = \int_0^\infty e^{-st} F(t)\, dt$

we have $\mathscr{L}\{\sin \omega t\} = \int_0^\infty e^{-st}\sin \omega t\, dt$ $\boxed{F(t) = \sin \omega t.}$

$$= \operatorname*{Lim}_{n\to\infty}\int_0^\infty e^{-st}\sin \omega t\, dt.$$

In Volume 2 we integrated by parts twice to find a solution. As an alternative we use complex numbers. We know that $\cos \omega t + j \sin \omega t = e^{j\omega t}$ where $\cos \omega t$ is the real part of $e^{j\omega t}$ and $\sin \omega t$ is the imaginary part of $e^{j\omega t}$.

$$\boxed{\begin{aligned} \cos \omega t &= \operatorname{Re} e^{j\omega t} \\ \sin \omega t &= \operatorname{Im} e^{j\omega t}. \end{aligned}}$$

Substituting we have

$$\mathscr{L}\{\sin \omega t\} = \operatorname{Im} \int_0^\infty e^{-st} e^{j\omega t}\, dt$$

$$= \lim_{n\to\infty} \operatorname{Im} \int_0^n e^{-(s-j\omega)t}\, dt$$

$$= \lim_{n\to\infty} \operatorname{Im} \left[-\frac{1}{(s-j\omega)} e^{-(s-j\omega)t} \right]_0^n$$

$$= \lim_{n\to\infty} \operatorname{Im} \left[-\frac{(s+j\omega)}{(s-j\omega)(s+j\omega)} e^{-(s-j\omega)t} \right]_0^n$$

$$\boxed{\begin{aligned}\text{Remember division} \\ \text{of complex numbers.}\end{aligned}}$$

$$= \lim_{n\to\infty} \operatorname{Im} \left[-\frac{(s+j\omega)}{s^2+\omega^2} e^{-(s-j\omega)t} \right]_0^n$$

$$\boxed{j^2 = -1.}$$

$$= \lim_{n\to\infty} \operatorname{Im} -\frac{(s+j\omega)}{s^2+\omega^2} \left[\frac{1}{e^{(s-j\omega)n}} - \frac{1}{e^{(s-j\omega)0}} \right]$$

$$\boxed{e^{(s-j\omega)0} = e^0 = 1.}$$

As $n \to \infty$, $(s-j\omega)n \to \infty$, $e^{(s-j\omega)n} \to \infty$ and so $\dfrac{1}{e^{(s-j\omega)n}} \to 0$.

Hence $\mathscr{L}\{\sin \omega t\} = \operatorname{Im} -\dfrac{(s+j\omega)}{s^2+\omega^2}[0-1]$

$$= \operatorname{Im} \frac{(s+j\omega)}{s^2+\omega^2}$$

i.e. $\mathscr{L}\{\sin \omega t\} = \dfrac{\omega}{s^2+\omega^2}$.

We can use a similar idea to find the Laplace transform of cosine, i.e. $\mathscr{L}\{\cos \omega t\}$, this time with the real part of $e^{j\omega t}$.

The following Exercise is optional. For a first reading you may wish to attempt only the early questions, or omit it completely.

▰▰▰ EXERCISE 16.1 ▰▰▰

Using the integral definition find the Laplace transforms of the following functions.

1 5

2 c, a constant

3 $4t$

4 t^2

5 e^{-2t}

6 $\cos \omega t$ where ω is a constant

7 $\sinh at$ where a is a constant

8 $\cosh at$ where a is a constant

9 te^{-2t}

10 $e^{-t} \sin 2t$

Similarly we may use the integral definition to find the Laplace transforms of derivatives; $\dfrac{dy}{dt}, \dfrac{d^2y}{dt^2}, \dfrac{d^3y}{dt^3}, \ldots$ Here we quote the transforms for y and the first and second derivatives.

$$\mathscr{L}\{y\} = \bar{y}$$

$$\mathscr{L}\left\{\frac{dy}{dt}\right\} = s\bar{y} - y_0 \qquad \text{where } y_0 \text{ is the value of } y \text{ at } t = 0.$$

$$\mathscr{L}\left\{\frac{d^2y}{dt^2}\right\} = s^2\bar{y} - sy_0 - y_1 \qquad \text{where } y_0 \text{ is the value of } y \text{ at } t = 0 \text{ and}$$

$$y_1 \text{ is the value of } \frac{dy}{dt} \text{ at } t = 0.$$

These show we are using initial (i.e. at $t = 0$) boundary conditions.

Using the the table of transforms

It is vital that you use the table at the end of this chapter. The first column lists a selection of frequently used functions. The second column gives their Laplace transforms. Referring to them we see that n is a power taking values of 0, 1, 2, 3, …; c, ω and a are constants. Notice the similarities when using sines and cosines. The transforms of $\sin \omega t$ and $\cos \omega t$ have the same denominators. They differ only in the numerators. Also check the $+/-$ signs in the denominators when comparing trigonometric and hyperbolic functions.

███████ **Examples 16.4** ███████

We use the transform table to find some Laplace transforms.

i) $\mathscr{L}\{7.5\}$ uses $\mathscr{L}\{c\} = \dfrac{c}{s}$ with $c = 7.5$,

    i.e. $\mathscr{L}\{7.5\} = \dfrac{7.5}{s}$.

ii) $\mathscr{L}\{2t^3\}$ or $2\mathscr{L}\{t^3\}$ uses $\mathscr{L}\{t^n\} = \dfrac{n!}{s^{n+1}}$ with $n = 3$,

    i.e. $\mathscr{L}\{2t^3\} = 2 \times \dfrac{3!}{s^{3+1}} = 2 \times \dfrac{3!}{s^4} = \dfrac{12}{s^4}$. $\boxed{3! = 3 \times 2 = 6.}$

iii) $\mathscr{L}\{e^{2t}\}$ uses $\mathscr{L}\{e^{ct}\} = \dfrac{1}{s-c}$ with $c = 2$,

    i.e. $\mathscr{L}\{e^{2t}\} = \dfrac{1}{s-2}$.

iv) $\mathscr{L}\{e^{-t}\}$ uses the same transform, this time with $c = -1$,

    i.e. $\mathscr{L}\{e^{-t}\} = \dfrac{1}{s--1} = \dfrac{1}{s+1}$.

Notice the opposite $+/-$ signs from the exponential and the transform.

v) $\mathscr{L}\{2t^3 + e^{-t}\}$ is the same as $\mathscr{L}\{2t^3\} + \mathscr{L}\{e^{-t}\}$.

We can simply add/subtract the transforms like we add/subtract different functions.

$$\mathscr{L}\{2t^3 + e^{-t}\} = \dfrac{12}{s^4} + \dfrac{1}{s+1}, \text{ using our earlier results.}$$

███████ **EXERCISE 16.2** ███████

Using the table of transforms write down the Laplace transforms of the following functions.

1 11.5

2 t

3 $12t$

4 $3t^2$

5 e^{3t}

6 $4e^{-3t}$

7 $2t^4 + e^{-2t}$

8 $7 + 5t - 4t^2$

9 $e^{t/2}$

10 $e^{-t/4}$

███ **Examples 16.5** ███

We use the transform table to find some Laplace transforms.

i) $\mathscr{L}\{3\sin t\}$ uses $\mathscr{L}\{\sin \omega t\} = \dfrac{\omega}{s^2 + \omega^2}$ with $\omega = 1$,

i.e. $\mathscr{L}\{3\sin t\} = 3 \times \dfrac{1}{s^2 + 1^2} = \dfrac{3}{s^2 + 1}$.

ii) $\mathscr{L}\{3\cosh 2t\}$ uses $\mathscr{L}\{\cosh at\} = \dfrac{s}{s^2 - a^2}$ with $a = 2$,

i.e. $\mathscr{L}\{3\cosh 2t\} = 3 \times \dfrac{s}{s^2 - 2^2} = \dfrac{3s}{s^2 - 4}$.

███ **EXERCISE 16.3** ███

Using the table of transforms write down the Laplace transforms of the following functions.

1 $\sin 3t$

2 $\cos t$

3 $\sin 4t - \cos t$

4 $2\sin 4t - 3\cos t$

5 $3\sin \dfrac{t}{2}$

6 $2\cosh 3t$

7 $\sinh 2t$

8 $4\cosh t$

9 $2\cosh t - \sinh 3t$

10 $2\sinh \dfrac{t}{2} + 3\sinh t + \cosh 2t$

███ **Examples 16.6** ███

We use the transform table to find some Laplace transforms.

i) $\mathscr{L}\{t^2 e^{-3t}\}$ uses $\mathscr{L}\{t^n e^{-ct}\} = \dfrac{n!}{(s+c)^{n+1}}$

with $n = 2$ and $-c = -3$, i.e. $c = 3$,

i.e. $\mathscr{L}\{t^2 e^{-3t}\} = \dfrac{2!}{(s+3)^{2+1}} = \dfrac{2}{(s+3)^3}$.

ii) $\mathscr{L}\{3e^{-2t}\sin t\}$ uses $\mathscr{L}\{e^{-ct}\sin \omega t\} = \dfrac{\omega}{(s+c)^2 + \omega^2}$

with $\omega = 1$ and $-c = -2$, i.e. $c = 2$,

i.e. $\mathscr{L}\{3e^{-2t}\sin t\} = 3 \times \dfrac{1}{(s+2)^2 + 1^2}$.

We could expand the denominator, but generally choose not to do so.

$$\mathscr{L}\{3e^{-2t}\sin t\} = \dfrac{3}{(s+2)^2 + 1} \quad \text{or} \quad \dfrac{3}{s^2 + 4s + 5}.$$

iii) $\mathscr{L}\{e^t \sinh 4t\}$ uses $\mathscr{L}\{e^{-ct} \sinh at\} = \dfrac{a}{(s+c)^2 - a^2}$

with $a = 4$ and $-c = 1$, i.e. $c = -1$

i.e. $\mathscr{L}\{e^t \sinh 4t\} = \dfrac{4}{(s-1)^2 - 4^2}$ or $\dfrac{4}{s^2 - 2s - 15}$

■ EXERCISE 16.4 ■

Using the table of transforms write down the Laplace transforms of the following functions.

1   $t^3 e^{-2t}$

2   $t^2 e^{3t}$

3   $t^2 e^{-2t}$

4   $e^{-t} \sin t$

5   $e^{-3t} \cos 4t$

6   $e^{-3t} \sinh 2t$

7   $e^{4t} \sin \dfrac{t}{3}$

8   $t^3 e^t$

9   $e^{-2t} \cosh \dfrac{t}{2}$

10   $e^{2t} \left(\cosh t - \sinh \dfrac{t}{2} \right)$

Inverse transforms

We use the symbol $\mathscr{L}^{-1}$ for the 'inverse Laplace transform of'. We always let the denominator dictate the format as we move from the second column to the first column. There are 2 important techniques to refresh; 'completing the square' (see Volume 1, Chapter 7) and partial fractions (see Volume 2, Chapter 12).

■ Examples 16.7 ■

We find the inverse Laplace transforms, moving from the s parameter in the second column to the t variable in the first column.

i) $\mathscr{L}^{-1}\left\{\dfrac{3}{s}\right\}$ uses $\mathscr{L}^{-1}\left\{\dfrac{c}{s}\right\} = c$ with $c = 3$,

i.e. $\mathscr{L}^{-1}\left\{\dfrac{3}{s}\right\} = 3$.

ii) $\mathscr{L}^{-1}\left\{\dfrac{4}{s+6}\right\}$ uses $\mathscr{L}^{-1}\left\{\dfrac{1}{s-c}\right\} = e^{ct}$ with $c = -6$,

i.e. $\mathscr{L}^{-1}\left\{\dfrac{4}{s+6}\right\} = 4\mathscr{L}^{-1}\left\{\dfrac{1}{s+6}\right\} = 4e^{-6t}$.

ii) $\mathcal{L}^{-1}\left\{\dfrac{14}{s^3}\right\}$ uses $\mathcal{L}^{-1}\left\{\dfrac{n!}{s^{n+1}}\right\}$ with $n+1=3$,

i.e. $n=2$, from the denominator.

Comparing the numerators we need $n!$, i.e. $2!$, and so adjust 14 to $7 \times 2 \times 1 = 7 \times 2!$

i.e. $\mathcal{L}^{-1}\left\{\dfrac{14}{s^3}\right\} = 7\mathcal{L}^{-1}\left\{\dfrac{2!}{s^{2+1}}\right\} = 7t^2.$

Examples 16.8

We use the transform table to find some inverse Laplace transforms.

Remember the sine and cosine transforms, $\sin \omega t$ and $\cos \omega t$, have the same denominator. The numerators differ only with s for $\cos \omega t$ and ω for $\sin \omega t$.

i) $\mathcal{L}^{-1}\left\{\dfrac{4}{s^2+16}\right\}$ uses $\mathcal{L}^{-1}\left\{\dfrac{\omega}{s^2+\omega^2}\right\}$ with $\omega = 4$,

i.e. $\mathcal{L}^{-1}\left\{\dfrac{4}{s^2+16}\right\} = \mathcal{L}^{-1}\left\{\dfrac{4}{s^2+4^2}\right\} = \sin 4t.$

ii) $\mathcal{L}^{-1}\left\{\dfrac{3s}{s^2+4}\right\}$ uses $\mathcal{L}^{-1}\left\{\dfrac{s}{s^2+\omega^2}\right\}$ with $\omega = 2$,

i.e. $\mathcal{L}^{-1}\left\{\dfrac{3s}{s^2+4}\right\} = 3\mathcal{L}^{-1}\left\{\dfrac{s}{s^2+2^2}\right\} = 3\cos 2t.$

iii) $\mathcal{L}^{-1}\left\{\dfrac{3s+6}{s^2+25}\right\}$ mixes both $\cos \omega t$ and $\sin \omega t$.

We split the numerator, each part using the common denominator.

i.e. $\mathcal{L}^{-1}\left\{\dfrac{3s+6}{s^2+25}\right\} = \mathcal{L}^{-1}\left\{\dfrac{3s}{s^2+5^2}\right\} + \mathcal{L}^{-1}\left\{\dfrac{6}{s^2+5^2}\right\}$

$= 3\mathcal{L}^{-1}\left\{\dfrac{s}{s^2+5^2}\right\} + \dfrac{6}{5}\mathcal{L}^{-1}\left\{\dfrac{5}{s^2+5^2}\right\}$

> Adjusting the numerator to the correct format.

$= 3\cos 5t + 1.2\sin 5t.$

EXERCISE 16.5

Using the table of transforms write down the inverse Laplace transforms of the following functions.

1 $\dfrac{1}{s^2}$

2 $\dfrac{1}{s-21}$

3	$\dfrac{3}{s^3}$		7	$\dfrac{s+4}{s^2+16}$
4	$\dfrac{3}{s+4}$		8	$\dfrac{2s+6}{s^2+9}$
5	$\dfrac{4}{s^4}$		9	$\dfrac{s-6}{s^2-25}$
6	$\dfrac{s}{s^2-16}$		10	$\dfrac{2\omega^2}{s^2+\omega^4}$

Examples 16.9

We use the transform table to find some inverse Laplace transforms. Again we concentrate on the denominator to dictate the format.

i) $\mathscr{L}^{-1}\left\{\dfrac{30}{(s+2)^4}\right\}$ uses $\mathscr{L}^{-1}\left\{\dfrac{n!}{(s+c)^{n+1}}\right\}$

with $c=2$ and $n+1=4$ from the denominator,

i.e. $\qquad\qquad n=3$.

Now comparing the numerators we need $n!$, i.e. 3! and so adjust 30 to give $30=5\times6=5\times3!$.

Then $\mathscr{L}^{-1}\left\{\dfrac{30}{(s+2)^4}\right\}=5\mathscr{L}^{-1}\left\{\dfrac{3!}{(s+2)^{3+1}}\right\}=5t^3e^{-2t}$.

ii) $\mathscr{L}^{-1}\left\{\dfrac{4(s+3)}{(s+3)^2+5^2}\right\}$ uses $\mathscr{L}^{-1}\left\{\dfrac{s+c}{(s+c)^2+\omega^2}\right\}$

with $c=3$ and $\omega=5$,

Then $\mathscr{L}^{-1}\left\{\dfrac{4(s+3)}{(s+3)^2+5^2}\right\}=4\mathscr{L}^{-1}\left\{\dfrac{s+3}{(s+3)^2+5^2}\right\}=4e^{-3t}\cos 5t$.

Suppose we have a quadratic denominator in the form as^2+bs+c, i.e. a different format from the previous example. It may be possible to factorise the quadratic expression. We will look at this soon. Alternatively, when we cannot factorise it we 'complete the square' to create a format similar to the previous example. Here we are going to work backwards using $(s+3)^2+5^2$.

Now $(s+3)^2+5^2=s^2+6s+3^2+25=s^2+6s+9+25$.

Notice $+6s$ when we have worked out the squared bracket and the original $+3$ in the bracket. Also notice 3^2 and the original $+3$ in the bracket.

Generally the relationships are $\left(\dfrac{1}{2} \times \text{coefficient of } s\right)$

and $\left(\dfrac{1}{2} \times \text{coefficient of } s\right)^2$.

███████ **Examples 16.10** ████████████████████████████

We find the inverse Laplace transforms.

i) $\mathscr{L}^{-1}\left\{\dfrac{s+4}{s^2+8s-33}\right\}$ has 8 as the coefficient of s,

i.e. $\dfrac{1}{2} \times$ coefficient of $s = 4$.

Then we use $+4$ in the bracket squared and subtract 4^2 to compensate, i.e.

$$s^2 + 8s - 33 = (s+4)^2 - 4^2 - 33 \qquad \boxed{\begin{aligned} -4^2 - 33 &= -16 - 33 \\ &= -49 \\ &= -7^2. \end{aligned}}$$

$$= (s+4)^2 - 7^2$$

$$\mathscr{L}^{-1}\left\{\dfrac{s+4}{s^2+8s-33}\right\} = \mathscr{L}^{-1}\left\{\dfrac{s+4}{(s+4)^2-7^2}\right\} = e^{-4t}\cosh 7t.$$

ii) $\mathscr{L}^{-1}\left\{\dfrac{3}{s^2-5s+15.25}\right\}$ has -5 as the coefficient of s,

i.e. $\dfrac{1}{2} \times$ coefficient of $s = -2.5$.

Then we use -2.5 in the bracket squared and subtract $(-2.5)^2$ to compensate, i.e.

$$s^2 - 5s + 15.25 = (s-2.5)^2 - (-2.5)^2 + 15.25$$

$$= (s-2.5)^2 + 3^2 \qquad \boxed{\begin{aligned} -(-2.5)^2 + 15.25 \\ = -6.25 + 15.25 \\ = 9 = 3^2. \end{aligned}}$$

$$\mathscr{L}^{-1}\left\{\dfrac{3}{s^2-5s+15.25}\right\} = \mathscr{L}^{-1}\left\{\dfrac{3}{(s-2.5)^2+3^2}\right\} = e^{2.5t}\sin 3t.$$

iii) $\mathscr{L}^{-1}\left\{\dfrac{4s+7}{s^2+6s+34}\right\}$ has 6 as the coefficient of s,

i.e. $\dfrac{1}{2} \times$ coefficient of $s = 3$.

Then we use 3 in the bracket squared and subtract 3^2 to compensate, i.e.

$$s^2 + 6s + 34 = (s+3)^2 - 3^2 + 34 \qquad \boxed{\begin{aligned} -3^2 + 34 &= -9 + 34 \\ &= 5^2. \end{aligned}}$$

$$= (s+3)^2 + 5^2$$

$$\mathcal{L}^{-1}\left\{\frac{4s+7}{s^2+6s+34}\right\} = \mathcal{L}^{-1}\left\{\frac{4s+7}{(s+3)^2+5^2}\right\}.$$

The format of the denominator compares with those in the table of transforms. However the numerator does not compare and so needs some adjustment. The numerator contains s but there is $(s+3)$ in the denominator. Hence we also need $(s+3)$ in the numerator. We also need some adjustment because of the 4 within the $4s$. The $(s+3)$ is important and we multiply it by 4 to create $4s$, as well as other terms. Now $4(s+3)$ gives us $4s+12$. This means we need to subtract 5 to return to our original 7,

i.e. $4s+7 = 4s+12-5$

$$= 4(s+3)-5.$$

Now $\mathcal{L}^{-1}\left\{\frac{4s+7}{s^2+6s+34}\right\}$

$$= \mathcal{L}^{-1}\left\{\frac{4s+7}{(s+3)^2+5^2}\right\}$$

$$= \mathcal{L}^{-1}\left\{\frac{4(s+3)-5}{(s+3)^2+5^2}\right\}$$

$$= 4\mathcal{L}^{-1}\left\{\frac{s+3}{(s+3)^2+5^2}\right\} - \mathcal{L}^{-1}\left\{\frac{5}{(s+3)^2+5^2}\right\}$$

$$= 4e^{-3t}\cos 5t - e^{-3t}\sin 5t$$

$$\text{or } e^{-3t}(4\cos 5t - \sin 5t).$$

iv) $\mathcal{L}^{-1}\left\{\dfrac{2s+15}{s^2+2s-8}\right\}$ needs 'completing the square' in the denominator. The numerator also needs some adjustment. The denominator has 2 as the coefficient of s, i.e. $\dfrac{1}{2} \times$ coefficient of $s = 1$.

Then we use 1 in the bracket squared and subtract 1^2 to compensate, i.e.

$$s^2+2s-8 = (s+1)^2-1^2-8$$

$$\boxed{\begin{aligned}-1^2-8 &= -1-8 \\ &= -3^2.\end{aligned}}$$

$$= (s+1)^2-3^2$$

We adjust the numerator to be consistent with the $(s+1)$ in the denominator, i.e. $2s+15 = 2(s+1)+13$.

Now $\mathscr{L}^{-1}\left\{\dfrac{2s+15}{(s+1)^2 - 3^2}\right\}$

$= \mathscr{L}^{-1}\left\{\dfrac{2(s+1)+13}{(s+1)^2 - 3^2}\right\}$

$= 2\mathscr{L}^{-1}\left\{\dfrac{s+1}{(s+1)^2 - 3^2}\right\} + \dfrac{13}{3}\mathscr{L}^{-1}\left\{\dfrac{3}{(s+1)^2 - 3^2}\right\}$

> Adjusting the numerator to the correct format.

$= 2e^{-t}\cosh 3t + \dfrac{13}{3}e^{-t}\sinh 3t$

$= e^{-t}\left(2\cosh 3t + \dfrac{13}{3}\sinh 3t\right).$

ASSIGNMENT

Later we will model an electrical circuit using Laplace transforms. Here we look at part of the solution, 'completing the square' in the denominator. Then we adjust the numerator to be consistent with the amended denominator, i.e.

$\mathscr{L}^{-1}\left\{\dfrac{31.2}{s^2 + 8s + 25}\right\} = \mathscr{L}^{-1}\left\{\dfrac{31.2}{(s+4)^2 + 3^2}\right\}$

$= \dfrac{31.2}{3} \times \mathscr{L}^{-1}\left\{\dfrac{3}{(s+4)^2 + 3^2}\right\}$

$= 10.4e^{-4t}\sin 3t.$

EXERCISE 16.6

Find the inverse transforms of the following functions in the s domain.

1 $\mathscr{L}^{-1}\left\{\dfrac{2}{(s+6)^2}\right\}$

2 $\mathscr{L}^{-1}\left\{\dfrac{3}{(s-1)^2}\right\}$

3 $\mathscr{L}^{-1}\left\{\dfrac{3}{(s+4)^2 + 9}\right\}$

4 $\mathscr{L}^{-1}\left\{\dfrac{s-6}{(s+4)^2 - 9}\right\}$

5 $\mathscr{L}^{-1}\left\{\dfrac{s+5}{(s+5)^2 + 16}\right\}$

6 $\mathscr{L}^{-1}\left\{\dfrac{24}{(s+2)^5}\right\}$

7 $\mathscr{L}^{-1}\left\{\dfrac{s+2}{s^2 + 4s + 2}\right\}$

8 $\mathscr{L}^{-1}\left\{\dfrac{s+4}{s^2 + 10s + 9}\right\}$

9 $\mathscr{L}^{-1}\left\{\dfrac{2s+6}{s^2-2s+2}\right\}$ | **10** $\mathscr{L}^{-1}\left\{\dfrac{3s-2}{s^2+2s}\right\}$

Our next set of Examples uses partial fractions. If necessary re-read the early sections of Volume 2, Chapter 12. Remember our aim is to split factors in the common denominator into separate denominators.

▬▬▬ Examples 16.11 ▬▬▬

We use some results from Volume 2, Chapter 12. You may wish to check the omitted partial fraction work as revision. Here we find some more inverse Laplace transforms.

i) $\mathscr{L}^{-1}\left\{\dfrac{30}{(s-1)(s+2)(s-3)}\right\}$

$= \mathscr{L}^{-1}\left\{\dfrac{-5}{s-1}\right\} + \mathscr{L}^{-1}\left\{\dfrac{2}{s+2}\right\} + \mathscr{L}^{-1}\left\{\dfrac{3}{s-3}\right\}$

$= -5\mathscr{L}^{-1}\left\{\dfrac{1}{s-1}\right\} + 2\mathscr{L}^{-1}\left\{\dfrac{1}{s+2}\right\} + 3\mathscr{L}^{-1}\left\{\dfrac{1}{s-3}\right\}$

$= -5e^t + 2e^{-2t} + 3e^{3t}.$

ii) $\mathscr{L}^{-1}\left\{\dfrac{5s^2-19s+5}{(s-1)^2(s+2)}\right\}$

$= \mathscr{L}^{-1}\left\{\dfrac{-2}{s-1}\right\} - \mathscr{L}^{-1}\left\{\dfrac{3}{(s-1)^2}\right\} + \mathscr{L}^{-1}\left\{\dfrac{7}{s+2}\right\}$

$= -2e^t - 3te^t + 7e^{-2t}.$

iii) This example combines the partial fractions and then the completion of the square techniques.

$\mathscr{L}^{-1}\left\{\dfrac{3s^2-10s-13}{(s^2+s+1)(s-2)}\right\} = \mathscr{L}^{-1}\left\{\dfrac{6s+5}{s^2+s+1}\right\} - \mathscr{L}^{-1}\left\{\dfrac{3}{s-2}\right\}.$

We need to complete the square for s^2+s+1,

i.e. $s^2+s+1 = (s+0.5)^2 - 0.5^2 + 1$

$= (s+0.5)^2 + 0.75$

$$\boxed{\begin{aligned} 0.75 &= \left(\sqrt{\dfrac{3}{4}}\right)^2 \\ &= \left(\dfrac{\sqrt{3}}{2}\right)^2 \\ &= 0.866^2. \end{aligned}}$$

Then $\mathscr{L}^{-1}\left\{\dfrac{3s^2 - 10s - 13}{(s^2 + s + 1)(s - 2)}\right\}$

$= \mathscr{L}^{-1}\left\{\dfrac{6s + 5}{(s + 0.5)^2 + 0.75}\right\} - \mathscr{L}^{-1}\left\{\dfrac{3}{s - 2}\right\}.$

$= \mathscr{L}^{-1}\left\{\dfrac{6(s + 0.5) + 2}{(s + 0.5)^2 + 0.75}\right\} - \mathscr{L}^{-1}\left\{\dfrac{3}{s - 2}\right\}$

$= 6\mathscr{L}^{-1}\left\{\dfrac{s + 0.5}{(s + 0.5)^2 + 0.75}\right\} + \mathscr{L}^{-1}\left\{\dfrac{2}{(s + 0.5)^2 + 0.75}\right\}$

$\qquad\qquad\qquad - \mathscr{L}^{-1}\left\{\dfrac{3}{s - 2}\right\}$

$= 6\mathscr{L}^{-1}\left\{\dfrac{s + 0.5}{(s + 0.5)^2 + 0.75}\right\} + \dfrac{2}{\sqrt{3}/2}\mathscr{L}^{-1}\left\{\dfrac{\sqrt{3}/2}{(s + 0.5)^2 + 0.75}\right\}$

$\qquad\qquad\qquad - \mathscr{L}^{-1}\left\{\dfrac{3}{s - 2}\right\}$

$= 6e^{-0.5t}\cos 0.866t + 2.309e^{-0.5t}\sin 0.866t - 3e^{2t}.$

ASSIGNMENT

This is another look at our electrical circuit Assignment. As we will see later this is based on a sinusoidal e.m.f. The solution eventually leads to

$\bar{i} = \dfrac{93.6s}{(s^2 + 9)(s^2 + 8s + 25)}$

$\equiv \dfrac{As + B}{s^2 + 9} + \dfrac{Cs + D}{s^2 + 8s + 25}$

where A, B, C and D are constants to be found.

With 4 constants to be found the method takes some time. We quote the results for you; $A = 1.8$, $B = 8.1$, $C = -1.8$ and $D = -22.5$. We substitute these numbers so that

$\bar{i} = \dfrac{1.8s + 8.1}{s^2 + 9} + \dfrac{-1.8s - 22.5}{s^2 + 8s + 25}$

$= \dfrac{1.8s + 8.1}{s^2 + 9} + \dfrac{-1.8s - 22.5}{(s + 4)^2 + 3^2}.$

Completing the square.

Remember the denominator dictates the format in the numerator, implying we need $(s + 4)$ and 3.

i.e. $\displaystyle \bar{i} = \frac{1.8s + 8.1}{s^2 + 9} + \frac{-1.8(s+4) - 15.3}{(s+4)^2 + 3^2}$

$\displaystyle = \frac{1.8s}{s^2 + 3^2} + \frac{8.1}{s^2 + 3^2} - \frac{1.8(s+4)}{(s+4)^2 + 3^2} - \frac{15.3}{(s+4)^2 + 3^2}$

$\displaystyle = 1.8\left\{\frac{s}{s^2 + 3^2}\right\} + 2.7\left\{\frac{3}{s^2 + 3^2}\right\} - 1.8\left\{\frac{s+4}{(s+4)^2 + 3^2}\right\}$

$\displaystyle \qquad\qquad\qquad\qquad - 5.1\left\{\frac{3}{(s+4)^2 + 3^2}\right\}$

Applying inverse Laplace transforms we get

$\qquad i = 1.8\cos 3t + 2.7\sin 3t - 1.8e^{-4t}\cos 3t - 5.1e^{-4t}\sin 3t.$

EXERCISE 16.7

Split up the following functions into partial fractions and find their inverse Laplace transforms.

1 $\displaystyle \mathscr{L}^{-1}\left\{\frac{6s + 2}{(s-1)(s+3)}\right\}$

2 $\displaystyle \mathscr{L}^{-1}\left\{\frac{11s^2 + 6s - 25}{(s+3)(s+1)(s-4)}\right\}$

3 $\displaystyle \mathscr{L}^{-1}\left\{\frac{3s^2 - 10s + 11}{(s+1)^2(s-5)}\right\}$

4 $\displaystyle \mathscr{L}^{-1}\left\{\frac{-7.5s - 19}{(s-4)(s+3)^2}\right\}$

5 $\displaystyle \mathscr{L}^{-1}\left\{\frac{5s^2 + 15s + 12}{(s+3)(s+1)^2}\right\}$

6 $\displaystyle \mathscr{L}^{-1}\left\{\frac{s^2 - 4s - 3}{(s^2 + 1)(s - 1)}\right\}$

7 $\displaystyle \mathscr{L}^{-1}\left\{\frac{6s^2 + 10}{s(s^2 + 2)}\right\}$

8 $\displaystyle \mathscr{L}^{-1}\left\{\frac{4s^2 - 50s - 10}{(s+1)(s^2 + 10)}\right\}$

9 $\displaystyle \mathscr{L}^{-1}\left\{\frac{-s - 4}{(s^2 - s + 2)s}\right\}$

10 $\displaystyle \mathscr{L}^{-1}\left\{\frac{3s^2 - 8}{(s-3)(s^2 + 2s + 4)}\right\}$

First order differential equations

Generally our differential equations involve y as a function of t. When we apply Laplace transforms to each term we transform from the t domain to the s domain. Use the table of transforms at the end of this chapter, particularly $\mathscr{L}\left\{\dfrac{dy}{dt}\right\} = s\bar{y} - y_0$ where y_0 is the value of y at $t = 0$ and $\mathscr{L}\{y\} = \bar{y}$. We manipulate the algebra to give $\bar{y}$ in terms of s. Finally we apply inverse transforms to quote a solution in the original domain.

■■■■■ **Example 16.12** ■■■■■■■■■■■■■■■■■■■■■■■■■■■■

Solve $\dfrac{dy}{dt} - 2y = 0$ given the initial boundary condition $y = 8$.

Remember we interpret this boundary condition as $y = 8$ at $t = 0$, i.e. $y_0 = 8$.

We apply Laplace transforms separately to $\dfrac{dy}{dt}$, $-2y$ and 0, i.e.

$$(s\bar{y} - y_0) - 2\bar{y} = \frac{0}{s}$$
$$s\bar{y} - 8 - 2\bar{y} = 0$$
$$s\bar{y} - 2\bar{y} = 8$$
$$(s - 2)\bar{y} = 8$$
$$\bar{y} = \frac{8}{s - 2} = 8 \times \frac{1}{s - 2}.$$

Applying an inverse Laplace transform we get

$$y = 8e^{2t}.$$

■■■■■ **ASSIGNMENT** ■■■■■■■■■■■■■■■■■■■■■■■■■■■■■

Let us look in detail at our electrical circuit. In Fig 16.1 we have a capacitor, C, a resistor, R, and an inductor, L, in series together with a constant e.m.f., E, and a current, i.

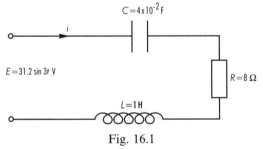

Fig. 16.1

The voltage across a capacitor is given by $\dfrac{1}{C} \displaystyle\int_0^t i \, dt$.

The voltage across a resistor is given by Ri.

The voltage across an inductor is given by $L\dfrac{di}{dt}$.

In our Assignment $C = 4 \times 10^{-2}$ F, $R = 8\,\Omega$, $L = 1$ H and $E = 31.2$ V. We describe (model) the circuit with a differential equation to find the current, i. The initial conditions are zero. The sum of the voltages across the components is the e.m.f, i.e.

$$\frac{1}{C} \int_0^t i \, dt + Ri + L\frac{di}{dt} = E.$$

Substituting for our circuit values we get

$$\frac{1}{4 \times 10^{-2}} \int_0^t i \, dt + 8i + 1\frac{di}{dt} = 31.2.$$

We apply Laplace transforms separately to each term (referring to the table of transforms),

$$\frac{25\bar{i}}{s} + 8\bar{i} + (s\bar{i} - i_0) = \frac{31.2}{s} \qquad \boxed{\text{Substituting for } i_0.}$$

i.e. $$\frac{25\bar{i}}{s} + 8\bar{i} + s\bar{i} - 0 = \frac{31.2}{s} \qquad \boxed{\begin{array}{l}\text{Multiplying through} \\ \text{by } s.\end{array}}$$

and then $$25\bar{i} + 8s\bar{i} + s^2\bar{i} = 31.2$$

$$(s^2 + 8s + 25)\bar{i} = 31.2$$

so that $$\bar{i} = \frac{31.2}{s^2 + 8s + 25}.$$

We saw previously the adjustments to this expression for $\bar{i}$ in terms of s. Applying the inverse Laplace transform we get

$$i = 10.4e^{-4t} \sin 3t$$

to be the expression for the current in the circuit.

Example 16.13

Solve $3\dfrac{dy}{dt} + 2y = 15e^t + 4e^{-t}$ given the boundary condition $y = -1$ at $t = 0$.

Applying Laplace transforms to each term separately we get

$$3(s\bar{y} - y_0) + 2\bar{y} = \frac{15}{s-1} + \frac{4}{s+1} \qquad \boxed{\begin{array}{l}\text{Substituting for} \\ y_0 = -1.\end{array}}$$

i.e. $$3(s\bar{y} - -1) + 2\bar{y} = \frac{15}{s-1} + \frac{4}{s+1}$$

$$3s\bar{y} + 3 + 2\bar{y} = \frac{15}{s-1} + \frac{4}{s+1}$$

$$3s\bar{y} + 2\bar{y} = -3 + \frac{15}{s-1} + \frac{4}{s+1}$$

$$(3s + 2)\bar{y} = \frac{-3(s-1)(s+1) + 15(s+1) + 4(s-1)}{(s-1)(s+1)}$$

$$\bar{y} = \frac{-3s^2 + 3 + 15s + 15 + 4s - 4}{(s-1)(s+1)(3s+2)}$$

$$\bar{y} = \frac{-3s^2 + 19s + 14}{(s-1)(s+1)(3s+2)}.$$

We split this compound fraction into partial fractions in the usual way.

$$\frac{-3s^2 + 19s + 14}{(s-1)(s+1)(3s+2)} \equiv \frac{A}{s-1} + \frac{B}{s+1} + \frac{C}{3s+2}$$
$$\equiv \frac{A(s+1)(3s+2) + B(s-1)(3s+2) + C(s-1)(s+1)}{(s-1)(s+1)(3s+2)}$$

i.e. $-3s^2 + 19s + 14$

$$\equiv A(s+1)(3s+2) + B(s-1)(3s+2) + C(s-1)(s+1).$$

In turn we choose values of s to make each bracket equate to 0. This allows us to find values for A, B and C.

Let $s+1 = 0$, i.e. $s = -1$,

$$-3(-1)^2 + 19(-1) + 14 = B(-2)(-1)$$
$$-3 - 19 + 14 = 2B$$

i.e. $$B = \frac{-8}{2}$$
$$= -4.$$

Let $s - 1 = 0$, i.e. $s = 1$,

$$-3(1)^2 + 19(1) + 14 = A(2)(5)$$
$$-3 + 19 + 14 = 10A$$

i.e. $$A = \frac{30}{10}$$
$$= 3.$$

Let $3s + 2 = 0$, i.e. $s = \frac{-2}{3}$,

$$-3\left(\frac{-2}{3}\right)^2 + 19\left(\frac{-2}{3}\right) + 14 = C\left(\frac{-5}{3}\right)\left(\frac{1}{3}\right)$$
$$0 = C\left(\frac{-5}{3}\right)\left(\frac{1}{3}\right)$$

i.e. $$C = 0.$$

Hence $$\bar{y} = \frac{3}{s-1} - \frac{4}{s+1} + \frac{0}{3s+2}$$

Obviously the last partial fraction is zero. When we apply inverse Laplace transforms we get

$$y = 3e^t - 4e^{-t}.$$

Let us look again at the algebra because the numerator, C, is zero. This means its denominator, $3s + 2$, is a factor of the original compound denominator. We can check this using algebraic long division, i.e.

$$\begin{array}{r} -s+7 \\ 3s+2\overline{)\,-3s^2+19s+14} \\ \underline{-3s^2-2s} \\ 21s+14 \\ \underline{21s+14} \\ 0 \end{array}$$

Now we have reduced our expression for $\bar{y}$ to $\bar{y}=\dfrac{-s+7}{(s-1)(s+1)}.$

We would attempt our partial fractions method on this simplified compound fraction. It would give exactly the same values for A and B as before.

ASSIGNMENT

We return to our Assignment with the same capacitor, C, resistor, R, and inductor, L, in series. This time the e.m.f., E, is sinusoidal. Again, in Fig. 16.2, we wish to find the current, i.

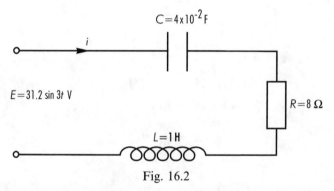

Fig. 16.2

$C=4\times10^{-2}$ F, $R=8\,\Omega$, $L=1$ H and $E=31.2\sin3t$ V. The initial conditions are zero. The sum of the voltages across the components is the e.m.f, i.e

$$\frac{1}{C}\int_0^t i\,dt + Ri + L\frac{di}{dt} = E.$$

Substituting for our circuit values we get

$$\frac{1}{4\times10^{-2}}\int_0^t i\,dt + 8i + 1\frac{di}{dt} = 31.2\sin3t.$$

We apply Laplace transforms separately to each term (referring to the table of transforms),

$$\frac{25\bar{i}}{s}+8\bar{i}+(s\bar{i}-i_0) = \frac{31.2\times3}{s^2+3^2}$$

i.e. $\quad 25\bar{i}+8s\bar{i}+s^2\bar{i}-0 = \dfrac{93.6s}{s^2+9}$ $\boxed{\text{Substituting for } i_0.\\ \text{Multiplying through by } s.}$

and then $\qquad (s^2 + 8s + 25)\bar{i} = \dfrac{93.6s}{s^2 + 9}$

so that $\qquad\qquad\qquad\qquad \bar{i} = \dfrac{93.6s}{(s^2 + 9)(s^2 + 8s + 25)}.$

We saw previously the adjustments to this expression for i in terms of s. Applying the inverse Laplace transforms we get

$\qquad i = 1.8\cos 3t + 2.7\sin 3t - 1.8e^{-4t}\cos 3t - 5.1e^{-4t}\sin 3t.$

to be the expression for the current in the circuit.

EXERCISE 16.8

Solve the following differential equations using Laplace transforms. In each case the initial boundary conditions are given.

1 $\dfrac{dy}{dt} + y = 9e^{2t}$ $\qquad\qquad$ given $y = -2$ at $t = 0$.

2 $2\dfrac{dy}{dt} - 4y + 3 = 0$ $\qquad\qquad$ with zero initial boundary conditions.

3 $\dfrac{dy}{dx} - 3y = 4e^{3x}$ $\qquad\qquad$ given $y = 0$ at $x = 0$.

4 $\dfrac{dy}{dt} - y = 6e^{-t}$ $\qquad\qquad$ with $y = -1$ initially.

5 $\dfrac{dx}{dt} - 2x = 2\sin t - \cos t$ $\qquad$ with $x = 1$ initially.

6 $\dfrac{dy}{dt} - 3y + 17 = 15t$ $\qquad\qquad$ given $y = 3$ at $t = 0$.

7 $5\dfrac{dy}{dt} + 2y = 29\cos t$ $\qquad\qquad$ with $y = 2$ initially.

8 $\dfrac{dy}{dt} - 3y = 3 - 9t$ $\qquad\qquad$ given $y = 0.5$ at $t = 0$.

9 $3\dfrac{dy}{dt} + 2y = e^{-t}(6\cos 2t - \sin 2t)$ $\qquad$ with zero initial conditions.

10 $\dfrac{dx}{dt} + 2x = 2t^2 + 2t + e^{-2t}$ $\quad$ given $x = 0$ at $t = 0$.

$\qquad$ In your solution you will get $\dfrac{s^3 + 2s^2 + 8s + 8}{s^3(s + 2)^2}$ which needs the

$\qquad$ partial fractions $\dfrac{A}{s} + \dfrac{B}{s^2} + \dfrac{C}{s^3} + \dfrac{D}{s + 2} + \dfrac{E}{(s + 2)^2}.$

We now turn our attention to 2 theorems. The algebra involved is very simple. However they do need to be applied with care as we shall see.

The initial value theorem

This theorem states that $\quad \underset{t \to 0}{\text{Lim}} \{f(t)\} = \underset{s \to \infty}{\text{Lim}} \{sf(s)\}.$

In it we know $f(s)$ to be the Laplace transform of $F(t)$. By looking at what happens to $sf(s)$ as s gets very large (i.e. as $s \to \infty$) we can find the initial value of $F(t)$ (i.e. as $t \to 0$).

Example 16.14

If
$$f(s) = \frac{s}{s^2 + 9}$$

then
$$sf(s) = s \times \frac{s}{s^2 + 9} = \frac{s^2}{s^2 + 9}.$$

When $s \to \infty$ we have no control; s is getting bigger and bigger. However as $s \to \infty$ so $\frac{1}{s} \to 0$, i.e. $\frac{1}{s}$ is getting smaller and smaller, and we do have control. In our expression for $sf(s)$ we divide each term by s^2 to create this controlled situation, i.e.

$$sf(s) = \frac{1}{1 + \dfrac{9}{s^2}}.$$

As $s \to \infty$, $\dfrac{1}{s^2} \to 0$, i.e. $\dfrac{9}{s^2} \to 0.$

Then $\quad \underset{s \to \infty}{\text{Lim}} \mathscr{L}\{sf(s)\} = \dfrac{1}{1 + 0} = 1$

i.e. $\quad \underset{t \to \infty}{\text{Lim}} \{F(t)\} = 1.$

We can verify this by checking the table of transforms, i.e.

$$\mathscr{L}^{-1}\left\{\frac{s}{s^2 + 9}\right\} = \cos 3t$$

i.e. $\quad F(t) = \cos 3t.$

$$\underset{t \to 0}{\text{Lim}} \{F(t)\} = \underset{t \to 0}{\text{Lim}} \{\cos 3t\} = 1,$$

confirming our earlier deduction that

$$\underset{s \to \infty}{\text{Lim}} \{sf(s)\} = 1.$$

The final value theorem

This theorem states that $\quad \underset{t \to \infty}{\text{Lim}} \{f(t)\} = \underset{s \to 0}{\text{Lim}} \{sf(s)\}.$

Again we know $f(s)$ to be the Laplace transform of $F(t)$. By looking at what happens to $sf(s)$ as s gets very small (i.e. as $s \to 0$) we can find the final value of $F(t)$ (i.e. as $t \to \infty$). Notice how similar it is to the initial value theorem, only the limiting values of 0 and ∞ are interchanged.

■■■■■ **Example 16.15** ■■■■■■■■■■■■■■■■■■■■■■■■■■■■■■■

If $$f(s) = \frac{2}{s+3}$$

then $$sf(s) = s \times \frac{2}{s+3} = \frac{2s}{s+3}.$$

As $s \to 0$, $s + 3 \to 3$ and so $\dfrac{2s}{s+3} \to 0$,

then $$\text{Lim}_{s \to \infty} \{sf(s)\} = 0$$

i.e. $$\text{Lim}_{t \to \infty} \{F(t)\} = 0.$$

We can verify this by checking the table of transforms, i.e.

$$\mathscr{L}^{-1}\left\{\frac{2}{s+3}\right\} = 2e^{-3t}$$

i.e. $$F(t) = 2e^{-3t}.$$

$$\text{Lim}_{t \to \infty} \{F(t)\} = 2\,\text{Lim}_{t \to \infty} \{e^{-3t}\} = 2 \times 0 = 0,$$

confirming our earlier deduction that

$$\text{Lim}_{s \to \infty} \{sf(s)\} = 0.$$

We need to be careful with both of these theorems. They do *not* always give the desired result. This is because the integral definition of the Laplace transform involves the parameter s. The value of s is chosen so that the integral actually has a value. This can contradict our theorems, as the next example shows.

■■■■■ **Example 16.16** ■■■■■■■■■■■■■■■■■■■■■■■■■■■■■■■

If $$f(s) = \frac{4}{s-2}$$

then $$sf(s) = s \times \frac{4}{s-2} = \frac{4s}{s-2}.$$

As $s \to 0$, $s - 2 \to -2$ and so $\dfrac{4s}{s-2} \to 0$,

then $$\text{Lim}_{s \to \infty} \{sf(s)\} = 0$$

i.e. $$\text{Lim}_{t \to \infty} \{F(t)\} = 0.$$

However, checking the table of transforms shows we have a contradiction.

$$\mathscr{L}\left\{\frac{4}{s-2}\right\} = 4e^{2t}$$

i.e. $$F(t) = 4e^{2t}.$$

Clearly as $t \to \infty$ $\{F(t)\} \to \infty$, differing from $\text{Lim}_{s \to 0} \{sf(s)\} = 0$.

Remember that the integral definition of the Laplace transforms came before the initial and final value theorems. It is the transforms that must override the theorems. Remember this when attempting the next Exercise.

■ EXERCISE 16.9 ■

In each case the question gives the expression for $f(s)$. For each function, $F(t)$, apply the

i)   initial value theorem to find the inital value,
ii) final value theorem to find the final value.

1   $\dfrac{1}{s-2}$

2   $\dfrac{5}{s+6}$

3   $\dfrac{2}{s^4}$

4   $\dfrac{2s}{s^2-25}$

5   $\dfrac{s}{s^2+49}$

6   $\dfrac{4}{s^2+16}$

7   $\dfrac{3}{(s+5)^2}$

8   $\dfrac{5}{(s-3)^2}$

9   $\dfrac{4}{(s+4)^2+16}$

10 $\dfrac{3s}{s^2+2s}$

Transfer functions

A **transfer function** changes an input into an output, i.e.

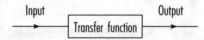

i.e. Output function = Transfer function operating on the input function

The transfer function can have many different forms. In this chapter of Laplace transforms it is given in terms of the parameter, s.

■ ASSIGNMENT ■

Let us look again at our electrical circuit. This time the capacitor, C, resistor, R, and inductor, L, are in series together with an unknown e.m.f., E. We use the same values as before for C, R and L together with zero initial conditions for the current, i. Again the sum of the voltages across the components is the e.m.f, i.e

$$\frac{1}{C}\int_0^t i\,dt + Ri + L\frac{di}{dt} = E.$$

Substituting for our circuit values we get

$$\frac{1}{4\times 10^{-2}}\int_0^t i\,dt + 8i + 1\frac{di}{dt} = E.$$

We apply Laplace transforms separately to each term (referring to the table of transforms),

$$\frac{25\bar{i}}{s} + 8\bar{i} + (s\bar{i} - i_0) = \bar{E}$$

> $\bar{E}$ is the Laplace transform of E.

i.e. $$\frac{25\bar{i}}{s} + 8\bar{i} + s\bar{i} - 0 = \bar{E}$$

> Substituting for i_0.

and then $$25\bar{i} + 8s\bar{i} + s^2\bar{i} = \bar{E}s$$

> Multiplying through by s.

$$(s^2 + 8s + 25)\bar{i} = \bar{E}s$$

so that $$\bar{i} = \left(\frac{s}{s^2 + 8s + 25}\right)\bar{E}.$$

In this case, having applied the Laplace transforms, the input is $\bar{E}$ and the output is $\bar{i}$. Hence the transfer function, $T(s)$ is

$$T(s) = \frac{s}{s^2 + 8s + 25}.$$

Poles and zeroes

A transfer function, as we have just seen in the Assignment, is an algebraic fraction. We may write it generally as

$$\text{Transfer function} = \frac{\text{Numerator as some function of } s}{\text{Denominator as some function of } s},$$

i.e. $$T(s) = \frac{N(s)}{D(s)}.$$

A **zero** exists where the value of s makes the numerator equal to zero, i.e. the value of s such that $N(s) = 0$.

A **pole** exists where the value of s makes the denominator equal to zero, i.e. the value of s such that $D(s) = 0$.

ASSIGNMENT

We look at the transfer function,

$$T(s) = \frac{s}{s^2 + 8s + 25},$$

and discuss the possible zero and poles.

For a zero we need $N(s) = 0$,

i.e. $s = 0.$

For poles we need $\quad D(s) = 0,$

i.e. $\qquad s^2 + 8s + 25 = 0$

$$(s+4)^2 + 3^2 = 0$$

$$(s+4)^2 = -3^2 = j^2 3^2$$

$$s + 4 = \pm j3$$

> Completing the square.
> $j^2 = -1.$
> Square root of both sides.

to give $\qquad\qquad s = -4 \pm j3$

$$\text{or} \ -4 + j3 \ \text{and} \ -4 - j3$$

as the positions of the poles.

Stability of poles

We need to know if the solution to a problem is stable or unstable. The transfer function and the associated poles are in the s domain, based on Laplace transforms. Remember the importance of the denominator. We know, from using the table of transforms, the nature of the function in the original t domain. Many of them involve exponential functions, both positive and negative. In Figs. 16.3 we remind you of the graphs for exponential growth (positive exponential power) and exponential decay (negative exponential power).

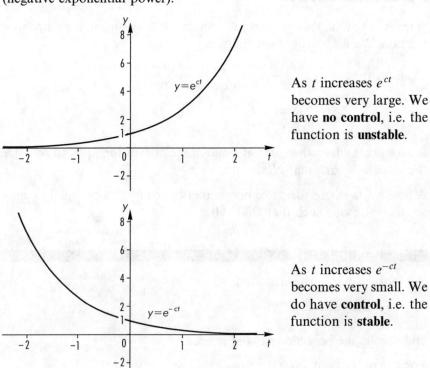

As t increases e^{ct} becomes very large. We have **no control**, i.e. the function is **unstable**.

As t increases e^{-ct} becomes very small. We do have **control**, i.e. the function is **stable**.

Figs. 16.3

Functions involving e^{ct} are associated with instability. Functions involving e^{-ct} are associated with stability. In the denominator of the transfer function, $D(s)$, we are looking for terms of the types $(s + c)$ and $(s + c)^2 + \omega^2$, ... We can plot the positions of the poles on a pair of real and imaginary axes. In Fig. 16.4 we show some algebraic examples.

If $\qquad s + c = 0$ $\qquad\qquad$ If $\qquad s - c = 0$

then $\qquad\qquad s = -c.$ $\quad$ ① $\quad$ then $\qquad\qquad s = c.$ $\qquad$ ④

If $\quad (s + c)^2 + \omega^2 = 0$ $\qquad\qquad$ If $\quad (s - c)^2 + \omega^2 = 0$

then $\qquad (s + c)^2 = -\omega^2 = j^2\omega^2$ $\qquad$ then $\qquad (s - c)^2 = -\omega^2 = j^2\omega^2$

$$\boxed{\text{square root of both sides and } j^2 = -1.}$$

i.e. $\qquad s + c = \pm j\omega$ $\qquad\qquad$ i.e. $\qquad s - c = \pm j\omega$

to give $\qquad s = -c \pm j\omega$ $\qquad$ to give $\qquad s = c \pm j\omega$

or $\qquad\qquad s = -c + j\omega$ $\quad$ ② $\quad$ or $\qquad\qquad s = c + j\omega$ $\qquad$ ⑤

$\qquad\qquad$ and $\quad s = -c - j\omega.$ $\quad$ ③ $\qquad\qquad\qquad$ and $\quad s = c - j\omega.$ $\quad$ ⑥

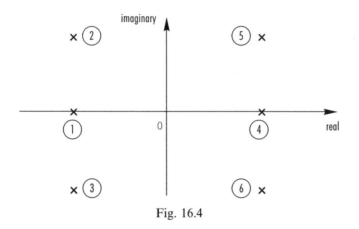

Fig. 16.4

The poles to the left of the imaginary (vertical) axis are stable and those to the right of it are unstable. For safer solutions we assume that poles lying on the vertical axis are unstable.

ASSIGNMENT

We look at the transfer function, $\quad T(s) = \dfrac{s}{s^2 + 8s + 25}$

and the poles at $\qquad\qquad\qquad s = -4 + j3 \text{ and } -4 - j3.$

In Fig. 16.5 we plot them and see that they are both to the left of the vertical axis, i.e. both are stable. This agrees with our earlier work. We know that $s^2 + 8s + 25$ may have its square completed and be associated with $e^{-4t} \sin 3t$ in the t domain.

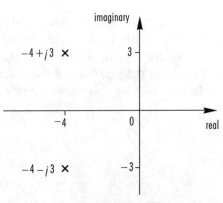

Fig. 16.5

▰▰▰▰ EXERCISE 16.10 ▰▰▰▰

In each case you are given a transfer function.
i)   Find any zeroes and poles.
ii) Plot the poles on a pair of axes.
iii) From your plot decide which poles are stable and which are unstable.

1   $\dfrac{3}{(s+2)^2 + 9}$

2   $\dfrac{s-2}{(s+2)^2 - 9}$

3   $\dfrac{4}{(s+1)^5}$

4   $\dfrac{3s-2}{s^2 + 4s}$

5   $\dfrac{s+1}{s^2 + 4s + 2}$

6   $\dfrac{s+4}{s^2 + 10s + 16}$

7   $\dfrac{s+2}{(s-2)(s+1)}$

8   $\dfrac{s^2 + 6s + 8}{(s+3)(s+1)(s-4)}$

9   $\dfrac{6s^2 - 10}{s(s^2 + 5)}$

10 $\dfrac{s^2 - 3s - 10}{(s+2)(s^2 + 16)}$

Applications

We have seen the techniques applied to our electrical circuit Assignment. There we mathematically modelled the problem with a differential equation. Using initial boundary conditions we solved the differential equation applying Laplace transforms and their inverses. We demonstrate the same complete technique in Example 16.17. You should use the same approach in Exercise 16.11.

███████ **Example 16.17** ████████████████████████████

This example deals with Newton's law of cooling. The rate of cooling is proportional to the temperature difference of a body and its surrounding environment. It can be applied to a human corpse, when the body is still warm, to estimate the time of death. In our case this law is represented by the differential equation

$$\frac{dT}{dt} = -k(T - 15).$$ T is the temperature of the body, (°C),

t is the time, (hours); and

k is the constant of proportionality.

The temperature of the surrounding environment is 15°C. This body cools from 37°C to 25°C in 8 hours. Using Laplace transforms solve this differential equation.

Remember k is simply a number. We will find its value later.

We start with $\dfrac{dT}{dt} = -k(T - 15).$

Applying Laplace transforms to each term separately we get

$$s\bar{T} - T_0 = -k\bar{T} + \frac{15k}{s}$$

i.e. $s\bar{T} - 37 = -k\bar{T} + \dfrac{15k}{s}$

> Substituting for
> $T = 37$ at $t = 0$.

$$s\bar{T} + k\bar{T} = 37 + \frac{15k}{s}$$

$$(s + k)\bar{T} = \frac{37s + 15k}{s}$$

to give $\bar{T} = \dfrac{37s + 15k}{s(s + k)}.$

We split this compound fraction into partial fractions in the usual way.

$$\frac{37s + 15k}{s(s + k)} \equiv \frac{A}{s} + \frac{B}{s + k}$$

$$\equiv \frac{A(s + k) + Bs}{s(s + k)}$$

i.e. $37s + 15k \equiv A(s + k) + Bs.$

In turn we choose values for s to find A and B.
Let $s = 0$,

$$15k = Ak$$

i.e. $A = 15.$

Let $s + k = 0$, i.e. $s = -k$,

$$-37k + 15k = -Bk$$

i.e. $B = 22$.

Hence $\bar{T} = \dfrac{15}{s} + \dfrac{22}{s+k}$.

When we apply inverse Laplace transforms we get

$$T = 15 + 22e^{-kt}.$$

We use the remaining information in the problem to find the value of k.
Using $T = 25$ at $t = 8$ we substitute to get

$$25 = 15 + 22e^{-k8}$$

i.e. $10 = 22e^{-k8}$

$$\dfrac{10}{22} = e^{-k8}$$

i.e. $-k8 = \ln\dfrac{10}{22} = -0.788\ldots$

    so that $k = 0.099$

to give a particular solution of

$$T = 15 + 22e^{-0.099t}.$$

EXERCISE 16.11

1   A large portion of a rocket's mass, m, is fuel so that during flight this
    mass changes significantly. The mass, m, is related to the velocity, v,
    of the rocket according to the differential equation

$$\frac{dm}{dv} + \frac{m}{2000} = 0.$$

   The original mass of the rocket, when resting on the launch pad, is
   15 000 kg. Using Laplace transforms solve this differential equation
   for m in terms of v. Explain why your solution is stable.

2   For an elastic spring the rate of working, $\dfrac{dW}{dx}$, is proportional to the
    extension, x, from the natural length. Write this as a differential
    equation and solve it using Laplace transforms and the following
    information. At the natural length there has been no work done.
    When $W = 2.5$ J the spring has been stretched by 0.1 m.

3   The needle deflection from the vertical, θ, in a meter is initially zero.
    Its movement is modelled by the differential equation

$$\frac{d\theta}{dt} = 3te^{-2t}.$$

   Using Laplace transforms solve this equation to find θ in terms of the
   time, t.

4   Storm tanks at a sewerage treatment plant store excess effluent following a heavy storm. V gallons is the volume of effluent stored in them. The rate of increase of volume, $\dfrac{dV}{dt}$, is related to time, t hours, after the start of the storm. We know that $\dfrac{dV}{dt} = k(t - 8)$. When $t = 0$ they still hold 200 000 gallons from the previous night's torrential downpour. Also the tanks are just empty 8 hours after the start of this storm. Show that $V = 3125t(t - 16) + 200000$.

5a) i)   The electrical circuit shows an e.m.f. of $10 \sin t$ V in series with an inductor of 4 H and a resistor of 3 Ω. The initial conditions are zero. Model this circuit using a differential equation with the current, i A, in terms of the time, t s. Using Laplace transforms solve your differential equation.

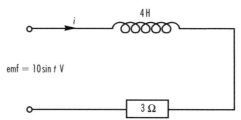

ii)   The circuit is now generalised to an e.m.f., $E \sin \omega t$, an inductor, L, and a resistor, R. It is modelled by the differential equation

$$L\frac{di}{dt} + Ri = E \sin \omega t.$$

Again apply Laplace transforms with zero initial conditions to get

$$\bar{i} = \frac{E\omega}{(s^2 + \omega^2)(Ls + R)}.$$

Using partial fractions and inverse transforms find an algebraic solution for i.

b)   The previous general circuit is amended to an e.m.f., $E \cos \omega t$, an inductor, L, and a capacitor, C.

It is modelled by the equation

$$L\frac{di}{dt} + \frac{1}{C}\int i\,dt = E \cos \omega t.$$

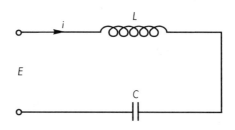

Again apply Laplace transforms with zero initial conditions to get

$$\bar{i} = \frac{ECs^2}{(s^2 + \omega^2)(CLs^2 + 1)}.$$

Using partial fractions expect two of your numerators to be 0. Find an algebraic solution for i using inverse Laplace transforms.

Table of Laplace Transforms

Function, $F(t)$	Transform, $\mathscr{L}\{F(t)\} = f(s)$	
c	$\dfrac{c}{s}$	where c is a constant
t^n	$\dfrac{n!}{s^{n+1}}$	for $n = 0, 1, 2, 3, \ldots$
e^{-ct}	$\dfrac{1}{s+c}$	
$\sin \omega t$	$\dfrac{\omega}{s^2 + \omega^2}$	
$\cos \omega t$	$\dfrac{s}{s^2 + \omega^2}$	
$\sinh at$	$\dfrac{a}{s^2 - a^2}$	
$\cosh at$	$\dfrac{s}{s^2 - a^2}$	
$t^n e^{-ct}$	$\dfrac{n!}{(s+c)^{n+1}}$	for $n = 0, 1, 2, 3, \ldots$
$e^{-ct} \sin \omega t$	$\dfrac{\omega}{(s+c)^2 + \omega^2}$	
$e^{-ct} \cos \omega t$	$\dfrac{s+c}{(s+c)^2 + \omega^2}$	
$e^{-ct} \sinh at$	$\dfrac{a}{(s+c)^2 - a^2}$	
$e^{-ct} \cosh at$	$\dfrac{s+c}{(s+c)^2 - a^2}$	
y	$\bar{y}$	
$\dfrac{dy}{dt}$	$s\bar{y} - y_0$	where y_0 is the value of y at $t = 0$.
$\dfrac{d^2 y}{dt^2}$	$s^2 \bar{y} - s y_0 - y_1$	where y_1 is the value of $\dfrac{dy}{dt}$ at $t = 0$ and y_0 is the value of y at $t = 0$.
$\displaystyle\int_0^t y\, dt$	$\dfrac{\bar{y}}{s}$	

17 Laplace Transforms: 2

The objectives of this chapter are to:

1   Find the Laplace transforms of first and second derivatives.
2   Apply Laplace transforms to solve second order differential equations.
3   Apply Laplace transforms to solve simultaneous first order differential equations.

Introduction

In this chapter we apply Laplace transforms to 2 types of differential equations:

1   second order differential equations,
2   simultaneous first order differential equations.

Having already looked at some of the detail around the transforms here we concentrate upon solving the equations. As usual we learn to apply the methods to engineering problems. Again partial fractions and 'completing the square' are important techniques within the solution. Always refer to the table of transforms at the end of Chapter 16 as necessary.

■■■■■■ ASSIGNMENT ■■■■■■

Our Assignment is a continuation of the previous one, i.e. an electrical circuit. As before we look at voltages.

The voltage across a capacitor is $\dfrac{1}{C}\displaystyle\int_0^t i\, dt$.

The voltage across a resistor is Ri.

The voltage across an inductor is $L\dfrac{di}{dt}$.

We describe (model) the circuit with a differential equation to find the charge, q, where $i = \dfrac{dq}{dt}$.

Using q instead of i affects our formats for the voltages across the components. Again we have zero initial conditions.

The second look at the Assignment includes a resistor in parallel with the capacitor to provide a damping effect. This, as we shall see, creates a pair of simultaneous equations.

In both cases the emphases are upon the Laplace transform techniques solving the differential equations. It is in preference to the values for the components in the circuits.

First and second order derivatives

We use our definition from Chapter 16,

$$\mathcal{L}\{F(t)\} = \int_0^\infty e^{-st} F(t)\, dt.$$

The usual notation for the first derivative is $f'(t)$ so that

$$\mathcal{L}\{f'(t)\} = \int_0^\infty e^{-st} f'(t)\, dt.$$

We need to use integration by parts to solve this integral.

Let $\quad u = e^{-st} \qquad$ and $\qquad \dfrac{dv}{dt} = f'(t)$

$\therefore \quad \dfrac{du}{dt} = -se^{-st} \qquad$ and $\qquad v = f(t).$

Using our formula for integration by parts

$$\int u \frac{dv}{dx}\, dx = uv - \int v \frac{du}{dx}\, dx$$

we get $\quad \mathcal{L}\{f'(t)\} = \left[e^{-st} f(t) \right]_0^\infty - \int_0^\infty -se^{-st} f(t)\, dt$

$$= \left[e^{-st} f(t) \right]_0^\infty + s \int_0^\infty e^{-st} f(t)\, dt$$

$$= \operatorname*{Lim}_{n \to \infty} \left[e^{-st} f(t) \right]_0^n + s\mathcal{L}\{f(t)\}$$

$$= \operatorname*{Lim}_{n \to \infty} \left[\frac{1}{e^{sn}} f(n) - \frac{1}{e^0} f(0) \right] + s\mathcal{L}\{f(t)\} \qquad \boxed{e^0 = 1.}$$

As $n \to \infty$, $sn \to \infty$, $e^{sn} \to \infty$ and so $\dfrac{1}{e^{sn}} \to 0$.

In the term $\dfrac{1}{e^{sn}} f(n)$, $\dfrac{1}{e^{sn}}$ dominates the $f(n)$. Hence this term tends to 0.

Hence $\mathscr{L}\{f'(t)\} = 0 - f(0) + s\mathscr{L}\{f(t)\}$

i.e. $\mathscr{L}\{f'(t)\} = s\mathscr{L}\{f(t)\} - f(0)$.

Alternatively if $y = f(t)$ then $\dfrac{dy}{dt} = f'(t)$

and so $\mathscr{L}\left\{\dfrac{dy}{dt}\right\} = s\mathscr{L}\{y\} - y_0$

i.e. $\mathscr{L}\left\{\dfrac{dy}{dt}\right\} = s\bar{y} - y_0$ where $y_0 = f(0)$

i.e. y_0 is the value of the function at $t = 0$.

You have seen this transform towards the bottom of the table and used it extensively already.

Now we find the transform of the second derivative where we use this result.

The usual notation for the second derivative is $f''(t)$ so that, in our definition,

$$\mathscr{L}\{f''(t)\} = \int_0^\infty e^{-st} f''(t)\, dt.$$

We use integration by parts to solve this integral.

Let $u = e^{-st}$ and $\dfrac{dv}{dt} = f''(t)$

$\therefore$ $\dfrac{du}{dt} = -se^{-st}$ and $v = f'(t)$

Using our formula for integration by parts

$$\int u\frac{dv}{dx}\,dx = uv - \int v\frac{du}{dx}\,dx$$

we get $\mathscr{L}\{f''(t)\} = \left[e^{-st}f'(t)\right]_0^\infty - \int_0^\infty -se^{-st}f'(t)\, dt$

$$= \left[e^{-st}f'(t)\right]_0^\infty + s\int_0^\infty e^{-st}f'(t)\, dt$$

$$= \operatorname*{Lim}_{n\to\infty} \left[e^{-st}f'(t)\right]_0^n + s\mathscr{L}\{f'(t)\}$$

$$= \operatorname*{Lim}_{n\to\infty} \left[\frac{1}{e^{sn}}f'(n) - \frac{1}{e^0}f'(0)\right] + s\mathscr{L}\{f'(t)\} \qquad \boxed{e^0 = 1.}$$

As $n \to \infty$, $sn \to \infty$, $e^{sn} \to \infty$ and so $\dfrac{1}{e^{sn}} \to 0$.

In the term $\dfrac{1}{e^{sn}} f'(n)$, $\dfrac{1}{e^{sn}}$ dominates the $f'(n)$. Hence this term tends to 0.

Hence $\mathscr{L}\{f''(t)\} = 0 - f'(0) + s\mathscr{L}\{f'(t)\}$.

We substitute for the Laplace transform of $f'(t)$ to give

$$\mathscr{L}\{f''(t)\} = s(s\bar{y} - y_0) - f'(0).$$

Alternatively if $y = f(t)$ then $\dfrac{dy}{dt} = f'(t)$ and $\dfrac{d^2y}{dt^2} = f''(t)$

and so $\mathscr{L}\left\{\dfrac{d^2y}{dt^2}\right\} = s^2\bar{y} - sy_0 - y_1$

where $y_0 = f(0)$

i.e. y_0 is the value of the function at $t = 0$

and $y_1 = f'(0)$

i.e. y_1 is the value of the first derivative at $t = 0$

This transform is at the end of the table. We shall use it extensively in this chapter. If you wish to find higher derivatives you can use integration by parts in the same way.

Second order differential equations

There are many types of differential equations. In a second order differential equation the highest derivative is the second derivative. Here we look at this type of equation with initial boundary conditions. As we have done with first order differential equations we apply Laplace transforms separately to each term. After some algebraic techniques we apply inverse transforms to return from the s domain to our original, generally t, domain.

Example 17.1

We solve the second order differential equation

$$\frac{d^2y}{dt^2} + 3\frac{dy}{dt} + 2y = 6e^t + 6.$$

The initial boundary conditions are that $y = 6$ (i.e. $y_0 = 6$) and that $\dfrac{dy}{dt} = -3$ (i.e. $y_1 = -3$).

In
$$\frac{d^2y}{dt^2} + 3\frac{dy}{dt} + 2y = 6e^t + 6$$

we apply Laplace transforms to each term separately to get

$$s^2\bar{y} - sy_0 - y_1 + 3(s\bar{y} - y_0) + 2\bar{y} = \frac{6}{s-1} + \frac{6}{s}$$

$$s^2\bar{y} - 6s - -3 + 3s\bar{y} - 18 + 2\bar{y} = \frac{6}{s-1} + \frac{6}{s}$$

> Substituting for
> $$y_0 = 6$$
> and $y_1 = -3$.

$$s^2\bar{y} + 3s\bar{y} + 2\bar{y} = 6s + 15 + \frac{6}{s-1} + \frac{6}{s}$$

$$(s^2 + 3s + 2)\bar{y} = \frac{6s^2(s-1) + 15s(s-1) + 6s + 6(s-1)}{s(s-1)}$$

$$(s+1)(s+2)\bar{y} = \frac{6s^3 - 6s^2 + 15s^2 - 15s + 6s + 6s - 6}{s(s-1)}$$

to give
$$\bar{y} = \frac{6s^3 + 9s^2 - 3s - 6}{s(s-1)(s+1)(s+2)}.$$

For this first example we concentrate on the general technique. Hence we do not work through all the algebraic techniques. In fact we could show, by long division, that $(s + 1)$ divides into the numerator. This simplifies our expression for $\bar{y}$ to

$$\bar{y} = \frac{6s^2 + 3s - 6}{s(s-1)(s+2)}.$$

The next, omitted stage, gives the partial fractions

$$\bar{y} = \frac{3}{s} + \frac{1}{s-1} + \frac{2}{s+2}$$

to which we apply Laplace transforms to get

$$y = 3 + e^t + 2e^{-2t}.$$

Remember you can always check your answer. Using this expression for y and differentiation find $\frac{dy}{dt}$ and $\frac{d^2y}{dt^2}$. When you substitute into the original differential equation on the left-hand side the algebra should simplify to the right-hand side.

Now we have seen the basic idea we work through an example completely and look at the Assignment.

████ **Example 17.2** ████

We solve the second order differential equation $\dfrac{d^2y}{dt^2} + 4y = 2(5t - 2)e^{-t}$.

The initial boundary conditions are that $y = 0$ (i.e. $y_0 = 0$) and that $\dfrac{dy}{dt} = 4$ (i.e. $y_1 = 4$).

We expand the brackets on the right-hand side of our differential equation, i.e.

$$\frac{d^2y}{dt^2} + 4y = 10te^{-t} - 4e^{-t}.$$

Applying Laplace transforms to each term separately we get

$$s^2\bar{y} - sy_0 - y_1 + 4\bar{y} = \frac{10 \times 1!}{(s+1)^2} - \frac{4}{s+1}$$

i.e. $s^2\bar{y} - 0 - 4 + 4\bar{y} = \dfrac{10}{(s+1)^2} - \dfrac{4}{s+1}$ | Substituting for $y_0 = 0$ and $y_1 = 4$.

$$s^2\bar{y} + 4\bar{y} = 4 + \frac{10}{(s+1)^2} - \frac{4}{s+1}$$

$$(s^2+4)\bar{y} = \frac{4s^2 + 8s + 4 + 10 - 4s - 4}{(s+1)^2}$$

to give $\bar{y} = \dfrac{4s^2 + 4s + 10}{(s+1)^2(s^2+4)}.$

We split this compound fraction into partial fractions in the usual way.

$$\frac{4s^2 + 4s + 10}{(s+1)^2(s^2+4)} = \frac{A}{s+1} + \frac{B}{(s+1)^2} + \frac{Cs+D}{s^2+4}$$

$$\equiv \frac{A(s+1)(s^2+4) + B(s^2+4) + (Cs+D)(s+1)^2}{(s+1)^2(s^2+4)}$$

i.e. $4s^2 + 4s + 10 \equiv A(s+1)(s^2+4) + B(s^2+4) + (Cs+D)(s+1)^2.$

In turn we could choose values of s enabling us to find values for A, B, C and D. As an alternative we expand the brackets on the right-hand side and equate like terms. This idea is similar to equating real and imaginary parts for complex numbers. We equate like terms in s^3, s^2, s and constant terms:

s^3:	$0 = A \qquad\quad + C$	①
s^2:	$4 = A + B + 2C + D$	②
s:	$4 = 4A \qquad + C + 2D$	③
constants:	$10 = 4A + 4B \qquad + D$	④

We solve this set of 4 simultaneous equations. Multiply equation ② by 4, then subtract equation ④ from it, i.e.

$$16 = 4A + 4B + 8C + 4D$$

and

$$10 = 4A + 4B \qquad + D$$

give

$$6 = \qquad 8C + 3D. \qquad ⑤$$

Equation ① gives $A = -C$ which we use in equation ③ to write

$$4 = \qquad -3C + 2D. \qquad ⑥$$

Multiply equation ⑤ by 2 and equation ⑥ by 3, then subtract them, i.e.

$$12 = 16C + 6D$$

and

$$12 = -9C + 6D$$

give

$$0 = 25C, \qquad \text{i.e.} \quad C = 0.$$

From equation ① we see that $\qquad A = 0.$
Substituting into equation ⑤ we get $\quad D = 2.$
Substituting into equation ④ we get $\quad B = 2.$

Linking together our numerator values in the partial fractions we have

$$\bar{y} = \frac{2}{(s+1)^2} + \frac{2}{s^2+4}$$

i.e.

$$\bar{y} = 2\left(\frac{1}{(s+1)^2}\right) + \frac{2}{s^2+2^2}.$$

We apply Laplace transforms to get

$$y = 2te^{-t} + \sin 2t.$$

ASSIGNMENT

Let us look in detail at our electrical circuit. In Fig 17.1 we have a capacitor, C, a resistor, R, and an inductor, L, in series together with a constant e.m.f., E. Remember that current, i, is the rate of change of charge, q.

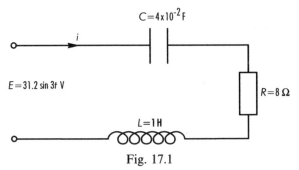

Fig. 17.1

The voltage across a capacitor is given by $\dfrac{1}{C}\displaystyle\int_0^t i\,dt = \dfrac{q}{C}$.

The voltage across a resistor is given by $Ri = R\dfrac{dq}{dt}$.

The voltage across an inductor is given by $L\dfrac{di}{dt} = L\dfrac{d^2q}{dt^2}$.

$C = 4 \times 10^{-2}$ F, $R = 8\ \Omega$, L = 1 H and E = 31.2 V. We describe (model) the circuit with a second order differential equation to find the charge, q. The initial conditions are zero. The sum of the voltages across the components is the e.m.f, i.e.

$$\frac{q}{C} + R\frac{dq}{dt} + L\frac{d^2q}{dt^2} = E.$$

Substituting for our circuit values we get

$$\frac{q}{4 \times 10^{-2}} + 8\frac{dq}{dt} + 1\frac{d^2q}{dt^2} = 31.2.$$

We apply Laplace transforms separately to each term (referring to the table of transforms),

$$25\bar{q} + 8(s\bar{q} - q_0) + (s^2\bar{q} - sq_0 - q_1) = \frac{31.2}{s}$$

i.e. $\qquad 25\bar{q} + 8s\bar{q} - 0 + s^2\bar{q} - 0 - 0 = \dfrac{31.2}{s}$ | Substituting for q_0, and q_1.

and then $\qquad\qquad\qquad 25\bar{q} + 8s\bar{q} + s^2\bar{q} = \dfrac{31.2}{s}$

i.e. $\qquad\qquad\qquad (s^2 + 8s + 25)\bar{q} = \dfrac{31.2}{s}$

so that $\qquad\qquad\qquad\qquad \bar{q} = \dfrac{31.2}{s(s^2 + 8s + 25)}.$

Notice how similar this expression for q is to the expression for i in Chapter 16. Remember the quadratic factor does not factorise further.

Again we will need to complete the square. As usual we use partial fractions in the form

$$\frac{31.2}{s(s^2 + 8s + 25)} = \frac{A}{s} + \frac{Bs + C}{s^2 + 8s + 25}.$$

For simplicity we omit the partial fractions and quote

$$\bar{q} = \frac{1.248}{s} + \frac{-1.248s - 9.984}{s^2 + 8s + 25}$$

$$= 1.248 \left(\frac{1}{s} + \frac{-s - 8}{(s+4)^2 + 3^2} \right) \qquad \boxed{\begin{array}{l} \text{Common factor of } 1.248, \\ \text{Completing the square.} \end{array}}$$

$$= 1.248 \left(\frac{1}{s} - \frac{(s+4)}{(s+4)^2 + 3^2} - \frac{4}{3} \times \frac{3}{(s+4)^2 + 3^2} \right)$$

We apply inverse Laplace transforms to get

$$q = 1.248 \left(1 - e^{-4t} \cos 3t - \frac{4}{3} e^{-4t} \sin 3t \right) \quad \text{for the charge.}$$

You can check this answer by substituting into the original second order differential equation. Alternatively you can check it by differentiation to see that it agrees with $i = 10.4e^{-4t} \sin 3t$, the expression for the current in the circuit.

■ EXERCISE 17.1 ■

Solve the following second order differential equations using the given boundary conditions.

1 $\dfrac{d^2y}{dt^2} + 2\dfrac{dy}{dt} - y = -10 \cos t - 2 \sin t$ given $y = 3$ and $\dfrac{dy}{dt} = -2$ at $t = 0$.

Hint: You will simplify the later algebra with a division by $(s^2 + 2s - 1)$

2 $\dfrac{d^2y}{dt^2} - \dfrac{dy}{dt} - 2y = 0$ given $y = 4$ and $\dfrac{dy}{dt} = -1$ initially.

3 $\dfrac{d^2y}{dt^2} + 4y = 12t - 5e^{-t}$ given $y_0 = 0$ and $y_1 = 4$

4 $2\dfrac{d^2y}{dt^2} + \dfrac{dy}{dt} - y = 2(2 - 3t)e^{-t}$ given $y = 1$ and $\dfrac{dy}{dt} = -1$ initially.

5 $2\dfrac{d^2y}{dt^2} + 3\dfrac{dy}{dt} + 2y = e^{-2t}(7 \cos t + 3 \sin t)$ given $y = 1$ and $\dfrac{dy}{dt} = -3$ initially.

EXERCISE 17.2

1 The circuit diagram shows a capacitor of 0.05 F, a resistor of 8 Ω and an inductor of 1 H in series with an e.m.f. of 125 V.

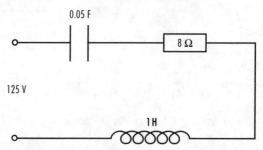

0.05 F

8 Ω

125 V

1 H

The second order differential equation models the charge, q, over time, t, $\dfrac{d^2q}{dt^2} + 8\dfrac{dq}{dt} + 20q = 125$. Find q in terms of t given zero initial conditions.

2 A mass, m (1 kg), is attached to a coiled spring. The force in a spring is proportional to its extension or compression, x, according to Hooke's law. In this case the proportionality constant is 25 Nm^{-1} so that the force is $25x$. The motion of the mass is damped by a force proportional to its velocity, $6\dfrac{dx}{dt}$. Using $F = m\dfrac{d^2x}{dt^2}$ to model this motion we create the differential equation

$$-25x - 6\frac{dx}{dt} = 1\frac{d^2x}{dt^2}.$$

You are given the initial boundary conditions that the extension is 0 m and the velocity is 6ms^{-1}. Solve this second order differential equation for x in terms of t.

3 The circuit diagram shows a capacitor of 0.025 F, a resistor of 40 Ω and an inductor of 10 H is series with an e.m.f. of 84.1 sin 5t V.

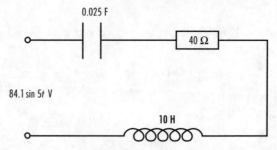

0.025 F

40 Ω

84.1 sin 5t V

10 H

The second order differential equation models the current, i over time, t,

$$10\frac{d^2i}{dt^2} + 40\frac{di}{dt} + 40i = 420.5\cos 5t.$$

Find i in terms of t given the initial conditions are zero.

4   Two capacitors (0.05 F and 0.2 F) each have a plate earthed. The two insulated plates are connected initially by a wire of resistance R (10 Ω) and inductance L (1 H). One capacitor has a charge q while the other capacitor is uncharged so that a current i flows in the wire. It is modelled by the second order differential equation

$$1\frac{d^2i}{dt^2} + 10\frac{di}{dt} + \left(\frac{1}{0.05} + \frac{1}{0.2}\right)i = 0.$$

Initially $i = 0$ and $\frac{di}{dt} = \alpha$, some general constant. Hence solve this differential equation.

5   The basis of this question has some similarities with Question **2**. A mass, m (2 kg), is attached to a coiled spring. The force in a spring is proportional to its extension or compression, x, according to Hooke's law. In this case the proportionality constant is 34 Nm^{-1} so that the force is $34x$. The motion of the mass is damped by a force proportional to its velocity, $4\frac{dx}{dt}$. Here we apply an external sinusoidal force, $13\sin 4t$. This causes forced vibrations. Using $F = m\frac{d^2x}{dt^2}$ to model this motion we create the differential equation

$$\frac{d^2x}{dt^2} + 2\frac{dx}{dt} + 17x = 6.5\sin 4t.$$

You are given the initial boundary conditions that the extension is 0 m and the velocity is 2 ms^{-1}. Solve this second order differential equation for x is terms of t.

Simultaneous first order differential equations

This technique can be rather long compared with many we have seen. However it is more a combination of earlier techniques rather than something particularly new and different. We have seen first order differential equations in a number of chapters, recently in terms of Laplace transforms. We have solved pairs of simultaneous equations in Volume 1, Chapters 9 and 14. To demonstrate we look at pairs of first order differential equations with x and y in terms of t. Here is an outline of the method.

- Apply Laplace transforms to both first order differential equations.
- Substitute for the initial boundary conditions.
- Gather together the unknowns in $\bar{x}$ and $\bar{y}$ in terms of the parameter, s.
- Eliminate $\bar{x}$ (or $\bar{y}$) to solve the pair of simultaneous equations for $\bar{y}$ (or $\bar{x}$) in terms of s.

- Apply inverse Laplace transforms to find y (or x) in terms of t.
- Use y or $\bar{y}$ (or x or $\bar{x}$) to find the other variable eventually in terms of t.

The last stage can be done in two ways. In the next set of Examples we complete a solution in stages, first finding y, and then finding x in different ways.

Example 17.3

We solve the pair of first order differential equations, for y only,

$$\frac{dx}{dt} - y = -2t \quad \text{and} \quad \frac{dy}{dt} + x + y = 3 + 2t - \sin t.$$

The initial boundary conditions are $x = 2$ and $y = 0$.

Applying Laplace transforms to each term in each equation we get

$$s\bar{x} - x_0 - \bar{y} = -\frac{2}{s^2}$$

and $s\bar{y} - y_0 + \bar{x} + \bar{y} = \dfrac{3}{s} + \dfrac{2}{s^2} - \dfrac{1}{s^2 + 1^2}$

i.e. $s\bar{x} - 2 - \bar{y} = -\dfrac{2}{s^2}$

Substituting for $x_0 = 2$
and $y_0 = 0$.

and $s\bar{y} - 0 + \bar{x} + \bar{y} = \dfrac{3}{s} + \dfrac{2}{s^2} - \dfrac{1}{s^2 + 1}$

gathering together the $\bar{x}$ and $\bar{y}$ terms so that

$$s\bar{x} - \bar{y} = 2 - \frac{2}{s^2}$$

and $\bar{x} + (s+1)\bar{y} = \dfrac{3}{s} + \dfrac{2}{s^2} - \dfrac{1}{s^2 + 1}.$

We can solve this pair of simultaneous equations by various methods. For example we can multiply the first equation by 1 and the second equation by s. This gives each equation a common term, $s\bar{x}$, which we eliminate by subtraction. A little algebraic manipulation reveals $\bar{y}$. Alternatively we can gather all the terms to the left and use determinants, i.e.

$$\frac{\bar{x}}{\begin{vmatrix} -1 & -2+\dfrac{2}{s^2} \\ s+1 & -\dfrac{3}{s} - \dfrac{2}{s^2} + \dfrac{1}{s^2+1} \end{vmatrix}} = \frac{-\bar{y}}{\begin{vmatrix} s & -2+\dfrac{2}{s^2} \\ 1 & -\dfrac{3}{s} - \dfrac{2}{s^2} + \dfrac{1}{s^2+1} \end{vmatrix}} = \frac{1}{\begin{vmatrix} s & -1 \\ 1 & s+1 \end{vmatrix}}$$

Of course you may wish to use an alternative method involving matrices.

Eventually $\bar{y} = \dfrac{s^4 + s^3 + 3s^2 + 2s + 2}{s^2(s^2 + 1)(s^2 + s + 1)}.$

We split this compound fraction into partial fractions, i.e.

$$\bar{y} = \frac{A}{s} + \frac{B}{s^2} + \frac{Cs + D}{s^2 + 1} + \frac{Es + F}{s^2 + s + 1}.$$

Using the usual partial fractions techniques we get $A = 0$, $B = 2$, $C = 0$, $D = -1$, $E = 0$ and $F = 0$. The many zeroes are because $s^2 + s + 1$ divides exactly into $s^4 + s^3 + 3s^2 + 2s + 2$. In fact

$$\bar{y} = \frac{s^4 + s^3 + 3s^2 + 2s + 2}{s^2(s^2 + 1)(s^2 + s + 1)}$$

simplifies to $\bar{y} = \dfrac{s^2 + 2}{s^2(s^2 + 1)}$

and then we use less complicated partial fractions.

By either method we get

$$\bar{y} = \frac{2}{s^2} - \frac{1}{s^2 + 1}.$$

We apply inverse Laplace transforms to get

$$y = 2t - \sin t.$$

Example 17.4

We solve the pair of first order differential equations, for x only,

$$\frac{dx}{dt} - y = -2t \quad \text{and} \quad \frac{dy}{dt} + x + y = 3 + 2t - \sin t.$$

The initial boundary conditions are $x = 2$ and $y = 0$.

We could start afresh with the same Laplace transform technique. However we can save ourselves time by using the first differential equation. Here we can easily substitute for y, i.e.

$$\frac{dx}{dt} - y = -2t$$

becomes $\dfrac{dx}{dt} - (2t - \sin t) = -2t$

i.e. $\dfrac{dx}{dt} = -\sin t.$

Integrating with respect to t we get

$$x = \cos t + c.$$

Substituting for $x = 2$ at $t = 0$,

$$2 = \cos 0 + c$$

i.e. $c = 1.$

Then our particular solution is

$$x = 1 + \cos t.$$

Example 17.5

We solve the pair of first order differential equations, for x only,

$$\frac{dx}{dt} - y = -2t \quad \text{and} \quad \frac{dy}{dt} + x + y = 3 + 2t - \sin t.$$

The initial boundary conditions are $x = 2$ and $y = 0$.
For this alternative method we use an expression for $\bar{y}$, i.e.

$$\bar{y} = \frac{s^4 + s^3 + 3s^2 + 2s + 2}{s^2(s^2 + 1)(s^2 + s + 1)},$$

substituting into $\quad s\bar{x} - \bar{y} = 2 - \dfrac{2}{s^2}$

or $\quad \bar{x} + (s + 1)\bar{y} = \dfrac{3}{s} + \dfrac{2}{s^2} - \dfrac{1}{s^2 + 1}.$

We choose the first of these equations because it is the simpler. Eventually, after some algebraic manipulation

$$\bar{x} = \frac{2s^4 + 2s^3 + 3s^2 + s + 1}{s^2(s^2 + 1)(s^2 + s + 1)}.$$

Further simplification gives $\quad \bar{x} = \dfrac{2s^2 + 1}{s^2(s^2 + 1)}$

and then $\quad \bar{x} = \dfrac{1}{s} + \dfrac{s}{s^2 + 1}.$

We apply inverse Laplace transforms to get

$$x = 1 + \cos t.$$

We can reach a complete solution by combining either Examples 17.3 and 17.4 or Examples 17.3 and 17.5.

ASSIGNMENT

We have looked, in this chapter and Chapter 16, at a capacitor, resistor and inductor in series with an e.m.f. In Fig. 17.2 we generalise this idea, suggesting a sinusoidal e.m.f., $e \sin \omega t$, where e and ω are constants.

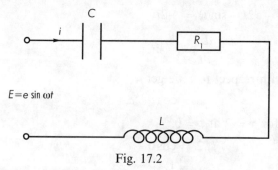

Fig. 17.2

Developing the circuit we include another resistor, R_2, in parallel with the capacitor, C (Fig. 17.3). For reference we label some important points W, X, Y and Z.

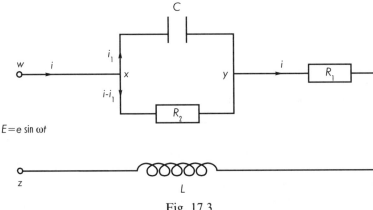

Fig. 17.3

At X the current splits into i_1 and $i - i_1$, recombining at Y. We look at the voltages across components in sections of the circuit.

In $WXCYZ$ we have the capacitor, C, resistor, R_1, and the inductor, L, in series with the e.m.f., $E = e \sin \omega t$. Our differential equation to model this is

$$\frac{1}{C}\int_0^t i_1 \, dt + R_1 i + L\frac{di}{dt} = e \sin \omega t. \qquad\text{①}$$

In $XCYR_2X$ we have only the capacitor, C, and the resistor, R_2, in series. Our differential equation to model this is

$$\frac{1}{C}\int_0^t i_1 \, dt - R_2(i - i_1) = 0. \qquad\text{②}$$

Notice XCY is the same direction as the current i_1. In YR_2X we oppose the current $i - i_1$, hence the negative sign.

In WXR_2YZ we have the resistors, R_1 and R_2, and the inductor, L, in series with the e.m.f., $E = e \sin \omega t$. Our differential equation to model this is

$$R_2(i - i_1) + R_1 i + L\frac{di}{dt} = e \sin \omega t. \qquad\text{③}$$

Notice the mixtures of unknown currents, i, i_1 and $i - i_1$ in all 3 equations. We could give specific values to e, ω, C, R_1, R_2 and L. Then equations ①, ② and ③ are simultaneous equations in i and i_1. In reality we have only 2 equations. Each equation is a combination of the other two.

We can apply Laplace transforms to them all, i.e.

$$\frac{\bar{i}}{Cs} + R_1\bar{i} + L(\bar{i} - i_0) = \frac{e\omega}{s^2 + \omega^2} \qquad\text{①a}$$

$$\frac{\bar{i_1}}{Cs} - R_2\bar{i} + R_2\bar{i_1} = 0 \qquad\text{②a}$$

$$R_2\bar{i} - R_2\bar{i_1} + R_1\bar{i} + L(\bar{i} - i_0) = \frac{e\omega}{s^2 + \omega^2} \qquad\text{③a}$$

Our solution continues, choosing the two simplest equations and solving simultaneously for $\bar{i}$ and $\bar{i}_1$. Then we apply the inverse Laplace transforms to find the currents i and i_1, and hence $i - i_1$.

We look at another use of simultaneous first order differential equations in Example 17.6.

▅▅▅▅ Example 17.6 ▅▅▅▅

Fig. 17.4 shows a primary circuit of self-inductance, L_1, and resistance, R_1, in series with a capacitor, C. The current is i_1. It is closely coupled to a secondary circuit of negligible resistance and self-inductance L_2. The current is i_2. M is the mutual inductance.

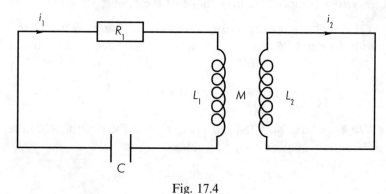

Fig. 17.4

We create our differential equations using the voltage drops across each component, i.e.

Primary $\quad L_1 \dfrac{di_1}{dt} + M \dfrac{di_2}{dt} + R_1 i_1 + \dfrac{1}{C} \displaystyle\int_0^t i_1 \, dt = 0$

Secondary $\quad\quad\quad\quad M \dfrac{di_1}{dt} + L_2 \dfrac{di_2}{dt} = 0.$

Again we can apply Laplace transforms and solve for i_1 and i_2.

▅▅▅▅ EXERCISE 17.3 ▅▅▅▅

Solve the following pairs of simultaneous first order differential equations.

1   For y only, solve the equations $\quad 2\dfrac{dx}{dt} + y = 6 - 3t$

and $\quad\quad\quad\quad\quad\quad\quad \dfrac{dy}{dt} + x + y = 3 - 2t$

using the boundary conditions that $x = 2$ and $y = 4$ at $t = 0$.

2   For x only, solve the equations $\quad 2\dfrac{dx}{dt} + y = 3e^{2t}$

    and $\qquad\qquad\qquad\qquad \dfrac{dy}{dt} + x - y = -3e^{-t}$

using the boundary conditions that $x = 2$ and $y = 1$ at $t = 0$.

3   Solve the equations $\quad \dfrac{dx}{dt} = 2(x + y)$

    and $\qquad\qquad\qquad \dfrac{dy}{dt} + x = 0$

using the initial boundary conditions that both x and y are 1.

4   Solve the equations $\quad \dfrac{dx}{dt} + y = 2 - te^{-t}$

    and $\qquad\qquad\qquad \dfrac{dy}{dt} + \dfrac{dx}{dt} + x = 2e^{-t}$

using the initial boundary conditions $x = 0$ and $y = 1$.

5   Solve the equations $\quad \dfrac{dy}{dt} + 2x = e^{-t}$

    and $\qquad\qquad\qquad \dfrac{dx}{dt} + 2y = e^{t}$

with zero initial boundary conditions.

18 Fourier Series

Introduction

We have looked at different types of series in Volume 2 and earlier in Volume 3, Chapter 10. Fourier developed his series to express a periodic function in terms of sines and/or cosines of different frequencies. Also we can use the reverse process. We can create a particular waveform by combining (adding and/or subtracting) those different sines and cosines. It involves integration, often integration by parts. Our early work concentrates upon series of period 2π for easy integration. Later we extend the techniques to any general period, 2ℓ.

We apply Fourier series techniques to periodic functions only. Non-periodic functions require Fourier transforms, beyond the scope of this volume.

ASSIGNMENT

We return to the Assignment ideas of Chapter 2 where we looked at functions. Here we look at 2 rectifications. In each case our input is a sine wave of period 2π and amplitude 1.

i) For the first part we have a half wave rectification. Fig. 18.1a shows the output where only the positive parts of the sine wave are retained. The input of the negative parts of the sine wave have zero outputs.

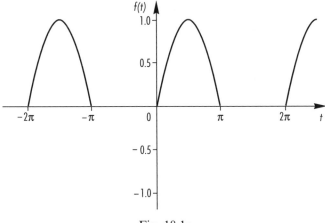

Fig. 18.1a

ii) For the second part we have a full wave rectification. Fig. 18.1b shows all the output as positive. The input of the negative parts of the sine wave are output as positive, i.e. those parts are reflections in the horizontal axis.

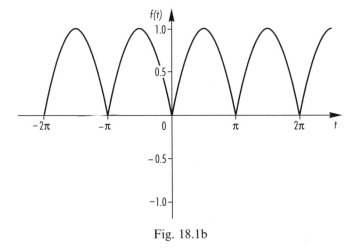

Fig. 18.1b

Functions

We looked in detail at many function types in Chapter 2. You need to remind yourself of the early parts of that chapter.

A periodic function is a function that repeats itself

████ Examples 18.1 ████

We look at a table of some simple trigonometric functions.

Function	Period
$\sin x$	2π
$\cos x$	2π
$\sin nx$	$\dfrac{2\pi}{n}$
$\cos nx$	$\dfrac{2\pi}{n}$

Later in the chapter you will find it useful to refer to the sketches of these functions in Figs. 18.2

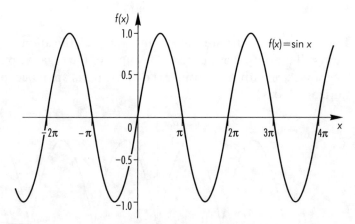

Fig. 18.2a

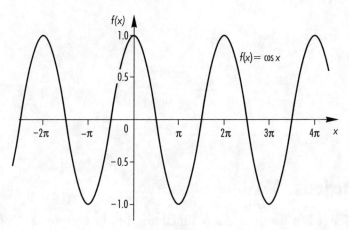

Fig 18.2b

For some function $f(x)$ **of period 2π** we write $f(x + 2\pi) = f(x)$. It means that at x and at the corresponding position 2π further along the horizontal axis (both towards the left and right) the function has the same value (on the vertical axis). Generally for $f(x)$ **of period ℓ** then $f(x + \ell) = f(x)$. In Fig. 18.3 we show this general periodicity.

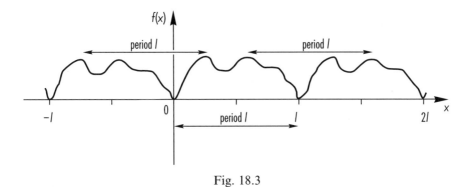

Fig. 18.3

f(x) is a single-valued function if one value of x corresponds to one value of f(x)

Example 18.2

In Fig. 18.4 we see $f(x) = \dfrac{x}{2}$ is a single-valued function. We show a specimen value of x leading to one value of $f(x)$.

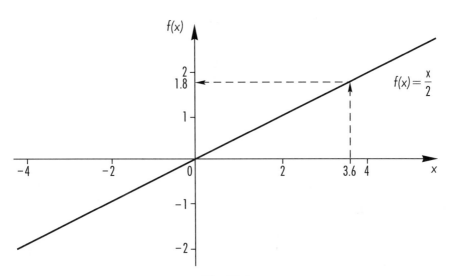

Fig. 18.4

If f(x) is a continuous function then its graph is unbroken.

■■■■ **Examples 18.3** ■■■■

i)   In Fig. 18.5 $f(x) = \sin 2x$ is a continuous function.

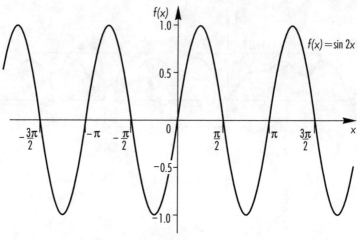

Fig. 18.5

ii)

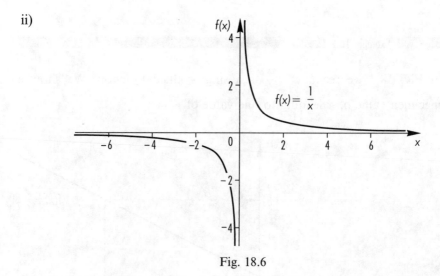

Fig. 18.6

In Fig. 18.6 we see $f(x) = \dfrac{1}{x}$ is *not* a continuous function because of the break at $x = 0$.

If $f(x)$ is a piecewise continuous function then its graph has some breaks. 'Piece' hints at the breaks. Then within each piece the function is continuous.

▓▓▓▓ **Examples 18.4** ▓▓▓▓▓▓▓▓▓▓▓▓▓▓▓▓▓▓▓▓▓▓▓▓▓▓▓▓▓

i) $f(x) = \tan x$ is piecewise continuous. You can sketch the graph as an exercise for yourself for confirmation. However this is *not* good enough in a Fourier series because the graph tends to infinity at the discontinuity.

ii)

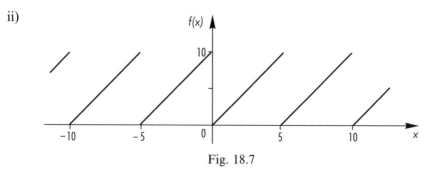

Fig. 18.7

Fig. 18.7 shows a piecewise continuous function. It is a sawtooth wave. We avoid drawing any connecting vertical lines, e.g. at $x = 5$. Such vertical lines are not single-valued functions. For reference only we may use dashed lines at the discontinuities.

We show some specimen waveforms together with their definitions. The definitions are often based upon the equation of a straight line, $y = mx + c$. You need to be able to
 i) sketch the graph from the given definition, and
ii) define the graph from the given sketch.

▓▓▓▓ **Examples 18.5** ▓▓▓▓▓▓▓▓▓▓▓▓▓▓▓▓▓▓▓▓▓▓▓▓▓▓▓▓▓

i)

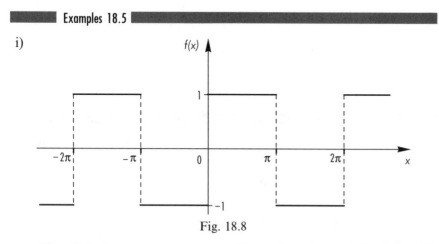

Fig. 18.8

Fig. 18.8 shows a square wave. We explain its period of 2π with $f(x + 2\pi) = f(x)$. The waveform is discontinuous so we use the inequality, $<$, i.e. excluding the end points of 0, π and 2π. We define each portion of the sketch separately, choosing sections close to the vertical axis for ease. In this case there are three parts to the definition; one for each part of the sketch and a third part for the period. Here are two alternatives.

Either $f(x) = -1$ for $-\pi < x < 0$

$f(x) = 1$ for $0 < x < \pi$

$f(x + 2\pi) = f(x)$.

or $f(x) = 1$ for $0 < x < \pi$

$f(x) = -1$ for $\pi < x < 2\pi$

$f(x + 2\pi) = f(x)$.

ii)

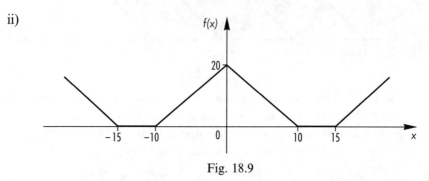

Fig. 18.9

The waveform in Fig. 18.9 is continuous in three parts. The continuity means we use $\leqslant$. Again we can find the equation for each part and the one describing the period of 25. Check for yourself the gradients for two parts are 2 and -2. Also their common vertical intercept is 20. We can define the function as

$f(x) = 2x + 20$ for $-10 \leqslant x \leqslant 0$

$f(x) = -2x + 20$ for $0 \leqslant x \leqslant 10$

$f(x) = 0$ for $10 \leqslant x \leqslant 15$

$f(x + 25) = f(x)$.

ASSIGNMENT

We need to look back at Figs. 18.1 and define the outputs for the half and full wave rectifications.

For the half wave rectification (Fig. 18.1a)

$f(t) = 0$ for $-\pi \leqslant t \leqslant 0$

$f(t) = \sin t$ for $0 \leqslant t \leqslant \pi$

$f(t + 2\pi) = f(t)$.

For the full wave rectification (Fig. 18.1b) the period is only π.

$f(t) = \sin t$ for $0 \leqslant t \leqslant \pi$

$f(t + \pi) = f(t)$.

■ EXERCISE 18.1 ■

In Questions **1–5** you are given the definitions of some periodic functions.
Sketch the graphs of each complete function on fully labelled axes.

1 $f(x) = 3x$ for $-\pi < x < \pi$
$f(x + 2\pi) = f(x)$.

2 $f(x) = -2$ for $0 < x < 5$
      $f(x) = 2$ for $5 < x < 10$
$f(x + 10) = f(x)$.

3 $f(x) = -4x$ for $-\pi \leqslant x \leqslant 0$
      $f(x) = 4x$ for $0 \leqslant x \leqslant \pi$
$f(x + 2\pi) = f(x)$.

4 $f(x) = -2x - 4$ for $-4 \leqslant x \leqslant -2$
      $f(x) = 0$ for $-2 \leqslant x \leqslant 2$
      $f(x) = 2x - 4$ for $2 \leqslant x \leqslant 4$
$f(x + 8) = f(x)$.

5 $f(\theta) = 0$ for $-\pi \leqslant \theta \leqslant -\dfrac{\pi}{2}$

      $f(\theta) = 2\cos\theta$ for $-\dfrac{\pi}{2} \leqslant \theta \leqslant \dfrac{\pi}{2}$

      $f(\theta) = 0$ for $\dfrac{\pi}{2} \leqslant \theta \leqslant \pi$

$f(\theta + 2\pi) = f(\theta)$.

In Questions **6–10** you are given the sketches of some periodic functions.
Write down the complete definitions.

6

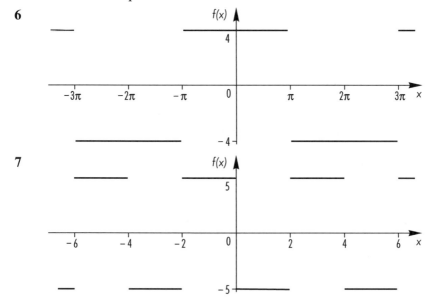

7

8

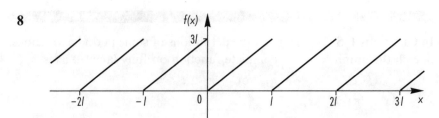

9

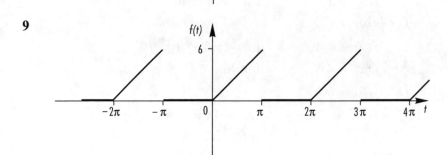

10

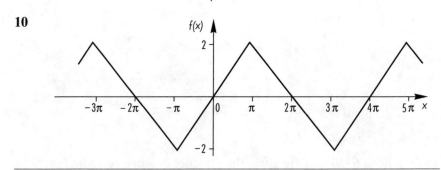

2 basic theorems

1   The order of summation, $\sum$, and integration, $\int$, does *not* matter, i.e.

$$\int \sum_{n=1}^{\infty} f(x)\, dx = \sum_{n=1}^{\infty} \int f(x)\, dx$$

2   The order of summation, $\sum$, and differentiation, $\dfrac{d}{dx}$, does *not* matter,

i.e. $\dfrac{d}{dx}\left\{ \sum_{n=1}^{\infty} f(x) \right\} = \sum_{n=1}^{\infty} \dfrac{d}{dx}\{f(x)\}$

Fourier series

$f(x)$, a single-valued function in the interval $-\pi \leqslant x \leqslant \pi$ that is piecewise continuous, may be expressed as a Fourier series of cosines and sines in the form

$$f(x) = \frac{1}{2}a_0 + \sum_{n=1}^{\infty} a_n \cos nx + \sum_{n=1}^{\infty} b_n \sin nx$$

$a_0, a_1, a_2, \ldots, a_n$ and $b_1, b_2, \ldots, b_n$ are the Fourier coefficients for us to find.

Alternatively in longhand notation this series is

$$f(x) = \frac{1}{2}a_0 + a_1 \cos x + a_2 \cos 2x + \ldots + b_1 \sin x + b_2 \sin 2x + \ldots$$

$a_1 \cos x + b_1 \sin x$ is the **first harmonic** or **fundamental**, $a_2 \cos 2x + b_2 \sin 2x$ is the **second harmonic**, $\ldots$

We have used $\leqslant$ in our definition. Alternatively we may use and apply $<$, as we shall see later. Also we have used $-\pi$ and π as the limits of our period. Alternatively we may use 0 and 2π, or any other multiples differing by 2π.

Our definition is a workable one. More details and rigour (Dirichlet conditions) are included in books solely about Fourier series.

The aim of the mathematics of Fourier series is to find the Fourier coefficients. This gives us the combination of cosines and/or sines we need to create the original waveform. To find them we integrate from $-\pi$ to π, i.e. over the interval of the periodic function. The integrals are chosen so that specific terms have a value of 0. In turn this gives us formulae for $\frac{1}{2}a_0$, a_n and b_n.

$$\frac{1}{2}a_0 = \frac{1}{2\pi} \int_{-\pi}^{\pi} f(x)\, dx \qquad \boxed{\text{mean value of } f(x).}$$

$$a_n = \frac{1}{\pi} \int_{-\pi}^{\pi} f(x) \cos nx\, dx \qquad \boxed{2 \times \text{mean value of } f(x) \cos nx.}$$

$$b_n = \frac{1}{\pi} \int_{-\pi}^{\pi} f(x) \sin nx\, dx \qquad \boxed{2 \times \text{mean value of } f(x) \sin nx.}$$

Example 18.6

In Fig. 18.10 we have a waveform defined by

$$f(x) = 0 \qquad \text{for } -\pi < x \leqslant 0$$
$$f(x) = 3x \qquad \text{for } 0 \leqslant x < \pi$$
$$f(x + 2\pi) = f(x).$$

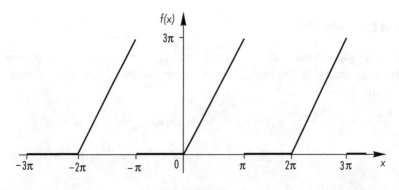

Fig. 18.10

Notice we use $\leqslant$ because there is a continuity in the middle of the complete function. At the extremes of the period we use $<$ because of the discontinuities. Our formulae for the Fourier coefficients show limits of $-\pi$ and π. We split the integrals. Each integral, its limits and the function within that part of the definition must be consistent.

Using
$$\frac{1}{2}a_0 = \frac{1}{2\pi}\int_{-\pi}^{\pi} f(x)\,dx$$

we have
$$\frac{1}{2}a_0 = \frac{1}{2\pi}\left\{\int_{-\pi}^{0} 0\,dx + \int_{0}^{\pi} 3x\,dx\right\}.$$

Where $f(x) = 0$ the mean value of 0 must itself be 0 between these limits.

Hence $\int_{-\pi}^{0} 0\,dx = 0$.

This simplification of the overall integration will occur in other cases.

$$\therefore \qquad \frac{1}{2}a_0 = \frac{1}{2\pi}\int_{0}^{\pi} 3x\,dx$$

$$= \frac{1}{2\pi}\left[\frac{3x^2}{2}\right]_{0}^{\pi}$$

$$= \frac{1}{2\pi}\left\{\frac{3}{2}(\pi^2) - \frac{3}{2}(0^2)\right\}$$

$$= \frac{1}{2\pi} \times \frac{3\pi^2}{2}$$

$$= \frac{3\pi}{4}.$$

Using
$$a_n = \frac{1}{\pi}\int_{-\pi}^{\pi} f(x)\cos nx\,dx$$

we have
$$a_n = \frac{1}{\pi}\left\{\int_{-\pi}^{0} 0\cos nx\,dx + \int_{0}^{\pi} 3x\cos nx\,dx\right\}.$$

Again our integration is simplified because $0 \cos nx = 0$ and $\displaystyle\int_{-\pi}^{0} 0 \, dx = 0$.

$$\therefore \qquad a_n = \frac{1}{\pi} \int_0^{\pi} 3x \cos nx \, dx.$$

Using integration by parts let $\quad u = 3x \quad$ and $\quad \dfrac{dv}{dx} = \cos nx$

$$\therefore \quad \frac{du}{dx} = 3 \quad \text{and} \quad v = \frac{1}{n} \sin nx.$$

$$\text{Now} \quad a_n = \frac{1}{\pi} \left\{ \left[\frac{3x}{n} \sin nx \right]_0^{\pi} - \int_0^{\pi} \frac{3}{n} \sin nx \, dx \right\} \qquad \boxed{\int u \frac{dv}{dx} \, dx = uv - \int v \frac{du}{dx} \, dx.}$$

$$= \frac{1}{\pi} \left\{ \left[\frac{3x}{n} \sin nx \right]_0^{\pi} + \left[\frac{3}{n^2} \cos nx \right]_0^{\pi} \right\}$$

$$= \frac{1}{\pi} \left\{ \frac{3\pi}{n} \sin n\pi - \frac{3(0)}{n} \sin 0 + \frac{3}{n^2} \cos n\pi - \frac{3}{n^2} \cos 0 \right\}.$$

Remember that n is an integer from the $\sum$ in the original formula. Also recall the details of the sine and cosine curves. $\sin 0 = 0$, $\cos 0 = 1$, $\sin n\pi = 0$ for integer multiples of π (i.e. $\sin 1\pi = 0$, $\sin 2\pi = 0$, ...). This simplifies a_n to

$$a_n = \frac{1}{\pi} \left\{ \frac{3}{n^2} \cos n\pi - \frac{3}{n^2} \right\}$$

$$= \frac{3}{n^2 \pi} \{ \cos n\pi - 1 \}.$$

We need to look more carefully at the cosine curve. When n is odd $\cos n\pi = -1$, (i.e. $\cos 1\pi$, $\cos 3\pi$, $\cos 5\pi$, ... all have values of -1). When n is even $\cos n\pi = 1$, (i.e. $\cos 2\pi$, $\cos 4\pi$, $\cos 6\pi$, ... all have values of 1).

For n odd, $\quad a_n = \dfrac{3}{n^2 \pi} \{ -1 - 1 \} = -\dfrac{6}{n^2 \pi}.$

For n even, $\quad a_n = \dfrac{3}{n^2 \pi} \{ 1 - 1 \} = 0.$

The method for finding b_n is similar to the method for finding a_n.

Using $\qquad b_n = \dfrac{1}{\pi} \displaystyle\int_{-\pi}^{\pi} f(x) \sin nx \, dx$

we have $\qquad b_n = \dfrac{1}{\pi} \left\{ \displaystyle\int_{-\pi}^{0} 0 \sin nx \, dx + \int_0^{\pi} 3x \sin nx \, dx \right\}.$

Again our integration is simplified because $0 \sin nx = 0$ and $\displaystyle\int_{-\pi}^{0} 0 \, dx = 0$.

$$\therefore \qquad b_n = \frac{1}{\pi} \int_0^{\pi} 3x \sin nx \, dx.$$

Using integration by parts let $\quad u = 3x \quad$ and $\quad \dfrac{dv}{dx} = \sin nx$

$$\therefore \quad \frac{du}{dx} = 3 \quad \text{and} \quad v = -\frac{1}{n}\cos nx.$$

$$\boxed{\int u\frac{dv}{dx}\,dx = uv - \int v\frac{du}{dx}\,dx.}$$

Now
$$b_n = \frac{1}{\pi}\left\{\left[(3x)\left(-\frac{1}{n}\cos nx\right)\right]_0^\pi - \int_0^\pi -\frac{3}{n}\cos nx\,dx\right\}$$

$$= \frac{1}{\pi}\left\{\left[-\frac{3x}{n}\cos nx\right]_0^\pi + \left[\frac{3}{n^2}\sin nx\right]_0^\pi\right\}$$

$$= \frac{1}{\pi}\left\{-\frac{3\pi}{n}\cos n\pi + \frac{3(0)}{n}\cos 0 + \frac{3}{n^2}\sin n\pi - \frac{3}{n^2}\sin 0\right\}.$$

Again remember that n is an integer from the $\sum$ in the original formula. Recall the details of the sine and cosine curves. $\sin 0 = 0$, $\cos 0 = 1$, $\sin n\pi = 0$ for integer multiples of π (i.e. $\sin 1\pi = 0$, $\sin 2\pi = 0$, ...). This simplifies b_n to

$$b_n = \frac{1}{\pi}\left\{-\frac{3\pi}{n}\cos n\pi\right\}$$

$$= -\frac{3}{n}\cos n\pi.$$

Again we need to look more carefully at the cosine curve. When n is odd $\cos n\pi = -1$, (i.e. $\cos 1\pi$, $\cos 3\pi$, $\cos 5\pi$, ... all have values of -1). When n is even $\cos n\pi = 1$, (i.e. $\cos 2\pi$, $\cos 4\pi$, $\cos 6\pi$, ... all have values of 1).

For n odd, $\quad b_n = -\dfrac{3}{n}(-1) = \dfrac{3}{n}.$

For n even, $\quad b_n = -\dfrac{3}{n}(1) = -\dfrac{3}{n}.$

We gather together our Fourier coefficient results;

$$\frac{1}{2}a_0 = \frac{3\pi}{4},$$

For n odd, $a_n = -\dfrac{6}{n^2\pi}$,

i.e. $\quad a_1 = -\dfrac{6}{1^2\pi} = -\dfrac{6}{\pi}, \; a_3 = -\dfrac{6}{3^2\pi} = -\dfrac{6}{9\pi},$

$$a_5 = -\frac{6}{5^2\pi} = -\frac{6}{25\pi}, \; \ldots$$

> Later we will remove a common factor of $-\dfrac{6}{\pi}$.

For n even $a_n = 0$,

i.e. $\quad a_2 = 0$, $a_4 = 0$, $a_6 = 0$, ...

For n odd, $b_n = \dfrac{3}{n}$,

i.e. $b_1 = \dfrac{3}{1}, b_3 = \dfrac{3}{3}, b_5 = \dfrac{3}{5}, \ldots$

> Later we will remove a common factor of 3.

For n even, $b_n = -\dfrac{3}{n}$,

i.e. $b_2 = -\dfrac{3}{2}, b_4 = -\dfrac{3}{4}, b_6 = -\dfrac{3}{6}, \ldots$

> Later we will remove a common factor of 3.

In $f(x) = \dfrac{1}{2}a_0 + \displaystyle\sum_{n=1}^{\infty} a_n \cos nx + \sum_{n=1}^{\infty} b_n \sin nx$

we substitute to get

$$f(x) = \frac{3\pi}{4} - \frac{6}{\pi}\left(\cos x + \frac{1}{9}\cos 3x + \ldots\right)$$
$$+ 3\left(\sin x - \frac{1}{2}\sin 2x + \frac{1}{3}\sin 3x - \frac{1}{4}\sin 4x \ldots\right).$$

Notice we show the patterns of the terms, rather than attempting to list too many of them. We show (Figs. 18.11) that the more terms we include the closer the series looks like the original function.

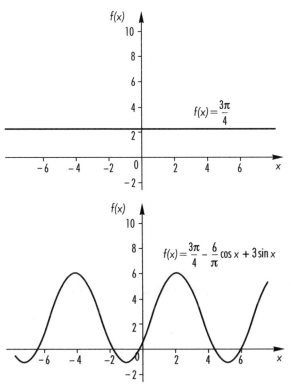

Figs. 18.11

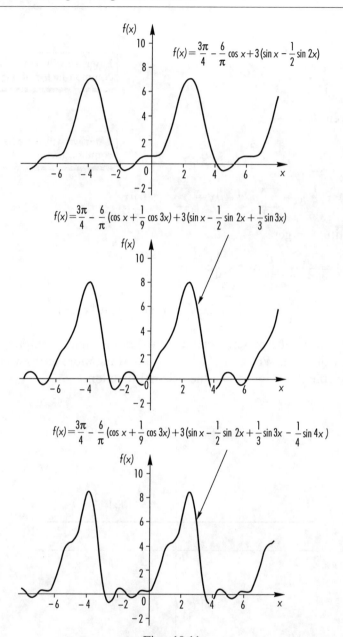

$$f(x) = \frac{3\pi}{4} - \frac{6}{\pi}\cos x + 3\left(\sin x - \frac{1}{2}\sin 2x\right)$$

$$f(x) = \frac{3\pi}{4} - \frac{6}{\pi}\left(\cos x + \frac{1}{9}\cos 3x\right) + 3\left(\sin x - \frac{1}{2}\sin 2x + \frac{1}{3}\sin 3x\right)$$

$$f(x) = \frac{3\pi}{4} - \frac{6}{\pi}\left(\cos x + \frac{1}{9}\cos 3x\right) + 3\left(\sin x - \frac{1}{2}\sin 2x + \frac{1}{3}\sin 3x - \frac{1}{4}\sin 4x\right)$$

Figs. 18.11

ASSIGNMENT

We have already worked out the definition for the half wave rectification output,

$$f(t) = 0 \quad \text{for } -\pi \leqslant t \leqslant 0$$
$$f(t) = \sin t \quad \text{for } 0 \leqslant t \leqslant \pi$$
$$f(t + 2\pi) = f(t).$$

Again we use the definitions for the Fourier coefficients, omitting some integration details. You can fill in those for yourself.

Using $\quad \dfrac{1}{2} a_0 = \dfrac{1}{2\pi} \displaystyle\int_{-\pi}^{\pi} f(t)\, dt$

we have $\quad \dfrac{1}{2} a_0 = \dfrac{1}{2\pi} \left\{ \displaystyle\int_{-\pi}^{0} 0\, dt + \displaystyle\int_{0}^{\pi} \sin t\, dt \right\}.$

$\therefore \qquad\qquad = \dfrac{1}{2\pi} \displaystyle\int_{0}^{\pi} \sin t\, dt$

$\qquad\qquad\quad = \dfrac{1}{\pi}.$

Using $\quad a_n = \dfrac{1}{\pi} \displaystyle\int_{-\pi}^{\pi} f(t) \cos nt\, dt$

we have $\quad a_n = \dfrac{1}{\pi} \left\{ \displaystyle\int_{-\pi}^{0} 0 \cos nt\, dt + \displaystyle\int_{0}^{\pi} \sin t . \cos nt\, dt \right\}.$

$\qquad\qquad = \dfrac{1}{\pi} \displaystyle\int_{0}^{\pi} \sin t . \cos nt\, dt.$

We use a trigonometric substitution from Volume 2, Chapter 4, $\sin x - \sin y = 2 \cos\left(\dfrac{x+y}{2}\right) \sin\left(\dfrac{x-y}{2}\right)$. Letting $\dfrac{x+y}{2} = nt$ and $\dfrac{x-y}{2} = t$ we solve this pair of simultaneous equations in x and y. Substituting into our integral we get

$$a_n = \dfrac{1}{2\pi} \int_{0}^{\pi} \left(\sin(n+1)t - \sin(n-1)t \right) dt.$$

We complete the integration and substitution to get

$$a_n = \dfrac{1}{2\pi} \left\{ -\dfrac{1}{(n+1)} \cos(n+1)\pi + \dfrac{1}{(n-1)} \cos(n-1)\pi \right.$$
$$\left. + \dfrac{1}{(n+1)} - \dfrac{1}{(n-1)} \right\}.$$

This needs care, valid only for $(n-1)$ being non-zero. We need to look at the separate case where $n = 1$.

When n is odd both $(n+1)$ and $(n-1)$ are even so that

$a_n = 0.$

> Check the substitutions for yourself.

When n is even both $(n+1)$ and $(n-1)$ are odd so that

$a_n = -\dfrac{2}{(n^2 - 1)\pi}.$

> Check the substitutions for yourself.

For $n = 1$, $a_1 = \dfrac{1}{\pi} \displaystyle\int_0^\pi \sin t . \cos t \, dt.$

> $\sin t . \cos nt = \sin t . \cos t$ for $n = 1$.

$$= \frac{1}{2\pi} \int_0^\pi \sin 2t \, dt$$

> $\sin 2t = 2 \sin t . \cos t.$

$$= \frac{1}{2\pi} \left[-\frac{1}{2} \cos 2t \right]_0^\pi$$

$$= -\frac{1}{4\pi} \left\{ \cos 2\pi - \cos 0 \right\}$$

$$= -\frac{1}{4\pi} \left\{ 1 - 1 \right\} = 0.$$

The method for finding b_n is similar to the method for finding a_n.

Using $b_n = \dfrac{1}{\pi} \displaystyle\int_{-\pi}^\pi f(t) \sin nt \, dt$

we have $b_n = \dfrac{1}{\pi} \left\{ \displaystyle\int_{-\pi}^0 0 \sin nt \, dt + \int_0^\pi \sin t . \sin nt \, dt \right\}.$

$\therefore$ $b_n = \dfrac{1}{\pi} \displaystyle\int_0^\pi \sin t . \sin nt \, dt.$

Again we use a trigonometric substitution from Volume 2, Chapter 4, $\cos x - \cos y = -2 \sin\left(\dfrac{x+y}{2}\right) \sin\left(\dfrac{x-y}{2}\right)$. Letting $\dfrac{x+y}{2} = nt$ and $\dfrac{x-y}{2} = t$ we solve this pair of simultaneous equations in x and y. Substituting into our integral we get

$$b_n = \frac{1}{2\pi} \int_0^\pi (\cos(n-1)t - \cos(n+1)t) \, dt.$$

We complete the integration and substitution to get

$$b_n = \frac{1}{2\pi} \left\{ \frac{1}{(n-1)} \sin(n-1)\pi - \frac{1}{(n+1)} \sin(n+1)\pi + 0 - 0 \right\}.$$

Again this needs care, valid only for $(n-1)$ being non-zero. We need to look at the separate case where $n = 1$.

When n is odd both $(n+1)$ and $(n-1)$ are even so that
$$b_n = 0.$$

> Check the substitutions for yourself.

When n is even both $(n+1)$ and $(n-1)$ are odd so that
$$b_n = 0.$$

> Check the substitutions for yourself.

For $n = 1$, $\quad b_1 = \dfrac{1}{\pi} \displaystyle\int_0^\pi \sin^2 t \, dt$

> $\sin t . \sin nt = \sin t . \sin t = \sin^2 t$
> for $n = 1$.
>
> $\sin^2 t = \frac{1}{2}(1 - \cos 2t)$.

$$= \dfrac{1}{2\pi} \int_0^\pi (1 - \cos 2t) \, dt$$

$$= \dfrac{1}{2\pi} \left[t - \dfrac{1}{2} \sin 2t \right]_0^\pi$$

$$= \dfrac{1}{2\pi} \left\{ \pi - \dfrac{1}{2} \sin 2\pi - 0 + \dfrac{1}{2} \sin 0 \right\}$$

$$= \dfrac{1}{2}.$$

In $\quad f(x) = \dfrac{1}{2} a_0 + \displaystyle\sum_{n=1}^\infty a_n \cos nx + \sum_{n=1}^\infty b_n \sin nx$

we substitute to get

$$f(t) = \dfrac{1}{\pi} + \dfrac{1}{2} \sin t - \dfrac{2}{\pi} \left(\dfrac{1}{3} \cos 2t + \dfrac{1}{15} \cos 4t \dots \right).$$

> Again check the substitutions for yourself.

After the next Exercise we reduce the work if the function is odd or even.

■ EXERCISE 18.2 ■

For Questions **1–5** find the Fourier series. For additional practice also sketch the functions.

1 $\qquad f(x) = 2 \qquad$ for $0 < x < \pi$
$\qquad f(x) = 0 \qquad$ for $\pi < x < 2\pi$
$\quad f(x + 2\pi) = f(x)$.

2 $\qquad f(x) = 2(x + \pi) \quad$ for $-\pi \leqslant x < 0$
$\qquad f(x) = 0 \qquad$ for $0 < x \leqslant \pi$
$\quad f(x + 2\pi) = f(x)$.

3 $\qquad f(x) = -2 \qquad$ for $-\pi < x < 0$
$\qquad f(x) = 4 \qquad$ for $0 < x < \pi$
$\quad f(x + 2\pi) = f(x)$.

4 $\qquad f(x) = x + \pi \qquad$ for $-\pi < x < \pi$
$\quad f(x + 2\pi) = f(x)$.

5 $\qquad f(x) = x + \pi \qquad$ for $-\pi < x \leqslant 0$
$\qquad f(x) = \pi \qquad$ for $0 < x \leqslant \pi$
$\quad f(x + 2\pi) = f(x)$.

Fourier series for odd functions

Remember for an odd function $f(-x) = -f(x)$ (p. 49). The definition for $f(x)$ remains as before, i.e.

$$f(x) = \frac{1}{2}a_0 + \sum_{n=1}^{\infty} a_n \cos nx + \sum_{n=1}^{\infty} b_n \sin nx$$

Remember the aim of the mathematics of Fourier series is to find the Fourier coefficients. For an odd function they are simplified to

$$\frac{1}{2}a_0 = 0, \qquad a_n = 0,$$

$$b_n = \frac{2}{\pi} \int_0^{\pi} f(x) \sin nx \, dx.$$

We could use the original integrals for the Fourier coefficients, but notice the reduced effort here. Hence it is vital to sketch the graph of the function before attempting any integration. Once we know the function is odd we can quote and apply the amended integrals. Notice the change for b_n, i.e. twice the integral but over only half of the period (in this case from 0 to π rather than from $-\pi$ to π).

Example 18.7

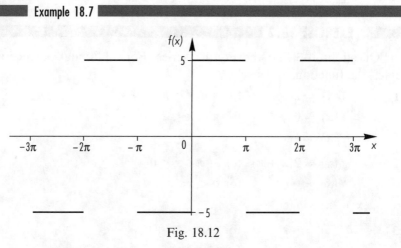

Fig. 18.12

In Fig. 18.12 we have a waveform defined by

$$f(x) = -5 \qquad \text{for } -\pi < x < 0$$
$$f(x) = 5 \qquad \text{for } 0 < x < \pi$$
$$f(x + 2\pi) = f(x).$$

Notice the following definition is equally valid

$$f(x) = 5 \qquad \text{for } 0 < x < \pi$$
$$f(x) = -5 \qquad \text{for } \pi < x < 2\pi$$
$$f(x + 2\pi) = f(x).$$

You can test for yourself that this is an odd function. Hence we can quote
$$\frac{1}{2}a_0 = 0, \ a_n = 0 \text{ and } b_n = \frac{2}{\pi}\int_0^\pi f(x)\sin nx\,dx.$$

We must be consistent with our integral, limits and function. From 0 to π we have $f(x) = 5$ so that

$$b_n = \frac{2}{\pi}\int_0^\pi 5\sin nx\,dx$$

$$= \frac{2}{\pi}\left[-\frac{5}{n}\cos nx\right]_0^\pi$$

$$= \frac{2}{\pi}\left\{-\frac{5}{n}\cos n\pi - -\frac{5}{n}\cos 0\right\}$$

$$= \frac{10}{n\pi}\{1 - \cos n\pi\}.$$

For n odd, $\quad b_n = \frac{10}{n\pi}\{1 - -1\} = \frac{20}{n\pi}.$

> Removing a common factor of $\frac{5}{n}$, and $\cos 0 = 1$.

For n even, $\quad b_n = \frac{10}{n\pi}\{1 - 1\} = 0.$

We gather together our Fourier coefficient results, though many of them are 0, and substitute into

$$f(x) = \frac{1}{2}a_0 + \sum_{n=1}^{\infty} a_n\cos nx + \sum_{n=1}^{\infty} b_n\sin nx$$

to get $\quad f(x) = \dfrac{20}{\pi}\left(\sin x + \dfrac{1}{3}\sin 3x + \dfrac{1}{5}\sin 5x\ldots\right).$

■■■■ **EXERCISE 18.3** ■■■■

For Questions **1–5** find the Fourier series. For additional practice also sketch the functions.

1
$$f(x) = -2.5 \qquad \text{for } -\pi < x < 0$$
$$f(x) = 2.5 \qquad \text{for } 0 < x < \pi$$
$$f(x + 2\pi) = f(x).$$

2
$$f(x) = 4x \qquad \text{for } -\pi < x < \pi$$
$$f(x + 2\pi) = f(x).$$

3
$$f(x) = -\frac{2}{\pi}x \qquad \text{for } -\pi < x < \pi$$
$$f(x + 2\pi) = f(x).$$

4 $f(x) = 7.5$ for $-\pi < x < 0$

       $f(x) = -7.5$ for $0 < x < \pi$

   $f(x + 2\pi) = f(x).$

5 $f(x) = -(x + \pi)$ for $-\pi \leqslant x < 0$

       $f(x) = -x + \pi$ for $0 < x \leqslant \pi$

   $f(x + 2\pi) = f(x).$

Fourier series for even functions

Remember for an even function $f(-x) = f(x)$ (p. 48). The definition for $f(x)$ remains as before, i.e.

$$f(x) = \frac{1}{2}a_0 + \sum_{n=1}^{\infty} a_n \cos nx + \sum_{n=1}^{\infty} b_n \sin nx$$

For an even function the Fourier coefficients are simplified to

$$\frac{1}{2}a_0 = \frac{2}{2\pi}\int_0^{\pi} f(x)\,dx = \frac{1}{\pi}\int_0^{\pi} f(x)\,dx,$$

$$a_n = \frac{2}{\pi}\int_0^{\pi} f(x)\cos nx\,dx,$$

$$b_n = 0.$$

We could use the original integrals for the Fourier coefficients, but notice the reduced effort here. Again it is vital to sketch the graph of the function before attempting any integration. Once we know the function is even we can quote and apply the amended integrals. Notice the change for $\frac{1}{2}a_0$ and a_n, i.e. twice the integral but over only half of the period (in this case from 0 to π rather than from $-\pi$ to π).

Example 18.8

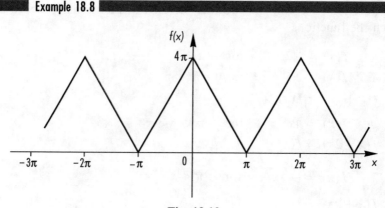

Fig. 18.13

In Fig. 18.13 we have a waveform defined by

$$f(x) = 4x + 4\pi \qquad \text{for } -\pi \leqslant x \leqslant 0$$
$$f(x) = -4x + 4\pi \qquad \text{for } 0 \leqslant x \leqslant \pi$$
$$f(x + 2\pi) = f(x).$$

You can test for yourself that this is an even function.

Using $\quad \dfrac{1}{2}a_0 = \dfrac{1}{\pi}\displaystyle\int_0^{\pi} f(x)\, dx$

we have $\quad \dfrac{1}{2}a_0 = \dfrac{1}{\pi}\displaystyle\int_0^{\pi} (-4x + 4\pi)\, dx$

$$= \frac{1}{\pi}\left[-\frac{4}{2}x^2 + 4\pi x \right]_0^{\pi}$$

$$= \frac{1}{\pi}\left[-2\pi^2 + 4\pi^2 - -0 - 0 \right]$$

$$= 2\pi.$$

Using $\quad a_n = \dfrac{2}{\pi}\displaystyle\int_0^{\pi} f(x)\cos nx\, dx$

we have $\quad a_n = \dfrac{2}{\pi}\displaystyle\int_0^{\pi} (-4x + 4\pi)\cos nx\, dx.$

Using integration by parts let $\quad u = -4x + 4\pi \quad$ and $\quad \dfrac{dv}{dx} = \cos nx$

$$\therefore \quad \frac{du}{dx} = -4 \qquad \text{and} \qquad v = \frac{1}{n}\sin nx$$

$$\boxed{\int u\frac{dv}{dx}\, dx = uv - \int v\frac{du}{dx}\, dx.}$$

Now $\quad a_n = \dfrac{2}{\pi}\left\{ \left[(-4x + 4\pi)\dfrac{1}{n}\sin nx \right]_0^{\pi} - \displaystyle\int_0^{\pi} -\dfrac{4}{n}\sin nx\, dx \right\}$

$$= \frac{2}{\pi}\left\{ \left[(-4x + 4\pi)\frac{1}{n}\sin nx \right]_0^{\pi} - \left[\frac{4}{n^2}\cos nx \right]_0^{\pi} \right\}$$

$$= \frac{2}{\pi}\left\{ (-4\pi + 4\pi)\frac{1}{n}\sin n\pi - (0 + 4\pi)\frac{1}{n}\sin 0 \right.$$

$$\left. - \frac{4}{n^2}\cos n\pi + \frac{4}{n^2}\cos 0 \right\}.$$

Remember that n is an integer from the $\sum$ in the original formula. Also recall the details of the sine and cosine curves. $\sin 0 = 0$, $\cos 0 = 1$, $\sin n\pi = 0$ for integer multiples of π (i.e. $\sin 1\pi = 0$, $\sin 2\pi = 0$, ...). This simplifies a_n to

$$a_n = \frac{2}{\pi}\left\{\frac{-4}{n^2}[\cos n\pi - \cos 0]\right\}$$

$$= \frac{8}{n^2\pi}[1 - \cos n\pi].$$

For n odd, $\quad a_n = \frac{8}{n^2\pi}[1 - -1] = \frac{16}{n^2\pi}.$

For n even, $\quad a_n = \frac{8}{n^2\pi}[1 - 1] = 0.$

Remember for an even function $b_n = 0$.

We gather together our Fourier coefficient results, though many of them are 0, and substitute into

$$f(x) = \frac{1}{2}a_0 + \sum_{n=1}^{\infty} a_n \cos nx + \sum_{n=1}^{\infty} b_n \sin nx$$

to get $\quad f(x) = 2\pi + \frac{16}{\pi}\left(\cos x + \frac{1}{9}\cos 3x + \frac{1}{25}\cos 5x \dots\right).$

Removing a common factor of $\frac{16}{\pi}$.

ASSIGNMENT

We have already worked out the definition for the full wave rectification output. Looking back to Figs. 18.1b) we see the function is even. However the period is only π, i.e.

$$f(t) = \sin t \qquad \text{for } 0 \leqslant t \leqslant \pi$$
$$f(t + \pi) = f(t).$$

We could apply our theory so far, but perhaps that is *not* the most efficient method. When we have amended the theory from a period of 2π to a more general period we will look again.

EXERCISE 18.4

For Questions 1–5 find the Fourier series. For additional practice also sketch the functions.

1 $\qquad f(x) = -2x \qquad$ for $-\pi \leqslant x \leqslant 0$
$\qquad f(x) = 2x \qquad$ for $0 \leqslant x \leqslant \pi$
$\qquad f(x + 2\pi) = f(x).$

2 $\qquad f(x) = \frac{3}{\pi}x + 3 \qquad$ for $-\pi \leqslant x \leqslant 0$
$\qquad f(x) = -\frac{3}{\pi}x + 3 \qquad$ for $0 \leqslant x \leqslant \pi$
$\qquad f(x + 2\pi) = f(x).$

3     $f(x) = -x + \pi$ for $-\pi \leqslant x \leqslant 0$

      $f(x) = x + \pi$ for $0 \leqslant x \leqslant \pi$

      $f(x + 2\pi) = f(x)$.

4     $f(x) = \dfrac{2}{\pi}x$ for $-\pi \leqslant x \leqslant 0$

      $f(x) = -\dfrac{2}{\pi}x$ for $0 \leqslant x \leqslant \pi$

      $f(x + 2\pi) = f(x)$.

5     $f(x) = 1$ for $-\pi \leqslant x < -\dfrac{\pi}{2}$

      $f(x) = 0$ for $-\dfrac{\pi}{2} < x < \dfrac{\pi}{2}$

      $f(x) = 1$ for $\dfrac{\pi}{2} < x \leqslant \pi$

      $f(x + 2\pi) = f(x)$.

Hint: You may need to look at alternate odd and alternate even values of n.

We have looked at Fourier series for odd and even functions. For the **odd functions** we have only **sine terms** (sometimes called a **sine series** in this context) and for the **even functions cosine terms** (sometimes called a **cosine series** in this context). The next section looks at examples where we are given the function over only half of the range.

Half-range series

In each case we are given the function over only half of the range and invited to extend it. We can extend it as an odd function (half-range sine series) or as an even function (half-range cosine series). The simplified Fourier coefficients continue to apply in each case.

████████ Examples 18.9 ████████

In Fig. 18.14 we have a function defined by

$f(x) = 0$ for $0 < x < \dfrac{\pi}{2}$

$f(x) = 3$ for $\dfrac{\pi}{2} < x < \pi$

$f(x + 2\pi) = f(x)$.

Notice the last part of the definition shows a period of 2π but the earlier parts of the definition cover only half of that range.

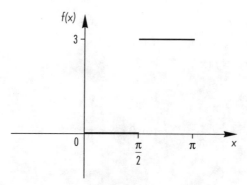

Fig. 18.14

We are going to extend the function as a   i) half-range sine series,
and a   ii) half-range cosine series.

i)   For the half-range sine series we know we have an odd function
(Fig. 18.15) so we quote $\frac{1}{2} a_0 = 0$, $a_n = 0$ and $b_n = \frac{2}{\pi} \int_0^\pi f(x) \sin nx \, dx$.

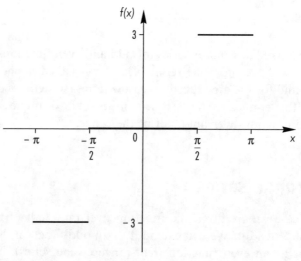

Fig. 18.15

i.e. $b_n = \frac{2}{\pi} \left\{ \int_0^{\pi/2} 0 \sin nx \, dx + \int_{\pi/2}^{\pi} 3 \sin nx \, dx \right\}$

$= \frac{2}{\pi} \left[-\frac{3}{n} \cos nx \right]_{\pi/2}^{\pi}$

Remember the first
integral of 0 has a
value of 0.

$= \frac{2}{\pi} \left\{ -\frac{3}{n} \cos n\pi - -\frac{3}{n} \cos \frac{n\pi}{2} \right\}$

$= \frac{-6}{n\pi} \left\{ \cos n\pi - \cos \frac{n\pi}{2} \right\}.$

Removing a common
factor of $\frac{3}{n}$.

Because of the $\dfrac{n}{2}$ we need to look at alternate even values of n.

For n odd,
$$b_n = \frac{-6}{n\pi}\{-1-0\}$$

$$\cos\frac{\pi}{2} = 0, \quad \cos\frac{3\pi}{2} = 0,$$
$$\cos\frac{5\pi}{2} = 0, \quad \ldots$$

$$= \frac{6}{n\pi}.$$

For $n = 2, 6, 10, 14, \ldots$
$$b_n = \frac{-6}{n\pi}\{1--1\} = \frac{-12}{n\pi}.$$

For $n = 4, 8, 12, \ldots$
$$b_n = \frac{-6}{n\pi}\{1-1\} = 0.$$

Gathering together our Fourier coefficient results we remove a common factor and substitute into

$$f(x) = \frac{1}{2}a_0 + \sum_{n=1}^{\infty} a_n \cos nx + \sum_{n=1}^{\infty} b_n \sin nx$$

to get
$$f(x) = \frac{6}{\pi}\left(\sin x - \sin 2x + \frac{1}{3}\sin 3x + \frac{1}{5}\sin 5x \ldots\right).$$

ii) For the half-range cosine series we know we have an even function (Fig. 18.16).

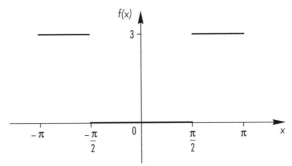

Fig. 18.16

Using
$$\frac{1}{2}a_0 = \frac{1}{\pi}\int_0^{\pi} f(x)\,dx$$

we have
$$\frac{1}{2}a_0 = \frac{1}{\pi}\left\{\int_0^{\pi/2} 0\,dx + \int_{\pi/2}^{\pi} 3\,dx\right\}$$

$$= \frac{1}{\pi}\int_{\pi/2}^{\pi} 3\,dx$$

$$= \frac{1}{\pi}\left[3x\right]_{\pi/2}^{\pi}$$

$$= \frac{1}{\pi}\left\{3\pi - \frac{3\pi}{2}\right\}$$

$$= \frac{3}{2}.$$

Also　$a_n = \dfrac{2}{\pi} \displaystyle\int_0^\pi f(x) \cos nx \, dx$

i.e.　$a_n = \dfrac{2}{\pi} \left\{ \displaystyle\int_0^{\pi/2} 0 \cos nx \, dx + \int_{\pi/2}^{\pi} 3 \cos nx \, dx \right\}$

> Remember the first integral of 0 has a value of 0.

$$= \dfrac{2}{\pi} \left[\dfrac{3}{n} \sin nx \right]_{\pi/2}^{\pi}$$

$$= \dfrac{2}{\pi} \left\{ \dfrac{3}{n} \sin n\pi - \dfrac{3}{n} \sin \dfrac{n\pi}{2} \right\}$$

$$= \dfrac{6}{n\pi} \left\{ \sin n\pi - \sin \dfrac{n\pi}{2} \right\}.$$

> Removing a common factor of $\dfrac{3}{n}$.

For all integer multiples of π we know $\sin n\pi = 0$ so that

$$a_n = \dfrac{-6}{n\pi} \sin \dfrac{n\pi}{2}.$$

For $n = 1, 5, 9, 13, \ldots$　$a_n = \dfrac{-6}{n\pi}(1) = \dfrac{-6}{n\pi}.$

For $n = 3, 7, 11, \ldots$　$a_n = \dfrac{-6}{n\pi}(-1) = \dfrac{6}{n\pi}.$

For even n there is cancellation with the 2 in the denominator so the sine is an integer multiple of π and $a_n = 0$.

Gathering together our Fourier coefficient results we remove a common factor and substitute into

$$f(x) = \dfrac{1}{2}a_0 + \sum_{n=1}^{\infty} a_n \cos nx + \sum_{n=1}^{\infty} b_n \sin nx$$

to get　$f(x) = \dfrac{3}{2} - \dfrac{6}{\pi} \left(\cos x - \dfrac{1}{3}\cos 3x + \dfrac{1}{5}\cos 5x \ldots \right).$

■■■ EXERCISE 18.5 ■■■

For Questions **1–5** find the half-range Fourier series. For additional practice also sketch the functions.

1　Extend the function and express it as a sine series.

$$f(x) = -4 \qquad \text{for } 0 < x < \pi$$
$$f(x + 2\pi) = f(x).$$

2　Extend the function and express it as a cosine series.

$$f(x) = x \qquad \text{for } 0 \leqslant x \leqslant \pi$$
$$f(x + 2\pi) = f(x).$$

3 Extend the function and express it as a cosine series.
$$f(x) = \frac{2}{\pi}x \qquad \text{for } -\pi \leqslant x \leqslant 0$$
$$f(x+2\pi) = f(x).$$

4 Extend the function and express it as a sine series.
$$f(x) = 2x + \pi \qquad \text{for } 0 < x < \pi$$
$$f(x+2\pi) = f(x).$$

5 Extend the function and express it as i) a cosine series,
ii) a sine series.
$$f(x) = -\frac{x}{2} \qquad \text{for } -\pi < x < 0$$
$$f(x+2\pi) = f(x).$$

Fourier series for a general period

All the techniques we have learned for the 2π period continue to apply. Only minor alterations to the trigonometric parts are necessary for this general period of 2ℓ, nx is replaced by $\dfrac{n\pi x}{\ell}$. The definition for $f(x)$ is based on a period of 2ℓ from $-\ell$ to ℓ;

$$f(x) = \frac{1}{2}a_0 + \sum_{n=1}^{\infty} a_n \cos\frac{n\pi x}{\ell} + \sum_{n=1}^{\infty} b_n \sin\frac{n\pi x}{\ell} \qquad \text{where}$$

$$\frac{1}{2}a_0 = \frac{1}{2\ell}\int_{-\ell}^{\ell} f(x)\, dx \qquad \boxed{\text{mean value of } f(x).}$$

$$a_n = \frac{1}{\ell}\int_{-\ell}^{\ell} f(x)\cos\frac{n\pi x}{\ell}\, dx \qquad \boxed{2 \times \text{mean value of } f(x)\cos\frac{n\pi x}{\ell}.}$$

$$b_n = \frac{1}{\ell}\int_{-\ell}^{\ell} f(x)\sin\frac{n\pi x}{\ell}\, dx \qquad \boxed{2 \times \text{mean value of } f(x)\sin\frac{n\pi x}{\ell}.}$$

We find the Fourier coefficients for an odd function with period 2ℓ and then take a final look at the Assignment.

Example 18.10

In Fig. 18.17 we have an odd waveform defined by
$$f(x) = 2 \qquad \text{for } -5 < x < 0$$
$$f(x) = -2 \qquad \text{for } 0 < x < 5$$
$$f(x+10) = f(x).$$
The period is 10, i.e. $2\ell = 10$ and so $\ell = 5$.

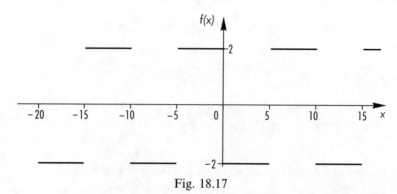

Fig. 18.17

You can test for yourself that this is an odd function. Hence we can quote $\frac{1}{2}a_0 = 0$, $a_n = 0$ and $b_n = \frac{2}{\ell}\int_0^\ell f(x)\sin\frac{n\pi x}{\ell}\,dx$. We must be consistent with our integral, limits and function. From 0 to ℓ we have $f(x) = -2$ so that

$$b_n = \frac{2}{5}\int_0^5 -2\sin\frac{n\pi x}{5}\,dx$$

$$= \frac{2}{5}\left[\frac{10}{n\pi}\cos\frac{n\pi x}{5}\right]$$

> Removing a common factor of $\dfrac{10}{n\pi}$ and simplifying
> $\dfrac{2}{5}\times\dfrac{10}{n\pi}$.

$$= \frac{4}{n\pi}\left\{\cos\frac{n\pi 5}{5} - \cos 0\right\}$$

$$= \frac{4}{n\pi}\{\cos n\pi - 1\}.$$

For n odd, $b_n = \frac{4}{n\pi}\{-1-1\} = -\frac{8}{n\pi}$.

For n even, $b_n = \frac{4}{n\pi}\{1-1\} = 0$.

We gather together our Fourier coefficient results, though many of them are 0, and substitute into

$$f(x) = \frac{1}{2}a_0 + \sum_{n=1}^\infty a_n\cos\frac{n\pi x}{\ell} + \sum_{n=1}^\infty b_n\sin\frac{n\pi x}{\ell}$$

to get $f(x) = -\frac{8}{\pi}\left(\sin\frac{\pi x}{5} + \frac{1}{3}\sin\frac{3\pi x}{5} + \frac{1}{5}\sin \pi x + \frac{1}{7}\sin\frac{7\pi x}{5}\cdots\right).$

◼ ASSIGNMENT ◼

We redraw the output for the full wave rectification (Fig. 18.18) and recall the definition

$$f(t) = \sin t \qquad \text{for } 0 \leqslant t \leqslant \pi$$
$$f(t+\pi) = f(t).$$

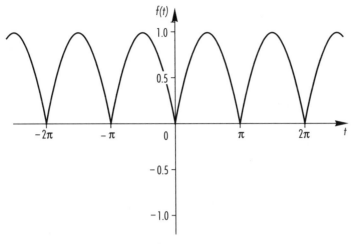

Fig. 18.18

This is an even function. Our definition is for $0 \leqslant t \leqslant \pi$, but equally valid is

$$f(t) = -\sin t \qquad \text{for } -\frac{\pi}{2} \leqslant t \leqslant 0$$

$$f(t) = \sin t \qquad \text{for } 0 \leqslant t \leqslant \frac{\pi}{2}$$

$$f(t + \pi) = f(t).$$

The period is π, i.e. $2\ell = \pi$ and so $\ell = \frac{\pi}{2}$.

Using $\qquad \frac{1}{2}a_0 = \frac{1}{\ell} \int_0^\ell f(t)\, dt$

we have $\qquad \frac{1}{2}a_0 = \frac{1}{\dfrac{\pi}{2}} \int_0^{\pi/2} \sin t\, dt$

$$= \frac{2}{\pi} \left[-\cos t \right]_0^{\pi/2}$$

$$= \frac{2}{\pi} \left\{ -\cos\frac{\pi}{2} - -\cos 0 \right\}$$

$$= \frac{2}{\pi}.$$

Using $\qquad a_n = \frac{2}{\ell} \int_0^\ell f(t) \cos\frac{n\pi t}{\ell}\, dt$

we have $\qquad a_n = \frac{2}{\dfrac{\pi}{2}} \int_0^{\pi/2} \sin t \cos 2nt\, dt.$

$$\frac{n\pi t}{\dfrac{\pi}{2}} = n\pi t \times \frac{2}{\pi} = 2nt.$$

We use a trigonometric substitution from Volume 2, Chapter 4,

$\sin x - \sin y = 2\cos\left(\dfrac{x+y}{2}\right)\sin\left(\dfrac{x-y}{2}\right)$. Letting $\dfrac{x+y}{2} = 2nt$ and $\dfrac{x-y}{2} = t$

we solve this pair of simultaneous equations in x and y. Substituting into our integral we get

$$a_n = \frac{4}{2\pi}\int_0^{\pi/2}(\sin(2n+1)t - \sin(2n-1)t)\,dt.$$

We complete the integration and substitution to get

$$a_n = \frac{2}{\pi}\left\{-\frac{1}{(2n+1)}\cos(2n+1)\frac{\pi}{2} + \frac{1}{(2n-1)}\cos(2n-1)\frac{\pi}{2}\right.$$
$$\left. + \frac{1}{(2n+1)} - \frac{1}{(2n-1)}\right\}.$$

When n is odd both $(2n+1)$ and $(2n-1)$ are odd so that

$$a_n = -\frac{4}{(4n^2-1)\pi}.$$

> Check the substitutions for yourself.

When n is even both $(2n+1)$ and $(2n-1)$ are odd so that

$$a_n = -\frac{4}{(4n^2-1)\pi}.$$

> Check the substitutions for yourself.

Remember for an even function $b_n = 0$.

We gather together our Fourier coefficient results, though many of them are 0, and substitute into

$$f(t) = \frac{1}{2}a_0 + \sum_{n=1}^{\infty} a_n \cos 2nt + \sum_{n=1}^{\infty} b_n \sin 2nt$$

to get $f(t) = \frac{2}{\pi} - \frac{4}{\pi}\left(\frac{1}{3}\cos 2t + \frac{1}{15}\cos 4t + \frac{1}{35}\cos 6t\ldots\right).$

> Removing a common factor of $\dfrac{-4}{\pi}$.

Here is a selection of questions in the last Exercise for Fourier series over a general period. They cover functions that are neither odd nor even, odd, even and half-range.

■■■■■ EXERCISE 18.6 ■■■■■

For Questions 1–5 find the Fourier series. For additional practice also sketch the functions.

1    $f(x) = 0$ for $-4 < x < 0$
     $f(x) = 1$ for $0 < x < 4$
   $f(x+8) = f(x).$

2 $f(x) = \pi$ for $-2 < x < 0$

$f(x) = -\pi$ for $0 < x < 2$

$f(x+4) = f(x)$.

3 $f(x) = 2x$ for $-1 < x < 1$

$f(x+2) = f(x)$.

4 $f(x) = -3x + 1$ for $-1 \leqslant x \leqslant 0$

$f(x) = 3x + 1$ for $0 \leqslant x \leqslant 1$

$f(x+2) = f(x)$.

5   Extend the half-range function and express it as i) a cosine series,

ii) a sine series.

$f(x) = 1 - x$ for $0 < x < 2$

$f(x+4) = f(x)$.

19 Discrete Probability Distributions

The objectives of this chapter are to:

1   Define probability in the range 0 to 1 and calculate simple probabilities.
2   Distinguish between dependent and independent events.
3   State and use the multiplication law for the probability of independent events.
4   State and use the addition law for probability.
5   Calculate successive probabilities.
6   Analyse a scenario, applying the binomial distribution if appropriate.
7   Relate the binomial distribution to $(p + q)^n$ and apply it.
8   State the mean is np and the standard deviation is $\sqrt{npq}$.
9   Relate binomial distribution examples to a histogram.
10 Analyse a scenario, applying the Poisson distribution if appropriate.
11 Calculate probabilities for a Poisson distribution.
12 State the mean is λ and the standard deviation is $\sqrt{\lambda}$.
13 Relate Poisson distribution examples to a histogram.

Introduction

This is the first of 2 chapters of statistics. The chapter has 3 main sections:
1   an introduction to the basic ideas of probability,
2   the binomial distribution,
and
3   the Poisson distribution.

Before looking at the binomial distribution section you may need to re-read Volume 2, Chapter 5. This chapter looks at discrete probability functions as opposed to continuous probability distributions (Chapter 20). In mathematics and statistics 'discrete' means countable, e.g. the number of printed circuit boards, the number of personnel.

▄▄▄ ASSIGNMENT ▄▄▄▄▄▄▄▄▄▄▄▄▄▄▄▄▄▄▄▄▄

Our Assignment looks at quality control on a building site, developing some tests to decide whether to accept or reject deliveries of bricks. We examine simple probability and then discuss alternative techniques.

Simple probability

Here we are looking at random events that may or may not occur. The result of an event is the outcome. In a quality control sample an item may or may not be faulty so dictating whether it fails or passes the control test. The opposite of this is that it may or may not be good. Notice the item passes or fails; i.e. the outcome is either pass or fail. There is no in-between, i.e 'maybe', category.

If the outcome of an event is A (e.g. a faulty item occurring in a quality control test) then $P(A)$ is the probability of the event occurring (e.g. the likelihood of there being a faulty item). We can split probability into

1   experimental probability,
and
2   theoretical probability.

▄▄▄ Examples 19.1 ▄▄▄▄▄▄▄▄▄▄▄▄▄▄▄▄▄▄▄▄

i)   By frequent, repeated, sampling in a quality control department we build up experimental information (data). It gives us some indication of the likelihood of future items passing or failing.

ii) An unbiased die has six sides numbered 1, 2, 3, 4, 5, and 6. Theoretically we can predict you will throw '4' once in every six times. This is because '4' appears once and there are six sides of the die. You can test this experimentally over many thousands of throws of the die before you get a result approaching the accuracy of $\frac{1}{6}$.

Usually we quote probability as a fraction or a decimal in the range 0 to 1 inclusive, i.e. $0 \leqslant P(A) \leqslant 1$. Alternatively we may use percentages so that $0 \leqslant P(A) \leqslant 100$. An event that is impossible has a probability of 0, i.e. $P(A) = 0$. An event that is certain has a probability of 1, i.e. $P(A) = 1$.

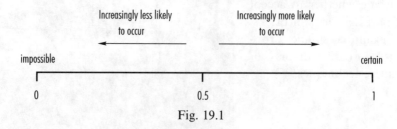

Fig. 19.1

Fig. 19.1 shows the probability scale.

We define the probability of an event, A, occurring to be

$$P(A) = \frac{n(A)}{n(S)}$$

where $n(A)$ is the number of ways that A can occur and $n(S)$ is the total number of ways that **possible** events can occur. S is the sampling space. If a day's quality control test selects from the day's production of 5000 components then this is the sampling space, i.e. $n(S) = 5000$.

The probability of an item, A, passing the quality control test can be the probability of success. Then the probability of failure is the probability of non-success. There can be *no* other options, i.e. it is certain that there is either success or non-success, i.e.

$$P(\text{success}) + P(\text{non-success}) = 1$$
$$\text{or} \quad p + q = 1$$
$$\text{i.e.} \quad q = 1 - p$$

> Notice the upper and lower case letters.

or
$$P(\text{non-success}) = 1 - P(\text{success}).$$

In Fig. 19.2 our diagram represents this as rectangle for S and a circle for an event A. The non-event is the difference between them, labelled A'.

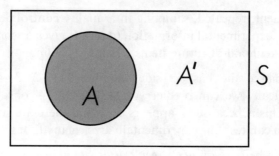

Fig. 19.2

━━━━━ **Example 19.2** ━━━━━

Suppose we have built up our experimental data and found that 1 in every 750 $\left(\text{i.e. } \dfrac{1}{750}\right)$ components fails the quality control test before the batch moves further along the production line,

i.e. $\qquad P(\text{failure}) \text{ or } P(\text{non-success}) = \dfrac{1}{750}$

and so using $\qquad\qquad P(\text{success}) = 1 - P(\text{non-success})$

$$= 1 - \frac{1}{750}$$

$$= \frac{749}{750}.$$

Most introductory work in probability looks at a coin, a die and a pack of 52 playing cards. All of them are unbiased. Though these are neither engineering nor science oriented they are ideal examples to show the early ideas.

━━━━━ **Examples 19.3** ━━━━━

i) A coin has 2 sides, i.e. $n(S) = 2$, one of which is heads (1 outcome) and the other tails (1 outcome). When tossing a coin

$$P(\text{head}) = \frac{1}{2} = 0.5 \text{ and } P(\text{tail}) = \frac{1}{2} = 0.5.$$

ii) A die has six sides labelled 1, 2, 3, 4, 5 and 6. As we indicated earlier, the probability of throwing a '4' is given by

$$P(\text{'4'}) = \frac{1}{6}.$$

Also $\qquad P(\text{odd number}) = \dfrac{3}{6} = \dfrac{1}{2}$

and $\quad P(\text{number } less \text{ than } 3) = \dfrac{2}{6} = \dfrac{1}{3}.$

> 1, 3 and 5 are the odd numbers, i.e. three possible outcomes.
>
> Only 1 and 2 are *less* than 3.

iii) There are 52 playing cards in a pack and we define the court cards to be the jacks, queens and kings. The probability of drawing the ten of hearts is given by

$$P(\text{ten of hearts}) = \frac{1}{52}.$$

Also $\qquad\qquad P(\text{ten}) = \dfrac{4}{52} = \dfrac{1}{13}$

> There are 4 tens; 1 in each suit.

and $\qquad\qquad P(\text{heart}) = \dfrac{13}{52} = \dfrac{1}{4}$

> Hearts is 1 of 4 suits.

and $\qquad P(\text{court card}) = \dfrac{12}{52} = \dfrac{3}{13}.$

> 4 jacks, 4 queens and 4 kings to give 12 cards altogether.

We distinguish between replacement and non-replacement in probability. Suppose we ask a person to pick a card from a pack of playing cards. The person chooses and then returns the card to the pack. A second person choosing from the pack has the same total of 52 cards to choose from. This is an example of replacement. Alternatively suppose the first person retains the card. When the second person chooses there are only 51 cards available. This is an example of non-replacement.

Let us return to the day's production run of 5000 components. In Example 19.2 we suggested, for the first quality control test, a failure rate of 1 in 750, i.e. in the long term of 750 components we expect 1 to fail. Or we may suggest that on average 1 fails in every 750. This is our expectation of the overall outcome. From the batch of 5000 we have an expectation of the number of failures, i.e

Expectation = sample size × probability

which we shorten to

$$E = np.$$

In the case of the components $n = 5000$ and $p = \dfrac{1}{750}$ so that

$$E = 5000 \times \frac{1}{750} = 6.\bar{6},$$

i.e. we expect that nearly 7 components will fail. This is an estimate for the average (mean) number of failures; *not* an accurate figure. On some days the result will be better and on some days it will be worse. Overall, in the long term when we average our results, it should approach this calculated figure of $6.\bar{6}$ failures each day.

■ ASSIGNMENT ■

Our building site has regular and frequent deliveries of facing bricks and other materials. The site manager can cope with some, but not too many, substandard bricks. He samples deliveries because he cannot check absolutely every item. A load is acceptable if no more than 5% of the bricks are substandard. Of couse he can apply similar conditions to all material types. From 1 sample the probability of rejecting a delivery is

$$P(\text{rejection}) = 5\% \text{ or } \frac{5}{100} \text{ or } \frac{1}{20} \text{ or } 0.05\%.$$

$$P(\text{acceptance}) = P(\text{non-rejection})$$

$$= 1 - 0.05$$

$$= 0.95 \text{ or } \frac{19}{20} \text{ or } \frac{95}{100} \text{ or } 95\%.$$

The bricks are delivered in 8000s, i.e. the site manager is sampling from $n = 8000$. Hence his expectation, E, of the number of substandard bricks is given by

$$E = np$$

i.e. $$E = 8000 \times 0.05 = 400.$$

■ EXERCISE 19.1 ■

1 97% of the day's aluminimum extrusions are perfect. Write down the probability of selecting a faulty one from stock.

2 A components tray contains only nuts and bolts. The probability of picking a nut is $\frac{7}{15}$. Write down the probability of picking a bolt.

3 8% of materials are wasted in the production process. What is the probability of the material being used. From a batch of 1500 l what volume can you expect to use?

4 Your company operates a monthly prize draw for personnel with 100% attendance and punctuality during that month. Each month 4 cash prizes are drawn. You are one of 80% of the 150 personnel entered in this month's draw. What is your probability of winning a prize? What is the probability of winning a prize for the other 20% of the personnel?

5 In your team are 2 apprentices, 7 technicians, 1 secretary, a manager and an assistant manager. All of you have an equal chance of promotion to your next grade. What is the probability of the scretary being promoted? What is the probability of any one of the technicians being promoted.

Dependent and independent events

We need to distinguish between these 2 types of events. It is likely that the reader and the author work in totally different places and have no influence upon each other's working lives. Events in each workplace should be independent of each other. In contrast the events for you in your workplace will be influenced by your colleagues. Events for you and events for a colleague are dependent events. In this chapter we tend to concentrate upon independent events. Textbooks devoted solely to statistics discuss both types of events in detail.

The multiplication law for probability

This law is applied to independent events. 'and' features in the wording of situations where we apply the multiplication law. If A and B are 2 independent events we understand the meaning of $P(A)$ and $P(B)$. The probability of both A and B occurring is given by

$P(A \text{ and } B) = P(A) \times P(B)$.

We represent this as the intersection of the 2 circles in Fig. 19.3.

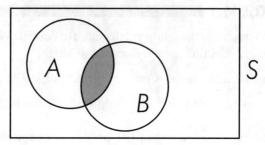

Fig. 19.3

▀▀▀ Example 19.4 ▀▀▀

The night shift lasts for 12 hours. The canteen serves hot drinks during an early short break and a late short break. Also it serves free hot and cold meals to all shift workers half-way through the night. The canteen manager notes the following data. Some workers prefer to bring their own alternative drinks for the short breaks. The percentage of workers having a first hot drink is 55% and the percentage of them having a second hot drink is 70%. 65% eat a hot meal, 33% eat a cold meal and 2% do not eat. In notational form, converted to decimals,

$$P(\text{first hot drink}) = 0.55.$$

$$P(\text{second hot drink}) = 0.70.$$

$\therefore$ $P(\text{not first hot drink}) = 1 - 0.55 = 0.45 = P(\text{cold first drink})$

and $P(\text{not second hot drink}) = 1 - 0.70 = 0.30 = P(\text{cold second drink})$.

$$P(\text{hot meal}) = 0.65$$

$\therefore$ $P(\text{not hot meal}) = 1 - 0.65 = 0.35.$ Includes cold meals and not eating.

$$P(\text{cold meal}) = 0.33.$$

$$P(\text{not eating}) = 0.02.$$

We can combine these pieces of information.

$$P(2 \text{ hot drinks}) = P(\text{first hot drink}) \text{ and } P(\text{second hot drink})$$
$$= 0.55 \times 0.70$$
$$= 0.385.$$

Notice we are multiplying figures that are individually less than 1. This dictates that our answer will be smaller than each of the original values.

$P(2$ hot drinks and a hot meal)

$\qquad = P(\text{first hot drink})$ and $P(\text{second hot drink})$ and $P(\text{hot meal})$

$\qquad = 0.55 \times 0.70 \times 0.65$

$\qquad = 0.25 \ldots$

> Actually 0.25025.

Obviously there are many more different combinations. We look at one more example.

$P(2$ cold drinks and a hot meal)

$\qquad = P(\text{first cold drink})$ and $P(\text{second cold drink})$ and $P(\text{hot meal})$

$\qquad = 0.45 \times 0.30 \times 0.65$

$\qquad = 0.08775.$

ASSIGNMENT

We return to the site manager's decisions to accept or reject brick deliveries. For the next phase of building he has been told to reduce the number of substandard bricks. 5% of each load is still substandard. He needs to reduce the probability of accepting them and so samples each delivery twice. A load is accepted only if both samples (i.e. Sample 1 **and** Sample 2) pass the test.

$P(\text{acceptance}) = P(\text{Sample 1 acceptance}) \times P(\text{Sample 2 acceptance})$

$\qquad = 0.95 \times 0.95$

$\qquad = 0.9025,$

i.e. 90.25% of the deliveries will be accepted rather than 95% as before.

EXERCISE 19.2

1   In your section are 2 lathes, A and B. The probability of lathe A breaking down today is 0.02 and of lathe B breaking down is 0.035. What is the probability of
    i)   Both lathes breaking down?
    ii) Lathe B breaking down while lathe A continues to work?
    iii) Both lathes working all day?

2   You are working an early shift in February. The probability of icy roads is $\frac{1}{8}$. The probability of you being late is $\frac{1}{45}$. The probability of you having a minor road accident is $\frac{1}{1800}$. On this particular morning what is the probability of arriving
    i)   Late because of a road accident due to icy roads?
    ii) Late because of a road accident?
    iii) On time though the roads are indeed icy?

3   In the maintenance department of the local hospital are 3 teams of technicians and apprentices. They are multi-skilled to deal with most routine and emergency maintenance. The probabilities of achieving this month's efficiency targets are for team A 90%, for team B 80% and for team C 85%. Work out the probabilities of meeting their targets for

   i) any 2 of the 3 teams,

   ii) all 3 teams,

   iii) none of them.

4   In a depleted spares tray are 9 nuts and 5 bolts. What is the probability of picking and retaining a nut? Then what is the probability of picking a bolt? What is the probability, without replacement, of picking a nut and then a bolt? What is the probability, without replacement, of picking a bolt and then a nut?

5   You are having difficulty sourcing a component. Your 3 usual suppliers could improve their service to your company. Supplier X has a 75% chance of delivering before the end of the week. For supplier Y this is 60% and for supplier C it is 50%. You need 2 of them to deliver to enable production to continue next week. What is the probability of this happening for each possible combination? If all 3 of them deliver you will need to rent expensive short term storage. The probability of being able to do so is 80%. What is the probability of needing and getting that extra storage?

The addition law for probability

'or' features in the application of the addition law. We are not concerned if both events occur. The aim is that one or other of them occurs. As we see in Fig. 19.4 if they both occur then our theory covers this option. The probability of an event A occurring is $P(A)$ and of an event B occurring is $P(B)$. The probability of either A or B occurring is given by

$$P(A \text{ or } B) = P(A) + P(B).$$

Really we saw this idea simply applied when we looked at the probabilities of success or failure in the formula $p + q = 1$.

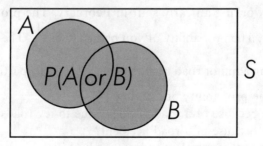

Fig. 19.4

━━━━ **Example 19.5** ━━━━━━━━━━━━━━━━━━━━━━━━━━━━━━━━━

We return to the canteen data of Example 19.4. The probability of a shift worker eating in the canteen covers the possibilities of hot or cold meals, i.e.

$$P(\text{eating a canteen meal}) = P(\text{hot meal or cold meal})$$
$$= P(\text{hot meal}) + P(\text{cold meal})$$
$$= 0.65 + 0.33$$
$$= 0.98.$$

Notice the answer is greater than the original probabilities, though never exceeding 1.

━━━━ **Example 19.6** ━━━━━━━━━━━━━━━━━━━━━━━━━━━━━━━━━

A small engineering company manufacturing types of meters has 4 partners, Alan, Baz, Chris and Dave. Alan spends 18% of his time in production. For Baz this is 30%, for Chris 27% and for Dave 25%. The remainder of their time is spent doing other duties, e.g. sourcing supplies, sales, maintenance, paperwork, . . . They produce 3 types of meters. Half of them are gas meters (G), one third of them are electricity meters (E) and the remainder are water meters (W). We look at some specimen probabilities.

We write down this information in fractional form.

Production probabilities	Meter type probabilities
$P(A) = \dfrac{18}{100}$	$P(G) = \dfrac{1}{2}$
$P(B) = \dfrac{30}{100}$	$P(E) = \dfrac{1}{3}$
$P(C) = \dfrac{27}{100}$	$P(W) = 1 - \dfrac{1}{2} - \dfrac{1}{3} = \dfrac{1}{6}$
$P(D) = \dfrac{25}{100}$	

i) We find the probability of a gas meter made by Dave, i.e.
$$P(D \text{ and } G) = P(D) \times P(G)$$
$$= \frac{25}{100} \times \frac{1}{2} = \frac{1}{8}.$$

ii) We find the probability of a water meter *not* made by Baz, i.e.
$$P(\text{not } B \text{ and } W) = P(\text{not } B) \times P(W)$$
$$= \left(1 - \frac{30}{100}\right) \times \frac{1}{6} = \frac{70}{100} \times \frac{1}{6} = \frac{7}{60}.$$

iii)   We find the probability of any meter made by Alan or Chris, i.e.

$$P(A \text{ or } C) = P(A) + P(C)$$

$$= \frac{18}{100} + \frac{27}{100} = \frac{45}{100} = \frac{9}{20}.$$

iv)   We find the probability of an electricity meter made by Alan or Chris, i.e.

$$P((A \text{ or } C) \text{ and } E) = (P(A) + P(C)) \times P(E)$$

$$= \frac{9}{20} \times \frac{1}{3} = \frac{3}{20}.$$

v)   Alan is equally likely to make any type of meter.

$$\therefore \quad P(G) = P(E) = P(W) = \frac{1}{3} \times \frac{18}{100} = \frac{3}{50}.$$

ASSIGNMENT

The brick supplier is unhappy with the site manager's decision. Accepting there are going to be 2 samples he suggests an alternative. The delivery should be acceptable ($p = 0.95$, $q = 0.05$) provided at least 1 of the samples is good. From the 2 samples being either accepted or rejected there are 4 different options. (We look at combinations in more detail soon.) They are

Sample 1:	acceptable	acceptable	rejected	rejected
Sample 2:	acceptable	rejected	acceptable	rejected

In pairs a decision is based upon 'sample 1 and sample 2', i.e. multiplication. Then a decision is based upon 'or', i.e. addition. We look at the supplier's suggestion in two different ways.

i) P(at least 1 acceptable sample)

$$= P(\text{acceptable, rejected}) + P(\text{rejected, acceptable})$$

$$+ P(\text{acceptable, acceptable})$$

$$= (0.95 \times 0.05) + (0.05 \times 0.95) + (0.95 \times 0.95)$$

$$= 0.0475 + 0.0475 + 0.9025$$

$$= 0.9975.$$

For such a high probability we see the supplier is asking for rather more than the site manager is likely to concede.

ii) P(at least 1 acceptable sample) $= 1 - P(\text{rejected, rejected})$

$$= 1 - 0.05 \times 0.05$$

$$= 0.9975, \text{ as before.}$$

■ EXERCISE 19.3 ■

Notice this Exercise uses the same type of information we saw in Exercise 19.2 with changed probability values. Here we ask for different probabilities.

1 In your section are 2 lathes, A and B. The probability of lathe A breaking down today is 0.025 and of lathe B breaking down is 0.040. What is the probability of either lathe breaking down?

2 You are working an early shift in February. The probability of icy roads is $\frac{1}{9}$. The probability of you being late is $\frac{1}{40}$. The probability of you having a minor road accident is $\frac{1}{2000}$. On this particular morning what is the probability of arriving late because of a road accident or due to icy roads?

3 In the maintenance department of the local hospital are 3 teams of technicians and apprentices. They are multi-skilled to deal with most routine and emergency maintenance. The probabilities of achieving this month's efficiency targets are for team A 90%, for team B 80% and for team C 85%. Work out the probabilities for
  i) only team A or team B meeting its target,
  ii) team A and either team B or team C meeting their targets.

4 In a depleted spares tray are 12 nuts and 8 bolts. What is the probability of picking and retaining a nut? Then what is the probability of picking a bolt? What is the probability, without replacement, of picking a nut and then a bolt? What is the probability, without replacement, of picking a bolt and then a nut? What is the probability of picking in either order?

5 You are having difficulty sourcing a component. Your 3 usual suppliers could improve their service to your company. Supplier X has a 50% chance of delivering before the end of the week. For supplier Y this is 75% and for supplier C it is 60%. You need 2 of them to deliver to enable production to continue next week. If all 3 of them deliver you will need to rent expensive short term storage. The probability of being able to do so is 70%. What is the probability of needing and getting that extra storage? (Parts of this question are simiilar to Exercise 19.2, Question **5**. Do you notice anything about some of your answers?)

Combinations

We need to look how different options combine. In the next section, the binomial distribution, we apply the technique. Most calculators have the function, $_nC_r$, but mathematically we write ^nC_r. From a list of n items, choosing r at a time, ^nC_r calculates how many different lists there are. It does not write them out and it does not take order into account.

We define $^nC_r = \dfrac{n!}{r!(n-r)!}$.

Because we are using factorials n and r *cannot* be negative or fractions or decimals. We saw factorials in Volume 2, Chapter 5. Remember $n! = n(n-1)(n-2)(n-3)\ldots \times 3 \times 2 \times 1$ and $1! = 1$ and $0! = 1$.

� ▬▬▬ **Example 19.7** ▬▬▬▬▬▬

We calculate some combinations using the formula and a calculator.

i) $^6C_2 = \dfrac{6!}{2!(6-2)!} = \dfrac{6!}{2!\,4!} = \dfrac{6 \times 5 \times 4 \times 3 \times 2 \times 1}{2!\,4!}$

$$= \dfrac{6 \times 5 \times 4!}{2!\,4!}$$

$$= \dfrac{6 \times 5}{2!} \qquad \boxed{\text{Notice the cancellation.}}$$

$$= 15,$$

i.e. there are 15 different ways of picking 2 items from 6 originals. Just for reference, in this first example only, we list them. Again notice the order within each selection is *not* important. We label our 6 items A, B, C, D, E and F so that our list is

$$AB, AC, AD, AE, AF, \quad BC, BD, BE, BF,$$
$$CD, CE, CF, \quad DE, DF, \quad EF.$$

ii)   Using the calculator to find $^6C_2$ the order of operations is

$\boxed{6}\ \boxed{_nC_r}\ \boxed{2}\ \boxed{=}$ to display 15.

iii) $^6C_4 = \dfrac{6!}{4!(6-4)!} = \dfrac{6!}{4!\,2!} = 15$ as before. $\boxed{\begin{array}{l}\text{The denominators are}\\ 2!\,4! = 4!\,2!.\end{array}}$

iv) $^6C_5 = \dfrac{6!}{5!(6-5)!} = \dfrac{6!}{5!\,1!} = \dfrac{6 \times 5 \times 4 \times 3 \times 2 \times 1}{5!\,1!}$

$$= \dfrac{6 \times 5!}{5!\,1!}$$

$$= \dfrac{6}{1!} \qquad \boxed{\text{Notice the cancellation.}}$$

$$= 6.$$

v) Using the calculator to find $^6C_5$ the order of operations is

   $\underline{6|}$ $\underline{_nC_r|}$ $\underline{5|}$ $\underline{=|}$ to display 6.

vi) For yourself check that $^7C_2 = {}^7C_5$ both with values of 21.

ASSIGNMENT

We return to the decision whether to accept or reject a delivery of bricks. The next suggestion is to take 3 samples and accept the delivery if 2 (or more) of them are acceptable. Remember $p = 0.95$ and $q = 0.05$. We are choosing 2 from 3, i.e. $^3C_2$, which gives 3 different ways of ppq, pqp and qpp. Each of these has a probability of $0.95 \times 0.95 \times 0.05$. Also there is the option of all 3 samples being acceptable, i.e. $0.95 \times 0.95 \times 0.95$. Combining these results we have

P(accepting the delivery) $= 3(0.95 \times 0.95 \times 0.05) + (0.95 \times 0.95 \times 0.95)$

$= 0.135375 + 0.857375$

$= 0.99275$

which is little different from before.

EXERCISE 19.4

For each question find the values using the formula and check them with a calculator.

1	$^5C_2$		**6**	$^4C_2$
2	$^8C_3$		**7**	$^6C_3$
3	$^{10}C_4$		**8**	$^5C_3$
4	$^8C_5$		**9**	$^7C_4$
5	$^7C_3$		**10**	$^9C_5$

The binomial distribution

We have met the binomial theorem in Volume 2, Chapter 5. You may need to re-read that chapter, or at least refer to it. For example we could use it to work out $(a + b)^4$. In the case of the binomial distribution we use p and q rather than a and b. p is the probability of an event occurring and q (or $\bar{p}$) is the probability of an event not occurring. (Remember $p + q = 1$.) There are no alternatives. It is similar to a light and a switch. The light is either on or off.

Generally $(p + q)^n$ looks at conducting trials of size n, with p and q defined as above. We expand such an expression using the previous binomial work, or Pascal's triangle. Recall the powers of p and q change throughout the expansion, one of them increasing to n and the other decreasing from n.

In Volume 1, Chapter 17, we calculated means and standard deviations. For the binomial distribution they are np and $\sqrt{npq}$ respectively. However they are usually referred to as the expectation and variance, i.e.

expectation $= np$ and   **variance** $= npq$.

Notice the standard deviation is the square root of the variance.

▮▮▮▮▮▮ Example 19.8 ▮▮▮▮▮▮

Your production team contains 6 people, i.e. $n = 6$. The probability of arriving for the start of the shift is p and of arriving late is q. We model this with $(p + q)^6$ and expand it to get

$$(p + q)^6 = p^6 + 6p^5q + 15p^4q^2 + 20p^3q^3 + 15p^2q^4 + 6pq^5 + q^6.$$

p^6 is the probability of all 6 people arriving for the start of the shift. p^5q is the probability of 5 arriving for the start and 1 arriving late. This can happen in 6 ways to give the probability for this category of $6p^5q$. p^2q^4 is the probability of 4 arriving for the start and 2 arriving late. This can happen in 15 ways to give the probability for this category of $15p^2q^4$. Notice that $^6C_2 = 15 = {}^6C_4$.

Similarly we can discuss the other terms in the expansion.

We can write our expansion using combination notation as

$$(p + q)^6 = p^6 + {}^6C_5p^5q + {}^6C_4p^4q^2 + {}^6C_3p^3q^3 + {}^6C_2p^2q^4 + {}^6C_1pq^5 + q^6.$$

> $^6C_6 = 1 = {}^6C_0.$

Notice the patterns of subscripts and superscripts we discussed in Volume 2, Chapter 5.

Suppose the probability of arriving for the start of the shift is 0.9, i.e. $p = 0.9$, and so of arriving late must be 0.1. This is based upon $q = 1 - p = 1 - 0.9$. We can substitute into our expansion to find the probabilities for each category. For clarity we write

$$p^6 \qquad = 0.9^6 \qquad\qquad = 0.53144\ldots$$
$$^6C_5p^5q \;= 6 \times 0.9^5 \times 0.1 \;= 0.35429\ldots$$
$$^6C_4p^4q^2 = 15 \times 0.9^4 \times 0.1^2 = 0.09841\ldots$$
$$^6C_3p^3q^3 = 20 \times 0.9^3 \times 0.1^3 = 0.01458$$
$$^6C_2p^2q^4 = 15 \times 0.9^2 \times 0.1^4 = 0.00121\ldots$$
$$^6C_1p\; q^5 \;= 6 \times 0.9 \times 0.1^5 \;\;= 0.00005\ldots$$
$$q^6 \;= 0.1^6 \qquad\qquad\quad = 1 \times 10^{-6}$$

Addition of the accurate probabilities gives a total probability of 1 as expected. Simply using the 5 decimal places gives 0.99998 which is so close to 1.

We can draw a histogram of these probabilities, the area underneath totalling 1 (Fig. 19.5).

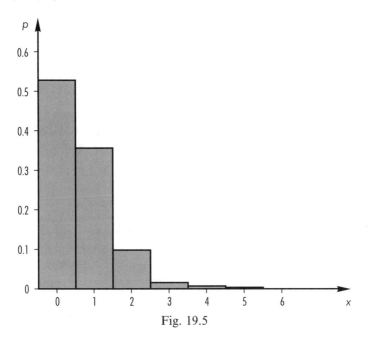

Fig. 19.5

Example 19.9

Using the data from the previous example we have $p = 0.9$, $q = 0.1$ and $n = 6$. Hence

$$\text{expectation} = np = 6 \times 0.9 = 5.4,$$

i.e. on average 5.4 people are on time to start the shift. We accept the figure and understand its interpretation relating to part of a person.

Also the $\qquad \text{variance} = npq = 6 \times 0.9 \times 0.1 = 0.54,$

and the standard deviation $= \sqrt{npq} = \sqrt{0.54} = 0.73\ldots,$

i.e. this is the spread of the distribution about the mean.

Usually we do not need all the terms, perhaps selecting only one or a few of them from the relevant expansion. We define $P(X = r) = {}^nC_r p^r q^{n-r}$ or ${}^nC_r p^r (1 - p)^{n-r}$ to be the probability of r events and $n - r$ non-events in a sample size of n. For many applications we need r good items and $n - r$ faulty items in that sample of n.

▌▌▌▌ ASSIGNMENT ▌▌▌▌

Last time we looked at the Assignment we worked upon 2 good samples from 3 (i.e. one term from the expansion). Using the binomial distribution this is $^3C_2p^2q = 3 \times 0.95^2 \times 0.05 = 0.135375$ as before. There is no need in this situation to discuss further terms. A site manager would not sample so diligently.

▌▌▌▌ EXERCISE 19.5 ▌▌▌▌

1   Your newly installed CNC milling machines are causing problems due to poor reliability. Generally it appears only 85% of them tend to be working. In your installation there are 6 of this new type. At any one time what is the probability of
   i)   4 working,
   ii) 4 or more working.

2   You are producing HD 3½″ computer disks. After a series of complaints concerning faulty disks you investigate. In a box of 10 disks the probability of a faulty one is 0.1. On average how many disks are faulty in each box? As a short term solution you package 11 disks hoping there will be no more than 1 faulty disk per box. Now what is the probability of 0 or 1 disks being faulty in each box of 11? What is the probability of 2 or more being faulty? What is the probability of exactly 2 being faulty?

3   Your engineering company is expanding rapidly and employees are expecting regular promotions. The probability of this for an employee in a year is 0.65. In your section of 9 people what is the probability of 1 or 2 people being promoted? Which is more likely; everybody being promoted or nobody being promoted?

4   In the production of brass internal door furniture your section produces the locking mechanism. In shrink wraps of 10 an anticipated 95% meet the production quality criteria. What is the probability of
   i)   at most 1 being faulty?
   ii) at least 9 being good?

5   The engineering company you work for provides subsidised meals for all employees who choose to eat in the canteen. 75% of them eat there. The personnel department are looking once again at the level of staff benefits. In a sample of 10 what is the probability of more than the average number of employees eating in the canteen?

The Poisson distribution

The 2 general uses of the Poisson distribution are
1   for the distribution of random independent events
and
2   as an approximation for the binomial distribution. (This is beyond the scope of a brief introduction to probability. In Chapter 20 we use the Normal distribution for approximations.)

Frequently used examples of the Poisson distribution are
1   flaws in lengths of material,
2   numbers of factory accidents,
3   telephone enquiries during a fixed time interval.

In **1** notice the implication for a continuous piece of material. This contrasts with the binomial distribution where we checked if single items were good or faulty.

The Poisson distribution has a mean of λ and a variance of λ (i.e. standard deviation of $\sqrt{\lambda}$). λ is the parameter for the distribution. We had a formula for the probability of individual items in the binomial distribution. Here we do the same, involving λ in

$$P(X = r) = \frac{e^{-\lambda}\lambda^r}{r!}.$$

We look at individual, and a few, probabilities. More detailed statistics textbooks use cumulative probabilities and the associated tables.

Example 19.10

Repairs have been made to a road. The top surfaces of tarmac have been removed and the basic structure of the road's foundation brought back to standard. Upon inspection by the Highways Department of the County Council some work remains to be done. The new top layer of tarmac averages 4 repairable flaws per 250 metres. In a given 250 metre stretch of road find the probability there will be i) no flaws, ii) exactly 4 flaws, iii) less than 4 flaws, iv) more than 4 flaws.

The fixed length of road being reviewed is a typical specimen of 250 metres. We are given a mean value of 4, i.e. $\lambda = 4$ so that

$$P(X = r) = \frac{e^{-\lambda}\lambda^r}{r!}$$

is amended to $P(X = r) = \dfrac{e^{-4}4^r}{r!}.$

i)   For no flaws $r = 0$ so that $P(X = 0) = \dfrac{e^{-4}4^0}{0!}$

$$= e^{-4} = 0.0183.$$

$$\boxed{\begin{array}{l} 4^0 = 1, \\ 0! = 1. \end{array}}$$

ii) For exactly 4 flaws $r = 4$ so that $P(X = 4) = \dfrac{e^{-4}4^4}{4!}$

$$= 0.0183\ldots \times \frac{256}{24}$$

$$= 0.1954.$$

iii) For less than 4 flaws we need to look at where there are 0, 1, 2 and 3 flaws, i.e.

$$P(X < 4) = P(0) + P(1) + P(2) + P(3)$$

$$= \frac{e^{-4}4^0}{0!} + \frac{e^{-4}4^1}{1!} + \frac{e^{-4}4^2}{2!} + \frac{e^{-4}4^3}{3!}$$

Common factor of e^{-4}.

$$= e^{-4}(1 + 4 + 8 + 10.\bar{6})$$

$$= 0.0183\ldots \times 23.\bar{6}$$

$$= 0.4335.$$

iv) The total probability must be 1. For more than 4 flaws we need to remove the lower probabilities, i.e.

$$P(X > 4) = 1 - \{P(0) + P(1) + P(2) + P(3) + P(4)\}$$

$$= 1 - \{0.4335 + 0.1954\}$$

$$= 0.3711.$$

We can draw a histogram of these individual probabilities ($P(0)$, $P(1)$, $P(2)$, ...) (Fig. 19.6).We omit the actual calculations but include a table of some results. After $P(10)$ the histogram becomes difficult to see in this Example. Notice the values increasing and then decreasing at the position where $X = 4$ ($\lambda = 4$ is no coincidence).

r	0	1	2	3	4	5
$P(X = r)$	0.0186	0.0737	0.1478	0.1959	0.195	0.156
r	6	7	8	9	10	
$P(X = r)$	0.104	0.060	0.030	0.013	0.005	

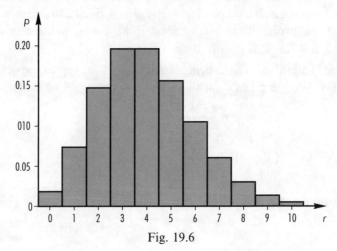

Fig. 19.6

███ **ASSIGNMENT** ███

In a health and safety conscious world the site manager is always monitoring the site safety record. In periods of 6 months on average there have been 5 accidents, i.e. $\lambda = 5$. The Personnel Director only becomes worried when the 6 monthly returns show an above average number of accidents, i.e. we are interested in $P(X > 5)$.

In
$$P(X = r) = \frac{e^{-\lambda}\lambda^r}{r!}$$

we substitute for $\lambda = 5$ so that $P(X = r) = \dfrac{e^{-5}5^r}{r!}$.

Now $P(X > 5) = P(6) + P(7) + P(8) + \ldots$

$$= 1 - \{P(0) + P(1) + P(2) + P(3) + P(4) + P(5)\}$$

$$= 1 - e^{-5}\left\{\frac{5^0}{0!} + \frac{5^1}{1!} + \frac{5^2}{2!} + \frac{5^3}{3!} + \frac{5^4}{4!} + \frac{5^5}{5!}\right\}$$

$$= 1 - e^{-5}\{1 + 5 + 12.5 + 20.8\bar{3} + 26.041\bar{6} + 26.041\bar{6}\}$$

$$= 1 - 0.0067\ldots \times 91.41\bar{6}$$

$$= 0.384,$$

i.e. the probability of exceeding the average number of accidents in a 6 month period is 0.384, or 38.4% of the accident returns will worry the Personnel Director.

███ **EXERCISE 19.6** ███

1 You work in the maintenance section of a wire company producing copper wire. There is a problem in the process. The average number of flaws in every 100 m of wire has risen to 2. What is the probability of your sample length of wire having no flaws?

2 On average during the first working hour of the day you receive 5 internal telephone requests for urgent maintenance. What is the probability of you being able to relax and take an early coffee break because you have received at most 2 telephone calls?

3 In a canning plant 1 in 2000 cans tends to be mis-filled. The cans are then packed and shrink-wrapped in 12000s. On average how many cans will be mis-filled? What is the probability of no more than half of the average mis-filled cans in a shrink-wrap?

4 In your daily morning mail you receive an average of 2½ letters of complaint. What is the probability of exceeding the average when you open this morning's mail?

5   As a national company in the engineering field you respect the experience of a mature and skilled workforce. Unfortunately this has a negative effect upon long term sickness records. An average of 4.5 employees are absent from work due to a heart attack in any month. (The Personnel Department are looking to improve the situation with regular health checks. They are closely monitoring the workforce to test for positive benefits of this new policy.) What is the probability of 3 or fewer employees being absent with this sickness in any month?

20 The Normal Distribution

The objectives of this chapter are to:

1 Analyse a scenario, applying the Normal distribution if appropriate.

2 State the percentage areas under a normal curve for integer standard deviations from the mean.

3 Convert data using the standardised form $z = \dfrac{x - \mu}{\sigma}$.

4 Calculate probabilities from tables using a mean (μ) of 0 and a standard deviation (σ) of 1.

5 Use the Normal distribution to solve problems.

6 Use the Normal distribution as an approximation for the binomial and Poisson distributions under specific conditions.

Introduction

In Chapter 19 we looked at some discrete probability distributions. Here the Normal distribution is a continuous probability distribution. Many measured quantities follow its charateristic bell-shaped curve, e.g. random errors, examination results. Under specific conditions we can approximate the binomial and Poisson distributions to the Normal distribution.

From Volume 1, Chapter 17, we recall that the mean is a measure of central tendency. The standard deviation is a measure of the spread of data.

▮▮▮▮ ASSIGNMENT ▮▮▮▮

For this Assignment we return to Volume 1, Chapter 17, and develop further our work on cement bags. Other production processes are equally valid applications for the Normal distribution. The cement company is looking at the accuracy of the machines it uses for bagging the cement. The production supervisor checked a test run on one machine and recorded the following masses (kg) correct to 2 decimal places:

471

49.95	50.01	50.23	50.11	50.09	50.19	50.03	50.31	50.07	50.10
50.15	49.95	50.10	50.17	50.04	50.22	49.92	50.25	50.18	50.16
50.08	50.08	50.12	50.40	49.81	50.25	50.16	50.15	49.93	50.12
50.15	50.23	50.41	50.16	50.32	50.14	50.47	50.26	50.09	50.18
50.28	50.17	49.97	50.09	50.26	50.35	50.11	50.33	50.30	50.11
50.13	50.14	50.21	50.13	50.04	50.22	50.52	49.84	50.49	50.24
50.27	50.22	50.18	50.38	50.29	50.27	50.44	50.10	50.26	50.08
49.64	50.15	50.29	49.99	50.15	50.09	50.10	50.12	50.20	50.30
49.87	50.06	50.00	50.03	50.56	50.37	50.66	50.07	50.21	49.86
50.20	50.05	49.76	50.08	50.16	49.90	50.22	50.10	50.14	50.02

The Normal distribution curve

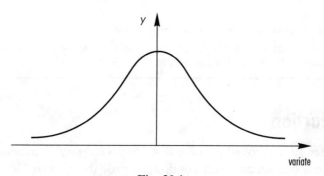

Fig. 20.1

In Fig. 20.1 we see the characteristic bell-shaped curve. Often we hope a set of data, when plotted, will look like this curve. An exact match is unlikely. We accept this on the basis the data curve is reasonably close to the bell-shape. Notice it is symmetrical about the mean and tails away both to the left and right. We include the equation of the curve for completeness only,

$$f(z) = \frac{1}{\sqrt{2\pi}} e^{-z^2/2} \qquad \text{where } z = \frac{x - \mu}{\sigma}.$$

We use tables of values worked out from the equation, rather than the equation itself.

The mean, μ, and the standard deviation, σ, dictate the shape of the curve, i.e. 'tall and thin' or 'low and spread out'. Remember the curve is symmetrical about the mean. Also the variate increases along the horizontal axis to the right. In Fig. 20.2 the mean for curve ② is greater than the mean for curve ①, i.e. $\mu_2 > \mu_1$. Otherwise the curves have the same shape, indicating the data are similarly spread out, i.e. $\sigma_2 = \sigma_1$.

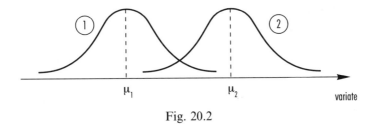

Fig. 20.2

We see (Fig. 20.3) that curves ① and ③ are symmetrical about the same mean. Curve ③ is taller, the data being more closely clustered around the mean than in curve ①. This tells us the standard deviation for curve ③ is less than the standard deviation for curve ①, i.e. $\sigma_3 < \sigma_1$.

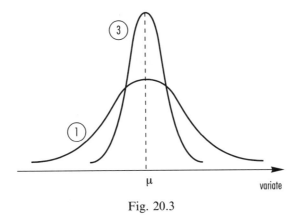

Fig. 20.3

It is likely, when comparing curves, that both the means differ and both the standard deviations differ (Fig. 20.4).

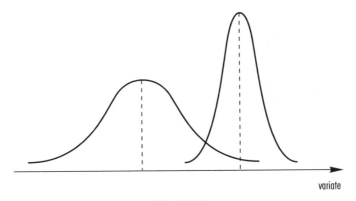

Fig. 20.4

This makes comparison between the distributions difficult for us. For easy comparison we standardise the data using $z = \dfrac{x - \mu}{\sigma}$. This transformation changes a Normal distribution from a mean of μ and a standard deviation of σ to a mean of 0 and a standard deviation of 1 (Fig. 20.5).

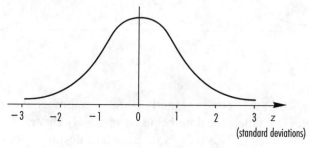

Fig. 20.5

The area under this curve is 1, i.e. it equates to the total probability.

	Original distribution	*Standardised distribution*
Variate	x	z where $z = \dfrac{x - \mu}{\sigma}$
Mean	μ	0
Standard deviation	σ	1

As a rough guide 68%, or just more than $\dfrac{2}{3}$, of the values lie within 1 standard deviation of the mean (Figs. 20.6), i.e. 34%, or just more than $\dfrac{1}{3}$ on each side of the mean.

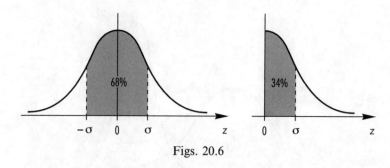

Figs. 20.6

Also approximately 95% of the values lie within 2 standard deviations of the mean. Approximately 99.75% (i.e. almost all) of the values lie within 3 standard deviations of the mean.

■■■■■■■ **ASSIGNMENT** ■■■■■■■■■■■■■■■■■■■■■■■■■■■

In the following table we have grouped our data.

Mass (kg)	Frequency
49.60–49.69	1
49.70–49.79	1
49.80–49.89	4
49.90–49.99	7
50.00–50.09	19
50.10–50.19	31
50.20–50.29	21
50.30–50.39	8
50.40–50.49	5
50.50–50.59	2
50.60–50.69	1

In Fig. 20.7 we draw a frequency curve of this data. It is a plot of the frequency against the mid-point of each class. You can see it approximates, rather than matches, the bell-shaped curve.

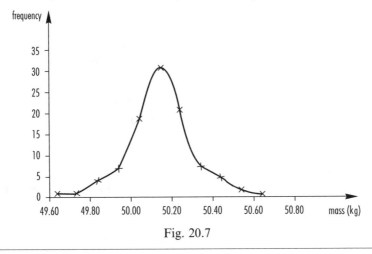

Fig. 20.7

Standardised values

We use $z = \dfrac{x - \mu}{\sigma}$ to standardise our original x values. As we saw in Fig. 20.5 negative values are to the left of the mean and positive values to the right, while maintaining the symmetry about the mean of 0. We show some calculations in the following Examples.

Design engineers are testing a new long-life battery. They have found the battery lifetimes (hours) to be Normally distributed with a mean of 145.5 hours and a standard deviation of 10 hours. We use this information to calculate some specimen random x and z values.

We are given $\mu = 145.5$ and $\sigma = 10$.

i) For $x = 159$ and using $z = \dfrac{x - \mu}{\sigma}$

we have $\qquad\qquad z = \dfrac{159 - 145.5}{10} = 1.35.$

ii) For $x = 124$ in $\qquad z = \dfrac{x - \mu}{\sigma}$

we have $\qquad\qquad z = \dfrac{124 - 145.5}{10} = -2.15.$

iii) For $x = 167$ in $\qquad z = \dfrac{x - \mu}{\sigma}$

we have $\qquad\qquad z = \dfrac{167 - 145.5}{10} = 2.15.$

Notice in ii) and iii) $|z| = 2.15$. In ii) the value is below the mean (i.e. to the left of the mean on the curve) and in iii) the value is above the mean (i.e. to the right of the mean on the curve).

iv) The majority of the battery lifetimes lie within 3 standard deviations of the mean, i.e. between $z = -3$ and $z = 3$. We find the corresponding x values (i.e. the actual lifetimes in hours).

For $z = 3$ in $\qquad\qquad z = \dfrac{x - \mu}{\sigma}$

we have $\qquad 3 \times 10 = x - 145.5$ $\qquad$ | Multiplying through by σ. |

i.e. $\qquad\qquad x = 175.5.$

Notice that $3\sigma = 3 \times 10 = 30$ and the upper extreme of 175.5 is 30 above the mean of 145.5. Hence the lower extreme of 115.5 is 30 below the mean, i.e. almost all the battery lifetimes lie between 115.5 hours and 175.5 hours.

EXERCISE 20.1

1   Screws are packed in 25s, though the actual number varies according to the Normal distribution. The mean number of screws/pack is indeed 25 and the standard deviation is 0.85 screws. Calculate the z values for 24 and 26 screws.

2 Excessive production time on a component needs some attention to ensure smooth and efficient overall production. Analysis of recent data shows the times to be Normally distributed. The mean time is 6 minutes and the standard deviation is 1.9 minutes. Find the z values for 3 and 4.5 minutes.

3 To remain competitive and retain valuable personnel a local engineering company supports its workers' part-time education and training. The weekly hours of study follows a Normal distribution with a mean of 9 hours and a standard deviation of 1.75 hours. Find the times of study that encompass approximately $\frac{2}{3}$ of the personnel.

What are the associated z values?

4 A batch of resistors has a nominal resistance of 15 Ω. Quality control checks reveal the actual resistances to be Normally distributed. The mean is 15.020 Ω and the standard deviation is 0.035 Ω. Find the z values for 14.975 Ω and 15.045 Ω.

5 The number of hours' overtime worked by employees at an auto-engineering firm in one month is recorded below:

Hours	1–5	6–10	11–15	16–20	21–25	26–30	31–35	36–40
Number of employees	6	7	18	9	5	4	3	2

Why is this data *not* normally distributed? Explain your decision, supporting it with a diagram if appropriate.

Use of tables

There are many variations in the presentation of Normal distribution tables. Some look at values from the mean while others look at values in the tail. We work from and above the mean. Remember that symmetry implies that the size of the values will be the same in the other half. There we only need to include a minus sign to make the distinction. The table on p. 478 gives z values combined in the first column and first row. The main body of the table gives the shaded area under the Normal curve, measured from the mean. Hence they start at 0 and tend towards 0.5000.

▬▬▬▬ **Examples 20.2** ▬▬▬▬

We recall the design engineers from Examples 20.1 looking at Normally distributed battery lifetimes with $\mu = 145.5$ and $\sigma = 10$.

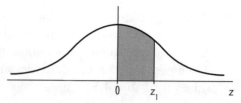

Area under the standard normal curve

z_1	0.00	0.01	0.02	0.03	0.04	0.05	0.06	0.07	0.08	0.09
0.0	0.0000	0.0040	0.0080	0.0120	0.0160	0.0199	0.0239	0.0279	0.0319	0.0359
0.1	0.0398	0.0438	0.0478	0.0517	0.0557	0.0596	0.0636	0.0675	0.0714	0.0753
0.2	0.0793	0.0832	0.0871	0.0910	0.0948	0.0987	0.1026	0.1064	0.1103	0.1141
0.3	0.1179	0.1217	0.1255	0.1293	0.1331	0.1368	0.1406	0.1443	0.1480	0.1517
0.4	0.1554	0.1591	0.1628	0.1664	0.1700	0.1736	0.1772	0.1808	0.1844	0.1879
0.5	0.1915	0.1950	0.1985	0.2019	0.2054	0.2088	0.2123	0.2157	0.2190	0.2224
0.6	0.2257	0.2291	0.2324	0.2357	0.2389	0.2422	0.2454	0.2486	0.2517	0.2549
0.7	0.2580	0.2611	0.2642	0.2673	0.2704	0.2734	0.2764	0.2794	0.2823	0.2852
0.8	0.2881	0.2910	0.2939	0.2967	0.2995	0.3023	0.3051	0.3078	0.3106	0.3133
0.9	0.3159	0.3186	0.3212	0.3238	0.3264	0.3289	0.3315	0.3340	0.3365	0.3389
1.0	0.3413	0.3438	0.3461	0.3485	0.3508	0.3531	0.3554	0.3577	0.3599	0.3621
1.1	0.3643	0.3665	0.3686	0.3708	0.3729	0.3749	0.3770	0.3790	0.3810	0.3830
1.2	0.3849	0.3869	0.3888	0.3907	0.3925	0.3944	0.3962	0.3980	0.3997	0.4015
1.3	0.4032	0.4049	0.4066	0.4082	0.4099	0.4115	0.4131	0.4147	0.4162	0.4177
1.4	0.4192	0.4207	0.4222	0.4236	0.4251	0.4265	0.4279	0.4292	0.4306	0.4319
1.5	0.4332	0.4345	0.4357	0.4370	0.4382	0.4394	0.4406	0.4418	0.4429	0.4441
1.6	0.4452	0.4463	0.4474	0.4484	0.4495	0.4505	0.4515	0.4525	0.4535	0.4545
1.7	0.4554	0.4564	0.4573	0.4582	0.4591	0.4599	0.4608	0.4616	0.4625	0.4633
1.8	0.4641	0.4649	0.4656	0.4664	0.4671	0.4678	0.4686	0.4693	0.4699	0.4706
1.9	0.4713	0.4719	0.4726	0.4732	0.4738	0.4744	0.4750	0.4756	0.4761	0.4767
2.0	0.4773	0.4778	0.4783	0.4788	0.4793	0.4798	0.4803	0.4808	0.4812	0.4817
2.1	0.4821	0.4826	0.4830	0.4834	0.4838	0.4842	0.4846	0.4850	0.4854	0.4857
2.2	0.4861	0.4864	0.4868	0.4871	0.4875	0.4878	0.4881	0.4884	0.4887	0.4890
2.3	0.4893	0.4896	0.4898	0.4901	0.4904	0.4906	0.4909	0.4911	0.4913	0.4916
2.4	0.4918	0.4920	0.4922	0.4925	0.4927	0.4929	0.4931	0.4932	0.4934	0.4936
2.5	0.4938	0.4940	0.4941	0.4943	0.4945	0.4946	0.4948	0.4949	0.4951	0.4952
2.6	0.4953	0.4955	0.4956	0.4957	0.4959	0.4960	0.4961	0.4962	0.4963	0.4964
2.7	0.4965	0.4966	0.4967	0.4968	0.4969	0.4970	0.4971	0.4972	0.4973	0.4974
2.8	0.4974	0.4975	0.4976	0.4977	0.4977	0.4978	0.4979	0.4979	0.4980	0.4981
2.9	0.4981	0.4982	0.4983	0.4983	0.4984	0.4984	0.4985	0.4985	0.4986	0.4986
3.0	0.4987	0.4987	0.4987	0.4988	0.4988	0.4989	0.4989	0.4989	0.4989	0.4990
3.1	0.4990	0.4991	0.4991	0.4991	0.4992	0.4992	0.4992	0.4992	0.4993	0.4993
3.2	0.4993	0.4993	0.4994	0.4994	0.4994	0.4994	0.4994	0.4995	0.4995	0.4995

i)   For $x = 159$ we know $z = 1.35$. From the table we use this value of z to find the associated area under the Normal curve and hence a probability. The first column uses 1 decimal place only. We look to 1.3. The top row accounts for the next decimal place, i.e. we look to 0.05 ($1.3 + 0.05 = 1.35$). From the body of the table we read 0.4115.

z_1	0.00	0.01	0.02	0.03	0.04	0.05	0.06	0.07	0.08	0.09
0.0	0.0000	0.0040	0.0080	0.0120	0.0160	0.0199	0.0239	0.0279	0.0319	0.0359
0.1	0.0398	0.0438	0.0478	0.0517	0.0557	0.0596	0.0636	0.0675	0.0714	0.0753
0.2	0.0793	0.0832	0.0871	0.0910	0.0948	0.0987	0.1026	0.1064	0.1103	0.1141
0.3	0.1179	0.1217	0.1255	0.1293	0.1331	0.1368	0.1406	0.1443	0.1480	0.1517
0.4	0.1554	0.1591	0.1628	0.1664	0.1700	0.1736	0.1772	0.1808	0.1844	0.1879
0.5	0.1915	0.1950	0.1985	0.2019	0.2054	0.2088	0.2123	0.2157	0.2190	0.2224
0.6	0.2257	0.2291	0.2324	0.2357	0.2389	0.2422	0.2454	0.2486	0.2517	0.2549
0.7	0.2580	0.2611	0.2642	0.2673	0.2704	0.2734	0.2764	0.2794	0.2823	0.2852
0.8	0.2881	0.2910	0.2939	0.2967	0.2995	0.3023	0.3051	0.3078	0.3106	0.3133
0.9	0.3159	0.3186	0.3212	0.3238	0.3264	0.3289	0.3315	0.3340	0.3365	0.3389
1.0	0.3413	0.3438	0.3461	0.3485	0.3508	0.3531	0.3554	0.3577	0.3599	0.3621
1.1	0.3643	0.366	0.3686	0.3708	0.3729	0.3749	0.3770	0.3790	0.3810	0.3830
1.2	0.3849	0.3869	0.3888	0.3907	0.3925	0.3944	0.3962	0.3980	0.3997	0.4015
1.3	0.4032	0.4049	0.4066	0.4082	0.4099	0.4115	0.4131	0.4147	0.4162	0.4177
1.4	0.4192	0.4207	0.4222	0.4236	0.4251	0.4265	0.4279	0.4292	0.4306	0.4319

We can interpret it in a number of ways.

The probability of lying between 145.5 and 159 is 0.4115.

41.15% of the batteries have lifetimes between 145.5 hours and 159 hours.

The probability of being 159 or below is 0.9115. Notice that this includes the other half of the Normal curve (0.5) to the left of the mean.

91.15% of the batteries have lifetimes of 159 hours or less.

The probability of being above 159 is $0.5 - 0.4115 = 0.0885$ or $1 - 0.9115 = 0.0885$.

8.85% of the batteries have lifetimes exceeding 159 hours.

ii) We look at the probability of lying between 159 hours and 167 hours, again using answers from Examples 20.1.

At $x_1 = 159$, $z_1 = 1.35$ and $P(z_1) = 0.4115$.

At $x_2 = 167$, $z_2 = 2.15$ and $P(z_2) = 0.4842$.

Both these probabilities are measured from the mean. The difference between the hours is the difference between the areas, i.e.

$$P(159 < x < 167)$$

or $P(1.35 < z < 2.15) = 0.4842 - 0.4115 = 0.0727$.

This tells us 7.27% of the battery lifetimes lie between 159 hours and 167 hours (Fig. 20.8). Notice the values are on the **same** side of the mean and we use subtraction.

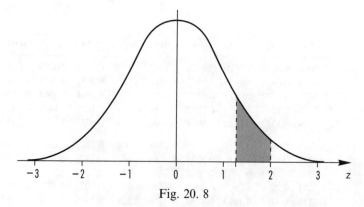

Fig. 20. 8

iii) We look at the probability of lying between 124 hours and 159 hours, again using answers from Examples 20.1.

At $x_1 = 159$, $z_1 = 1.35$ and $P(z_1) = 0.4115$.

At $x_3 = 124$, $z_3 = -2.15$ and $P(z_3) = 0.4842$.

Again both these probabilities are measured from the mean. The negative sign implies we are to the left of the mean. We ignore it when we use the table. Remember the Normal distribution is symmetrical, so the left and right sides of the mean are mirror images of each other. This time we add the areas under the curve, i.e.

$P(124 < x < 159)$

or $P(-2.15 < z < 1.35) = 0.4842 + 0.4115 = 0.8957$.

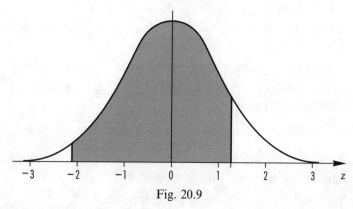

Fig. 20.9

This tells us that 89.57% of the battery lifetimes lie between 124 hours and 159 hours (Fig. 20.9). Notice the values are on **different sides** of the mean and we use addition.

iv) Finally we look at the probability of lying in the tails, i.e.

$P(x < 124 \text{ or } x > 159)$

or $P(z < -2.15 \text{ or } z > 1.35) = 1 - 0.8957 = 0.1043$.

This tells us 10.43% of the battery lifetimes lie **outside** the range 124 hours to 159 hours (Fig. 20.10).

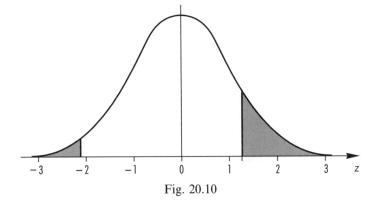

Fig. 20.10

ASSIGNMENT

We look at our data on the 50 kg cement bags, remembering the data does *not* exactly match a Normal distribution. Hence all our calculations will give answers approximating to the truth. In Volume 1, Chapter 17, we found $\mu = 50.16$ kg and $\sigma = 0.17$ kg. We show some specimen calculations.

i) We find the probability of a cement bag being more than 50.40 kg.

For $x = 50.40$ in $z = \dfrac{x - \mu}{\sigma}$

we have $z = \dfrac{50.40 - 50.16}{0.17} = 1.41$.

From the body of the table we read the corresponding area of 0.4207. Now we want the probability of a cement bag being more than 50.40 kg and so need the area in the tail, i.e.

$$P\,(> 50.40 \text{ kg}) = 0.5 - 0.4207 = 0.0793,$$

i.e. 7.93% of the cement bags exceed a mass of 50.40 kg.

ii) Next we look at the probability of a cement bag being close to the mean. We are interested in the mass limits accounting for 25% of the cement bags lying above and 25% lying below the mean, i.e. the middle 50%. We concentrate our attention above the mean and then use the symmetrical properties of the Normal distribution. In the body of the table we use 0.25 rather than 25%.

z_1	0.00	0.01	0.02	0.03	0.04	0.05	0.06	0.07	0.08	0.09
0.0	0.0000	0.0040	0.0080	0.0120	0.0160	0.0199	0.0239	0.0279	0.0319	0.0359
0.1	0.0398	0.0438	0.0478	0.0517	0.0557	0.0596	0.0636	0.0675	0.0714	0.0753
0.2	0.0793	0.0832	0.0871	0.0910	0.0948	0.0987	0.1026	0.1064	0.1103	0.1141
0.3	0.1179	0.1217	0.1255	0.1293	0.1331	0.1368	0.1406	0.1443	0.1480	0.1517
0.4	0.1554	0.1591	0.1628	0.1664	0.1700	0.1736	0.1772	0.1808	0.1844	0.1879
0.5	0.1915	0.1950	0.1985	0.2019	0.2054	0.2088	0.2123	0.2157	0.2190	0.2224
0.6	0.2257	0.2291	0.2324	0.2357	0.2389	0.2422	0.2454	0.2486	0.2517	0.2549

0.25 is not exact in the body of the table. We notice it must lie between 0.2486 and 0.2517. 0.25 is approximately at the mid-point between them, i.e. at $z = 0.675$.

For $z = 0.675$ in $\qquad z = \dfrac{x - \mu}{\sigma}$

we have $\qquad 0.675 \times 0.17 = x - 50.16$ | Multiplying through by σ.

i.e. $\qquad\qquad\qquad x = 50.27$.

You can check that 50.27 is 0.11 kg (0.675×0.17) above the mean. This imples the lower limit is 0.11 kg below the mean at 50.05 kg. Alternatively

for $z = -0.675$ in $\qquad z = \dfrac{x - \mu}{\sigma}$

we have $\quad - 0.675 \times 0.17 = x - 50.16$ | Multiplying through by σ.

i.e. $\qquad\qquad\qquad x = 50.05$.

Using either method we see the middle 50% lie between 50.05 kg and 50.27 kg. Written in terms of probabilities this is

$\qquad P(50.05 \text{ kg} < x < 50.27 \text{ kg}) = 0.5$

or $\qquad P(-0.675 < z < 0.675) = 0.5$.

EXERCISE 20.2

In Questions **1–10** use the given range of z values to find the probabilities.

1 $P(0 < z < 1.92)$

2 $P(0 < z < 1.545)$

3 $P(-0.65 < z < 0)$

4 $P(-0.65 < z < 0.65)$

5 $P(|z| < 0.75)$

6 $P(0.5 < z < 1.75)$

7 $P(-0.5 < z < 1.75)$

8 $P(z > 1.5)$

9 $P(-1.3 < z)$

10 $P(|z| > 1.25)$

In Questions **11–15** find the z_1 values given the probabilities. Take care to notice the appropriate region of the Normal curve for each question.

11 $P(0 < z < z_1) = 0.3340$

12 $P(z_1 < z < 0) = 0.4750$

13 $P(|z| < z_1) = 0.6$

14 $P(0 < z < z_1) = 0.1517$

15 $P(z_1 < z < 0) = 0.1255$

16 An engineering company is producing bolts nominally measuring 200 mm with a standard deviation of 10 mm. What percentage of bolts lie between 185 mm and 210 mm? A customer, for a lower price, will accept bolts between 185 mm and 215 mm rather than within the previous range. What extra percentage of production can the engineering firm sell to this customer?

17 A brand of electric light bulbs have Normally distributed lifetimes with a mean of 2000 hours and a standard deviation of 160 hours. Estimate the probability of a bulb shining for more than 2200 hours. The manufacturer intends to tighten up the quality of its production methods. By doing so it reduces the standard deviation. Investigate the probability of lasting for more than 2200 hours when the standard deviation is reduced to i) 150 hours, ii) 135 hours, iii) 120 hours.

18 A tyre manufacturer expects car tyres to last for 35 000 miles on average with a standard deviation of 5000 miles. Accepting the life expectancies to be Normally distributed what percentage of tyres will travel for 40 000 miles or more? Tyres are returned for a compensatory payment if they wear out, under general usage, below 15 000 miles. What is the probability of this happening to you?

19 The lifetimes of types *A* and *B* television tubes are Normally distributed. Type *A* has a mean of 48 months and a standard deviation of 4 months. Type *B* has a mean of 45 months and a standard deviation of 8 months. Your television tube lasts for 50 or more months. Find the probability of it being type *A* and of being type *B*. Which is the more likely?

20 A canner fills tin cans with 410 g of catfood. This is the mean mass of a Normally distributed production line. The standard deviation is 20 g. Complaints tend to occur if the masses drop below 375 g. What is the probability of this happening? To reduce the complaints should the supermarket buyers insist upon a higher or lower standard deviation? During routine maintenance you can adjust the production in line with the supermarket's wishes. For virtually no complaints all cans must lie within 3 standard deviations of the mean. Link this with the previous 375 g to find the new required standard deviation.

The Normal approximation to the binomial distribution

Remember for the binomial distribution $p + q = 1$, $\mu = np$ and $\sigma = \sqrt{npq}$ where n is the number in the sample. The Normal distribution is a good approximation for large n (say greater than 20) and p close to 0.5. When $p = 0.5$ the binomial distribution is symmetrical. When n gets large we can allow p to slightly drift away (larger or smaller) from 0.5. We treat these conditions with some latitude, remembering it is an approximation. Also the binomial distribution is a discrete distribution, yet the Normal distribution is continuous. We need to make corrections for this.

We consider a prototype packing machine under-going early development trials. In samples of 1000 packing trays it appears to mispack 15% of them. We look at the probability of mispacking some specimen numbers of trays.

Using our initial data in decimals rather than percentages we have

$$P(\text{mispack}) = p \quad = 0.15$$

$$\therefore \qquad q = 1 - p = 0.85.$$

Also $\qquad n = 1000.$

Then $\qquad \mu = np = 150$

and $\qquad \sigma = \sqrt{npq} = \sqrt{127.5} = 11.29\ldots$

i) We find the probability of mispacking less than 125 in the batch of 1000. We need to correct for continuity, accepting that 125 has limits of 124.5 to 125.5. For less than 125 we use the lower limit, $x = 124.5$.

For $x = 124.5$ in $\quad z = \dfrac{x - \mu}{\sigma}$

we have $\qquad z = \dfrac{124.5 - 150}{11.29\ldots} = -2.26.$

From the table we read 0.4881. Because we are looking at 'less than 125' we use the left tail of the Normal distribution, i.e.
$$P(\text{mispacking} < 125) = 0.5 - 0.4881 = 0.0119.$$

ii) We find the probability of mispacking more than 170 in the batch of 1000. Again we need to correct for continuity, accepting that 170 has limits of 169.5 to 170.5. For 'more than 170' we use the upper limit, $x = 170.5$.

For $x = 170.5$ in $\quad z = \dfrac{x - \mu}{\sigma}$

we have $\qquad z = \dfrac{170.5 - 150}{11.29\ldots} = 1.82.$

From the table we read 0.4656. Because we are looking at 'more than 170' we use the right tail of the Normal distribution, i.e.
$$P(\text{mispacking} > 170) = 0.5 - 0.4656 = 0.0344.$$

iii) We look at the probability of mispacking 170 or more in the batch of 1000. This time we need to include, rather than exclude, 170. This indicates we use the lower limit, 169.5. You can check for yourself that we get
$$P(\text{mispacking 170 or more}) = 0.5 - 0.4582 = 0.0418.$$

iv) We find the probability of mispacking between 125 and 170 in the batch of 1000. Now 125 goes as low as 124.5 and 170 goes as high as 170.5. Using our earlier answers we have a probability of 0.4881 to the left of the mean and a probability of 0.4656 to the right of the mean. The different sides of the mean indicate we add these probabilities, i.e.

$$P(125 < x < 170) = 0.4881 + 0.4656 = 0.9537.$$

■■■■ EXERCISE 20.3 ■■■■

In the following questions apply the Normal approximation to the binomial distribution.

1 10% of the screws in a particular batch are faulty. Express this as a probability, p. Express the probability of a screw being good, q. Find the mean and standard deviation of faulty screws in batches of 1000. Use the Normal distribution as an approximation to the binomial distribution. What is the probability of between 90 and 110 screws being faulty in a batch? What is the probability of more than 110 screws being faulty?

2 Business is booming and continued expansion of the engineering company means there is reduced on-site parking. Overspill parking is available on nearby narrow, congested, streets. You have a 60% chance of finding on-site parking each day. Excluding holidays and sickness you work for 225 days in a year. What is the probability of finding on-site parking for at least 150 working days in a year?

3 Four-fifths of the workforce eat in the canteen; the remainder bring their own lunch. This electronics company employs 150 people. On average how many people eat in the canteen on this particular day? The canteen has 130 seats. What is the probability of *not* finding a seat once you have purchased your meal?

4 The probability of a component being faulty is 0.05. What is the probability of it being good? In a batch of 500 the batch will be rejected if it contains more than 35 faulty components. What is the likelihood of this happening?

5 35% of production is for export. On a continuous shift system, 365 days/year, on average how many days of production will be exported? What is the probability of this rising to more than 150 days in any year?

The Normal approximation to the Poisson distribution

Remember for the Poisson distribution the parameter is λ. The mean (μ) is λ and the standard deviation (σ) is $\sqrt{\lambda}$. The Normal distribution is a good approximation for large λ, say greater than 20. As with the previous approximation again we need to make corrections for continuity.

Examples 20.4

A software house provides the usual level of technical support with a dedicated telephone hot-line. The mean number of calls/hour is 30. Using the Normal approximation to the Poisson distribution we look at some specimen calls/hour. Our basic data gives $\mu = \lambda = 30$ and
$$\sigma = \sqrt{\lambda} = \sqrt{30} = 5.477\ldots$$

i) We find the probability of there being more than 32 calls in an hour. For our continuity correction 32 lies between 31.5 and 32.5. For 'more than 32' we use $x = 32.5$.

   For $x = 32.5$ in $z = \dfrac{x - \mu}{\sigma}$

   we have $z = \dfrac{32.5 - 30}{5.477\ldots} = 0.456$.

   0.456 splits the distance between 0.45 and 0.46 in the ratio 6:4. From the table we read correspondingly 0.1736 and 0.1772. We need to split the distance between the table values in this same ratio of 6:4. Doing so we get a table value of 0.1758. Because we are looking at 'more than 32' we use the right tail of the Normal distribution, i.e.
   $$P(> 32 \text{ calls/hour}) = 0.5 - 0.1758 = 0.3242.$$

ii) We find the probability of there being between 28 and 32 calls in an hour. For our continuity corrections we use 27.5 and 32.5, i.e. 2.5 either side of the mean. Using our previous answer $z = 0.456$ and the probability is 0.1758. Remember the symmetry of the Normal distribution so that
   $$P(28 < x < 32 \text{ calls/hour}) = 2 \times 0.1758 = 0.3516.$$

ASSIGNMENT

Let us return to our cement bags. This time we look at a different aspect of production; accidents. On average the cement works has an accident once every 10 weeks. More realistically we look over a 5 year period, i.e. 260 weeks (5 × 52). Hence on average there will be 26 accidents in 5 years. Using the Normal approximation to the Poisson distribution we have
$$\mu = \lambda = 26 \text{ and } \sigma = \sqrt{\lambda} = \sqrt{26} = 5.099\ldots$$

We find the probability of there being less than 15 accidents in this period. For our continuity correction 15 lies between 14.5 and 15.5. For 'less than 15' we use $x = 14.5$.

For $x = 14.5$ in $\quad z = \dfrac{x - \mu}{\sigma}$

we have $\quad z = \dfrac{14.5 - 26}{5.099\ldots} = -2.26.$

The table value is 0.4881 and we are looking at the left tail of the Normal distribution, i.e.

$\quad P(< 15 \text{ accidents}/5 \text{ years}) = 0.5 - 0.4881 = 0.0119.$

This is a small probability, implying that such a low accident record is unlikely for this company.

■ EXERCISE 20.4 ■

In the following questions apply the Normal approximation to the Poisson distribution.

1 Your engineering company is launching a new product. Previous product launches suggest that the marketing department expects on average 45 telephone enquiries/hour. Why are 25 and 65 suitable approximate lower and upper limits for this distribution? What is the probability of receiving 55 or more enquiries/hour and hence needing to employ temporary staff? What is the probability of receiving less than 35 enquiries/hour and hence needing to re-deploy staff?

2 A company produces one hundred thousand high quality alloy bolts each year. On average 250 of those fail in the first year. What is the probability of between 250 and 275 failing? What is the probability of more than 275 failing?

3 Factory accidents for this manufacturer average 2 every 5 months. What is the average over 5 years? What is the probability of there being 30 or more in 5 years? What is the probability of there being less than 15 in 5 years? If 39 occurred in this period should it be considered a rare event? Explain your reasoning.

4 A person enters information into a computer to source parts for production. On average that person makes 4 errors in $10\,000$ character inputs. Hence in 10^6 character inputs 400 errors are expected on average. Find the probability of 375 or less errors in 10^6. Find the probability of more than 445 errors in 10^6. Why should you expect the majority of errors to be between 340 and 460 in 10^6?

5 You are managing a chemical process plant, in a densely populated area, subject to very strict monitoring. Active environmental campaigners are trying to associate the chemical process with

regional deaths from a rare disease. The annual average number of deaths in the region is 20. It is suggested that a Poisson distribution accurately models this.

Production is then increased and the following year there are 26 deaths. What is the probability of there being 26 or more deaths? Is there sufficient evidence to link these deaths with the production increase? If the number of annual deaths rose to 32 would you suggest there was any link between them and chemical production.

Answers to Exercises

Chapter 1

Exercise 1.1

1	$-3 - j$	**2**	$-0.5 - j5.5$
3	$9.5(1 - j)$	**4**	$-9 - j5$
5	$9 + j5$	**6**	$13 - j2$
7	$5 + j12$	**8**	$-9.5(1 - j)$
9	$9.5 - j10.5$	**10**	$-1.5 - j3.5$

Exercise 1.2

1	$-21 + j14$	**2**	$-13 + j47$
3	$51 + j7$	**4**	50
5	$29 - j50$	**6**	100
7	$102 + j14$	**8**	$-47 - j13$
9	$81 + j167$	**10**	$25(1 - j)$

Exercise 1.3

1	$-0.52 + j1.36$	**2**	$-0.077 + j1.615$
3	$-0.26 + j0.68$	**4**	$0.20 + j0.21$
5	$-0.16 + j3.88$	**6**	$0.385 - j2.077$
7	$22 + j4$	**8**	$9.4 + j13.2$
9	$0.18 + j1.71$	**10**	$0.075 - j0.084$

Exercise 1.4

1	$10, \underline{/53.13^\circ}$ or $10\underline{/0.927}$	**2**	$9.90\underline{/45^\circ}$ or $9.90\underline{/0.785}$
3	$6.40\underline{/141.34^\circ}$ or $6.40\underline{/2.467}$	**4**	$7.07\underline{/-81.87^\circ}$ or $7.07\underline{/-1.429}$
5	$5\underline{/-143.13^\circ}$ or $5\underline{/-2.498}$	**6**	$0.68 + j1.88$
7	$-1.71 + j4.70$	**8**	$0.42 - j0.91$
9	$-1.69 - j3.63$	**10**	$0 - j2.5$

Exercise 1.5

1 $12(\cos(-75°)+j\sin(-75°))$ **2** $96(\cos 65°+j\sin 65°)$
3 $240(\cos(-10°)+j\sin(-10°))$ **4** $0.75(\cos 100°+j\sin 100°)$
5 $0.4(\cos 75°+j\sin 75°)$ **6** $1.5(\cos 145°+j\sin 145°)$
7 $0.3(\cos 175°+j\sin 175°)$ **8** $0.6(\cos(-145°)+j\sin(-145°))$
9 $0.083(\cos 75°+j\sin 75°)$ **10** $0.0083(\cos 55°+j\sin 55°)$

Exercise 1.6

1 $12\underline{/-120°}$ **2** $48\underline{/0°}$
3 $40\underline{/-90°}$ **4** $0.5\underline{/90°}$
5 $1.2\underline{/90°}$ **6** $3\underline{/120°}$
7 $0.6\underline{/180°}$ **8** $0.3\underline{/-120°}$
9 $0.083\underline{/120°}$ **10** $0.15\underline{/120°}$

Exercise 1.7

1 $5e^{-j2\pi/3}$ **2** $25e^{-j5\pi/12}$
3 $50e^{-j11\pi/12}$ **4** $0.5e^{j11\pi/12}$
5 $0.5e^{j\pi/2}$ **6** $5e^{j7\pi/12}$
7 $0.25e^{-j7\pi/12}$ **8** $0.2e^{-j7\pi/12}$
9 $0.2e^{j2\pi/3}$ **10** $0.04e^{-j\pi/6}$

Exercise 1.8

1 $\cos(-60°)+j\sin(-60°)$ **2** $\cos 0+j\sin 0$
3 $64\underline{/60°}$ **4** $\cos(-160°)+j\sin(-160°)$
5 $1\underline{/-\dfrac{5\pi}{6}}$ **6** $\cos\dfrac{\pi}{2}+j\sin\dfrac{\pi}{2}$
7 $\cos\pi+j\sin\pi$ **8** $\cos(-30°)+j\sin(-30°)$
9 $1\underline{/-60°}$ **10** $64\underline{/\pi}$
11 $-j8$ **12** $-2(1+j)$
13 $-237-j3116$ **14** $-8.00-j13.86$
15 $-341525+j145668$

Exercise 1.9

1 $5(\cos(-165°)+j\sin(-165°))$, $5(\cos 15°+j\sin 15°)$
2 $3(\cos(-140°)+j\sin(-140°))$, $3(\cos(-20°)+j\sin(-20°))$,
$3(\cos 100°+j\sin 100°)$

3   $1.26\left(\cos\left(-\dfrac{\pi}{2}\right) + j\sin\left(-\dfrac{\pi}{2}\right)\right)$, $1.26\left(\cos\dfrac{\pi}{6} + j\sin\dfrac{\pi}{6}\right)$,

    $1.26\left(\cos\dfrac{5\pi}{6} + j\sin\dfrac{5\pi}{6}\right)$

4   $1.78\underline{/-155°}$, $1.78\underline{/-65°}$, $1.78\underline{/25°}$, $1.78\underline{/115°}$

5   $2\underline{/-114°}$, $2\underline{/-42°}$, $2\underline{/30°}$, $2\underline{/102°}$, $2\underline{/174°}$

6   $9\underline{/-\dfrac{3\pi}{10}}$, $9\underline{/\dfrac{7\pi}{10}}$

7   $3(\cos(-120°) + j\sin(-120°))$, $3(\cos(-30°) + j\sin(-30°))$,
    $3(\cos 60° + j\sin 60°)$, $3(\cos 150° + j\sin 150°)$

8   $4\left(\cos\left(-\dfrac{7\pi}{8}\right) + j\sin\left(-\dfrac{7\pi}{8}\right)\right)$, $4\left(\cos\dfrac{\pi}{8} + j\sin\dfrac{\pi}{8}\right)$

9   $5\left(\cos\left(-\dfrac{\pi}{3}\right) + j\sin\left(-\dfrac{\pi}{3}\right)\right)$, $5\left(\cos\dfrac{\pi}{3} + j\sin\dfrac{\pi}{3}\right)$, $5(\cos\pi + j\sin\pi)$

10   $2\underline{/-\dfrac{17\pi}{20}}$, $2\underline{/-\dfrac{9\pi}{20}}$, $2\underline{/-\dfrac{\pi}{20}}$, $2\underline{/\dfrac{7\pi}{20}}$, $2\underline{/\dfrac{3\pi}{4}}$

11   $3.61\underline{/-168.7°}$, $3.61\underline{/11.3°}$

12   $2.24\underline{/-108.4°}$, $2.24\underline{/-18.4°}$, $2.24\underline{/71.6°}$, $2.24\underline{/161.6°}$

13   $1.12\underline{/-105°}$, $1.12\underline{/15°}$, $1.12\underline{/135°}$

14   $1.24\underline{/-159.4°}$, $1.24\underline{/-99.4°}$, $1.24\underline{/-39.4°}$, $1.24\underline{/20.6°}$, $1.24\underline{/80.6°}$,
    $1.24\underline{/140.6°}$

15   $1.58\underline{/-172.6°}$, $1.58\underline{/-100.6°}$, $1.58\underline{/-28.6°}$, $1.58\underline{/43.4°}$, $1.58\underline{/115.4°}$

Exercise 1.10

1   -1

2   $4\cos^3\theta - 3\cos\theta$, $3\sin\theta - 4\sin^3\theta$

3   $4\cos\theta\sin\theta(1 - 2\sin^2\theta)$ or $2\sin 2\theta(1 - 2\sin^2\theta)$ -

4   0.5

5   $32\cos^6\theta - 48\cos^4\theta + 18\cos^2\theta - 1$,
    $2\cos\theta\sin\theta(3 - 16\sin^2\theta + 16\sin^4\theta)$ or $\sin 2\theta(3 - 16\sin^2\theta + 16\sin^4\theta)$

Exercise 1.11

1   $5\underline{/53.13°}$ or $5\underline{/0.927}$, $30\underline{/113.13°}$ or $30\underline{/1.974}$

2   $2\underline{/135°}$, $13\underline{/67.38°}$; $0.059 + j0.142$, $0.154\underline{/67.62°}$,
    $0.154(\cos 67.62° + j\sin 67.62°)$, $0.154e^{j1.18}$

3   $-j318.3\ \Omega$, $240\underline{/0°}$ V, $0.754\underline{/90°}$ A; halved, halved, doubled

4   No, $-j2.5$, no

5   $31.23\underline{/-51.34°}$ A, 3902 W

6   $5\underline{/36.87°}$, $200.06\underline{/88.57°}$, $3.163 \times 10^{-3}\underline{/62.72°}$, $(1.45 + j2.81)10^{-3}$

7   $547.7\underline{/-0.1°}$, $547.7\underline{/179.9°}$

8   *AN*, 0.125, $0.125\underline{/0°}$; *CN*, $0.25 - j0.25$, $0.354\underline{/-45°}$; *DN*, $0.1 - j0.3$, 0.316, $\underline{/-71.57°}$; *AB*, $0.027\underline{/-3.09°}$; *BC*, $0.076\underline{/-48.09°}$; *CD*, $0.121\underline{/-66.53°}$; *AC*, $0.048\underline{/5.04°}$; *AD*, $0.043\underline{/-21.53°}$; *BD*, $0.068\underline{/-74.66°}$

9   $R = \dfrac{C_2 R_2}{C_1} - R_1, \; L = C_2 R_2 R_3$

10   50, $50\underline{/0°}$; $25 - j\,318.3$, $319.3\underline{/-85.51°}$; $98.53\underline{/-4.33°}$, $327.02\underline{/-76.74°}$, $179.5\underline{/-40.5°}$

Chapter 2

Exercise 2.1

1	2, 0, −2, 1	2	6, 2, 3.75
3	3, 11, $\sqrt{5}$ or 2.236	4	0.5, 0.5
5	−0.707, 0.707	6	2.718, 7.389, 1, 0.135
7	0.368, 0.135, 1, 7.389	8	0.8, −0.8
9	$\sqrt{2}$ or 1.414, 0	10	1.543, 1.543

Exercise 2.2

1	1-1	2	many-to-one
3	1-1	4	1-1
5	not a function	6	1-1
7	many-to-one	8	many-to-one
9	many-to-one	10	1-1
11	not a function	12	1-1
13	many-to-one	14	not a function
15	many-to-one		

Exercise 2.3

1	even	2	even
3	odd	4	neither odd nor even
5	neither odd nor even	6	neither odd nor even
7	even	8	odd

9	neither odd nor even	**10**	odd
11	even	**12**	neither odd nor even
13	odd	**14**	even
15	odd		

Exercise 2.4

1	continuous	**2**	continuous
3	discontinuous, e.g. at $x = \dfrac{\pi}{2}$	**4**	continuous
5	continuous	**6**	discontinuous, e.g. at $x = 0$
7	discontinuous, e.g. at $x = \dfrac{\pi}{2}$	**8**	continuous
9	discontinuous, e.g. at $x = 1$	**10**	continuous

Exercise 2.5

1 $y = \sin 4x$

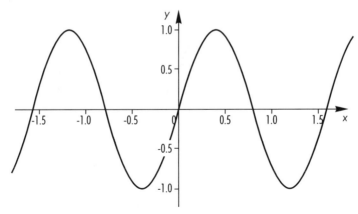

2

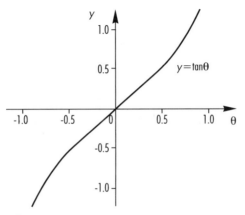

Period is π

3 $y = \cos \frac{1}{2} x$

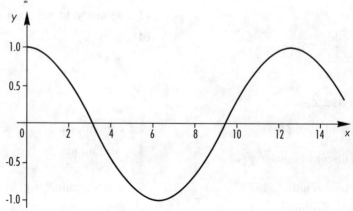

4 $y = 2 \sin \frac{1}{2} x$

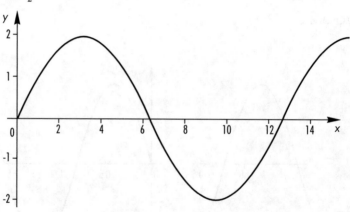

5   1   **6**   1   **7**   5

8

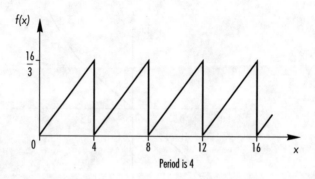

Period is 4

9

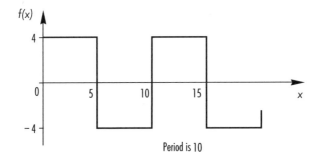

Period is 10

10

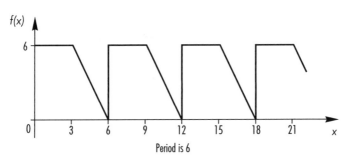

Period is 6

Exercise 2.6

1 $f^{-1}(x) = \dfrac{x}{3}$

2 $f^{-1}(x) = 2x$

3 $f^{-1}(x) = \dfrac{x-1}{2}$

4 $f^{-1}(x) = x$

5 $f^{-1}(x) = \dfrac{2}{x}$

6 $f^{-1}(x) = x^{1/3}$

7 $f^{-1}(x) = \dfrac{x^2}{9}$

8 $f^{-1}(x) = \dfrac{x^2}{3}$

9 $f^{-1}(x) = \dfrac{x^4}{16}$

10 $f^{-1}(x) = \dfrac{1}{2}e^x$

Exercise 2.7

1 71.81° or 1.253 rad

2 108.7° or 1.897 rad

3 58.78° or 1.026 rad

4 −26.74° or −0.467 rad

5 60° or 1.047 rad

6 41.81° or 0.730 rad

7 53.13° or 0.927 rad

8 53.06° or 0.926 rad

9 66.42° or 1.159 rad

10 36.87° or 0.644 rad

11 60° or 1.047 rad

12 36.87° or 0.644 rad

13 90° or 1.571 rad

14 134.43° or 2.346 rad

15 −20.49° or −0.358 rad

16 38.68° or 0.675 rad

17 56.31° or 0.983 rad

18 30° or 0.524 rad

19 $-21.80°$ or -0.381 rad

20 $72.90°$ or 1.272 rad

Exercise 2.8

1

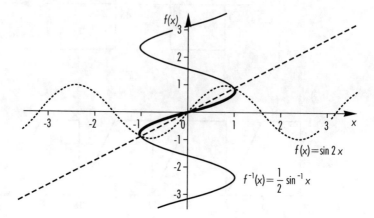

$f(x) = \sin 2x$

$f^{-1}(x) = \dfrac{1}{2} \sin^{-1} x$

2

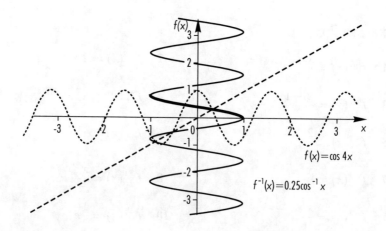

$f(x) = \cos 4x$

$f^{-1}(x) = 0.25 \cos^{-1} x$

3

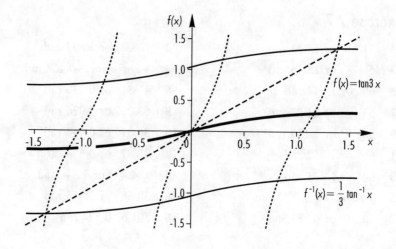

$f(x) = \tan 3x$

$f^{-1}(x) = \dfrac{1}{3} \tan^{-1} x$

4

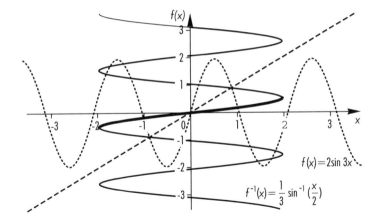

$f(x) = 2\sin 3x$

$f^{-1}(x) = \dfrac{1}{3}\sin^{-1}\left(\dfrac{x}{2}\right)$

5

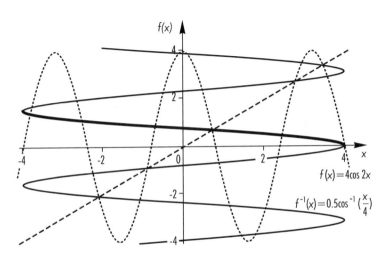

$f(x) = 4\cos 2x$

$f^{-1}(x) = 0.5\cos^{-1}\left(\dfrac{x}{4}\right)$

6

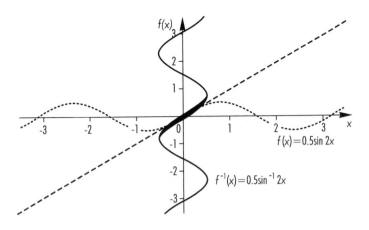

$f(x) = 0.5\sin 2x$

$f^{-1}(x) = 0.5\sin^{-1} 2x$

7

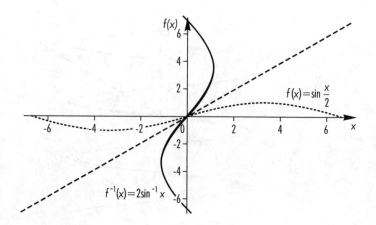

$f(x) = \sin \dfrac{x}{2}$

$f^{-1}(x) = 2\sin^{-1} x$

8

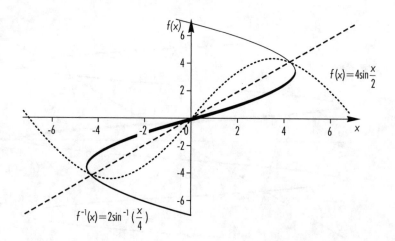

$f(x) = 4\sin\dfrac{x}{2}$

$f^{-1}(x) = 2\sin^{-1}\left(\dfrac{x}{4}\right)$

9

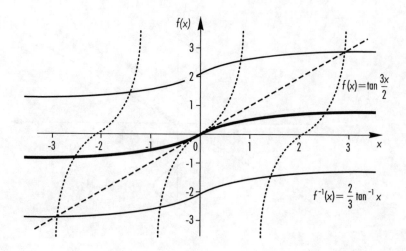

$f(x) = \tan\dfrac{3x}{2}$

$f^{-1}(x) = \dfrac{2}{3}\tan^{-1} x$

10

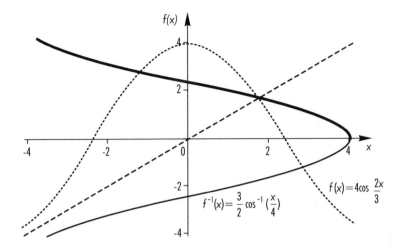

$$f^{-1}(x) = \frac{3}{2}\cos^{-1}\left(\frac{x}{4}\right)$$

$$f(x) = 4\cos\frac{2x}{3}$$

Exercise 2.9

1 $\dfrac{2}{\sqrt{1-4x^2}}$

2 $-\dfrac{3}{\sqrt{1-9x^2}}$

3 $\dfrac{\frac{1}{3}}{1+\dfrac{x^2}{9}}$

4 $\dfrac{\frac{1}{4}}{\sqrt{1-\dfrac{x^2}{16}}}$

5 $\dfrac{\frac{1}{2}}{\sqrt{1-\dfrac{x^2}{16}}}$

6 $-\dfrac{\frac{1}{2}}{\sqrt{1-\dfrac{x^2}{16}}}$

7 $\dfrac{6}{1+4x^2}$

8 $\dfrac{\frac{1}{2}}{\sqrt{1-4x^2}}$

9 $-\dfrac{\frac{15}{4}}{\sqrt{1-\dfrac{25x^2}{16}}}$

10 $\dfrac{\frac{15}{4}}{\sqrt{1-\dfrac{9x^2}{16}}}$

11 5.77 **12** 0.539

13 −0.436, −0.436 **14** 0.385

15 −0.414, 0.414; 1.707, 1.707

Exercise 2.10

1 $\pm\dfrac{\dfrac{1}{2x^2}}{\sqrt{1-\dfrac{1}{4x^2}}}$

2 $\pm\dfrac{\dfrac{1}{x^2}}{\sqrt{1-\dfrac{1}{x^2}}}$

3 $\pm \dfrac{3}{2\sqrt{x-x^2}}$

4 $\pm \dfrac{\frac{5}{2x^2}}{\sqrt{1-\frac{1}{4x^2}}}$

5 $\pm \dfrac{\frac{2}{x^2}}{\sqrt{1-\frac{4}{x^2}}}$

6 ± 0.577

7 ± 4.5

8 -1.6

9 -0.042

10 $(0.007, 0.145)$

Exercise 2.11

1 $\theta = \sin^{-1} 50A, \dfrac{50}{\sqrt{1-2500A^2}}, 114.7 \text{ rad m}^{-2}$

2 $\theta = \tan^{-1}\left(\dfrac{v^2}{gr}\right), \theta = \tan^{-1}\left(\dfrac{v^2}{1177.2}\right), 8.23 \times 10^{-4}$

3 $t = \dfrac{1}{100\pi} \sin^{-1}\left(\dfrac{v}{250}\right), 2.92 \times 10^{-5}$

4 $\dfrac{50x}{\sqrt{1-(1.25-25x^2)^2}}, 10.33$

5 $\dfrac{\frac{g}{2v^2}}{\sqrt{1-\frac{g^2R^4}{v^4}}}$

Chapter 3

Exercise 3.1

1	3.63	**2**	0.91	**3**	1.13	**4**	1.13
5	-3.63	**6**	45.00	**7**	-0.91	**8**	1.97
9	1.94	**10**	-5.40	**11**	1.19	**12**	0.76
13	1.61	**14**	1.99	**15**	0.52	**16**	0.26
17	-1.19	**18**	0.126	**19**	-0.52	**20**	0

Exercise 3.2

1	0.060	**2**	1.129	**3**	0.337	**4**	0.337
5	1.879	**6**	-0.060	**7**	-1.129	**8**	0.930
9	-0.060	**10**	2.001	**11**	1.205	**12**	0.414
13	0.362	**14**	-0.414	**15**	0.179	**16**	2.993
17	1.474	**18**	0.286	**19**	-0.362	**20**	0.277

Exercise 3.3

10 i) $\cosh(x - y)$ ii) $\cosh 2x$

Exercise 3.4

1 $\cos 2x = 1 - 2\sin^2 x$

2 $\sin(x - y) = \sin x \cos y - \cos x \sin y$

3 $\sin 2x = 2\sin x \cos x$

4 $\sec^2 x = 1 + \tan^2 x$

5 $\tan(x + y) = \dfrac{\tan x + \tan y}{1 - \tan x \tan y}$

6 $\cosh(x - y) = \cosh x \cosh y - \sinh x \sinh y$

7 $\cosh 2x = 2\cosh^2 x - 1$

8 $\tanh 2x = \dfrac{2\tanh x}{1 + \tanh^2 x}$

9 $\sinh(x + y) = \sinh x \cosh y + \cosh x \sinh y$

10 $\sinh 2x = \dfrac{2\tanh x}{1 - \tanh^2 x}$

Exercise 3.5

1 $4\cosh 4x$

2 $3\sinh 3x$

3 $3\operatorname{sech}^2 3t$

4 $\dfrac{1}{2}\sinh \dfrac{x}{2}$

5 $2\sinh t \cosh t$ or $\sinh 2t$

6 $2\cosh t \sinh t$ or $\sinh 2t$

7 $-\dfrac{\sinh x}{\cosh^2 x}$ or $-\tanh x \operatorname{sech} x$

8 $-2\dfrac{\cosh 2x}{\sinh^2 2x}$ or $-2\coth 2x \operatorname{cosech} 2x$

9 $-a\operatorname{cosech}^2 ax$

10 $\cosh 2x$

11 0

12 $2\sinh 2x$

13 $2\operatorname{sech}^2 2x$

14 $3\tanh 3t$

15 $3\coth 3t$

16 $\sinh x(\operatorname{sech}^2 x + 1)$

17 $\cosh x$

18 $\sinh x$

19 $\dfrac{\operatorname{sech}^2 t}{\tanh t}$ or $\dfrac{2}{\sinh 2t}$

20 $2\tanh t \operatorname{sech}^2 t$

21 4.77

22 0.521

23 -12.71

24 57.94

25 It is a constant, i.e. 1.

Exercise 3.6

1 $\frac{1}{3}\sinh 3x + c$

2 $2\cosh\frac{1}{2}x + c$

3 $3\cosh\frac{x}{3} + \frac{2}{3}\cosh\frac{3}{2}x + c$

4 $\frac{1}{4}\tanh 2x + c$

5 $\frac{1}{12}\cosh 6x + c$

6 7.254

7 0.762

8 0.613

9 5.102

10 0.632

Exercise 3.7

1 1.0109

2 93.35 m. When $x = 0$ we need $y = 75$.

3 $7.5\sinh 0.25t + 240\cosh 0.25t$, 243 V

4 2.05. Odd function

5 b) 2.129 unit^2, 3.529 unit^2, 1.40 unit^2

Chapter 4

Exercise 4.1

1 explicit

2 $xy - 24 = 0$, implicit; $y = \frac{24}{x}$, explicit

3 $x^2 + y^2 = 9$, implicit; $y = \sqrt{9 - x^2}$, explicit, $y = -\sqrt{9 - x^2}$, explicit

4 implicit

5 $x^2 + y^2 - 2x - 4y = 0$, implicit; $y = 2 + \sqrt{5 - (x - 1)^2}$, explicit,

$y = 2 - \sqrt{5 - (x - 1)^2}$, explicit

6 explicit

7 implicit   **8** implicit   **9** implicit   **10** implicit

Exercise 4.2

1 $-\frac{x}{y}$

2 $\frac{1 - x}{y - 2}$

3 $\frac{-y}{x}$

4 $\frac{4}{3x^3 y^2}$

5 $-\dfrac{1}{3(y^2 + e^{3y})}$

6 $-\dfrac{25x}{4y}$

7 $\dfrac{2y - 3x^2}{3y^2 - 2x}$

8 $\dfrac{\sin x}{1 + \cos y}$

9 $-\dfrac{(3x + 4y)x}{2x^2 + 3y^2}$

10 $\dfrac{\cos y}{1 + x \sin y}$

Exercise 4.3

1 $\dfrac{12x + 1 - 3\cos(3x + y)}{\cos(3x + y)}$

2 $\dfrac{1 + 2e^{(2x+y)}}{1 - e^{(2x+y)}}$

3 $\dfrac{\sin(x + 5y) - 9}{1 - 5\sin(x + 5y)}$

4 $\dfrac{-\sec^2(x + y)}{\sec^2(x + y) + \tan y}$

5 $\dfrac{3e^{(3x-y)} + 8x + 1}{3 + e^{(3x-y)}}$

6 $\dfrac{2e^{(3y-2x)} - 4x + y}{3e^{(3y-2x)} - x - 2y}$

7 $\dfrac{1 - y\cos(xy)}{5 + x\cos(xy)}$

8 $-\dfrac{1 + y^2 \sin(xy^2)}{1 + 2xy \sin(xy^2)}$

9 $2(4x^3 - 3x^2 + 2y)$

10 $\dfrac{y(6 - 2y^2)}{-y - 6x + 2xy^2}$

11 $\dfrac{(4x^2 - 1)y}{(2 - y)x}$

12 $\dfrac{7 - ye^{xy}}{1 + xe^{xy}}$

13 $\dfrac{2(3x - y)e^{(3x^2y)}}{xe^{(3x^2y)}}$

14 $\dfrac{(2x - 1)y}{(4y - 1)x}$

15 $\dfrac{4x(1 - y^3 e^{(2x^2y^3)})}{5 + 6x^2y^2 e^{(2x^2y^3)}}$

Exercise 4.4

1 $\dfrac{2t - xe^t}{e^t}$

2 $-\dfrac{6}{\pi}\left(\dfrac{3}{\pi} + \sqrt{3}\right)$

3 $49e^{-2t} - 2y$

4 8.22 ms^{-2}

5 $\dfrac{2(5 - (3y - 2)(t - 24))}{3(t - 24)^2}$, 0.027 mh^{-1}

Exercise 4.5

1 i) $-\dfrac{1}{\sin y}$,

ii) $-\dfrac{1}{\sqrt{1 - x^2}}$

2 i) $\dfrac{1}{1 + \tan^2 y}$,

ii) $\dfrac{1}{1 + x^2}$

3 i) $-\dfrac{\tan y}{x}$,

ii) $-\dfrac{1}{x\sqrt{x^2 - 1}}$

4 i) $-\dfrac{\sin y}{\sin y + x\cos y}$ or

$-\dfrac{1}{1 + x\cot y}$,

ii) $-\dfrac{1}{1 + x^2}$

5 i) $\dfrac{1}{3\cos 3y}$,

ii) $\dfrac{1}{3\sqrt{1 - x^2}}$

6 i) $-\dfrac{2}{\sin y}$,

ii) $-\dfrac{2}{\sqrt{1 - 4x^2}}$

7 0.25

8 not defined

9 −0.77

10 11.31

Exercise 4.6

1 max $(0.125, 0.25)$, min $(0.125, -0.25)$

2 max $(0.464, 0.354)$

3 $y = -27$, max

4 min $(0, 1)$

5 max $(0.469, 0.039)$, min $(1.516, -0.023)$

Chapter 5

Exercise 5.1

1 t, $y^2 = 4x$

2 t, $2y^2 = 9x$

3 t, $y = x^2 - 1$

4 θ, $x^2 + y^2 = 25$

5 θ, $x^2 + \dfrac{y^2}{4} = 1$

6 t, $xy = 4$

7 ϕ, $x^2 + y^2 = 9$

8 t, $xy = 8$

9 θ, $\dfrac{x^2}{4} + y^2 = 1$

10 t, $27y^2 = 2x^3$

Exercise 5.2

1 $\dfrac{3}{2t}$

2 $\dfrac{4t}{3}$

3 t

4 $-\tan\theta$

5 $-4\cot\theta$

6 $-\dfrac{1}{t^2}$

7 $-0.5\tan\phi$

8 $-\dfrac{2}{t^4}$

9 $-0.5 \tan 3\theta$

10 $\dfrac{1}{t}$

11 $\dfrac{\sin \theta - 1}{\cos \theta}$ or $\tan \theta - \sec \theta$, -0.577

12 $-t \sin t$, $t \cos t$, 1.5

13 $i = -0.2 e^{-50t}$, $-400\ \mathrm{VA}^{-1}$

14 $\dfrac{t^2 - 1}{t^2 + 1}$, 1, -1

15 10, $35 - 30t$, $\dfrac{7}{6}$

Exercise 5.3

1 0.25

2 $-\dfrac{3}{4t^3}$

3 $-\dfrac{8}{\sin^3 \theta}$

4 $-\dfrac{1}{12} \sec^3 \phi$

5 $\dfrac{3}{16} t^5$

6 $-4\left(\dfrac{t+2}{t^2+4t}\right)^3$

7 $\left(\dfrac{t^2+1}{t^2-1}\right)^3$

8 $\dfrac{\sin \theta \cos \theta - \theta}{\sin^3 \theta}$

9 $\dfrac{\sin \theta - 1}{\cos \theta}$, $\dfrac{\sin \theta - 1}{\cos^3 \theta}$, -0.414, -0.828

10 $t \cos t$, $-t \sin t$; $0, \pi, 2\pi \ldots$; $-\tan t$, $-\dfrac{\sec^3 t}{t}$, -3.40

Chapter 6

Exercise 6.1

1 $\left(\dfrac{6x^2 + 10x}{2x^3 + 5x^2} + \dfrac{2x + 28x^3}{x^2 + 7x^4}\right) y$

or $\left(\dfrac{6x^2 + 10x}{2x^3 + 5x^2} + \dfrac{2x + 28x^3}{x^2 + 7x^4}\right)(2x^3 + 5x^2)(x^2 + 7x^4)$, 56, 338

2 $\left(\dfrac{6t^2}{1 + 2t^3} + \dfrac{\cos t}{\sin t}\right) y$ or $\left(\dfrac{6t^2}{1 + 2t^3} + \dfrac{\cos t}{\sin t}\right)(1 + 2t^3) \sin t$, 14.01

3 $(1 - \tan \theta) y$ or $(1 - \tan \theta) e^{\theta} \cos \theta$, -1.04

4 $\left(\dfrac{-\frac{1}{2} x^{-1/2}}{7 - x^{1/2}} + \dfrac{2 + 3x^2}{2x + x^3}\right) y$ or $\left(\dfrac{-\frac{1}{2} x^{-1/2}}{7 - x^{1/2}} + \dfrac{2 + 3x^2}{2x + x^3}\right)(7 - x^{1/2})(2x + x^3)$,

360, 232

5 $2\left(1 + \dfrac{\cos(2t + \pi)}{\sin(2t + \pi)}\right) y$ or $2\left(1 + \dfrac{\cos(2t + \pi)}{\sin(2t + \pi)}\right) e^{2t} \sin(2t + \pi)$, -7.51

Exercise 6.2

1 $\left(\dfrac{3+2x}{1+3x+x^2}+\dfrac{2x}{1-x^2}\right)y$ or $\left(\dfrac{3+2x}{1+3x+x^2}+\dfrac{2x}{1-x^2}\right)\left(\dfrac{1+3x+x^2}{1-x^2}\right)$,

8.71, 40.2

2 $\left(\dfrac{\cos t}{\sin t}-\dfrac{1}{1+t}\right)y$ or $\left(\dfrac{\cos t}{\sin t}-\dfrac{1}{1+t}\right)\dfrac{\sin t}{(1+t)}$, -0.278

3 $\left(\dfrac{3\cos 3\theta}{\sin 3\theta}-2\right)y$ or $\left(\dfrac{3\cos 3\theta}{\sin 3\theta}-2\right)\dfrac{2\sin 3\theta}{e^{2\theta}}$, -1.47

4 $\left(\dfrac{2\cos 2t-\sin t}{\sin 2t+\cos t}-\dfrac{1}{t}\right)\theta$ or $\left(\dfrac{2\cos 2t-\sin t}{\sin 2t+\cos t}-\dfrac{1}{t}\right)\left(\dfrac{\sin 2t+\cos t}{3t}\right)$,

0.244, -0.875

5 $\left(-\dfrac{\sin\theta}{\cos\theta}-\dfrac{\cos\theta}{\sin\theta}\right)y$ or $-\dfrac{1}{\sin^2\theta}$, -4.35

Exercise 6.3

1 $\left(\dfrac{1}{x+2}-\dfrac{2x}{3-x^2}+\dfrac{\cos x}{\sin x}\right)y$ or

$(3-4x-3x^2)\sin x+(x+2)(3-x^2)\cos x$

2 $\left(\dfrac{2}{2x-1}-\dfrac{1}{x+2}-\dfrac{4}{3+4x}\right)y$ or

$\dfrac{2}{(x+2)(3+4x)}-\dfrac{2x-1}{(x+2)^2(3+4x)}-\dfrac{4(2x-1)}{(x+2)(3+4x)^2}$

3 $\left(\dfrac{2t}{t^2-2}+\sin t+t\cos t\right)y$ or $\left(\dfrac{2t}{t^2-2}+\sin t+t\cos t\right)(t^2-2)e^{t\sin t}$

4 $\left(\dfrac{1}{\theta}-2-4\tan 4\theta\right)y$ or $2(\cos 4\theta-2\theta\cos 4\theta-4\theta\sin 4\theta)e^{-2\theta}$

5 $\left(\dfrac{\cos t}{\sin t}+\cos t-t\sin t\right)y$ or $(\cos t+\cos t\sin t-t\sin^2 t)e^{t\cos t}$

6 $-\left(\tan t+\dfrac{1}{t}+1\right)y$ or $-\left(\sin t+\dfrac{\cos t}{t}+\cos t\right)\dfrac{e^{-t}}{t}$

7 $\left(\dfrac{1}{\theta}+\dfrac{2\cos 2\theta}{\sin 2\theta}-\dfrac{2\theta}{\theta^2+2}\right)y$ or $\left(\dfrac{1}{\theta}+\dfrac{2\cos 2\theta}{\sin 2\theta}-\dfrac{2\theta}{\theta^2+2}\right)\dfrac{\theta\sin 2\theta}{(\theta^2+2)}$

8 $\left(\dfrac{1}{1+2x}+\dfrac{\cos 2x}{\sin 2x}\right)y$ or $\left(\dfrac{1}{1+2x}+\dfrac{\cos 2x}{\sin 2x}\right)\sqrt{(1+2x)\sin 2x}$

9 $2\left(\dfrac{1}{1+2x}-\tan 2x-2\right)y$ or $2\left(\dfrac{1}{1+2x}-\tan 2x-2\right)\dfrac{(1+2x)\cos 2x}{e^{4x}}$

10 $\dfrac{1}{2}\left(-\dfrac{\sin x}{1+\cos x}-\dfrac{(1+\cos x)}{x+\sin x}\right)y$ or

$\dfrac{1}{2}\left(-\dfrac{\sin x}{1+\cos x}-\dfrac{(1+\cos x)}{x+\sin x}\right)\sqrt{\dfrac{1+\cos x}{x+\sin x}}$

Exercise 6.4

1 $\dfrac{-2(1+\tan(2t+\pi/4))5\cos(2t+\pi/4)}{e^{2t}}$, 0.930

2 $\left(1.5-\dfrac{2}{t^2}+\dfrac{6}{t}+4.5t\right)e^{3t}$

3 $3(2\cos^2\theta-\sin^2\theta)\sin\theta$, 1.06; 0, $\dfrac{\pi}{2}$ radians; 0, -3

4 $0.6\left(2\cos 3t-\dfrac{\sin 3t}{t+1}\right)\dfrac{\sin 3t}{(t+1)^3}$, 0.00115 rads^{-1}

5 $\left(\dfrac{1}{t}-0.25-6\tan 6t\right)y$, 3.733; $\left(\dfrac{1}{t}-0.25+\dfrac{6\cos 6t}{\sin 6t}\right)x$, -8.647

Chapter 7

Exercise 7.1

1 i) 4, ii) 4, iii) 4   **2** 2.73

3 16   **4** 20.9 unit^3

5 2.36 unit^2 **6** £665 233

7 E, t are independent; i is dependent

8 259   **9** 1.78

10 0.25 m^3; same due to symmetry of r and R.

Exercise 7.2

1 $5x^4y, x^5$ **2** $1, 5y^4$

3 $\dfrac{1}{y}, -\dfrac{x}{y^2}$ **4** $2x\ln y, \dfrac{x^2}{y}$

5 $y\cos xy, x\cos xy$ **6** $3x^2y^2+2xy^3, 2x^3y+3x^2y^2$

7 $3\sin y, 3x\cos y$ **8** $\dfrac{1}{x+y}, \dfrac{1}{x+y}$

9 $\dfrac{2}{2x+3y}, \dfrac{3}{2x+3y}$ **10** $\dfrac{1}{x}, \dfrac{1}{y}$

11 $\dfrac{2}{3}\pi rh$, 0.34 m^2 **12** $\sqrt{1+\mu^2}$, 1.04

13 $-\dfrac{1}{4\pi\sqrt{L^3 C}}$, -0.32

14 $\dfrac{BD^2}{4}$, 0.037 m^3

15 $-\dfrac{kAt}{x^2}$, -4.4×10^6 Wm^{-1}

Exercise 7.3

1 $2x\cos(x^2 + 3y)$, $3\cos(x^2 + 3y)$

2 $3y^2 e^{3xy^2}$, $6xy e^{3xy^2}$

3 $-8\sin(2x - 5y^2)$, $40y\sin(2x - 5y^2)$

4 $\dfrac{xy}{x - y} + y\ln(x - y)$, $-\dfrac{xy}{x - y} + x\ln(x - y)$

5 $\sin 2xy + 2(x + y)y\cos 2xy$, $\sin 2xy + 2(x + y)x\cos 2xy$

6 $8x(x^2 - y^2)^3$, $-8y(x^2 - y^2)^3$

7 $\dfrac{xy(x + 2y)}{(x + y)^2}$, $\dfrac{x^3}{(x + y)^2}$

8 $\dfrac{1 - (x - y)y}{e^{xy}}$, $\dfrac{-(1 + (x - y)x)}{e^{xy}}$

9 $\dfrac{x^2 - 2xy - y^2}{(x - y)^2}$, $\dfrac{x^2 + 2xy - y^2}{(x - y)^2}$

10 $\dfrac{2x(y^2 - xy - x^2)}{(x + y)^2}$, $\dfrac{2x^3}{(x + y)^2}$

11 $\dfrac{C_2{}^2}{(C_1 + C_2)^2}$, $\dfrac{C_1{}^2}{(C_1 + C_2)^2}$, 0.224, 0.277

12 $\dfrac{\pi D^3}{8}$, 0.036 m^3

13 $\dfrac{V_R}{\sqrt{V_R{}^2 + (V_L - V_C)^2}}$

14 $\dfrac{\pi a}{\sqrt{\tfrac{1}{2}(a^2 + b^2)}}$, 4.2

15 $\dfrac{1}{2}\sqrt{\dfrac{g\tan\theta}{r}}$, $\dfrac{1}{2}gr\sec^2\theta(gr\tan\theta)^{-1/2}$, 0.06 s^{-1}, 42.1 ms^{-1}rad^{-1};

$gr\left(\dfrac{1 + \mu^2}{(\cos\theta - \mu\sin\theta)^2}\right)$

Exercise 7.4

1 $12x\ln y$, $-\dfrac{2x^3}{y^2}$, $\dfrac{6x^2}{y}$

2 $-\cos(x + y)$, $-\cos(x + y)$, $-\cos(x + y)$

3 $16e^{4x-3y}$, $9e^{4x-3y}$, $-12e^{4x-3y}$

4 $-4y^2\sin 2xy$, $-4x^2\sin 2xy$, $2\cos 2xy - 4xy\sin 2xy$

5 $4\cos y$, $-2x^2\cos y$, $-4x\sin y$

6 $24(2x+3y)$, $54(2x+3y)$, $36(2x+3y)$

7 $12xy$, $12xy$, $6(x^2+y^2)$

8 $-\dfrac{(2-(x+y)y)y}{e^{xy}}$, $-\dfrac{(2-(x+y)x)x}{e^{xy}}$, $\dfrac{(x+y)(xy-2)}{e^{xy}}$

9 $2y^2(3x+y)$, $2x^2(3y+x)$, $6xy(x+y)$

10 $\dfrac{2y}{x^3}$, $\dfrac{2x}{y^3}$, $-\dfrac{(x^2+y^2)}{x^2y^2}$

Exercise 7.5

1 -0.12 m^2

2 $-\dfrac{1}{4\pi\sqrt{CL^3}}$, $-\dfrac{1}{4\pi\sqrt{LC^3}}$, -5.855×10^6

3 0.034

4 -2.25%

5 $-\dfrac{kAT}{x^2}$, -4.4×10^6; $\dfrac{kT}{x}$, $110\,000$; $\dfrac{kA}{x}$, 2200; -2200 W

Exercise 7.6

1 0.027 m^{3}s^{-1} **2** 630 W

3 7.2×10^{-3} As^{-1} **4** 0.362 ms^{-2}

5 -0.025 ms^{-1}

Chapter 8

Exercise 8.1

1 18 **2** 12 **3** -4 **4** 36

5 108 **6** 108 **7** 48 **8** -28

9 6 **10** 48

Exercise 8.2

1 $10.9°$ **2** $68.6°$ **3** $122.6°$ **4** $133.9°$

5 $59.2°$ **6** $90°$ **7** $31.4°$ **8** $83.5°$

9 $123.6°$ **10** $135.5°$

Exercise 8.3

1	-1.11	**2**	-3.04	**3**	7.21	**4**	-0.866
5	1.35			**6**	-0.707 and 3.54		
7	3.58 and -2.68			**8**	0.707 and 3.54		
9	0 and 3.61			**10**	-2.22 and 3.88		

Exercise 8.4

1 24 J; 0 because F and s are perpendicular.

2 -73

3 -8 J

4 21 W, 1.125 J

Exercise 8.5

1	$23i + 0.5j + 3.5k$	**2**	$-4i - 19j - 2.5k$
3	$2.5i + 20.5j + 3k$	**4**	$46i + j + 7k$
5	$345i + 7.5j + 52.5k$	**6**	$345i + 7.5j + 52.5k$
7	$60i + 24j - 6k$	**8**	$-35i + 54.25j - 42k$
9	$7.5i + 61.5j + 9k$	**10**	$-60i - 24j + 6k$

Exercise 8.6

1	$7i - 6j - k$	**2**	$-7i + 1.5j - 0.5k$
3	$12i + 6j - 66k$ or $6(2i + j - 11k)$	**4**	$-4.5j + 9k$
5	$6i - 2k$	**6**	$4i - 5j + k$
7	$16i - 11j + 21k$	**8**	$2i - 18j - 24k$
9	$-13.5i + 5j - 3k$	**10**	$22i - 21j + 61k$

Exercise 8.7

1 i) 9.87 unit^2, ii) 20 unit^2 **4** $-0.42i + 0.525j - 1.05k$ ms^{-1}

5 $60.5i - 7j - 5k$ Nm

Exercise 8.8

1	19	**2**	9	**3**	2	**4**	-10
5	29	**6**	19	**7**	76	**8**	-21
9	19.5	**10**	-152				

Exercise 8.9

1    $-18i - 76j - 7k$

2    $-37i + 29j - 50k$

3    $-27.75i + 16.25j - 21k$

4    $-8i - 10j - 15k$

5    $-46.5i + 84j + 52k$

Exercise 8.10

1    $3x^2i + 6xj + 4x^3k$

2    $3x^2i + (4x + 1)j - 2k$

3    $i - (2\sin 2\theta)j + (2\cos 2\theta)k$

4    $3t^2i - 4t^3j + 10tk$

5    $-2xi + 6xj + 4x^3k$

6    $3(e^{3t}i + (\cos 3t)k), 9(e^{3t}i - (\sin 3t)k)$

7    $3t^2j + (6t + 1)k, 6(tj + k)$

8    $9t^2i + (8t - 1)j - 7k, 18ti + 8j$

9    $(6t^2 + 1)i + (2 - 6t)j + tk, 12ti - 6j + k$

10   $e^{3t}\{(3\cos t - \sin t)i + (3\sin t + \cos t)j\} + k,$
     $2e^{3t}\{(4\cos t - 3\sin t)i + (4\sin t + 3\cos t)j\}$

Exercise 8.11

1    $3i + \dfrac{1}{t}j, -\dfrac{1}{t^2}j; 3i + 0.25j, -0.0625j$

2    $p(1.73i - k), -p^2(i + 1.73k); p\sin 2pt(i - k), 2p^2\cos 2pt(i - k)$

3   4.46

4    $(\cos t)i + j + (\sin t)k, -(\sin t)i + (\cos t)k, 1.414, 1, (1 + t^2)^{1/2},$
     $t(1 + t^2)^{-1/2}, (1 + t^2)^{-3/2}$

6    $2\{-(\sin t + 1)j + (\cos t - t)k\}, 2\sqrt{2 + 2\sin t - 2t\cos t + t^2}$

7    $45°$

9    $(-a\omega \sin \theta)i + a\omega(1 + \cos \theta)j, -a\omega^2\{(1 + 2\cos \theta)i + 2(\sin \theta)j\}$

Exercise 8.12

1    $2(xy + z)i + x^2j + 2xk$

2    $(3x^2y^2z + 3y^3z^2)i + (2x^3yz + 9xy^2z^2)j + (x^3y^2 + 6xy^3z)k$

3    $(3\cos 3x + 2xz^3)i + 2j + 3x^2z^2k$

4    $(2e^{2x}\cos 4y)i - (4e^{2x}\sin 4y)j$

5    $\dfrac{2x(y^2 + z)i + 2y(z - x^2)j - (x^2 + y^2)k}{(x^2 + y^2)^2}$

6   3

7   0

8 $x(1 + 3y)$

9 $\cos(x + y) - \sin(y - z) + 3xy$

10 $ye^{xy} + ze^{yz}$

11 $(1 - x)\mathbf{k}$

12 $-z\mathbf{j}$

13 $-z\mathbf{i} + (y - 1)\mathbf{k}$

14 $\mathbf{i} - \mathbf{j} - (y \sin xy + \sin(x - y))\mathbf{k}$

15 $-(e^{y+z}\mathbf{i} + e^{z+x}\mathbf{j} + e^{x+y}\mathbf{k})$

16   i) vector,   ii) scalar,   iii) scalar,   iv) vector,   v) vector,   vi) scalar

17 $16(3\mathbf{i} - 4\mathbf{j})$

18 $2x^2 + y^2 - z^2$; they both need a vector rather than a scalar to operate upon; $4x\mathbf{i} + 2y\mathbf{j} - 2z\mathbf{k}$

19 $\dfrac{-(x\mathbf{i} + y\mathbf{j} + z\mathbf{k})}{(x^2 + y^2 + z^2)^{3/2}}$

20 $2 - (x \sin z)$, $-(\cos z)\mathbf{j} - (\cos y)\mathbf{k}$, $(\sin y - \sin z)\mathbf{i}$, grad operates on a scalar only.

Exercise 8.13

3   irrotational   **4**   0   **5**   yes

Chapter 9

Exercise 9.1

1 $\dfrac{(2x - 1)^4}{8} + c$ **2** $\dfrac{(2x - 1)^4}{6} + c$

3 $-\dfrac{2}{7(7x + 3)} + c$ **4** $\dfrac{10(x - 3)^{3/2}}{3} + c$

5 $\dfrac{8(3x + 2)^{1/2}}{3} + c$ **6**   5.133

7   18.078   **8**   0.342   **9**   0.095   **10**   0.685

Exercise 9.2

1   0.305   **2**   0.178   **3**   0.424   **4**   0.270

5   0.196

Exercise 9.3

1 $\dfrac{(3x^2-5)^4}{4}+c$

2 $-\dfrac{(3x^2-5)^4}{4}+c$

3 $\dfrac{4(x^2+7)^{7/4}}{7}+c$

4 $\dfrac{(2x^2-1)^3}{12}+c$

5 $\dfrac{(x^3-5)^5}{30}+c$

6 24.8

7 2.727

8 0.002

9 0.005

10 1.173

Exercise 9.4

1 1.179

2 0.223

3 0.203

4 0.346

5 1.881

Exercise 9.5

1 6.246

2 0.218

3 0.077

4 5.311

5 0.636

Exercise 9.6

1 0.203

2 0.051

3 0.486

4 0.102

5 0.549

Exercise 9.7

1 $\arcsin\dfrac{x}{5}+c$

2 $-7\arcsin x+c$

3 $2.5\arctan\dfrac{x}{2}+c$

4 $4\arcsin\dfrac{x}{3}+c$

5 $\dfrac{1}{16}\arctan\dfrac{x}{4}+c$

6 5.358

7 -0.306

8 0.015

9 3.248

10 0.040

Exercise 9.8

1 $\dfrac{1}{3}\arctan\dfrac{x}{3}+\ln(x^2+9)+c$

2 $\arcsin\dfrac{x}{2}-8(4-x^2)^{1/2}+c$

3 $\dfrac{1}{4}\ln(x^2+9)-\dfrac{2}{3}\arctan\dfrac{x}{3}+c$

4 $\arcsin x+(1-x^2)^{1/2}+c$

5 $1.25\arctan\dfrac{x}{2}+0.5\ln(x^2+4)+c$

Exercise 9.9

1 0.5   **2** 0.068   **3** $0.\overline{3}$ **4** 134.5

5 1.62

Exercise 9.10

1 4.89 m, 6.92 m

2 $(1 + 9x)^{1/2}$, 8.36

3 $3(5t + 1)(5t^2 + 2t)^{1/2}$, $3(5t + 1)(5t^2 + 2t)^{1/2}$; 1186 N

4 $\dfrac{C}{1 - n}(V_2^{1-n} - V_1^{1-n})$, $\dfrac{C}{1 - n}V_1^{1-n}(2^{1-n} - 1)$

5 i) 1.528 unit^3,   ii) 2.585 unit^3,   iii) 1.698 unit^3

Chapter 10

Exercise 10.1

1 not convergent	**2** convergent
3 convergent	**4** not convergent
5 convergent	**6** strictly monotonic decreasing
7 strictly monotonic decreasing	**8** strictly monotonic increasing
9 strictly monotonic increasing	**10** strictly monotonic decreasing

Exercise 10.2

1 1   **2** $\dfrac{1}{2}$ **3** $\dfrac{2}{3}$ **4** 2

5 $\dfrac{4}{5}$ **6** 1   **7** 0   **8** ∞

9 1   **10** 2

Exercise 10.3

1 divergent	**2** divergent
3 convergent	**4** convergent
5 convergent	**6** convergent
7 divergent	**8** divergent
9 convergent	**10** divergent

Exercise 10.4

1 $\cosh x = \cosh 1 + (x-1)\sinh 1 + \dfrac{(x-1)^2}{2!}\cosh 1 + \dfrac{(x-1)^3}{3!}\sinh 1 \ldots$

2 $\dfrac{1}{x} = \dfrac{1}{a} - \dfrac{(x-a)}{a^2} + \dfrac{(x-a)^2}{a^3} - \dfrac{(x-a)^3}{a^4} \cdots$

3 a)   i) $\cos(x+\alpha) = \cos x - \alpha\sin x - \dfrac{\alpha^2}{2!}\cos x + \dfrac{\alpha^3}{3!}\sin x \ldots$

      ii) $\sin(x+\alpha) = \sin x + \alpha\cos x - \dfrac{\alpha^2}{2!}\sin x - \dfrac{\alpha^3}{3!}\cos x \ldots$

      iii) $\cos(x-\alpha) = \cos x + \alpha\sin x - \dfrac{\alpha^2}{2!}\cos x - \dfrac{\alpha^3}{3!}\sin x \ldots$

      iv) $\sin(x-\alpha) = \sin x - \alpha\cos x - \dfrac{\alpha^2}{2!}\sin x + \dfrac{\alpha^3}{3!}\cos x \ldots$

   b)   i) -0.035 ii) -0.996 iii) -0.999 iv) -0.044

4 $x^2\left((x-1) - \dfrac{(x-1)^2}{2} + \dfrac{(x-1)^3}{3} - \dfrac{(x-1)^4}{4} \cdots \right)$

5 $(1+\ln x)x^x$, $(1+\ln x)^2 x^x + x^{x-1}$, $x^x = 1 + (x-1) + (x-1)^2 \ldots$

Exercise 10.5

1 $2x - \dfrac{(2x)^3}{3!} + \dfrac{(2x)^5}{5!} \ldots$ or $2x - \dfrac{4}{3}x^3 + \dfrac{4}{15}x^5 \ldots$

2 $1 - \dfrac{(3x)^2}{2!} + \dfrac{(3x)^4}{4!} \ldots$ or $1 - \dfrac{9}{2}x^2 + \dfrac{27}{8}x^4 \ldots$

3 $1 + 2x + \dfrac{(2x)^2}{2!} + \dfrac{(2x)^3}{3!} + \dfrac{(2x)^4}{4!} + \dfrac{(2x)^5}{5!} \ldots$ or

    $1 + 2x + 2x^2 + \dfrac{4}{3}x^3 + \dfrac{2}{3}x^4 + \dfrac{4}{15}x^5 \ldots$

4 $x - \dfrac{x^2}{2} + \dfrac{x^3}{3} - \dfrac{x^4}{4} + \dfrac{x^5}{5} \ldots$

5 $1 - 2x + \dfrac{(2x)^2}{2!} - \dfrac{(2x)^3}{3!} + \dfrac{(2x)^4}{4!} - \dfrac{(2x)^5}{5!} \ldots$ or

    $1 - 2x + 2x^2 - \dfrac{4}{3}x^3 + \dfrac{2}{3}x^4 - \dfrac{4}{15}x^5 \ldots$

6 $1 - x + \dfrac{x^2}{2!} - \dfrac{x^3}{3!} + \dfrac{x^4}{4!} - \dfrac{x^5}{5!} \ldots$

7 $1 + nx + \dfrac{n(n-1)x^2}{2!} + \dfrac{n(n-1)(n-2)x^3}{3!} + \dfrac{n(n-1)(n-2)(n-3)x^4}{4!}$

    $+ \dfrac{n(n-1)(n-2)(n-3)(n-4)x^5}{5!} \ldots$

8 $-x - \dfrac{x^2}{2} - \dfrac{x^3}{3} - \dfrac{x^4}{4} - \dfrac{x^5}{5} \ldots$ or $-\left(x + \dfrac{x^2}{2} + \dfrac{x^3}{3} + \dfrac{x^4}{4} + \dfrac{x^5}{5} \ldots\right)$

9 $2x + \dfrac{(2x)^3}{3!} + \dfrac{(2x)^5}{5!} \ldots$ or $2x + \dfrac{4}{3}x^3 + \dfrac{4}{15}x^5 \ldots$

10 $1 + \dfrac{(3x)^2}{2!} + \dfrac{(3x)^4}{4!} \ldots$ or $1 + \dfrac{9}{2}x^2 + \dfrac{27}{8}x^4 \ldots$

11 $1 - \dfrac{(3x)^2}{2!} + \dfrac{(3x)^4}{4!} \ldots$ or $1 - \dfrac{9}{2}x^2 + \dfrac{27}{8}x^4 \ldots$

12 $\dfrac{x}{2} - \dfrac{(x/2)^3}{3!} + \dfrac{(x/2)^5}{5!} \ldots$ or $\dfrac{x}{2} - \dfrac{x^3}{48} + \dfrac{x^5}{3840} \ldots$

13 $1 - x + x^2 - x^3 + x^4 - x^5 \ldots$

14 $1 + \dfrac{x}{2} + \dfrac{(x/2)^2}{2!} + \dfrac{(x/2)^3}{3!} + \dfrac{(x/2)^4}{4!} + \dfrac{(x/2)^5}{5!} \ldots$ or

$1 + \dfrac{x}{2} + \dfrac{x^2}{8} + \dfrac{x^3}{48} + \dfrac{x^4}{384} + \dfrac{x^5}{3840} \ldots$

15 $2x - \dfrac{(2x)^2}{2} + \dfrac{(2x)^3}{3} - \dfrac{(2x)^4}{4} + \dfrac{(2x)^5}{5} \ldots$ or

$2x - 2x^2 + \dfrac{8}{3}x^3 - 4x^4 + \dfrac{32}{5}x^5 \ldots$

Exercise 10.6

1 $2\left(x + \dfrac{x^3}{3} + \dfrac{x^5}{5} \ldots\right)$

2 $2x + 4x^2 + \dfrac{2}{3}x^3 - \dfrac{8}{3}x^4 - \dfrac{16}{15}x^5 \ldots$

3 $x^2 - \dfrac{x^4}{3} \ldots$

4 $-x^2 - \dfrac{x^4}{2} \ldots$

5 $1 + \dfrac{x^2}{2} - \dfrac{x^3}{3} + \dfrac{3}{8}x^4 - \dfrac{11}{30}x^5 \ldots$

6 $1 - x^2 + \dfrac{x^4}{3} \ldots$

7 $2x - x^2 + \dfrac{2}{3}x^3 - \dfrac{x^4}{2} + \dfrac{2}{5}x^5 \ldots$

8 $1 + 2x^2 + \dfrac{10}{3}x^4 \ldots$

9 $1 - 2x - \dfrac{5}{2}x^2 + \dfrac{23}{3}x^3 - \dfrac{119}{24}x^4 - \dfrac{61}{60}x^5 \ldots$

10 $-2x - \dfrac{2}{3}x^3 - \dfrac{2}{5}x^5 \ldots$

Exercise 10.7

1 i) $\sin(x - \alpha) = \sin x . \cos \alpha - \cos x . \sin \alpha$

   ii) $\cos(x + \alpha) = \cos x . \cos \alpha - \sin x . \sin \alpha$

   iii) $\cos(x - \alpha) = \cos x . \cos \alpha + \sin x . \sin \alpha$

4 $\sin 2x = 2x - \dfrac{(2x)^3}{3!} + \dfrac{(2x)^5}{5!} - \dfrac{(2x)^7}{7!} \cdots,$

   $\cos 2x = 1 - \dfrac{(2x)^2}{2!} + \dfrac{(2x)^4}{4!} - \dfrac{(2x)^6}{6!} \cdots,$

   $\sin ax = ax - \dfrac{(ax)^3}{3!} + \dfrac{(ax)^5}{5!} - \dfrac{(ax)^7}{7!} \cdots,$

   $\cos ax = 1 - \dfrac{(ax)^2}{2!} + \dfrac{(ax)^4}{4!} - \dfrac{(ax)^6}{6!} \cdots$

5 i) $\tan ax = ax + \dfrac{(ax)^3}{3} + \dfrac{2}{15}(ax)^5 \cdots,$

   $\sec^2 ax = 1 + (ax)^2 + \dfrac{2}{3}(ax)^4 \cdots,$

   $\sec^2 3x = 1 + (3x)^2 + \dfrac{2}{3}(3x)^4 \cdots$

   ii) $\ln(\cos x) = -\dfrac{x^2}{2} - \dfrac{x^4}{12} - \dfrac{x^6}{45} \cdots$

6 $1 + x + x^2 + x^3 \cdots,\ 2 + x + x^2 + x^3 \cdots,\ 2.87$ N

7 $10 + s - 0.00\bar{6}s^3 \cdots,\ 133.\bar{3}$ J

8 0.478

9 $2t^2 - \dfrac{t^4}{3} + \dfrac{t^6}{60} \cdots,\ 0.602$ V

10 $5s^2 - 5s^3 + 2.5s^4 \cdots,\ 10.42$ N

Chapter 11

Exercise 11.1

1 1.784 s

2 40.1 mm

3 $-0.475, 1.395$

4 ± 0.693

5 1.562

6 -0.565

7 $-0.540, 1.497$

9 1.352, 6.76

10 0.0114, i.e. 1.14%

Chapter 12

Exercise 12.1

1 $x = 0.18$, $y = 0.06$, $z = 0.16$

2 $9V_1 + V_2 = 10$, $7V_2 - 2V_3 = 5$, $V_1 - V_2 + 7V_3 = 7$; $V_1 = 1$, $V_2 = 1$, $V_3 = 1$

3 $i_1 = 1.12$ A, $i_2 = 0.60$ A, $i_3 = 0.65$ A

4 $x = 1$, $y = 3$, $z = 2$

Exercise 12.2

1 $x = 3.0$, $y = -0.5$, $z = 1.5$

2 $x = 4$, $y = 10$, $z = 3$

3 $I_1 = 3$ A, $I_2 = 2$ A, $I_3 = 6$ A

4 $x = 1$, $y = 3$, $z = 2$

Exercise 12.3

1 $x = 0.5$, $y = 1.0$, $z = 1.5$

2 $x = -10$, $y = 7$, $z = 29$

3 $x = 1.5$, $y = 2$, $z = 3$

4 $x = 15$, $y = 25$, $z = 25$

5 $I_1 = 4$ A, $I_2 = 2$ A, $I_3 = 1$ A

Chapter 13

Accept that the last decimal places may differ slightly depending upon the quality of your calculations.

Exercise 13.1

1 x	$f(x)$	**2** x	$f(x)$	**3** x	$f(x)$
0	1.500	0	0.000	1.0	2.5000
0.2	1.800	0.1	0.000	1.1	2.6400
0.4	2.200	0.2	0.010	1.2	2.7817
0.6	2.720	0.3	0.028	1.3	2.9248
0.8	3.384	0.4	0.052	1.4	3.0693
1.0	4.221	0.5	0.082	1.5	3.2149

4

x	f(x)
0	0.8000
0.05	0.7800
0.10	0.7661
0.15	0.7548
0.20	0.7457
0.25	0.7382
0.30	0.7322

5

t	f(t)
1.0	0.00000
1.1	0.08415
1.2	0.15941
1.3	0.22797
1.4	0.29103
1.5	0.34931

Exercise 13.2

1

x	f(x)
1.0	2.150
1.2	2.887
1.4	3.891
1.6	5.238
1.8	7.022
2.0	9.355

2

x	f(x)
0	1.5000
0.1	2.0275
0.2	2.7600
0.3	3.7682
0.4	5.1472
0.5	7.0250

3

x	f(x)
1.0	1.0000
1.1	1.2325
1.2	1.5543
1.3	2.0197
1.4	2.7433
1.5	4.0115

4

t	f(t)
1	0.5000
1.2	0.5750
1.4	0.6577
1.6	0.7471
1.8	0.8423
2.0	0.9427

5

x	f(x)
0.5	2.000
0.6	2.231
0.7	2.428
0.8	2.602
0.9	2.757
1.0	2.898

Exercise 13.3

1

x	f(x)
1.0	2.1500
1.2	2.8930
1.4	3.9065
1.6	5.2681
1.8	7.0725
2.0	9.4356

2

x	f(x)
0.5	1.0000
0.6	1.0877
0.7	1.2044
0.8	1.3567
0.9	1.5525

3

x	f(x)
0	2.0000
0.1	1.9761
0.2	1.9542
0.3	1.9341

4

x	$f(x)$
0.50	4.8000
0.52	4.9267
0.54	5.0547
0.56	5.1841
0.58	5.3149
0.60	5.4471

5

θ	$f(\theta)$
0	1.5000
0.1	1.5673
0.2	1.6354
0.3	1.7037

Exercise 13.4

1

t (h)	T (°C)
0	65.00
0.25	62.22
0.50	59.56
0.75	57.03
1.00	54.61

2

v (ms⁻¹)	m (kg)
0	13 500
10	13 163
20	12 178
30	10 659

3

t (s)	θ (rad)
0	0.000
0.1	0.001
0.2	0.007
0.3	0.019
0.4	0.036
0.5	0.057

4

t (s)	y (mm)
0	1.750
0.2	1.332
0.4	0.995
0.6	0.726

5

θ (°C)	R (Ω)
75.0	45.60
77.5	45.70
80.0	45.80
82.5	45.89
85.0	45.99

Chapter 14

Exercise 14.1

1 $x^2 + 4xy = k$

2 $4xy + y^2 = k$

3 $x^2 = 4e^{y/x}$

4 $y - x = x\ln(xy^2)$

5 $2x - 4y = 3(x+y)\ln x$

Exercise 14.2

1 $2ye^x = x - 1$

2 $xy = 2x + 1$

3 $y = \cos x - \sin x + e^{-x}$

4 $y = 0.5(e^{2x} - 3 + x)$

5 $8y\sin x = 5 - 2\cos 2x$

Exercise 14.3

1   $i = 25(1 - e^{-5t})$, 5.53 A

2   $v = 200 - 195e^{-t/400}$, 7.42 ms^{-1}, 9.81 ms^{-1}, 12.18 ms^{-1}, 32 s

3   yes

4   0.0009 C, $q = 10^{-4}(10 - e^{-200t})$

5   $v^2 = \dfrac{a^2}{2k^2}(1 - 2kx) - \dfrac{a^2}{2k^2}(1 - 2kb)e^{2k(b-x)}$

Chapter 15

Exercise 15.1

1   $y = 0.25e^{2x} + 0.08x^4 + c_1x + c_2$

2   $y = 1 - x + \dfrac{x^3}{6} - 2\ln x$

3   $y = -0.25\cos 2x + e^{-x} - 0.29$

4   $y = -\ln(\cos t)$ or $\ln(\sec t)$

5   $x = 1.59t - 4\sin\dfrac{t}{2}$

Exercise 15.2

1   $y = \ln\left(\dfrac{1}{2-x}\right)$, $y = \ln\left(\dfrac{1}{x}\right)$

2   $y^2 = 2(2 \pm x)$

3   $y = \sin\left(\dfrac{\pi}{6} \pm x\right)$

4   $2\tan y = 1 + x$, $2\tan y = 3 - x$

5   $y = 2\ln x$, $y = 2\ln(2 - x)$

Exercise 15.3

1   $y = Ae^{2x} + Be^{3x}$

2   $y = Ae^{2x} + Be^{-4x}$

3   $y = (Ax + B)e^{-3x}$

4   $y = Ae^{-3.56x} + Be^{0.56x}$

5   $x = e^t(A\cos 3t + B\sin 3t)$

6   $y = Ae^{-x} + Be^{-2x}$

7   $y = (Ax + B)e^{5x}$

8   $y = e^{-3x}(A\cos x + B\sin x)$

9   $x = Ae^{0.15t} + Be^{0.45t}$

10   $y = e^{-2t}(A\cos t + B\sin t)$

11   $y = (2x + 1)e^{x/2}$

12   $x = 2e^{-3t} + 3e^{-4t}$

13   $x = e^{-t}\cos 2t$

14   $y = e^{-2x} + e^{5x}$

15   $y = e^{1.62t} - 2.5e^{-0.62t}$

Exercise 15.4

1 $y = Ae^{-2x} + Be^{-3x} + \dfrac{1}{3}e^x$

2 $y = Ae^x + (B + 3x)e^{2x}$

3 $y = \dfrac{2}{16}xe^{-5x} + \dfrac{1}{16}e^{-x}$

4 $y = e^{-5x} + \dfrac{2}{7}(3 + x)e^{2x}$

5 $y = e^{-2t}(\cos t + \sin t) + \dfrac{1}{2}e^{-3t}$

Exercise 15.5

1 $y = e^x(A\cos 3x + B\sin 3x) + \dfrac{3}{26}\cos 2x - \dfrac{1}{13}\sin 2x$

2 $y = Ae^{-4x} + Be^{6x} - (0.037\cos x + 0.043\sin x)$

3 $y = 0.75\{(2t + 1)e^{-2t} - \cos 2t\}$

4 $y = 10.60e^{-3t}\sin t + 2\cos 3t + \sin 3t$

5 $y = -\cos 2t - 2.828\sin 2t + 3\cos t + \sin t$

Exercise 15.6

1 $y = (Ax + B)e^{-4x} - 0.625 + 0.75x$

2 $y = (Ax + B)e^{-4x} - \dfrac{5}{3} + \dfrac{19}{6}x - \dfrac{5}{2}x^2 + x^3$

3 $y = e^{-x} - e^{-2x} + 4 - 3x + x^2$

4 $y = 0.74e^t\sin 3t + 0.4 + 2t$

5 $x = 6.94e^{-3t} - 6e^{-4t} + \dfrac{5}{9} - \dfrac{2}{3}t + \dfrac{1}{2}t^2$

Exercise 15.7

1 $q = 6.25\{1 - e^{-4t}(\cos 2t + 2\sin 2t)\}$

2 $x = 1.5e^{-3t}\sin 4t$

3 $i = (1.05 - 2.9t)e^{-2t} - 1.05\cos 5t + \sin 5t$

4 $i = \alpha te^{-5t}$

5 $x = e^{-t}(0.8\cos 4t + 0.4\sin 4t) + 0.1\sin 4t - 0.8\cos 4t$

Chapter 16

Exercise 16.1

1 $\dfrac{5}{s}$ **2** $\dfrac{c}{s}$ **3** $\dfrac{4}{s^2}$ **4** $\dfrac{2}{s^3}$

5 $\dfrac{1}{s+2}$ **6** $\dfrac{s}{s^2+\omega^2}$ **7** $\dfrac{a}{s^2-a^2}$ **8** $\dfrac{s}{s^2-a^2}$

9 $\dfrac{1!}{(s+2)^2}$ **10** $\dfrac{2}{(s+1)^2+2^2}$ or $\dfrac{2}{s^2+2s+5}$

Exercise 16.2

1 $\dfrac{11.5}{s}$ **2** $\dfrac{1}{s^2}$

3 $\dfrac{12}{s^2}$ **4** $\dfrac{6}{s^3}$

5 $\dfrac{1}{s-3}$ **6** $\dfrac{4}{s+3}$

7 $\dfrac{48}{s^5}+\dfrac{1}{s+2}$ **8** $\dfrac{7}{s}+\dfrac{5}{s^2}-\dfrac{8}{s^3}$

9 $\dfrac{1}{s-1/2}$ or $\dfrac{2}{2s-1}$ **10** $\dfrac{1}{s+1/4}$ or $\dfrac{4}{4s+1}$

Exercise 16.3

1 $\dfrac{3}{s^2+9}$ **2** $\dfrac{s}{s^2+1}$

3 $\dfrac{4}{s^2+16}-\dfrac{s}{s^2+1}$ **4** $\dfrac{8}{s^2+16}-\dfrac{3s}{s^2+1}$

5 $\dfrac{1.5}{s^2+0.25}$ or $\dfrac{6}{4s^2+1}$ **6** $\dfrac{2s}{s^2-9}$

7 $\dfrac{2}{s^2-4}$ **8** $\dfrac{4s}{s^2-1}$

9 $\dfrac{2s}{s^2-1}-\dfrac{3}{s^2-9}$ **10** $\dfrac{4}{4s^2-1}+\dfrac{3}{s^2-1}+\dfrac{s}{s^2-4}$

Exercise 16.4

1 $\dfrac{6}{(s+2)^4}$ **2** $\dfrac{2}{(s-3)^3}$

3 $\dfrac{2}{(s+2)^3}$ **4** $\dfrac{1}{(s+1)^2+1^2}$ or $\dfrac{1}{s^2+2s+2}$

5 $\dfrac{s+3}{(s+3)^2+4^2}$ or $\dfrac{s+3}{s^2+6s+25}$

6 $\dfrac{2}{(s+3)^2-2^2}$ or $\dfrac{2}{s^2+6s+5}$

7 $\dfrac{1/3}{(s-4)^2+1/9}$

8 $\dfrac{6}{(s-1)^4}$

9 $\dfrac{s+2}{(s+2)^2-1/4}$

10 $\dfrac{s-2}{(s-2)^2-1}-\dfrac{1/2}{(s-2)^2-1/4}$

Exercise 16.5

1 t

2 e^{21t}

3 $1.5t^2$

4 $3e^{-4t}$

5 $\dfrac{2}{3}t^3$

6 $\cosh 4t$

7 $\cos 4t + \sin 4t$

8 $2(\cos 3t + \sin 3t)$

9 $\cosh 5t - 1.2\sinh 5t$

10 $2\sin \omega^2 t$

Exercise 16.6

1 $2te^{-6t}$

2 $3te^t$

3 $e^{-4t}\sin 3t$

4 $e^{-4t}\left(\cosh 3t - \dfrac{10}{3}\sinh 3t\right)$

5 $e^{-5t}\cos 4t$

6 $t^4 e^{-2t}$

7 $e^{-2t}\cosh\sqrt{2}t$

8 $e^{-5t}\left(\cosh 4t - \dfrac{1}{4}\sinh 4t\right)$

9 $2e^t(\cos t + 4\sin t)$

10 $e^{-t}(3\cosh t - 5\sinh t)$

Exercise 16.7

1 $4e^{-3t}+2e^t$

2 $4e^{-3t}+2e^{-t}+5e^{4t}$

3 $-4te^{-t}+2e^{-t}+e^{5t}$

4 $-0.5te^{-3t}+e^{-3t}-e^{4t}$

5 $3e^{-3t}+te^{-t}+2e^{-t}$

6 $4\cos t - 3e^t$

7 $\cos\sqrt{2}t+5$

8 $4e^{-t}-5\sqrt{10}\sin\sqrt{10}t$

9 $2(e^{0.5t}\cos 1.323t - 0.756e^{0.5t}\sin 1.323t - 1)$

10 $2e^{-t}\cos\sqrt{3}t + 1.155e^{-t}\sin\sqrt{3}t + e^{3t}$

Exercise 16.8

1 $y = 3e^{2t}-5e^{-t}$

2 $y = 0.75(1-e^{2t})$

3 $y = 4xe^{3x}$

4 $y = 2e^t - 3e^{-t}$

5 $x = e^{2t}-\sin t$

6 $y = 4 - 5t - e^{3t}$

7 $y = 2\cos t + 5\sin t$

8 $y = 3t + \dfrac{1}{2}e^{3t}$

9 $y = e^{-t}\sin 2t$

10 $x = t^2 + te^{-2t}$

Exercise 16.9

1	i) 1,	ii)	final value theorem fails to apply	
2	i) 5,	ii) 0		
3	i) 0,	ii) ∞		
4	i) 2,	ii)	final value theorem fails to apply	
5	i) 1,	ii)	final value theorem fails to apply	
6	i) 0,	ii)	function oscillates, theorem fails	
7	i) 0,	ii) 0		
8	i) 0,	ii)	final value theorem fails to apply	
9	i) 0,	ii) 0		
10	i) 3,	ii) 0		

Exercise 16.10

	Zeroes (at $s =$)	Poles (at $s =$)
1	no zeroes	$-2 + j3$ (stable), $-2 - j3$ (stable)
2	2	-5 (stable), 1 (unstable)
3	no zeroes	-1 (stable)
4	$\dfrac{2}{3}$	-4 (stable), 0 (unstable)
5	-1	-3.414 (stable), -0.586 (stable)
6	-4	-8 (stable), -2 (stable)
7	-2	-1 (stable), 2 (unstable)
8	$-4, -2$	-3, (stable), -1 (stable), 4 (unstable)
9	$-1.291, 1.291$	0 (unstable) $-j2.236$ (unstable), $j2.236$ (unstable)
10	5	$-j4$ (unstable), $j4$ (unstable)

Exercise 16.11

1 $m = 15000e^{-v/2000}$, stable because of the negative exponential

2 $\dfrac{dW}{dx} = kx$, $W = 250x^2$

3 $\theta = \dfrac{3}{4}\left(1 - e^{-2t} - 2te^{-2t}\right)$

5 a)   i) $i = 1.6e^{-0.75t} - 1.6\cos t + 1.2\sin t$

   ii) $i = \dfrac{E\omega}{L^2\omega^2 + R^2}\left(-L\cos \omega t + \dfrac{R}{\omega}\sin \omega t + Le^{-Rt/L}\right)$

   b) $i = \dfrac{EC}{1 - LC\omega^2}\left(-\omega \sin \omega t + \dfrac{1}{\sqrt{LC}}\sin \dfrac{t}{\sqrt{LC}}\right)$

Chapter 17

Exercise 17.1

1 $y = 3\cos t - 2\sin t$

2 $y = e^{2t} + 3e^{-t}$

3 $y = 3t - e^{-t} + \cos 2t$

4 $y = e^{-t}(1 + t^2)$

5 $y = e^{-2t}(\cos t - \sin t)$

Exercise 17.2

1 $q = 6.25\{1 - e^{-4t}(\cos 2t + 2\sin 2t)\}$

2 $x = 1.5e^{-3t}\sin 4t$

3 $i = (1.05 - 2.9t)e^{-2t} - 1.05\cos 5t + \sin 5t$

4 $i = \alpha t e^{-5t}$

5 $x = e^{-t}(0.8\cos 4t + 0.4\sin 4t) + 0.1\sin 4t - 0.8\cos 4t$

Exercise 17.3

1 $y = 4 - 3t$

2 $x = e^{2t} + e^{-t}$

3 $x = e^{t}(\cos t + 3\sin t). \ y = e^{t}(\cos t - 2\sin t)$

4 $x = te^{-t}, \ y = 2 - e^{-t}$

5 $x = \dfrac{2}{3}e^{-t} - \dfrac{1}{3}e^{t} - \dfrac{2}{3}e^{-2t} + \dfrac{1}{3}e^{2t}, \ y = \dfrac{1}{3}e^{-t} + \dfrac{2}{3}e^{t} - \dfrac{2}{3}e^{-2t} - \dfrac{1}{3}e^{2t}$

Chapter 18

Exercise 18.1

1

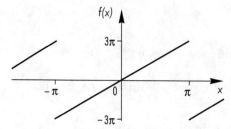

2

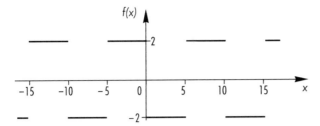

3

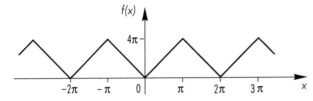

4

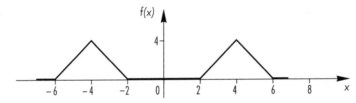

5

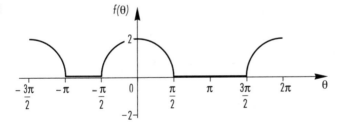

6 $f(x) = 4$ for $-\pi < x < \pi$
          $f(x) = -4$ for $\pi < x < 3\pi$
     $f(x + 4\pi) = f(x)$

7 $f(x) = 5$ for $-2 < x < 0$
          $f(x) = -5$ for $0 < x < 2$
     $f(x + 4) = f(x)$

8 $f(x) = 3x$ for $0 < x < \ell$
     $f(x + \ell) = f(x)$

9        $f(t) = 0$ for $-\pi < t \leqslant 0$

         $f(t) = \dfrac{6t}{\pi}$ for $0 \leqslant t < \pi$

    $f(t + 2\pi) = f(t)$

10        $f(x) = \dfrac{2x}{\pi}$ for $-\pi \leqslant x \leqslant \pi$

         $f(x) = 4 - \dfrac{2x}{\pi}$ for $\pi \leqslant x \leqslant 3\pi$

    $f(x + 4\pi) = f(x)$

Exercise 18.2

1   $f(x) = 1 + \dfrac{4}{\pi}\left(\sin x + \dfrac{1}{3}\sin 3x \ldots\right)$

2   $f(x) = \dfrac{\pi}{2} + \dfrac{4}{\pi}\left(\dfrac{1}{1^2}\cos x + \dfrac{1}{3^2}\cos 3x \ldots\right)$

    $\qquad\quad -2\left(\dfrac{1}{1}\sin x + \dfrac{1}{2}\sin 2x + \dfrac{1}{3}\sin 3x \ldots\right)$

3   $f(x) = 1 + \dfrac{12}{\pi}\left(\dfrac{1}{1}\sin x + \dfrac{1}{3}\sin 3x + \dfrac{1}{5}\sin 5x \ldots\right)$

4   $f(x) = \pi + 2\left(\sin x - \dfrac{1}{2}\sin 2x + \dfrac{1}{3}\sin 3x - \dfrac{1}{4}\sin 4x \ldots\right)$

5   $f(x) = \dfrac{3\pi}{4} + \dfrac{2}{\pi}\left(\cos x + \dfrac{1}{3^2}\cos 3x + \dfrac{1}{5^2}\cos 5x \ldots\right)$

    $\qquad\quad +\left(\sin x - \dfrac{1}{2}\sin 2x + \dfrac{1}{3}\sin 3x \ldots\right)$

Exercise 18.3

1   $f(x) = \dfrac{10}{\pi}\left(\sin x + \dfrac{1}{3}\sin 3x + \dfrac{1}{5}\sin 5x \ldots\right)$

2   $f(x) = 8\left(\sin x - \dfrac{1}{2}\sin 2x + \dfrac{1}{3}\sin 3x - \dfrac{1}{4}\sin 4x \ldots\right)$

3   $f(x) = -\dfrac{4}{\pi}\left(\sin x - \dfrac{1}{2}\sin 2x + \dfrac{1}{3}\sin 3x - \dfrac{1}{4}\sin 4x \ldots\right)$

4   $f(x) = -\dfrac{30}{\pi}\left(\sin x + \dfrac{1}{3}\sin 3x + \dfrac{1}{5}\sin 5x \ldots\right)$

5   $f(x) = 2\left(\sin x + \dfrac{1}{2}\sin 2x + \dfrac{1}{3}\sin 3x \ldots\right)$

Exercise 18.4

1 $f(x) = \pi - \dfrac{8}{\pi}\left(\dfrac{1}{1^2}\cos x + \dfrac{1}{3^2}\cos 3x + \dfrac{1}{5^2}\cos 5x \ldots\right)$

2 $f(x) = \dfrac{3}{2} + \dfrac{12}{\pi^2}\left(\dfrac{1}{1^2}\cos x + \dfrac{1}{3^2}\cos 3x + \dfrac{1}{5^2}\cos 5x \ldots\right)$

3 $f(x) = \dfrac{3}{2}\pi - \dfrac{4}{\pi}\left(\dfrac{1}{1^2}\cos x + \dfrac{1}{3^2}\cos 3x + \dfrac{1}{5^2}\cos 5x \ldots\right)$

4 $f(x) = -1 + \dfrac{8}{\pi^2}\left(\dfrac{1}{1^2}\cos x + \dfrac{1}{3^2}\cos 3x + \dfrac{1}{5^2}\cos 5x \ldots\right)$

5 $f(x) = \dfrac{1}{2} + \dfrac{2}{\pi}\left(-\dfrac{1}{1}\cos x + \dfrac{1}{3}\cos 3x - \dfrac{1}{5}\cos 5x + \dfrac{1}{7}\cos 7x \ldots\right)$

Exercise 18.5

1 $f(x) = -\dfrac{16}{\pi}\left(\sin x + \dfrac{1}{3}\sin 3x + \dfrac{1}{5}\sin 5x \ldots\right)$

2 $f(x) = \dfrac{\pi}{2} - \dfrac{4}{\pi}\left(\dfrac{1}{1^2}\cos x + \dfrac{1}{3^2}\cos 3x + \dfrac{1}{5^2}\cos 5x \ldots\right)$

3 $f(x) = -1 + \dfrac{8}{\pi^2}\left(\dfrac{1}{1^2}\cos x + \dfrac{1}{3^2}\cos 3x + \dfrac{1}{5^2}\cos 5x \ldots\right)$

4 $f(x) = 8\sin x - \dfrac{4}{2}\sin 2x + \dfrac{8}{3}\sin 3x - \dfrac{4}{4}\sin 4x \ldots$

5 i) $f(x) = \dfrac{\pi}{4} - \dfrac{2}{\pi}\left(\dfrac{1}{1^2}\cos x + \dfrac{1}{3^2}\cos 3x + \dfrac{1}{5^2}\cos 5x \ldots\right)$

ii) $f(x) = -\sin x + \dfrac{1}{2}\sin 2x - \dfrac{1}{3}\sin 3x \ldots$

Exercise 18.6

1 $f(x) = \dfrac{1}{2} + \dfrac{2}{\pi}\left(\sin x + \dfrac{1}{3}\sin 3x + \dfrac{1}{5}\sin 5x \ldots\right)$

2 $f(x) = -4\left(\sin x + \dfrac{1}{3}\sin 3x + \dfrac{1}{5}\sin 5x \ldots\right)$

3 $f(x) = \dfrac{4}{\pi}\left(\sin x - \dfrac{1}{2}\sin 2x + \dfrac{1}{3}\sin 3x \ldots\right)$

4 $f(x) = \dfrac{5}{2} - \dfrac{12}{\pi^2}\left(\dfrac{1}{1^2}\cos x + \dfrac{1}{3^2}\cos 3x + \dfrac{1}{5^2}\cos 5x \ldots\right)$

5 i) $f(x) = \dfrac{8}{\pi^2}\left(\dfrac{1}{1^2}\cos x + \dfrac{1}{3^2}\cos 3x + \dfrac{1}{5^2}\cos 5x \ldots\right)$

ii) $f(x) = \dfrac{4}{\pi}\left(\dfrac{1}{2}\sin x + \dfrac{1}{4}\sin 4x \ldots\right)$

Chapter 19

Exercise 19.1

1   0.03

2 $0.5\bar{3}$

3   0.92, 1380 ℓ

4 $\dfrac{1}{30}$, 0

5 $\dfrac{1}{12}$, $\dfrac{7}{12}$

Exercise 19.2

1   i) 7×10^{-4}, ii) 0.0343, iii) 0.9457

2   i) 1.543×10^{-6}, ii) $1.23\ldots \times 10^{-5}$, iii) 0.12

3   i) 0.108, 0.153, 0.068, ii) 0.612, iii) 0.003

4   0.643, 0.385, 0.247, 0.247

5   0.225, 0.150, 0.075, 0.180

Exercise 19.3

1   0.063

2   0.003

3   i) 0.039,   ii) 0.261

4   0.600, 0.421, 0.253, 0.253, 0.505

5   0.45, 0.1575

Exercise 19.4

1   10

2   56

3   210

4   56

5   35

6   6

7   20

8   10

9   35

10   126

Exercise 19.5

1   i) 0.1762, ii) 0.9527

2   1, 0.6974, 0.3026, 0.2131

3   0.0111, all being promoted

4   i) 0.9139,   ii) 0.9139

5   0.5256

Exercise 19.6

1   0.1353

2   0.1247

3   6/shrink wrap, 0.1512

4   0.4562

5   0.3423

Chapter 20

Exercise 20.1

1 −1.176, 1.176   **2** −1.579, −0.789

3 7.25 and 10.75 hours, −1 and 1   **4** −1.286, 0.714

5 Does not closely resemble the bell-shaped curve.

Exercise 20.2

1	0.4726	**2**	0.4388	**3**	0.2422	**4**	0.4844
5	0.5468	**6**	0.2684	**7**	0.6514	**8**	0.0668
9	0.9032	**10**	0.2112	**11**	0.97	**12**	−1.96
13	0.84	**14**	0.39	**15**	−0.32		

16 77.45%, 9.19%

17 0.1056, i) 0.0918, ii) 0.0694, iii) 0.0475

18 15.87%, virtually 0

19 0.3085, 0.266, *A*

20 0.04, lower, 11.6 g

Exercise 20.3

1 0.1, 0.9, 100, 9.48 ..., 0.733, 0.1335

2 0.0244

3 120, 0.0162

4 0.95, 0.0158

5 127.75, i.e. 128; 0.0062

Exercise 20.4

1 3 standard deviations either side of the mean, 0.0784, 0.0588

2 0.4466, 0.0534

3 24, 0.1307, 0.0262, yes, it differs from the mean by more than 3 standard deviations

4 0.1102, 0.0115, 3 standard deviations from the mean

5 0.1093, 0.0037

Index